VCP6-DCV
Official Cert Guide
(Exam #2VO-621)

VMware Press is the official publisher of VMware books and training materials, which provide guidance on the critical topics facing today's IT professionals and students. VMware virtualization and cloud infrastructure technologies simplify IT complexity and streamline operations, helping organizations of all kinds and sizes to become more agile, efficient, and profitable.

VMware Press provides proven, technically accurate information that will help you achieve your goals for customizing, building, and maintaining a virtual environment—from the data center to mobile devices to the public, private, and hybrid cloud.

With books, certification and study guides, video training, and learning tools produced by world-class architects and IT experts, VMware Press helps you master a diverse range of topics on virtualization and cloud computing and is the official source of reference materials for preparing for the VMware Certified Professional certifications.

VMware Press is also pleased to have localization partners that can publish its products into more than 42 languages, including, but not limited to, Chinese (Simplified), Chinese (Traditional), French, German, Greek, Hindi, Japanese, Korean, Polish, Russian, and Spanish.

For more information about VMware Press, please visit **vmwarepress.com**.

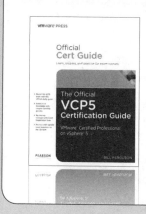  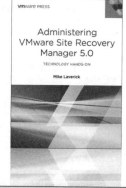 

VCP6-DCV
Official Cert Guide
(Exam #2VO-621)

John A. Davis
Steve Baca
Owen Thomas

vmware® PRESS

Hoboken, NJ • Boston • Indianapolis • San Francisco
New York • Toronto • Montreal • London • Munich • Paris • Madrid
Capetown • Sydney • Tokyo • Singapore • Mexico City

VCP6-DCV Official Cert Guide (Exam #2VO-621)

ISBN-10: 0-7897-5648-X

ISBN-13: 978-0-7897-5648-0

Library of Congress Control Number: 2016903596

1   16

Warning and Disclaimer

Every effort has been made to make this book as complete and as accurate as possible, but no warranty or fitness is implied. The information provided is on an "as is" basis. The authors, VMware Press, VMware, and the publisher shall have neither liability nor responsibility to any person or entity with respect to any loss or damages arising from the information contained in this book or from the use of the DVD or programs accompanying it.

The opinions expressed in this book belong to the author and are not necessarily those of VMware.

Special Sales

For information about buying this title in bulk quantities, or for special sales opportunities (which may include electronic versions; custom cover designs; and content particular to your business, training goals, marketing focus, or branding interests), please contact our corporate sales department at corpsales@pearsoned.com or (800) 382-3419.

For government sales inquiries, please contact governmentsales@pearsoned.com.

For questions about sales outside the U.S., please contact intlcs@pearson.com.

EDITOR-IN-CHIEF
Mark Taub

EXECUTIVE EDITOR
Mary Beth Ray

VMWARE PRESS PROGRAM MANAGER
Karl Childs

DEVELOPMENT EDITOR
Ellie Bru

MANAGING EDITOR
Sandra Schroeder

PROJECT EDITOR
Mandie Frank

COPY EDITOR
Kitty Wilson

PROOFREADER
Debbie Williams

INDEXER
Ken Johnson

EDITORIAL ASSISTANT
Vanessa Evans

COVER DESIGNER
Chuti Prasertsith

COMPOSITOR
Studio GaLou

We Want to Hear from You!

As the reader of this book, *you* are our most important critic and commentator. We value your opinion and want to know what we're doing right, what we could do better, what areas you'd like to see us publish in, and any other words of wisdom you're willing to pass our way.

We welcome your comments. You can email or write us directly to let us know what you did or didn't like about this book—as well as what we can do to make our books better.

Please note that we cannot help you with technical problems related to the topic of this book.

When you write, please be sure to include this book's title and author as well as your name, email address, and phone number. We will carefully review your comments and share them with the author and editors who worked on the book.

Email: VMwarePress@vmware.com

Mail: VMware Press
            ATTN: Reader Feedback
            800 East 96th Street
            Indianapolis, IN 46240 USA

Reader Services

Visit our website at www.pearsonitcertification.com/title/9780789756480 and register this book for convenient access to any updates, downloads, or errata that might be available for this book.

Dedication

She came to us in such a whirl,

This precious little angel girl.

A fragile life, doctors would say,

Yet perfect to us in every way.

She changed us all from the very start.

Touching each and every heart.

God loves us all, I'll always believe.

He sent his angel of proof to you and me.

Everything I see, Everything I do,

Madison Hope I think of you.

You now see us clearly, that I know,

For God has brought his angel home.

Dedicated to my oldest granddaughter,
Madison Hope Stith,
03/20/2000 to 01/17/2012

—With Love, Grampy (John Davis)

First and foremost, I would like to dedicate this book to my loving wife, Sharyl. Without your support I would not be able to commit the time necessary to co-author a book. Thank you for believing in me and allowing me to have the time for my many endeavors. I would also like to dedicate this book to my children: Zachary, Brianna, Eileen, Susan, Keenan, and Maura. Also a shout-out to my dog, Baxter, who helps me clear my head on our 3:00 walks to the park and back.

—Steve Baca

I would like to dedicate this book to my wife, Angela, and our daughter, Emma Jean. You have been very patient with the amount of time it has taken me to write, rewrite, re-search, and make sure that I have been as thorough as possible in my contributions to this book. Thank you for putting up with my nerding out and delving deeper into the world of VMware through all these years.

—Owen Thomas

About the Authors

John A. Davis, now a product architect at Rackspace, became a VMware Certified Instructor (VCI) and VMware Certified Professional (VCP) in 2004. Since then, all of his work has been completely focused on VMware-based technologies. He has experience in teaching official VMware curriculum in five countries and delivering VMware professional services throughout the United States. Recently, his work has involved designing solutions based on vRealize Operations and Site Recovery Manager. He has authored several white papers and co-authored the *VCAP5-DCA Cert Guide* (VMware Press). He holds several advanced certifications, including VCAP5-DCA, VCAP5-DCD, VCAP5-DTD, VCAP5-CID, and VCIX-NV. He has been a vExpert since 2014. He is author of the vLoreBlog.com and can be found on Twitter @johnnyadavis.

Steve Baca, VCAP, VCI, VCP, and NCDA, has been in the computer industry for more than 20 years. Originally a computer programmer and a system administrator working on Unix and Windows systems, he migrated over to technical training and wrote a course for Sun Microsystems. After teaching various courses for Sun, he eventually transitioned to VMware about 8 years ago, doing technical training and consulting as well as teaching for NetApp. Currently he lives in Omaha, Nebraska, and does a number of worldwide engagements. He thoroughly enjoys teaching and writing and believes that the constant evolution of the computer industry requires continuously learning to stay ahead. Steve can be found on Twitter @scbaca1.

Owen Thomas, VCI Level 2, VCP-DCV, VCP-Cloud, VCP-DT, VCAP-DCA, has been teaching various VMware classes since 2008. His first major IT position was in an enterprise-level NOC in Louisville, Kentucky, where he started in 2000 as a backup operator and transitioned to the role of NOC analyst. As his experience increased, he was tasked with training new staff. Introduced to VMware as of version 2 and trained in VI3, he became a VMware Certified Instructor at the end of 2007. Since then, he has taught hundreds of VMware classes for open enrollment and onsite classes for customers. Owen is a VMware partner and solutions provider as well as a technical trainer and performs JumpStarts, Audits, HealthChecks, Capacity Planning, and P2V migrations for SMBs.

About the Reviewers

Dave Davis has spent his career carrying out expert management and engineering innovations for corporate leaders in the virtualization space. Over the past 12 years, he has gained extensive experience and knowledge in the IT industry, backed by a abroad range of in-depth professional certifications like VCAP-DCD 5, VCAP-DCA 5, VCP5-DCV, VCP6-DCV, Cisco CCNA, and MCSA/E, with hopes of obtaining the VCDX in data center virtualization. Dave recently received VMware's vExpert 2016 for his contributions at www.virtualizestuff.com, where he talks about various VMware topics and about his home lab configuration.

As a VMware subject matter expert, **Jordan Roth** currently designs and builds VMware's VCA, VCP, and VCAP certification exam curriculum. Jordan's passion for virtualization started in 2006, with the release of VMware GSX. Ever since then, he has been at the forefront of architecture design and implementation for small business, healthcare, financing, and classified/unclassified federal, state, and local government entities. Jordan is a VMware Certified Professional on vSphere versions 3, 4, 5, and 6 as well as a VMware Certified Sales Professional with specialization in server sprawl reduction.

Acknowledgments

I would like to thank my wife and best friend Delores, who supports my late-night writing and gives me reason to be happy every day.

I would like to thank my parents, Monica and Norman Davis, who ensured that I received a solid education and learned from their great work ethics. My siblings and I did not attend preschool or kindergarten; my Mom taught us to read.

Thank you to Charlie Hagerty, the president of New Age Technologies, for molding me into a strong instructor and consulting engineer.

I would like to thank my co-authors Steve Baca and Owen Thomas, who were great partners in this adventure. Thanks to our technical editors, Dave Davis and Jordan Roth, for their hard work and dedication. Special thanks to Mary Beth Ray (executive editor) and Ellie Bru (development editor) for coordinating everything and keeping this project moving in spite of all of our obstacles.

Finally, I would like to thank my granddaughter and grandson, Emma and Jaxon Rosebush. They put a lot of joy in Delores's and my lives. I know I will be able to stay focused to complete my day's work on time whenever I plan to spend the afternoon or weekend with them. All work and no play makes Grampy a dull boy.

—John Davis

There are so many people to acknowledge and thank for making this book possible. First, thanks to my wife and family for supporting me while writing this book. I would also like to thank my fellow co-authors John Davis and Owen Thomas, who spent many hours working on this book, and contributing to our bi-weekly conference call with Ellie and Mary Beth. Thank you to the production team and editors at VMware Press/Pearson Publishing, Ellie Bru and Mary Beth Ray, and the rest of the team at Pearson Publishing, who do a tremendous amount of work from the initial planning of the book to the final printing.

—Steve Baca

I want to thank my wife and daughter for letting me have the time to contribute to this book. I would also like to thank John Davis and Steve Baca for allowing me to tag along with them on this book. Despite the blueprint changing halfway through, I think it has been a positive experience. I'd like to thank John Davis for starting me down the path to not just VMware but instruction as well. Who knows where my life would have taken me had I not taken his class all of those years ago? Thank you to Mary Beth Ray and Ellie Bru for keeping us all on track. I want to finally thank VMware for being this amazing ever-growing thing that has captivated my imagination and managed to hold onto it in a way that no other technology has.

—Owen Thomas

Contents at a Glance

Contents

Introduction

This book focuses on one major goal: helping you prepare to pass the VCP6-DCV exam (2V0-621). You may find this book useful for other purposes, such as learning how to troubleshoot vSphere or as a tool to partially prepare for other exams, but primarily you should use this book to prepare for the 2V0-621 exam.

The rest of this introduction focuses on two topics: the 2V0-621 exam and a description of this book.

The VMware Certified Professional 6—Data Center Virtualization (VCP6-DCV) Exam

The VCP6-DCV Exam is the second exam that is required to achieve VCP6-DCV certification. The exam became available August 30, 2015. The primary objective of the VCP6-DCV exam is to demonstrate that you have mastered the skills to successfully install, deploy, scale, and manage the VMware vSphere 6 environments. The format of the exam is multiple-choice questions in a proctored environment.

Contents of the VCP6-DCV Exam

Every student who ever takes an exam wants to know what's on the exam. For all of its exams, VMware publishes a set of exam topics that give general guidance about what's on the exam.

You can find the exam topics at vmware.com. A good way to find the topics is to navigate to `www.vmware.com/certification` and look for the VCP6-DCV certification.

A big goal of this book is to make sure you are prepared for any topic you might encounter on the VCP6-DCV exam. Therefore, in addition to covering topics in the official recommended course list, this book covers topics not found in the list of courses.

Table I-1 lists the topics on the VCP6-DCV exam blueprint, with a reference to the chapter or chapters of this book that covers the topic.

Table I-1 VCP6-DCV Exam Topics and Chapter References

Exam Section/ Objective	Chapter Where Covered
Section 1: Configure and Administer vSphere 6.x Security	
Objective 1.1: Configure and Administer Role-based Access Control	Chapter 1
Objective 1.2: Secure ESXi, vCenter Server, and vSphere Virtual Machines	Chapter 1
Objective 1.3: Enable SSO and Active Directory Integration	Chapter 1
Section 2: Configure and Administer Advanced vSphere 6.x Networking	
Objective 2.1: Configure Advanced Policies/Features and Verify Network Virtualization Implementation	Chapter 2
Objective 2.2: Configure Network I/O Control (NIOC)	Chapter 3
Section 3: Configure and Administer Advanced vSphere 6.x Storage	
Objective 3.1: Manage vSphere Storage Virtualization	Chapter 4
Objective 3.2: Configure Software-defined Storage	Chapter 5
Objective 3.3: Configure vSphere Storage Multi-pathing and Failover	Chapter 5
Objective 3.4: Perform Advanced VMFS and NFS Configurations and Upgrades	Chapter 6
Objective 3.5: Setup and Configure Storage I/O Control	Chapter 6
Section 4: Upgrade a vSphere Deployment to 6.x	
Objective 4.1: Perform ESXi Host and Virtual Machine Upgrades	Chapter 7
Objective 4.2: Perform vCenter Server Upgrades	Chapter 7
Section 5: Administer and Manage vSphere 6.x Resources	
Objective 5.1: Configure Advanced/Multilevel Resource Pools	Chapter 8
Section 6: Backup and Recover a vSphere Deployment	
Objective 6.1: Configure and Administer a vSphere Backups/Restore/ Replication Solution	Chapter 9
Section 7: Troubleshoot a vSphere Deployment	
Objective 7.1: Troubleshoot vCenter Server, ESXi Hosts, and Virtual Machines	Chapter 10
Objective 7.2: Troubleshoot vSphere Storage and Network Issues	Chapter 11
Objective 7.3: Troubleshoot vSphere Upgrades	Chapter 11

Exam Section/ Objective	Chapter Where Covered
Objective 7.4: Troubleshoot and Monitor vSphere Performance	Chapter 12
Objective 7.5: Troubleshoot HA and DRS Configurations and Fault Tolerance	Chapter 13
Section 8: Deploy and Consolidate vSphere Data Center	
Objective 8.1: Deploy ESXi Hosts Using Autodeploy	Chapter 14
Objective 8.2: Customize Host Profile Settings	Chapter 14
Objective 8.3: Consolidate Physical Workloads using VMware Converter	Chapter 14
Section 9: Configure and Administer vSphere Availability Solutions	
Objective 9.1: Configure Advanced vSphere HA Features	Chapter 15
Objective 9.2: Configure Advanced vSphere DRS Features	Chapter 15
Section 10: Administer and Manage vSphere Virtual Machines	
Objective 10.1: Configure Advanced vSphere Virtual Machine Settings	Chapter 16
Objective 10.2: Create and Manage a Multi-site Content Library	Chapter 16
Objective 10.3: Configure and Maintain a vCloud Air Connection	Chapter 16

How to Take the VCP6-DCV Exam

At this time, VMware exclusively uses testing vendor Pearson Vue (www.vue.com) for delivery of all VMware career certification exams. See Chapter 17, "Final Preparation," for details on registering for the exam. Be sure to use the advice in Chapter 17 to finish your preparation prior to registering for the exam.

Who Should Take This Exam and Read This Book?

The VCP-DCV certification is the most popular certification at VMware, with more than 100,000 professionals certified around the world. This book is intended for anyone wanting to prepare for the 2V0-621 exam, which is a required exam for the certification. The audience includes IT professionals who use VMware for virtualization. This book will help prepare you for the exam by explaining the objectives listed in the exam blueprint.

Candidates who are preparing for the VCP6-DCV exam fall into two categories: those who currently hold a VMware Certified Professional (VCP) certification and those who are new to VMware certification (or hold only expired VCP certifications). New candidates are required to take a qualifying course and pass the vSphere 6 Foundation Exam. Candidates who are holders of current VCP certification in any track (data center virtualization, desktop/mobility, cloud management or networking) and new candidates who already passed the vSphere 6 Foundation Exam are good candidates to take the VCP6-DCV exam and are the expected readers of this book.

Format of the VMware Certified Professional 6–Data Center Virtualization Exam

The VCP6-DCV exam follows the same general format as the other VMware exams. When you get to the testing center and check in, the proctor will give you some general instructions and then take you into a quiet room with a PC. When you're at the PC, you have a few things to do before the timer starts on your exam; for example, you can take a sample quiz to get accustomed to the PC and to the testing engine. Anyone who has user-level skills in getting around a PC should have no problems with the testing environment.

As mentioned previously, the exam is composed purely of multiple-choice questions, where each question either requires you to select a single choice or a specified number of choices from a list of provided choices. See Chapter 17 for more information on the exam and advice on taking it, such as good time management.

Book Features and Exam Preparation Methods

This book uses several key methodologies to help you discover the exam topics on which you need more review, to help you fully understand and remember those details, and to help you prove to yourself that you have retained your knowledge of those topics. This book does not try to help you pass the exam only by memorization but by truly learning and understanding the topics.

The book includes many features that provide different ways to study so you can be ready for the exam. If you understand a topic when you read it but do not study it any further, you probably will not be ready to pass the exam with confidence. The features included in this book give you tools that help you determine what you know, review what you know, better learn what you don't know, and be well prepared for the exam. These tools include:

- **"Do I Know This Already?" Quizzes:** Each chapter begins with a quiz that helps you determine the amount of time you need to spend studying that chapter.

- **Foundation Topics:** These are the core sections of each chapter. They explain the protocols, concepts, and configuration for the topics in that chapter.

- **Exam Preparation Tasks:** This section of each chapter lists a series of study activities that should be done after reading the "Foundation Topics" section. Each chapter includes the activities that make the most sense for studying the topics in that chapter. The activities include the following:

  - **Key Topics Review:** The Key Topic icon appears next to the most important items in the "Foundation Topics" section of the chapter. The "Key Topics Review" section lists the key topics from the chapter and their page numbers. Although the contents of the entire chapter could be on the exam, you should definitely know the information listed in each key topic. Review these topics carefully.

  - **Memory Tables:** To help you exercise your memory and memorize some important facts, memory tables are provided. The memory tables contain only portions of key tables provided previously in the chapter, enabling you to complete the table or list. Appendix B, "Memory Tables," provides the incomplete tables, and Appendix C, "Memory Tables Answer Key," includes the completed tables (answer keys). These appendixes are also provided on the Companion Website that is provided with your book.

  - **Definition of Key Terms:** The VCP6-DCV exam requires you to learn and know a lot of related terminology. This section lists some of the most important terms from the chapter and asks you to write a short definition and compare your answer to the Glossary.

- **Practice Exams:** The companion website contains an exam engine

Companion Website

Register this book to get access to the Pearson IT Certification test engine and other study materials plus additional bonus content. Check this site regularly for new and updated postings written by the authors that provide further insight into the more troublesome topics on the exam. Be sure to check the box that you would like to hear from us to receive updates and exclusive discounts on future editions of this product or related products.

To access this companion website, follow the steps below:

1. Go to www.pearsonITcertification.com/register and log in or create a new account.

2. Enter the ISBN: 9780789756480.

3. Answer the challenge question as proof of purchase.

4. Click on the "Access Bonus Content" link in the Registered Products section of your account page to be taken to the page where your downloadable content is available.

Please note that many of our companion content files can be very large, especially image and video files.

If you are unable to locate the files for this title by following the steps at left, please visit www.pearsonITcertification.com/contact and select the "Site Problems/ Comments" option. Our customer service representatives will assist you.

Pearson IT Certification Practice Test Engine and Questions

The companion website includes the Pearson IT Certification Practice Test engine—software that displays and grades a set of exam-realistic multiple-choice questions. Using the Pearson IT Certification Practice Test engine, you can either study by going through the questions in Study Mode, or take a simulated exam that mimics real exam conditions. You can also serve up questions in a Flash Card Mode, which will display just the question and no answers, challenging you to state the answer in your own words before checking the actual answers to verify your work.

The installation process requires two major steps: installing the software and then activating the exam. The website has a recent copy of the Pearson IT Certification Practice Test engine. The practice exam (the database of exam questions) is not on this site.

NOTE The cardboard case in the back of this book includes a piece of paper. The paper lists the activation code for the practice exam associated with this book. Do not lose the activation code. On the opposite side of the paper from the activation code is a unique, one-time-use coupon code for the purchase of the Premium Edition eBook and Practice Test.

Install the Software

The Pearson IT Certification Practice Test is a Windows-only desktop application. You can run it on a Mac using a Windows virtual machine, but it was built specifically for the PC platform. The minimum system requirements are as follows:

- Windows 10, Windows 8.1, or Windows 7

- Microsoft .NET Framework 4.0 Client

- Pentium-class 1GHz processor (or equivalent)

- 512MB RAM

- 650MB disk space plus 50MB for each downloaded practice exam

- Access to the Internet to register and download exam databases

The software installation process is routine as compared with other software installation processes. If you have already installed the Pearson IT Certification Practice Test software from another Pearson product, there is no need for you to reinstall the software. Simply launch the software on your desktop and proceed to activate the practice exam from this book by using the activation code included in the access code card sleeve in the back of the book.

The following steps outline the installation process:

1. Download the exam practice test engine from the companion site.

2. Respond to windows prompts as with any typical software installation process.

The installation process will give you the option to activate your exam with the activation code supplied on the paper in the cardboard sleeve. This process requires that you establish a Pearson website login. You need this login to activate the exam, so please do register when prompted. If you already have a Pearson website login, there is no need to register again. Just use your existing login.

Activate and Download the Practice Exam

After the exam engine is installed, you should then activate the exam associated with this book (if you did not do so during the installation process) as follows:

1. Start the Pearson IT Certification Practice Test software from the Windows Start menu or from your desktop shortcut icon.

2. To activate and download the exam associated with this book, from the My Products or Tools tab, click the **Activate Exam** button.

3. At the next screen, enter the activation key from paper inside the cardboard sleeve in the back of the book. Once entered, click the **Activate** button.

4. The activation process will download the practice exam. Click **Next**, and then click **Finish**.

When the activation process completes, the My Products tab should list your new exam. If you do not see the exam, make sure that you have selected the **My Products** tab on the menu. At this point, the software and practice exam are ready to use. Simply select the exam and click the **Open Exam** button.

To update a particular exam you have already activated and downloaded, display the **Tools** tab and click the **Update Products** button. Updating your exams will ensure that you have the latest changes and updates to the exam data.

If you want to check for updates to the Pearson Cert Practice Test exam engine software, display the **Tools** tab and click the **Update Application** button. You can then ensure that you are running the latest version of the software engine.

Activating Other Exams

The exam software installation process, and the registration process, only has to happen once. Then, for each new exam, only a few steps are required. For instance, if you buy another Pearson IT Certification Cert Guide, extract the activation code from the cardboard sleeve in the back of that book; you do not even need the exam engine at this point. From there, all you have to do is start the exam engine (if not still up and running) and perform Steps 2 through 4 from the previous list.

Assessing Exam Readiness

Exam candidates never really know whether they are adequately prepared for the exam until they have completed about 30 percent of the questions. At that point, if you are not prepared, it is too late. The best way to determine your readiness is to work through the "Do I Know This Already?" quizzes at the beginning of each chapter and review the foundation and key topics presented in each chapter. It is best to work your way through the entire book unless you can complete each subject without having to do any research or look up any answers.

Premium Edition eBook and Practice Tests

This book also includes an exclusive offer for 70% off the Premium Edition eBook and Practice Tests edition of this title. Please see the coupon code included with the cardboard sleeve for information on how to purchase the Premium Edition.

Book Organization

This book contains 17 chapters, plus appendixes. The topics all focus in some way on VCP6-DCV, making the topics somewhat focused but with deep coverage on those topics:

- **Chapter 1: "Security:"** This chapter discusses the security-related topics covered in the exam.

- **Chapter 2: "Networking, Part 1:"** This chapter discusses advanced policies and features of network virtualization as well as verifying existing configurations.

- **Chapter 3: "Networking, Part 2:"** This chapter delves into Network I/O Control (NIOC) and the changes to NIOC in vSphere 6.

- **Chapter 4: "Storage, Part 1:"** This chapter provides details on how to set up and use NFS, iSCSI, FC, and FCoE protocols. This chapter also discusses how to set up and configure these protocols.

- **Chapter 5: "Storage, Part 2:"** This chapter discusses VMware's software-defined storage solutions Virtual SAN (VSAN) and Virtual Volumes (VVOL). In addition, there is a section on multipathing and failover using Pluggable Storage Architecture.

- **Chapter 6: "Storage, Part 3:"** This chapter takes a closer look at file systems such as VMFS and NFS. Both of these types of file systems have different properties that affect how a datastore interacts with an ESXi Host. There is also a section on how to set up and configure Storage I/O Control (SIOC) for prioritization of virtual machines.

- **Chapter 7: "Upgrade a vSphere Deployment to 6.x:"** This chapter provides the information needed to upgrade the vSphere environment. Upgrading vCenter Server, ESXi Hosts, and other parts of vSphere are discussed.

- **Chapter 8: "Resource Pools:"** This chapter explains the benefits of using resource pools and explores features and settings, as well as how to plan for properly utilizing them.

- **Chapter 9: "Backup and Recovery:"** This chapter discusses how to provide data protection for your virtual machines using VMware Data Protection and vSphere Replication.

- **Chapter 10: "Troubleshoot Common Issues:"** This chapter discusses how to troubleshoot common vSphere issues.

- **Chapter 11: "Troubleshoot Storage, Networks, and Upgrades:"** This chapter discusses how to troubleshoot storage, network, and upgrade issues in vSphere.

- **Chapter 12: "Troubleshoot Performance:"** This chapter discusses how to troubleshoot performance-related issues.

- **Chapter 13: "Troubleshoot Clusters:"** This chapter covers the various issues that can occur with HA and DRS clusters, as well as fault tolerance (FT) and the changes to FT in vSphere 6.

- **Chapter 14: "Deploy and Consolidate:"** This chapter looks at the many pieces involved in configuring a successful Auto Deploy environment, and the host profiles that make this possible. The chapter then discusses VMware Converter for virtualizing workloads.

- **Chapter 15: "Configure and Administer vSphere Availability Solutions:"** This chapter provides information on the features of high availability (HA). Admission control and advanced cluster features are discussed in this chapter. Distributed Resource Scheduler (DRS), which is a vSphere cluster used to provide load balancing and VM placement, is also discussed.

- **Chapter 16: "Virtual Machines:"** This chapter discusses advanced settings, content libraries, and vCloud Air connectors.

- **Chapter 17: "Final Preparation:"** This chapter provides advice from the authors for final preparation. It discusses how to get ready to take the exam and tips for taking the exam.

In addition to the core chapters of the book, the book has several appendixes. Some appendixes exist in the printed book, whereas others exist on the Companion Website included with the book.

The following appendixes are printed in the book:

- **Appendix A, "Answers to the 'Do I Know This Already?' Quizzes and Review Questions:"** This appendix includes the answers to all the questions from Chapters 1 through 16.

The following appendixes are included on the the Companion Website:

- **Appendix B, "Memory Tables:"** This appendix holds the key tables and lists from each chapter, with some of the content removed. You can print this appendix and, as a memory exercise, complete the tables and lists. The goal is to help you memorize facts that can be useful on the exams.

- **Appendix C, "Memory Tables Answer Key:"** This appendix contains the answer key for the exercises in Appendix B.

- **Appendix D, "Study Planner:"** This appendix contains a study table to help guide the study process.

- **Glossary:** The glossary contains definitions for all the terms listed in the "Define Key Terms" sections at the conclusions of Chapters 1–16.

This chapter covers the following objectives:

- **Objective 1.1: Configure and Administer Role-based Access Control**
  - Compare and contrast propagated and explicit permission assignments
  - View/sort/export user and group lists
  - Add/modify/remove permissions for users and groups on vCenter Server inventory objects
  - Determine how permissions are applied and inherited in vCenter Server
  - Create/clone/edit vCenter Server roles
  - Configure VMware Directory Service
  - Apply a role to a user/group and to an object or group of objects
  - Change permission validation settings
  - Determine the appropriate set of privileges for common tasks in vCenter Server
  - Compare and contrast default system/sample roles
  - Determine the correct permissions needed to integrate vCenter Server with other VMware products
- **Objective 1.2: Secure ESXi, vCenter Server, and vSphere Virtual Machines**
  - Harden virtual machine access
  - Harden a virtual machine against denial-of-service attacks
  - Harden ESXi Hosts
  - Harden vCenter Server
  - Understand the implications of securing a vSphere environment
- **Objective 1.3: Enable SSO and Active Directory Integration**
  - Describe SSO architecture and components
  - Differentiate available authentication methods with VMware vCenter
  - Perform a multi-site SSO installation
  - Configure/manage Active Directory authentication
  - Configure/manage Platform Services Controller (PSC)
  - Configure/manage VMware Certificate Authority (VMCA)
  - Enable/disable Single Sign-On (SSO) users
  - Upgrade a single/multi-site SSO installation
  - Configure SSO policies and manage SSO identity sources
  - Add an ESXi Host to an AD domain

## CHAPTER 1

Security

This chapter covers exam topics related to hardening the vSphere environment.

"Do I Know This Already?" Quiz

The "Do I Know This Already?" quiz allows you to assess whether you should study this entire chapter or move quickly to the "Exam Preparation Tasks" section. Regardless, the authors recommend that you read the entire chapter at least once. Table 1-1 outlines the major headings in this chapter and the corresponding "Do I Know This Already?" quiz questions. You can find the answers in Appendix A, "Answers to the 'Do I Know This Already?' Quizzes and Review Questions."

Table 1-1 "Do I Know This Already?" Foundation Topics Section-to-Question Mapping

Foundation Topics Section	Questions Covered in This Section
Determine How Permissions Are Applied and Inherited in vCenter Server	1
Configure VMware Directory Service	2
Determine the Appropriate Set of Privileges for Common Tasks in vCenter Server	3
Harden Virtual Machine Access	4
Harden ESXi Hosts	5, 6
Describe SSO Architecture and Components	7
Configure/Manage Active Directory Authentication	8
Configure/Manage VMware Certificate Authority (VMCA)	9
Enable/Disable Single Sign-On (SSO) Users	10

1. Which of the following is true concerning the effective privileges for User-01, who is a member of Group-A and Group-B, where Group-A is assigned the Administrator role on Cluster-X, and Group-B is assigned the Read Only role on Host-01, which resides in Cluster-X? (Choose two.)

    a. User-01 can modify Host-01.

    b. User-01 can only view information on Host-01.

    c. User-01 can modify Cluster-X.

    d. User-01 can only view information on Cluster-X.

2. Which of the following commands can be used to stop the VMware Directory Service?

    a. `service stop`

    b. `service-control stop`

    c. `service --stop`

    d. `service-control --stop`

3. Which of the following tasks do not require the `Datastore.Allocate Space` privilege? (Choose two.)

    a. Install a guest operating system

    b. Migrate a virtual machine with vMotion

    c. Create a virtual machine snapshot

    d. Migrate a virtual machine with Storage vMotion

4. Which of the following is a setting that VMware recommends for most environments?

    a. `isolation.tools.copy.enable = "FALSE"`

    b. `isolation.tools.paste.enable = "FALSE"`

    c. `isolation.tools.diskWiper.disable = "TRUE"`

    d. `isolation.tools.diskReclaim.disable = "TRUE"`

5. Which of the following summarizes the steps that may be used to enable lockdown mode on an ESXi host using the vSphere Web Client?

    a. Set **Lockdown Mode** to `Enable`.

    b. Deselect the **Lockdown Mode** check box.

    c. Set Lockdown Mode to `YES`.

    d. In the **Lockdown Mode** panel, select **Strict**.

6. Which of the following is an advanced system setting that can be used to disable Managed Object Browsing on an ESXi Host?

    a. `Config.HostAgent.plugins.solo.disableMob`

    b. `disableDebugBrowse`

    c. `enableDebugBrowse`

    d. `Config.HostAgent.plugins.solo.enableMob`

7. Which of the following is not a vCenter Single Sign-On (SSO) component?

    a. STS

    b. vmdir

    c. SAML Service

    d. Identity Management Service

8. Which of the following is an identity source that requires you to choose to use a machine account or to specify an SPN and a UPN when adding to SSO?

    a. Active Directory (Integrated Windows Authentication)

    b. Active Directory over LDAP

    c. Local OS

    d. All of the above

9. Which of the following is used to store ESXi certificates?

    a. VMCA

    b. VECS

    c. `/etc/vmware/ssl`

    d. Database

10. Which of the following is an SSO group that has the ability to manage the VMCA?

    a. `SolutionUsers`

    b. `CAAdmins`

    c. `SystemConfiguration.Administrators`

    d. `Administrators`

Foundation Topics

Objective 1.1—Configure and Administer Role-based Access Control

This section describes how to configure and administer role-based access control. It provides details on configuring roles, applying permissions, understanding effective permissions, and determining required settings.

Compare and Contrast Propagated and Explicit Permission Assignments

Permissions can be set explicitly on vCenter Server inventory objects, such as ESXi Hosts, virtual machines, and folders. Permissions can also be inherited, so that a permission that is set on an ancestor object can propagate to its child object down to other descendant objects. When you set permissions on an object, you have the option to deselect the Propagate to Children option, which is enabled by default. If you deselect this box, then the permission is applied only to the selected object.

For details on how permissions are applied as they propagate to descendants, see the section "Determine How Permissions Are Applied and Inherited in vCenter Server," later in this chapter.

You can use the vSphere Client to connect directly to an ESXi Host and set permissions that are applied only when users connect directly the ESXi server. These permissions are separate from vCenter Server permissions but use a similar role-based model.

View/Sort/Export User and Group Lists

You can view, sort, and export lists of ESXi Host local users to files in HTML, XML, Microsoft Excel, or CSV format by using this procedure:

Step 1. Log onto the ESXi Host using the vSphere Client.

Step 2. Click the **Local Users and Groups** tab.

Step 3. Click **Users**.

Step 4. Optionally, sort the table by any column by clicking the column heading.

Step 5. Optionally, select which columns to show or hide by right-clicking each column and selecting or deselecting the column name.

Step 6. Right-click anywhere in the table and click **Export List**.

Step 7. Provide the location and filename and click **OK**.

You can use a similar procedure to export ESXi local groups, except that you choose Groups in step 3.

To export Single Sign-On (SSO) users, use this procedure:

Step 1.   Log onto the vSphere Web Client.

Step 2.   Select **Home > Administration**.

Step 3.   Select **Single Sign On > Users and Groups**.

Step 4.   Select the Users tab.

Step 5.   Click the **Export List** icon in the lower-right corner, as shown in Figure 1-1.

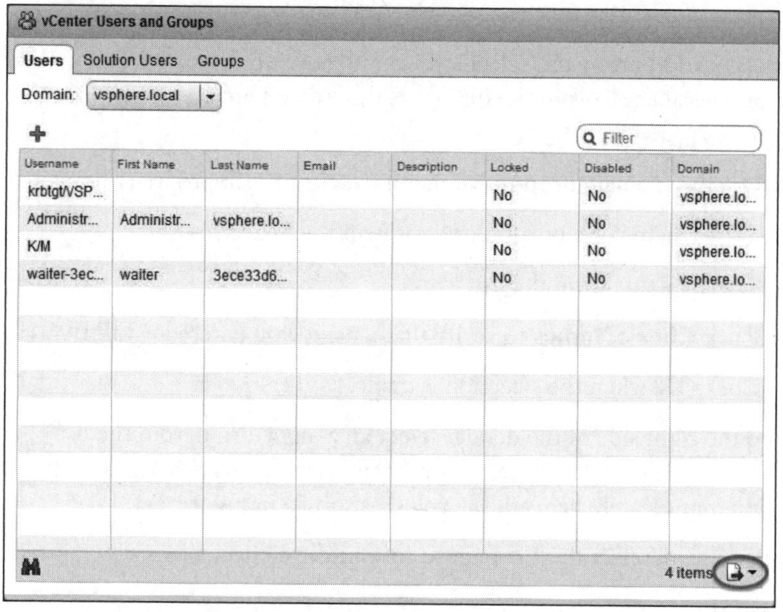

Figure 1-1   Export SSO Users List

You can use a similar procedure to export SSO groups, except that you choose Groups in step 4.

Add/Modify/Remove Permissions for Users and Groups on vCenter Server Inventory Objects

To authorize users to access and manipulate vSphere objects, you can configure role-based permissions in vCenter Server. A permission associates a user group (or user) and a role to a vCenter Server inventory object. To authorize a user or group of users to have specific privileges on an object, such as an ESXi Host, virtual machine, or datastore, you add a permission that assigns a role containing the privileges to the user or group on the object. For example, you can create a permission that assigns the Read Only role to a Single Sign-On user on the virtual datacenter object to allow the user to view information about the datacenter object and its descendants. The following procedure can be used to create a permission:

Step 1.   Select an object, such as an ESXi Host or virtual machine, in the vCenter Server inventory.

Step 2.   Click **Manage > Permissions**.

Step 3.   Click the **Add Permission** icon (+), which opens the Add Permission dialog.

Step 4.   From the left side of the dialog, in the **Users and Groups** section, click the **Add** button and select a user or group. To do so, you can make use of several controls in the dialog, as described here and shown in Figure 1-2.

- Use the Domain drop-down menu to select the appropriate domain.

- Type a name or a portion of a name in the **Search** box.

- Select a name from the list.

- Click **Check Names** to verify that a name you entered is valid.

- Click **OK** when the selection is made.

Step 5.   From the right side of the dialog, select an assigned role from the list of available roles. You can select a role and examine its privileges in the section immediately beneath the roles, as shown in Figure 1-3.

Step 6.   Optionally, deselect the **Propagate to Children** check box.

Step 7.   Click **OK**.

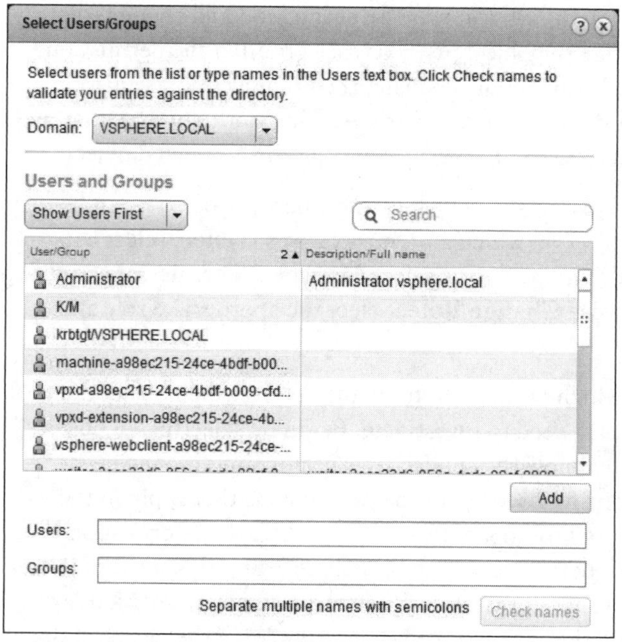

Figure 1-2   Select a Users/Groups Dialog

Figure 1-3   Assigned Roles and Privileges

To modify an existing permission, you can edit the permission and change role assignment. You cannot change the object, user, or user group in the permission, but you can change the role. If this is not adequate, then remove the permission and create a new permission with the correct settings. This work must be done as a user with sufficient privileges to change permissions on the associated objects.

The challenge in editing permissions may be locating a permission so it can be modified. If you know the object on which a permission was created, select the object in the vSphere Web Client inventory, select **Manage** > **Permissions**, right-click the permission, and choose **Change Role**. Select the appropriate role and click OK.

If you do not already know which permission to modify or on which object the permission is assigned, you may need to investigate. Begin by selecting an object in the inventory on which you know the applied user permissions are incorrect. Select **Manage** > **Permissions** to discover all the permissions that apply to the object. Use the **Defined In** column to identify where each applied permission is actually defined. Some of the permissions may be assigned directly on the object, and some may be assigned to ancestor objects. Determine which permissions are related to the issue and where they are assigned. For example, in the next section, which explains permission inheritance, review the provided scenario. In the scenario, if you want User-E to have the ability to view the host-02 object, then modify the permission on host-02 that assigns the No Access role to assign Read Only to Group-04. In many cases, you will decide that you do not want to actually change any existing permission but should instead add a new permission. For example, in the same scenario, if you want User-C to have administrator control on host-02, you may consider changing the existing permission on host-02 that assigns Read Only to Group-02. But if you change that permission, that change also impacts other users, such as User-A. So the solution may be to add a new permission on host-02 that assigns the Administrator role to just User-C. For more details, read the following section.

Determine How Permissions Are Applied and Inherited in vCenter Server

You need to know how permissions are applied and inherited when multiple permissions are applied that impact the same user but that involve different roles. As you assign each permission, you can choose whether to allow the permission to propagate to child objects. This setting is made per permission. It cannot be universally applied. The default setting is to allow propagation to child objects. The propagation is applied to the vSphere Inventory Hierarchy, as shown in Figure 1-4.

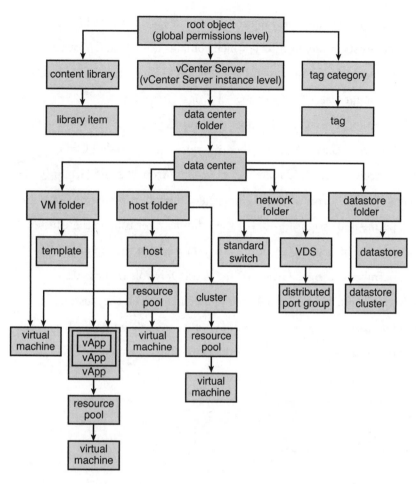

Figure 1-4 vSphere Inventory Hierarchy

An object may have only one distinct path from which permissions may be inherited. For example, a library item can only inherit permissions from a Content Library, which can inherit permissions only from the global root. Other objects have multiple paths from which permissions may be inherited. For example, a virtual machine may inherit permissions from a VM folder and from a resource pool.

Permissions that are assigned at a lower-level object in the inventory hierarchy override permissions assigned at a higher-level object. Permissions assigned on the same object are joined, such that the union of their privileges is applied to users affected by both permissions. Permissions that are inherited from different paths, such as virtual machine permissions inherited from a VM folder and a resource pool, are also joined. Permissions assigned to a user override permissions assigned to groups containing the user, when the permissions are applied to the same object. The No Access permission has precedence over all other privileges.

To illustrate this, consider the following scenario, which is illustrated in Figure 1-5:

- One cluster exists in the inventory, which contains host-01 and host-02.
- The user account User-A is a member of groups Group-01 and Group-02.
- The user account User-B is a member of group Group-01.
- The user account User-C is a member of group Group-02.
- The user account User-D is a member of groups Group-01 and Group-03.
- The user account User-E is a member of groups Group-02 and Group-04.
- **Propagate to Children** is enabled for each of the following permissions:
    - A permission assigns Group-01 the Administrator role on the Cluster.
    - A permission assigns Group-02 the Administrator role on host-01.
    - A permission assigns Group-02 the Read Only role on host-02.
    - A permission assigns User-D the Read Only role on the cluster.
    - A permission assigns Group-03 the No Access role on host-02.
    - A permission assigns Group-04 the Read Only role on host-01.
    - A permission assigns Group-04 the No Access role on host-02.

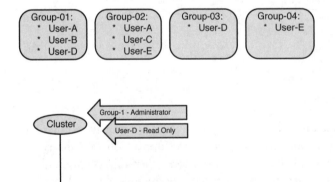

Figure 1-5 Permissions Scenario

In this scenario, the following effective permissions apply:

- User-A:
  - Can perform all tasks on the cluster object
  - Can perform all tasks on the host-01 object
  - Can only view the host-02 object
- User-B:
  - Can perform all tasks on the cluster object
  - Can perform all tasks on the host-01 object
  - Can perform all tasks on the host-02 object
- User-C:
  - Cannot view or perform any task on the cluster object
  - Can perform all tasks on the host-01 object
  - Can only view the host-02 object
- User-D:
  - Can only view the cluster object
  - Can only view the host-01 object
  - Cannot view or perform any task on the host-02 object
- User-E:
  - Cannot view or perform any task on the cluster object
  - Can perform all tasks on the host-01 object
  - Cannot view or perform any task on the host-02 object

Most entities that appear in the vCenter inventory are managed objects, whose access can be controlled using permissions. A few entities are considered to be global entities. You cannot modify permissions on global entities, which include:

- Custom fields
- Licenses
- Roles
- Statistics intervals
- Sessions

The global root object is used to assign permissions across solutions. The vCenter Server is an example of a solution, and it is attached as a child to the global root object in the hierarchy. The Content Library and Tag Category objects are also attached as children to the global root object. This means that user access to the Content Library is controlled by global permissions.

Global permissions are permissions that are applied to the global root object and span solutions. For example, a global permission can be applied to both vCenter Server and vCenter Orchestrator. Each solution has its own root object in the hierarchy, whose parent is the global root object. In some cases, you may assign a global permission and choose not to propagate to child objects. This may be useful for providing a global functionality, such as creating roles. To assign a global permission, you should use the vSphere Web Client with a user account that has the **Permission > Modify Permission** privilege on the root object of all inventory hierarchies. Select **Administration > Global Permissions > Manage** and use the Add Permission icon (green plus sign) dialog to select the desired user group (or user) and role, as described previously in this chapter.

NOTE By default, the administrator account in the SSO domain, such as `administrator@vsphere.local`, can modify global permissions, but the vCenter Server appliance `root` account cannot.

NOTE Be careful when applying a global permission. Decide if you truly want the permission to apply to all solutions and to all objects in all inventory hierarchies.

Create/Clone/Edit vCenter Server Roles

vCenter Server provides many roles out of the box. You cannot modify the vCenter Server System Roles, which are Administrator, Read Only, and No Access. You can modify the Sample Roles, but VMware recommends that you not modify these roles directly but instead clone the roles and modify the clones to suit your case.

NOTE Changes to roles take effect immediately, even for users who are currently logged into vCenter Server. One exception is with searches, where the change is not realized until the next time the user logs into vCenter Server.

To create a role in vCenter Server using the vSphere Web Client, you can use this procedure:

Step 1.   Click **Administration > Roles**.

Step 2. Click **Manage** > **Permissions**.

Step 3. Click the **Create Role Action** (+) button.

Step 4. Provide a name for the role.

Step 5. Select the desired privileges.

Step 6. Click **OK**.

After you create custom roles, you can assign the roles to permissions in the same manner as you assign the vCenter Server system roles and sample roles.

To clone a sample role or custom role in the vSphere Web Client, select the role at **Administration** > **Roles**, click the **Clone Role Action** icon, and provide a name for the new role. To edit a sample role or custom role in the vSphere Web Client, select the role at **Administration** > **Roles**, click the **Edit Role Action** icon, and modify the set of privileges in the role.

Much like vCenter Server, each ESXi Host uses role-based permission for users who log on directly to the ESXi Host rather than access the ESXi Host through vCenter Server. ESXi allows the creation of custom roles, but these roles are applied only when a user logs directly onto the host, such as when the user uses the vSphere Client to connect to the host directly. In most cases, managing roles and permissions at the host level should be avoided or minimized. To create roles on an ESXi Host, log onto the host directly using the vSphere Client (not the vSphere Web Client).

Configure VMware Directory Service

The VMware Directory Service (vmdir) is the component of SSO 6.0 that provides the SSO domain (directory service) that you create during the installation of SSO. The vmdir service is included on each Platform Services Controller (PSC), including each embedded vCenter Server deployment. It is a multi-tenanted, multi-mastered directory service that provides an LDAP directory on port 389. It also uses port 11711 for backward compatibility with vSphere 5.5.

In environments with multiple instances of PSC, updates to vmdir data in one instance are replicated to the other instances. Starting in vSphere 6.0, vmdir stores not only SSO data but certificate information as well.

If you decide to use a new VMCA root certificate and you un-publish the VMCA root certificate that was used initially, you must replace the machine certificates, the solution user certificates, and some internal services certificates. You must replace the SSL signing certificate that is used by SSO. You must also replace the VMware Directory Service (vmdir) certificate.

You can use the follow procedure to replace the VMware Directory Service certificate. Each step provides details for Linux-based deployments of SSO and Windows-based deployments of SSO.

Step 1. Stop vmdir:

Linux: `service-control --stop vmdird`

Windows: `service-control --stop VMWareDirectoryService`

Step 2. Copy the certificate and key to the vmdir location:

Linux:
```
cp vmdir.crt /usr/lib/vmware-vmdir/share/config/vmdircert.pem
cp vmdir.priv /usr/lib/vmware-vmdir/share/config/vmdirkey.pem
```

Windows:
```
copy vmdir.crt C:\programdata\vmware\vCenterServer\cfg\vmdird\
vmdircert.pem
copy vmdir.priv C:\programdata\vmware\vCenterServer\cfg\vmdird\
vmdirkey.pem
```

Step 3. Restart vmdir:

Linux: `service-control --start vmdird`

Windows: `service-control --start VMWareDirectoryService`

If vmdir replication is interrupted due to a broken link, it should resume once the root cause is fixed. Once the root cause is fixed, the nodes should begin replication and eventually reach a converged state, but this may take some time. Do not be concerned unless it does not reach its consistent state in an hour.

Apply a Role to a User/Group and to an Object or a Group of Objects

The section "Add/Modify/Remove Permissions for Users and Groups on vCenter Server Inventory Objects," earlier in this chapter, already explained how to set permissions that apply roles to users (and groups) on inventory objects. This section adds details for assigning permissions on containers such as folders and resource pools.

VMware recommends that instead of assigning identical permissions to similar objects, you should group objects into a folder. Folders can be used to organize many types of objects, such as virtual machines, ESXi Hosts, datastores, networks, datacenters, and clusters. A great use case for folders is to organize a set of objects into folders based on user access requirements and to assign permissions to the folders. For example, if your organization has a group of software developers who require the ability to access test and development virtual machines but cannot be allowed to access any other virtual machine, then you may decide to implement virtual machine folders. In this case, you could create a folder named Test and Dev, drag all the appropriate virtual machines into the folder, and assign permissions on the folder to provide the appropriate privileges.

NOTE   Folders can be used to set permissions on groups of datacenters, datastores, hosts, virtual machines, and networks but not on groups of vCenter Servers.

NOTE   As discussed previously, the permissions that an object inherits may come from multiple paths. For example, a virtual machine may inherit permissions from a virtual machine folder and from a resource pool. Be sure to examine all the permissions that apply to an object prior to deciding what changes to make to change a user's effective permissions.

Change Permission Validation Settings

Periodically, vCenter Server validates its user and group lists against the users and groups in the Windows Active Directory domain. It removes users and groups that no longer exist in the domain. You can change the behavior of this validation by using the vSphere Web Client to edit the general settings of the vCenter Server and change the **Validation** and **Validation Period** options. If you want to want to disable the validation, deselect the **Validation** > **Enabled** check box, shown in Figure 1-6. If you want to adjust the frequency at which this validation is performed, enter a value in the **Validation Period** text box to specify a time, in minutes, between validations.

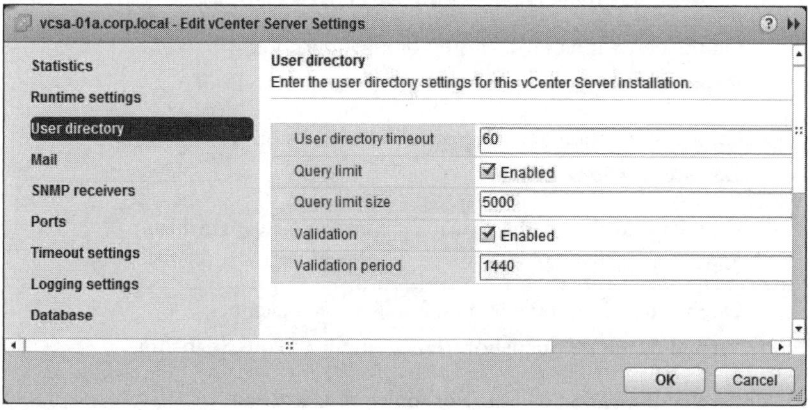

Figure 1-6   User Directory Validation Settings

Determine the Appropriate Set of Privileges for Common Tasks in vCenter Server

Table 1-2 provides the minimum permissions required for common tasks.

Table 1-2 Required Permissions for Common Tasks

Task	Required Privileges
Create a virtual machine	On the destination folder or datacenter: **Virtual Machine.Inventory.Raw Create New** **Virtual Machine.Configuration.Add New Disk** **Virtual Machine.Configuration.Add Existing Disk** **Virtual Machine.Configuration.Raw Device** On the destination host, cluster, or resource pool: **Resource. Assign Virtual Machine to Resource Pool** On the destination datastore or datastore folder: **Datastore.Allocate Space** On the network: **Network.Assign Network**
Deploy a virtual machine from a template	On the destination folder or datacenter: **Virtual Machine.Inventory.Create from Existing** **Virtual Machine.Configuration.Add New Disk** On a template or template folder: **Virtual Machine.Provisioning.Deploy Template** On the destination host, cluster, or resource pool: **Resource.Assign Virtual Machine to Resource Pool** On the destination datastore or folder of datastores: **Datastore.Allocate Space** On the network that the virtual machine will be assigned to: **Network.Assign Network**
Take a virtual machine snapshot	On the virtual machine or a folder of virtual machines: **Virtual Machine.Snapshot Management.Create Snapshot** On the destination datastore or folder of datastores: **Datastore.Allocate Space**

Task	Required Privileges
Move a virtual machine into a resource pool	On the virtual machine or folder of virtual machines: **Resource.Assign Virtual Machine to Resource Pool** **Virtual Machine.Inventory.Move** On the destination resource pool: **Resource.Assign Virtual Machine to Resource Pool**
Install a guest operating system on a virtual machine	On the virtual machine or folder of virtual machines: **Virtual Machine.Interaction.Answer Question** **Virtual Machine.Interaction.Console Interaction** **Virtual Machine.Interaction.Device Connection** **Virtual Machine.Interaction.Power Off** **Virtual Machine.Interaction.Power On** **Virtual Machine.Interaction.Reset** **Virtual Machine.Interaction.Configure CD Media** **Virtual Machine.Interaction.Configure Floppy Media** **Virtual Machine.Interaction.Tools Install** On a datastore containing the installation media ISO image: **Datastore.Browse Datastore** On the datastore to which you upload the installation media ISO image: **Datastore.Browse Datastore** **Datastore.Low Level File Operations**
Migrate a virtual machine with vMotion	On the virtual machine or folder of virtual machines: **Resource.Migrate Powered on Virtual Machine** **Resource.Assign Virtual Machine to Resource Pool** On the destination host, cluster, or resource pool: **Resource.Assign Virtual Machine to Resource Pool**
Cold migrate (relocate) a virtual machine	On the virtual machine or folder of virtual machines: **Resource.Migrate Powered Off Virtual Machine** **Resource.Assign Virtual Machine to Resource Pool** On the destination host, cluster, or resource pool: **Resource.Assign Virtual Machine to Resource Pool** On the destination datastore: **Datastore.Allocate Space**

Task	Required Privileges
Migrate a virtual machine with Storage vMotion	On the virtual machine or folder of virtual machines: **Resource.Migrate Powered On Virtual Machine** On the destination datastore: **Datastore.Allocate Space**
Move a host into a cluster	On the host: **Host.Inventory.Add Host to Cluster** On the destination cluster: **Host.Inventory.Add Host to Cluster**

For more details, such as the predefined vCenter Server roles that best fit each of these tasks, see the "Required Privileges for Common Tasks" sections in the *vSphere Security (ESXi 6.0/vCenter Server 6.0)* guide.

Compare and Contrast Default System/Sample Roles

VMware vCenter Server 6.0 provides system roles and sample roles out of the box.

The system roles cannot be modified. System roles are organized as a hierarchy, where each role inherits privileges from another role. For example, the Administrator role inherits privileges from the Read Only role. The system roles are:

- **Administrator:** Allows full control of the associated objects.

- **Read Only:** Allows the user to only view information on the associated objects.

- **No Access:** Prevents the user from viewing or accessing the associated objects in any manner.

The sample roles are intended to be examples of roles, which may be handy in some environments for assigning permissions to perform common tasks. Instead of using these roles directly, you could clone a sample role and customize the cloned role to suit your needs. The default sample roles are:

- Resource Pool Administrator (sample)

- Virtual Machine User (sample)

- VMware Consolidated Backup User (sample)

- Datastore Consumer (sample)

- Network Administrator (sample)

- Virtual Machine Power User (sample)

- Content Library Administrator (sample)

New roles in vSphere 6.0 are Tagging Admin and Content Library Administrator (sample). Although the Tagging Admin role does not contain *sample* in its name, it appears to be a sample role because it can be edited. The Tagging Admin role includes only a few privileges, all of which reside in the Inventory Service > vSphere Tagging category, but it does not include all the privileges in this category. It does not include privileges related to managing the tagging scope. Likewise, the Content Library Administrator role contains only privileges in the Content Library category but does not include all the privileges in the category.

To get familiar with the privileges in a sample role, edit the role and explore the privileges that are included in the role. For example, if you edit the VMware Consolidated Backup User role, you see that it only includes some privileges in the Virtual Machine category and no other privileges. Specifically, it includes only these privileges:

- Virtual Machine > Configuration > Disk Lease

- Virtual Machine > Provisioning > Allow Read-Only Disk Access

- Virtual Machine > Provisioning > Allow Virtual Machine Download

- Virtual Machine > Snapshot Management > Create Snapshot

- Virtual Machine > Snapshot Management > Remove Snapshot

Determine the Correct Permissions Needed to Integrate vCenter Server with Other VMware Products

Each unique VMware product may have unique permission requirements for vCenter Server integration. Here are some examples:

- **vCenter Orchestrator:** Log into the vSphere Web Client as a user who has at least View and Execute permissions in Orchestrator. The user must also have permission to manage vCenter Server objects.

- **Horizon View:** Create a role that contains at least the following privileges. When creating the role, navigate into each category as indicated here by an arrow (>) and locate and select the underlying privilege:

    - Folder >

        - Create Folder

        - Delete Folder

- Datastore >
  - Allocate Space
- Virtual Machine >
  - Configuration >
    - Add or Remove Device
    - Advanced
    - Modify Device Settings
- Interaction >
  - Power Off
  - Power On
  - Reset
  - Suspend
- Inventory >
  - Create New
  - Create from Existing
  - Remove
- Provisioning
- Customize >
  - Deploy Template
  - Read Customization Specifications
- Resource >
  - Assign Virtual Machine to Resource Pool
- Global >
  - Act as vCenter Server
- Host
  - Configuration
  - Advanced Settings

- **vRealize Operations:** When you install vRealize Operations Manager and register a vCenter Server, new privileges are automatically added to vCenter Server and are available for use. The only existing vCenter Server role that is automatically modified to include the vRealize Operations privileges is the Administrator role. You can modify or create other roles to include privileges from vRealize Operations Manager.

Objective 1.2—Secure ESXi, vCenter Server, and vSphere Virtual Machines

This section describes how to harden components in vSphere including the ESXi Hosts, vCenter Server, and virtual machines.

Harden Virtual Machine Access

To harden a virtual machine, you should control the VMware Tools installation, control virtual machine access, and configure virtual machine security policies. Here are some virtual machine security best practices:

- **General protection:** In most respects, treat the virtual machine as you would a physical server when it comes to applying security measures. For example, be sure to install guest operating systems patches, protect with antivirus software, and disable unused serial ports.

- **Templates:** Carefully harden the first virtual machine deployment of each guest OS and verify hardening completeness. Convert the virtual machine into a template and use the template to deploy virtual machines as needed.

- **Virtual machine console:** Minimize the use of this console. Use it only when required. Use remote tools, such as SSH and Remote Desktop, to access virtual machines. Consider limiting the number of console connections to just one.

- **Virtual machine resource usage:** Prevent virtual machines from taking over resources on the ESXi Host to minimize the risk of denial of service to other virtual machines. Configure each virtual machine with sufficient virtual hardware but not much more virtual hardware resources than needed. For example, configure each virtual machine with sufficient virtual memory to handle its workload and meet application vendor recommendations but do provide much more memory than you expect it will need. Consider setting reservations or shares to ensure that critical virtual machines have access to a sufficient amount of CPU and memory.

- **Disable unnecessary services:** Disable or uninstall any function for the guest OS that is not required to reduce the number of components that can be attacked and to reduce its resource demand. For example, turn off screen savers, disable unneeded guest operating system services, and disconnect the CD/DVD drive.

Control VMware Tools Installation

After upgrading an environment to vSphere 6.0, you should consider upgrading virtual machines. The first step in upgrading virtual machines is to upgrade VMware Tools to the most recent version that is compatible with the ESXi Host. VMware provides two methods for upgrading virtual machines. One is to use the vSphere Web Client. The other is to user VMware Update Manager.

NOTE   Do not use `vmware-vmupgrade.exe` to upgrade virtual machines.

When using the vSphere Web Client method, you could manually upgrade each virtual machine, one by one, as needed. To install a VMware Tools upgrade, you can use the same procedure that you initially used to install VMware Tools. Upgrading VMware Tools actually installs a new version. To manually upgrade a set of virtual machines, you can select an ESXi Host or cluster in the inventory, use the **Related Objects** > **Virtual Machines** tab to select a set of virtual machines, and choose **Guest OS** > **Install/Upgrade VMware Tools** in the **Actions** menu.

Alternatively, you can configure virtual machines to automatically check and install newer versions of VMware Tools, as needed. As each virtual machine is started, the guest operating system checks the version of VMware Tools. The virtual machine status in the vSphere Web Client displays a message when a new version is available.

In Windows virtual machines, you can set VMware Tools to notify the Windows user when an upgrade is available by placing a yellow caution icon with the VMware Tools icon in the Windows taskbar.

For Windows and Linux guest operating systems, you can configure the virtual machine to automatically upgrade VMware Tools. Although the version check is performed when you power on the virtual machine, on Windows guest operating systems, the automatic upgrade occurs when you power off or restart the virtual machine. The status bar displays the message `Installing VMware Tools` when an upgrade is in progress.

For Linux guest operating systems, when you upgrade VMware Tools, new network modules are available but not used until you restart the virtual machine or reload the associated networking kernel modules. This approach avoids network interruptions and allows you to install VMware Tools over SSH, but it limits the benefit of auto-matically upgrading VMware Tools without restarting the virtual machine.

Using VMware Update Manager, you can perform an orchestrated upgrade of vir-tual machines at the folder or datacenter level. For details, see Chapter 7, "Upgrade a vSphere Deployment to 6.x."

The Default VM Compatibility settings can be set on the cluster. In Figure 1-7, the Default VM Compatibility setting is **Use Datacenter Setting and Host Version**, so it is impacted by the associated datacenter setting and ESXi Host version.

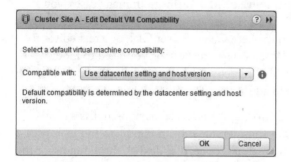

Figure 1-7   Edit the Default VM Compatibility

Alternatively, you could specify a particular version for the cluster, such as ESXi 5.5 and later. The virtual machine compatibility options are identified in Table 1-3, including the maximum number of virtual CPU cores and the maximum amount of memory that each one supports.

Table 1-3   Virtual Machine Compatibility Options

Compatibility	Description	Maximum Virtual Cores	Maximum Memory (GB)
ESXi 6.0 and later	This virtual machine (hardware version 11) is compatible with ESXi 6.0 and later.	128	4080
ESXi 5.5 and later	This virtual machine (hardware version 10) is compatible with ESXi 5.5 and later.	64	1011
ESXi 5.1 and later	This virtual machine (hardware version 9) is compatible with ESXi 5.1 and later.	64	1011
ESXi 5.0 and later	This virtual machine (hardware version 8) is compatible with ESXi 5.0 and 5.1.	32	1011
ESX/ESXi 4.0 and later	This virtual machine (hardware version 7) is compatible with ESX/ESXi 4.x, ESXi 5.0, and ESXi 5.1.	8	255

Compatibility	Description	Maximum Virtual Cores	Maximum Memory (GB)
ESX/ESXi 3.5 and later	This virtual machine (hardware version 4) is compatible with ESX/ESX 3.5, ESX/ESX 4.x, and ESXi 5.1. It is also compatible with VMware Server 1.0 and later. You cannot create a virtual machine with ESX/ESXi 3.5 compatibility on ESXi 5.0.	4	64

Virtual machines provide settings that impact VMware Tools. In many cases, you should change a virtual machine's VMware Tools settings to provide better security. You can use the vSphere Web Client, vSphere Client Power CLI, or a text editor to change the VMware Tools settings. When using a text editor, you need to modify the virtual machine configuration file (VMX) directly. Changes to the following VMware Tools settings should be considered to address specific potential security threats:

- **Disk shrinking:** Because disk shrinking, which reclaims unused disk space from a virtual machine, can take considerable time to complete and its invocation can result in a temporary denial of service, disable disk shrinking using the following lines in the VMX file:

```
isolation.tools.diskWiper.disable = "TRUE"
isolation.tools.diskShrink.disable = "TRUE"
```

- **Copy and paste:** This ability is disabled by default in new virtual machines. In most cases, retain this default setting to ensure that one user of the virtual machine console cannot paste data that was originally copied from a previous user. Ensure that the following lines remain in the VMX files:

```
isolation.tools.copy.disable = "TRUE"
isolation.tools.paste.disable = "TRUE"
```

- **Connecting devices:** By default, the ability to connect and disconnect devices is disabled. One reason for this is to prevent one user from accessing a sensitive CD-ROM that was left in the drive. Another reason is to prevent users from disconnecting the network adapter, which could produce a denial of service. Ensure that the following lines remain in the VMX file:

```
isolation.device.connectable.disable = "TRUE"
isolation.device.edit.disable = "TRUE"
```

- **Logging:** Uncontrolled virtual machine logging could lead to denial of service if the associated datastore runs out of disk space. VMware recommends keeping 10 log files. To set this on a virtual machine, set the following in the VMX file:

```
vmx.log.keepOld = "10"
```

Alternatively, to limit the number of log files for virtual machines on an ESXi Host, add the previous line to the host's `/etc/vmware/config` file. A more aggressive measure is to disable virtual machine logging with the following statement in the VMX file:

```
logging = "FALSE"
```

- **VMX file size:** By default, the size of each VMX file is 1 MB because uncontrolled file sizes can lead to a denial of service if the datastore runs out of disk space. Occasionally, `setinfo` messages that define virtual machine characteristics or identifiers are sent as name/value pairs from the virtual machine to the VMX file. If needed, you can increase the size of the VMX file limit by using the following statement in the VMX file but replacing the numeric value with a larger value:

```
tools.setInfo.sizeLimit = "1048576"
```

In most cases, though, keep the default setting as a security measure.

- **Performance counters:** VMware Tools provides performance counters on CPU and memory from the ESXi Host into the virtual machine for use by PerfMon. This feature is disabled by default because an adversary could potentially make use of this information to attack the host. Ensure that the following line remains in the VMX files to block some, but not all, performance metrics:

```
tools.guestlib.enableHostInfo = "FALSE"
```

- **Unexposed vSphere features:** Because VMware Tools is used in many VMware products, not just vSphere, the VMX file may contain parameters that do not apply in a vSphere environment. To secure the virtual machine and reduce the number of vectors through which a guest operating system could access an ESXi Host, implement the following lines in the VMX file:

```
isolation.tools.unity.push.update.disable = "TRUE"
isolation.tools.ghi.launchmenu.change = "TRUE"
isolation.tools.ghi.autologon.disable = "TRUE"
isolation.tools.hgfsServerSet.disable = "TRUE"
isolation.tools.memSchedFakeSampleStats.disable = "TRUE"
isolation.tools.getCreds.disable = "TRUE"
```

Control VM Data Access

The best practices stated at the beginning of this section, the VMware Tools settings in the previous section, and the risk profiles in the next section can all be applied to control virtual machine data access.

Configure Virtual Machine Security Policies

VMware's vSphere 6.0 Hardening Guide provides guidelines for address vulnerabilities based on risk profiles. When you can apply the hardening guide to your environment, the first step is to apply the appropriate risk profile based on the sensitivity of your environment and data. The hardening guide offers three risk profiles:

- **Risk Profile 1:** Intended to be implemented in just the most secure environments, such as top-secret government environments.

- **Risk Profile 2:** Intended to be implemented in sensitive environments to protect sensitive data such as data that must adhere to strict compliance rules.

- **Risk Profile 3:** Intended to be implemented in all production environments.

For example, Table 1-4 contains the Risk Profile 3 guidelines from the hardening guide that directly impact virtual machines. Many of these guidelines are associated with the VMware Tools Configuration Parameters discussed previously in this chapter.

Table 1-4   Risk Profile 3 Virtual Machine Guidelines

Guideline	Configuration Parameter
VM.disable-console-copy	isolation.tools.copy.disable
VM.disable-console-drag-n-drop	isolation.tools.dnd.disable
VM.disable-console-gui-options	isolation.tools.setGUIOptions.enable
VM.disable-console-paste	isolation.tools.paste.disable
VM.disable-disk-shrinking-shrink	isolation.tools.diskShrink.disable
VM.disable-disk-shrinking-wiper	isolation.tools.diskWiper.disable
VM.limit-setinfo-size	tools.setInfo.sizeLimit
VM.minimize-console-VNC-use	RemoteDisplay.vnc.enabled
VM.prevent-device-interaction-connect	isolation.device.connectable.disable
VM.prevent-device-interaction-edit	isolation.device.edit.disable
VM.TransparentPageSharing-inter-VM-Enabled	sched.mem.pshare.salt
VM.verify-network-filter	ethernetn.filtern.name = filtername

For more details, see the vSphere 6.0 Hardening Guide.

Harden a Virtual Machine Against Denial-of-Service Attacks

The vCenter Server and its related components involve many services. One of these services is the vCenter Server Service, which can be managed using the native operating system. For example, a Windows-based vCenter Server Service can be stopped and restarted by using the Services Management Console from within Windows.

Control VM–VM Communications

Virtual Machine Communication Interface (VMCI) is a high-speed communication mechanism for virtual machine—to–ESXi Host communication. In some VMware products, including ESXi 4.x, VMCI also provides high-speed communication between virtual machines on the same ESXi Host. In ESXi 5.1, the guest-to-guest VMCI is removed. In a VMX file, the `vmci0.unrestricted` parameter is used to control VMCI isolation for virtual machines running on ESX/ESXi 4.x and ESXi 5.0 but has no effect on virtual machines running on ESXi 5.1 and later.

Control VM Device Connections

As discussed previously in this chapter, the ability to connect and disconnect devices is disabled by default for new virtual machines. In most cases, you should not change this behavior. You should verify that the following settings exist in your VMX files, especially if the virtual machines were deployed from a non-hardened template or were originally built on older ESXi Hosts:

```
isolation.device.connectable.disable = "TRUE"
isolation.device.edit.disable = "TRUE"
```

If these parameters are set to FALSE, then in a guest operating system, all users and processes, with or without root or administrator privileges, could use VMware Tools to change device connectivity and settings. They could connect or disconnect devices, such as network adapters and CD-ROM drives. They could modify device settings. This functionality could allow them to connect a CD-ROM with sensitive data. It could allow them to disconnect a network adapter, which could cause denial of service to other users.

Configure Network Security Policies

You should connect virtual machines to a standard virtual switch port group or distributed virtual switch port group that is configured with an appropriate security policy. The network security policy provides three options, which may be set to Reject or Accept, as described in Table 1-5.

Table 1-5   Network Security Policies

Guideline	Setting	Description
Promiscuous mode	Accept	The virtual switch forwards all frames to the virtual network adapter in compliance with the associated VLAN policy
	Reject	The virtual switch forwards only the frames that are addressed to the virtual network adapter.
MAC address changes	Accept	If the guest operating system changes the effective MAC address of the virtual adapter to a value that differs from the MAC address assigned to the adapter in the VMX file, the virtual switch allows the inbound frame to pass.
	Reject	If the guest operating system changes the effective MAC address of the virtual adapter to a value that differs from the MAC address assigned to the adapter in the VMX file, the virtual switch drops all inbound frames to the adapter. If the guest OS changes the MAC address back to its original value, the virtual switch stops dropping the frames and allows inbound traffic to the adapter.
Forged transmits	Accept	The virtual switch does not filter outbound frames. It permits all outbound frames, regardless of source MAC address.
	Reject	The virtual switch drops any outbound frame from a virtual machine virtual adapter that uses a source MAC address that differs from the MAC address assigned to the virtual adapter in the VMX file.

On a distributed virtual switch, you can override the security policy per virtual port.

Harden ESXi Hosts

To harden an ESXi Host, you should consider disabling some services, changing the default user access, implementing directory services, using host profiles, enabling lockdown, and controlling host access.

Enable/Configure/Disable Services in the ESXi Firewall

Several optional services that are provided in an ESXi Host are disabled by default. VMware disables these services in an effort to provide strong security out of the box. In some circumstances, you may wish to configure and enable these services. A good example of an optional service that you may decide to configure and enable in most environments is NTP because solid time synchronization is vital for many services. An example of a service that you may want to configure and enable temporarily for troubleshooting is Secure Shell (SSH). You can edit the security profile of an ESXi Host to enable, disable, and configure the services that it provides.

The ESXi software firewall is enabled by default. It should never be disabled while the ESXi host is running production virtual machines. In rare cases, such as with a temporary troubleshooting measure, you can disable the ESXi firewall using the `esxcli network firewall set --enabled false` command.

By default, the ESXi firewall is configured to block incoming and outgoing traffic, except traffic for services that are enabled in the host's security profile. Prior to opening any ports on the firewall, you should consider the impact that doing so might have for potential attacks and unauthorized user access. You can reduce this risk by configuring the firewall to only allow communication on the port with authorized networks. To modify the firewall's rule set, use the vSphere Web Client and follow this procedure:

Step 1.   Select the ESXi Host in the inventory and click **Manage** > **Settings**.

Step 2.   Click **Security Profile**.

Step 3.   In the Firewall section, click **Edit**.

Step 4.   Examine the rule set. Change the state of any rule by selecting the rule (placing a check in the rule's box) to enable the rule or deselect the rule to disable it.

Step 5.   Optionally, uncheck the **Allow Connections from Any IP Address** box and enter specific IP addresses in the accompanying text box to restrict use to only those IP addresses, as illustrated in Figure 1-8.

Step 6.   Click **OK**.

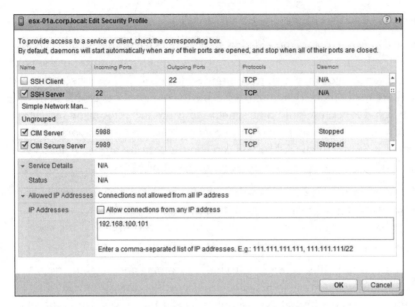

Figure 1-8   Restrict IP Addresses for a Firewall Rule

You can also use a security profile to modify the settings for the associated services:

Step 1.   Select the ESXi Host in the inventory and click **Manage** > **Settings**.

Step 2.   Click **Security Profile**.

Step 3.   In the Services section, click **Edit**.

Step 4.   Examine the set of services. Select a service that you wish to modify and use its Service Details pane to make changes. Click the **Start, Stop**, or **Restart** button to immediately change the state of the service.

Step 5.   Use the **Startup Policy** menu to change the status permanently. You can choose from the following options:

- **Start Automatically if Any Ports Are Open and Stop When All Ports Are Closed:** This is the default setting for the defined services. If at least one of the associated ports is open, the service starts, but it might fail if at least one associated port is closed. If all associated ports are closed, the service stops.

- **Start and Stop with Host:** The service starts automatically each time the host starts. The service stops automatically each time a host shutdown begins.

- **Start and Stop Manually:** The service does not start automatically when the host starts or when ports are opened. It does not stop automatically when ports are closed. But it does shut down automatically each time a host shutdown begins.

Step 6. Click **OK**.

Table 1-6 lists the can be impacted by the currently installed vSphere Installation Bundles (VIBs).

Table 1-6 Typical ESXi Firewall Services and Ports

Firewall Service	Incoming Port(s)	Outgoing Port(s)
CIM Server	5988 (TCP)	
CIM Secure Server	5989 (TCP)	
CIM SLP	427 (TCP, UDP)	427 (TCP, UDP)
DHCPv6	546 (TCP, UDP)	547 (TCP, UDP)
DVSSync	8301, 8302 (UDP)	8301, 8302 (UDP)
HBR		44046, 31031 (TCP)
NFC	902 (TCP)	902 (TCP)
WOL		9 (UDP)
Virtual SAN Clustering Service	12345, 23451 (UDP)	12345, 23451 (UDP)
DCHP Client	68 (UDP)	68 (UDP)
DNS Client	53 (UDP)	53 (TCP, UDP)
Fault Tolerance	8100, 8200, 8300 (TCP, UDP)	8100, 8200, 8300 (TCP, UDP)
NSX Distributed Logical Router Service	6999 (UDP)	6999 (UDP)
rabbitmqproxy		5671 (TCP)
Virtual SAN Transport	2233 (TCP)	2233 (TCP)
SNMP Server	161 (UDP)	
SSH Server	22 (TCP)	
vMotion	8000 (TCP)	8000 (TCP)
VMware vCenter Agent		902 (UDP)
vSphere Web Client	902, 443 (TCP)	
vsanvp	8080 (TCP)	8080 (TCP)

Change Default Account Access

One step involved in hardening an ESXi Host is to harden the password required to use its predefined local administrator account, which is called `root`. By default, the ESXi Host enforces passwords for its local user accounts, which may be used to access the host via the Direct Console User Interface (DCUI), the ESXi Shell, Secure Shell (SSH), or the vSphere Client. Starting with ESXi 6.0, the default password policy must contain characters from at least three character classes (from the four character classes lowercase letters, uppercase letters, numbers, and special characters) and must be at least seven characters long.

> **NOTE**   An uppercase character that begins a password and a number that ends a password do not count toward the number of used character classes. The password cannot contain a dictionary word or part of a dictionary word.

For example, `xQaT3!A` is an acceptable password because it contains 4 character classes and 7 characters. But, `Xqate!3` is not an acceptable password because it contains only 2 character classes (the leading `x` and ending `3` do not count toward the number of used character classes).

You can modify the ESXi password requirements by using the ESXi Host `Security.PasswordQualityControl` advanced option. You can also use `Security.PasswordQualityControl` to configure the ESXi Host to accept passphrases, which it does not accept by default. The key to changing the password and passphrase requirements is understanding the syntax and functionality of the `Security.PasswordQualityControl` parameter, whose default value is:

```
retry=3 min=disabled,disabled,disabled,7,7
```

The first part of the value used for this parameter identifies the number of retries allowed for the user following a failed logon attempt. In the default value, `retry=3` indicates that three additional attempts are permitted following a failed logon. The remainder of the value can be abstracted as:

```
min=N0,N1,N2,N3,N4
```

where:

- `N0` is the minimum number of accepted characters for passwords that contain characters from only one class or `disabled` to disallow passwords that contain characters from only one class.

- `N1` is the minimum number of accepted characters for passwords that contain characters from only two classes or `disabled` to disallow passwords that contain characters from only two classes.

- N2 is the minimum number of accepted characters for passphrases or `dis-abled` to disallow passphrases. In addition, to require a passphrase, append `passphrase=N` to the end of the value, where N specifies the minimum number of words, separated by spaces, in the passphrase.

- N3 is the minimum number of accepted characters for passwords that contain characters from only three classes or `disabled` to disallow passwords that contain characters from only three classes.

- N4 is the minimum number of accepted characters for passwords that contain characters from all four classes.

For example, to require a passphrase with a minimum of 16 characters and 3 words, set the `Security.PasswordQualityControl` to:

```
retry=3 min=disabled,disabled,16,7,7,passphrase=3
```

The password requirements in ESXi 6.0 are implemented by `pam_passwdqc`. For more details, see the man pages for `pam_passwdqc`.

Add an ESXi Host to a Directory Service

You can add an ESXi Host to a directory service, such as Active Directory, and configure permissions to allow the associated users to connect directly to the ESXi host using DCUI, ESXi Shell, SSH, or the vSphere Client. The main reason for this is to reduce the number of local ESXi user accounts that you have to create and manage. Another reason is to provide people with the means to access ESXi directly with user accounts that are already used for other purposes and are already hardened.

To configure an ESXi Host to use Active Directory, you can use these steps:

Step 1. Verify that an Active Directory domain is available.

Step 2. Ensure that the hostname of the ESXi Host is fully qualified with the domain name that matches the domain name of the Active Directory forest. For example, if the Active Directory domain name is `mydomain.com` and the ESXi Host hostname is `Host-01`, then the host fully qualified name is `Host-01.domain.com`.

Step 3. Synchronize time between the ESXi Host and domain controllers using NTP. For details, see VMware KB 1035833.

Step 4. Ensure that the DNS servers that are configured for the ESXi Host can resolve the hostnames of the Active Directory domain controllers.

Step 5. In the vSphere Web Client, select the ESXi Host and select **Authentication Services** on the **Manage** > **Settings**.

Step 6.   Click the **Join Domain** button.

Step 7.   In the dialog box, specify the domain and user credentials. Optionally, specify a proxy server.

Step 8.   Enter a domain, either in the form `name.tld` or `name.tld/container/path`, where `name.tld` is the domain name and `/container/path` is an optional path to an organization unit, where the host computer object should be created. For example, you can use `domain.com/ou01/ou02.` to add the host to an organization unit named `ou02` that resides in an organization unit named ou01 in a domain named `domain.com`.

Step 9.   Click **OK**.

Apply Permissions to ESXi Hosts Using Host Profiles

You can use host profiles to apply ESXi Host permissions to be used when users access the host directly. To configure a host profile with the appropriate permissions, you can use the vSphere Client (not the vSphere Web Client) and follow this procedure:

Step 1.   Select **View > Management > Host Profiles**.

Step 2.   Select an existing profile and click **Edit Profile**.

Step 3.   In the profile tree, locate and expand **Security Configuration**.

Step 4.   Right-click on the **Permission Rules** folder and click **Add Profile**.

Step 5.   Expand **Permissions Rules** and **select Permission**.

Step 6.   On the **Configuration Details** tab, click the **Configure Permission** drop-down menu and select **Require a Permission Rule**.

Step 7.   Enter the name of a user or group. Use the format `domain\name`, where `domain` is the domain name and `name` is the user or group name.

Step 8.   If a group name is used, select the **Name Refers to a Group of Users** check box.

Step 9.   Enter the assigned role name, which is case sensitive. This can be the name of a built-in role on the host or a custom role that you created on the host. For system roles, use the non-localized role name, such as `Admin` for the Administrator role or `ReadOnly` for the Read Only role.

Step 10.   Optionally, select **Propagate Permission**.

Step 11.   Click **OK**.

After configuring the host profile, you can use it to apply the permissions to new or existing ESXi Hosts, as described in Chapter 14, "Deploy and Consolidate."

Enable Lockdown Mode

ESXi 6.0 provides different levels of lockdown and introduces the Exception Users list. In strict lockdown, the DCUI is disabled, and no one can use it. In normal lockdown, some users can use the DCUI. Exception Users, who are administrators and users who are identified in the DCUI.Access advanced system setting, can access the DCUI.

Exception Users, who have administrator privileges, can use the ESXi Shell or SSH, if these services are enabled, even if the host is placed in strict or normal lockdown mode. For all other users, ESXi Shell or SSH access is disallowed when a host is in strict or normal lockdown mode. Starting with vSphere 6.0, ESXi or SSH sessions for users who do not have administrator privileges are terminated when lockdown mode is enabled.

To enable lockdown mode, use the vSphere Web Client and follow this procedure:

Step 1.   In the inventory pane, select the ESXi Host.

Step 2.   In the middle pane, select **Manage** > **Settings** > **Security Profile**.

Step 3.   In the **Lockdown Mode** panel, click the Edit button.

Step 4.   Click Lockdown Mode and choose either **Normal** or **Strict**.

Step 5.   Click **OK**.

To disable lockdown mode, repeat this procedure but choose **Disabled** for the lockdown mode in step 4.

NOTE   In vSphere 5.0 and earlier, only the root account can log into the DCUI on an ESXi Host that is in lockdown mode.

In vSphere 5.1 and later, you can add a user to the DCUI.Access advanced system setting to grant the user access to the DCUI on a host that is in lockdown mode, even if the user is not granted the Administrator role on the host. The main purpose of this feature is to prepare for catastrophic failures of vCenter Server.

vSphere 6.0 also includes an Exception Users list, whose main purpose is to support the use of lockdown mode, but still support service accounts, which must log on directly to the ESXi Host. User accounts in the Exception Users list, who have administrator privileges can log onto the DCUI and ESXi Shell.

By default, the `root` account is included in `DCUI.Access`. You could consider removing the `root` account from `DCUI.Access` and replacing it with another account for better auditability.

Control Access to Hosts (DCUI/Shell/SSH/MOB)

In addition to using lockdown mode, `Exception Users`, and `DCUI.Access`, as described in the previous section, you can use other mechanisms to control direct access to ESXi Hosts.

The `dcui` user acts as an agent for the direct console and cannot be used by interactive users. It acts as a user with Administrator rights and cannot be modified. Its primary purpose is to configure hosts for lockdown mode from the DCUI.

You can configure smart card authentication for DCUI using these steps:

Step 1. Ensure that you have the necessary infrastructure to handle smart card authentication, such as Active Directory user accounts, smart card readers, and smart cards.

Step 2. Configure the ESXi Host to join an Active Directory domain that supports smart card authentication.

Step 3. Use the vSphere Web Client authentication services to enable smart card authentication for the host and to add root certificates.

When Active Directory is unavailable, the authentication reverts to username and password authentication until Active Directory is available. You can switch to username and password authentication from the DCUI by pressing F3. The chip on the smart card locks after a few consecutive incorrect PIN entries (usually three). When a smart card is locked, only selected personnel can unlock it,

To prevent intruders from using an idle session, set the ESXi Shell Timeouts. For the ESXi Shell, you can set two timeouts, the Availability Timeout and the Idle Timeout. The Availability Timeout is used to set the amount of time that can elapse before someone must log in after the ESXi Shell is enabled. If the allowed time expires prior to a login, the service is disabled. The Idle Timeout is used to set the amount of time that can elapse before a user of an idle session is logged out of the interactive session. Changes to the Idle Timeout do not apply to existing sessions but do apply to each interactive session the next time a user logs into the ESXi Shell. These timeouts can be set from the vSphere Web Client and from the DCUI.

As described previously in this section, you can use the vSphere Web Client to manage the SSH, ESXi Shell, and DCUI services. For example, you can start and stop these services, and you can enable and disable related ports in the ESXi firewall.

The Managed Object Browser (MOB), which is a tool that can be used to explore the VMkernel object model, could be exploited by attackers. Starting in vSphere 6.0, the MOB is disabled by default. You may need to enable the MOB, at least temporarily, to perform certain tasks, such as extracting an old certificate from a host. You can use the vSphere Web Client to enable or disable the `Config.HostAgent.plugins.solo.enableMob` advanced system setting.

You can configure authorized keys to enable access to an ESXi Host through SSH without requiring user authentication. This functionality is useful for running unattended remote scripts, but it should be used with care. One step in permitting the use of authorized keys is to store one or more keys in `/etc/ssh/keys-username/authorized_keys`. To increase the ESXi Host hardening, ensure that the file is empty, which prevents users from accessing the host using authorized keys instead of user authentication. For more details, see VMware KB 1002866.

By default, the `root` account cannot access the ESXi Host via SSH. To enable `root` access via SSH, change the `PermitRootLogin no` statement in the `/etc/ssh/sshd_config` file to `PermitRootLogin yes`.

Harden vCenter Server

To harden a vCenter Server, you should consider controlling datastore browser access, managing the security certificates, controlling MOB access, changing default account access, and restricting administrative privileges.

Control Datastore Browser Access

Assign the **Datastore.Browser** datastore privilege only to users and user groups who truly require the privilege.

Create/Manage vCenter Server Security Certificates

You can use the vSphere Certificate Manager utility to replace certificates with custom certificates. To begin, use the Certificate Manager utility to create the Certificate Signing Requests (CSRs) that you need to send to your trusted Certificate Authority (CA). You could choose to replace only the machine SSL certificates and use the solution user certificates that are provisioned by the VMware Certificate Authority (VMCA). Solution user certificates are used only for communication between vSphere components. When using custom certificates, you must replace the VMCA-signed certificates that are provisioned by VMCA on each node with custom certificates. You can use the vSphere Certificate Manager utility or command-line interface to replace the certificates. Certificates are stored in the VMware Endpoint Certificate Store (VECS).

Control MOB Access

The vCenter Server MOB provides a means to explore the vCenter Server object model. Its primary use is for debugging. It provides the ability to make some configuration changes, so it may be considered a vulnerability for malicious attacks. As a step in hardening the vCenter Server, you can disable the MOB by setting the `enableDebugBrowse` parameter to `FALSE` in the `vpxd.cfg` file. You can use the vSphere Web Client to examine the value of `config.vpxd.enableDebugBrowe` to determine whether it is `FALSE`, but the setting is read-only in the vSphere Web Client. After making the change to the `vpxd.cfg` file, restart the vCenter Server.

Change Default Account Access

When you install vCenter Server 5.1 and later, you must specify the initial vCenter Server administrator user or group. For deployments where vCenter Server and Single Sign-On are deployed on the same server, you can identify a local operating system group as the initial administrator group. For example, on a Windows deployment, you can set the local Windows `Administrators` group as the initial administrator group. After the installation, you can change the default permissions in vCenter Server to assign the Administrator role to at least one other user account or group and then delete the default permission.

In situations where an external Platform Services Controller (PSC) is used, local operating system accounts cannot be used. Instead, you should assign the Administrator role to user groups provided by SSO identity sources, such as the SSO domain (such as `vsphere.local`), an Active Directory domain, or an OpenLDAP domain.

Restrict Administrative Privileges

As mentioned in the previous paragraphs, you can use permissions to assign the Administrator role to specific users and groups in vCenter Server. You should restrict the assignment of the Administrator role to just those users and groups who truly require it. You should use roles with only necessary privileges when creating permissions. In other words, you should apply the principle of least privileges when configuring permissions in vCenter Server.

Understand the Implications of Securing a vSphere Environment

Each of the settings discussed previously in this chapter has implications, most of which have been discussed here. Generally speaking, the implication of each setting is that the environment is more secure, but some additional steps may be involved. For example, in small environments, administrators may enjoy the simplicity of sharing the use of the vCenter Server Appliance `root` account to manage the vSphere environment, but this is certainly not considered to be secure. To harden such an environment, they could replace the default permissions such that only user groups in the SSO domain and Active Directory domains are assigned the Administrator role. Besides the extra steps to configure the identity sources and new permissions, the implication is that you must carefully manage the domains and user accounts to ensure that at least one account is available to manage the environment.

Objective 1.3—Enable SSO and Active Directory Integration

This section provides details for configuring Single Sign-On (SSO) and Active Directory integration.

Describe SSO Architecture and Components

VMware vCenter Single Sign-On (SSO) has many components, including the Security Token Service (STS), the Administration Server, the VMware Directory Service (vmdir), and Identity Management Service.

STS issues Security Assertion Markup Language (SAML) tokens, which represent the identity of users from its identity sources. The tokens allow users who successfully authenticate to SSO to use any vCenter service that SSO supports without needing to authenticate again to each service. SSO signs each token with a signing certificate, which it stores on disk.

Administration Server allows users with administrator privileges in SSO to use the vSphere Web Client to configure SSO and to configure SSO users and groups. Initially, only the administrator account in the SSO domain can configure SSO. In vSphere 5.5, this user was `administrator@vsphere.local`, but in vSphere 6.0, you can change the SSO domain during the vCenter Server installation.

The vmdir service is associated with the domain that was created during the vCenter Server installation. It is included in each embedded deployment and on each Platform Services Controller (PSC). It is a multi-tenanted, multi-mastered directory service that makes an LDAP directory available on port 389. It also uses port 11711 for backward compatibility with vSphere 5.5 and earlier systems. For environments with multiple PSC instances, the vmdir content of one instance is replicated to the other. Starting with vSphere 6.0, the vmdir service stores not only SSO information but also certificate information.

The Identity Management Service handles the identity sources and STS authentication requests.

Differentiate Available Authentication Methods with VMware vCenter

To access vCenter Server, users log in with SSO domain user accounts or user accounts from identity sources registered in SSO. The acceptable identity sources are Active Directory (Integrated Windows Authentication), Active Directory as a LDAP Server, Open LDAP, and Local OS.

The Local OS identity source is available immediately following the installation of SSO. It refers to all local user accounts on the SSO operating system. For example, on a vCenter Server appliance with embedded PSC, the local `root` account may be available to vCenter Server via the Local OS identity source.

The SSO domain is also available immediately as an identity source. This domain was called `vsphere.local` in vSphere 5.5, but you may set a different name during the SSO installation.

Perform a Multi-site SSO Installation

Two deployment models are available for vCenter Server 6.0. You can deploy vCenter Server with an embedded Platform Services Controller (PSC), where all PSC services are deployed on the same server as vCenter Server, as illustrated in Figure 1-9. During the installation of vCenter Server into a Windows server, you can choose the Embedded deployment. Or you can deploy vCenter Server with an external PSC, where the PSC and vCenter Server are deployed on different servers, as illustrated in Figure 1-10. Prior to installing vCenter Server on a Windows server, install the PSC on a different server.

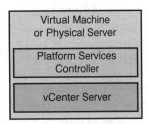

Figure 1-9   vCenter Server with Embedded PSC

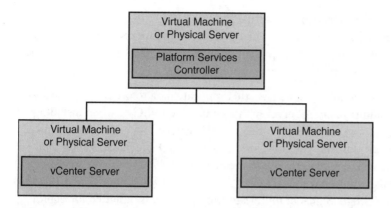

Figure 1-10   vCenter Server with External PSC

The advantages of deploying vCenter Server with an embedded PSC are:

- Communication between the vCenter Server and PSC is directly within the server and is not over the network. It is not prone to outages due to network connectivity or name resolution issues.

- When deployed on Windows Severs, fewer Windows licenses are required.

- Fewer servers need to be managed.

- No load balancer is required for the PSC.

The disadvantages of deploying vCenter Server with an embedded PSC are:

- An instance of PSC is required for each vCenter Server, which may consume more resources.

- The model may not be suitable for large environments.

The advantages of deploying vCenter Server with an external PSC are:

- Fewer resources are consumed by the combined services in PSC.

- It supports multiple vCenter Server instances.

The disadvantages of deploying vCenter Server with an external PSC are:

- The connection between the vCenter Server and PSC is susceptible to network issues.

- When deployed on Windows servers, additional Windows licenses may be required.

- Additional servers must be managed.

When using vCenter Server with an external PSC, the PSC can be used to manage multiple vCenter Server instances, which may be a mixture of Windows-based vCenter Servers and vCenter Server appliances. In this case, the PSC itself could be deployed in a Windows server or in a PSC appliance.

You can deploy multiple instances of PSC that replicate data to provide high availability. When installing vCenter Server with an embedded PSC or when installing an external PSC, you can choose to create a new domain or join an existing domain. When creating a new domain, you must specify a new SSO site name. When joining an existing domain, you may choose to create a new SSO site or join an existing SSO site. Specifying additional sites is key to installing SSO in a multi-site deployment. The vCenter Single Sign-On multi-site configuration is designed for deployments with multiple physical locations.

A typical multi-site deployment involves a vCenter Server with an external PSC implemented at each site, where the PSCs share a common SSO domain. The vCenter Server at each site is aware of the site topology and uses the local PSC in normal circumstances. This topology allows for the use of Enhanced Linked Mode. Optionally, a second instance of PSC could be deployed to each site to provide high availability. At each site, a load balancer is used for connecting to the PSC nodes. Optionally, Windows-based vCenter Server nodes could be clustered with Windows Server Failover Cluster (WSFC) at each site.

NOTE   Replication between embedded PSC instances is not supported.

Enhanced Linked Mode uses one or more PSC instances to link multiple vCenter Servers, allowing users to view and search across the linked vCenter Servers. Enhanced Linked Mode provides the following features:

- It works with Windows-based vCenter Servers as well as vCenter Server appliances.

- Users can log onto all linked vCenter instances simultaneously with a single username and password.

- Users can view and search the inventories of multiple linked vCenter Server instances, using the vSphere Web Client (not the vSphere Client).

- It replicates roles, permissions, licenses, tags, and policies.

To join vCenter Server instances in Enhanced Linked Mode, connect them to the same PSC or to PSC instances that share the same SSO domain. Enhanced Linked

Mode requires vCenter Server standard licensing. It is not supported with vCenter Server Foundation or vCenter Server Essentials.

In vSphere 5.5 and earlier, Linked Mode relies on Microsoft ADAM to provide replication. Starting in vSphere 6.0, the PSC provides the replication for Enhanced Linked Mode, and ADAM is no longer required. Because of this change, you must isolate vCenter Server 5.5 instances from any Linked Mode groups prior to upgrade.

Configure/Manage Active Directory Authentication

To permit Active Directory authentication in vSphere, add one or more Active Directory domains as identity sources in SSO. In scenarios where the SSO server is a member of an Active Directory domain, that domain may be added as an **Active Directory (Integrated Windows Authentication)** identity source. You can add other Active Directory domains to SSO as **Active Directory LDAP Server** identity sources.

You can use the vSphere Web Client (not the vSphere Client) to add SSO identity sources. To add an Active Directory domain as an identity source, select **Administration > Single Sign-On > Configuration**, click **Add Identity Source**, and choose either **Active Directory (Integrated Windows Authentication)** or **Active Directory as an LDAP Server**. Set the appropriate identity source parameters.

Using the vSphere Web Client to add SSO identity sources requires an account that is a member of the Administrators group in the SSO domain (vsphere.local), which contains only the administrator account by default. You have the ability to add additional user accounts from other identity sources. To add additional user accounts from other identity sources to the Administrators group in the SSO domain, follow these steps:

Step 1. Log into vSphere Web Client with the SSO domain administrator account.

Step 2. Select **Administration > Users/Groups**.

Step 3. Select **Group > Administrators > Add Member** from the Group Members section (see Figure 1-11).

Step 4. Select the additional identity source from the Domain drop-down menu.

Step 5. Select the account you would like to add (see Figure 1-12).

Step 6. Click **OK**.

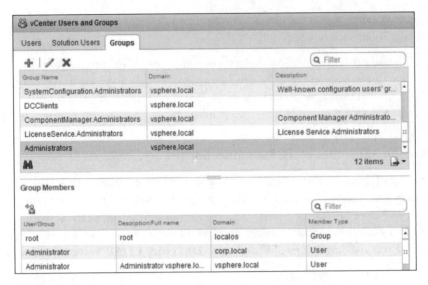

Figure 1-11   Users/Groups

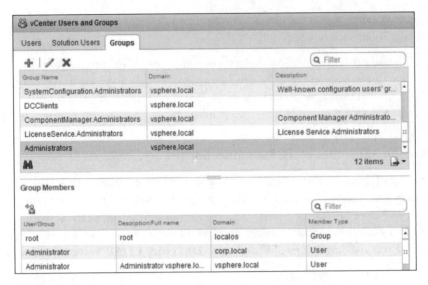

Figure 1-12   Add Member

When adding an Active Directory (Integrated Windows Authentication) identity source, provide the following information:

- **Domain Name:** Specify the FDQN of the domain.

- **Use Machine Account:** Select this option to use the local machine account as the Service Principal Name (SPN). Do not use this option if you plan to rename the machine.

- **Use Service Principal Name (SPN):** Select this option, instead of Use Machine Account, if you prefer to specify a unique SPN instead of using the machine name as the SPN. If you choose this option, then you must also provide the SPN, UPN, and password as described below.

- **Service Principal Name (SPN):** If you selected the Use Service Principal Name option, then provide a unique name that includes the domain name, such as STS/*domain*.com.

- **User Principal Name (UPN):** If you selected the Use Service Principal Name option, then provide a username that can authenticate to the Active Directory domain.

- **Password:** If you selected the Use Service Principal Name option, then provide a password that is associated with the UPN.

When adding an Active Directory over LDAP identity source, provide the following information:

- **Name:** The logical name for the identity source

- **Base DN for users:** The base distinguished name for users

- **Domain Name:** The FDQN of the domain

- **Domain Alias:** The domain's NetBIOS name

- **Base DN for groups:** The base distinguished name for groups

- **Primary Server URL:** The primary domain controller's URL, in the form ldap://hostname:port or ldaps://hostname:port

- **Secondary Server URL:** The secondary domain controller's URL, in the form ldap://hostname:port or ldaps://hostname:port

- **Choose certificate:** When using LDAPS in the URL parameters, the certificate

- **Username:** The username in the domain that has at least read access to the specified user and group base DNs

- **Password:** The password that is associated with the username

As a requirement to add an integrated Active Directory identity source, you need to ensure that the server where SSO is installed is in the domain. For a Windows server, you should ensure that the server is added to the Active Directory domain prior to installing SSO. For a PSC appliance or vCenter Server appliance, you can add the appliance to the domain using the following procedure:

Step 1. Log onto the vSphere Web Client using the SSO domain administrator account, such as `administrator@vsphere.local`.

Step 2. In the left pane, select **Administration > System Configuration > Nodes**.

Step 3. Select the appropriate node and click the **Manage** tab.

Step 4. Select **Active Directory** and click **Join**.

Step 5. Enter the Active Directory details such as **Domain**, **Organizational Unit**, **Username**, and **Password**.

Step 6. Click **OK**.

Step 7. Right-click the node and select **Reboot**.

After the appliance reboots, you add it as an Active Directory (Integrated Windows Authentication) identity source.

Configure/Manage Platform Services Controller (PSC)

To use external PSC instances, you need to install PSC in a Windows server or deploy a PSC appliance. The PSC provides required services, such as SSO, VMCA, and License Service, which can be shared by multiple vCenter Servers. When deploying multiple PSC instances to share the same SSO domain, you must deploy the instances one at a time. VMware does not support concurrent deployments of PSC in the same SSO domain.

You can use the following procedure to deploy a PSC appliance on an ESXi Host using a web browser and the Client Integration plug-in:

Step 1. Double-click **vcsa-setup.html** and allow the Client Integration plug-in to run.

Step 2. In the web page, click **Install**.

Step 3. Accept the license agreement and click **Next**.

Step 4. Provide the hostname and user credentials for an ESXi host and click **Next**. Accept any certificate warnings.

Step 5. On the Setup Virtual Machine page, provide a PSC appliance name, assign a root account password, and click **Next**.

Step 6.   In the Select a Deployment Type page, select **Install Platform Services Controller** and click **Next**.

Step 7.   On the next page, either create a new SSO domain or join an existing domain:

To create a new domain, provide a new domain name, assign an administrator password, and provide a new site name.

To join a domain, enter an existing SSO domain name and appropriate administrator password. Either create a new SSO site name or specify an existing SSO site to join.

Click **Next**.

Step 8.   On the Select Appliance Size page, click **Next** to deploy an appliance with two CPUs and 2 GB memory.

Step 9.   Select the datastore, optionally select **Enable Thin Disk Mode**, and click **Next**.

Step 10.   On the Network Settings page, set each of these options:

Choose a Network: Select the appropriate virtual switch port group.

IP Address Family: Specify IPv4 or select IPv6.

Network Type: Specify a static IP address or select DHCP.

FQDN: Specify a fully qualified domain name.

Click **Next**.

Step 11.   Configure the time settings, optionally select Enable SSH, and click **Next**. The time setting can be set to **Synchronize appliance time with ESXi Host** or **Use NTP servers**.

Step 12.   Click **Finish**.

NOTE   The supported characters for SSO site names are alphanumeric characters and dash (-). Site names cannot be changed after the PSC installation.

To install an external PSC in a Windows server, you can use this procedure:

Step 1.   Log onto the Windows server and double-click on **autorun.exe**.

Step 2.   Select **vCenter Server for Windows** and click **Install**.

Step 3.   Follow the prompts in the wizard to review the welcome page and accept the license agreement.

Step 4.   Select **Platform Services Controller** and click **Next**.

Step 5.   Follow the prompts in the wizard to configure the system name, SSO domain, and SSO site name, much as in the previous procedure. In addition, either accept or modify the default ports.

Step 6.   When prompted, optionally change the installation folder path and click **Next**.

Step 7.   On the Summary page, click **Install**.

Step 8.   After the installation completes, click **Finish**.

To install vCenter Server and Embedded PSC in a Windows server, use similar steps as in the previous procedure, but in step 4, select **vCenter Server and Embedded Platform Services Controller**. Also, follow the additional prompts in the wizard to configure the vCenter Server options, including the service user account and database.

Configure/Manage VMware Certificate Authority (VMCA)

The VMware Certificate Authority (VMCA), which runs in the PSC, is responsible for issuing certificates for VMware solution users, machine certificates for machines on which services run, and ESXi Host certificates. The VMware Endpoint Certificate Store (VECS) is a local repository for certificates and private keys. VECS is a mandatory component that is used when VMCA is not signing certificates. The VECS includes a set of keystores, including machine SSL certificates, trusted roots, CRLs, and solution users (`machine`, `vpxd`, `vpx-extension`, `vSphere-webclient`). VECS does not store ESXi certificates. ESXi certificates are stored locally on the ESXi Host, in the `/etc/vmware/ssl` directory.

With VMCA, you can deal with certificates in three different manners. First, you can let VMCA operate in a default manner, where it uses a self-signed root certificate, issues certificates to the vSphere components, and serves as the Certificate Authority (CA) to vSphere. Second, you can configure VMCA to operate as a subordinate CA on behalf of the enterprise's CA and use a subordinate CA signing certificate. Third, you can bypass VMCA and use only third-party certificates, which you need to store in the VECS, except for ESXi Hosts certificates. When necessary, you can use `vecs-cli` commands to explicitly manage certificates and keys.

NOTE   The VMCA in vSphere 6.0 does *not* support the use of CRLs, nor does it have the concept of certificate revocation. If you suspect that one certificate has been compromised, you should remove it and consider replacing all certificates.

When you use VMCA in the default manner, where it acts as the CA for vSphere, no real configuration is required other than to configure web browsers to trust VMCA. The VMCA can handle all certificate management in vSphere environments, where historically the administrator has elected not to replace certificates. During an upgrade to vSphere 6.0, all self-signed certificates are replaced with certificates signed by VMCA.

Using VMCA in a subordinate CA manner requires you to replace the VMCA root certificate with a certificate signed by a third-party CA, making the VMCA certificate an intermediate certificate of the CA. To use VMCA in the subordinate CA manner, follow this procedure:

Step 1. Launch the vSphere 6.0 Certificate Manager.

Step 2. Select **Option 2**, which is to replace the VMCA root certificate with a custom signing certificate and replace all certificates.

Step 3. When prompted, provide the password for the SSO domain administrator account.

Step 4. Select **Option 1** to generate a Certificate Signing Request (CSR) and key. When prompted, provide a directory to save the CSR and key.

Step 5. Provide the CSR (`root_signing_cert.csr`) to your CA to generate the subordinate signing certificate.

Step 6. Use a text editor to copy the contents of the intermediate CA certificates and the root CA certificate into a single file (`root_signing_chain.cer`).

Step 7. In the Certificate Manager, select **Option 1** to continue to the step to import custom certificates.

Step 8. Import the root signing certificate (`root_sigining_chain.cer`) and root signing key (`root_signing_cert.key`).

Step 9. When prompted, provide a value for each item, such as country, name, and organization.

After you complete these steps, the VMCA root certificate is replaced with a custom signing certificate. For more details on this procedure, see VMware KB 2112016.

If company policy does not allow intermediate certificates in the certificate chain, then you must explicitly replace certificates with third-party CA–signed certificates.

Enable/Disable Single Sign-On (SSO) Users

To manage SSO users, you should use the vSphere Web Client (not the vSphere Client). To create an SSO user, follow these steps:

Step 1.   Click on **Administration > Single Sign-On > Users and Groups**.

Step 2.   Select the **Users** tab and click the green plus sign (+).

Step 3.   Provide the **Username** and **Password**. Optionally provide values for the other fields.

Step 4.   Click **OK**.

In a similar manner, you can create an SSO group by using the **Groups** tab in step 2 and providing a group name in step 3. You can also use the **Groups** tab to select a group and use the **Add Member** icon (in the details section) to add users to the group. When adding a user to a group, use the Domain drop-down to select the SSO domain or another identity source and select a user account from the provided list.

To disable an SSO user account, select the user account on the **Users** tab at **Administration > Single Sign-On > Users and Groups** and click the **Disable User** icon (red circle with a slash through it). To enable an SSO account, select the user account and click the **Enable User** icon (checkmark).

The SSO domain (vsphere.local in vSphere 5.5, but it may be named differently in vSphere 6.0) provides several predefined groups. You can add users from Active Directory domains or other identity sources to these predefined groups. Some SSO privileges are determined solely by the membership of these groups. For example, a user who is a member of the CAAdmins group can manage VMCA, and a user who is a member of the LicenseService.Administrators group can manage licenses.

The SSO domain contains many predefined groups, including the following:

- **Users:** Contains all users in the SSO domain.

- **DCAdmins:** Members can perform domain controller administrator actions on the VMware Directory Service.

- **SolutionUsers:** Each solution user authenticates individually to vCenter Single Sign-On with a certificate. By default, VMCA provisions solution users with certificates. Do not add members to this group explicitly.

- **CAAdmins:** Members have administrator privileges for VMCA. Adding members to this group is not usually recommended, but a user must be a member of this group to perform most certificate management operations, such as using the certool command.

- **SystemConfiguration.BashShellAdministrators:** Only applies to vCenter Server appliance deployments. Members can enable and disable access to the BASH Shell.

- **SystemConfiguration.Administrators:** Members can view and manage the system configuration and perform tasks such as restarting services.

- **LicenseService.Administrators:** Members have full write access to all licensing-related data and can add, remove, assign, and unassign serial keys for all product assets registered in the licensing service.

- **Administrators:** Members can perform SSO administration tasks for the VMware Directory Service (vmdir).

Upgrade a Single/Multi-site SSO Installation

An upgrade of vCenter Server 5.5 that is deployed in the same server as SSO 5.5 is automatically upgraded to vCenter Server 6.0 with an embedded PSC. An upgrade of a Single Sign-On 5.5 instance that is deployed on a separate server than vCenter Server is upgraded to an externally deployed PSC 6.0. In this case, the vCenter Server remains at version 5.5 but continues to operate as normal with SSO, which is now running within the external PSC 6.0. This is considered a mixed environment. Everything in this paragraph is also true for upgrading SSO 5.1 and vCenter Server 5.1.

During the upgrade of an SSO 5.5 instance to a PSC instance, if it is the first SSO instance, then upgrade it to a new standalone PSC instance by configuring a new SSO domain and site name. In this case, the data from the original domain is migrated into the domain. If it is the second or an additional SSO instance, join it to the SSO domain of the first PSC instance. The upgrade of the SSO 5.5 procedure to external PSC is similar to the installation process covered in the "Configure/Manage Platform Services Controller (PSC)" section of this chapter.

Upgrade from the vCenter Server Appliance 5.1 Update 3 to vCenter Server Appliance 6.0 is supported. To upgrade a vCenter Server 5.0 appliance, you must first upgrade it to version 5.1 Update 3.

When upgrading environments that involve more than one SSO node, VMware typically recommends upgrading the complete SSO environment before restarting the SSO services. But during the upgrade of some environments, you may want to temporarily use SSO version 5.5 and SSO version 6.0 together, such that they are replicating vmdir data. VMware calls this a mixed-mode environment. In this case, you may still plan to replace the default VMCA signed (default) SSL certificate with custom SSL certificates. Here is the procedure to replace the VMware Directory Service Certificate in a mixed-mode environment:

Step 1.   On the SSO 6.0 node, stop the vmdir service.

Step 2.   On the SSO 6.0 node, copy the new certificate and key to the vmdir location.

Step 3. On the SSO 6.0 node, start the vmdir service.

Step 4. On the SSO 5.5 node, back up the contents of the `vmdird` directory.

Step 5. On the SSO 6.0 node, copy the `vmdircert.pem` file and rename it `fqdn.pem`, where `fqdn` is the fully qualified name of the SSO 6.0 node.

Step 6. Copy the renamed file from the SSO 6.0 node to the `vmdird` directory on the SSO 5.5 node to replace the existing certificate.

Step 7. Restart the vmdir service on the SSO 5.5 node.

Configure SSO Policies

SSO provides policies that enforce security rules in the environment. You can configure SSO password policies, SSO lockout policies, and SSO token policies. To configure these policies, use the vSphere Web Client to select **Administration > Single Sign-On > Configuration** and then select **Password Policies, Lockout Policies,** or **Token Policies** and click **Edit.** For each set of policies, set the appropriate password policy parameters, as described in Table 1-7.

Table 1-7 SSO Policies and Parameters

SSO Policy Type	Policy Parameter	Details
Password policy	Description	Password policy description.
	Maximum lifetime	Maximum number of days that a password can exist before the user must change it.
	Restrict reuse	Number of the user's previous passwords that cannot be selected.
	Maximum length	Maximum number of characters that are allowed in the password.
	Minimum length	Minimum number of characters that are allowed in the password, which must be no less than the combined minimum of alphabetic, numeric, and special character requirements.
	Character requirements	Minimum number of different character types that are required in the password. The types include special, alphabetic, uppercase, lowercase, and numeric.
	Identical adjacent characters	The number of identical adjacent characters that are supported in a password. The value must be greater than 0.

SSO Policy Type	Policy Parameter	Details
Lockout policy	Description	Description of the lockout policy.
	Max number of failed login attempts	Maximum number of failed login attempts that are allowed before the account is locked.
	Time interval between failures	Time period in which failed login attempts must occur to trigger a lockout.
	Unlock time	The amount of time the account stays locked. The value 0 specifies that an administrator must explicitly unlock the account.
Token policy	Clock tolerance	Time difference in milliseconds that SSO tolerates between a client clock and a domain controller clock. If the time difference is greater than the specified value, SSO declares the token to be invalid.
	Maximum token renewal count	Maximum number of times a token may be renewed before a new security token is required.
	Maximum token delegation count	Maximum number of times a single holder-of-key token can be delegated.
	Maximum bearer token lifetime	The lifetime value of a bearer token before the token has to be reissued.
	Maximum holder-of-key token lifetime	The lifetime value of a holder-of-key token before the token is marked invalid.

Add/Edit/Remove SSO Identity Sources

To remove an SSO identity source, use the vSphere Web Client to select the identity source on the **Identity Sources** tab at **Administrator > Single Sign-On > Configuration** and click the **Delete Identity Source** icon. When prompted, click **Yes** to confirm.

You can configure a default SSO domain. The default SSO domain allows users to authenticate without identifying a domain name. Users from other identity sources must identify the domain name during authentication. To configure a default domain, select the identity source on the **Identity Sources** tab at **Administrator > Single Sign-On > Configuration** and click the **Set as Default Domain** icon.

Add an ESXi Host to an AD Domain

Previously in this chapter, in the "Harden ESXi Hosts" section, details are provided for adding an ESXi Host to an Active Directory domain.

Summary

You have now read the chapter covering exam topics related to hardening vSphere components. You should use the information in the following sections to complete your preparation for exam Objectives 1.1, 1.2, and 1.3.

Exam Preparation Tasks

Review All the Key Topics

Table 1-8 provides a reference to each of the key topics identified in this chapter. Take a few moments to review each of these specific items.

Table 1-8   Key Topics for Chapter 1

Key Topic Element	Description	Pages
Paragraph	How permissions are inherited and applied	11
List	Sample roles in vCenter Server	20
Procedure	Modify ESXi firewall rules	31
Procedure	Enable lockdown mode	37
Paragraph	SSO components	41
Procedure	Deploy a PSC appliance	48

Complete the Tables and Lists from Memory

Print a copy of Appendix B, "Memory Tables" (found on the CD), or at least the section for this chapter, and complete the tables and lists from memory. Appendix C, "Memory Tables Answer Key," also on the CD, includes completed tables and lists to check your work.

Definitions of Key Terms

Define the following key terms from this chapter and check your answers in the glossary.

Virtual Machine Communication Interface (VMCI), Managed Object Browser (MOB), Mware Directory Service (vmdir), VMware Endpoint Certificate Store (VECS)

Answer Review Questions

The answers to these review questions can be found in Appendix A.

1. Which of the following is true concerning the effective privileges for User-01, who is a member of Group-A and Group-B, where Group-A is assigned the Administrator role on Host-01 and Group-B is assigned the No Access role on Host-01 and User-01 is assigned the Read Only role on Host-01?

   a. User-01 can perform administrative tasks on Host-01.

   b. User-01 can only view information on Host-01.

   c. User-01 cannot even view Host-01.

   d. User-01 can only view Host-01 by default, but has the ability to change the permission.

2. Which of the following users can access the ESXi Shell on an ESXi Host that is in strict lockdown mode?

   a. Only the administrator

   b. No one

   c. Members of the `Exception Users` group

   d. Members of the `Exception Users` group who also have administrator privileges

3. Which of the following is valid syntax for specifying the secondary server URL when adding Active Directory over an LDAP identity source?

   a. `ldaps://hostname:port`

   b. `hostname`

   c. `hostname:port`

   d. all of the above

4. Which of the following is a correct statement describing the size of an external PSC appliance?

   a. Its size is customizable during its deployment.

   b. It is configured with two vCPUs and 4 GB memory.

   c. It is configured with one vCPUs and 2 GB memory.

   d. It is configured with two vCPUs and 2 GB memory.

5. Which of the following are valid SSO policies? (Choose three.)

   a. Password policy

   b. Token policy

   c. Certificate policy

   d. Lockout policy

   e. User policy

This chapter covers the following objective:

- **Objective 2.1—Configure Advanced Policies/Features and Verify Network Virtualization Implementation.**

  - Create/delete a vSphere distributed switch

  - Add/remove ESXi Hosts from a vSphere distributed switch

  - Add/configure/remove dvPort groups

  - Add/remove uplink adapters to dvUplink groups

  - Configure vSphere distributed switch general and dvPort group settings

  - Create/configure/remove virtual adapters

  - Migrate virtual machines to/from a vSphere distributed switch

  - Configure LACP on vDS given design parameters

  - Describe vDS security policies/settings

  - Configure dvPort group blocking policies

  - Configure load balancing and failover policies

  - Configure VLAN/PVLAN settings for VMs given communication requirements

  - Configure traffic shaping policies

  - Enable TCP segmentation offload support for a virtual machine

  - Enable jumbo frames support on appropriate components

  - Recognize behavior of vDS Auto-Rollback

  - Configure vDS across multiple vCenter Servers to support long-distance vMotion

  - Compare and contrast vSphere distributed switch (vDS) capabilities

## CHAPTER 2

Networking, Part 1

This chapter explores the differences between vSphere standard switches (vSS) and vSphere distributed switches (vDS). vDS was introduced in vSphere 4.0, but these virtual switches have received increasing functionality with each vSphere release. vSphere 5, for example, included the ability to back up the configuration of a vSphere distributed switch and all the associated port groups and VMkernel ports to a single file. Even though this information is stored in the vCenter database, it is nice to be able to restore vDS data independently of the vCenter database (and not have to worry about the restoration of the entire database).

"Do I Know This Already?" Quiz

The "Do I Know This Already?" quiz allows you to assess whether you should study this entire chapter or move quickly to the "Exam Preparation Tasks" section. Regardless, the authors recommend that you read the entire chapter at least once. Table 2-1 outlines the major headings in this chapter and the corresponding "Do I Know This Already?" quiz questions. You can find the answers in Appendix A, "Answers to the 'Do I Know This Already?' Quizzes and Review Questions."

Table 2-1 "Do I Know This Already?" Foundation Topics Section-to-Question Mapping

Foundation Topics Section	Questions Covered in This Section
Create/Delete a vSphere Distributed Switch	5
Add/Remove ESXi Hosts from a vSphere Distributed Switch	8
Add/Configure/Remove dvPort Groups	6, 7
Add/Remove Uplink Adapters to dvUplink Groups	2
Migrate Virtual Machines to/from a vSphere Distributed Switch	4
Configure LACP on vDS Given Design Parameters	9
Describe vDS Security Policies/Settings	10

Foundation Topics Section	Questions Covered in This Section
Configure Load Balancing and Failover Policies	11
Configure VLAN/PVLAN Settings for VMs Given Communication Requirements	3
Enable TCP Segmentation Offload Support for a Virtual Machine	12
Compare and Contrast vSphere Distributed Switch (vDS) Capabilities	1

1. Which of the following is a policy setting that is available only on a vSphere distributed switch?

   a. Source and Destination IP-Hash Load Balancing Mechanism

   b. To CDP Support

   c. VLAN Tagging

   d. Outbound Traffic Shaping

2. What is the maximum number of dvUplinks that can be configured on a vSphere distributed switch?

   a. 16

   b. 1

   c. 32

   d. 4

3. Which of the following is not a valid secondary PVLAN?

   a. Isolated

   b. Private

   c. Promiscuous

   d. Community

4. By what method could you move multiple virtual machines from a port group on a standard vSwitch to one on a distributed vSwitch?

   a. In the networking inventory view, select the Standard vSwitch port group and select the **Related Objects>Virtual Machines** tab. Select the first VM in the list and, while holding down the Shift key, select the bottom VM in the list. Then drag and drop the VMs to the vDS port group.

    b. In the networking inventory view, right-click the vDS or datacenter object, select **Migrate VM to Another Network**, and then use the wizard to define source and destination networks and which VMs you choose to move.

    c. You cannot move more than one VM from a standard port group to one on a distributed vSwitch.

    d. In the VMs and templates inventory view, select the folder or higher object containing the VMs you wish to move and then select the **Related Objects>Virtual Machines** tab. Select the first VM in the list and, while holding down the Shift key, select the bottom VM in the list. Right-click the selected VMs, select **Migrate Virtual Machine Networking**, and choose source and destination networks.

5. Which of the following is the maximum number of uplink adapters each ESXi server can contribute to a vSphere distributed switch?

    a. 1

    b. 8

    c. 32

    d. 64

6. Which of the following are the three types of port binding?

    a. Static, dynamic, and ephemeral

    b. Static, automatic, and ephemeral

    c. Static, distributed, and encrypted

    d. Physical, virtual, and dynamic

7. The vCenter Server in your organization has failed and needs to be replaced with a new vCenter Server, but the database is still intact on a different server. The vCenter Server was a virtual machine and resided on a vDS, and there are no standard switches in the environment. Which of the following would prevent a new vCenter virtual machine from connecting to the network?

    a. The dvPort group is using the Load Based Teaming load balancing policy.

    b. The dvPort group has NetFlow enabled.

    c. The dvPort group is not in promiscuous mode.

    d. The port binding on the dvPort group is set to static.

8. When modifying a vDS, which of the following cannot be done by using the Add and Manage Hosts wizard?

   a. Adding new VMkernel ports for ESXi servers

   b. Creating dvPort groups

   c. Adding physical uplinks from ESXi Hosts

   d. Moving virtual machines

9. When configuring LACP on a vDS, which of the following cannot be configured on the vDS?

   a. NetQueue

   b. Port Mirroring

   c. Split RX

   d. NetFlow

10. In the security policy of a vDS, what are the default settings for promiscuous mode, MAC address changes, and forged transmits?

   a. Reject, accept, accept

   b. Reject, reject, accept

   c. Reject, reject, reject

   d. Accept, reject, reject

11. Which of the following load balancing mechanisms is present only on a vDS?

   a. Source and destination IP hash

   b. Round Robin

   c. Source MAC hash

   d. Load-based teaming

12. The vSphere administrator has enabled TCP Segmentation Offload (TSO) on an ESXi Host and for a virtual machine. Which file would have to be modified on an ESXi server to allow TSO to remain enabled after an ESXi Host reboots?

   a. `/etc/rc.local.d/local.sh`

   b. `/etc/opt/init.d`

   c. `/etc/opt/profile.local`

   d. `/etc/rc.local`

Foundation Topics

Objective 2.1—Configure Advanced Policies/Features and Verify Network Virtualization Implementation

There are many differences between standard and distributed virtual switches, and it is important to realize the differences in terms of features and options and how these differences function.

Compare and Contrast vSphere Distributed Switch (vDS) Capabilities

vSphere distributed switches (vDS) have numerous advantages over vSphere standard switches (vSS). They require Enterprise Plus licensing but yield many extra configuration options. Many of the Enterprise Plus features benefit large "plus-sized" enterprises, and when you look at the features and benefits that vDS has over vSS, this becomes evident.

Table 2-2 provides a side-by-side comparison of the features that are available in vSS and vDS:

Table 2-2 vSphere Standard Switches Versus vSphere Distributed Switches

Feature	vSS	vDS
Layer 2	×	×
VLAN tagging (802.1q)	×	×
IPv6	×	×
NIC teaming	×	×
Outbound traffic shaping	×	×
Inbound traffic shaping		×
VM network port block		×
Private VLANs		×
Load-based teaming		×
Datacenter level management		×
Network vMotion		×
Per-port policy settings		×
Port state monitoring		×
NetFlow		×

Feature	vSS	vDS
Port mirroring		×
Network I/O Control		×

Next we explore the features specific to vDS in more detail:

- **Inbound traffic shaping:** Distributed virtual switches can do both inbound and outbound traffic shaping, whereas standard virtual switches handle just outbound traffic shaping. The settings that are available on inbound (average bandwidth in Kbps, peak bandwidth in Kbps, and burst size in KB) are available on vDS for both directions.

- **VM network port block:** On a vDS, network admins or whoever has access to the vDS can block individual vDS ports if needed. This may be useful if a virtual machine starts broadcasting a lot of traffic, as a result of a broken application, for example, and starts consuming a large portion of the network bandwidth. A network admin who has access to the vDS could block the individual switch port much as on a physical switch. One of the arguments against this is that if a virtual machine starts broadcasting traffic, why not disconnect the virtual network adapter from the port group? The problem with this argument is the assumption that the virtual network administrator (who may also be responsible for managing the physical network) has access to modifying virtual machine hardware. This might be something that is not desired, especially in large organizations with delegated control over different components within vSphere.

- **Private VLANs:** Private VLANs are an extension of the VLAN standard (802.1q). Packets are sent with VLAN tags, but private VLANs allow further segmentation by allowing VLANs to be carved up into smaller private VLANs, allowing for a primary private VLAN (PVLAN) and one or more secondary PVLANs. We explore the functionality of PVLANs later in this chapter.

- **Load-based teaming:** In addition to the three load-balancing mechanisms that standard virtual switches offer (originating virtual port ID, source MAC hash, and source and destination IP hash), vDS offers a fourth load-balancing mechanism, load-based teaming, which does load balancing based on actual physical network adapter load. The VMkernel tracks the send and receive traffic for each physical uplink on the team and determines the load average in 30-second increments. Load-based teaming offers lower overhead than IP-based load balancing as well, and it doesn't require the physical switches to support 802.3ad (Etherchannel/link aggregation).

- **Datacenter-level management:** vDS makes it easy to both create virtual switches and update the configuration on existing distributed virtual switches. vDS can be pushed down to as many as 1000 ESXi servers, demonstrating the capability of updating and configuring networking for large environments.

- **Network vMotion:** A virtual machine can effectively maintain its switch connection when migrating to a different ESXi server host. The vDS port number is still the same, as are the policies and statistics that are tied to that switch port. As far as the operating system is concerned, the virtual machine hasn't moved. When you perform a migration of a virtual machine using standard virtual switches, the policies and statistics change in favor of the new switch that the VM gets connected to after the migration (and the VM gets attached to a new switch port on the second switch).

- **Per-port policy settings:** In addition to the ability to define security, traffic shaping, and teaming and failover policies at the virtual switch and port group level, with vDS you can define these policies for individual switch ports—effectively for individual virtual machines. As an administrator, you can allow or deny the ability to define per-port policies at the port group level on a vDS.

- **Port state monitoring:** In the vSphere Client or Web Client, administrators can see not only which vDS ports are in use but also some general information about the ports, such as the current state of the port (link up, link down, blocked, or information unavailable).

- **NetFlow:** NetFlow allows administrators to forward network flows—internal VM-to-VM traffic flows, or VM–to–physical device traffic flows and vice versa—to a centralized NetFlow collector. This collector can be a physical device on the network or a virtual machine. In either case, the collector is gathering the network traffic flows for the purpose of analyzing usage patterns for network monitoring and troubleshooting. Network flows can be sent at a sampled rate, and there is also the possibility of sending unsampled data as well.

- **Port mirroring:** Port mirroring allows administrators to duplicate everything that is happening on one virtual switch port to then be visible on a completely different virtual switch port. The vSphere Web Client allows you to create a mirroring session and determine the port to be mirrored and on which switch port to duplicate the traffic.

- **Network I/O Control:** NIOC allows prioritization of network traffic in the event of contention.

Create/Delete a vSphere Distributed Switch

Now that we have taken a look at the features that vDS make available, we can look at the steps involved in creating a vDS. When creating a vSphere distributed switch, it is important to determine whether you are working with a mixed environment of multiple different versions of vSphere. When building a vDS, you can define the compatibility of the switch. It is also important to be aware of the licensing restrictions: Distributed virtual switches are available only with Enterprise Plus vSphere licensing.

To create a vDS, you need to be in the networking inventory view of the vSphere Client or Web Client (see Figure 2-1).

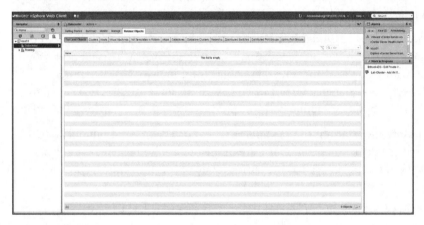

Figure 2-1 Networking Inventory View

In the networking inventory view, right-click the datacenter object and select **Distributed Switch > New Distributed Switch** (see Figure 2-2).

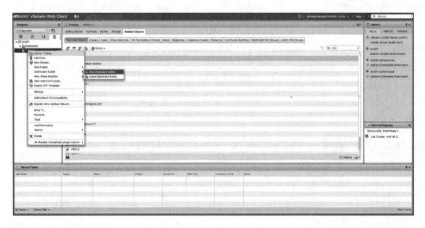

Figure 2-2 New vDS

In the New Distributed Switch wizard that appears, enter the name of the new vDS (see Figure 2-3) and then select the version (see Figure 2-4). The version selection is critical if you are working with an environment of mixed ESXi versions. If all of the ESXi servers are at version 6, then you can safely select Distributed Switch 6.0.0. If, however, some of the ESXi servers are older versions, then in order to have vDS functionality, you must choose only the version of vDS that matches the lowest version of ESXi that is in the environment. If your environment has some ESXi 5.1, 5.5, and 6.0 servers, for example, you need to choose Distributed Switch: 5.1.0.

Figure 2-3   New vDS

Figure 2-4   New vDS Wizard

The next screen of the wizard is the Edit Settings screen (see Figure 2-5). In this screen, you define the number of uplinks, enable/disable Network I/O Control, and create a VM port group. The number of uplinks defined on this screen determines the maximum number of physical uplinks each ESXi server can contribute to the vDS. The default value here is 4, which allows every ESXi server (a maximum of 1000 per vDS) to contribute up to 4 physical uplinks to the vDS. The minimum value here is 1, and the maximum value is 32. By defining a maximum, you restrict future growth by only allowing ESXi servers to be able to contribute up to the maximum number of uplinks defined here. This value can, however, be modified after the creation of the distributed switch. This would allow for delegation. For example, a vSphere networking admin may be responsible for building and maintaining/modifying virtual switches but may be unable to modify ESXi servers or their physical uplinks. In this case, the network admin might need to restrict the number of uplinks. If at some point in the future it is determined that each ESXi server needs to contribute more physical uplinks to the switch, the vSphere network admin can then adjust the maximum number of uplinks per host.

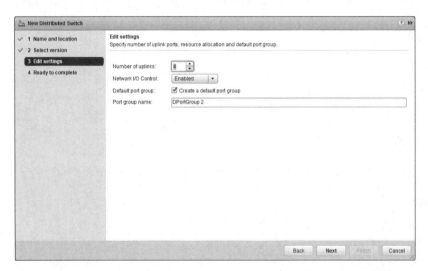

Figure 2-5   Edit Settings

Network I/O Control allows prioritization of network traffic if there is contention on the network. This setting is enabled by default, and administrators can create network resource pools. There are several network resource pools configured by default: one for each different type of VMkernel network traffic, and one for all of the virtual machines. Administrators can create additional network resource pools for varying levels of priorities for virtual machines as needed. Network resource pools prioritize network traffic by utilizing a share mechanism (the same mechanism used for prioritization in the event of CPU, memory, or storage contention). They can also be used to define limits, if needed.

The last setting, Create a Default Port Group, creates a virtual machine port group on the new vDS during creation. By default, this option is selected and the port group name is DPortGroup; you can modify the name either in this wizard or after the vDS has been created.

At the end of the wizard is a completion screen that indicates what is going to be created and also gives tips on next steps. These suggestions include creating new port groups and adding ESXi servers to the vDS (see Figure 2-6).

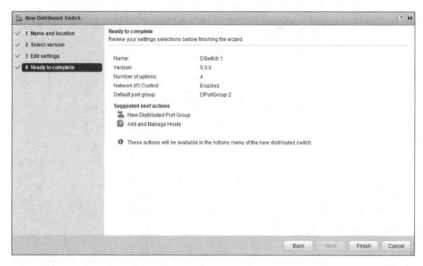

Figure 2-6   vDS Wizard Review Screen

Once the vDS has been created, it shows up in the networking inventory view, along with two port groups: one for virtual machines (the one that was created by default) and one for the physical uplinks, with a name in the format ***vDS name>-DVUp-links-<number>*** (see Figure 2-7).

To delete a vDS, you simply right-click the vDS and choose Delete. However, if it has been pushed to ESXi servers first and has virtual machines residing on it, you have to migrate them off first and remove the vDS from the ESXi servers.

Figure 2-7   vDS dvPort Groups

Add/Remove ESXi Hosts from a vSphere Distributed Switch

Once a vDS has been created, the next step is to either create a virtual machine port group (if one has not already been created) or attach ESXi servers to the vDS. This section looks at adding ESXi servers to the newly created vDS.

Step 1.   There are a couple different ways to add one or more ESXi servers to a vDS. If the Getting Started tabs are still present in the vSphere Web Client, you can select **Basic Tasks** > **Add and Manage Hosts**. Otherwise, right-click the vDS itself in the Navigator pane (the left-hand pane of the Web Client, where the inventory is listed) and select **Add and Manage Hosts** (see Figure 2-8).

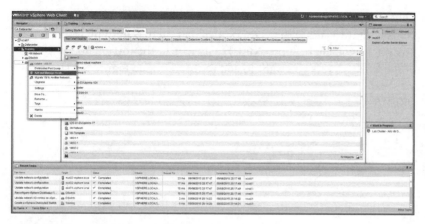

Figure 2-8   Add and Manage Hosts

Step 2.   As shown in Figure 2-9, the Add and Manage Hosts wizard appears. The first screen allows you to not only add ESXi servers to the new vDS but migrate VMkernel ports from standard virtual switches, migrate physical uplinks from standard virtual switches, migrate both at the same time (which is very useful when you need to migrate a management VMkernel port and do not want to disconnect yourself from the ESXi server), or remove ESXi servers from the vDS. For now, you want to just add the hosts, so click **Next**.

Figure 2-9   Add and Manage Hosts Wizard

Step 3.   On the next screen (see Figure 2-10), you select which of the ESXi servers you want to add to the vDS. Notice that there is nothing listed in this box yet, so you click on the **New Hosts** icon at the top to choose which of the ESXi servers you want to add to the vDS (see Figure 2-11).

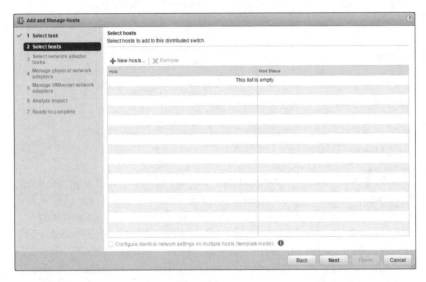

Figure 2-10   ESXi Servers

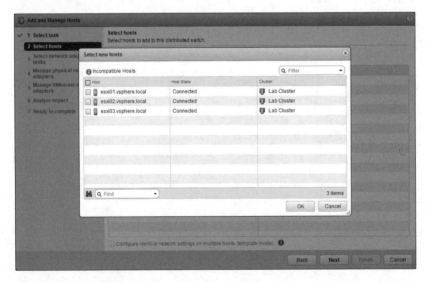

Figure 2-11   New Hosts

Step 4.   In the Select New Hosts screen, you can either select individual ESXi servers by selecting the check box next to each one or you can select the check box at the top of the host column and select all of the ESXi servers listed. This box can be a little confusing because at the top, you see a message that says Incompatible Hosts. In this case, none of the ESXi servers are incompatible because if they were, you would see a circle with an i in the middle of it, indicating incompatibility. You could expect to see that appear if an ESXi server were a version below what the vDS is configured for; for example, an ESXi 5.5 server would show incompatible if you tried to add a vDS 6.0 to it.

Step 5.   Once all the ESXi servers that should be added to the vDS have been selected, you can click OK to go back to the Select Hosts part of the Add and Manage Hosts wizard. At the bottom of the wizard is the Configure Identical Network Settings on Multiple Hosts (Template Mode) check box. This setting allows you to use one of the ESXi servers as a template, and vSphere then uses the configuration of that template ESXi server to configure physical uplinks and VMkernel ports on the other ESXi servers in the list. This template mode is only present in this instance of the wizard and is lost once the wizard is completed. An alternative to this option would be to utilize host profiles to accomplish the same goal. Be aware that this makes sense only if all the ESXi servers are configured identically.

Step 6.   The next screen, Select Network Adapter Tasks (see Figure 2-12), allows you to add physical uplinks from each of the selected ESXi servers to the vDS, move VMkernel adapters from standard virtual switches, move virtual machines from standard virtual machine port groups, and adjust the number of ports for older vDS.

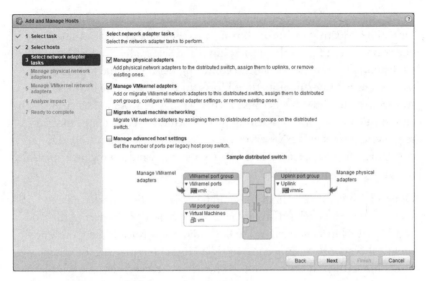

Figure 2-12   Select Network Adapter Tasks

You might want to migrate physical uplinks from standard vSwitches and VMkernel adapters from standard vSwitches in a scenario like this: Consider an environment with no management network redundancy, at least initially, where you want to move from a standard virtual switch to a distributed virtual switch. There wouldn't be an easy way to do this otherwise. You could add another physical uplink to the standard virtual switch for redundancy first, but what would happen if you removed the only management VMkernel port from an ESXi server? If you were to remove a management VMkernel port, and that VMkernel port were the only one marked for management, vCenter would have no way to connect to the ESXi server, and it would be disconnected. Interestingly, the interface does not allow this to happen. The other way to think about it is if you removed `vmnic0`, the only physical uplink attached to `vSwitch0` by default, you would have the same problem: vCenter would no longer be able to connect to the ESXi server and, again, the interface does not allow this to happen.

We discuss migrating VMkernel ports and virtual machine networking later. For now, we look at just adding one physical uplink per ESXi server to the vDS and then adding additional ones afterward.

Step 7.   If you deselect Manage VMkernel Adapters and click Next to be able to choose to add physical uplinks to the vDS, then you would be presented with the Manage Physical Network Adapters screen (see Figure 2-13).

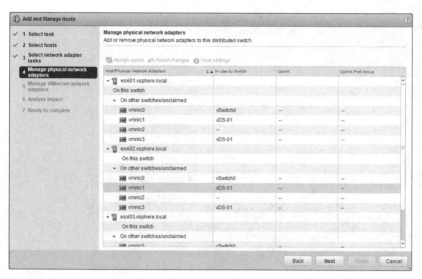

Figure 2-13   Manage Physical Network Adapters

Step 8.   If all the ESXi servers are configured identically, this part is easy. However, if they are not all configured identically, this can be challenging. Once in a while, you might see inconsistencies from one ESXi server to another. For example, on one particular server, instead of following the normal convention of vmnic0, vmnic1, vmnic2, and vmnic3 for a system with four physical uplinks, you might observe vmnic0, vmnic1, vmnic4, and vmnic5—especially if there were some hardware failures at some point in the past. One of the advantages with distributed virtual switches is that the ESXi servers don't have to all be identical. You just need to know which physical uplinks are attached to the same physical networks. Notice that this screen tells you which vmnics are in use by which virtual switches so you don't accidentally disconnect networking—unless, of course, you are migrating both VMkernel ports and physical uplinks at the same time. To choose a physical uplink to use, you select the physical uplink by vmnic number under an ESXi server and select the Assign Uplink option at the top. If the vDS was built with the default of four uplinks, you see four uplink slots listed (again, allowing each ESXi server to contribute, by default, up to four uplinks to the vDS). It doesn't really matter which uplink is selected, but uniformity makes troubleshooting and documenting a lot easier (see Figure 2-14).

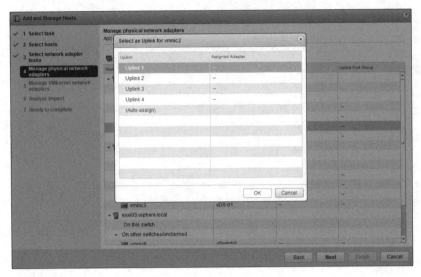

Figure 2-14   Assign Uplinks

Step 9.   Once all the physical uplinks (vmnics) have been assigned to uplinks, you see in the Manage Physical Network Adapters window's Uplink and Uplink Port Group fields populated with the names of the uplink chosen (see Figure 2-15).

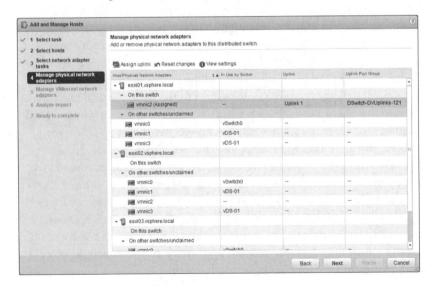

Figure 2-15   Uplink Port Group

Step 10.   The next screen, Analyze Impact, identifies whether there will be disruption to iSCSI storage traffic. This is a helpful check because if you were moving a physical uplink or VMkernel port that was currently being used for iSCSI traffic, moving it would cause at least temporary interruption, so you would probably want to plan such a move to occur during off-peak hours (see Figure 2-16).

Figure 2-16   Analyze Impact

Step 11.   At the end of the wizard is a summary of the changes that will be taking place. It is always good to verify that you are doing everything you intended to. In this example, you see a number of ESXi servers that are going to be added to the vDS and the number of physical uplinks (see Figure 2-17).

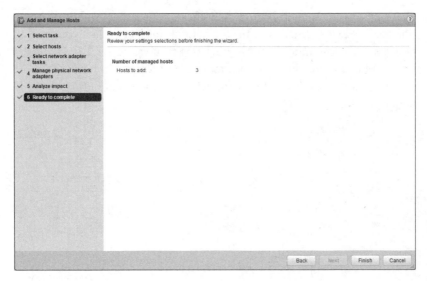

Figure 2-17   Physical Uplinks

One thing that is useful about distributed virtual switches is that it is relatively easy to see the configuration on each ESXi server. Each vDS has a Topology view that allows you to see which VMkernel ports or VM port groups reside on the switch and which physical uplinks have been assigned. To see the topology, select the vDS from the inventory tree in the Navigator pane and select **Manage > Settings > Topology** (see Figure 2-18).

Figure 2-18   vDS Topology

Once a vSphere distributed switch has been pushed to ESXi servers, you can remove the ESXi servers from the vDS if needed. To do so, right-click the vDS from the Navigator pane and choose **Add and Manage Hosts** again. In the Add and Manage Hosts wizard that appears, instead of selecting Add Hosts, you just need to select **Remove Hosts**. You then see an empty window much like the one you saw when we selected **Add Hosts** to determine which ESXi servers you wanted to add to the vDS. However, this time you see the option **Attached Hosts** at the top (see Figure 2-19). You can click this to see a list of the ESXi servers that are attached, and you can select one, many, or all of the ESXi servers, and then click **OK** (see Figure 2-20). You can then verify that you have all the ESXi servers you want to remove from the vDS (see Figure 2-21) and finish out the wizard.

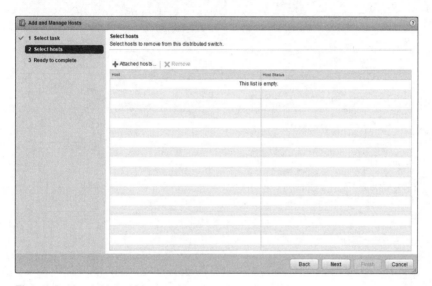

Figure 2-19   Add and Manage Hosts

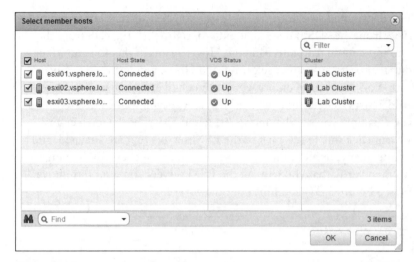

Figure 2-20   Select Hosts

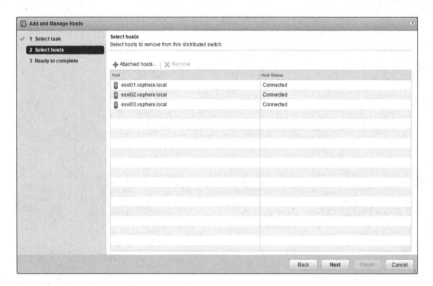

Figure 2-21   Remove Selected Hosts

Add/Configure/Remove dvPort Groups

Whether a virtual machine port group was created on a vDS during creation or not, you can create or modify additional ones after the fact. To create a dvPort group (distributed virtual port group), you need to be in the networking inventory view of the vSphere Client or vSphere Web Client.

Right-click the vDS and select **Distributed Port Group > New Distributed Port Group** (see Figure 2-22).

Figure 2-22 New dvPort Group

The first screen of the New Distributed Port Group wizard that appears asks you for a name. The default dvPort group name is DPortGroup#. If there is already one dvPort Group on the virtual switch, the vSphere Client starts appending numbers at the end of new dvPort group names, such as DPortGroup1, DPortGroup2, and so on. In this example, you need to create a dvPort group with the name Production (see Figure 2-23).

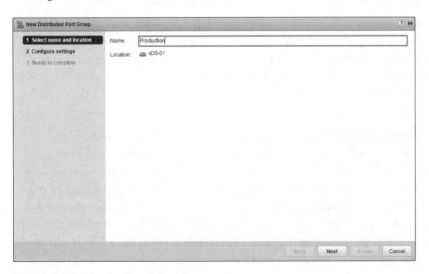

Figure 2-23 Production dvPort Group

The next screen of the wizard (see Figure 2-24) allows you to determine how virtual machines will be bound to virtual switch ports, how you want the virtual switch ports to be allocated, what default number of virtual switch ports you want, whether you want to tie the port group to a network resource pool, whether you want to define a VLAN for the port group, and whether you want to modify the default security, traffic shaping, or teaming and failover policies.

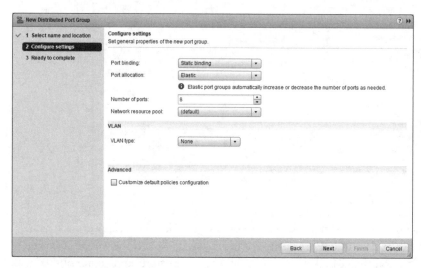

Figure 2-24 Port Binding

The first option on this screen, Port Binding, determines how virtual machines are bound or attached to virtual switch ports. It has three possible settings:

- **Static Binding:** With Static Binding (which is the default), when a virtual machine's network adapter is attached to a dvPort group, that connection is static—meaning the virtual machine is always attached to the virtual switch port, regardless of power state. The VM never releases or is disconnected from the virtual switch port, so the statistics and policies migrate with the virtual machine during a migration.

- **Dynamic Binding:** The next option, Dynamic Binding, means that virtual machine network adapters are only connected to the dvPort when the virtual machine is powered on. Powering off the virtual machine disconnects it from a virtual switch port. As a result, you could potentially have more virtual machines than virtual switch ports as long as there aren't any more virtual machines powered on than there are virtual switch ports. It is important to realize that dynamic port binding has been deprecated as of vSphere 5.0. So although it is still available as an option, using it is no longer recommended.

- **Ephemeral:** The third option, Ephemeral, means there is no binding. With this setting, virtual switch ports are created and deleted on demand. In the past, the Ephemeral setting seemed like the easiest way to go because it required the least administrative effort to address an ever growing environment. However, as of vSphere 5.1, static port binding is also "elastic" by default.

The first option on this screen, Port Allocation, is set to Elastic by default. This essentially has the same effect as ephemeral port binding: Ports are created and removed on demand. This means a virtual switch with only eight ports configured by default will automatically expand and add more ports as you try to attach more virtual machines to it. If you remove virtual machines from the vDS, the ports are automatically removed.

If you set Port Allocation to **Static**, then once the ports defined on the dvPort group are consumed by virtual machines (powered on or not), there will not be any additional ports created or available for new virtual machines to use, which means you can effectively run out of ports. So you can see why the default is eight ports, with elastic static port binding: to allow the lowest amount of overhead by not configuring a virtual switch with a lot of ports unused up front and allowing an automatic expansion of switch ports as needed, as well as the ability of virtual machines to always maintain which dvPort they are attached to, regardless of power state or which ESXi server the VM resides on. The default settings work well, without requiring vSphere administrators to have any additional knowledge or training on how port binding should be configured.

Another thing to be aware of is the maximum number of ports that can be configured. The maximum number of static or dynamic ports that can be defined per vDS is 10,000, while each ESXi server can manage only up to 4096 total switch ports (for standard as well as distributed virtual switches). The maximum number of ephemeral ports per vDS is only 1016, which may be another reason the default static port binding seems to be a better option.

NOTE If a vCenter Server is a virtual machine attached to a vDS, it is recommended that the port group the vCenter Server is attached to be configured for ephemeral port binding. With static or dynamic port binding, vCenter is responsible for assigning virtual switch ports, and if the vCenter Server needs to be replaced with a new VM, this wouldn't be possible. With ephemeral port binding, the new VM would be able to attach to the vDS, however.

The next option is Network Resource Pool. There are no network resource pools defined for virtual machines other than the default (which groups all virtual machine traffic together in the event of contention). You can modify this only when a different network resource pool has been defined. (We look at creating network resource pools in Chapter 3, "Networking, Part 2.")

VLAN Type is, by default, set to None. You can define VLANs for logical segmentation on dvPort groups, as you can with standard virtual switch port groups, but there is more functionality available for distributed virtual switches, as we explore later in this chapter, in the section "Configure VLAN/PVLAN Settings for VMs Given Communication Requirements."

If you want to customize the policies (security, traffic shaping, and teaming and failover policies), you can select the last check box in the Configure Settings screen. Otherwise, you can always define these settings after the new port group has been created.

The last screen of the New Distributed Port Group wizard allows you to check all the selections that have been made for the new port group.

Once a dvPort group has been created, you can remove it, as long as you move all the virtual machines off the dvPort group first. An interesting thing to be aware of is that if you try to remove a dvPort group when there are virtual machines attached to it, even if those virtual machines aren't powered on, you receive an error message that the selected resource is in use. The easiest way to see what VMs are attached to the dvPort group is to select the port group, select the **Related Objects** tab, and select **Virtual Machines**. You get a list of all the VMs attached to the dvPort group, and you can then move them to another dvPort group or standard vSwitch port group. Once there are no virtual machines attached to the dvPort group, you right-click the dvPort group under the vDS in the Navigator pane and select **Delete**.

Add/Remove Uplink Adapters to dvUplink Groups

Once a vDS has been created and at least one dvPort group has been created, you may need to add additional physical uplinks to the vDS for one or more ESXi servers. In earlier examples, you created a vDS with only one uplink being contributed per ESXi server, vmnic1. In this section, you will add vmnic3 from each ESXi server to the vDS.

In the past, if you wanted to add additional physical uplinks to a vDS in the Windows vSphere Client, you would have had to go to each ESXi server from the hosts and clusters inventory view and add physical uplinks to the vDS from there. Fortunately, the vSphere Web Client enables you to manipulate a large number of objects with relative ease.

Right-click the vDS from the Navigator pane in the vSphere Web Client and choose **Add and Manage Hosts**. Then select **Manage Host Networking** and click **Next**. Once again, you can select from the attached hosts. Once all the ESXi servers have been selected, you can move onto the next part of the wizard, where you deselect **Manage VMkernel Adapters** so that only the **Manage Physical Adapters** check box is selected (see Figure 2-25).

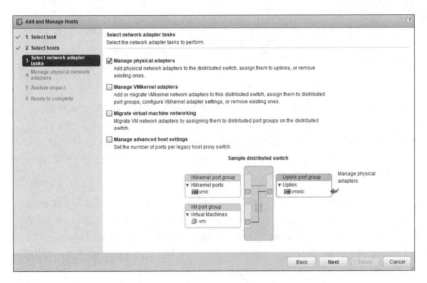

Figure 2-25   Manage Physical Adapters

The next screen looks almost identical to the screen where you selected the physical uplinks to add from each ESXi server to the vDS. You go through the same process here: Select one of the physical uplinks from each host and click **Assign Uplink**. As shown in Figure 2-26, vmnic1 has already been added from each ESXi server, so you should select vmnic3 instead.

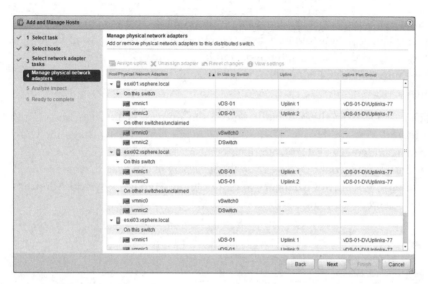

Figure 2-26   Assign Uplink

Instead of adding physical uplinks, you could also remove physical uplinks from multiple ESXi servers by using this method. At the top of the Manage Physical Network Adapters window is the Unassign Adapter option. To remove vmnic1 from each ESXi server on the vDS, you could simply select vmnic1 from each ESXi server host and then click **Unassign Adapter**.

In Figure 2-26, you can see that vmnic3 is assigned to the dvUplink slot Uplink 2 for each ESXi server. You then see a screen that identifies whether there is any impact to the iSCSI storage. In this case there is none because vmnic1 and vmnic3 are attached to a physical network that is not being utilized for IP-based storage. The final screen of the wizard allows you to check your selections.

As you have now seen, adding physical uplinks from each ESXi server is easier to do in the vSphere Web Client than in the vSphere Client. However, you could certainly use the vSphere Client per host if so desired by going to the hosts and clusters inventory view, selecting one of the ESXi servers, selecting **Manage > Networking**, selecting **Virtual Switches**, and clicking the **Manage Physical Adapters** icon (see Figure 2-27).

Figure 2-27   Manage Physical Adapters

This is the same screen that you can use to then remove physical uplinks from the vDS for each ESXi server. You just select one of the physical uplinks and click the red **X** icon at the top (see Figure 2-28).

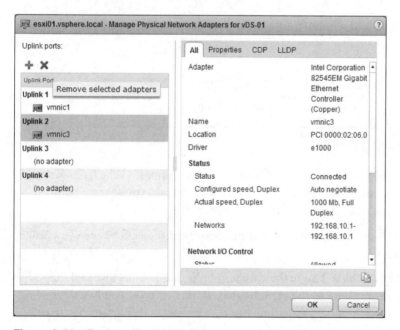

Figure 2-28   Remove Physical Uplink

Configure vSphere Distributed Switch General and dvPort Group Settings

When a vDS or dvPort group is created, as discussed earlier in this chapter, you can define some of the general settings. Of course, you can also adjust those settings after creation of a vDS or dvPort group.

To view the settings that can be modified on a vDS, right-click the vDS from the Navigator pane (in the networking inventory view) and select **Settings > Edit Settings** (see Figure 2-29). You then see additional options, such as **Edit Private VLAN**, **Edit NetFlow**, **Edit Health Check**, **Export Configuration**, and **Restore Configuration**. (We explore VLANs and PVLANs later in this chapter, in the section "Configure VLAN/PVLAN Settings for VMs Given Communication Requirements.")

Figure 2-29   Edit Settings for a vDS

In the Edit Settings window for the vDS, you see two options on the left: General and Advanced. Under General, which is selected by default, you see five options, some of which can't be modified here (see Figure 2-30):

- **Name:** This option was defined during creation of the vDS but can be changed here if needed.

- **Number of Uplinks:** This is the number of physical uplinks that each ESXi server can contribute to the vDS. By default, it is set to 4. You had the option to set that number at the time the vDS was created and can change it here if needed, to a minimum of 1 or a maximum of 32. Next to the number of uplinks is the link Edit Uplink Names, which you can click to modify the individual names of the dvUplinks if you don't want to use the default naming convention Uplink1, Uplink2, and so on (see Figure 2-31). Say that you need to configure one vDS for two or more types of traffic and two or more physical networks. You could label the dvUplinks vMotion and IP Storage,

for example. You would then know to contribute the physical uplinks from
each ESXi server that are on the physical network for vMotion to the vMotion
dvUplink, and the two adapters for IP storage to the IP Storage dvUplinks.
This is just one possibility. If one vDS were to only be used by one type of
traffic, or if you didn't want to use multiple physical networks on one vDS,
you could just have one vDS for vMotion, and still it may be useful to call the
dvUplinks something else like vMotion dvUplink to make it easy to know
which physical networks to use.

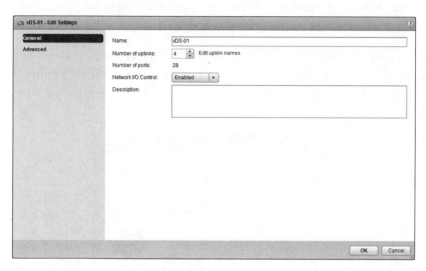

Figure 2-30   vDS General Settings

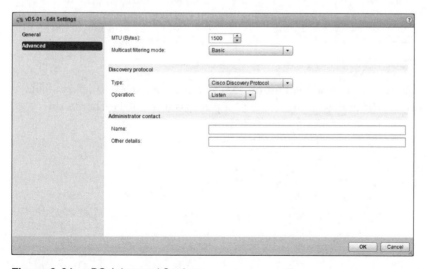

Figure 2-31   vDS Advanced Settings

- **Number of Ports:** On a vDS, this is set to 28 by default. This isn't modifiable from here, but you can define the numbers of ports per dvPort group, and since they are elastic by default, the number of ports on the vDS is not static.

- **Network I/O Control:** This option is enabled by default, provided that it was not changed during the creation of the vDS. Notice that the only options here are to enable and disable this setting. To further configure Network I/O Control, you need to go to the Manage tab of the vDS.

- **Description:** You can use this box to define information about the purpose of this vDS, what networks will be used by this vDS.

You can also modify the dvPort groups that exist on the vDS, either at time of creation or afterward. To modify a dvPort group's settings, expand the vDS in the Navigator pane, right-click the dvPort group, and choose **Settings > Edit Settings** (see Figure 2-32).

Figure 2-32   dvPort Group Settings

In the Edit Settings window (see Figure 2-33), you see the same settings available when you create the dvPort group in the first place, as discussed earlier in this chapter.

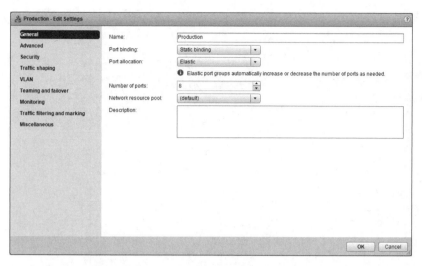

Figure 2-33   Edit Settings for a dvPort Group

Create/Configure/Remove Virtual Adapters

When you add ESXi servers to a vDS, there is an option to migrate VMkernel ports, and we discussed earlier why this is beneficial. If you were replacing all standard virtual switches with distributed virtual switches, you could migrate all physical uplinks and VMkernel ports at the same time to the new vDS. We now look at creating VMkernel ports on a vDS, configuring them, and removing them.

You can use the Add and Manage Hosts wizard to add VMkernel ports to an existing vDS. To launch the wizard, right-click a vDS and choose **Add and Manage Hosts**. Then choose **Select Task > Manage Host Networking**. On the Select Hosts screen, click the **Attached Hosts** link at the top and then select which ESXi servers you want to modify. You can select all or some of the ESXi servers. Once the ESXi servers have been selected, move to the **Select Network Adapter Tasks** screen.

To add new VMkernel ports, make sure only the **Manage VMkernel Adapters** check box is selected. You then see the Manage VMkernel Network Adapters screen in the Add and Manage Hosts wizard (see Figure 2-34).

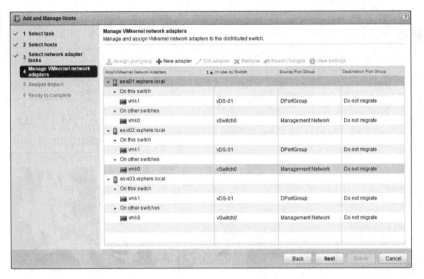

Figure 2-34   Add and Manage Hosts

Click **New Adapter** at the top of the window to bring up the Add Networking wizard (which we could also access by navigating to each individual ESXi server through the hosts and clusters inventory view and selecting **Manage > Networking > Add Networking**). Here, you select an existing network and choose the distributed virtual switch (see Figure 2-35).

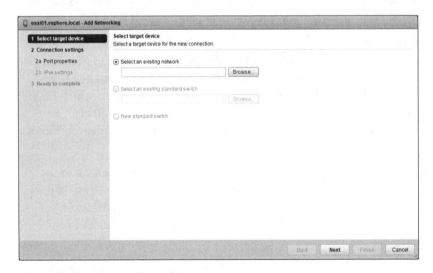

Figure 2-35   Manage Networking

Notice that on the Select Network screen (see Figure 2-36), the wizard only gives you the ability to choose from existing port groups. Unlike when you create a new VMkernel port on a standard vSwitch or when you create a VMkernel port via the hosts and clusters inventory view for a vDS, you do not have the ability to name a new VMkernel port here. You could always cancel this part of the wizard, minimize the task, and create a dvPort group. Or, because you can always rename dvPort groups later, you could simply choose the default dvPort group that was created for now since you created the Production dvPort group for use by your virtual machines. Once you have selected which network to use and clicked **Next**, you are presented with the **Port Properties** screen to define which type of VMkernel traffic this port will be used for (see Figure 2-37). Notice that from here, the option to define the network label and, interestingly, choose a different TCP/IP stack to use are disabled.

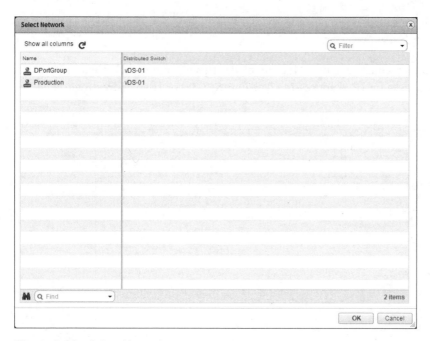

Figure 2-36 Select Network

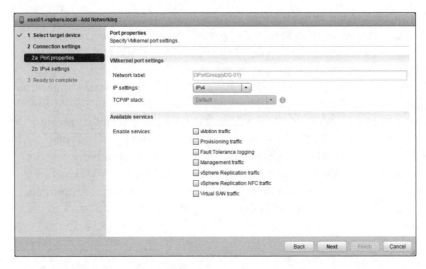

Figure 2-37   VMkernel Traffic Type

You can select which type of VMkernel traffic this is for and click **Next**. The
next screen asks for IPv4 addressing (see Figure 2-38) or IPv6 addressing (see
Figure 2-39).

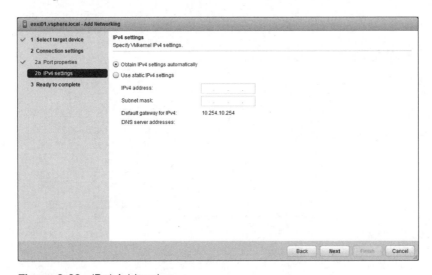

Figure 2-38   IPv4 Addressing

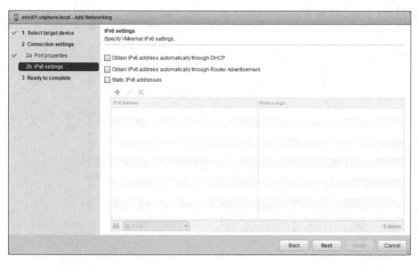

Figure 2-39 IPv6 Addressing

As you complete the wizard, you see that there is now a new VMkernel port listed under the first ESXi server listed. Now, for each of the other ESXi servers in the list, you can select the server and choose **New Adapter** again. This is just as time-consuming as the same process in the hosts and clusters inventory view, but you do not have to keep switching hosts in the Navigator pane. Once all the ESXi servers have been configured, you can go to the next screen of the Add and Manage Hosts wizard to see an analysis of the impact; if no adapters are being utilized for iSCSI, you do not see any errors. Finally you get the validation screen.

You can not only create VMkernel ports on a vDS but migrate existing VMker-nel ports from a standard vSwitch to a distributed vSwitch. This process is fairly straightforward: Right-click a vDS, choose **Add and Manage Hosts**, and choose **Manage Host Networking**. Then select the ESXi server(s) from the attached hosts and choose **Manage VMkernel Adapters** from the Select Network Adapter Tasks screen. This time, instead of choosing an ESXi server and choosing **New Adapter**, you choose a VMkernel port and click **Assign Port Group** at the top. If you are go-ing to migrate a VMkernel port from a standard virtual switch, it is a good idea to also move a physical uplink at the same time. Otherwise, as long as you have enough physical uplinks, make sure at least one is attached to the same physical network on the new vDS before trying to migrate a VMkernel port. You may notice that the ability to remove a VMkernel port is available from this view, as long as you are not removing vmk0. As long as you want to remove a VMkernel port that is not being used for management, you can do so from this view. To remove a VMkernel port marked for management from a vDS altogether, you have to go back to the hosts and clusters inventory view, select an ESXi server from the Navigator pane, go to **Manage > Networking > VMkernel Adapters**, and delete the VMkernel port from there (see Figure 2-40).

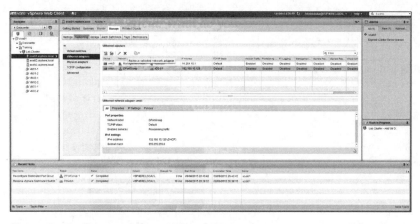

Figure 2-40   Remove Selected Network Adapter

Migrate Virtual Machines to/from a vSphere Distributed Switch

Moving virtual machines to or from a vSphere distributed switch can be a very easy operation, or it can be time-consuming. There are many ways to perform this task. The following sections look at the options available, from the most labor-intensive to the fastest way to perform this move on multiple virtual machines at once.

Migrating Virtual Machines Individually

This method requires the most administrative effort but is useful when you want to move just one virtual machine to/from a vDS. Right-click a virtual machine in the Navigator pane and choose **Settings > Edit Settings** (see Figure 2-41).

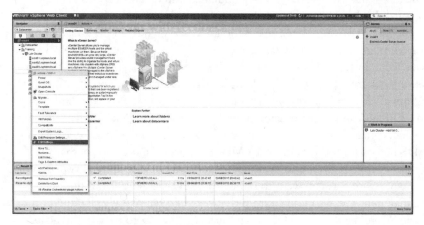

Figure 2-41   Edit Settings

In the Edit Settings window (see Figure 2-42), select the drop-down next to the virtual network adapter that you need to attach to the vDS and choose the dvPort group. The interface tries to assist with the decision of where to move the virtual machine by indicating which port groups are on standard vSwitches and which ones are on distributed vSwitches.

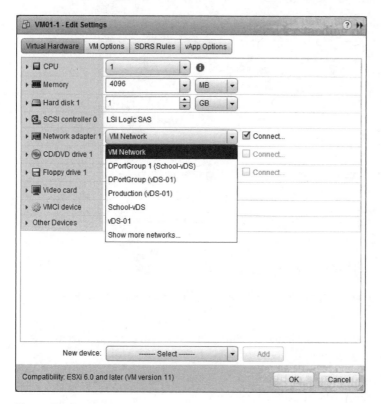

Figure 2-42   VM Network Adapter

Once the correct dvPort group has been selected, and the **Connected** check box has been selected, click **OK** to apply the change. To remove a virtual machine from a vDS, you can duplicate these steps but choose a standard virtual machine port group instead of the dvPort group.

NOTE   The virtual machine drops a few packets when you move it from a port group on a standard vSwitch to a vSphere distributed switch.

Migrating Multiple Virtual Machines

You can migrate multiple virtual machines to a vDS using a much faster method—
via the Migrate Virtual Machine Networking wizard. To access this wizard, you
must be in the networking inventory view. You then right-click the vDS and choose
Migrate VM to Another Network (see Figure 2-43).

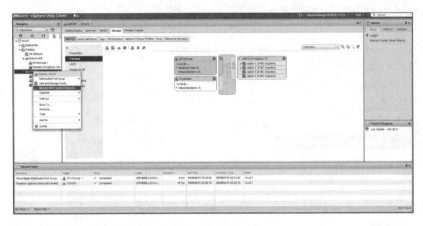

Figure 2-43   Migrate VM to Another Network

Notice these options in the wizard that appears (see Figure 2-44):

- **Specific network:** Allows you to browse for an existing virtual machine port
  group.

- **No network:** Specifies the virtual machine's network adapters that are not attached to a VM port group.

- **Destination network:** Allows you to browse the available dvPort groups to migrate the VMs from the chosen source network.

In the next screen you choose which virtual machines to migrate to the destination
network. You only see virtual machines that are attached to the source network in
this view and can select individual virtual machines or all of them on the source network (see Figure 2-45). Notice that the top of the window identifies which networks
the selected virtual machines are moving from and to. When you finish the wizard,
all the selected virtual machines are migrated to the new dvPort group.

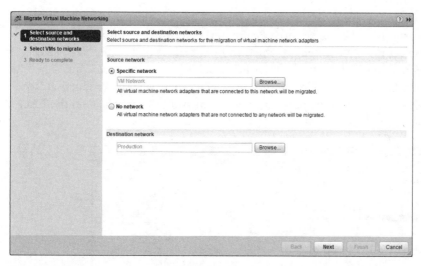

Figure 2-44   Migrate Virtual Machine Networking

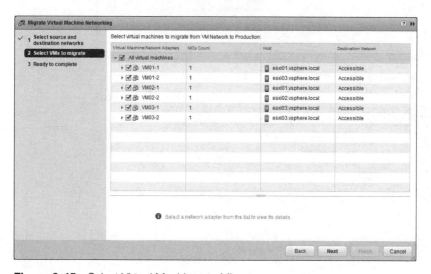

Figure 2-45   Select Virtual Machines to Migrate

Configure LACP on dvUplink and dvPort Groups

Only vDS support Link Aggregation Control Protocol (LACP). This support was first introduced in vSphere 5.1 and, as with all features introduced in 5.1 or later, is accessible only via the vSphere Web Client. LACP allows a logical grouping of physical network links to achieve greater bandwidth by using the multiple links as one logical connection. Unfortunately, when LACP is utilized, you cannot configure port mirroring, and you cannot include LACP in host profiles.

In order to configure uplink port groups for LACP, you must create a link aggregation group (LAG). Make sure you are in the networking inventory view and then select the vDS switch on which you want to set up LACP. Next, select **Manage > Settings > LACP** (see Figure 2-46). Now click the green plus sign to create the LAG and provide a descriptive name, such as LAG-Production (see Figure 2-47). Then select the number of ports you want to participate in the LAG group and set Mode to Passive.

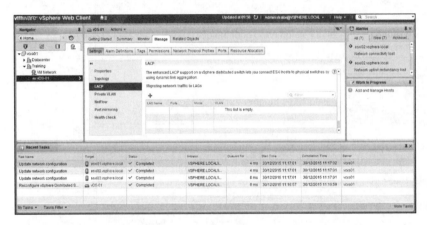

Figure 2-46   LACP Settings

New Link Aggregation Group

Name:	LAG-Production
Number of ports:	2
Mode:	Passive
Load balancing mode:	Source and destination IP address, TCP/UDP port and VLAN

Port policies

You can apply VLAN and NetFlow policies on individual LAGs within the same uplink port group. Unless overridden, the policies defined at uplink port group level will be applied.

VLAN type:	Override	VLAN trunking
VLAN trunk range:		0-4094
NetFlow:	Override	Disabled

OK   Cancel

Figure 2-47   Descriptive name

The other setting for Mode is Active, which means that all LAG ports are in an active negotiating mode. The LAG ports initiate negotiations with the LACP port channel on the physical switch by sending LACP packets.

LAG ports that are in passive negotiating mode respond to LACP packets they receive but do not initiate LACP negotiation.

Then select the desired option from the Load Balancing Mode drop-down. In this case, you want the setting Source and Destination IP Address (see Figure 2-48), but there are many other options, including the following:

- Destination, Source, or Source and Destination IP Address

- Destination, Source, or Source and Destination IP Address and TCP/UDP Port

- Destination, Source, or Source and Destination IP Address and VLAN

- Destination, Source, or Source and Destination IP Address, TCP/UDP Port and VLAN

- Destination, Source, or Source and Destination MAC Address

- Destination, Source, or Source and Destination TCP/UDP Port

- Source Port ID

- VLAN

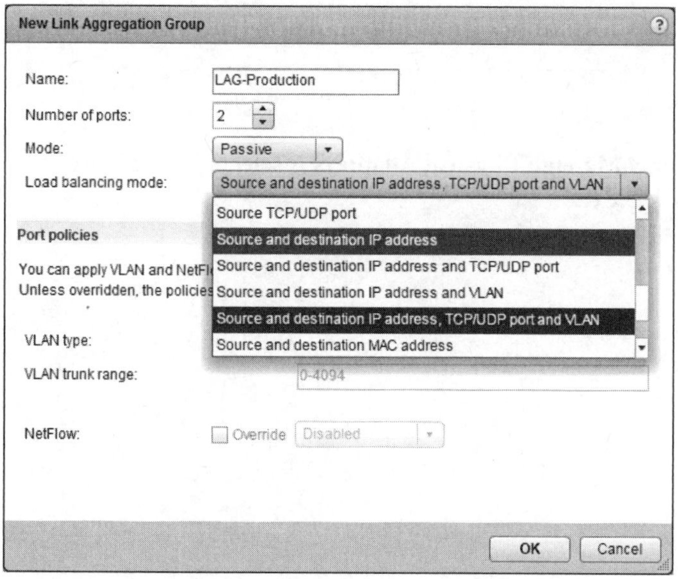

Figure 2-48   Source and Destination IP Address

NOTE LACP must be configured on a physical switch in order to successfully establish a connection.

To configure LACP on the dvUplink:

Step 1. Right-click **vDS-01** and select **Add and Manage Hosts.**

Step 2. Select **Manage Host Networking** and click **Next.**

Step 3. Click the **Attached Hosts icon** and select **esxi03.vsphere.local** (see Figure 2-49).

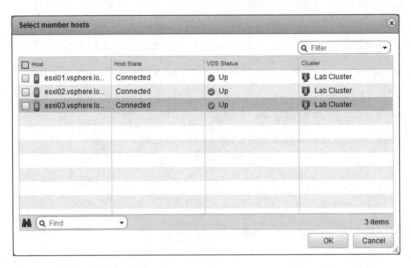

Figure 2-49 Attached Hosts

Step 4. Ensure that only **Manage Physical Adapters** is selected (see Figure 2-50) and click **Next.**

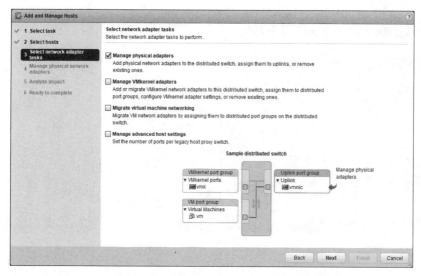

Figure 2-50   Manage Physical Adapters

Step 5.   Select **vmnic1** and click **Assign Uplink** (see Figure 2-51).

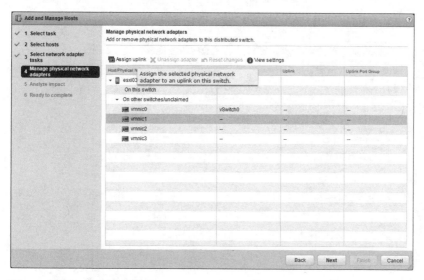

Figure 2-51   Assign Uplink

Step 6. Select **LAG-Production-0**, where **0** is the first port in the LAG group (see Figure 2-52), and click **OK**.

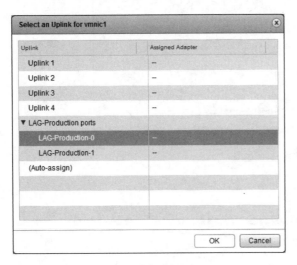

Figure 2-52 Select LAG for Uplink

Step 7. Select **vmnic2** and click **Assign Uplink** (see Figure 2-53).

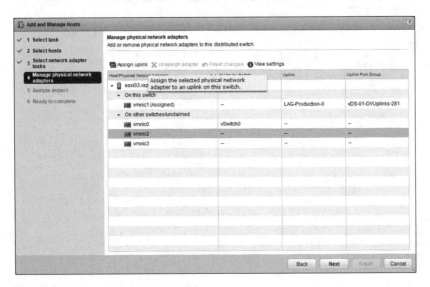

Figure 2-53 Assign Another Uplink

Step 8.   Select **LAG-Production-1**, where **1** is the second port in the LAG group (see Figure 2-54), and click **OK**.

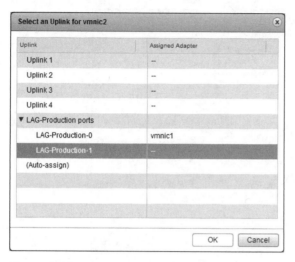

Figure 2-54   Select LAG-Production-1

Step 9.   Select **Next > Next > Finish** to complete the wizard.

Follow these steps to configure LACP on the dvPort group:

Step 1.   Right-click **Production** and click **Edit Settings** (see Figure 2-55).

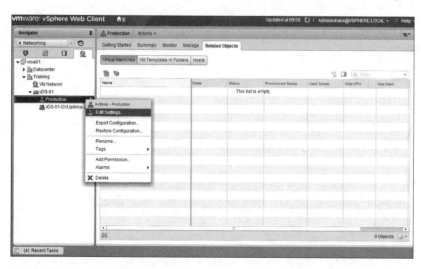

Figure 2-55   Edit Settings

Step 2.   Select **Teaming and Failover.** You now see **LAG-Production** in the
Unused Uplinks section (see Figure 2-56).

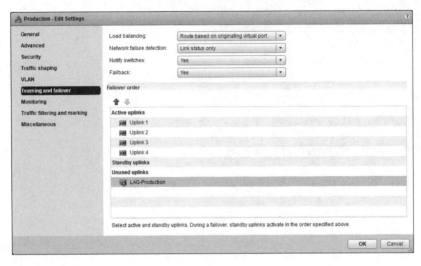

Figure 2-56   Unused Uplinks

Step 3.   Select **LAG-Production** and click the up arrow until it's at the top of the
list (see Figure 2-57).

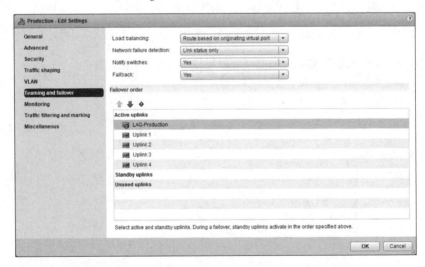

Figure 2-57   LAG-Production

Step 4.   Move the other items from the **Active Uplinks** section down to the
Unused Uplinks section (because standalone uplinks and LAGs are
not supported in a mixed configuration, as noted by the ◆ shown in
Figure 2-57).

NOTE   Notice the 🛈 . It informs you that the LAG's load-balancing mode over-rides the load-balancing mode of the port group (see Figure 2-58).

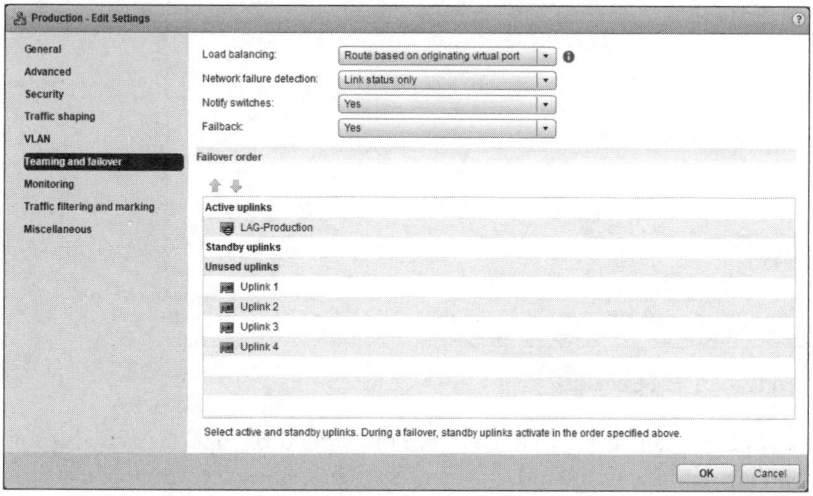

Figure 2-58   LAG Overriding Load-Balancing Mechanism

Describe vDS Security Policies/Settings

vDS security policy settings are almost exactly the same as vSphere standard switch policy settings. There are defaults for all dvPort groups and VMkernel ports on the vDS, or the policies can be overridden at the dvPort group or even port level. To modify the definitions, you have to modify the dvPort groups individually. Right-click a dvPort group in the Navigator pane and choose **Settings > Edit Settings**. The default is the General view, but you should select the **Security** option from the list on the left instead (see Figure 2-59).

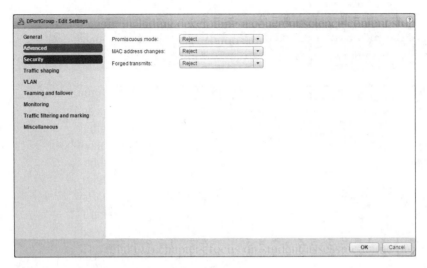

Figure 2-59 dvPortGroup Edit Settings

Just like on a vSphere standard switch, you have the same three options available for the security policy. Unlike with standard virtual switches, however, vSphere distributed switches default to Reject as the setting for all three options. This is an important distinction to be aware of. Otherwise, the functionality is the same. These are the three security policy options:

- **Promiscuous Mode:** If enabled, allows virtual machines to receive packets not destined for them, thus allowing tools such as TCPDump or Wireshark to be able to be utilized inside a guest operating system.

- **MAC Address Changes:** Allows a guest OS to change its own MAC address.

- **Forged Transmits:** Allows a guest OS to send a packet that appears to come from a different MAC address; this spoofing could be necessary if a virtual machine is doing something such as Microsoft Network Load Balancing or Microsoft Clustering Services.

These settings only allow functionality inside a guest operating system and have no impact on vSphere functions.

An interesting setting, available in the advanced policy for the dvPort group, is to allow overrides at the individual port level (see Figure 2-60). If only one virtual machine in a port group needs to analyze traffic, you can enable promiscuous mode for just that one switch port.

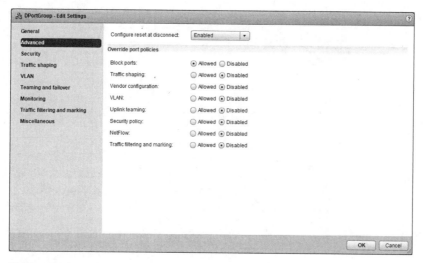

Figure 2-60   dvPortGroup Advanced Settings

Configure dvPort Group Blocking Policies

One of the advantages of utilizing vSphere distributed switches is that for large organizations, you can delegate control: The department that is responsible for managing the virtual switches/networking may be a different department from the one responsible for managing virtual machines—or, for that matter, for managing storage or ESXi servers or clusters. If a virtual machine started broadcasting traffic and consuming a large amount of network bandwidth, causing collisions or even dropped packets, the networking team could block a virtual switch port on a vDS even though that department may not have access to modify any of the virtual machine hardware (such as virtual network adapters). As you may have noticed in Figure 2-60, the ability to block individual vDS ports is enabled by default. This, of course, could be disabled if needed. It is also possible to block all switch ports on a dvPort group, cutting off everything attached to that dvPort group from the network (see Figure 2-61).

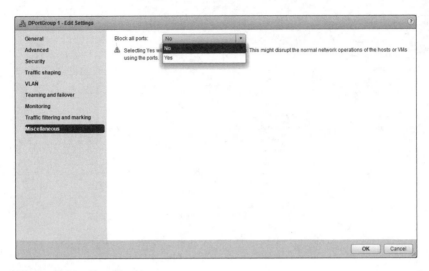

Figure 2-61   Port Blocking

Remember that a dvPort group can be used by virtual machines or by VMkernel ports, which is why the interface displays the warning message that this action could cause disruption of VMkernel traffic as well.

To block individual dvPorts and to see the ports in use and some general information on the ports, select the vDS from the Navigator pane and click the **Ports** button on the Manage tab (see Figure 2-62).

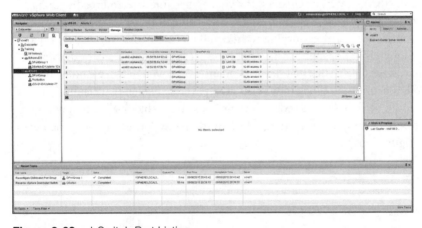

Figure 2-62   dvSwitch Port Listing

From here, you can select an individual port and see information about that port in the pane at the bottom, such as state, policy settings, etc. To block a port or to define any of the settings available at the dvPort group level to the port specifically, select a port (you can see which ports are in use by which virtual machines by looking at the Connected column) and select the pencil icon at the top of the window. Moving your mouse cursor over to the icon reveals the pop-up **Edit Distributed Port Settings**. Another **Edit Settings** window appears, allowing you to define at the port level the same things you saw at the dvPort level. Notice that if **Allow VM Overrides** is not selected for certain items, the options here are grayed out. To block a virtual switch port, select **Miscellaneous** from the left and choose the check box next to **Block Port: Override**. Then you can block the switch port by changing the drop-down selection from **No** to **Yes** (see Figure 2-63).

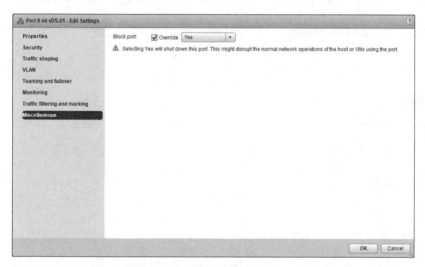

Figure 2-63   Block an Individual dvPort

Configure Load Balancing and Failover Policies

Much as when you define the load-balancing policies on vSphere standard switches, on a vDS, you have a fourth load-balancing mechanism, load-based teaming, and you can also define the load balancing not just at the dvPort level but at the individual port level as well.

As with defining the security policy at a dvPort level, the defaults that are set on the vDS are not configurable at the vDS level itself, but rather at the dvPort group level. Just like with vSS, the load-balancing mechanism set on a vDS by default is Originating Virtual Port ID because this has the lowest overhead and works regardless of the type of physical switches in the environment. In most cases, though, load-based teaming makes the most sense of any of the load-balancing mechanisms because unlike with the source and destination IP hash load-balancing mechanism, you don't need to configure the physical switches for link aggregation or Etherchannel, which means less administrative overhead/maintenance. It is important to note, however, that a virtual machine's effective bandwidth cannot exceed that of one physical net-work port, so if a virtual machine needs more bandwidth than one physical uplink can provide for it, the virtual machine needs more than one virtual network adapter. Typically, this is not an issue, especially with the rise of 10 Gbps and even 40 Gbps network adapters.

To access the load-balancing options available at the dvPort level, you once again go to the **Edit Settings** screen of the dvPort groups, but this time you choose the **Teaming and Failover** option from the left side of the window (see Figure 2-64).

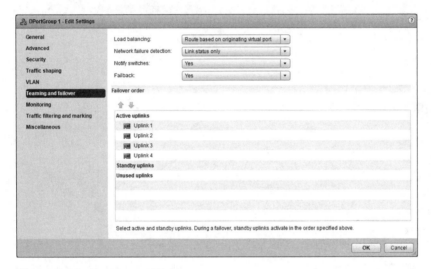

Figure 2-64   Teaming and Failover

Configure VLAN/PVLAN Settings for VMs Given Communication Requirements

Like vSphere standard switches, vSphere distributed switches can be configured to logically segment traffic by way of 802.1q VLAN tagging. The settings are more granular on vDS, however. To access the VLAN settings on a dvPort group, right-click the dvPort group in the Navigator pane under the vDS and choose **Settings > Edit Settings**. This once again opens the Edit Settings window for the dvPort group. Select the **VLAN** policy from the left, and you see several available options (see Figure 2-65):

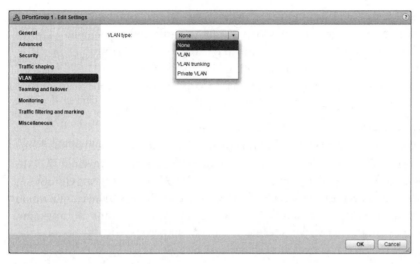

Figure 2-65   VLAN Tagging

- **VLAN:** The VLAN option allows the definition of a VLAN ID to be associated with the selected dvPort group, as with standard vSwitches. The difference is the VLAN ID range. On a standard port group, the valid VLAN ID range is 1 to 4094, with 4095 being identified as all traffic. 4095 on a standard vSwitch allows all tagged traffic to go through the port group with VLAN 4095 defined. If that port group also has promiscuous mode enabled, a virtual machine attached to that port group can see all traffic on the vSwitch, regardless of VLAN. On a dvPort group, the valid VLAN ID range is absolutely 1 to 4095. If you attempt to define VLAN 4095 on a dvPort group, the VLAN ID simply drops to 4094 as soon as you click out of the text box.

- **VLAN Trunking:** In order to achieve the same goal as VLAN 4095 on a dvPort group, we would have to select the VLAN Trunking option. This option gives you far more flexibility than simply having an "all or one" option that you have on standard vSwitches. With VLAN trunking, you can define a range of VLANs that are to be trunked or potentially visible to the dvPort group (or even an individual port). For example, to achieve exactly the same functionality that VLAN 4095 on a standard vSwitch yields, the VLAN trunking range is simply 1 to 4094, indicating that the selected dvPort group should be able to receive all VLANs worthy of traffic. However, the flexibility comes in the ability to subdivide which VLANs you want to be visible.

Say that an organization has VLANs defined for production traffic (VLAN 101), test/development traffic (VLAN 102), QA traffic (VLAN 103), IP storage traffic (VLAN 300), vMotion traffic (VLAN 310), and management traffic

(VLAN 500). A vDS administrator wants a virtual machine running Wire-Shark to be able to receive all virtual machine traffic and management traffic but doesn't want the virtual machine to be able to receive IP storage or vMotion traffic. The vDS administrator could then enter, 101 to 103,500 for the VLAN trunking range. Or if you wanted to only exclude vMotion and IP storage traffic, you could define the range 1 to 103,500 to 4094.

- **Private VLANs:** Private VLANs are an extension of the VLAN standard. They are not double encapsulation but do allow a VLAN to effectively be subdivided into other VLANs. This is useful, for example, for a hosting provider that has run out of VLANs or any environment where 4094 VLANs is not enough. vSphere supports private VLANs (and has since vSphere 4.0) because there are many organizations that employ private VLANs. vSphere administrators need to work with the networking teams to implement private VLANs because they affect traffic on the entire physical network as well.

A VLAN that is to be subdivided becomes known as the primary private VLAN. This primary PVLAN is then carved up into one or multiple secondary PVLANs that exist only within the primary. When a virtual machine or VMkernel port sends a packet, that packet is tagged at the dvPort group level on the vDS. Because this is not double encapsulation, packets only travel with one VLAN tag at a time. However, physical switches could be confused by seeing MAC addresses tagged with more than one VLAN tag, unless the physical switches are PVLAN aware and have their PVLAN tables configured appropriately. If the physical network is configured correctly, it identifies that the secondary PVLAN exists as part of the primary. This is defined in PVLAN tables on the physical networking switches themselves.

PVLANs are defined at the vDS level before they become available to define at the dvPort level. If PVLANs have not been defined at the vDS level, the properties of the dvPort display the error message `Private VLAN is not configured for this distributed switch`. To configure PVLANs on the vDS, right-click the vDS and select **Settings > Edit Private VLAN**. This brings up the Edit Private VLAN Settings window (see Figure 2-66).

Figure 2-66 Edit Private VLAN Settings

The first thing that has to be defined is the primary PVLAN. In this example, you define VLAN 10 as the primary PVLAN (see Figure 2-67). Once this has been defined, at least one secondary PVLAN can be defined. There are three different types of secondary PVLANs:

- **Promiscuous:** This type of secondary PVLAN is created by default when a primary PVLAN is defined on the distributed switch. The reason for this is that it might be necessary to place a virtual machine in the primary PVLAN in order to allow it to see all the traffic in other secondary PVLANs, but a VM cannot be connected directly to a distributed switch and can only be attached to a dvPort group. As a result, the VM can be placed in the promiscuous secondary PVLAN, effectively placing it in the primary PVLAN itself. VMs in a promiscuous secondary PVLAN can see all other VMs in other secondary PVLANs, regardless of whether they are in a community or isolated secondary PVLAN, as long as they are all in the same primary PVLAN.

- **Community:** VMs in a community secondary PVLAN are able to communicate with other VMs in the same community as well as virtual machines that are in the promiscuous secondary PVLAN because they are in the same primary PVLAN. Multiple community secondary PVLANs can be created in the same primary, and each community is unable to see other communities or isolated PVLANs.

- **Isolated:** Virtual machines in an isolated secondary PVLAN are unable to communicate with other VMs in the isolated secondary PVLAN or any VM in a community secondary PVLAN, but they are able to see and communicate with VMs in the promiscuous secondary PVLAN because they are in the same primary PVLAN.

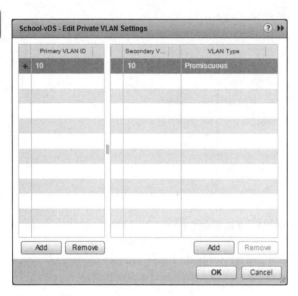

Figure 2-67 Edit Private VLAN

PVLANs and the types of secondary PVLANs become very useful when there is a need to isolate multiple VMs. If an organization needs to logically segment more than 4096 virtual machines from each other, there isn't a way to do it with regular VLANs. But by using PVLANs—specifically isolated secondary PVLANs—all those virtual machines and more can be logically isolated. Another example is if there is a forward-facing web server that you want to be accessed from multiple secondary PVLANs; you could place that web server in the promiscuous secondary PVLAN. Then an app server and database server could be placed in a community secondary PVLAN. Instead of a web server, a router could be used to illustrate a similar need for this type of communication.

As a further example of how some of these PVLANs could be put in use, think of a school that is using only virtual desktops. There could be zero clients at every student desk, at the teacher's desks, in the computer labs, and in the main office. There may also be security requirements; for example, you may want the front desk to be able to see all of the virtual desktops, the student virtual desktops to be able to only see the front desk and not each other, and all the virtual desktops in each computer lab to be able to see just the virtual desktops in each lab room. To implement this scenario, you might want the main office to be in a promiscuous secondary PVLAN, to be able to see all virtual desktops in the school, the student virtual desktops to be in an isolated secondary PVLAN, and each computer lab to be in a community secondary PVLAN.

You could define a primary PVLAN of 10 to the vDS for the school. Then you could define the additional PVLANs that will be used for the dvPort groups. As discussed earlier, the PVLANs have to be defined on the vDS before they can be used on the dvPort groups (see Figure 2-68). After the primary PVLAN is defined, you can then click the **Add** button in the right-hand side of the window to add additional secondary PVLANs in addition to the promiscuous one. You define the secondary PVLAN ID and then click the drop-down to set whether it's a community or isolated PVLAN. Then you can define secondary PVLAN 10 for the main office, secondary PVLANs 21 to 23 for the computer labs, and secondary PVLAN 24 for the students.

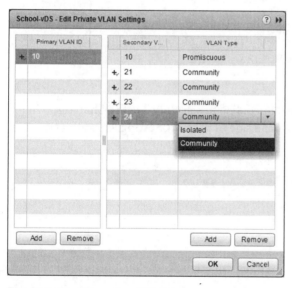

Figure 2-68   Secondary PVLANs

Configure Traffic Shaping Policies

Traffic shaping can be configured on vSphere standard switches or vSphere distributed switches. On standard switches, it can only be configured for outbound traffic, and it can be configured at the switch or VMkernel port/VM port group level. On a distributed switch, traffic shaping can be configured for outbound and inbound traffic, and it can be defined at the dvPort group or port level.

To define the traffic shaping policies for a VMkernel or virtual machine port group level on a standard virtual switch, select the ESXi server from the Navigator pane of the hosts and clusters inventory view and select **Manage > Networking > Virtual Switches**. Select the virtual switch where the port group resides and in the switch diagram, select the virtual machine port group or VMkernel port and click the pencil icon (see Figure 2-69).

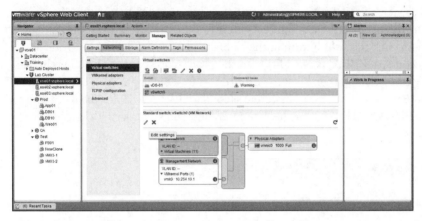

Figure 2-69 Edit Settings

You can then define the traffic shaping policy by selecting **Traffic Shaping** from the list of policies in the left-hand side of the **Edit Settings** window (see Figure 2-70).

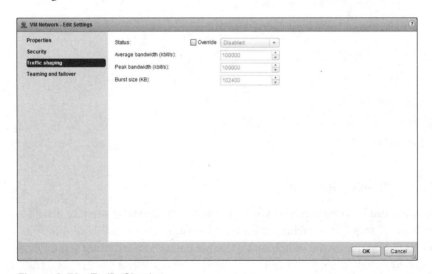

Figure 2-70 Traffic Shaping

As you can see in Figure 2-70, the port group is currently inheriting the traffic shaping policy defined on the virtual switch itself, and that policy is turned off by default. You can override the switch policy here and define average and peak bandwidth as well as burst size. What this means is that you can define an average bandwidth allotment for the VMs within this port group. If they haven't used all the average bandwidth, you can allow them to be able to "burst" to the peak bandwidth. The way this mechanism works is that if a VM has not used all the bandwidth defined in the average, if there is not contention on the network, the VM attached to the port group can have a burst bonus and is then able to use bandwidth up to the peak—but only with the given burst size. Once the burst size has been reached, the bonus ends, and the port group restricts the bandwidth back to the average.

To define this policy on a dvPort group, you need to go back to the networking inventory view. Expand the vDS in the Navigator pane and right-click the port group you want to modify. This is the same place you defined the private VLAN in the prior section. Select **Traffic Shaping** from the policies on the left. This time, because you are looking at a dvPort group on a vDS, you see the ability to define inbound and outbound traffic shaping (see Figure 2-71).

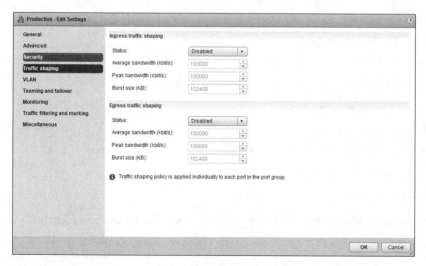

Figure 2-71   Inbound/Outbound Traffic Shaping

The part of this that can be confusing is that because these traffic shaping policies are defined at the dvPort group or port level, they are affecting the traffic through a dvPort. In other words, you are not defining limitations on the physical network adapters because doing so would require a setting on the dvUplink instead. You are only defining limitations for the dvPort or port group on a vDS. On a vSS, the same is true, except that, again, you can only define outbound traffic.

Enable TCP Segmentation Offload Support for a Virtual Machine

TCP segmentation offload (referred to as large segment offload or large send offload [LSO] in VMXNET3's latest attributes) allows the segmentation of traffic to be offloaded from the VM and from the VMkernel to the physical network adapter itself. The result is less overhead and better performance. ESXi servers are configured by default to be able to utilize this functionality as long as the physical network adapters themselves support this feature.

Since this is enabled by default, you can disable or reenable it via the vSphere Web Client or through the command line if necessary. You also have the ability to enable or disable this feature at the physical network adapter. To change the TSO setting via the Web Client, you start from the hosts and clusters inventory view. Select an ESXi server and then select the **Manage > Settings> Advanced System Settings**. Then set the option **Net.UseHWTSO** to **1** to enable the feature or **0** to disable it.

To enable or disable TSO using the ESXi Shell or SSH directly to the ESXi server, you use the following commands:

- On vSphere 4.x hosts, enable TSO like this:

  ```
  # esxcfg-advcfg -s 1 /Net/UseHwTSO
  ```

  and disable TSO like this:
  ```
  # esxcfg-advcfg -s 0 /Net/UseHwTSO
  ```

- On vSphere 5.x and newer hosts, enable TSO like this:

  ```
  # esxcli system settings advanced set -o /Net/UseHwTSO -i 1
  ```

  and disable TSO like this:
  ```
  # esxcli system settings advanced set -o /Net/UseHwTSO -i 0
  ```

- On vSphere 4.x hosts, identify whether TSO is enabled like this:

  ```
  # esxcfg-advcfg -g /Net/UseHwTSO
  ```

- On vSphere 5.x and higher hosts, identify whether TSO is enabled like this:

  ```
  # esxcli system settings advanced list -o /Net/UseHwTSO
  ```

If the `Int Value` value is `1`, TSO is enabled.

Here is how you enable TSO on physical network adapters:

```
# ethtool -K vmnic# tso on
```

replacing # with the physical uplink number.

Here is how you disable TSO on physical network adapters:

```
# ethtool -K vmnic# tso off
```

> **NOTE** This command is not persistent across reboots. When the physical ESXi server is rebooted, the physical uplinks revert back to the defaults. In order to force this command to persist across reboots of the ESXi server host, the command has to be added manually to the `/etc/rc.local.d/local.sh` file on the ESXi server.

Here is how you enable TSO on Linux:

```
# ethtool -K eth# tso on
```

replacing # with the virtual network adapter number.

Here is how you disable TSO on Linux:

```
# ethtool -K eth# tso off
```

To enable TSO on Windows, power off the virtual machine and add the following line to the .vmx file:

```
# ethernet#.features = "0x2"
```

replacing # with the virtual network adapter number.

If the guest OS is Windows 2000, ensure that the following registry setting is defined:

```
My Computer\HKEY_LOCAL_MACHINE\SYSTEM\CurrentControlSet\Services\
Tcpip\Parameters
```

Add this value:

```
DisableLargeSendOffload
```

and set it to 0. Once this has been defined in the registry, after the OS is rebooted, the virtual machine makes use of TSO.

Enable Jumbo Frames Support on Appropriate Components

Ethernet packets, or frames, are 1500 bytes by default. This is for cross-compatibility with all physical networking infrastructure, from older or unmanaged switches to brand-new high-end physical switches. Some organizations have their networking components set to reject or block jumbo frames, or large-sized packets. If configured end-to-end, however (meaning all interconnecting networking between source and destination), jumbo frames can allow better utilization of a fast network link, such as a 10 Gbps link.

In order to make use of jumbo frames, you must enable them on the virtual switch (standard or distributed), inside guest operating systems that need to make use of this feature, and/or on VMkernel ports that need this enabled (those for IP storage, vMotion, fault tolerance, VSAN, etc.). To configure jumbo frames for a standard virtual switch, from the hosts and clusters inventory view, select an ESXi server and select **Manage > Networking**. Then select the virtual switch you need to enable jumbo frames for and click the pencil icon (see Figure 2-72).

Figure 2-72   Manage Networking

The properties of the virtual switch come up, and you need to define the default maximum transmission unit (MTU) as a 9000-byte packet size (see Figure 2-73).

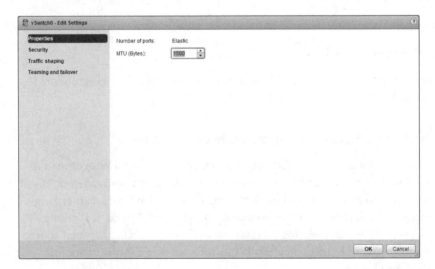

Figure 2-73   MTU Setting

To enable jumbo frames on a vSphere distributed switch, you need to be in the networking inventory view, right-click the vSphere distributed switch on which you choose to enable jumbo frames, and select **Settings > Edit Settings**. From here, you click on **Advanced** on the left and then define the MTU size, as you do with a standard vSwitch (see Figure 2-74).

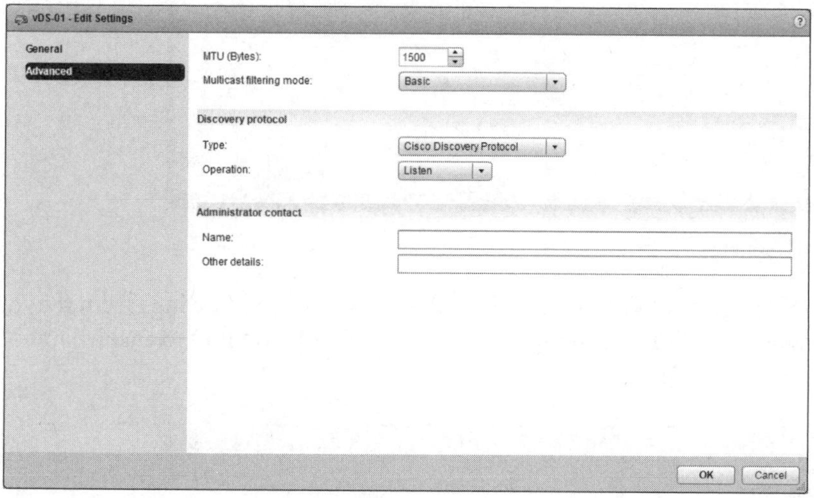

Figure 2-74 Advanced vDS Settings

Once jumbo frames has been enabled on the standard or distributed switch, you have to enable it on the VMkernel ports you want to use with jumbo frames, and/or the virtual machines.

To enable jumbo frames for VMkernel ports on vSS or vDS, you go through the same process, since VMkernel ports are defined on the ESXi servers: In the hosts and clusters inventory view, select an ESXi server and again select **Manage > Networking** but this time select **VMkernel Adapters** from the left. Then select the VMkernel port you wish to modify and click the pencil icon (see Figure 2-75).

Figure 2-75   Edit Settings

In the Edit Settings window of the VMkernel port, select **NIC Settings** from the left, and change the MTU setting from the default of 1500 to **9000** to enable jumbo frames (see Figure 2-76).

Figure 2-76   VMkernel MTU Setting

You can find many blog posts and white papers on the merits of enabling jumbo frames and whether doing so is truly as beneficial as one may surmise when it comes to vMotion, IP storage, fault tolerance, or VSAN. In the end, a lot of times it comes down to testing it in your environment to determine whether there is enough benefit to make it worth making the change. In most cases, the benefit can be realized when you are dealing with moving large amounts of data, as is the case for vMotion migrations, fault tolerance logging, or storage traffic, but, of course, it depends on the usage and characteristics of the virtual machines and their application workloads. In any case, there wouldn't be any benefit to enabling jumbo frames for small traffic loads, such as management traffic.

To enable jumbo frames for a virtual machine, you first have to make sure the VM is using a VMXNET3 adapter because the E1000 and E1000E do not support the use of jumbo frames. Once the virtual machine is configured with a virtual network adapter that supports jumbo frames and the vSwitch the virtual machine is attached to has this enabled, you can then configure the operating system to use jumbo frames. This chapter does not go into depth about how to enable jumbo frames for all of the various different operating systems in use today. Refer to your OS vendor's documentation for instructions on how to enable jumbo frames for that specific operating system.

Determine Appropriate VLAN Configuration for a vSphere Implementation

VLANs, as discussed earlier, allow a logical segmentation of a network when physical segmentation is not possible. Since VLANs defined in a virtual network affect and are affected by the physical network as well, a vSphere administrator needs to coordinate with a networking administrator to determine how VLANs (and which VLAN IDs) will be used in a virtual environment. In a lot of cases, defining how many and which VLANs to use is very similar to deciding how many physical networks (physical uplinks, physical switches, etc.) should be used. For example, is the organization bound by regulatory requirements, or is there a management directive that the management network be physically segmented from regular traffic? Is physical segmentation required, or is logical segmentation using VLANs acceptable? A big deciding factor can simply be the number of physical uplinks available for use on an ESXi server. If there are only two, for example, then it would be very difficult to achieve physical segmentation between just management and regular virtual machine traffic, to say nothing of other VMkernel or different tiers of virtual machine traffic. In a system with two physical uplinks, for example, you would have very few choices, and ideally you would want to configure a single virtual switch with both physical uplinks attached and then utilize VLAN tagging at the VMkernel port and VM port group level to logically segment the traffic. The more physical uplinks that are on the ESXi server, of course, the more options are available.

Recognize Behavior of vDS Auto-Rollback

vSphere 5.1 introduced the ability to offer rollback options in the event that the management VMkernel network becomes disconnected. For standard virtual switches, if an administrator misconfigures the management network, causing an ESXi server to be unreachable, the network can be reset using the DCUI. However, on vDS environments, misconfigurations could cause potentially hundreds of ESXi servers to become disconnected, as they all share the same network configuration. When anyone misconfigures a vDS, causing the management network to become disconnected, the ESXi servers automatically roll back to the last configuration.

Automatic network rollback is enabled by default, and the following events can trigger such a rollback (see the VMware KB 2032908):

- Host networking rollbacks:
  - Updating the speed or duplex of a physical NIC (such as updating DNS and routing settings)
  - Updating teaming and failover policies or traffic shaping policies of a standard port group that contains the management VMkernel network adapter
  - Updating the VLAN of a standard port group that contains the management VMkernel network adapter
  - Increasing the MTU of management VMkernel network adapters and their switches to values not supported by the physical infrastructure
  - Changing the IP settings of management VMkernel network adapters
  - Removing the management VMkernel network adapter from a standard or distributed switch
  - Removing a physical NIC of a standard or distributed switch containing the management VMkernel network adapter
- Distributed switch rollbacks:
  - Changing the MTU of a distributed switch
  - Changing the following settings in the distributed port group of the management VMkernel network adapter: Teaming and Failover, VLAN, and Traffic Shaping
  - Blocking all ports in the distributed port group containing the management VMkernel network adapter
  - Overriding the policies above for the distributed port to which the management VMkernel network adapter is connected

The process for restoring a vDS from the DCUI is as follows:

Step 1.   Connect to the DCUI from a crash cart or management card.

Step 2.   Log into the DCUI.

Step 3.   Select **Network Restore Options**.

Step 4.   Select **Restore vDS**.

Step 5.   Enter the appropriate values for VLAN uplink and blocked settings.

Step 6.   Press **Enter**.

The operations that take place when the vDS is restored from the DCUI are as follows:

- A new local (host-only) VMkernel port gets created, using the VLAN and blocking settings defined in the DCUI.

- The management network uses this new VMkernel port, and vCenter is then able to contact the ESXi server.

- vCenter's database is updated with the new VMkernel port information.

- vCenter creates a new VMkernel port connected to the management network.

NOTE   Network recovery is not supported on an auto deployed ESXi server with a stateless configuration (installed to RAM).

Configure vDS Across Multiple vCenter Servers to Support Long-Distance vMotion

Numerous improvements have been made to vMotion in vSphere 6. Two of the major improvements are long-distance vMotion and Cross vCenter vMotion. Long-distance vMotion allows vMotion migrations across up to a 150-ms round-trip latency link. In vSphere 6, any or all of the following can be changed for a virtual machine with vMotion:

- Computing resource location (ESXi Host)

- Datastore location

- Network:

  - From standard virtual switch to distributed virtual switch

  - From standard virtual switch to standard virtual switch

  - From distributed virtual switch to distributed virtual switch

- vCenter

The requirements for long-distance vMotion include:

- VM networking should have Layer 2 network connectivity.

- The IP address of the VM must be available at the destination.

- The vMotion network (VMkernel network designated for vMotion) needs Layer 3 connectivity.

- There should be 250 Mbps for each vMotion migration.

- There should be a maximum of 150 ms round-trip latency.

- The vMotion network should be secure, either via physical segmentation and/or link layer encryption.

In order to perform Cross vCenter vMotion migrations, the vCenter Servers must be in enhanced linked mode, and they also must be sharing the same SSO information. This can be done by either having the two vCenter Servers connecting to the same Platform Services Controller, or Platform Services Controllers that are replicating between them. The license required to configure Enhanced Linked Mode is vCenter Standard (not Foundation or Essentials).

Linking vCenter Servers together using enhanced linked mode is a very easy process: When you install a second vCenter Server, during the installation, you point to the existing SSO environment (via the already created or replicated Platform Services Controller). The rest of the install is like normal. Once the new vCenter Server is installed, when you log into the vSphere Web Client, you see both vCenter Servers in the inventory.

Once the vCenter Servers have been linked together, you need to evaluate the VM-kernel ports designated for vMotion and ensure that their configuration meets the requirements. (See the requirements for long-distance vMotion.) To ensure that the configurations match, host profiles can be created on one of the ESXi servers on one vCenter and then exported and imported to the other vCenter Server. If vSphere distributed switches are used, the vDS configuration can be exported as well and imported on the new vCenter Server. In addition to the normal checks that vCenter performs prior to a vMotion migration, if a Cross vCenter vMotion migration is attempted, vCenter performs checks and displays errors if any of the following occurs:

- The MAC address is not available at the destination.

- A vMotion migration is attempted from a distributed to a standard switch.

- A vMotion migration is attempted between vSphere distributed switches of different versions.

- A vMotion migration is attempted to an internal-only network.

Summary

You have now read the chapter covering exam topics on vDS and vSS settings, configurations, migrations, and use and functionality. You should now use information in the following sections to complete your preparation for Objective 2.1.

Exam Preparation Tasks

Review All the Key Topics

Table 2-3 provides a reference to each of the key topics identified in this chapter. Take a few moments to review each of these specific items.

Table 2-3   Key Topics for Chapter 2

Key Topic Element	Description	Pages
Figure 2-7	vDS dvPort Groups	72
Section	Add/Configure/Remove dvPort Groups	82
Figure 2-34	Add and Manage Hosts	94
Paragraph	Configure load-balancing and failover policies	113
Figure 2-67	Edit Private VLAN Paragraph	118
Paragraph	Traffic shaping policies	121
Section	Recognize Behavior of vDS Auto-Rollback	127

Complete the Tables and Lists from Memory

Print a copy of Appendix B, "Memory Tables" (found on the CD), or at least the section for this chapter, and complete the tables and lists from memory. Appendix C, "Memory Tables Answer Key," also on the CD, includes completed tables and lists to check your work.

Definitions of Key Terms

Define the following key terms from this chapter and check your answers in the glossary.

vDS, vSS, dvPort group, dvUplink, PVLAN

Answer Review Questions

The answers to these review questions can be found in Appendix A.

1. Which type of virtual network adapter is needed to support jumbo frames inside a VM?

   a. Flexible

   b. VMXNET3

   c. E1000

   d. E1000E

2. Which type of secondary private VLAN would be defined for a group of virtual machines if you wanted them to be able to communicate to each other but not to any of the other secondary private VLANs that are defined under the same primary PVLAN?

   a. Community

   b. Promiscuous

   c. Isolated

   d. Company

3. When can an ESXi server be added to a vDS?

   a. In the vDS creation wizard, you can select which ESXi servers you want to push the vDS to and choose physical uplinks from each.

   b. ESXi servers cannot be added to a vDS.

   c. After the vDS is created, you can drag the ESXi servers to the vDS.

   d. After the vDS is created, you can use the Add and Manage Hosts wizard.

4. Which of the following is only a vDS capability?

   a. NIC teaming

   b. Outbound traffic shaping

   c. Port state monitoring

   d. Port forwarding

5. Which vDS security policy would prevent Microsoft Network Load Balancing (MSNLB) from functioning properly?

   a. Promiscuous mode set to accept

   b. MAC address changes set to accept

   c. Promiscuous mode set to reject

   d. Forged transmits set to reject

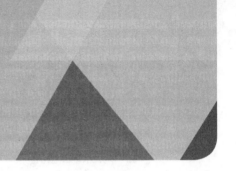

This chapter covers the following objective:

- **Objective 2.2—Configure Network I/O Control (NIOC)**

  - Define Network I/O Control

  - Explain Network I/O Control capabilities

  - Configure NIOC shares/limits based on VM requirements

  - Explain the behavior of a given Network I/O Control setting

  - Determine Network I/O Control requirements

  - Differentiate Network I/O Control capabilities

  - Enable/disable Network I/O Control

  - Monitor Network I/O Control

## CHAPTER 3

Networking, Part 2

This chapter expands on the discussions in the previous chapter and goes into Network I/O Control (NIOC) and its capabilities and requirements. Administrators may need to configure NIOC, especially in cases where the physical ESXi servers may not have many physical network adapters or where multiple types of traffic need to pass through few physical uplinks, making it necessary to prioritize different types of traffic if there is network congestion. For example, if vMotion and IP Storage are on the same network, there is a possibility of poor storage performance when a vMotion migration is performed as a result of vMotion consuming a large amount of network bandwidth. NIOC can allow administrators to prioritize workloads accordingly.

"Do I Know This Already?" Quiz

The "Do I Know This Already?" quiz allows you to assess whether you should study this entire chapter or move quickly to the "Exam Preparation Tasks" section. Regardless, the authors recommend that you read the entire chapter at least once. Table 3-1 outlines the major headings in this chapter and the corresponding "Do I Know This Already?" quiz questions. You can find the answers in Appendix A, "Answers to the 'Do I Know This Already?' Quizzes and Review Questions."

Table 3-1 "Do I Know This Already?" Foundation Topics Section-to-Question Mapping

Foundation Topics Section	Questions Covered in This Section
Define Network I/O Control	6
Explain Network I/O Control Capabilities	1
Configure NIOC Shares/Limits Based on VM Requirements	4, 7
Explain the Behavior of a Given Network I/O Control Setting	5
Determine Network I/O Control Requirements	2
Differentiate Network I/O Control Capabilities	9
Enable/Disable Network I/O Control	3
Monitor Network I/O Control	8

1. Which version of Network I/O Control (NIOC) was introduced in vSphere 6?

    a. Version 3

    b. Version 12

    c. Version 6

    d. NIOC is not available in vSphere 6.

2. Which feature cannot be configured for a virtual machine to be able to make use of NIOC?

    a. Independent virtual disks

    b. Raw device mappings

    c. SR-IOV

    d. Processor affinity

3. On a vDS, network bandwidth can be allocated for different types of traffic. Which of the following are valid types of system traffic that can have this defined? (Choose three.)

    a. iSCSI

    b. Management

    c. vSA

    d. High availability

    e. vSphere data protection

4. What is the range for share values that can be defined on network resource pools?

    a. 1–50

    b. 1–100

    c. 1000–10000

    d. There is no upper limit on shares because they are just a relative priority.

5. How high can a reservation be set on virtual machine traffic when setting up the system traffic for virtual machines?

    a. 75% of the total bandwidth

    b. 50% of the total bandwidth

    c. 100% of the total bandwidth

    d. You cannot define reservations for virtual machine traffic.

6. What does NIOC allow?

   a. NIOC allows direct use of physical network adapters, bypassing the virtualization layer.

   b. NIOC allows the prioritization of network traffic through defining reservations, limits, and shares for virtual machine and VMkernel traffic.

   c. NIOC allows the prioritization of network traffic through defining reservations, limits, and shares for virtual machines only.

   d. NIOC allows the prioritization of network traffic through defining reservations, limits, and shares for VMkernel traffic only.

7. Where would reservations for user-defined network resource pools be defined?

   a. Reservations only need to be set on the user-defined network resource pool.

   b. Reservations are not supported on NIOC.

   c. Reservations are set on the vDS for all traffic before it can be defined for a user-defined network resource pool.

   d. A reservation needs to be defined for virtual machine traffic under system traffic for the vDS before a reservation can be defined for user-defined network resource pools.

8. What information could an administrator obtain about NIOC for a vDS through the Resource Allocation tab of the Manage tab of a vDS? (Choose three.)

   a. Number of physical uplinks configured for NIOC

   b. Network speed of the slowest physical uplink

   c. Current reservations set

   d. Network speed of the fastest physical uplink

   e. Minimum reservation allowed

9. Which of the following is not supported on NIOC version 3 but is supported on NIOC version 2?

   a. CoS

   b. User-defined network resource pools

   c. Reservations

   d. Limits

   e. Shares

Foundation Topics

Objective 2.2—Configure Network I/O Control (NIOC)

This section defines how to configure Network I/O Control (NIOC), the requirements to enable it, the capabilities of what NIOC can do, and how to monitor NIOC.

Define Network I/O Control

Network I/O Control (NIOC) was created to allow vSphere administrators to be able to control which type of traffic has priority over other types of traffic in the event of network contention. There are a couple main versions of NIOC, and it is important to understand the capabilities and changes between versions. NIOC allows you to define shares, reservations, and limits for network traffic and can be defined for virtual machines and VMkernel traffic.

Explain Network I/O Control Capabilities

Network I/O Control (NIOC) was enabled by way of vSphere Distributed Switches (vDSs) as early as vDSs were first supported—in vSphere 4. It is useful to identify the changes to NIOC through the versions, however. vSphere 4 has predefined network resource pools and offers no ability to add additional ones. In vSphere 4, on vDSs, administrators can define shares and limits for each type of VMkernel traffic, as well as for all virtual machine traffic. The advantage here is that if you are working with ESXi server hosts with very few physical network adapters, and you need to have everything—or multiple dvPorts—using the same physical uplinks, it would be useful to prioritize which processes are more important or more sensitive to network latency than others. The big problem, however, is that this means grouping all virtual machine traffic together, so test or development virtual machines are just as important as production virtual machines. vSphere 5 introduced the concept of user-defined network resource pools, which can align with dvPort groups. With vSphere 5 it is possible to define different priorities to test in dev and production, which makes a lot more sense for most environments. In vSphere 6 and vDS 6.0.0, reservations have been added to allocate minimum acceptable bandwidth to VMs or groups of VMs.

It is possible to upgrade from NIOC version 2 to version 3 in vSphere 6, but there you lose functionality when you perform this upgrade. The VMware document http://tinyurl.com/nukbmm9 describes the following losses:

- User-defined network resource pools, including all associations between them and existing distributed port groups

- Existing associations between ports and user-defined network resource pools

- CoS tagging of the traffic that is associated with a network resource pool

If an administrator is deciding to upgrade to NIOC version 3, it is a good idea to back up the existing vDS configuration first in case there is a need to roll back. Remember that once a vDS has been upgraded, there is no way to downgrade unless you revert to a previously backed up configuration.

To perform the upgrade from NIOC version 2 to version 3 (which must be done in the vSphere Web Client):

Step 1.   Ensure that the vDS is at version 6.0.0:

- Select the vDS from the Navigator pane on the left.

- Select the **Summary** tab at the top.

- Under Version, verify that 6.0.0 is listed. If it is not, the vDS needs to be upgraded first, as follows:

    1. In the Navigator pane, right-click the vDS that needs to be upgraded.

    2. Select **Upgrade** > **Upgrade Distributed Switch**.

    3. Ensure that the **Version 6.0.0** radio button is selected and click **Next**.

    4. Verify that all the ESXi servers attached to the vDS are compatible (at ESXi version 6) and click **Next**.

    5. Review the **Ready to Complete** screen (see Figure 3-1). Notice that there is a section on this screen that mentions feature conversion. This is where administrators can upgrade Network I/O Control to version 3 (which can also be done after the vDS has been upgraded). Also, note that enhanced LACP support can be enabled at this time. (We discuss LACP and enhanced LACP in more detail later in this chapter.) Click **Finish**.

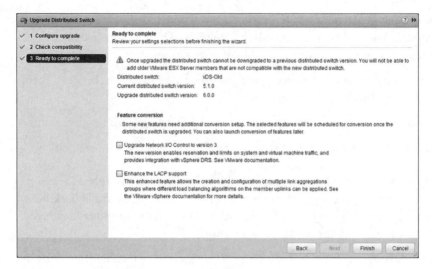

Figure 3-1 vDS Upgrade Ready to Complete

Step 2. Right-click the vDS in the Navigator pane.

Step 3. Choose **Upgrade** > **Upgrade Network I/O Control**. This brings up the Upgrade Network I/O Control wizard. Be aware of the warning message at the top of this wizard, which reminds you to back up the configuration of the distributed switch prior to upgrading.

Step 4. Click **Next**.

Step 5. In the Validate Prerequisites screen (see Figure 3-2), the wizard identifies whether there are any potential issues with the upgrade process. The validation identifies the following:

- **Port Group Accessibility:** This verifies whether all port groups on the vDS are able to be modified by the current administrative user account (that is, whether sufficient privileges exist to modify dvPort groups).

- **Host State:** This verifies that all the ESXi servers attached to the vDS are connected.

- **CoS Priority Tag for System Traffic:** This identifies whether CoS has been defined for VMkernel ports. CoS is not supported on NIOC version 3. When a NIOC is upgraded to version 3, any CoS priority tags defined on network resource pools are removed. It is still possible to define a CoS tag at the dvPort group level of the vDS, so if this is required, you should take note of the current CoS definition so that it can be defined after the upgrade.

- **User-Defined Network Resource Pools:** If there are existing network resource pools built by administrators, they will be removed when the vDS is upgraded. It is then useful to take note of what settings have been defined on existing user-defined network resource pools before the upgrade.

- **Resource Allocation Policy Override:** This identifies whether administrators have allowed resource allocation overrides per port. (They would be removed if this were the case.)

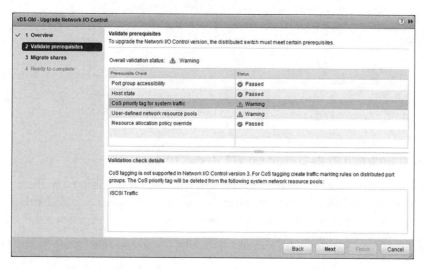

Figure 3-2   Validate Prerequisites

Once you are aware of the potential issues, you can either proceed or cancel the wizard to document the existing vDS configuration as it pertains to user defined network resource pools and CoS tags. When ready, click **Next**.

Step 6.   If existing user-defined network resource pools still exist, you are prompted to migrate the shares. The wizard allows you to automatically change the individual virtual machine shares to match those of the user-defined resource pools before destroying them. Click **Next** when ready.

Step 7.   At the final **Ready to Complete** screen of the wizard, you have a final chance to validate the changes that will take place during the upgrade. Take note of the next steps listed at the bottom of the wizard (see Figure 3-3).

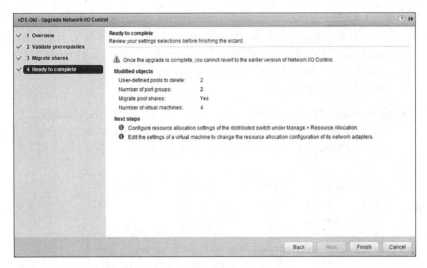

Figure 3-3   Ready to Complete and Next Steps

Configure NIOC Shares/Limits Based on VM Requirements

To define network resource pools for the different types of virtual machine traffic that may be on a virtual switch, you can select the network resource pools under the Resource Allocation tab. From here, click the green plus sign to create a new network resource pool (see Figure 3-4).

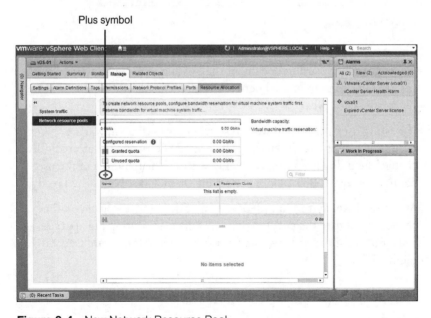

Figure 3-4   New Network Resource Pool

When you create a new network resource pool, you may notice that you are only able to define a reservation quota (a guaranteed amount of bandwidth to allocate). It is important to be aware of the total number of reservations in place. Once a resource pool has been created, you see the available unreserved capacity that is left. This allows administrators to keep track of reservations in place in order to avoid trying to reserve too many network resources. It is interesting to note that resource pools do not allow you to define a higher reservation than what is available.

Once enabled on the vDS, individual virtual machines can be configured specifically with shares, reservations, and limits. This is done from the virtual hardware through the Edit Settings window of the virtual machine, under the specific virtual network adapters. Shares allow the definition of a relative priority (from 1 to 100) only when there is network competition. Reservations define the minimum acceptable bandwidth available to this virtual machine all the time. If there is a period of time the virtual machine is not using this amount of physical network bandwidth, no other virtual machine can use it. A limit defines an upper limit or cap on how much physical network bandwidth a virtual machine can achieve.

You may notice that when you try to create a new network resource pool, the interface, by default, lists the reservation quota to be a maximum quota of 0 Mbit/s (see Figure 3-5). Any number you type in here generates the following error: The resource allocation settings of the network resource pool are invalid. Correct them to proceed. This is because the default virtual machine traffic defined under System Traffic (**Manage > Resource Allocation > System Traffic**) must have a reservation defined, and there is no reservation defined by default. Once a reservation has been defined for the virtual machine traffic as a whole, you can then define a reservation for a resource pool out of the reserved bandwidth for all virtual machines. To do this, under System Traffic, right-click the **Virtual Machines** field and select **Edit**. This brings up the **Edit Resource Settings for Virtual Machine Traffic** window, where you can define a reservation for all VMs. Be aware that the largest amount of bandwidth that can be reserved is 75% of the maximum bandwidth the physical uplink can provide (see Figure 3-6).

Max. quota: 0 Mbit/s

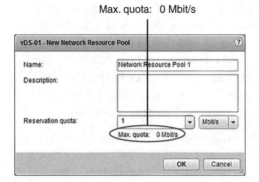

Figure 3-5 Reservation Quota

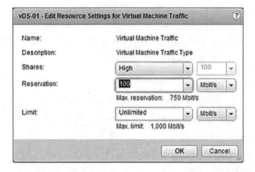

Figure 3-6 Reservations for Virtual Machine Bandwidth

Network resource pools then need to be associated with dvPort groups. To do this:

Step 1. Right-click the dvPort group in the Navigator pane of the networking inventory view.

Step 2. Select **Edit Settings**.

Step 3. Select the appropriate network resource pool from the drop-down box (see Figure 3-7).

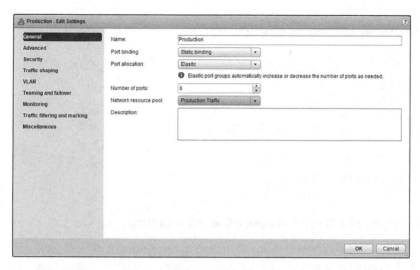

Figure 3-7 Network Resource Pool Selection

It is possible to set shares, reservations, and limits on multiple virtual machines at the same time. In a vDS's **Manage** tab > **Resource Allocation** > **Network Resource Pools**, there are three tabs at the bottom of the window: **Details**, **Distributed Port Groups**, and **Virtual Machines**. The **Details** tab shows the name of the network resource pool and the current reservation quota. The **Distributed Port Groups** tab shows which dvPort group or groups is currently associated with this network resource pool. The **Virtual Machines** tab shows which virtual machines are currently associated with this network resource pool (as per their associated dvPort group). Very much like how a compute resource pool on the hosts and clusters inventory view allows administrators to change virtual machines' shares, reservations, and limits without having to modify each individual virtual machine, the same is true of network resource pools:

Step 1.   On the **Virtual Machines** tab (of the **Manage** tab > **Resource Allocation** > **Network Resource Pools**), left-click one virtual machine and either hold down the **Shift** key and select the last virtual machine you wish to modify or hold down the **Ctrl** key while selecting multiple VMs.

Step 2.   Select the pencil/edit icon.

Step 3.   Modify the shares, reservations, or limits. In the title of the window, you should see the number of virtual network adapters that you have chosen to modify. The example in Figure 3-8 shows two because there are two virtual machines selected.

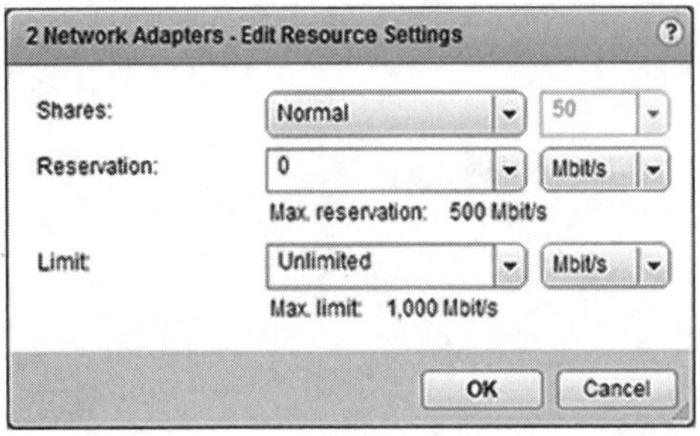

Figure 3-8   Modify Virtual Network Adapters

Explain the Behavior of a Given Network I/O Control Setting

Network I/O Control allows definitions of the relative priorities of different types of traffic under contention and also allows the definitions of minimums and maximums. The settings available in NIOC are similar to the settings available for general resource controls for memory, CPU, and storage.

The three main settings that can be defined in NIOC are shares, reservations, and limits. As stated earlier in this chapter, NIOC version 3, introduced in vSphere 6, now allows administrators the ability to define reservations.

On the **Manage** tab > **Resource Allocation Setting** of a vDS, you can define these settings for system traffic and for network resource pools. *System traffic* refers to all VMkernel traffic, and each type of VMkernel traffic can have different settings. This becomes useful when a vDS has multiple VMkernel connections on it for things like vMotion, IP Storage, vSAN, etc. A look at the default settings under the system traffic reveals that, as with resource controls in general, there are no limits or reservations set, and all VMkernel traffic has the same number of shares (normal, or 50 shares), except for virtual machine traffic. It is interesting that virtual machine traffic is listed as system traffic, but it is grouping all VMs together by default. Virtual machine traffic has 100 shares, or high shares by default. This is fine if all the virtual machines have the same relative priority, but if there are various different types of virtual machines attached to the vDS, it may be useful to define network resource pools. We will explore creating network resource pools later in this chapter.

A big change in NIOC version 3 is that in order to create a user-defined network resource pool, a reservation must be defined under the virtual machine traffic listed under system traffic. This allows a certain amount of bandwidth to be set aside specifically for virtual machine traffic as a bare minimum. Note that you cannot define a reservation for the full amount of network bandwidth; you are capped at 75% of the total bandwidth of the physical uplinks, so if the vDS has 1 Gbps physical uplinks contributed by each of the ESXi servers, the bandwidth reservation cannot be any higher than 750 Mbps, or 75% of the available bandwidth.

As stated earlier, all virtual machine traffic can be grouped together (and will be at least initially), but then individual network resource pools can be created to set reservations (of the total reservation defined for the total of virtual machine traffic).

Once NIOC is enabled on the vDS, individual virtual machines can be configured with shares, reservations, and limits specifically. Interestingly, you do not configure this through network resource pools. Network resource pools simply allow you to define a reservation of the virtual machine traffic that this selected resource pool is guaranteed. Network resource pools are then assigned to dvPort groups on the vDS. Changing a virtual machine's shares, reservations, or limits has to be done on a per-virtual machine basis. This is done from the virtual hardware through the Edit Settings window of the virtual machine, under the specific virtual network adapters. These are the available settings:

- **Shares:** Shares allow the definition of a relative priority (from 1 to 100) only when there is network competition. For example, if a VMkernel process or other virtual machine has higher shares but is not currently consuming any network bandwidth, then the higher shares are ignored; there is no contention. If one virtual machine has 30 shares, and another virtual machine has 70 shares, for example, and both virtual machines are sending a large amount of traffic, the VM with 70 shares will get 70% of the available bandwidth, and the virtual machine with 30 shares will get 30% of the bandwidth.

- **Reservations:** Reservations define the minimum acceptable bandwidth available to this virtual machine all of the time. If there is a period of time when the virtual machine is not using this amount of physical network bandwidth, no other virtual machine can use it. As in the case with reservations for CPU and memory, setting too many reservations too high can impose limitations, so it is important to set a reservation only to be the absolute minimum amount of bandwidth that is needed 100% of the time. However, if virtual machines are not using their allocated reservation, the unused bandwidth can be used for other types of system traffic. Unused bandwidth from a reservation cannot be used to allow new virtual machines to power on, though. If a virtual machine has a higher reservation than is currently unreserved (used or not) and the virtual machine is powered off, it will not be allowed to power on as this would violate admission control.

■ **Limits:** Limits define an upper limit or cap on how much physical network bandwidth this virtual machine can achieve.

Determine Network I/O Control Requirements

The first and easiest requirement for using NIOC is vSphere Distributed Switches (vDSs). Since vDSs are required, the Enterprise Plus vSphere license is required, which is the second requirement. vSphere Standard Switches (vSSs) cannot utilize NIOC. vSphere 6 and vDS version 6.0.0 introduce NIOC version 3, which adds the ability to define reservations in addition to the shares and limits that can be defined in prior versions.

The last requirement is that virtual machines cannot be utilizing SR-IOV (Single Root I/O Virtualization), where a physical device is visible and usable from multiple virtual machines. SR-IOV would bypass virtual switches, so if it is configured, you lose the ability to make use of virtual switch functions.

Differentiate Network I/O Control Capabilities

As stated earlier in this chapter, there are two main versions of NIOC: version 2, introduced in vSphere 5, and version 3, introduced in vSphere 6. Version 2 has the ability to define many of the same things that can be defined in version 3, with some key differences. As mentioned earlier, version 2 of NIOC only allows the ability to define limits and shares—but not reservations. Also, version 2 allows the definition of a CoS tag for network prioritization at Layer 2, at the network resource pool level. Again, it is possible to define CoS at the dvPort group on vSphere 6 and on vDS 6.0.0, but it is a setting of the dvPort group and not of the network resource pool.

Enable/Disable Network I/O Control

When a vDS is created, NIOC can be enabled at that time. (In the Create New Distributed Switch Wizard, there is a check box to enable NIOC.) NIOC can also be enabled or disabled after creation of the vDS. To enable NIOC after a vDS has been created or to verify that it is enabled:

Step 1.   Right-click the vDS in the Networking Inventory.

Step 2.   Select **Settings**.

Step 3.   Select **Edit Settings**.

The **General** view of the **Edit Settings** window has a section for **Network I/O Control**. This is where the setting can be enabled/disabled (see Figure 3-9).

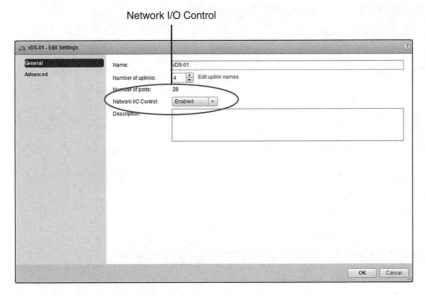

Figure 3-9   Enable/Disable NIOC

Once NIOC is enabled on the vDS, navigate to **Manage > Resource Allocation**. From here, define network resource management for system traffic and define network resource pools. System traffic allows the definition of shares, reservations, and limits for all types of VMkernel traffic:

- Fault tolerance

- Management

- NFS

- Virtual machines

- vSAN

- iSCSI

- vMotion

- vSphere data protection

- vSphere replication

An interesting thing to be aware of here is that there is a predefined allocation for virtual machine traffic (see Figure 3-10).

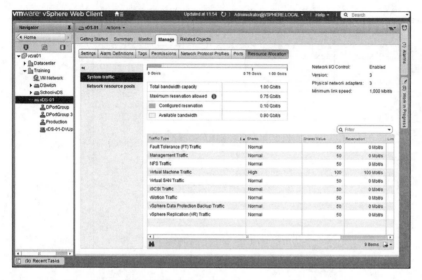

Figure 3-10   vDS Default Traffic Allocations

By default, all virtual machine traffic is grouped together. However, if multiple different types of virtual machine traffic will reside on this vDS, then administrators can define additional network resource pools to differentiate them.

It is possible to exclude a physical network adapter from participating in Network I/O Control:

Step 1.   In the hosts and clusters inventory view, select an ESXi server.

Step 2.   Select **Manage** > **Settings**.

Step 3.   Expand the **System** option on the left and select **Advanced System Settings**.

Step 4.   Select **Net.IOControlPnicOptOut** and select the pencil/edit icon.

Step 5.   Enter the physical uplink name or names that you wish to exclude from NIOC, using commas (not spaces) to separate them if there is more than one. For example, if you wanted to exclude vmnic1 and vmnic2 from NIOC, enter vmnic1,vmnic2.

Monitor Network I/O Control

One of the interesting things to be aware of with NIOC and how the vSphere Web Client displays information regarding vDS network bandwidth is that it displays an aggregate of all physical uplinks attached to the vDS. For example, for a vDS with three ESXi servers attached, and each ESXi server host contributing 1 Gbps physical uplink to the vDS, the vSphere Web Client displays a total bandwidth capacity of 3 Gbps because this is the maximum throughput all three physical uplinks could provide.

To see the total bandwidth capacity, reservations, and the network resource pool utilization:

Step 1. Left-click the vDS in the Navigator pane of the networking inventory view to select it.

Step 2. Click the **Manage** tab.

Step 3. Click the **Resource Allocation** tab.

Step 4. Select **System Traffic** or **Network resource pools**.

You now see information about the system traffic (refer to Figure 3-10) or network resource pools (see Figure 3-11).

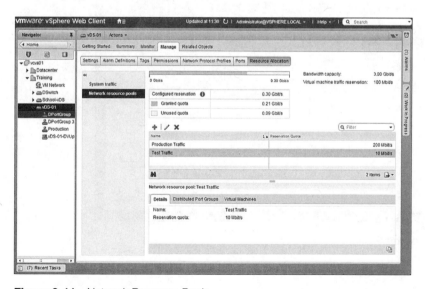

Figure 3-11   Network Resource Pools

With system traffic selected, you can easily identify several key pieces of information:

- Total bandwidth capacity, in Gbps, of the physical network

- Maximum reservation allowed (which is 75% of the total bandwidth)

- Configured reservation (that is, the configured reservation that is currently defined)

- Available bandwidth (that is, the amount of unreserved bandwidth)

- Whether NIOC is enabled or disabled

- The version of NIOC configured (up to version 3, the latest version)

- The number of physical uplinks currently contributing to the vDS

- The slowest physical uplink attached to the vDS

When you have network resource pools selected, you can select one of them (or create new ones) and see some general information, such as the name and quota defined for the selected resource pool. Also, there are additional tabs at the bottom of the window, titled Distributed Port Groups (see Figure 3-12) and Virtual Machines (see Figure 3-13).

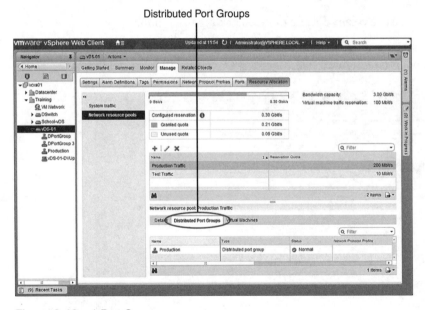

Figure 3-12   dvPort Groups

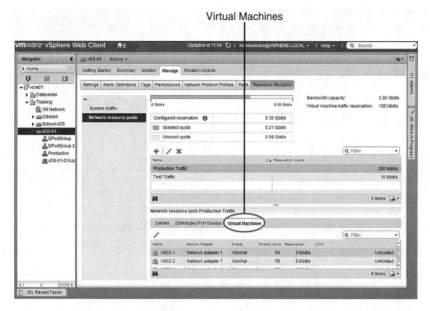

Figure 3-13   Virtual Machines

It is also possible to right-click virtual machines from here and modify their individual reservations, limits, and shares without having to go back to the VMs and templates inventory view. (This is very similar to how you change compute reservations, limits, and shares for virtual machines in resource pools or ESXi cluster objects.)

Summary

You have now read the chapter covering exam topics on NIOC, the comparisons of features in NIOC versions 2 and 3, the different settings available, and the upgrade process. It is useful to become familiar with these settings and review how to configure the different settings for NIOC and then how to monitor utilization on a day-to-day basis. You should now use information in the following sections to complete your preparation for Objective 2.2.

Exam Preparation Tasks

Review All the Key Topics

Table 3-2 provides a reference to each of the key topics identified in this chapter. Take a few moments to review each of these specific items.

Table 3-2   Key Topics for Chapter 3

Key Topic Element	Description	Pages
Paragraph	Evolution of NIOC	138
Paragraph	Back up the existing vDS configuration before upgrading NIOC version 3	139
Paragraph	When NIOC can be enabled/disabled	148
Step List	Excluding a physical network adapter from NIOC	150

Complete the Tables and Lists from Memory

Print a copy of Appendix B, "Memory Tables" (found on the CD), or at least the section for this chapter, and complete the tables and lists from memory. Appendix C, "Memory Tables Answer Key," also on the CD, includes completed tables and lists to check your work.

Definitions of Key Terms

Define the following key terms from this chapter and check your answers in the glossary.

vSphere Distributed Switch (vDS), dvPort group, Network I/O Control (NIOC), Class of Service (CoS)

Answer Review Questions

The answers to these review questions can be found in Appendix A.

1. When looking at the resource allocation of a vDS and analyzing the system traffic, which of the following is *not* listed?

   a. Whether NIOC is enabled or disabled

   b. Which version of NIOC is configured for this vDS

   c. Configured reservation

   d. Consumed bandwidth

2. The finance department has virtual machines that need to be prioritized in the event of network contention. There is one vDS defined, and each ESXi server has four physical uplinks, all attached to the single vDS. How would you define shares and/or reservations for the finance department's virtual machines? (Choose the answer that would be easiest to implement in a large environment.)

   a. In the hosts and clusters view or the VMs and templates inventory view, select one of the virtual machines, right-click the VM in the inventory, and select **Edit Settings**. Expand the network adapter and define the shares, reservations, and limits here. Repeat for each of the finance virtual machines.

   b. In the networking inventory view, right-click the dvPort group in which the finance VMs reside and select **Edit Settings**. Select **Network Resource Pools** on the left and then modify the shares, reservations, and limits.

   c. In the networking inventory view, select the vDS on the left and then select **Manage > Resource Allocation** and select **Network Resource Pools** on the left. Select the network resource pool associated with the finance department's virtual machines and select the pencil/edit icon. Modify the share value for the network resource pool.

   d. In the networking inventory view, select the vDS on the left and then select **Manage > Resource Allocation** and select **Network Resource Pools** on the left. Select the network resource pool associated with the finance department's virtual machines. Select the **Virtual Machines** tab at the bottom of the window and modify individual virtual machines' reservations limits and shares here.

3. How could you remove a physical uplink (vmnic3) from each ESXi server from participating in NIOC?

    a. NIOC cannot be excluded for a physical uplink; it can only be enabled/disabled for the vDS.

    b. Modify the advanced system setting `Net.IOControlPnicOptOut` for each ESXi server and add the value vmnic3.

    c. Modify the advanced system setting `Net.IOControlvmnicOptOut` for each ESXi server and add the value vmnic3.

    d. On the hosts and clusters inventory view, select each ESXi server and go to **Manage** > **Networking** > **Network Adapters**. Right-click vmnic3 and select **Remove from NIOC**.

4. Which of the following is lost when upgrading from NIOC version 2 to version 3?

    a. vMotion ability

    b. VMkernel system-defined network priorities

    c. User-defined network resource pools

    d. Traffic shaping

5. Which is the lowest version of ESXi needed to support NIOC version 3?

    a. ESXi 5.5

    b. ESXi 6.0

    c. ESXi 5.0

    d. NIOC has been deprecated in vSphere 6.

This chapter covers the following objective:

- **Objective 3.1—Manage vSphere Storage Virtualization**

  - Discover new storage LUNs

  - Configure FC/iSCSI/FCoE LUNs as ESXi boot devices

  - Create an NFS share for use with vSphere

  - Enable/configure/disable vCenter Server storage filters

  - Configure/edit software iSCSI initiator settings

  - Configure iSCSI port binding

  - Enable/configure/disable iSCSI CHAP

  - Determine use cases for Fibre Channel zoning

  - Compare and contrast array and virtual disk thin provisioning

## CHAPTER 4

Storage, Part 1

In this chapter we will begin the first of three chapters related to storage. In vSphere storage can be either a block-based Storage Area Network (SAN) or a file-based Network Attached Storage (NAS) device. This chapter will concentrate on the requirements and capabilities of storage devices. The SAN protocols that an administrator will need to know are Fibre Channel, Fibre Channel over Ethernet, and iSCSI. The NAS protocol that VMware supports is Network File System (NFS). These protocols can be enabled, modified, and deleted in different ways. In addition, there are properties and features that you will need to know for the exam.

"Do I Know This Already?" Quiz

The "Do I Know This Already?" quiz allows you to assess whether you should study this entire chapter or move quickly to the "Exam Preparation Tasks" section. Regardless, the authors recommend that you read the entire chapter at least once. Table 4-1 outlines the major headings in this chapter and the corresponding "Do I Know This Already?" quiz questions. You can find the answers in Appendix A, "Answers to the 'Do I Know This Already?' Quizzes and Review Questions."

Table 4-1 "Do I Know This Already?" Foundation Topics Section-to-Question Mapping

Foundations Topics Section	Questions Covered in This Section
Discover New Storage LUNs	1, 2
Configure FC/iSCSI/FCoE LUNs as ESXi Boot Devices	3
Create an NFS Share for Use with vSphere	4
Enable/Configure/Disable vCenter Server Storage Filters	5
Enable/Disable Software iSCSI Initiator	10
Configure iSCSI Port Binding	9
Enable/Configure/Disable iSCSI CHAP	6

Foundations Topics Section	Questions Covered in This Section
Determine Use Cases for Fibre Channel Zoning	7
Compare and Contrast Array and Virtual Disk Thin Provisioning	8

1. ESXi Host does not need a VMkernel port for which type of network adapter?

   a. ESXi Host always requires a VMkernel port for iSCSI.

   b. Software iSCSI initiator

   c. Dependent hardware iSCSI initiator

   d. Independent hardware iSCSI initiator

2. What is the best approach for discovering new storage LUNs.?

   a. You do not need to do anything; storage is automatically presented to the ESXi Host.

   b. To scan for new storage, select **Home** > **Hosts and Clusters** > **Datacenter** > right-click **Storage** > **Rescan Storage** > **OK**.

   c. After the ESXi Host boots up, select the **Scan for New Storage** button.

   d. Highlight the LUN, right-click, and select **Scan for New Storage**.

3. Which of the following is an incorrect statement?

   a. In order for Fibre Channel (FC) to boot from a SAN, the /etc/vmware/fc.conf file must designate the FC adapter as a boot controller.

   b. When you boot from a SAN, each ESXi Host must have exclusive access to its own boot LUN.

   c. With FCoE, during the ESXi boot process, the parameters to find the boot LUN over the network are loaded into the system memory.

   d. If you are using a dependent hardware iSCSI or software iSCSI initiator, you must have an iSCSI boot-capable network adapter that supports the iSCSI Boot Firmware Table (iBFT) format.

4. The virtual disks that are created on an NFS datastore are _____.

   a. in a format dictated by the NFS server

   b. thin provisioned

   c. thick eager-zeroed

   d. thick lazy-zeroed

5. vCenter Server uses storage filters to prevent LUN filtering corruption. If you need VMs to access the same LUN, then they must share the same RDM mapping file. To set up a SCSi-3 quorum disk for MSCS, which configuration parameter filter would you need to disable in the advanced settings of vSphere Client?

   a. `config.vpxd.filter.rdmFilter` set to `false`

   b. `config.vpxd.filter.vmfsFilter` set to `false`

   c. `config.vpxd.filter.rdmFilter` set to `true`

   d. `config.vpxd.filter.vmfsFilter` set to `true`

6. Which CHAP security level is not supported with Independent Hardware iSCSI?

   a. Do Not Use CHAP

   b. Use Unidirectional CHAP if Required by Target

   c. Use Unidirectional CHAP Unless Prohibited by Target

   d. Use Unidirectional CHAP

7. If you are following best practices, where should LUN masking be configured?

   a. On the ESXi Host

   b. On the switch

   c. On the storage array

   d. On vCenter Server

   e. LUN masking is not supported in vSphere 6

8. Which statement about thin provisioning is incorrect?

   a. When a thin virtual disk is created, it does not preallocate capacity and does not zero out the data block on the VMFS file system.

   b. When you use Storage vMotion, there is an option to enable thin provisioning on a storage array.

   c. When writes occur and more space is needed, the VMkernel grows storage for VMFS 1 MB at a time.

   d. If the file system is NFS, which is by default thin provisioned, it grows 4 KB at a time.

9. Which of the following statement about iSCSI port binding is incorrect?

   a. You need to associate a VMkernel port with a specific iSCSI adapter in order to configure iSCSI port binding.

   b. For multipathing purposes, it is best to have two active network adapters connected to one VMkernel port.

   c. The iSCSI initiator for an ESXi Host can be either hardware or software based.

   d. Best practices say to designate a separate network adapter for iSCSI; this is done for performance and security.

10. Which of the following statements about iSCSI initiators is incorrect?

    a. The steps to enable a software iSCSI initiator begin with browsing to the host using the vSphere Web Client. Click **Manage** > **Storage** > **Storage Adapters** > **Add.**> **Storage** > **Storage Adapters** > **Add**.

    b. You need to activate a minimum of two software iSCSI adapters on each host.

    c. If the iSCSI software adapter was used to boot the ESXi Host, it will be reenabled the next time the host boots.

    d. The steps to disable the software iSCSI initiator begin with browsing to the host using the vSphere Web Client. Click the **Manage** tab and then click **Storage**. Click **Storage Adapters** and then highlight the iSCSI software adapter that you want to disable.

Foundation Topics

Objective 3.1—Manage vSphere Storage Virtualization

This section provides details on how to set up and use storage area network (SAN) and network access server (NAS) storage in a virtualized environment. vSphere storage virtualization combines APIs and features built into vSphere, which abstracts the physical layer of storage into storage space that can be managed and utilized by virtual machines. A virtual machine (VM) uses a virtual disk or disks to store files that it needs to run an operating system and an application or applications. The files comprising a virtual machine are detailed in Chapter 16, "Virtual Machines." One of the files that encompass a VM is a virtual disk, which contains the data for the VM.

This chapter concentrates on SAN- and NAS-based storage. A SAN is a block-based storage protocol that makes data available over the Ethernet or Fibre Channel network, using the Fibre Channel, FCoE, or iSCSI protocols. On the other hand, a NAS is a file-based storage system that makes data available over an Ethernet network, using the Network File System (NFS) protocol. Both a SAN and a NAS are shared devices that connect to an ESXi Host through a network or storage adapter. Now let's discuss how to configure and manage these shared storage protocols.

Storage Protocols

Storage is a resource that vSphere uses to store virtual machines. Four main protocols can be used within vSphere: Fibre Channel (FC), Fibre Channel over Ethernet (FCoE), Internet Small Computer System Interface (iSCSI), and Network File System (NFS). These protocols can be used to connect the ESXi Host with a storage device.

Identify Storage Adapters and Devices

A storage adapter connects the ESXi Host and a storage SAN/NAS device. There are different adapters, and interaction is dependent on how much intelligence is built into the card. Some adapters have firmware or integrated circuitry on the card that can improve performance between the ESXi Host and the storage device. A VM resides on a storage device and needs a software driver to control communication with the ESXi Host. No matter which protocol you use, the VM residing on the storage device relies on a SCSI device driver to communicate to the ESXi Host. The VM uses a virtual SCSI controller to access the virtual disks of the virtual machine. One factor that determines which storage adapter to use is what protocol is being utilized for the communication between the ESXi Host and the storage device. Before we discuss each of the storage protocols, this chapter shows how to find the storage adapters and devices within vSphere using the vSphere Web Client. Then it describes each of these protocols and identifies important characteristics to consider when using each of these options.

NOTE   You cannot use IDE/ATA or USB drives to store virtual machines that are powered on in vSphere 6.

Display Storage Adapters for a Host

The procedure to display all of a host's storage adapters using the vSphere Web Client is to highlight the ESXi Host in the hosts and clusters inventory. Then click the **Manage** tab, click **Storage**, and select **Storage Adapters**. In Figure 4-1 you can see four adapters. The last listed adapter, vmhba33, is a software-based iSCSI initiator.

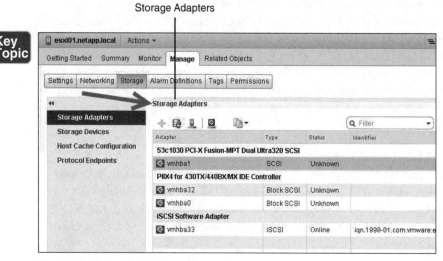

Figure 4-1   Storage Adapters

Storage Devices for an Adapter

Figure 4-1 shows connections between storage and the ESXi Host. You can have multiple storage devices reserved, and they can contain VMs. One method to distinguish one storage device from another is to use a logical unit number (LUN). A LUN is the identifier of a device that is being addressed by the SCSI protocol or similar protocols, such as Fibre Channel and iSCSI. The protocol may be used with any device that supports read/write operations, such as a tape drive, but the term is most often used to refer to a disk drive, and these terms are, in fact, often used synonymously. Tapes, CD-ROMs, and even scanners and printers can be connected to a SCSI bus and may therefore appear as LUNs.

NOTE   The same LUN cannot be presented to an ESXi Host through different storage protocols, such as iSCSI and Fibre Channel.

A VMware VMDK (Virtual Machine Disk) becomes a LUN when it is mapped to a VM using the virtual SCSI adapter. *LUN* is one of the many terms that are used incorrectly most of the time. A SAN is structured just the same way as a traditional SCSI bus except that the old ribbon cable has been replaced with a network. This is why LUN masking is needed: SCSI is a master/slave architecture (initiator/target), and there is no authentication mechanism in the SCSI protocol to dictate which hosts can acquire a particular LUN; hence LUN masking "masks" (hides) LUNs from all hosts except the ones it is configured for.

The procedure to display a list of storage devices for a storage adapter on an ESXi Host is to highlight the ESXi Host in the hosts and clusters inventory. Then click the **Manage** tab, click **Storage**, and select **Storage Adapters**. Once you select the storage adapter, the storage devices that can be accessed through the adapter are displayed in the Adapter Details section by selecting **Devices**. In Figure 4-2, the iSCSI software adapter has been selected and is displaying three iSCSI LUN devices.

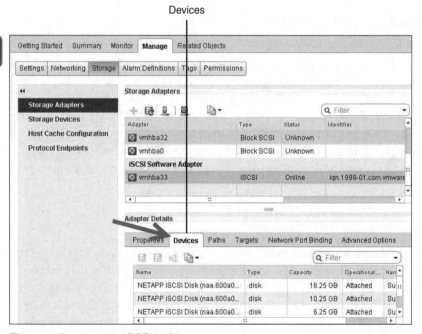

Figure 4-2   Available iSCSI LUNs

Fibre Channel Protocol

Fibre Channel (FC) is a transport layer that can be used to transmit data on a SAN. Many devices can communicate with each other on a SAN, such as switches, hubs, initiator HBAs, and storage adapters using the Fibre Channel Protocol (FCP). The protocol has been around since the mid-1980s, so it is a well understand topology, and it has been popular due to its excellent performance. Fibre Channel replaced Small Computer Systems Interface (SCSI) as the primary means of host-to-storage communication. In order to facilitate the compatibility, the FC frame encapsulates the SCSI protocol. Thus, FC is moving SCSI packets around its network.

The terms *initiator* and *target* were originally SCSI terms. FCP connects the actual initiator and target hardware, which must log into the fabric and be properly zoned (like VLANs) for storage discovery by the ESXi Host. The host operating system communicates via SCSI commands with the disk drives in a SAN. The cabling that FC uses can be either copper cables or optical cables. Using optical cables, the SCSI protocol is serialized (that is, the bits are converted from parallel to serial, one bit at a time) and transmitted as light pulses across the optical cable. Data runs at the speed of light, without the limitations of short-distance SCSI cables. Fibre Channel is like a SAN highway where other protocols such as SCSI and IP can drive.

Fibre Channel over Ethernet Protocol

The Fibre Channel over Ethernet (FCoE) is a protocol that takes a Fibre Channel (FC) packet and puts it over an Ethernet network of 10 Gbps or higher speeds. Each FC frame is encapsulated into an Ethernet frame with a one-to-one mapping. ESXi servers connect to a SAN fabric using host bus adapters (HBAs). Connectivity to FCoE fabrics is enabled through converged network adapters (CNAs). Each HBA/CNA can run as either an initiator (ESXi Host) or a target (storage array). Each adapter has a global unique address referred to as a World Wide Name (WWN). Each WWN must be known in order to configure LUN access on a NetApp storage array.

iSCSI Protocol

The Internet Small Computer System Interface (iSCSI) protocol provides access to storage devices over Ethernet-based TCP/IP networks. iSCSI enables data transfers by carrying SCSI commands over an IP network. Routers and switches can be used to extend the IP storage network to the wide area network—or even through the Internet with the use of tunneling protocols. The iSCSI protocol establishes communication sessions between initiators (clients) and targets (servers). The initiators are devices that request commands be executed. Targets are devices that carry out the commands. The structure used to communicate a command from an application client to a device server is referred to as a *Command Descriptor Block* (*CDB*). The basic functions of the SCSI driver are to build SCSI CDBs from requests issued by the application and forward them to the iSCSI layer.

NFS Protocol

The Network File System (NFS) service lets you share files over a network between a storage device and an ESXi Host. The files are centrally located on the NFS server, which enables the NFS client access using a client/client architecture. The NFS server is the storage array, and it provides not only the data but also the file system. The NFS client is the ESXi Host, and the client code has been built into the VMkernel since 2002, running NFS version 3. Because the NFSv3 client is automatically loaded into the ESXi Host, it was the only version of NFS that VMware supported. What is new in vSphere 6.0 is that VMware reworked the source code to add support for both NFSv3 and NFSv4.1. NFS version 4.1 adds additional features that aid in interactions between the storage and the ESXi Host.

Authentication NFSv4.1 with Kerberos Authentication

NFSv4.1 supports both Kerberos and non-`root` user authentication. With NFSv3, remote files are accessed with `root` permissions, and servers have to be configured with the `no_root_squash` option to allow `root` access to files. This is known as an `AUTH_SYS` mechanism.

Native Multipathing and Session Trunking

The ability to add multiple IP addresses associated with a single NFS mount for redundancy is known as *session trunking*, or *multipathing*. In the server field, you add a comma to separate the IP addresses in a list to do load balancing or multipathing.

In-band, Mandatory, and Stateful Server-Side File Locking

In NFSv3 VMware does not use the standard lockd daemon because of how VMware's high availability conflicts with the standard server lock daemon. Thus, in NFSv3, VMware uses its own client-side locking mechanism for file locking. In NFSv4.1, VMware now uses the standard server-side lockd daemon.

NOTE vSphere 6.0 does not support pNFS (parallel NFS), which is a feature of NFSv4.1.

Identify Storage Naming Conventions

In the previous sections, you have learned that various protocols can be presented to vSphere. If you want to create a virtual machine, you need a place to store the virtual machine files, and thus you need a datastore. The naming convention is based on which protocol you use. In order to create a datastore, you need to ask the storage administrator to create either a LUN or an NFS server. If you are using local drives, iSCSI, or Fibre Channel, then the device naming begins with vmhba. If you are using NFS, the device naming includes the NFS export name. Each LUN or storage device can be identified by several names.

The procedure to display the storage paths using the vSphere Web Client is to highlight the ESXi Host in the hosts and clusters inventory. Then click the **Manage** tab, click **Storage**, and select **Storage Adapters**. Once you select the storage adapter, the storage devices that can be displayed through the adapter are displayed in the Adapter Details section when you select **Paths**. In Figure 4-3 the iSCSI software adapter is selected and showing three iSCSI LUN devices:

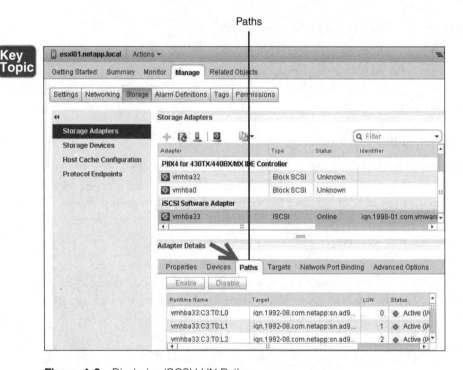

Figure 4-3   Displaying iSCSI LUN Paths

- **Runtime name:** vmhbaAdapter:CChannel:TTarget:LLUN

  - vmhbaAdapter is the name of the storage adapter. The name refers to the physical adapter on the host, not to the SCSI controller used by the virtual machine. In vmhba in Figure 4-3, vm refers to the VMkernel, and hba is the host bus adapter.

  - CChannel is the storage channel, if the adapter has multiple connections, the first channel is channel 0. Software iSCSI adapters and dependent hardware adapters use the channel number to show multiple paths to the same target.

  - TTarget is the target number. The target number might change if the mappings of targets visible to the host change or if the ESXi Host reboots.

  - LLun is the LUN, which shows the position of the LUN within the target. If a target has only one LUN, the LUN is always 0.

    For example, vmhba2:C0:T2:L3 would be LUN 3 on target 2, accessed through the storage adapter vmhba2 and channel 0.

  - The target name shows the Network Address Authority (NAA) ID, which can appear in different formats, based on the device itself. In Figure 4-3, the target name is for a software-based iSCSI device that is using the iqn scheme.

- **LUN number:** This is the LUN for the device.

To display all device names using the CLI, type in the following command (see Figure 4-4):

```
# esxcli storage core device list
```

Display Name: NETAPP iSCSI Disk (naa. 600a09807737555a473f476b466b5778)

naa. 600a09807737555a473f476b466b5778

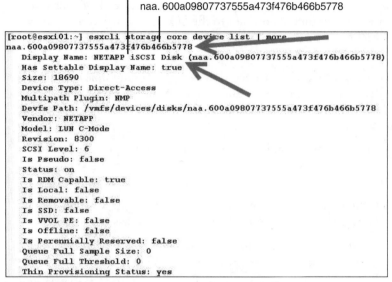

```
[root@esxi01:~] esxcli storage core device list | more
naa.600a09807737555a473f476b466b5778
    Display Name: NETAPP iSCSI Disk (naa.600a09807737555a473f476b466b5778)
    Has Settable Display Name: true
    Size: 18690
    Device Type: Direct-Access
    Multipath Plugin: NMP
    Devfs Path: /vmfs/devices/disks/naa.600a09807737555a473f476b466b5778
    Vendor: NETAPP
    Model: LUN C-Mode
    Revision: 8300
    SCSI Level: 6
    Is Pseudo: false
    Status: on
    Is RDM Capable: true
    Is Local: false
    Is Removable: false
    Is SSD: false
    Is VVOL PE: false
    Is Offline: false
    Is Perennially Reserved: false
    Queue Full Sample Size: 0
    Queue Full Threshold: 0
    Thin Provisioning Status: yes
```

Figure 4-4   Use the CLI to Display Storage Device Information

Identify Hardware/Dependent Hardware/Software iSCSI Initiator Requirements

The ESXi Host uses the iSCSI protocol to access LUNs on the storage system and is the initiator over a standard Ethernet interface. The host needs a network adapter to send and receive the iSCSI packets over TCP/IP. There are three iSCSI initiator options available, as shown in Figure 4-5:

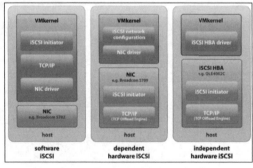

Figure 4-5   iSCSI Initiators

- **Software iSCSI initiator:** A software iSCSI initiator is a standard 1 GbE or 10 GbE NIC. There is nothing special about the network interface. A `Send Targets` command creates an iSCSI session between the initiator and the target on TCP port 3260. The VMkernel on the ESXi Host is responsible for discovering the LUNs by issuing the `Send Targets` request.

- **Dependent hardware iSCSI initiator:** A dependent hardware iSCSI initiator is a network interface card that has some built-in intelligence. It could be a chip or firmware, but either way, the card can "speak" iSCSI, which means the TCP offload function is on the card. However, not everything is done on the NIC; you must configure networking for the iSCSI traffic and bind the adapter to an appropriate VMkernel iSCSI port.

- **Independent hardware iSCSI initiator:** An independent hardware iSCSI initiator handles all network and iSCSI processing and management for the ESXi Host. For example, QLogic makes adapters that provide for the discovery of LUNs as well as the TCP offload engine (TOE). The ESXi Host does not need a VMkernel port for this type of card. This type of card is more expensive than the other types of NICs, but it also gets better performance.

Discover New Storage LUNs

When an ESXi Host boots up, it scans or sends a signal down its bus path, which discovers all the LUNs that are connected to the host. Then the host stops scanning for any new LUNs. I like to think of the host as being on siesta, taking a break from scanning for any new LUNs. While the host is on siesta, if the storage administrator presents any new LUNs to the ESXi Host, they will not be seen. So you need to wake up the ESXi Host by selecting Rescan Storage, as shown in Figure 4-6.

Figure 4-6 Rescan Storage

After you click **OK**, a new box pops up, with check boxes for **Scan for New Storage Devices** (to scan all host bus adapters looking for new LUNs) and **Scan for New VMFS Volumes** (to rescan all known storage devices for new VMFS volumes that have been added since the last scan).

Configure FC/iSCSI/FCoE LUNs as ESXi Boot Devices

You can set up your ESXi Host to boot from a FC or iSCSI LUN instead of booting from a local hard disk. The host's boot image is stored on the LUN that is being used exclusively for that ESXi Host. Thus, vSphere supports an ESXi Host's ability to boot from a LUN on a SAN. The ability of an ESXi Host to boot from a SAN is supported using FC and iSCSI. This capability does require that each host have unique access to its own LUN. You also need to enable the boot adapter in the host BIOS.

NOTE When you boot from a SAN, each host must have its own boot LUN.

FC

In order for a Fibre Channel (FC) device to boot from a SAN, the BIOS of the FC adapter must be configured with the World Wide Name (WWN) and LUN of the boot device. In addition, the system BIOS must designate the FC adapter as a boot controller.

iSCSI

It is possible to boot an ESXi Host using an independent hardware iSCSI, dependent hardware iSCSI, or software iSCSI initiator. If your ESXi Host uses an independent hardware iSCSI initiator, you need to configure the adapter to boot from the SAN. How you configure the adapter varies, depending on the vendor of the adapter.

If you are using a dependent hardware iSCSI or software iSCSI initiator, you must have an iSCSI boot-capable network adapter that supports the iSCSI Boot Firmware Table (iBFT) format. iBFT is a protocol defined in Advanced Configuration and Power Interface (ACPI) that defines parameters used to communicate between the storage adapter and the operating system. This is needed because the ESXi Host needs to load up enough information from the firmware to discover the iSCSI LUN over the network.

FCoE

You can boot an ESXi Host from a Fibre Channel over Ethernet (FCoE) network adapter. The FCoE initiator must support the FCoE Boot Firmware Table (FBFT) or FCoE Boot Parameter Table (FBPT). During the ESXi boot process, the parameters to find the boot LUN over the network are loaded into the system memory.

Create an NFS Share for Use with vSphere

The Network File System (NFS) is a client/server service that allows users to view, store, and modify files on a remote system as though they were on their own local computer. NFS allows systems of different architectures running different operating systems to access and share files across a network. The ESXi Host is the NFS client, while typically a SAN device such as EMC or NetApp acts as an NFS server. The NFS server shares the files, and the ESXi Host accesses the shared files over the network. How you create an NFS server and set up NFS shares depend on the system that is being used as the NFS server.

Enable/Configure/Disable vCenter Server Storage Filters

vCenter Server provides storage filters to avoid presenting storage that should be avoided due to performance problems or unsupported storage devices. The vSphere environment provides four storage filters that can affect the action of the vCenter Server when scanning storage. Without these filters, when vCenter Server is scanning for storage, all storage that is found could be presented to vSphere, even if it is in use. The filters prevent this type of unwanted activity. However, some specific use cases can affect what storage devices are found during scanning. By default, the storage filters are set to `true` and are designed to prevent specific storage datastore problems. Except in certain situations, it is best to leave the storage filters in their enabled state. Table 4-2 displays the vCenter Server storage filters and their respective Advanced Setting keys:

Table 4-2   vCenter Server Storage Filters

Filter	Advanced Setting Key
RDM	`config.vpxd.filter.rdmFilter`
VMFS	`config.vpxd.filter.vmfsFilter`
Host Rescan	`config.vpxd.filter.hostRescanFilter`
Same Host and Transports	`config.vpxd.filter.SameHostAndTransportsFilter`

- **RDM filter:** Filters out LUNs that have been claimed by any RDM on any ESXi Host managed by vCenter Server. This storage filter can be used in a situation such as when using Microsoft Cluster Server. When set to `false`, the filter is disabled, allowing a LUN to be added as an RDM, even though the LUN is already being utilized as an RDM by another VM. To set up a SCSI-3 quorum disk for MSCS, this storage filter needs to be disabled.

- **VMFS filter:** Filters out LUNs that have been claimed and VMFS formatted on any ESXi Host managed by vCenter Server. Thus, in the vSphere client, when you go to the Add Storage Wizard, you do not see any VMFS-formatted LUNs. If the setting is switched to `false`, the LUN is seen as available by the vSphere Client, and any ESXi Host could attempt to format it and claim it.

- **Host Rescan filter:** By default, when a VMFS volume is created, an automatic rescan occurs on all hosts connected to the vCenter Server. If the setting is switched to `false`, the automatic rescan is disabled when creating a VMFS datastore on another host. For example, you could run a PowerCLI `cmdlet` to add 100 datastores; you should wait until the `cmdlet` is finished before scanning all the hosts in the cluster.

- **Same Host and Transports filter:** Filters out LUNs that cannot be used as VMFS datastore extents due to host or storage incompatibility. If the setting is switched to `false`, an incompatible LUN could be added as an extent to an existing volume. An example of an incompatible LUN would be adding a LUN as an extent that is not seen by all of the hosts.

As an example, the Host Rescan filter could be set to `false` to stop an automatic rescan when you create a new datastore. Since you are going to run a PowerCLI `cmdlet` to add 100 datastores, you would want to turn this off until the `cmdlet` is finished running. Thus, after the 100 datastores are added, you could scan to discover all of the new storage. Figure 4-7 displays the vCenter Advanced Settings screen, which is where storage filters can be enabled. The steps to turn off the filter begin by using the vSphere Web Client navigator and starting at **Home** and selecting **Hosts and Clusters**. Then highlight your vCenter Server, click the **Manage** tab, and click **Settings**. To disable a filter, first add it by clicking **Advanced Settings** and then **Edit**. This opens the Edit Advanced vCenter Server Settings window. At the bottom of the window, in the **Key** box, type in the storage filter **config. vpxd.filter.hostRescanFilter** and add the Value **false** to enable the storage filter, as shown in Figure 4-7.

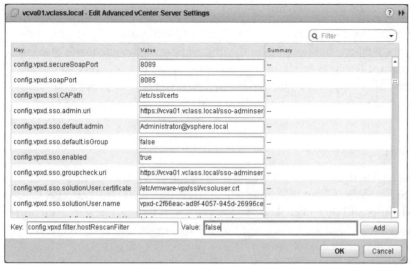

Figure 4-7   Enable a Storage Filter

iSCSI

vSphere provides support for several different methods of booting up using an iSCSI LUN. An independent hardware iSCSI adapter, such as a QLogic iSCSI HBA, first needs to boot from the VMware installation media, which loads an iSCSI HBA configuration menu. The HBA config menu allows you to configure host adapter settings.

In addition to the independent hardware adapter, the ESXi Host can boot from a software adapter or dependent hardware iSCSI adapter. The network adapter must support the iSCSI Boot Firmware Table (iBFT) format to deploy an ESXi Host from an iSCSI SAN. The iBFT allows for communicating parameters about the iSCSI boot device to an operating system.

Configure/Edit Hardware/Dependent Hardware Initiators

A hardware initiator or a dependent initiator is a network adapter that has either firmware or a chip built in to the adapter that speaks iSCSI. The network adapter can handle standard networking as well as the iSCSI offload engine. After you install the hardware initiator, it appears in the list of network adapters. However, you need to associate a VMkernel port with the adapter before you can configure the iSCSI settings.

Enable/Disable Software iSCSI Initiator

A software iSCSI initiator is a standard 1 GB or 10 GB network adapter. It is simply a supported adapter, but nothing on the physical card is designed with SCSI in mind. The network adapter relies on the VMkernel to handle discovery and sends the processing of encapsulation and de-encapsulation of network packets up to the kernel. You need to activate only one software iSCSI adapter on the ESXi Host.

Enable a Software iSCSI Initiator

The steps to enable the software iSCSI initiator begin with browsing to the host using the vSphere Web Client. Click the **Manage** tab and then click **Storage**. Click **Storage Adapters** and then click **Add**. As you can see in Figure 4-8, select **Software iSCSI Adapter** and confirm that you want to add the driver to your ESXi Host.

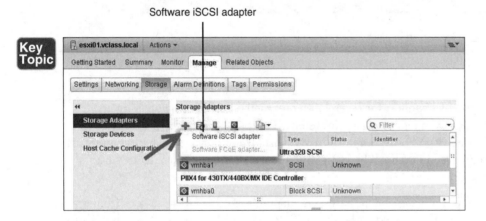

Software iSCSI adapter

Figure 4-8   Enable a Software iSCSI Initiator

Disable a Software iSCSI Initiator

The steps to disable the software iSCSI initiator begin with browsing to the host using the vSphere Web Client. Click the **Manage** tab and then click **Storage**. Click **Storage Adapters** and then highlight the iSCSI software adapter that you want to disable. Underneath Storage Adapters is the Adapter Details section; click **Properties** and click the **Disable** button. Disabling the adapter marks it for removal, but the adapter is not removed until the next host reboot. Figure 4-9 shows the iSCSI initiator being disabled. After you reboot the host, the iSCSI adapter no longer appears in the list of storage adapters.

> **NOTE** If the iSCSI software adapter was used to boot the ESXi Host, it is reenabled the next time the host boots.

vmhba33

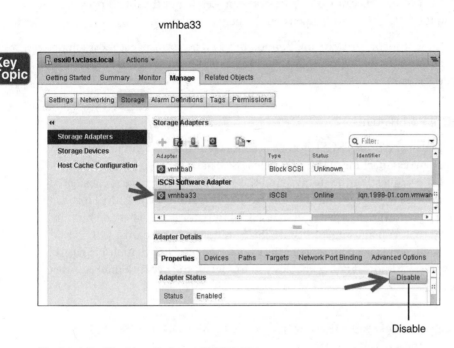

Figure 4-9   Disable a Software iSCSI Initiator

Configure/Edit Software iSCSI Initiator Settings

There are several different settings you can make on an iSCSI initiator. The settings can be configured in the Adapter Details section. One option is to enable and disable paths for the iSCSI adapter. Another option when you are editing an iSCSI initiator is to use dynamic or static discovery. With dynamic discovery, the iSCSI initiator sends a Send Targets request to the storage array, which returns a list of available targets to the initiator. The other option is to use static discovery, where you manually add targets. Also, you can set up CHAP authentication, which is discussed in an upcoming section of this chapter.

Determine Use Case for Hardware/Dependent Hardware/Software iSCSI Initiator

A good reason to use a software iSCSI initiator is that you do not need to purchase a specialized network adapter. You only need to buy a standard 1 GB or 10 GB network adapter. Another reason you might use a software initiator is that it is the only initiator that supports bidirectional CHAP.

The benefit of a dependent hardware iSCSI initiator is that part of the processing happens on the network adapter and part on the CPU. The adapter offloads iSCSI processing to the adapter, which speeds up processing of the iSCSI packets. It also reduces CPU overhead because only part of the processing of the iSCSI packets happens on the CPU, and part happens on the network adapter.

You use an independent hardware iSCSI initiator when performance is most important. This adapter handles all its own networking, iSCSI processing, and management of the interface.

Configure iSCSI Port Binding

For most implementations, iSCSI storage is connected to the ESXi Hosts and is used to host virtual machines. The ESXi Host is then considered to be the initiator because it is requesting the storage, and the iSCSI storage device is considered the target because it is delivering the storage. The initiator for the ESXi Host can be software or hardware based. A software iSCSI initiator is included and built in to the VMkernel. When using a software iSCSI initiator, a standard 1 GB or 10 GB network adapter is used for storage transport. You might have multiple network adapters, and iSCSI port binding enables you to specify the network interface that iSCSI can use.

NOTE iSCSI ports of the storage array must reside in the same broadcast domain and IP subnet as the VMkernel adapters.

A VMkernel port must be configured on the same network as the storage device to use the software iSCSI initiator. This is because you need to associate a VMkernel port with a specific iSCSI adapter in order to configure iSCSI port binding. The initiator uses the first network adapter port it finds that can see the storage device and use it exclusively for transport. This means that just having multiple adapter ports is not enough to balance storage workloads. However, you can achieve load balancing by configuring multiple VMkernel ports and binding them to multiple adapter ports.

After you load the software iSCSI kernel module, the next step is to bind the iSCSI driver to a port. There is a one-to-one relationship between the VMkernel port and the network adapter. This is a requirement for iSCSI port binding and multipathing. Only one port can be in the active state for a VMkernel adapter. Because only one port can be in the active state, you need to make sure that all other ports are set to Unused.

From the **Home** page, go to **Hosts and Clusters**. Select the ESXi Host in the inventory, click the **Manage** tab, and click the **Networking** tab. Choose the virtual switch that you want to use to bind the VMkernel port to a physical adapter. Next, choose the VMkernel adapter by highlighting the network label as shown in Figure 4-10 (step 1), which turns the VMkernel adapter blue. Then click the **Edit Settings** icon, shown as step 2 in Figure 4-10, which opens the Edit Settings window.

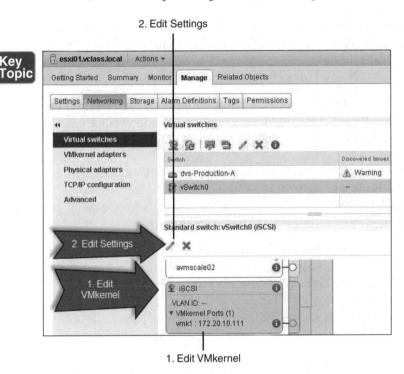

Figure 4-10 Select the VMkernel Port to Bind

The final step is to bind the VMkernel port to a network adapter. This can be accomplished by selecting the override switch failover order option, where one port is active and all of the other ports are set to the Unused state. The Edit Settings for the iSCSI VMkernel adapter then appear. To modify the vmnics, click **Teaming and Failover**. Select the check box for failover order **Override**. Then highlight all vmnics except for the one vmnic that will remain active. Move all other vmnics to Unused adapters using the blue down arrow. Then click **OK**.

NOTE   Designate a separate network adapter for iSCSI for performance and security.

Enable/Configure/Disable iSCSI CHAP

There is an optional security feature you can enable for iSCSI, called Challenge Handshake Authentication Protocol (CHAP). CHAP is a method for authenticating the ESXi Host and a storage device using password authentication. The authentication can be either one-way (unidirectional CHAP) or two-way (bidirectional, or mutual, CHAP):

- **Unidirectional:** Also called one-way CHAP. The storage array or target authenticates the ESXi Host or initiator. With unidirectional CHAP, the ESXi Host does not authenticate the storage device. The ESXi Host authenticates by sending the CHAP secret to the storage target.

- **Bidirectional:** Also called mutual CHAP. Authentication is done both ways, and the secret is different in the two directions. vSphere supports this method for software and dependent hardware iSCSI adapters only.

CHAP is a three-way handshake used to authenticate the ESXi Host, and bidirectional CHAP also authenticates the storage array. The CHAP secret is nothing more than a password. For both software iSCSI and dependent hardware iSCSI initiators, ESXi also supports per-target CHAP authentication.

As shown in Figure 4-11, in order to enable and configure iSCSI CHAP on ESXi Host, begin at **Home** then **Hosts and Clusters** and select the host on which you want to configure CHAP. Then select **Manage**, click **Storage**, and then **Storage Adapters**. Highlight **iSCSI Software Adapter**, and in the Adapter Details section, select the **Properties** tab and click the **Edit** button for authentication to set up CHAP.

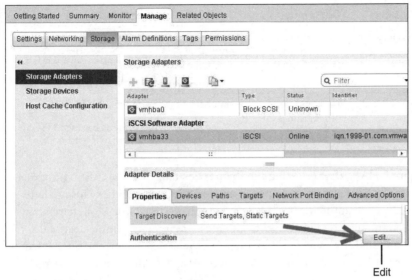

Edit

Figure 4-11 iSCSI CHAP's Edit Button

The CHAP authentication method needs to match the storage array's CHAP implementation and is vendor specific. You need to consult the storage array's documentation to help determine which CHAP security level is supported. When you set up the CHAP parameters, you need to specify which security level for CHAP should be utilized between the ESXi Host and the storage array. The different CHAP security levels, descriptions, and their corresponding supported adapters are listed in Table 4-3.

Table 4-3 CHAP Security Levels

CHAP Security Level	Description	Supported
None	CHAP authentication is not used. Select this option to disable authentication if it is currently enabled.	Software iSCSI Dependent hardware iSCSI Independent hardware iSCSI
Use Unidirectional CHAP if Required by Target	Host prefers non-CHAP connection but can use CHAP if required by the target.	Software iSCSI Dependent hardware iSCSI
Use Unidirectional CHAP Unless Prohibited by Target	Host prefers CHAP but can use non-CHAP if the target does not support CHAP.	Software iSCSI Dependent hardware iSCSI Independent hardware iSCSI

CHAP Security Level	Description	Supported
Use Unidirectional CHAP	Host requires CHAP authentication. The connection fails if CHAP negotiation fails.	Software iSCSI
		Dependent hardware iSCSI
		Independent hardware iSCSI
Use Bidirectional CHAP	Host and target both support bidirectional CHAP.	Software iSCSI
		Dependent hardware iSCSI

To configure CHAP, after selecting the **Properties** tab, click the **Edit** button to open up the Edit Authentication window, as shown in Figure 4-12. This is where you set up CHAP to authenticate. Keep in mind that CHAP does not encrypt anything; the communication between the initiator and target are in the clear. The CHAP name should not exceed 511 alphanumeric characters, and the CHAP secret should not exceed 255 alphanumeric characters. Also note that some hardware-based iSCSI initiators might have lower limits. For example, the QLogic adapter limits the CHAP name to 255 alphanumeric characters and the CHAP secret to 100 alphanumeric characters.

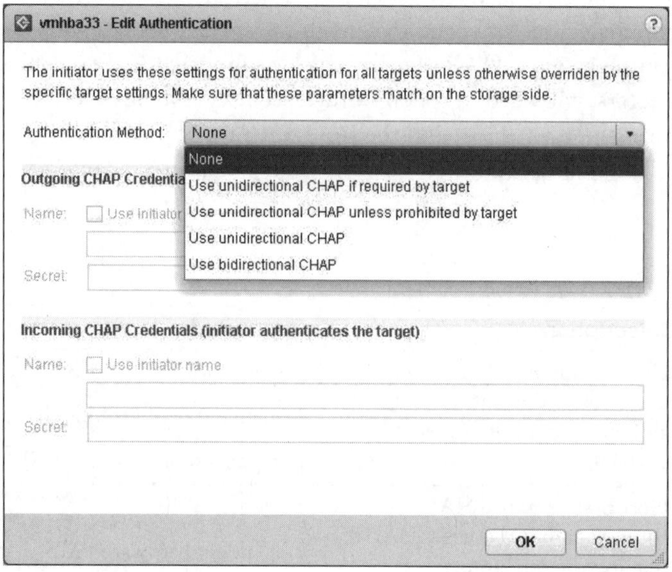

Figure 4-12 CHAP Setup Options

Determine Use Cases for Fibre Channel Zoning

One goal in storage is to make sure the host communicates with the correct storage and the storage communicates with the correct host. This can be challenging because many devices and nodes can be attached to a SAN. FC and FCoE switches use zoning and LUN masking to isolate communication between ESXi Hosts and storage devices. Zoning blocks communication between targets and initiators to isolate traffic to scan only devices that should be seeing each other. There are two kinds of zoning: hard zoning, which uses the physical switch port IDs, and soft zoning, which uses the WWPNs of the initiators and targets. Hardware and software zoning both attempt to reduce the number of targets and LUNs presented to the host. The best practice with LUN masking is to configure it on the storage array. The storage administrator configures which hosts have access to a LUN using masking. As a VMware best practice, LUN masking should be done on the ESXi Host using CLI but not in the vSphere client.

Compare and Contrast Array and Virtual Disk Thin Provisioning

Thin provisioning involves presenting more storage space to the hosts connecting to the storage system than is actually available on the storage system. For example, say that a storage system has usable capacity of 500 GB. The storage administrator then presents two hosts, each with a LUN of 300 GB. The mapping of these two LUNs means the storage array is presenting more storage to both hosts than is physically available on the storage array. When a LUN is created, the storage array does not dedicate specific blocks out of the volume for the LUN at the time of provisioning; rather, blocks are allocated when the data is actually written to the LUN. In this way, it is possible to provision more storage space, as seen from the connected ESXi Hosts, than actually physically exists in the storage array.

Array Thin Provisioning

ESXi supports thin-provisioned LUNs. *Array thin provisioning* simply means that the thin provisioning is done on the storage array, which reports the LUN's logical size instead of the real physical capacity of the LUN. When a LUN is thin provisioned, the storage array does not assign specific blocks for the LUN; instead, it waits until blocks are going to be written to zero out the data blocks and then performs the write. The storage array vendor uses its own file system and bookkeeping for the LUN, thus filling the LUN capacity on demand and saving storage space. By promising more storage space than the LUN actually has, you can overallocate storage. One built-in advantage that many storage array vendors have is the ability to grow the volume automatically when it is running out of space. Many storage vendors have automatic processes to grow the volume or delete certain file system constructs such as array-based snapshots.

Virtual Disk Thin Provisioning

When a thin virtual disk is created, it does not preallocate capacity, and it does not zero out the data block on the VMFS file system and the backend storage. Instead, the virtual disk consumes storage space only when data is required due to write to a disk. Initially, the VMDK's actual space usage starts out small and grows as more writes to disk occur. However, the guest OS sees the full allocated disk size at all times. The VMDK hides from the guest OS the fact that it is has not actually claimed all of the data blocks. The virtual machine's disk consumes only the amount of space that is needed for the current files in the file system. When writes occur and more space is needed, the VMkernel grows storage for VMFS 1 MB at a time. So as writes are committed and the 1 MB data block fills up, another 1 MB is allocated to the virtual disk. If the file system is NFS, which is by default thin provisioned, it grows 4 KB at a time, which is the size of its data block. Since the VMFS datastore is shared, SCSI locking needs to be performed by VMware vStorage API for Array Integration (VAAI). The metadata operation of SCSI locking is accomplished by VAAI.

To put array-based and virtual disk thin provisioning into perspective, the new data block or blocks need to be zeroed out when you are working with a virtual thin disk and new writes occur. However, before this operation can occur, the thin disk might have to obtain additional capacity from the datastore. Therefore, the storage array's math depends on how much space it has available compared to the ESXi Host. Thus, the thin provisioning is working at different levels.

Determine Use Case for and Configure Array Thin Provisioning

The ESXi Host can use storage arrays that present thin-provisioned storage. When a LUN is thin provisioned, it reports the logical size of the LUN and not its actual physical size. The storage array can promise more storage than its physical capacity. For example, an array may report that the LUN has 3 TB of space, when it really physically has 2 TB of disk space. The VMFS datastore is going to believe it has 3 TB of disk space that it can use. Thin provisioning is useful in virtual desktop environments where the system disk is shared among a number of users. You can save money by not having to reserve storage for each desktop's system disk. On the server side, thin provisioning can also be useful when you want to save money. However, be careful to monitor growth because running out of space with certain types of applications can be hazardous to your employment.

NOTE   Array-based thin provisioning is dependent on the storage array itself. If the LUN becomes full, the storage array decides what action to take. It is most likely to go offline. ESXi does not support enabling and disabling of thin provisioning on a storage device.

Summary

You have now read the chapter covering exam topics on storage. You should use information in the following sections to complete your preparation for Objective 3.1.

Exam Preparation Tasks

Review All the Key Topics

Table 4-4 provides a reference to each of the key topics identified in this chapter. Take a few moments to review each of these specific items.

Table 4-4   Key Topics for Chapter 4

Key Topic Element	Description	Pages
Note	No IDE/ATA/USB support to store VMs	164
Figure 4-1	Displaying storage adapters	164
Note	LUN presentation	165
Figure 4-2	iSCSI LUNs that are available	165
Note	Parallel NFS not supported	167
Figure 4-3	Displaying iSCSI LUN paths	168
Figure 4-4	Using CLI to display storage device information	170
Figure 4-5	iSCSI initiators	170
Figure 4-6	Rescanning storage	171
Note	SAN booting, with each host having its own boot LUN	172
Bulleted list	vCenter Server storage filters	174
Figure 4-7	Enabling storage filter	175
Figure 4-8	Enabling a software iSCSI initiator	176
Note	iSCSI adapter reenabled after boot	177
Figure 4-9	Disabling software iSCSI initiator	177
Note	iSCSI ports in the same domain and subnet as adapters	178
Figure 4-10	Selecting the VMkernel port to bind	179
Note	Separate network adapter for iSCSI	179

Key Topic Element	Description	Pages
Figure 4-11	iSCSI CHAP's Edit button	181
Figure 4-12	CHAP setup options	182
Note	No support for modifying thin provisioning at a storage device	184

Complete the Tables and Lists from Memory

Print a copy of Appendix B, "Memory Tables" (found on the CD), or at least the section for this chapter, and complete the tables and lists from memory. Appendix C, "Memory Tables Answer Key," also on the CD, includes completed tables and lists to check your work.

Definitions of Key Terms

Define the following key terms from this chapter and check your answers in the glossary.

Small Computer Systems Interface (SCSI), Fibre Channel (FC), Fibre Channel over Ethernet (FCoE), Internet Small Computer System Interface (iSCSI), Network File System (NFS), Kerberos, Parallel NFS (pNFS), software iSCSI initiator, independent hardware iSCSI initiator, dependent hardware iSCSI initiator, vCenter Server storage filters, Challenge Handshake Authentication Protocol (CHAP)

Answer Review Questions

The answers to these review questions can be found in Appendix A.

1. Which device cannot appear as a LUN?

   a. Tape device

   b. iSCSI

   c. FC

   d. NFS

2. Which of the following statements is not correct?

   a. A CD-ROM can be connected to a SCSI bus and appear as a LUN.

   b. You do not need to configure networking for a dependent hardware iSCSI initiator.

   c. A software iSCSI initiator is a standard 1 GbE or 10 GbE NIC.

   d. The ESXi Host does not need a VMkernel port for an independent hardware iSCSI initiator.

3. What TCP port is the default iSCSI port?

   a. 3620

   b. 3720

   c. 3270

   d. 3260

4. Which NFS protocols are not supported in vSphere 6.0? (Choose two.)

   a. NFSv3

   b. NFSv4.0

   c. NFSv4.1

   d. pNFS

5. Which of the following statements about iSCSI is incorrect?

   a. CHAP is a method for authenticating the ESXi Host and a storage device using password authentication.

   b. CHAP is a required security feature for iSCSI.

   c. With unidirectional CHAP, the ESXi Host does not authenticate the storage device.

   d. vSphere supports bidirectional CHAP for software and dependent hardware iSCSI adapters only.

This chapter covers the following objectives:

- **Objective 3.2: Configure Software-defined Storage**
  - Explain VSAN and VVOL architectural components
  - Determine the role of storage providers in VSAN
  - Determine the role of storage providers in VVOLs
  - Explain VSAN failure domains functionality
  - Configure/manage VMware Virtual SAN
  - Create/modify VMware Virtual Volumes (VVOLs)
  - Configure storage policies
  - Enable/disable Virtual SAN fault domains
  - Create Virtual Volumes given the workload and availability requirements
  - Collect VSAN Observer output
  - Create storage policies for workloads and availability requirements
  - Configure VVOLs protocol endpoints

- **Objective 3.3: Configure vSphere Storage Multipathing and Failover**
  - Explain common multipathing components
  - Differentiate APD and PDL states
  - Given a scenario, compare and contrast Active Optimized vs. Active Non-Optimized port group states
  - Explain features of Pluggable Storage Architecture (PSA)
  - Understand the effects of a given claim rule on multipathing and failover
  - Explain the function of claim rule elements
  - Change the path selection policy using the UI
  - Determine required claim rule elements to change the default PSP
  - Determine the effect of changing PSP on multipathing and failover
  - Determine the effects of changing SATP on relevant device behavior
  - Configure/manage storage load balancing
  - Differentiate available storage load balancing options and multipathing policies
  - Configure storage policies
  - Locate failover events in the UI

## CHAPTER 5

Storage, Part 2

In the second chapter on storage, Software Defined Storage and multipathing are the topics that will be discussed as they relate to the VCP exam. The first objective is Software Defined Storage, which details Virtual SAN (VSAN) and Virtual Volumes (VVOLs). Both types of software defined storage rely upon using storage providers to communicate the storage capabilities between vSphere and the storage device. VSAN and VVOLs are two different ways of delivering storage to virtual machines than traditional storage methods. The second objective that is covered is multipathing and failover; including the components that are a part of multipathing, such as claim rules and features of Pluggable Storage Architecture (PSA). Both objectives will be presented with information that you need to know for the exam.

"Do I Know This Already?" Quiz

The "Do I Know This Already?" quiz allows you to assess whether you should study this entire chapter or move quickly to the "Exam Preparation Tasks" section. Regardless, the authors recommend that you read the entire chapter at least once. Table 5-1 outlines a sampling of the major headings in this chapter and the corresponding "Do I Know This Already?" quiz questions. You can find the answers in Appendix A, "Answers to the 'Do I Know This Already?' Quizzes and Review Questions."

Table 5-1 "Do I Know This Already?" Foundation Topics Section-to-Question Mapping

Foundation Topics Section	Questions Covered in This Section
Explain VSAN and VVOL Architectural Components	1, 2
Configure/Manage VMware Virtual SAN	3
Enable/Disable Virtual SAN Fault Domains	4
Configure VVOLs Protocol Endpoints	5
Differentiate APD and PDL States	6, 7

Foundation Topics Section	Questions Covered in This Section
Explain Features of Pluggable Storage Architecture (PSA)	8, 10
Differentiate Available Storage multipathing Policies	9

1. Which feature is not needed for a VVOL to communicate with a virtual machine?

   a. VASA provider 2.0

   b. VVOL Observer

   c. Storage container

   d. VM storage policy

2. A VSAN cluster is being set up, but there appears to be a problem. There are four ESXi Hosts in the cluster, and each host has one 200 GB HDD for persistent storage. The problem appears when you check the Virtual SAN datastore, which shows only 200 GB of total capacity. Why is the total capacity not correct?

   a. DRS has been enabled on the same cluster as VSAN.

   b. There are four storage providers registered instead of one.

   c. The VSAN VMkernel ports are not set up correctly.

   d. The VASA provider 2.0 has been installed.

3. Which of the following statements is incorrect?

   a. A network requires a vSphere distributed switch.

   b. vSphere HA must be enabled before a VSAN cluster is created.

   c. Before a VSAN cluster can be created, the VMkernel port network needs to be set up on every ESXi Host in the cluster.

   d. The VSAN network is a critical component, and all the ESXi Hosts must be able to access it.

4. Which of the following statements is incorrect?

   a. *Number of disk stripes per object* is the number of physical disks of storage that the VMDK will be written across.

   b. A custom VSAN storage policy has been created. The first rule is number of failures to tolerate, with `NumberOfFailuresToTolerate` set to `1`.

This means the VSAN cluster can tolerate one ESXi Host, network, or disk failure and not lose access to the VM.

   c. In VSAN 6.0, you create fault domains and deploy virtual machines across the fault domains so that if a rack fails, it will not make the virtual machine inaccessible.

   d. vSphere 5.5 introduced VSAN fault domains as a new feature.

5. Which of the following statements is incorrect?

   a. The protocol endpoint is created during virtual machine creation.

   b. If a VM is not configured with a storage policy, the VM uses the default storage policy.

   c. ESXi uses protocol endpoints to establish a data path from virtual machines to their Virtual Volumes.

   d. A VVOL is bound to a protocol endpoint when it is accessed by a VM from an ESXi Host.

6. Which of the following is not an option for Permanent Device Loss (PDL)?

   a. Disabled

   b. Issue Events

   c. Power Off VMs

   d. Power Off and Restart VMs

7. Which statements are correct? (Choose two.)

   a. If an ESXi Host does not receive a SCSI sense code reply within the APD default timeout of 140 seconds, the ESXi Host begins to fail any non-virtual machine I/O traffic that is being sent to the storage device.

   b. An All Paths Down condition can occur when the ESXi Host receives an error message saying the path is going to be temporarily down.

   c. A good example of a PDL is the LUN failing but the storage array remaining functional. The storage array sends a SCSI sense code to inform the ESXi Host that the LUN is permanently disabled.

   d. If an ESXi Host does not receive a SCSI sense code reply within the PDL default timeout of 140 seconds, the ESXi Host begins to fail any non-virtual machine I/O traffic that is being sent to the storage device.

8. Which of these tasks would be performed by the Pluggable Storage Architecture (PSA)? (Choose two.)

  a. Discover available storage and the physical paths to that storage only.

  b. Discovery and removal of available storage and their physical paths.

  c. Assign each storage device a multipathing Plug-in (MPP) by using pre-defined claim rules.

  d. Assign each storage device a multipathing Plug-in (MPP) by using the predefined port binding.

9. Which of the following path selection policies (PSPs) has a preferred path setting for the plug-in?

  a. `VMW_PSP_RR`

  b. `VMW_PSP_IO`

  c. `VMW_PSP_FIXED`

  d. `VMW_PSP_MRU`

10. Which of the following statements is not true?

  a. PSA discovers the storage and then figures out which multipathing driver will be in charge of communicating with that storage.

  b. The Native multipathing Plug-in (NMP) is the default MPP in vSphere and is used when the storage array does not have a third-party MPP solution.

  c. The SATP monitors the health of each physical path and can respond to error messages from the storage array to handle path failover.

  d. The NMP assigns a default PSP based on the multipathing policies.

Foundation Topics

Objective 3.2—Configure Software-defined Storage

A number of components have been added to accomplish VMware's vision of software-defined storage. The virtualization layer needs to have the ability to automate and pool storage. Whether you are using VSAN or VVOL is a factor in how the physical storage is presented to vSphere. Using vSphere, one of the components needed is policy-based management, which allows for automation of storage administration. Thus, when storage needs to be provisioned for VMs, it is done using policies. In this chapter, you will see how Storage Policy Based Management (SPBM) can be utilized to provision and manage VSAN and VVOL. Storage policies enable you to provision virtual machines on storage that matches their requirements.

Explain VSAN and VVOL Architectural Components

VMware has two software-based storage solutions: Virtual SAN (VSAN), introduced in vSphere 5.5, and Virtual Volumes (VVOL), introduced in vSphere 6.0. These two different solutions solve different problems, and really VSAN can be used by VVOL to provide storage for virtual machines.

VSAN

Virtual SAN (VSAN) is a distributed layer of software that runs on the ESXi hypervisor and uses direct-attached storage across ESXi Hosts to form a virtual datastore. VSAN has been built into the vSphere hypervisor as a kernel module since vSphere 5.5. The ESXi hypervisor allows Virtual SAN to run natively. VSAN uses local storage from the ESXi Hosts to present a shared datastore. The datastore appears to the ESXi Hosts to be like any other shared datastore. You do not need to install any additional software or drivers to utilize VSAN. You need ESXi installed on between 3 and 64 physical hosts that are on the hardware compatibility list (HCL). In addition, you need either the Windows or Linux (virtual appliance) version of vCenter Server installed with version 5.5 or 6.0. As with many other new features that VMware has introduced, you can use the vSphere Web Client but not the Windows vSphere Client to manage VSAN.

One of the main parts of the hardware that you need for a Virtual SAN cluster is at least three ESXi Hosts that are contributing to the available storage capacity. In addition to HDs used for capacity, you need SSDs for performance. Another hardware component is the disk controller, which needs to run in passthrough mode or HBA mode.

Finally, networking hardware is needed for Virtual SAN. VSAN requires a VMkernel port running on either a 1 Gbps or 10 Gbps network for VSAN communication between the ESXi Hosts. However, a 10 Gbps network is recommended, and it is required for all-flash configurations.

NOTE   VSAN does not support IPv6.

VVOL

Virtual Volumes (VVOLs) are new in vSphere 6.0, and they change how storage is delivered. The traditional models tend to focus on LUNs and NFS exports. If you need storage for a virtual machine, you request a LUN from the storage administrator. But is that LUN optimized for a particular VM? You may not know. The vSphere client only tells you the size of the LUN. It does not tell you any additional information, like stripe size or whether the LUN is replicated. Thus, a VMware administrator has no hard knowledge about how the LUN is set up but only knows the LUN's size. In addition, each ESXi Host is limited to 256 LUNs, which can be a problem in large environments that have hundreds of LUNs. The ability of virtual volumes to go beyond 256 LUNs may entice some companies to look at using VVOLs.

The components that are needed for VVOLs start with at least one ESXi Host running vSphere 6.0, which contains a set of APIs called vSphere APIs for Storage Awareness 2.0 (VASA). Originally, VASA 1.0 was introduced in vSphere 5.0 to advertise the capabilities of the storage array. VMware worked with the storage vendors to release a version of VASA that would be acceptable and supported by those vendors. Each storage vendor can implement the VASA provider in whatever method works for the particular environment. Some vendors implement the storage provider as a virtual appliance, while others build it into their software operating system.

The VASA storage provider communicates with the storage container, which is a virtual datastore. The storage administrator defines storage containers on the storage side, which is a pool of raw storage that serves as a virtual volume store. Each storage vendor can implement storage containers using its own implementation method. The storage container needs to be registered with the VASA storage provider, which allows the vCenter Server to discover all the configured storage containers, along with their storage capability profiles. The capabilities include features such as high availability, deduplication, and IOPS.

Think of the VASA provider as the matchmaker between the storage container and the VM. The VASA provider reports to vSphere the storage that is available and the capabilities that the storage options possess. In addition, the VASA provider can verify whether the VM requirements are being met, based on those capabilities. The virtual machine uses storage policies to define its storage policy requirements, and the storage container advertises its abilities with its storage capability profile. The VM sees only storage containers that match its requirements due to the VASA provider.

Determine the Role of Storage Providers in VSAN

The Virtual SAN cluster during the creation process automatically registers a storage provider for each host. Once a storage provider is registered, the VASA storage provider (SP) communicates to the vCenter Server the underlying capabilities of the storage. Ideally, the storage provider should be registered on each ESXi Host in case a host goes down, so another ESXi Host can deliver the VSAN capabilities to vSphere. In addition, even though all the ESXi Hosts register a storage provider, only one of the VASA providers is online, and the others are there for failover.

The storage provider needs to be loaded for the VSAN cluster in order to work with the VM storage policy. The virtual machine storage policy is basically a list of storage features that are demanded for the VM. The VASA provider is the middleman between the storage and the VM. The SP wants to find storage that will meet the demands of the VM storage policy. Because the storage policy has already learned what the storage is advertising for features, it just needs to find the right virtual machine to match the storage container. Using the vSphere Web Client, you can view the storage providers by highlighting the vCenter Server in the left pane. Then, as shown in Figure 5-1, select the **Manage** tab and then **Storage Providers** view to see all of the VSAN registered storage providers.

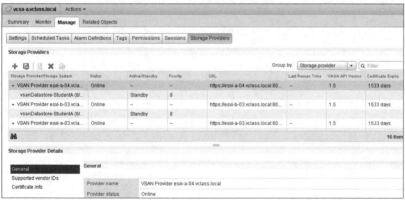

Figure 5-1 Example of VSAN Storage Providers

Determine the Role of Storage Providers in VVOLs

One of the main parts of Virtual Volumes (VVOLs) is the VMware APIs for Storage Awareness (VASA) storage provider. The VASA provider is software that is written and developed by the storage vendors. It is the middleman between the storage container and the ESXi Host's VM. The storage system uses a storage capability profile to advertise the capabilities of the storage that comes from the storage provider. The storage provider works with the built-in Storage Monitoring Service (SMS) to communicate with the vCenter Server. Without the storage provider, the VM would not know which storage container best matches its requirements.

The storage provider that is integrated with vSphere is certified by VMware and is either added to the software of the storage array or can be provided as a virtual appliance. In addition, the storage provider must be registered with vCenter Server, which creates an I/O path so the ESXi Host can communicate with the VVOL storage container through the VASA bind request.

The virtual appliance needs some configuration, and it needs to be powered on to function as the middleman between NetApp and VMware. Using the vSphere Web Client, you can view the storage providers by highlighting the vCenter Server in the left pane. Then, as shown in Figure 5-2, select the **Manage** tab and then **Storage Providers** to see all the registered storage providers.

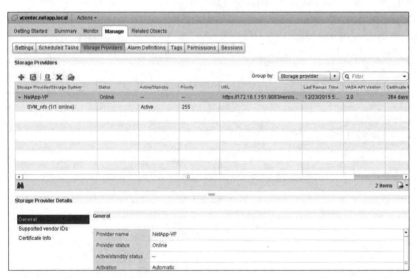

Figure 5-2   Example of a Registered NetApp VASA 2.0 Service Provider

Explain VSAN Failure Domains Functionality

The concept of VSAN failure domains was introduced in vSphere 5.5. The idea is that if a host fails, you need to know the impact on availability of data. In order to understand failure domains, you need to first define a disk group—a logical container of one to seven HDDs, with at least one SSD device. The key is that the SSD or flash device is the caching or buffer layer for the HDDs, so if the SSD fails, the disk group and its data become unavailable until VSAN rebuilds the disk group. Therefore, when designing a VSAN, keep in mind that having a smaller disk group decreases the time it takes to rebuild a disk group in the event of a flash device failure, and a larger disk group size increases the time it takes for VSAN to rebuild the disk group or failure domain.

Configure/Manage VMware Virtual SAN

The configuration of a VSAN cluster begins by designing the VSAN environment and adding all the appropriate licenses. The cluster can have between 3 and 64 ESXi Hosts, and each host can have up to a maximum of 200 VMs. The ESXi Hosts need to communicate over the VSAN network, and the network requires a vSphere distributed switch. The minimum network uplink for the VSAN network is 1 Gbps, and the recommended uplink is 10 Gbps. VSAN cluster communication between the hosts utilizes a VMkernel port type called Virtual SAN traffic. Before the VSAN cluster can be created, the VMkernel port network needs to be set up on every ESXi Host in the cluster. In Figure 5-3 you can see that the VMkernel network had been created with four hosts added to the Virtual SAN port group VSAN-studentB. The VSAN network is a critical component, and all the ESXi Hosts must be able to access it. In this VSAN cluster, there are four ESXi Hosts. If an ESXi Host does not have access to the VSAN network, it is excluded from the VSAN cluster, which decreases the size of the VSAN datastore.

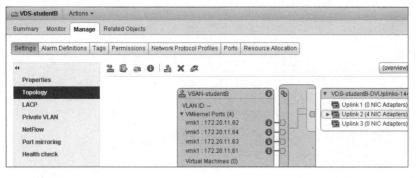

Figure 5-3 Virtual SAN Network

Once you have the VSAN network set up, you can begin to set up the VSAN cluster. You can use the vSphere Web Client to enable the Virtual SAN cluster. In the vSphere Web Client's left pane, right-click the data center and select **New Cluster** in the Actions menu. The New Cluster Wizard appears (see Figure 5-4). Type the name of the cluster in the **Name** text box. In this example, select the **Turn ON** check box for DRS. Then select the Virtual SAN **Turn ON** check box to enable VSAN.

NOTE   When a VSAN cluster is enabled, vSphere HA must be disabled.

When you enable the VSAN cluster, the last option on the page indicates whether you want vSphere to automatically discover all the local disks on the hosts and add them to the VSAN datastore or whether you want the VMware administrator to manually choose the disks that will be added to the cluster. In this example, select **Manual** from the **Add Disks to Storage** option to select the mode for claiming host storage devices for the VSAN cluster. The first choice is **Automatic**, which claims all local devices on the hosts for the VSAN cluster. The other choice, **Manual**, means that the storage devices on the ESXi Hosts will be manually claimed by the VSAN cluster (see Figure 5-4). The VSAN cluster contains the local hard disks of the hosts that are included in the Virtual SAN cluster.

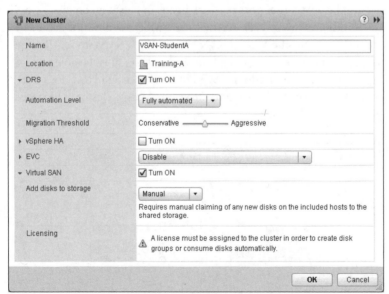

Figure 5-4   Creating a New VSAN Cluster

You can add ESXi Hosts before or after creating the VSAN cluster. Figure 5-5 shows manually claiming the disks for the VSAN cluster. As you can see, the VSAN cluster has been created and enabled with four hosts. However, Figure 5-5 shows no disks claimed for the Virtual SAN cluster because **Data Disks in Use** is 0. Therefore, the Virtual SAN has no capacity.

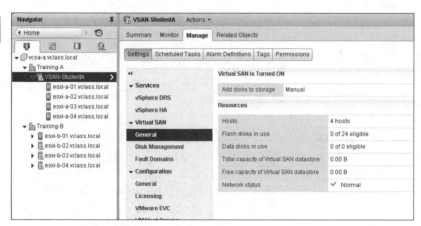

Figure 5-5   VSAN Cluster with Four ESXi Hosts but No Disks

The VSAN cluster currently has zero disk capacity. You need to manually add disks from each ESXi Host, which will help to form disk groups. vSphere defines a *disk group* as a unit of storage or container on an ESXi Host that includes one SSD and one or more HDDs. A disk group uses the SSD flash device for performance and the HDDs for permanent storage. In vSphere 6.0, you can have a maximum of five VSAN disk groups per host, with up to seven HDDs per disk group and a maximum of one SSD per disk group. Therefore, VSAN can use an aggregate of disk groups to back up a single datastore that is created when you enable Virtual SAN.

Next, you need to manually claim the disks for the VSAN cluster by creating disk groups. Select the VSAN cluster in the left pane. In the center pane, shown in Figure 5-6, select **Manage > Settings > Disk Management**. Then click on the **Claim Disks** icon.

Claim disks

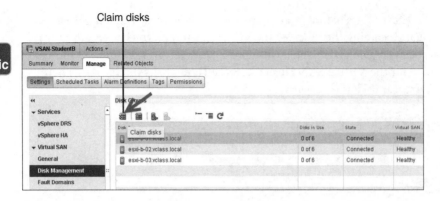

Figure 5-6   Manually Claim Disks

After you click the **Claim Disks** icon, you have several options. You can either select all the disks, or you can manually claim disks to create a disk group on each ESXi Host in the cluster. Figure 5-7 shows the Claim Disks window, where you select at least one drive type of flash and one or more HDDs of drive type HDD for capacity on each ESXi Host. After you click **OK**, vSphere begins to create the disk groups for the VSAN cluster.

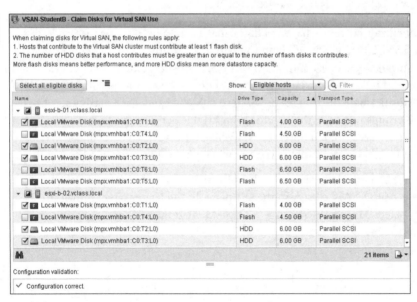

Figure 5-7   Create a Disk Group on Each ESXi Host by Claiming Disks

Create/Modify VMware Virtual Volumes (VVOLs)

Virtual Volumes (VVOLs) are software-defined storage that is different from traditionally managed storage. When you create a VVOL, you do not also create the underlying storage objects, so depending on the storage vendor, the underlying storage objects need to be created ahead of time. A traditional datastore was either a LUN (VMFS) or a volume (NFS). VVOLs are a new way of looking at storage.

To begin to create a VVOL, you need to set up the VASA storage provider according to the storage vendor because each storage vendor can set up the VASA provider differently. You need to check with the storage vendor on how to configure the VASA provider. Once the VASA provider and VVOL storage containers are set up, the storage capability profile or storage policy is then set up. In a VVOL environment, the underlying storage is presented as a virtual storage system. During VVOL creation, only the storage containers that meet the storage capability profile requirements are presented as acceptable storage for VVOLs. In Figure 5-8, a VVOL datastore creation is being initiated by selecting **Storage** from the **Actions** menu of the datacenter.

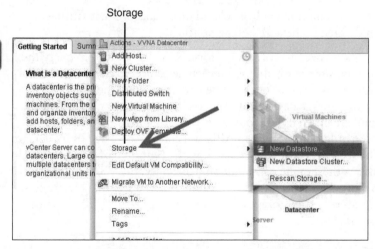

Figure 5-8   Create a VVOL Datastore on a VVOL Container

After the VVOL is created, you can check the status of the VVOL datastore by using the vSphere Web Client. Highlight the VVOL datastore and select the **Summary** tab. The datastore type is VVOL, as shown in Figure 5-9. In this figure, you can see other pertinent information about the VVOL datastore, such as the storage capability profile.

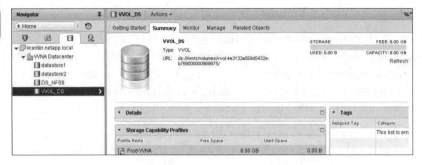

Figure 5-9 Display a VVOL Datastore

Configure Storage Policies

Virtual machine storage policies (SPs) are an important part of virtual machine provisioning with VVOLs. Storage policies were introduced in vSphere 5.0, but until version 6.0, they lacked the ability to query the storage for the capabilities that are defined in rule sets. A storage policy outlines the storage requirements and capabilities that the VM expects of a datastore. Each storage policy is a set of constraints that are defined by a set of rule sets. When you create, clone, or migrate a VM, the SP requires that the virtual machine only be placed on a datastore that satisfies all rules that have been defined in the VM storage policy.

VMware APIs for Storage Awareness (VASA) provides the technology to query the datastores and return the storage capabilities of each datastore. Each storage vendor decides how the VASA provider is to be implemented. The VASA provider is the middleman between the storage device and vSphere. Therefore, no matter how the VASA provider is implemented, it has the task of translating between the storage vendor's APIs and constructs and vSphere's APIs and constructs. The VSAN default storage policy can be seen in Figure 5-10. Changing the **Number of Failures to Tolerate** setting affects the storage consumption. Currently, the VSAN cluster can tolerate two disks failing. If you decreased the Number of Failures to Tolerate setting to 1, that would decrease the storage consumption by one-third. The storage space would then be 200.00 GB.

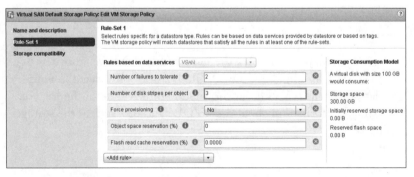

Figure 5-10 VM Default Storage Policy

Enable/Disable Virtual SAN Fault Domains

In VSAN 5.5, there is an issue of how to spread the replicas of virtual machines across multiple racks. You need to set the VSAN variable `NumberOfFailuresToTolerate` to a high value to make a number of copies of the virtual machine to spread across the racks. A new feature in vSphere 6.0 is VSAN fault domains, which ensure that virtual machine replica data is not duplicated on hosts in the same domain. In VSAN 6.0 you deploy virtual machines across the fault domains so that if a rack fails, it does not make the virtual machines inaccessible.

To create or enable a VSAN fault domain, you need to first configure the VSAN fault domains, which can be done by highlighting the **VSAN cluster** > **Manage** tab > **Settings** > **Fault Domains**. You can see in Figure 5-11 that three fault domains have been created. In the third fault domain, StudentA-ThirdFD, there are two ESXi Hosts. Only one replica or copy of a VM will be stored within that fault domain. Ideally, one copy of a virtual machine will be stored on each of the three fault domains. And in the physical world, each FD would be in a separate physical rack.

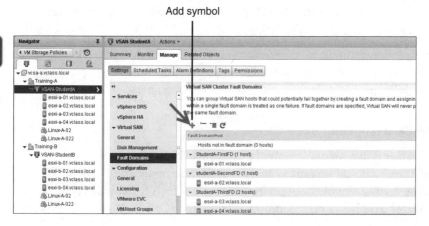

Figure 5-11   VSAN Cluster Fault Domain Configuration

The example in Figure 5-11 shows a VSAN cluster with three fault domains using four ESXi Hosts. In order to increase availability and performance for the VM, you could use either the default VSAN storage policy or create a custom VSAN storage policy. Figure 5-12 shows how to create a custom VSAN storage policy. The first rule is **Number of Failures to Tolerate**, which is set to 1. This indicates the number of ESXi Host, network, or disk failures that can happen in the cluster without losing access to the VM. You can think of this as creating a mirror or Raid-1 of your VM.

The second rule created here is **Number of Disk Stripes per Object**, which is set to 3. This indicates the number of physical disks of storage that the storage object (VMDK) will be written across. In this case, the VMDK will be written across three disks.

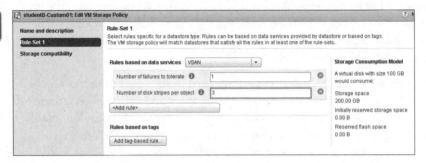

Figure 5-12 VSAN VM Storage Policy

Create Virtual Volumes Given the Workload and Availability Requirements

Virtual Volumes (VVOLs) are designed to be created on storage containers. You or the storage administrator create different storage containers that can meet different workload and availability requirements. During VVOL datastore creation, you use storage capability profiles to match available storage containers.

Collect VSAN Observer Output

VSAN Observer is designed to capture performance statistics that can be used by you or VMware technical support to analyze performance statistics. VSAN Observer can be used to troubleshoot performance issues for VSAN. It can provide an in-depth snapshot of performance information such as IOPS, latency, and other statistics for different layers of the VSAN.

Figure 5-13 shows VSAN statistics from the viewpoint of the VSAN client running on each host. In other words, this view represents the VSAN performance as seen by VMs running on the hosts for which statistics are shown.

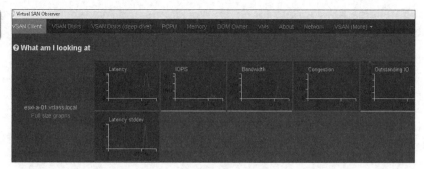

Figure 5-13   Virtual SAN Observer Client View

Figure 5-14 offers a deep view into the physical disk layer of a VSAN host. It offers an aggregate view across all disks and disk groups, as well as details about every physical disk. Using this view, you can get insight into how VSAN is splitting the I/O work between the SSDs and HDDs.

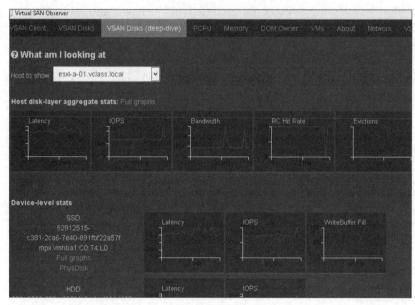

Figure 5-14   VSAN Disks (Deep Dive) View

Create Storage Policies Appropriate for Given Workloads and Availability Requirements

The VASA storage provider presents the storage capabilities of the storage device. Storage capability features can be based on capacity, availability, performance, and other factors. During storage setup, you combine the capabilities into what the storage policies or storage capability profiles. For example, if a VM storage policy includes the requirement to have thin provisioning and deduplication, then during VVOL creation, only storage containers that have both capabilities are presented as potential containers.

Configure VVOLs Protocol Endpoints

A protocol endpoint (PE) is the logical path that an ESXi Host uses to communicate between a VVOL and a virtual machine. The PE is created during VVOL creation. ESXi uses protocol endpoints to establish a data path from virtual machines to their VVOLs. When you map a storage container to a VVOL or when you perform a storage rescan, protocol endpoints are discovered. The I/O path to a VVOL to a VM traverses and is bound through the PE. The VVOL is bound to a protocol endpoint when it is accessed by a VM from an ESXi Host. For example, when a VM powers on, it becomes bound to a VVOL. To view protocol endpoints in the vSphere Web Client, highlight the ESXi Host. Select the **Manage** tab, click **Storage**, and select **Protocol Endpoints** (see Figure 5-15).

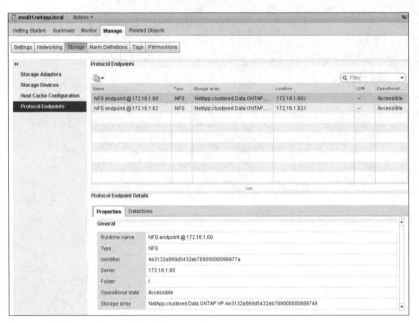

Figure 5-15   VVOL Protocol Endpoints

NOTE   If a virtual machine is not configured with a storage policy, then the VM uses the default storage policy.

Data is not equal, and vSphere uses storage policies to enforce virtual machine storage requirements. The policies help define how the storage handles capacity, availability, and performance. For example, how redundant do you want data to be? In other words, how many copies of data do you want written across the ESXi Hosts in case a host fails? Having more copies of data results in more availability. However, using more storage for redundancy results in less total capacity. Each virtual machine that uses VSAN is going to be assigned at least one storage policy. Therefore, when a virtual machine uses Virtual SAN for its storage, it is distributed across the VSAN datastore based on its storage policy.

Objective 3.3—Configure vSphere Storage Multipathing and Failover

Objective 3.3 discusses how vSphere configures and manages multipathing and failover using Pluggable Storage Architecture (PSA). In addition to discussing PSA, this section also looks at other means of protection, such as Virtual Machine Component Protection (VMCP), which can be used to protect against All Paths Down (APD) and Permanent Device Loss (PDL) issues.

Explain Common Multipathing Components

The common multipathing components are adapters, switches, and cables. If these parts fail, ESXi can switch to a functioning physical path, in a process known as *path failover*. A configuration that consists of more than one path, or *multipathing*, provides path failover and also allows for load balancing. *Load balancing* is the process of distributing I/O across the physical paths.

Differentiate APD and PDL States

Virtual Machine Component Protection (VMCP) is a vSphere high availability feature that is new in vSphere 6.0 and used to protect virtual machines when storage issues occur. The VMCP was created to protect against All Paths Down (APD) and Permanent Device Loss (PDL) situations.

An APD situation can occur when an ESXi Host cannot access a storage device. During normal communication between the ESXi Host and a storage device, communication happens via SCSI sense codes. When an ESXi Host is no longer receiving communication from the storage device, the host does not know if the device loss is going to be temporary or permanent. Without an acknowledgment from the storage device, the ESXi Host continues to try to reestablish communication by sending I/O commands until the APD timeout has been reached. If the ESXi Host does not receive a SCSI sense code reply within the APD default timeout of 140 seconds, the ESXi Host begins to fail any non-virtual machine I/O traffic that is being sent to the storage device. For example, if an administrator issues a rescan of the SAN, the hostd worker threads wait indefinitely for I/O to return from the device when it is in an APD condition. This is a problem because hostd has a limited number of worker threads available to perform its functions. The hostd daemon manages virtual machine operations such as vMotion, LUN discovery, power on/off, etc. So if all of the hostd worker threads are exhausted because of an APD condition, then other operations that hostd would normally perform are affected.

The PDL condition was added in vSphere 5.0. The storage device sends a SCSI sense code to the ESXi Host, specifying that the storage device has become unavailable. A good example of a PDL is a LUN failing but the storage array continuing to function. The storage array sends a SCSI sense code to inform the ESXi Host that the LUN is permanently disabled. Once this occurs, the ESXi Host stops sending I/O requests to the storage array. Figure 5-16 shows the options for PDL: **Disabled**, **Issue Events**, and **Power Off and Restart VMs**.

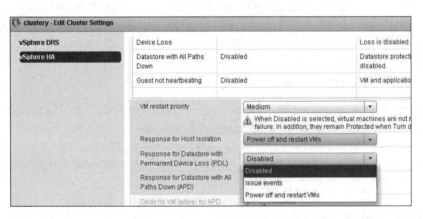

Figure 5-16   The Options for Path Device Loss (PDL)

Compare and Contrast Active Optimized vs. Active non-Optimized Port Group States

Asymmetrical Logical Unit Access (ALUA) is associated with an asymmetric active/active array. *Asymmetric* means that one storage processor can issue I/O to the LUN, and *active/active* means both controllers can receive I/O. The controller that can issue commands is called the *managing controller*, and paths to the LUN via ports on this controller are called *optimized paths*. The controller that cannot issue I/O is the *non-optimized port*.

Explain Features of Pluggable Storage Architecture (PSA)

In vSphere 4.0, VMware changed how it did multipathing when it introduced Pluggable Storage Architecture (PSA). PSA is simply a set of APIs that third-party vendors can use to add their multipathing software into vSphere to manage multipathing and access to storage. Before vSphere 4.0, the only choices for multipathing policies were VMware's **Fixed** or **Most Recently Used (MRU)**. PSA solved this problem by giving third-party storage vendors a means to add policies and to recognize the type of storage deployed. The PSA has two primary tasks. The first task is to discover available storage and the physical paths to that storage as well as removal of the paths. The second task is to assign each storage device a multipathing Plug-in (MPP) by using predefined claim rules, including handling I/O queuing to the logical devices. Therefore, PSA discovers the storage and then figures out which multipathing driver will be in charge of communicating with that storage. All the error codes, I/O requests, and I/O queuing to the HBA are handled by the MPP.

MPP

The top-level plug-in in PSA is the Multipathing Plug-in (MPP). The MPP can be either the internal MPP, which is called the Native Multipathing Plug-in (NMP), or a third-party MPP supplied by a storage vendor. Examples of third-party MPPs are Symantec DMP and EMC PowerPath/VE. Therefore, all storage is accessed through an MPP, whether it is VMware's built-in MPP or one of the third-party MPPs. The MPP combines NMP, SATP, and PSP, which are the pieces that make up the process.

Say that you have a NetApp storage array that you want to connect to VMware. You first make sure that the NetApp array is supported by VMware by checking the hardware compatibility list (HCL). If it is on the HCL, you could simply use the built-in NMP to handle all the multipathing and load balancing. Or you could switch to Symantec's Dynamic Multipathing (DMP), which is a supported third-party MPP. Symantec's DMP solution can handle the path discovery and path management of the ESXi Host to the NetApp storage array. This third-party MPP solution might provide better load-balancing performance than the built-in solution. With the following command line. you can list the multipathing modules for an ESXi Host:

```
esxi> esxcli storage core plugin list -plugin-class=MP
Plugin name  Plugin class
NMP                   MP
```

In this example, you can see that the internal Native Multipathing Plug-in (NMP) is loaded on the ESXi Host.

NMP

The Native Multipathing Plug-in (NMP) is the default MPP in vSphere and is used when the storage array does not have a third-party MPP solution. VMware has a default claim rule that applies to storage that has not been claimed by a claim rule; it defaults to NMP. The NMP contains a Storage Array Type Plug-in (SATP) and a Path Selection Plug-in (PSP). One of the tasks of NMP is to associate physical storage paths with an SATP and to associate a PSP that chooses the best available path.

SATP

VMware provides a Storage Array Type Plug-in (SATP) for every type of array that VMware supports in the HCL. For example, VMware provides an SATP for supported storage arrays such as the IBM SVC, which uses the VMW_SATP_SVC SATP provided by VMware. The SATP monitors the health of each physical path and can respond to error messages from the storage array to handle path failover. There are third-party SATPs that the storage vendor can provide to take advantage of unique storage properties.

PSP

The Path Selection Plug-in (PSP) performs the task of selecting which physical path to use for storage transport. One way to think of PSP is which multipathing solution you are using for load balancing. There are three built-in PSPs: Fixed, MRU, and Round Robin (which was added with vSphere 4.1). The NMP assigns a default PSP from the claim rules, based on the SATP associated with the physical device. If you need to override the default PSP, you create a claim rule to assign a different PSP to the device.

Understand the Effects of a Given Claim Rule on Multipathing and Failover

When you power on an ESXi Host or manually choose to rescan for storage devices, the ESXi Host sends a signal down the physical bus paths and discovers any storage available to the host. The ESXi Host then assigns each storage device an MPP based on the claim rules listed in the /etc/vmware/esx.conf file. When the storage device has a proper MPP assigned, the multipathing driver is responsible for managing the path selection for the storage device. By default, every 5 minutes the ESXi Host resends a signal down the physical bus paths, looking for any unclaimed paths to be claimed by the appropriate MPP. This process of associating a storage device with a plug-in is referred to as *claiming the device*, and the MPP claims a storage device by finding an appropriate claim rule in the `/etc/vmware/esx.conf` file.

To get a list of the current claim rules, use the `esxcli storage core claimrule list` command, as shown in Figure 5-17.

```
ESX01.vclass.local - PuTTY
[root@esxi01:~] esxcli storage core claimrule list
Rule Class   Rule Class   Type        Plugin     Matches                           XCOPY Use Array Reported Values   XCOPY Use Multiple Segme
nts  XCOPY Max Transfer Size
-----------  -----   -------  ----------  ---------  --------------------------------  -------------------------------   ------------------------
---  -----------------------
MP             0   runtime  transport   NMP        transport=usb                               false                              fa
lse                       0
MP             1   runtime  transport   NMP        transport=sata                              false                              fa
lse                       0
MP             2   runtime  transport   NMP        transport=ide                               false                              fa
lse                       0
MP             3   runtime  transport   NMP        transport=block                             false                              fa
lse                       0
MP             4   runtime  transport   NMP        transport=unknown                           false                              fa
lse                       0
MP           101   runtime  vendor      MASK_PATH  vendor=DELL model=Universal Xport           false                              fa
lse                       0
MP           101   file     vendor      MASK_PATH  vendor=DELL model=Universal Xport           false                              fa
lse                       0
MP         65535   runtime  vendor      NMP        vendor=* model=*                            false                              fa
lse                       0
```

Figure 5-17   List the Current Claim Rules for an ESXi Host

Figure 5-17 shows the list of the current claim rules on the ESXi Host. You can use any claim rule number that is not being used, with the exception of rules 0 through 100, which are reserved for VMware's internal use. By default, PSA claim rule 101 masks Dell array pseudo-devices and should not be removed unless you need to un-mask these types of devices. Claim rules can be created a number of ways, including by manually masking based on the HBA adapter (`C:#T:#L:#`).

Explain the Function of Claim Rule Elements

Claim rules can be created based on the following elements:

- **vendor string:** A claim rule can be set up using the `vendor` string, which must be an exact match. An example would be `vendor=DELL`.

- **model string:** A claim rule can be set up using the `model` string, which must be an exact match. An example would be `model=Universal Xport`.

- **transport type:** A claim rule can be created to mask all LUNs based on the transport type. Valid transport types are `block`, `fc`, `iscsi`, `iscsivendor`, `ide`, `sas`, `sata`, `usb`, `parallel`, and `unknown`.

- **Driver type:** A driver name can be used to create a claim rule. Figure 5-18 lists all the drivers that can be used in a claim rule. You can set up a claim rule masking all paths to devices attached to an HBA using a driver such as the `iscsi_vmk` driver:

```
# esxcli storage core adapter list
```

iSCSi_vmk

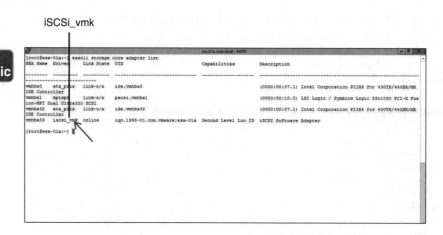

Figure 5-18   ESXi Driver Types

Let's look at an example of creating a claim rule using the `transport` type element. Figure 5-19 shows masking all LUNs that are of `transport` type `fc` (Fibre Channel). The example uses rule number 200 because that number was not being used and is greater than 100. The first two command lines in Figure 5-19 show the successful addition of the claim rule because no error message is given. Line 2 shows the command line to load the claim rule into the runtime environment. Line 3 shows executing the claim rule.

As a result of running these command lines, the fifth command line lists all the claim rules. The rules 0 through 3 show that the NMP claims all paths connected to storage devices that use the USB, SATA, IDE, and Block SCSI transportation. The new claim rule 200 can be seen in the output masking all LUNs that use the `transport` type of `fc`.

200 runtime

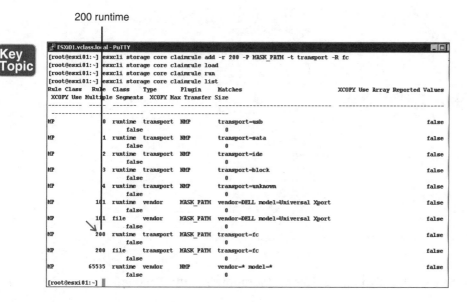

Key
Topic

```
ESXi01.vclass.local - PuTTY
[root@esxi01:~] esxcli storage core claimrule add -r 200 -P MASK_PATH -t transport -R fc
[root@esxi01:~] esxcli storage core claimrule load
[root@esxi01:~] esxcli storage core claimrule run
[root@esxi01:~] esxcli storage core claimrule list
Rule Class  Rule  Class    Type      Plugin     Matches                          XCOPY Use Array Reported Values
  XCOPY Use Multiple Segments  XCOPY Max Transfer Size
----------  ----  -------  ---------  ---------  -------------------------------  --------------------------------
----------  -------------  -----------------------
MP           0  runtime  transport  NMP        transport=usb                                                false
                false                                  0
MP           1  runtime  transport  NMP        transport=sata                                               false
                false                                  0
MP           2  runtime  transport  NMP        transport=ide                                                false
                false                                  0
MP           3  runtime  transport  NMP        transport=block                                              false
                false                                  0
MP           4  runtime  transport  NMP        transport=unknown                                            false
                false                                  0
MP         101  runtime  vendor     MASK_PATH  vendor=DELL model=Universal Xport                            false
                false                                  0
MP         101  file     vendor     MASK_PATH  vendor=DELL model=Universal Xport                            false
                false                                  0
MP         200  runtime  transport  MASK_PATH  transport=fc                                                 false
                false                                  0
MP         200  file     transport  MASK_PATH  transport=fc                                                 false
                false                                  0
MP       65535  runtime  vendor     NMP        vendor=* model=*                                             false
                false                                  0
[root@esxi01:~]
```

Figure 5-19   LUN Masking for All FC Devices on an ESXi Host

Change the Path Selection Policy Using the UI

VMware supports three built-in path selection policies (PSPs) or multipathing drivers: Most Recently Used (MRU), Fixed, and Round Robin. If you want to change the PSP you are currently using, in the vSphere Web Client highlight the datastore as shown in Figure 5-20, select the **Manage** tab, and then select **Settings**. Next, choose **Connectivity and Multipathing** and then select the host to view the multipathing details. Under the Multipathing Details header you see the multipathing policies and the button **Edit Multipathing**, which you click to see the list of multipathing policies. Select the multipathing policy that you want to utilize. If you select **Fixed**, you need to specify the preferred path by right-clicking it. Click **OK** to save the selections and exit the dialog box.

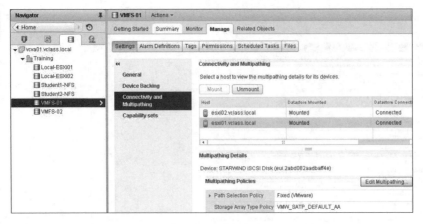

Figure 5-20   vSphere Web Client Displaying Multipathing Details

Determine the Effect of Changing PSP on Multipathing and Failover

You can use `esxcli` commands to modify the default Path Selection Policy (PSP)
for a Storage Array Type Plug-in (SATP), as shown in Figure 5-21. Any device that
is currently using an SATP that is going to be modified has to have all its paths unclaimed and then reclaimed. The following `esxcli` command changes the default
PSP for VMW_SATP_CX SATP from **MRU** to **Round Robin**:

```
# esxcli storage nmp satp set -s VMW_SATP_CX -P VMW_PSP_RR
```

For this modification to take effect, you still must reboot the ESXi Host. After the
default PSP has been changed, you can execute the following command to verify
that the default PSP has been changed (see Figure 5-21):

```
# esxcli storage nmp satp list
```

However, changing the default pathing policy for an SATP when there are other
storage arrays utilizing the same PSP can create issues for those storage arrays
because the other storage array pathing policy and failover will change.

```
ESXi01.vclass.local - PuTTY
[root@esxi01:~] esxcli storage nmp satp set -s VMW_SATP_CX -P VMW_PSP_RR
Default PSP for VMW_SATP_CX is now VMW_PSP_RR
[root@esxi01:~] esxcli storage nmp satp list
Name                  Default PSP    Description
--------------------  -------------  ------------------------------------------
VMW_SATP_MSA          VMW_PSP_MRU    Placeholder (plugin not loaded)
VMW_SATP_ALUA         VMW_PSP_MRU    Placeholder (plugin not loaded)
VMW_SATP_DEFAULT_AP   VMW_PSP_MRU    Placeholder (plugin not loaded)
VMW_SATP_SVC          VMW_PSP_FIXED  Placeholder (plugin not loaded)
VMW_SATP_EQL          VMW_PSP_FIXED  Placeholder (plugin not loaded)
VMW_SATP_INV          VMW_PSP_FIXED  Placeholder (plugin not loaded)
VMW_SATP_EVA          VMW_PSP_FIXED  Placeholder (plugin not loaded)
VMW_SATP_ALUA_CX      VMW_PSP_RR     Placeholder (plugin not loaded)
VMW_SATP_SYMM         VMW_PSP_RR     Placeholder (plugin not loaded)
VMW_SATP_CX           VMW_PSP_RR     Placeholder (plugin not loaded)
VMW_SATP_LSI          VMW_PSP_MRU    Placeholder (plugin not loaded)
VMW_SATP_DEFAULT_AA   VMW_PSP_FIXED  Supports non-specific active/active arrays
VMW_SATP_LOCAL        VMW_PSP_FIXED  Supports direct attached devices
[root@esxi01:~]
```

Figure 5-21   Use an `esxcli` Command to Modify a PSP Plug-in to Round Robin

Determine the Effect of Changing SATP on Multipathing and Failover

VMware provides a Storage Array Type Plug-in (SATP) for every type of array that VMware supports in the HCL. The SATP monitors the health of each physical path and can respond to error messages from the storage array to handle path failover. If you change the SATP for an array, it may change the PSP, which may create unexpected failover results.

Configure/Manage Storage Load Balancing

The goal of storage load balancing is to provide an equal balance of I/O requests using all paths between the storage array and the ESXi Host. There are different methods or multipathing options because storage arrays are designed to handle multipathing differently. Using the vSphere Web Client, you can configure or manage storage load balancing by highlighting the datastore in Storage view, as shown in Figure 5-22. Select the **Manage** tab and then select **Settings**. Next choose **Connectivity and Multipathing** and then select the host to view the multipathing details. The path selection policy in Figure 5-22 has been set to Round Robin. Also, two active paths are being used for load balancing.

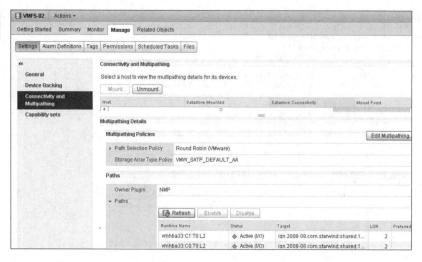

Figure 5-22 Configure/Manage Multipathing Using vSphere Web Client

Differentiate Available Storage Load Balancing Options

The ESXi Host discovers all the paths to the storage devices when there is a reboot or when you rescan the storage adapter. During this process, the Multipathing Plug-in (MPP) is determined based on claim rules. The MPP helps determine the path selection policy (PSP) to use. If the PSP is Fixed, then the option Preferred Path can be set. However, if the PSP is Round Robin or Most Recently Used (MRU), then the Preferred Path option is not set.

Differentiate Available Storage Multipathing Policies

The PSA is used to take control of the path failover and load-balancing operations for specific storage devices. These multipathing operations do not apply to NFS, which relies on networking over multiple TCP sessions. PSPs are included with the VMware NMP to determine the physical path for I/O requests. By default, three PSPs are included with vSphere:

- **Round Robin:** VMW_PSP_RR

  The ESXi Host uses Round Robin as an algorithm that rotates through all the active paths and can be used with active/active and active/passive arrays. On supported arrays, multiple paths can be active simultaneously; otherwise, the default is to rotate between the paths.

- **Most Recently Used (MRU):** VMW_PSP_MRU

  With this setting, the ESXi Host selects the path that was most recently used. If the active path fails, then an alternative path will become active and take over. When the original path comes back online, it is now the alternative path. MRU is the default for most active/passive storage arrays. In addition, by default, MRU is also selected for ALUA devices.

- **Fixed:** `VMW_PSP_FIXED`

The ESXi Host may use a designated preferred path, or fixed path. Otherwise, it selects the first working path discovered at boot time. Fixed is the default for active/active storage arrays, iSCSI, and Fibre Channel.

Configure Storage Policies

A virtual machine needs a datastore for its files. As a VMware systems administrator, you need to request from the storage administrator a LUN to create a SAN datastore. The storage administrator then works magic to present the LUN to the ESXi Host. Next, the VMware administrator creates a datastore by using the Add Storage Wizard. When choosing the LUN, the administrator sees only the size of the LUN. The VMware administrator does not know anything else about the LUN except its size, so how does he or she know if the LUN has ideal characteristics for the VM? That is the problem: There is no way in the vSphere Client to have a definitive idea of which LUN has the proper characteristics. This is where the concept of storage policies comes into play. The idea is to add intelligence to virtual machine placement. Storage policies allow you to create your own storage policies based on features and characteristics of the storage. Then you can choose the storage policy that best matches the characteristics of your virtual machine and place the VM in the matching storage. Figure 5-23 shows storage policies.

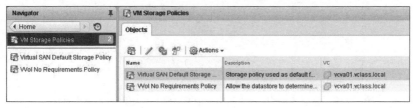

Figure 5-23   VM Storage Policies

Storage policies are a key element of Virtual Volumes (VVOLs) because a VMware administrator wants virtual machines to be located on storage that matches characteristics of the VM. Storage policies are created to include features such as protocol and disk speed. For example, a storage administrator could create a storage policy that says include storage that has compression, where the disk type is SSD, and where the disk speed is 7200 rpms. Then only LUNs that match those characteristics would be associated with that storage policy. Thus, for example, when you create a VM, you could say that you want a VM's files to be located only on storage that matches a particular storage policy.

Locate Failover Events in the UI

When failover events occur, you can use the vSphere Web Client to view details about the events. Using the vSphere Web Client, highlight the vCenter Server in the Navigator pane. Select **Monitor** and then the **Events** tab. In Figure 5-24 you can see events that have occurred within the vCenter Server.

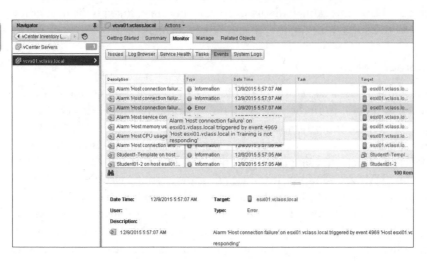

Figure 5-24   Failover Events for the vCenter Server in the vSphere Web Client

NOTE   Array-based thin provisioning is dependent on the storage array itself. If a LUN becomes full, the storage array decides what action to take. It is most likely to go offline. ESXi does not support enabling and disabling of thin provisioning on a storage device.

Summary

You have now read the chapter covering exam topics on configuring software-defined storage and configuring vSphere storage multipathing and failover. You should now use information in the following sections to complete your preparation for Objectives 3.2 and 3.3.

Exam Preparation Tasks

Review All the Key Topics

Table 5-2 provides a reference to each of the key topics identified in this chapter. Take a few moments to review each of these specific items.

Table 5-2 Key Topics for Chapter 5

Key Topic Element	Description	Pages
Note	VSAN does not support IPv6	194
Figure 5-1	Example of VSAN storage providers	195
Figure 5-2	Example of a registered NetApp VASA 2.0 SP	196
Figure 5-3	Virtual SAN network	197
Note	When a VSAN cluster is enabled, vSphere HA must be disabled	198
Figure 5-4	Creating a new VSAN cluster	198
Figure 5-5	VSAN cluster with 4 ESXi Hosts but no disks	199
Figure 5-6	Manually claim disks	200
Figure 5-7	Create a disk group on each ESXi Host by claiming disks	200
Figure 5-8	Creating a VVOL datastore on a VVOL container	201
Figure 5-9	Displaying a VVOL datastore	202
Figure 5-10	Displaying VM default storage policy	202
Figure 5-11	VSAN cluster fault domain configuration	203
Figure 5-12	VSAN VM storage policy	204
Figure 5-13	Virtual SAN Observer client view	205
Figure 5-14	VSAN disks (deep dive) view	205
Figure 5-15	Displaying VVOL protocol endpoints	206
Note	If a virtual machine is not configured with a storage policy, then the VM uses the default storage policy	207
Figure 5-16	The options for Path Device Loss (PDL)	208
Figure 5-17	List the current claim rules for an ESXi Host	211
List	Claim rule elements	211
Figure 5-18	ESXi driver types	212

Key Topic Element	Description	Pages
Figure 5-19	Steps showing LUN masking for all FC devices on an ESXi Host	213
Figure 5-20	vSphere Web Client displaying multipathing details	214
Figure 5-21	Using an `esxcli` command to modify a PSP plug-in to round robin	215
Figure 5-22	Configure/manage multipathing using vSphere Web Client	216
Figure 5-23	VM storage policies	217
Figure 5-24	Failover events for the vCenter Server in the vSphere Web Client	218
Note	Array-based thin provisioning is dependent on the storage array itself	218

Complete the Tables and Lists from Memory

Print a copy of Appendix B, "Memory Tables" (found on the CD), or at least the section for this chapter, and complete the tables and lists from memory. Appendix C, "Memory Tables Answer Key," also on the CD, includes completed tables and lists to check your work.

Definitions of Key Terms

Define the following key terms from this chapter and check your answers in the glossary.

Virtual SAN (VSAN), Virtual Volume (VVOL), vSphere APIs for Storage Awareness (VASA), storage provider (SP), protocol endpoint (PE), Virtual Machine Component Protection (VMCP), All Paths Down (APD), Permanent Device Loss (PDL), Asymmetrical Logical Unit Access (ALUA), Pluggable Storage Architecture (PSA), Multipathing Plug-in (MPP), Native Multipathing Plug-in (NMP), Storage Array Type Plug-in (SATP), Path Selection Plug-in (PSP), Round Robin, Most Recently Used (MRU), Fixed

Answer Review Questions

The answers to these review questions can be found in Appendix A.

1. Which of the following is an incorrect statement?

   a. You do not need to install any additional software or drivers to use VSAN.

   b. You can manage VSAN using either the Windows vSphere Client or the vSphere Web Client.

   c. To use VSAN, you need either the Windows or Linux (virtual appliance) version of vCenter Server installed with either version 5.5 or 6.0.

   d. VSAN requires a VMkernel port running on either a 1 Gbps or 16 Gbps network for VSAN communication between the ESXi Hosts.

2. Which of the following statements is not true about VSAN fault domains?

   a. VSAN fault domains ensure that virtual machine replica data is not duplicated on hosts in the same domain.

   b. Fault domains are used to deploy virtual machines across the fault domains so that if a rack fails, it does not make the virtual machines inaccessible.

   c. If the rule `Number of Failures to Tolerate` is set to `1`, this setting is the number of failures of fault domains that the VSAN can tolerate.

   d. If the rule `Number of Disk Stripes per Object` is set to `3`, this setting is the number of physical disks of storage that the storage object (VMDK) will be written across.

3. In Pluggable Storage Architecture, a claim rule can be created to mask all LUNs based on the `transport` type. Which of the following is not a supported `transport` type?

   a. `nfs`

   b. `fc`

   c. `unknown`

   d. `block`

4. If the path selection policy (PSP) is Round Robin or Most Recently Used (MRU), no preferred path will be set. Which of the following statements is incorrect in regards to PSP and preferred paths?

   a. PSA applies to both SAN- and NAS-based storage.

   b. Fixed is the default for active/active storage arrays, iSCSI, and Fibre Channel.

   c. PSPs are included with the VMware NMP that determines the physical path for I/O requests.

   d. By default, there are three PSPs built in to vSphere: Round Robin, MRU, and Fixed.

5. You can choose the storage policy that best matches the characteristics of your virtual machine and place the VM in the matching storage. Which of the following statements is incorrect in regards to storage policies?

   a. If you use storage policies, you do not need to ask the storage administrator for a LUN.

   b. When creating a virtual machine, you can use a storage policy to help pick the storage that best matches the characteristics of the VM.

   c. Storage policies are used to create Virtual Volumes (VVOLs).

   d. Storage policies are created to include features such as protocol and disk speed.

This chapter covers the following objectives:

- **Objective 3.4—Perform Advanced VMFS and NFS Configurations and Upgrades**
  - Describe VAAI primitives for block devices and NAS
  - Differentiate VMware file system technologies
  - Upgrade VMFS3 to VMFS5
  - Compare functionality of new and upgraded VMFS5 datastores
  - Differentiate physical mode and virtual mode RDMs
  - Create virtual/physical mode RDMs
  - Differentiate NFS 3.X And 4.1 capabilities
  - Compare and contrast VMFS and NFS datastore properties
  - Configure bus sharing
  - Configure multi-writer locking
  - Connect an NFS 4.1 datastore using Kerberos
  - Create/rename/delete/unmount VMFS datastores
  - Extend/expand VMFS datastores
  - Place a VMFS datastore in maintenance mode
  - Select the preferred path/disable a path to a VMFS datastore
  - Enable/disable vStorage APIs for Array Integration (VAAI)
  - Given a scenario, determine a proper use case for multiple VMFS/NFS datastores
- **Objective 3.5—Set Up and Configure Storage I/O Control**
  - Describe the benefits of SIOC
  - Enable SIOC
  - Configure/manage/monitor SIOC
  - Differentiate between SIOC and dynamic queue depth throttling features
  - Given a scenario, determine a proper use case for SIOC

## CHAPTER 6

Storage, Part 3

This chapter is the third part of the storage topics for the VCP exam. The two storage objectives that are covered in this chapter are related to advanced VMFS and NFS and Storage I/O Control. The advanced VMFS and NFS section discusses topics for the VCP exam such as how to set up NAS- and SAN-based storage and features such as VAAI and upgrading VMFS. The second objective in this module involves Storage I/O Control. This section covers setup and configuration of SIOC, as well as how to monitor Storage I/O Control.

"Do I Know This Already?" Quiz

The "Do I Know This Already?" quiz allows you to assess whether you should study this entire chapter or move quickly to the "Exam Preparation Tasks" section. Regardless, the authors recommend that you read the entire chapter at least once. Table 6-1 outlines the major headings in this chapter and the corresponding "Do I Know This Already?" quiz questions. You can find the answers in Appendix A, "Answers to the 'Do I Know This Already?' Quizzes and Review Questions."

Table 6-1 "Do I Know This Already?" Foundation Topics Section-to-Question Mapping

Foundation Topics Section	Questions Covered in This Section
Describe VAAI Primitives for Block Devices and NAS	1
Differentiate VMware File System Technologies	2
Upgrade VMPFS3 to VMFS5	3
Differentiate Physical Mode and Virtual Mode RDMs	4
Differentiate NFS 3.x and 4.1 Capabilities	5
Configure Bus Sharing	6
Connect an NFS 4.1 Datastore Using Kerberos	7
Create/Rename/Delete/Unmount/VMFS Datastores	8
Select the Preferred Path/Disable a Path to a VMFS Datastore	9

Foundation Topics Section	Questions Covered in This Section
Given a Scenario, Determine a Proper Use Case for Multiple VMFS/NFS Datastores	10
Describe the Benefits of SIOC	11
Differentiate Between SIOC and Dynamic Queue Depth Throttling Features	12

1. Which of the following is not a VAAI primitive?

   a. SCSI extended copy

   b. Full copy

   c. Block zeroing

   d. Hardware-assisted locking

2. Which of the following is not a file system technology supported by vSphere 6.0?

   a. VMFS

   b. NFSv3

   c. NFSv4

   d. NFSv4.1

3. Which of the following are supported block sizes if you upgrade a VMFS3 datastore to a VMFS5 datastore? (Choose three.)

   a. 1 MB

   b. 2 MB

   c. 4 MB

   d. 8 KB

   e. 4 KB

4. Which of the following is a supported feature for a physical mode RDM?

   a. Virtual machine snapshots

   b. Virtual machine cloning

   c. SAN-aware application

   d. NFS

5. Which of the following is not a difference in capabilities between NFS version 3 and NFS version 4.1?

   a. Session trunking

   b. Improved security

   c. Improved locking

   d. AUTH_SYS for authentication

6. Which of the following, when combined with a third-party solution, enables VMs on the same or different physical ESXi Hosts to access the same VMDK?

   a. Multi-writer lock

   b. VMs on different physical ESXi Hosts cannot access the same VMDK.

   c. Virtual compatibility mode

   d. Physical compatibility mode

7. Which of the following protocols is supported for NFSv4.1 for encryption on AD?

   a. RC4

   b. AES 128-bit

   c. AES 256-bit

   d. DES-CBC-MD5

8. What is the vSphere Web Client's limit on the number of characters in the datastore name?

   a. 32

   b. 42

   c. 48

   d. 108

9. Which of the following is not a built-in Path Selection Plug-in with vSphere 6.0?

   a. MRU

   b. NMP

   c. Fixed

   d. Round Robin

10. Which of the following is not a benefit of a NFS datastore?

    a. Direct I/O between each VMDK on the NFS server and the ESXi Host.

    b. The NFS client is easy to install.

    c. Less storage provisioning because NFS datastores can be larger than VMFS.

    d. NFS has greater scalability of VM density due to the lack of LUN queues.

11. Which of the following is not an accurate statement about Storage I/O Control (SIOC)?

    a. You can achieve more benefits during times of contention by setting reservations, shares, and limits for the VM.

    b. The mClock scheduler algorithm allocates storage resources to the VM in proportion to its shares.

    c. During periods of I/O congestion, the more important VMs get more IOPS and have less latency in proportion to the number of shares.

    d. The ESXi Host starts monitoring the device latency of the datastore when the ESXi Host completes the boot process.

12. Company ABC has vSphere set up, with DRS fully automated. You notice that memory and CPU are load balancing VMs properly, thanks to DRS. However, one VM appears to have more storage activity than other VMs. What could you enable to ensure equal access to storage for all virtual machines?

    a. Storage DRS

    b. Storage I/O Control

    c. High availability

    d. VAAI support

Foundation Topics

Objective 3.4—Perform Advanced VMFS and NFS Configurations and Upgrades

This section provides details on advanced features of VMFS and NFS datastores. There are a number of different configurations that both datastores utilize in presenting storage. Upgrading and many other options and capabilities of VMFS and NFS are addressed. Both versions of NFS 3 and 4.1 are compared and contrasted, as well as new features of NFS 4.1 are presented. There is also information provided about VAAI and its capabilities.

Describe VAAI Primitives for Block Devices and NAS

The vSphere APIs for Array Integration (VAAI) was first introduced in vSphere 4.1 as a method for offloading specific storage operations from the ESXi Host to the storage array. VAAI was ratified by the IEEE T10 committee and is based on running certain SCSI commands on the storage array instead of the ESXi Host. In order for that to happen, the storage vendor is required to add VAAI to the storage array's operating system. In the case of NAS, an additional plug-in needs to be installed to help perform the offloading. VAAI defines a set of storage primitives, which in essence replace select SCSI operations with VAAI operations that are performed on the storage array instead of the ESXi Host. VAAI offloads the processing to the storage system where it belongs instead of processing on the ESXi Host, because storage is where SCSI is most efficiently handled. This offloading of the operations to run directly on the storage array can significantly improve performance for certain operations, such as zeroing, storage migration, and cloning.

In environments without VAAI, the original SCSI commands run directly on the ESXi Host, which defaults back to the old performance issues of additional CPU cycles and network bandwidth consumption. VAAI has three main built-in capabilities:

- **Full copy:** The SCSI Extended Copy command is replaced by the VAAI XCOPY command, which enables the storage array to perform full copies of data completely within the storage array without having to communicate with the ESXi Host during the reading and writing of data. This saves the ESXi Host from having to perform the read and then write of data, which reduces the time needed to clone VMs or perform Storage vMotion operations.

- **Block zeroing**: When a new virtual disk is created with VMFS as an eager-zeroed thick disk, the disk must be formatted and the blocks must be zeroed out before data can be written on them. Block zeroing removes this task from the ESXi Host by moving the function down to the storage array with VAAI. This increases the speed of the block zeroing process.

- **Hardware-assisted locking**: VMFS is a shared cluster file system that requires file locking to ensure that only one host can write to the data at a time. VAAI uses a single atomic test and set operation (ATS), which is an alternative method to VMware's SCSI-2 reservations. ATS allows a VMFS datastore to scale to more VMs per datastore, and more ESXi Hosts can attach to each LUN.

For vSphere to take advantage of VAAI, the storage array has to support VAAI hardware acceleration. One way to check whether the storage array is supported for VAAI hardware acceleration is to check the hardware configuration list (HCL), which lists all the supported storage arrays. Hardware acceleration for VAAI is supported for both SAN and NAS storage devices in vSphere 6.0.

Enable/Disable vStorage APIs for Array Integration (VAAI)

VMFS3 was built on and followed the SCSI2 specifications. When vSphere 5 was released, it included a new version of the file system, referred to as VMFS5. The upgrade to VMFS extended the SCSI protocol, which was rather like putting a bandage on SCSI2. The bandage that extended the SCSI2 protocol is called the vStorage APIs for Array Integration (VAAI).

VMware began the process of upgrading the file system in vSphere 4.1 by asking storage vendors to add VAAI support to their storage array operating systems, even though VAAI would not be a fully functional storage feature until the vSphere 5.0 release. VAAI enables the ESXi Host to offload certain storage operations to the storage array, where they can be performed faster and consume less CPU and memory resources on the host. The three main built-in capabilities for VAAI are full copy, block zeroing, and hardware-assisted locking.

By default, the ESXi Host supports VAAI hardware acceleration for block devices, which means no configuration is needed for block devices. If a storage device supports T10 SCSI commands, then by default the ESXi Host can use VAAI.

To view whether VAAI is enabled or disabled, run the following commands, and if the value that is returned is 0, it is disabled, and if the value returned is 1, then it is enabled:

```
# esxcfg-advcfg -g /DataMover/HardwareAcceleratedMove
# esxcfg-advcfg -g /DataMover/HardwareAcceleratedInit
# esxcfg-advcfg -g /VMFS3/HardwareAcceleratedLocking
```

To disable VAAI for a dedicated primitive, use the option -s 0:

```
# esxcfg-advcfg -s 0 /DataMover/HardwareAcceleratedMove
# esxcfg-advcfg -s 0 /DataMover/HardwareAcceleratedInit
# esxcfg-advcfg -s 0 /VMFS3/HardwareAcceleratedLocking
```

To enable VAAI for a dedicated primitive, use the option -s 1:

```
# esxcfg-advcfg -s 1 /DataMover/HardwareAcceleratedMove
# esxcfg-advcfg -s 1 /DataMover/HardwareAcceleratedInit
# esxcfg-advcfg -s 1 /VMFS3/HardwareAcceleratedLocking
```

Differentiate VMware File System Technologies

A system administrator for Windows, Unix, or VMware needs a storage device to house data. In the case of a VMware system administrator, the storage device is a virtual construct. VMware calls this construct a *datastore*, and it can be located either on shared storage or on local disks. VMware uses a datastore as the primary location for storing virtual machine files and ISO images. The semantics of file access from guests is the same, regardless of whether the VMDK is on local disk, VMFS, NFS, or VVOL; only the host access is different. Four different file system technologies can be used with vSphere 6.0. All four of them are utilized to contain the virtual disks and configuration files for VMs:

- **VMFS:** This cluster-aware file system is designed for virtual machines. It is used on block-based storage, which allows a number of virtual machines to be stored and accessed using VMware's proprietary file system. VMFS uses a uniform block size of 1 MB and allows up to 64 ESXi Hosts the ability to access the datastore. The maximum volume size is 64 TB. VMFS provides SCSI access directly to the virtual machine files to efficiently allow read and write requests to the storage disks.

- **NFSv3:** This file-based storage system allows the ESXi Host to access files from an NFSv3 server. You can use Network File System (NFS) volumes to store and boot virtual machines in the same way that you use VMFS datastores. NFSv3 uses a proprietary lock daemon that resides on the ESXi Host.

- **NFSv4.1:** This is a file-based storage system that allows the ESXi Host to access files from an NFSv4.1 server. NFSv4.1, introduced with vSphere 6.0, has several differences from Version 3. File locking for NFSv4.1 is controlled by the NFS server, which reduces the overhead on the VMkernel.

- **VVOL:** This is a new method in vSphere 6.0 for working with storage. The traditional models of storage focus on providing LUNs. Virtual Volume (VVOL) is a management and integration framework to virtualize external storage such as SAN and NAS and enable VM-centric operations.

Compare and Contrast VMFS and NFS Datastore Properties

VMFS and NFS are very similar in many ways, but there are some differences in the properties of these two datastores. One difference is that the maximum size of a VMFS datastore is 64 TB, while the maximum size of an NFS datastore is 100 TB. Another difference is that VMFS uses SCSI queuing and has a default queue length of 32 outstanding I/Os at a time, while with NFS, each VM gets its own I/O data path. Thus, the VM density of active virtual machines in a datastore is twice as many with NFS as with VMFS.

Upgrade VMFS3 to VMFS5

When block-based protocols are used, VMware can create a VMFS file system by writing its own signature and partition on a LUN. The VMware File System (VMFS) is currently at version 5, or VMFS5. VMFS is VMware's proprietary file system and can be used to store VM files on any SCSI-based local or networked storage device, such as Fibre Channel or iSCSI. The VMFS file system logic and control run on the ESXi Host and communicate with the storage device's SAN LUN using SCSI commands.

When you upgrade VMFS3 to VMFS5, it is an online and non-disruptive upgrade operation, which means the virtual machines continue to run on the datastore. There are a couple different methods for upgrading a VMFS3 file system to a VMFS5 file system. One method, using the vSphere Web Client and the Upgrade button, creates limitations on the file system:

Step 1. In the vSphere Web Client navigator, select **vCenter Inventory Lists > Datastores.**

Step 2. Click the datastore to upgrade.

Step 3. Click **Manage > Settings**.

Step 4. Click **Upgrade to VMFS5.**

Step 5. Verify that the host accessing the datastore supports VMFS5.

Step 6. Click **OK** to start the upgrade.

The easiest and cleanest method to upgrade the file system to VMFS5 is to create a new VMFS5 file system and then Storage vMotion the old VMFS3 datastore to the new VMFS5 datastore. Table 6-2 illustrates the differences between a newly formatted VMFS5 datastore and a VMFS5 datastore migrated from VMFS3.

Table 6-2 Comparing Upgraded and Newly Formatted VMFS5 Datastores

Characteristic	Upgraded VMFS5	Formatted VMFS5
File block size	1 MB, 2 MB, 4 MB, and 8 MB	1 MB
Sub-block size	64 KB	8 KB
Partition format	Originally MBR format. The datastore size needs to expand beyond 2 TB for conversion to GPT format.	GPT format
Datastore limits	Retains limitations of the original VMFS3 file system.	Utilizes the new VMFS5 limits.
VMFS locking mechanism	Uses ATS+SCSI	Uses ATS only on hardware that supports ATS. Uses ATS and SCSI on hardware that does not support ATS.

Compare Functionality of New and Upgraded VMFS5 Datastores

If you migrate from a VMFS3 datastore to a VMFS5 datastore, there can be limitations. However, if you create a brand-new VMFS5 file system, it will have the ability to utilize all the features of a VMFS5 datastore. Another option for upgrading to VMFS5 is to migrate the VM that originally was on a VMFS3 datastore to a datastore formatted with VMFS5, using Storage vMotion. When you utilize Storage vMotion, the VM's files utilize the format of VMFS5 and do not have any of the old VMFS3 limitations. However, if you click on the Upgrade to VMFS5 button mentioned in the previous section, you have limitations. You can see the comparison between upgrading and creating a new VMFS5 datastore in Table 6-2.

Differentiate Physical Mode and Virtual Mode RDMs

Using a Raw Device Map (RDM) is the primary method of presenting a VM direct access and ownership of a LUN. The RDM connects directly to the virtual machine's virtual SCSI adapter for direct access to the storage device.

There are two different compatibility modes to choose from when creating an RDM: physical compatibility mode (`rdmp`) and virtual compatibility mode (`rdm`). The key difference between these two options is the amount of SCSI virtualization that occurs at the VM level.

The physical compatibility (passthrough) mode is the default format. In this format, the SCSI commands pass directly through to the hardware during communication between the guest operating system and the LUN or SCSI device. This allows for unsupported features such as SCSI3 clustering. Another use case is if the application in the virtual machine is SAN-aware and needs to communicate directly to storage devices on the SAN. However, this mode does not support virtual machine snapshots, VMware cloning, and several other features that require hypervisor support.

Virtual compatibility mode supports a subset of SCSI commands to be passed through the hypervisor for communication between the guest operating system and a mapped physical raw LUN or SCSI disk. Virtual compatibility mode fully virtualizes the mapped device, which enables an RDM virtual disk to appear to the virtual machine as a typical VMFS-based virtual disk. Because this mode allows some SCSI commands to be passed through the hypervisor, VMware features that physical compatibility mode will not allow, such as VMware snapshots, cloning, or storage migration, are supported.

In addition to allowing the passthrough of SCSI commands for use cases previously described, the use of an RDM can be beneficial for performance reasons. This is due to the fact that a typical VMFS datastore is shared by multiple virtual machines, which have to share the available I/O operations of the underlying LUN. Some applications might have specific I/O requirements and might be critical enough to require guaranteed I/O. An RDM is presented directly to a single virtual machine and cannot be used by any other virtual machine; it also is presented with the I/O characteristics defined by the storage administrator. It is important to note that similar performance requirements can be gained by placing a single VM on a VMFS datastore that fully utilizes the datastore.

A final reason to use RDMs is that it allows you to use N-Port ID Virtualization (NPIV), which is covered in the next section.

Create a Virtual/Physical Mode RDM

A Raw Device Map (RDM) disk gives your VM direct access to a raw SAN LUN. You can create an RDM when you are initially creating the virtual machine, or you can add an RDM to an existing VM. When you create an RDM, the important steps are which LUN is going to be mapped and whether you are creating a physical compatibility mode (rdmp) or virtual compatibility mode (rdm) RDM. The following procedure creates an RDM on an existing VM:

Step 1.   Highlight the virtual machine for which you want to create an RDM, right-click in the vSphere Web Client, and choose **Edit Settings**.

Step 2.   The Edit Settings Wizard appears in the vSphere Web Client. Within the Virtual Hardware tab at the bottom of the window you will see **New Device** and an arrow to open up options to select. From the options, select **RDM Disk** and then click on the **Add** button.

Step 3.   When you see the list of the LUNs that can be used for an RDM, high-light the LUN that you choose to use as an RDM device and then click on the **OK** button.

Step 4.   In the Edit settings window, click on the new hard disk to see the options for the RDM. Notice that for Compatibility Mode you can choose either Virtual or Physical. After setting the options to set up the RDM as shown in Figure 6-1, click the **OK** button on the bottom to create the RDM.

Figure 6-1   Edit Hard Disk Settings

Differentiate NFS 3.x and 4.1 Capabilities

One of the main new features in vSphere 6.0 is the addition of the NFSv4.1 client. The NFSv4.1 client adds a number of new features and overcomes many of the limitations in NFSv3. The following are several of the main differences in capabilities:

- **Session trunking and multipathing:** The NFSv3 client supports only one path and has no multipathing built in. Therefore, NFSv3 relies on ESXi to provide multipathing. With NFSv4.1, you can use native multipathing and session trunking. Support has been added for multiple IP addresses to be configured, which creates the ability to load balance and have failover. The added support of session trunking and multipathing can improve performance because of the parallel access to data along with the improved availability provided by multiple paths.

- **Improved security:** One of the limitations of version 3 is the use of AUTH_SYS for authentication, which means only the root user is allowed access to the virtual disk. In NFSv4.1, VMware is trying to eliminate the root user–only requirement by adding support for Microsoft's Kerberos. The current NFSv4.1 client defaults to AUTH_SYS, but each datastore can now choose which authentication method it requires.

NOTE NFSv4.1 does not support simultaneous AUTH_SYS and Kerberos mounts.

- **Improved locking:** VMware does not use the lockd daemon that is incorporated into the NFSv3 server. VMware wrote its own locking mechanism that resides on the ESXi Host (NFSv3 client) to handle file locking for the NFSv3 server. One of the problems with VMware's locking mechanism is that it increases the overhead on the VMkernel because the ESXi Host has to keep refreshing the file locks. In NFSv4.1, file locking is controlled by the NFSv4.1 server lockd, which is located on the storage array. This helps decrease the overhead because you no longer have to keep updating the file locks.

Configure Bus Sharing

In vSphere 6.0, VMware has enhanced the ability to share disks. You can configure bus sharing and work with the new multi-writer option to create some additional functionality.

By default, a virtual disk cannot be shared by other virtual machines. However, you can modify disk sharing on a VM basis. To configure bus sharing, highlight and right-click the virtual machine and select **Edit Settings**. Then highlight the SCSI controller for the VM. You then see the SCSI bus sharing option and can change the setting to your preference, as shown in Figure 6-2. These are the options for SCSI bus sharing:

- **None:** Virtual disks cannot be shared by other virtual machines.
- **Virtual:** Virtual disks can be shared by virtual machines on the same server.
- **Physical:** Virtual disks can be shared by virtual machines on any server.

The idea is that you want to be able to share a VMDK to multiple virtual machines. The virtual mode is used when attaching a VMDK to VMs running on the same host. The physical mode is used when attaching a VMDK to VMs running on different hosts. An example of using SCSI bus sharing in vSphere 6.0 is allowing a physical RDM to be able to work with Windows Server Failover Cluster (WSFC) and vMotion. In the past, if a VMDK was running in the physical compatibility mode, you would not be able to perform vMotion without creating a failure in WSFC. Now with vSphere 6.0 you can provide support for high availability using WSFC features and provide virtual machine vMotion.

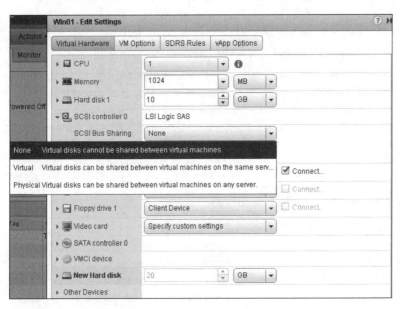

Figure 6-2 SCSI Bus Sharing Options

Configure Multi-writer Locking

In previous versions of vSphere, there was a limitation on the ability to virtualize virtual machines that were using cluster-based software such as Microsoft Cluster Server (the old name for WSFC). This was the case because only one host had the ability to own the write lock of a VMDK disk, and vSphere inserts VMFS and VMDK between the cluster-based software and the physical storage for cluster-based applications. The side effect of this insertion is that it stops the cluster-based software from functioning and controlling the VMDK, since VMFS has a locking mechanism that limits access.

In previous versions of vSphere, you needed to use a physical compatibility mode RDM to bypass the hypervisor and get around the incompatibility of how vSphere handled file locking for the VMDK. The RDM would allow direct access to the storage. Unfortunately, bypassing the hypervisor means that hypervisor features that VMs use, like vMotion, are bypassed as well. Thus, to accomplish clustering using RDMs and third-party clustering software, you have to sacrifice virtualization features such as vMotion and VMware snapshots to allow for multiple VMs to write to the same VMDK file.

vSphere 6.0 has a new multi-writer option that, when combined with a third-party solution, enables VMs on the same or different physical ESXi Hosts to access the same VMDK. The multi-writer option makes virtualizing applications using third-party clustering software possible. In prior versions of vSphere, the ability to have multiple VMs write to the same VMDK was not allowed to prevent accidental data corruption of one host or VM overriding another host's or VM's data.

It is important to understand that you should not turn on the multi-writer flag when you create a new VMDK because enabling the multi-writer option abandons control of the VMDK by vSphere and gives it to the guest OS of the virtual machine. In addition, any VM in the cluster can now access any VMDK in the cluster. However, when the multi-writer option is turned on, an RDM can use hypervisor features such as vMotion.

Connect an NFS 4.1 Datastore Using Kerberos

A few prerequisites are required when setting up an environment to use NFSv4.1. You need to define a user account in Active Directory that will be used to connect to the NFSv4.1 mount point. An Active Directory server must be present, and a user account needs to be created for NFS access. The user account must have Kerberos DES encryption enabled, and the account should be set to never expire. Also, each ESXi Host must be added to the AD domain.

Another prerequisite is that anytime you deal with Kerberos, clocks need to be within 5 minutes of each other. Kerberos requires the NFS server and the ESXi Host to be time synchronized. Authentication fails if any significant drift exists between the devices.

NOTE   VMware supports only DES-CBC-MD5 as the protocol for encryption on AD.

There are various versions of Kerberos available, but VMware is currently only supporting Microsoft Active Directory (AD). The Remote Procedure Call (RPC) request and response sent to and from the ESXi Host can be cryptographically authenticated by the server. However, in the packet frame in vSphere 6.0, only the header is encrypted, not the data.

Create/Rename/Delete/Unmount VMFS Datastores

In this section we look at different actions that can be performed on VMFS and NFS datastores, including creating, renaming, deleting, and unmounting the datastores.

VMFS datastores are repositories for virtual machines. You can create, rename, delete, and unmount VMFS datastores as necessary. In order to create a VMFS datastore, you need either a local disk, Fibre Channel, or an iSCSI LUN, and you use the New Datastore Wizard to create a VMFS datastore.

Create a VMFS Datastore

Use the following procedure to create a VMFS datastore:

Step 1. In the vSphere Web Client navigator, select **vCenter Inventory Lists > Datastores**.

Step 2. Click the **Create a New Datastore** icon (see Figure 6-3).

Create a new datastore

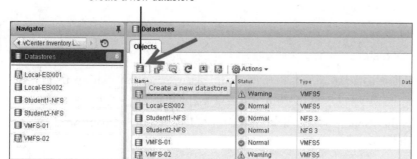

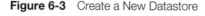

Figure 6-3   Create a New Datastore

Step 3. Select the new placement location for the datastore, which could be a datacenter, cluster, or datastore folder.

Step 4. On the Type page, select **VMFS** as the datastore type.

Step 5. On the Name and Device selection page, specify the name of the datastore and select the device (LUN) to use for the datastore.

NOTE The vSphere Web Client enforces a 42-character limit on the datastore name.

Step 6. Specify the partition configuration and click **Next** if you want to use all of the LUN space in the datastore.

Step 7.   In the Ready to Complete page, review the datastore configuration information and click **Finish**.

NOTE   You cannot create VMFS3 datastores in vSphere 6.0, but existing VMFS3 datastores continue to be available and usable; however, you must upgrade them to VMFS5.

Rename a VMFS Datastore

You can use the vSphere Web Client to change the name of an existing datastore, as described in the following procedure:

Step 1.   In the vSphere Web Client navigator, select **vCenter Inventory Lists > Datastores**.

Step 2.   Right-click the datastore you want to rename and select **Rename**.

Step 3.   Type a new datastore name. The new name appears on all hosts that have access to the datastore.

Delete a VMFS Datastore

When you delete a datastore, it is destroyed and disappears from all hosts that have access to the datastore. The following procedure explains how to delete a datastore:

Step 1.   In the vSphere Web Client navigator, select **vCenter Inventory Lists > Datastores**.

Step 2.   Right-click the datastore you want to remove and select **Delete Datastore**.

Step 3.   Confirm that you want to remove the datastore.

Unmount a VMFS Datastore

When you unmount a VMFS datastore, it remains intact but can no longer be seen from the hosts that you specify. After you unmount a VMFS datastore from all hosts, the datastore is marked as inactive. The following is the procedure to unmount a VMFS datastore:

Step 1.   In the vSphere Web Client navigator, select **vCenter Inventory Lists > Datastores**.

Step 2.   Right-click the datastore you want to unmount and select **Unmount Datastore**.

Step 3. If the datastore is shared, specify which hosts should no longer access the datastore.

Step 4. Confirm that you want to unmount the datastore.

Mount/Unmount an NFS Datastore

ESXi can access an NFS volume located on an NFS server. When you mount an NFS datastore, the steps are similar to the steps for mounting a VMFS datastore by using the New Datastore Wizard, with the ESXi Host acting as the NFS client and accessing virtual machine virtual disks stored on the NFS server. In vSphere 6, an NFS volume cannot be mounted as NFSv3 on one ESXi Host and as NFSv4.1 on another ESXi Host. This is due to the different file locking mechanisms: NFSv3 uses proprietary client-side cooperative file locking, while NFSv4.1 uses server-side file locking.

Mount an NFS Datastore

To mount an NFS datastore, use the following procedure:

Step 1. In the vSphere Web Client navigator, select **vCenter Inventory Lists > Datastores**.

Step 2. Click the **Create a New Datastore** icon.

Step 3. Select the new placement location for the datastore, which could be a datacenter, cluster, or datastore folder.

Step 4. Select **NFS** as the datastore type.

Step 5. Specify the version of NFS.

NOTE You must use the same NFS protocol on all hosts that access the same datastore.

Step 6. On the Name and Location page, type the datastore name you want for the datastore within the ESXi Host. Under NFS Share Details, type the NFS mount point folder name. Next, type in the server name or IP address of the NFS server. Under Access Mode, check the **Mount NFS as Read-only** box if you want to mount the datastore as read-only.

Step 7. If you use Kerberos authentication with NFS 4.1, enable Kerberos on the datastore.

Step 8. On the Host Accessibility page, if you are creating a datastore at the data center or cluster level, select the ESXi Hosts that will mount the NFS datastore.

Step 9. Review the configuration options and click **Finish**.

Unmount an NFS Datastore

The files on an NFS server remain intact when an NFS datastore is unmounted, but they are no longer accessible on the ESXi Host. Before you can unmount an NFS datastore, you must stop all virtual machines that reside on the datastore and follow these steps:

Step 1. In the vSphere Web Client navigator, select **vCenter Inventory Lists > Datastores**.

Step 2. Right-click the datastore you want to unmount and select **Unmount Datastore**.

Step 3. If the datastore is shared, specify which hosts should no longer access the datastore.

Step 4. Confirm that you want to unmount the datastore.

Extend/Expand VMFS Datastores

If you need to add more capacity for a VMFS datastore, you can increase its size using several different methods. The methods listed here allow you to dynamically increase the capacity by growing a datastore extent or by adding a new extent. In addition, another method not listed here is to use Storage vMotion, which is covered thoroughly in Chapter 13, "Troubleshoot Clusters."

Expandable

One method for increasing capacity is to grow an existing datastore. This expands the datastore extent. Dynamically growing the datastore extent fills the available adjacent capacity. The extent is considered expandable when the underlying storage device has free space immediately after the extent.

Extending

Another method for increasing capacity is to add a new extent (LUN) to an existing VMFS datastore, as shown in the following procedure. The datastore can span up to 32 extents—and each extent can be more than 2 TB—yet appear as a single volume.

The spanned VMFS datastore can use any or all of its extents at any time. It does not need to fill up a particular extent before using the next one.

Step 1.   In the vSphere Web Client navigator, select **vCenter Inventory Lists > Datastores**.

Step 2.   Select the datastore you want to grow and click the **Increase Datastore Capacity** icon (see Figure 6-4).

Increase datastore capacity

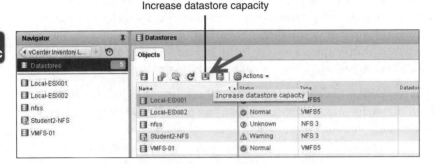

Figure 6-4   Increase Datastore Capacity

Step 3.   Select a device (LUN) from the list of storage devices. If the value in the Expandable column is Yes, you can expand the existing extent. If the Expandable column's value is No, then you have the option to extend the existing datastore by adding another extent (LUN) to the datastore (see Table 6-3).

Table 6-3   Selection in Wizard Expand or Extend VMFS Datastore

Option	Description
Expand an existing extent	Select the device if the Expandable column reads Yes.
Extend an existing datastore	Select the device if the Expandable column reads No.

Step 4.   Review the current disk layout to ensure that the available configurations are correct and click **Next**.

Place a VMFS Datastore in Maintenance Mode

If you need to take a VMFS datastore out of service, you can put the datastore into maintenance mode. One of the requirements for datastore maintenance mode is that the datastore must be a member of a storage DRS cluster that contains at least two datastores.

NOTE The virtual machines must be moved off of the datastore before it enters maintenance mode.

Select the Preferred Path/Disable a Path to a VMFS Datastore

When an ESXi Host reboots or when you rescan the storage adapter of the host, a signal is sent down all the physical paths, looking for storage devices. The storage device sends a signal back, along with information such as the vendor name for that storage device. Then the ESXi Host assigns the storage device with a claim rule, based on the best match. After matching the storage device to a claim rule, the host determines which Multipathing Plug-in (MPP) to load for the storage device. All the error codes, I/O requests, and I/O queuing to the HBA are handled by the MPP.

One part of the MPP is the Path Selection Plug-in (PSP), which selects which physical path to use for storage transport. One way to think of PSP is that it chooses which multipathing solution you are going to use to load balance. There are three built-in PSPs: Fixed, MRU, and Round Robin (which was added with vSphere 4.1). The NMP assigns a default PSP from the claim rules based on the Storage Array Type Policy (SATP) associated with the physical device. You can use the following command line to list multipathing modules:

```
esxcli storage core plugin list -plugin-class=MP
```

If you need to override the default PSP, you can create a claim rule to assign a different PSP to the device. Figure 6-5 shows a VMFS datastore that is using Round Robin as its PSP, with one path displayed in the screenshot.

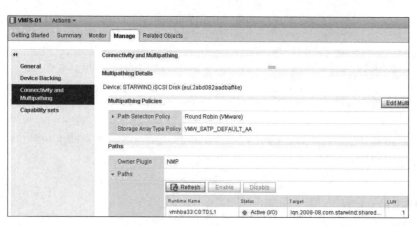

Figure 6-5 Multipathing Details for a VMFS Datastore

Given a Scenario, Determine a Proper Use Case for Multiple VMFS/NFS Datastores

VMware administrators have to make a decision about how they want to utilize their datastores. You could have a datastore for every VM. That would keep the storage administrators busy, since they would have to create a LUN for each datastore. The good news about each datastore having its own LUN is that you don't have to worry about one of the VMs that would be sharing the datastore using up all the storage capacity. However, the problem is that as you add more and more VMs, each with its own datastore, you can start running into storage and LUN limits that you might not expect.

Another option is to have one large giant datastore for all of the VMs. The positive here is that you need to create only one LUN on one datastore. The negative is that you get no load balancing with Storage vMotion. Therefore, a common option is to use multiple datastores in a cluster. This gives you the ability to use Storage vMotion and to do load balancing on VMs with DRS.

Using VMFS datastores is a simple method for provisioning shared storage pools, and datastores can be used with any of the supported storage protocols. But there can be issues with VMFS, such as overloading the datastore with too many VMs. Often, large VMFS datastores reach their I/O performance limit before their capacity limit has been reached. Therefore, you can use VMFS for a datastores but you need to be aware that there are limits on the number of VMs that can be utilized in a VMFS datastore.

If the ESXi Host generates more commands to a LUN than the LUN queue depth permits, the excess commands are queued in the VMkernel. This increases the latency, or the time that is takes to complete I/O requests. The host takes longer to complete I/O requests, and this can lead to virtual machines displaying unsatisfactory performance. You can remedy this by adjusting the LUN queue depth.

SCSI device drivers have a configurable parameter called the LUN queue depth that determines how many commands to a given LUN can be active at one time. If the sum of active commands from all virtual machines within the LUN consistently exceeds the LUN queue depth, you should increase the queue depth.

An alternative to SAN storage is NAS using the NFS protocol. One of the main benefits of NFS is greater scalability of VM density due to the lack of LUN queues and direct I/O between each VMDK on the NFS server and ESXi Hosts.

Because vSphere creates a VM as a set of files, managing a VMware environment with NFS is simply a matter of managing those files. With NFS, you can provision a large number of VMs per datastore, thus reducing the number of datastores required and management efforts around datastores. Ease of management is a major benefit for enterprise customers running VMware over NFS.

With fewer NFS datastores, less storage provisioning is needed, and a simple GUI configuration in vSphere creates an NFS volume and mounts it on the appropriate ESXi servers. In addition, NFS datastores can grow or shrink on the fly by changing the size of the storage at the storage array.

Objective 3.5—Set Up and Configure Storage I/O Control

Storage I/O Control (SIOC) is used to provide I/O prioritization for virtual machines. Other resources, such as CPU and memory, use shares, limits, and reservations to help determine resource access. SIOC also can use those types of constructs to provide priority access for more important VMs.

Describe the Benefits of SIOC

VMware introduced the Storage I/O Control (SIOC) feature in vSphere 4.1. It is enabled on the datastore to throttle back VMs that are monopolizing storage I/O during times of congestion. By default, SIOC is disabled on the datastore. When you enable SIOC, it begins by monitoring the device latency at the datastore level. If all virtual machines are considered equal—that is, with an equal number of shares—then each VM will have equal access to the datastore.

You can achieve more benefits during times of contention by setting reservations, shares, and limits for the VMs. You can give virtual machines more storage resources during periods of I/O congestion by setting their share values higher for periods of I/O congestion. This ensures that more important VMs get preference over less important virtual machines.

The left side of Figure 6-6 shows that without SIOC, any VM or VMs could begin to monopolize access to the storage, and this could continue during periods of contention. Maybe these are not the virtual machines that are most important, but they are using more than their fair share of storage I/O. The right side of Figure 6-6 shows SIOC enabled on the shared storage. The VMs that you want to prioritize are granted more shares at the VMDK level and receive more storage I/O proportionally than other less important virtual machines. During periods of I/O congestion, the more important VMs get more IOPS and have less latency in proportion to the number of their shares.

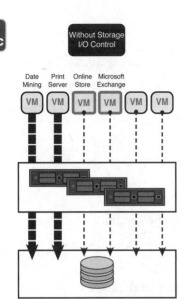
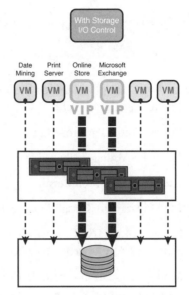

Figure 6-6 Storage I/O Control

Enable and Configure SIOC

The ESXi Host starts monitoring the device latency of the datastore when you enable Storage I/O Control. When device latency exceeds the set threshold, the datastore is considered to be congested, and each virtual machine that accesses that datastore is allocated I/O resources in proportion to its shares. Shares and limits can be allocated for each virtual machine's VMDK based on level of importance. The more important a VM, the more shares you should assign to the virtual machine reservations with SIOC. Earlier versions of SIOC only set shares and limits on the VMDK. Additional reservation capability was added when VMware introduced the mClock scheduler algorithm in vSphere 5.5.

The mClock scheduler algorithm allocates storage resources to the VM in proportion to its shares, allocating its minimum guarantee reservation and not going above its limit. The algorithm is designed to handle the challenges of scheduling storage I/O with many diverse storage requirements. Simple storage I/O allocation is more difficult when storage capacity fluctuates dynamically. Thus, the mClock scheduler guarantees that VMs receive at least their minimum reservation and are held to their limit in the time interval. After enforcing the minimum and maximum, the mClock scheduler focuses on allocating the remaining throughput proportionally using shares.

NOTE   When a datastore utilizes storage DRS, Storage I/O Control is enabled by default.

Since Storage I/O Control is disabled by default, you need to enable it for each datastore. The procedure to enable SIOC is as follows:

Step 1.   Browse to the datastore in the vSphere Web Client inventory.

Step 2.   Click the **Manage** tab.

Step 3.   Click **Settings** > **General**.

Step 4.   In the Datastore Capabilities section, click the **Edit** button.

Step 5.   In the Storage I/O Control window that opens, check the **Enable Storage I/O Control** check box.

Step 6.   Modify congestion threshold by selecting either **Percentage of Peak Throughput** or **Manual**, as shown in Figure 6-7.

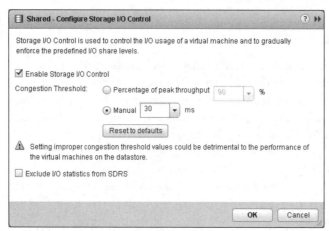

Figure 6-7   Enabling SIOC

The congestion threshold value for a datastore is the point where SIOC begins to assign importance to the virtual machine workloads on the datastore according to their shares. The throttling of VMs occurs when the overall latency exceeds the congestion threshold that is set or when a very low latency value is set, such as lower than 20 ms (which could potentially decrease throughput for the datastore). Therefore, you need to either use the defaults or do some testing and adjust any thresholds if necessary.

Configure/Manage SIOC

Configuring Storage I/O Control is a five-step process:

Step 1.   Enable Storage I/O Control for a datastore as described in the previous procedure.

Step 2.   To allocate storage I/O resources to a virtual machine, right-click the VM and select **Edit Settings**.

Step 3.   In the Edit Settings window that appears, select the VMDK of the virtual machine you want to modify. For example, Figure 6-8 shows changing the default shares value of 1000 to 2000.

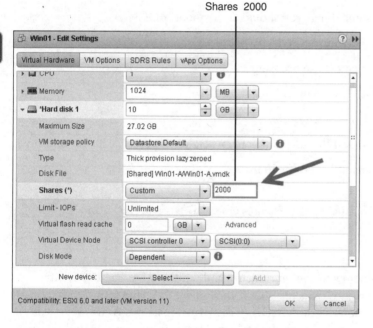

Figure 6-8   Customizing the Shares Value for SIOC

Step 4.   Set the number of storage I/O shares and the upper limit of I/O operations per second (IOPS) for the VMDK file of the virtual machine.

Step 5.   You can check how SIOC shares for the datastore compare by selecting **Home > Storage** > highlight the datastore > **Related Objects > Virtual Machines** (see Figure 6-9).

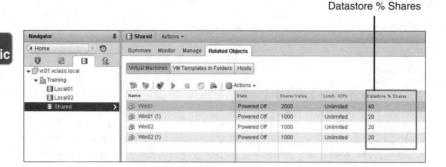

Figure 6-9 Datastore % Shares of SIOC

The following are some things you should know about SIOC:

- SIOC was initially introduced in vSphere 4.1

- SIOC requires enterprise licensing.

- SIOC is disabled by default.

- SIOC is enabled on a datastore.

- SIOC monitors and throttles VMs only when latency exceeds the set threshold.

- SIOC has a default latency of 30 ms.

NOTE By default, all virtual machine shares are set to Normal (1000) and Limit IOPS (Unlimited).

So far you have seen how to configure shares and limits for Storage I/O Control. How do you set up reservations for SIOC? In vSphere 6, VMware introduced the ability to set reservations on the VMDK of the virtual machine. At this time, you cannot configure it in the vSphere Web Client. However, vSphere's API does have a data object called `StorageIOAllocationInfo` that can be set at the datastore level only. You can add the reservation value for SIOC using PowerCLI `cmdlets` using the `StorageIOAllocation.reservation` property.

Monitor SIOC

In the vSphere Web Client, a number of built-in charts for SIOC are easily accessible and can help with monitoring SIOC. After you enable Storage I/O Control, it begins to monitor the latency of the datastore. SIOC monitors the storage I/O, and when the latency is higher than the configured latency threshold, it begins to take action due to contention. It begins to limit the I/O a host can issue by throttling the host device queue. To monitor SIOC, go to the SIOC Performance Charts in the vSphere Web Client and select a datastore. Then click on the **Monitor** tab and select the **Performance** tab. In the **View** drop-down menu, select **Performance**. Figure 6-10 shows the SIOC performance charts.

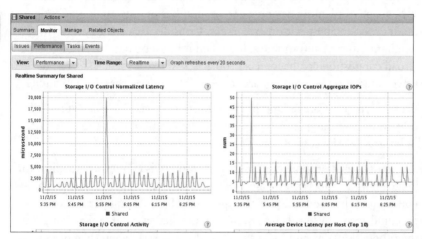

Figure 6-10   SIOC Performance Charts

The following built-in SIOC charts are available, and you can see that there are a number of available ways to see how SIOC is working within the datastore:

- Storage I/O Control Normalized Latency
- Storage I/O Control Aggregate IOPS
- Storage I/O Control Activity
- Average Device Latency per Host (Top 10)
- Max Queue Depth per Host (Top 10)
- Read IOPS per Host (Top 10)
- Write IOPS per Host (Top 10)
- Average Read Latency per Virtual Machine Disk (Top 10)
- Average Write Latency per Virtual Machine Disk (Top 10)
- Read IOPS per Virtual Machine Disk (Top 10)
- Write IOPS per Virtual Machine Disk (Top 10)

Differentiate Between SIOC and Dynamic Queue Depth Throttling Features

Storage I/O Control and Dynamic Queue Depth Throttling are two features that are used in vSphere to manage the queue depth of the ESXi Host. The LUN queue is used to determine the number of outstanding I/Os that can be sent to a disk. During normal disk activity, ESXi Hosts make SCSI requests to the shared disk device, and the LUN queue can handle having a certain number of outstanding SCSI commands without experiencing performance issues. Consider this analogy: A road can handle a certain number of automobiles, but when it hits a certain threshold of too many cars, road congestion can become a problem. Just like a road, a storage device can experience congestion when there are more SCSI requests than it can handle.

Both SIOC and Dynamic Queue Depth Throttling can be used to alleviate SCSI congestion by throttling the queue depth. But the two technologies use different methodologies to solve the congestion problem.

Storage I/O Control uses proportional shares when there is congestion to allow for a proportional amount of I/Os. For example, if you had a production VM and a test VM, and you wanted the production VM to get more I/Os during periods of congestion, you could accomplish this by assigning more shares. So if you assign 2000 shares to the production VM and 1000 shares to the test VM, when there is congestion, the production VM will be allowed to queue twice as many I/Os as the test VM in the storage device queue.

Dynamic Queue Depth Throttling, otherwise known as Adaptive Queue Depth Algorithm, can adjust the LUN queue depth. The algorithm engages when storage I/O congestion returns QUEUE FULL or BUSY status codes. When these error codes are received, the queue depth is cut in half. This algorithm modifies the values of the QFullSampleSize and QFullThreshold parameters, which can be accomplished using the following at the command line:

```
# esxcfg-advcfg -s 32 /Disk/QFullSampleSize
# esxcfg-advcfg -s 8 /Disk/QFullThreshold
```

Given a Scenario, Determine a Proper Use Case for SIOC

As you probably already know, virtual machines are not all created equal. Some VMs are more important than other VMs. By default, VMs are supposed to get equal access to resources, since all virtual machines have shares equal to Normal (1000) when Storage I/O Control (SIOC) is disabled.

However, that is not always the case. For example, one issue is the "noisy neighbor," where one VM (the noisy neighbor) can get more than its fair share of storage I/O than other VMs. Since SIOC has not been enabled, the noisy neighbor VM can continue to use more than its fair share of resources. To combat this issue, Storage I/O Control is enabled on a datastore to control the storage I/O usage of virtual machines. In vSphere 6, you can set reservations, share, and limits to control the amount of storage I/O that is allocated to virtual machines.

When SIOC is enabled on a datastore, it prevents any one VM from dominating the datastore by monitoring the device latency of the datastore. If the latency is higher than the configured value, SIOC reduces the latency by throttling back VMs that are using excessive I/O. Enabling SIOC solves the noisy neighbor problem, and adding controls can further benefit performance.

Compare and Contrast the Effects of I/O Contention in Environments With and Without SIOC

With SIOC enabled, virtual machines will receive equal device queue depth and equal access to the same datastore. The proportional algorithm comes into effect just by enabling SIOC, and with additional settings, such as reservations, shares, and limits, you can further manage storage I/O allocation on the datastore.

Without SIOC, you can encounter the noisy neighbor problem, where one VM could use more storage I/O than its allotment. This is especially true when a VM requests I/O in bursts and workloads arrive at different times.

Summary

You have now read the chapter covering exam topics for Advanced Storage operations and Storage I/O Control. You should now use information in the following sections to complete your preparation for Objectives 3.4 and 3.5.

Exam Preparation Tasks

Review All the Key Topics

Table 6-4 provides a reference to each of the key topics identified in this chapter. Take a few moments to review each of these specific items.

Table 6-4   Key Topics for Chapter 6

Key Topic Element	Description	Pages
List	VAAI primitives	229
List	File system technologies	231
Figure 6-1	Editing hard disk settings	235
List	NFS version 3 and 4.1 differences	235
Note	NFSv4.1 AUTH_SYS and Kerberos	236
Figure 6-2	SCSI bus sharing options	237
Note	CDES-CBC-MD5 support for encryption	238
Figure 6-3	Create a new datastore	239
Note	vSphere Web Client 42-character name limit	239
Note	VMFS3 no longer supported for creation	240
Note	Use same NFS protocol all host access to same datastore	241
Figure 6-4	Increase datastore capacity	243
Note	VM must be moved off datastore before entering maintenance mode	244
Figure 6-5	Multipathing details for a VMFS datastore	244
Figure 6-6	Storage I/O Control	247
Note	SIOC enabled by default with storage DRS	248
Figure 6-7	Enabling SIOC	248
Figure 6-8	Customizing the shares value for SIOC	249
Figure 6-9	Datastore % shares of SIOC	250
Note	VM shares normal (1000) and limit IOPS (unlimited)	250
Figure 6-10	SIOC performance charts	251

Complete the Tables and Lists from Memory

Print a copy of Appendix B, "Memory Tables" (found on the CD), or at least the section for this chapter, and complete the tables and lists from memory. Appendix C, "Memory Tables Answer Key," also on the CD, includes completed tables and lists to check your work.

Definitions of Key Terms

Define the following key terms from this chapter and check your answers in the glossary.

> vSphere APIs for Array Integration (VAAI), Virtual Machine File System (VMFS), Virtual Volumes (VVOL), Network File System (NFS), DES-CBC-MD5, Multipathing Plug-in (MPP), Native Multipathing Plug-in (NMP), Storage Array Type Plug-in (SATP), Path Selection Plug-in (PSP), Storage I/O Control (SIOC)

Answer Review Questions

The answers to these review questions can be found in Appendix A.

1. Which of the following statements is incorrect?

   a. VAAI supports SAN storage but not NAS storage.

   b. VAAI uses Atomic Test and Set Operations (ATS) instead of SCSI-2 reservations.

   c. VAAI offloads specific storage operations from the ESXi Host to the storage array.

   d. VAAI is based on running certain SCSI commands on the storage array instead of the ESXi Host.

2. Which of the following features is not supported with virtual compatibility mode RDM?

   a. VMware snapshots

   b. VMware SCSI3 clustering

   c. VMware cloning

   d. Storage migration

3. Which of the following is not an option for SCSI bus sharing?

   a. None

   b. One

   c. Virtual

   d. Physical

4. Which of the following statements about SIOC is incorrect?

   a. Shares, reservations, and limits for SIOC are configured using the vSphere Web Client.

   b. By default, SIOC is disabled on a datastore.

   c. You can achieve more benefits during times of contention by setting reservations, shares, and limits for the VMs.

   d. During periods of I/O congestion, the more important VMs get more IOPS and have less latency in proportion to the number of their shares.

5. Which of the following statements about SIOC and Dynamic Queue Depth Throttling is incorrect?

   a. Dynamic Queue Depth Throttling uses proportional shares when there is congestion.

   b. Dynamic Queue Depth Throttling is also known as Adaptive Queue Depth.

   c. Both SIOC and Dynamic Queue Depth Throttling can be used to alleviate the SCSI congestion by throttling the queue depth.

   d. Storage I/O Control and Dynamic Queue Depth Throttling are two features that are used in vSphere to manage queue depth of the ESXi Host.

This chapter covers the following objectives:

- **Objective 4.1: Perform ESXi Host and Virtual Machine Upgrades**

    - Configure download source(s)

    - Set up UMDS to set up download repository

    - Import ESXi images

    - Create baselines and/or baseline groups

    - Attach baselines to vSphere objects

    - Scan vSphere objects

    - Stage patches and extensions

    - Remediate an object

    - Upgrade vSphere

    - Align appropriate baselines with target inventory objects

- **Objective 4.2: Perform vCenter Server Upgrades**

    - Compare the methods of upgrading vCenter Server

    - Back up vCenter Server database, configuration, and certificate datastore

    - Perform update as prescribed for appliance or installable

    - Upgrade vCenter Server Appliance (vCSA)

    - Given a scenario, determine the upgrade compatibility of an environment

    - Determine correct order of steps to upgrade a vSphere implementation

## CHAPTER 7

Upgrade a vSphere Deployment to 6.x

This chapter provides you with the knowledge and skills to successfully upgrade a vSphere environment. This chapter covers upgrading the many parts of vSphere, such as ESXi Hosts and the vCenter Server, with an emphasis on ensuring that you have the skills to successfully answer questions that might be a part of the VMware Certified Professional 6—Data Center Virtualization Exam. As you read this chapter, take time to practice the steps that are provided and understand how the upgrade process works.

"Do I Know This Already?" Quiz

The "Do I Know This Already?" quiz allows you to assess whether you should study this entire chapter or move quickly to the "Exam Preparation Tasks" section. Regardless, the authors recommend that you read the entire chapter at least once. Table 7-1 outlines the major headings in this chapter and the corresponding "Do I Know This Already?" quiz questions. You can find the answers in Appendix A, "Answers to the 'Do I Know This Already?' Quizzes and Review Questions."

Table 7-1 "Do I Know This Already?" Foundation Topics Section-to-Question Mapping

Foundation Topics Section	Questions Covered in This Section
Set Up UMDS to Set Up Download Repository	1
Upgrade a vSphere Distributed Switch	2
Upgrade VMware Tools	3
Upgrade Virtual Machine Hardware	4
Upgrade an ESXi Host Using vCenter Update Manager	5
Stage Multiple ESXi Host Upgrades	6
Compare the Methods of Upgrading vCenter Server	7
Back Up vCenter Server Database, Configuration, and Certificate Datastore	8

Foundation Topics Section	Questions Covered in This Section
Perform Update as Prescribed for Appliance or Installable	9
Upgrade vCenter Server Appliance (VCSA)	10

1. Which of the following steps is not used to perform an upgrade of an ESXi Host using vSphere Update Manager 6.0 directly from the Internet?

   a. Scan vSphere objects.

   b. Attach baseline to vSphere objects.

   c. Remediate an object.

   d. Set up UMDS to download repository.

2. Which of the following statements about upgrading a vSphere Distributed Switch configuration is incorrect?

   a. A prerequisite to upgrading Distributed Switch is to ensure that vCenter Server and all of the ESXi Hosts are upgraded before the virtual switch.

   b. vSphere Distributed Switch must be rebooted in order for the upgrade to take effect.

   c. It is best practice to back up the Distributed Switch configuration before upgrading in case there is a failure.

   d. When vSphere Distributed Switch is upgraded to Distributed Switch version 6.0, the virtual machines lose connection, and thus a reboot of the VMs is required.

3. An Advanced Options text box allows you to add options to the VMware Tools upgrade. To perform a silent upgrade of VMware Tools for a Windows operating system, which command do you enter into the Advanced Options text box?

   a. `/s /v "qn" /l "c:\windows\filename.log"`

   b. `/s /v "qn" "up"`

   c. `/s /v "c:\windows\filename.log"`

   d. `/s /qn /v "c:\windows\filename.log"`

4. Which of the following is not a prerequisite that your environment must meet before you can upgrade the virtual machine hardware version?

   a. Verify that the virtual machines running on Distributed Switch are stored on VMFS3, VMFS5, or NFS datastores.

   b. Upgrade to the latest version of VMware Tools before upgrading hardware version.

   c. The standard ISO image for VMware Tools for all guest operating systems must be installed on all virtual machines.

   d. Verify that all .vmdk files are available to ESXi Host on VMFS3, VMFS5, or NFS datastores.

5. Which of the following is not a step used in upgrading an ESXi Host using Update Manager?

   a. Scan ESXi Hosts for available updates.

   b. Create a host upgrade baseline or baseline group.

   c. Remediate ESXi Hosts or clusters against the baseline or baseline group.

   d. Import the host upgrade image or images.

6. An upgrade script contains the installation settings for ESXi. Which of the following is not a supported location for an upgrade script?

   a. FTP server

   b. HTTP/HTTPS

   c. USB flash drive

   d. PXE

7. Which of the following components does not run on the Platform Services Controller?

   a. vSphere Auto Deploy

   b. VMware Single Sign-on

   c. Lookup service

   d. Certificate store

8. Which of the following statements is incorrect?

   a. The VMware Certificate Authority (VMCA) is where the certificates are stored.

   b. The following command could be used to back up a Windows vCenter Server database.

```
python.exe c:\backup_win.py -p "s_PJmbGzC83QRYlp" -f c:\
   vcdb_backup.bak
```

   c. The VMware Certificate Authority (VMCA) issues certificates to all VMware services that need them and uses a self-signed root certificate.

   d. If a Windows or Linux vCenter Server is running an external database such as SQL or Oracle, then the DBA is utilizing a third-party backup solution.

9. Which of the following is not a step used in performing updates for a Linux vCenter Server Appliance?

   a. Before you upgrade vCenter Server Appliance, you need to download the pre-update checker application.

   b. Download the vCenter Server Appliance installer and Client Integration Plug-In ISO file from the VMware website, at `https://my.vmware.com/web/vmware/downloads`.

   c. Mount the ISO image to a Windows VM and then configure the ISO image as a datastore for the CD/DVD drive of the virtual machine.

   d. Install the Client Integration Plug-in by navigating to the `vcsa` directory and double-clicking `VMware-ClientIntegrationPlugin-6.0.0.exe`. The Client Integration Plug-in Installation Wizard appears. Follow its steps, and when the installation completes, click **Finish**.

10. When you are upgrading vCenter Server Appliance, if you do not deploy the vCSA with the correct FQDNs, what must you do?

   a. Regenerate the FQDNs with the `fqdn-app` script.

   b. Modify the `/etc/hosts` file with the correct FQDNs.

   c. Regenerate the certificates.

   d. Enable HA for vCenter Server Appliance.

Foundation Topics

Objective 4.1—Perform ESXi Host and Virtual Machine Upgrades

There are various methods to upgrade the VMware environment from vSphere 5.x to vSphere 6.0. This section first looks at vSphere Update Manager 6.0 (VUM) and the different parts of VUM that are utilized in the upgrade process. Then this section goes through the process of upgrading different parts of vSphere, such as the ESXi Host and virtual machines. When upgrading, you need to perform all the procedures in the proper order to prevent data loss and limit downtime. To show that the Windows vSphere Client is a usable option, the examples for Update Manager use it instead of Web Client. Web Client can be used to view scan results and compliance states.

Update Manager

You can perform the following tasks with Update Manager:

- Upgrade and path ESXi Hosts.

- Install and update third-party software on hosts.

- Upgrade virtual machine hardware, VMware Tools, and virtual appliances.

Update Manager 6.0 is a Windows-based application designed to centralize and automate patch and version management. A server and web-based client piece needs to be installed and configured. Update Manager can run on either a Windows vCenter Server or a separate Windows-based VM. To manage the VUM server, you need the Update Manager plug-in that interacts with either the vSphere Windows client or the web-based client.

NOTE The Update Manager server and client plug-ins must be the same version.

You begin the Update Manager process by downloading the software needed for patching or upgrading. A group of patch(es) or upgrade(s) form a baseline group, which consists of a baseline or a group of baselines. You can associate a baseline or baseline group with an ESXi Host or cluster of hosts. Then you scan to see if the host is up to date with the patch(es), and if the host is not compliant with the patches, you remediate the hosts.

Update Manager is software for upgrading, migrating, and patching clustered hosts, virtual machines, and guest operating systems. Update Manager can be used for these different processes. VMware recommends using VUM, but there are several other update methods that are discussed in this section as well. After setting up Update Manager, you either need to download the software that you want to upgrade or copy it from a media drive and save it on a local or shared network drive. For example, to download the ESXi installer from the VMware website, go to `https://my.vmware.com/web/vmware/downloads`. There you find ESXi labeled VMware vSphere under Datacenter & Cloud Infrastructure. After downloading vSphere and any other necessary software, you can begin to set up VUM to begin the upgrade process.

There are two deployment models that Update Manager can use to upgrade vSphere. With the Internet-connected model, you configure download sources from the Internet to gather upgrade software. Without an Internet connection, you cannot download upgrade software, so you use the other method: Use UMDS to download and store patch metadata and patch binaries in a shared repository.

Configure Download Source(s)

To upgrade vSphere while using Update Manager, you can download the vSphere upgrade from VMware's website or, if you have already obtained a copy, you can set up a shared repository. You can use either the Web vSphere Client or the Windows vSphere Client to add download sources. For example, using the Windows vSphere Client, go to **Home** > **Solutions and Applications** > **Update Manager** > your vCenter Server. Select the **Configuration** tab, and in the Settings pane select **Download Settings**. Click **Download Now** to run the VMware vSphere Update Manager Update Download task and download all updates from the sources listed (see Figure 7-1).

Download Now

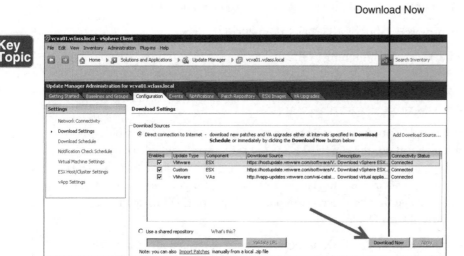

Figure 7-1 Download vSphere Upgrade Sources

Set Up UMDS to Set Up Download Repository

Another option to upgrade vSphere is to utilize an optional module for Update
Manager called vSphere Update Manager Download Service (UMDS). In some
environments where security does not allow Internet access, you can use a separate
computer system on the other side of the DMZ to obtain upgrade software. That
computer system needs to run UMDS to help download the upgrade software and
then export the downloaded software to help prepare it to become accessible to the
Update Manager Server. This process can be automated to help transfer the upgrade software from UMDS to the Update Manager Server.

NOTE You cannot download updates from the Internet and use a shared repository
at the same time. Choose one or the other.

Import ESXi Images

To upgrade ESXi to version 6.0, the hardware and system resources must meet the
minimum hardware and software requirements:

- 64-bit x86 CPU processor, released after September 2006

- At least two CPU cores

- NX/XD bit enabled for the CPU in the BIOS

- A minimum of 4 GB of physical RAM (8 GB recommended)
- One or more 1 Gbps or 10 Gbps Ethernet controllers
- Boot device with minimum 1 GB

For a list of supported systems, see the VMware Compatibility Guide at `http://www.vmware.com/resources/compatibility`.

There are a couple options you can use when upgrading to a new version of the ESXi Host. You can use the standard ESXi 6.0 ISO image available on the VMware website. The standard image distributed by VMware has the name format `VMware-VMvisor-Installer-6.0.0-build_number.x86_64.iso`. Or you can use a custom ESXi 6.0 ISO image that has been created using vSphere ESXi Image Builder, which is a part of Auto Deploy.

The procedure to import an ESXi image can be started using either the Windows vSphere Client or the vSphere Web Client. Pick your client and then connect to vCenter Server 6.0, where Update Manager 6.0 has been registered and set up. For example, using the Windows vSphere Client, go to **Home** > **Solutions and Applications** > **Update Manager** > your vCenter Server. Select the **ESXi Images** tab (see Figure 7-2). To import an image, select Import ESXi Image and browse for the ESXi ISO image that you are going to use to upgrade the ESXi Host. After you import the ESXi image, it appears in the Imported ESXi Images pane. After you have uploaded the ESXi image, you can see additional information about the software package in the Software Packages pane.

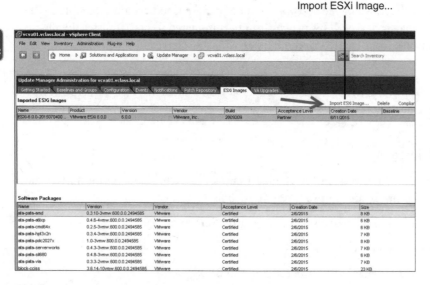

Figure 7-2 Import ESXi Image

Create Baselines and/or Baseline Groups

Once you have imported the ESXi image, the next thing you need to do is create an ESXi Host upgrade baseline. It is a requirement to create a baseline to upgrade an ESXi Host. To create the baseline using the Windows vSphere Client, go to **Home > Solutions and Applications > Update Manager >** your vCenter Server. Select the **Baselines and Groups** tab (see Figure 7-3). Click on the **Create** hyperlink to open the New Baseline window. Then find the ESXi ISO image to load into VUM to form the baseline.

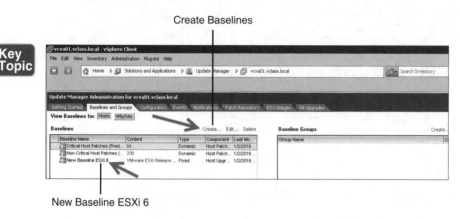

Figure 7-3   Create ESXi Host Baseline

Attach Baselines to vSphere Objects

Once you have the ESXi Host upgrade baseline, you need to attach the baseline to the ESXi Host that you want to upgrade. If you are using the Windows vSphere Client, go to **Home > Solutions and Applications > Update Manager >** your vCenter Server. You are now in the admin view, as shown in Figure 7-4. In the admin view you can see all the baselines and baseline groups for hosts or VMs/VAs. Select the **Baselines and Groups** tab and click the **Compliance View** hyperlink to change the screen appearance and options.

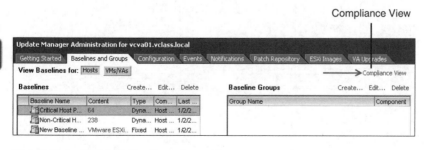

Figure 7-4   Switch to the Compliance View

Once you have switched over to the compliance view, you can see the hosts and clusters in the left pane inventory. Highlight in the left pane inventory the objects to which you want to attach an existing baseline or baseline group.

After you click **Attach** (see Figure 7-5), the selected baseline attaches to the selected object—in this case, the Lab cluster of ESXi Hosts.

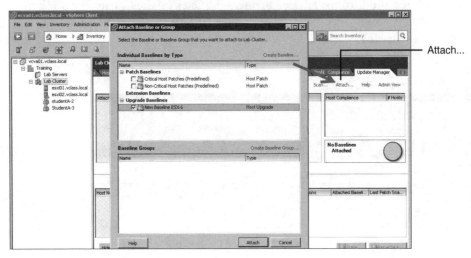

Figure 7-5 Attach Baseline to a Host or Cluster

Figure 7-6 shows the result. When you attach the baseline, you can see the status of whether the host is up to date or in need of updating. Currently, the two ESXi Hosts are in the unknown state, which means you do not know the state of the hosts since the hosts have not been scanned for compliance.

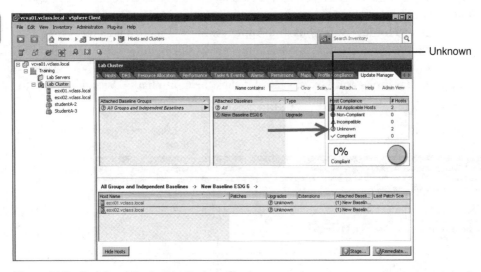

Figure 7-6 Baseline Attached to the Lab Cluster

Scan vSphere Objects

Scanning is the process in which the ESXi Host is evaluated against the upgrade ISO in the attached baseline. You can either schedule Update Manager to scan for compliance or manually click **Scan** to begin the process to check for compliance. If you click Scan, in the Confirm Scan window, click the **Upgrades** check box and click **Scan**. The scanning process checks whether the ESXi Host is up to date. In Figure 7-7 you can see that the ESXi Hosts are non-compliant and need to be upgraded to the new version.

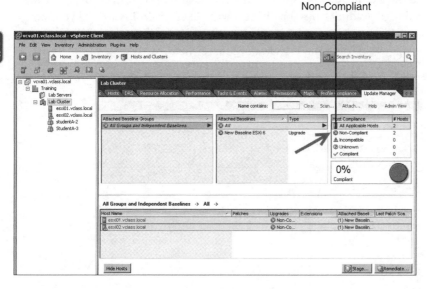

Figure 7-7   After Scanning, ESXi Hosts Are Shown to Be Non-Compliant

Stage Patches and Extensions

The staging process is not used for upgrading ESXi Hosts. It is used if you are patching ESXi Hosts or adding an extension baseline. When you click the **Stage** button, you open the Stage Wizard. By staging the remediation process, you will reduce the time needed for patching because the host will have to enter maintenance mode. After remediation of the staged patches and extensions, all the patches and extensions are deleted from the host.

Remediate an Object

After scanning the host or cluster of hosts, remediation is the next step in the upgrade of the ESXi Host process. Remediation can also be used when you need to patch or add an extension to a host. If you are remediating a cluster of ESXi Hosts and there is a failure during the upgrade process with one of the hosts, the remediation process stops, and no further hosts are upgraded. However, the hosts that have already been successfully upgraded remain upgraded. If you are going to upgrade a cluster of hosts, remediation requires that you temporarily disable cluster features such as high availability (HA), distributed power management (DPM), and fault tolerance (FT).

You can upgrade a cluster of ESXi Hosts one at a time, or you can upgrade them in parallel. If you are remediating a cluster of hosts in parallel, and a host encounters an error during the upgrade process, the remediation process continues for the other hosts, but upgrading stops for the host with an error. In Figure 7-8 you can see the remediation steps in the left pane, as well as the baseline and ESXi Hosts selected to be upgraded using the Windows vSphere client.

Remediation Selection

Figure 7-8   Remediation Selection

Upgrade a vSphere Distributed Switch

vSphere Distributed Switch can be upgraded to Distributed Switch version 6.0 to match the vCenter Server and ESXi Hosts, with no downtime for the virtual machines attached to the Distributed Switch. It is best practices to back up the Distributed Switch configuration before upgrading in case there is a failure. A prerequisite to upgrading Distributed Switch is that vCenter Server and all of the ESXi Hosts must be upgraded before the virtual switch. To upgrade Distributed Switch in the vSphere Web Client, go to **Home** > **Networking**. In the left inventory pane, highlight the vSphere Distributed Switch that you want to upgrade. Then right-click the switch and select **Upgrade** > **Upgrade Distributed Switch** (see Figure 7-9). The

Upgrade Distributed Switch Wizard appears and asks which version of Distributed Switch you would like to upgrade; it then checks compatibility with the ESXi Hosts.

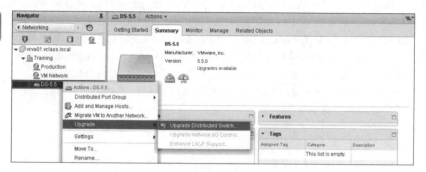

Figure 7-9   Upgrade vSphere Distributed Switch

Upgrade VMware Tools

VMware Tools provides device drivers and services for virtual machines (VMs). When you install VMware Tools in a VM's guest operating system, the OS can take advantage of device drivers that are compiled to run in a virtual environment. This can provide a performance benefit in most cases. The VMware Tools service starts immediately after the guest operating system has finished starting.

After you perform an ESXi upgrade, you can manually upgrade VMware Tools for all of the virtual machines. You can also configure your virtual machines to automatically check for and install newer versions of VMware Tools.

The manual process is one option for installing VMware Tools. The installers for VMware Tool are ISO image files, and there is a different ISO image for each guest operating system. The installation process for VMware Tools differs for different operating systems. Thus, the installation for VMware Tools for Windows is different than the installation for VMware Tools for Solaris. In a Windows virtual machine, there is a VMware Tools option that can notify you when an upgrade is available. You see a yellow caution icon in the Windows taskbar, indicating that a VMware Tools upgrade is needed. To upgrade VMware Tools, you perform the same steps as for installing VMware Tools.

The automated approach can start an automatic upgrade of VMware Tools. During the automated process, the previous version of VMware Tools is automatically uninstalled and the new version is installed.

NOTE   Automated VMware Tools is supported only for VMs running Windows or Linux guest operating systems.

To automatically upgrade VMware Tools, the virtual machine must be powered on, and the guest OS must be running. You can determine whether the VM is running the latest version of VMware Tools by viewing the **Summary** tab of the virtual machine (see Figure 7-10). If VMware Tools needs to be upgraded, you see the message **Automatic Tools Upgrade**, which you can click to open up a window to begin the process. The **Advanced Options** text box allows you to add options to the VMware Tools Upgrade. For example, if you want to perform a silent upgrade of VMware Tools for a Windows operating system, you could enter the following in the **Advanced Options** text box:

```
/s /v "qn" /l "c:\windows\filename.log"
```

The silent upgrade of VMware Tools creates a log file in the specified location on the guest operating system.

VMware Tools: Running, version:9536 (Current)

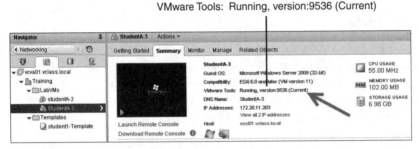

Figure 7-10   VMware Tools Version Information

Upgrade Virtual Machine Hardware

The version of the virtual machine hardware determines what virtual hardware is supported for the VM. You can think of the virtual machine hardware as a virtual motherboard. If your motherboard is limited to four CPUs, but the new version of the motherboard supports eight CPUs, if you need eight CPUs, you need to upgrade the motherboard. So when you upgrade your motherboard, you typically have new supported devices, and in many cases more CPU and/or RAM supported. Similarly, with virtual machine hardware, the newer the version, the more devices and the greater the amount of CPU and RAM supported. The VM hardware version can be upgraded using either the vSphere Update Manager or the vSphere Web Client.

You can upgrade the virtual machine hardware version to match the most current version, or you can use an older version. Since it is not necessary to use the latest version, maybe you need to have compatibility with older versions of ESXi Hosts. Consider the following when you upgrade the virtual machine hardware:

- Create a backup or snapshot of the virtual machine.

- Upgrade to the latest version of VMware Tools.

- Verify that all .vmdk files are available to ESXi Host on VMFS3, VMFS5, or NFS datastores.

- Verify that the virtual machine is stored on VMFS3, VMFS5, or NFS datastores.

Upgrade an ESXi Host Using vCenter Update Manager

You can use Update Manager 6.0 to upgrade using a single baseline or using a baseline group. Make sure to check that the ESXi Hosts you are going to upgrade meet all of the requirements before attempting to upgrade. Here are the steps for upgrading an ESXi Host using Update Manager:

Step 1.   Import the host upgrade image or images.

The ESXi host image can be downloaded from VMware or you can use the Image Builder to build a unique ESXi host image.

Step 2.   Create the host upgrade baseline.

You can create an upgrade baseline after you have imported the ESXi image into the Update Manager repository.

Home > Update Manager > ESXi Images > Import ESXi Image > Next.

After the file is uploaded > Next > Finish.

Step 3.   Attach the baseline or baseline group to the host or cluster of hosts.

After you have created a baseline or a baseline group you need to attach it to either an ESXi host or a cluster of hosts.

Home > Inventory > Hosts and Clusters > Update Manager > Attach > select Baseline > click Attach.

Step 4.   Manually scan the ESXi Host or cluster of hosts.

Before you can remediate the ESXi hosts, you need to scan them against the attached baseline or baseline groups.

Step 5.   View the compliance information.

After scanning the ESXi host or cluster you can review the compliance feedback from scanning the host.

Home > Inventory > Hosts and Clusters

Then select the Host to see the status of the compliance information.

Step 6. Remediate the ESXi Host or cluster against the baseline or the baseline group.

You can remediate ESXi hosts against a baseline to upgrade the host.

Home > Hosts and Clusters > Update Manager

Right-click the inventory object you want to remediate and select Remediate.

Stage Multiple ESXi Host Upgrades

The previous section discusses how to upgrade an ESXi Host using Update Manager 6.0, but that is just one method for upgrading a host. Here is a list of the supported methods to upgrade an ESXi Host to version 6.0:

- Use Update Manager 6.0

- Do an interactive upgrade from CD, DVD, or USB drive

- Use vSphere Auto Deploy to redeploy the host with an ESXi 6.0 image

- Use the esxcli command-line utility

- Do a scripted upgrade

Using Update Manager, as discussed in the previous section, is a recommended method for upgrading ESXi Hosts. The interactive upgrade by using an ESXi installer ISO image on CD, DVD, or USB drive is useful for small deployments, so we do not discuss it here. Although you can use Auto Deploy to upgrade an ESXi Host, it really just involves redeploying the host with a new ESXi 6.0 image. Next we look at the last two methods, running the esxcli command and doing a scripted upgrade.

The esxcli command is a command-line method that can be used to upgrade an ESXi Host. If you are using the esxcli command to upgrade an ESXi Host, you need to understand VIBs, image profiles, and software depots. A vSphere installation bundle (VIB) is a software package that could be the core hypervisor components, drivers, and other software necessary to form an ESXi image. Third parties can add drivers and applications that can form a VIB. Thus, an ESXi image is based on a standard VMware ESXi deployment image combined with optional VIBs. The standard image can be downloaded from VMware's website. An image profile is a collection of VIBs. You begin with the base ESXi VIB, and you might add additional VIBs to extend vSphere. A *software depot* is a collection of VIBs and image profiles.

You need to download the ESXi image and place it into a datastore that can be accessed by the ESXi Host you want to upgrade. For example, the ESXi image file is named `VMware-ESXi-6.0.0-26718293.zip`, and the location of the file is `/vmfs/volumes/SAN3/VMware-ESXi-6.0.0-2671893.zip`. Now that you have the ESXi image in a location that you can access, you can use the following command line to determine which VIBs are installed on the ESXi Host:

```
esxcli -server=ESX1 software vib list
```

In addition, you can use the `-rebooting-image` option to list the VIBs and profiles that are installed on the ESXi Host and that will be active after the next host reboot. Next, the host needs to enter maintenance mode, and then you `ssh` into the host. Then run the `esxcli` upgrade command. Note that you must use the full path to the ESXi zip file, like this, or the process will stop with an error:

```
esxli software vib update -d /vmfs/volumes/ SAN3/
   VMware-ESXi-6.0.0-2671893.zip
```

When the script finishes running, reboot the host and exit maintenance mode.

Another method you can use to upgrade hosts from ESXi 5.x to ESXi 6.0 is to run an upgrade script for an unattended upgrade. The upgrade script process begins by powering on the host. During the boot process, the Loading ESXi Installer window appears. At that point, press Shift+O to edit the boot options. A command prompt appears, where you need to type in the necessary kickstart command to begin the upgrade process. For example, you could type in the following command:

```
ks=http://10.10.10.11/kickstart/ks-script.cfg nameserver=10.20.20.20
   ip=10.20.30.30 netmask=10.20.30.40 gateway=10.10.1.1
```

where `ks` is the location of the installation script plus the boot command-line options.

The upgrade script contains the installation settings for ESXi. You can apply the script to all hosts that you want to have a similar configuration. The script syntax must consist of supported commands and options. You can edit the script to change settings for each host as needed. The upgrade script can reside in one of the following locations:

- FTP server
- HTTP/HTTPS server

- NFS server
- USB flash drive
- CD-ROM drive

The upgrade script is a text file (for example, `ks.cfg`) that contains the supported commands. One of the commands in the `ks.cfg` script must be `upgrade` in order to upgrade the ESXi Host. There are also lines in the upgrade script that accept the license agreement, set the root password, and set network information.

Objective 4.2—Perform vCenter Server Upgrades

vCenter Server is an application or service that performs a number of features, such as vMotion, high availability (HA), and Distributed Resource Scheduler (DRS), and it is a main component of a vSphere deployment.

Before vSphere 5.0, it was simple to perform the upgrade on a Windows-based vCenter Server application because there were not a lot of things to consider in the upgrade process. vCenter Server is still a service, but now there are a number of different configuration issues to consider when performing an upgrade.

One of the main things to consider is that the vCenter Server system can run on Windows as a virtual machine or physical server or as a Linux vCenter Server Appliance. Both the Windows and Linux Appliance have the same features and are configured the same way.

Compare the Methods of Upgrading vCenter Server

Upgrade methods for vCenter Server depend on your existing deployment and version of vCenter Server. One of the big changes in vSphere 6.0 is how the components of the vCenter Server can be deployed. Since vSphere 5.1, you can have vCenter Server running on four different systems. You can have a separate Single Sign-On server, web client, inventory server, and vCenter Server service itself. You can also bundle these together into one system or several systems. Customers found this confusing and difficult to manage, though, so in vSphere 6.0, VMware simplified the choices: Use two nodes at most or install all the vCenter Server components into one node. If you have all of the vCenter components running on one VM or physical system, you are using the Embedded Deployment. The other option is to deploy the vCenter Single Sign-On server on a separate VM or physical system than the vCenter Server service. The Platform Service Controller contains all the components that are needed for authentication. By separating the authentication pieces from the vCenter Server service, you make it possible to do a number of things, such as linking multiple vCenter Servers together. The following are the components of the Platform Service Controller:

- VMware Single Sign-On
- VMware license server
- Lookup service
- VMware Certificate Authority (VMCA)
- Certificate store

The other node that makes up the vCenter Server is for the vCenter Server Services, and it contains the following:

- vCenter Server
- vSphere Web Client (server)
- vSphere Auto Deploy (optional)
- vSphere ESXi Dump Collector (optional)
- vSphere Syslog Collector (optional)

Thus, you can break down the vCenter Server into two separate deployment models, with two different ways to upgrade. Another thing that affects the method used to upgrade is the existing version of the vCenter Server in your current deployment:

- If you currently have a Windows vCenter Server 5.0 deployment, you can use either the embedded or external architecture deployment.
- If you currently have a Windows vCenter Server version 5.1 or version 5.5 deployment with all components on a single virtual machine or physical host, you must use an embedded architecture deployment.
- If you currently have a Windows vCenter Server version 5.1 or version 5.5 deployment with the vCenter Single Sign-On deployed on a different virtual machine or physical server than the vCenter Server, you must use an external architecture deployment.
- If the vCenter Server is running the Linux operating system as a virtual appliance, you need to be aware of the requirements discussed later in this chapter for the Linux-based virtual appliance vCenter Server.

The two methods of upgrading vCenter Server are embedded deployment and external deployment.

Embedded Architecture Deployment

In the embedded deployment model, both the Platform Service Controller and vCenter Server service are deployed on the same virtual machine or physical server. Thus, the Platform Service Controller and the vCenter Server service run or are embedded onto one system (see Figure 7-11).

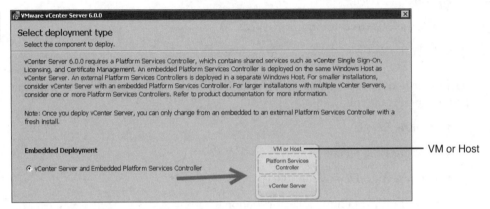

VM or Host

Figure 7-11   Embedded Deployment Option

External Architecture Deployment

With the external or distributed system, the Platform Service Controller and the vCenter Server are deployed on different virtual machines or physical servers (see Figure 7-12).

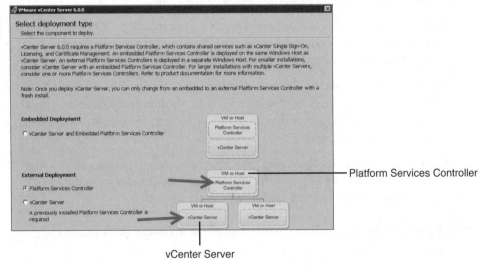

Platform Services Controller

vCenter Server

Figure 7-12   External Deployment Option

Back Up vCenter Server Database and Certificates

How the database for a vCenter Server is backed up depends on which vCenter Server database you are using. If the Windows or Linux vCenter Server is running an external database such as SQL or Oracle, the DBA is utilizing a third-party backup solution. But if the Windows or Linux vCenter Server is running an embedded database, the method for backing up the database depends on the operating system.

Embedded Windows vCenter Server

You can back up the embedded vPostgres database for an embedded Windows vCenter Server. In this case, *embedded* means the database resides within the same VM as the vCenter Server application. You need to download a script to perform the backup. Follow these steps to run the backup process:

Step 1.   Log in to the vCenter Server as administrator.

Step 2.   Locate the `vcdb.properties` file in the `%VMWARE_CFG_DIR%\vmware-vpx\` folder and open the file using a text editor.

Step 3.   In the `vcdb.properties` file, locate the password of the `vc` database user and record it.

Step 4.   Download the Windows backup and restore file `windows_backup_restore.zip` from KB 2091961 and unzip it on the vCenter Server.

Step 5.   Change directory to `%VMWARE_CIS_HOME%\Python\` and run the script `backup_win.py`, providing the password of the `vc` database user that was recorded in step 3, and the location of the backup file. To save the database in the file `c:\vcdb_backup.bak` and use the `vc` password `s_PJmbGzC83QRYlp`, run this command:

```
python.exe c:\backup_win.py -p "s_PJmbGzC83QRYlp" -f c:\
   vcdb_backup.bak
```

You see a message when the backup successfully completes.

Embedded Linux vCenter Server Appliance Database

You can back up the embedded vPostgres database for an embedded Linux vCenter Server. Remember that *embedded* means that the database resides in the same VM as the vCenter Server application. There is a different script than the one used for the Windows Server. The Linux script needs to be downloaded to the Linux server to perform the backup. Follow these steps to run the backup process:

Step 1.   Log in to the Linux vCenter Server console as the `root` user.

Step 2.   Download the Linux backup and restore file
`2091961_linux_backup_restore.zip` from the KB 2091961 and unzip it
on the Linux host.

Step 3.   Add the execute permission to the backup file:

```
chmod 700 /tmp/backup_lin.py
```

Step 4.   Run the backup script and save the backup as `/tmp/vcdb_backup.bak`:

```
python /tmp/backup_lin.py -f /tmp/backup_VCDB.bak
```

You see a message when the backup successfully completes.

Certificates

When you do an upgrade to vSphere 6.0, the certificates change. Certificates are
created and managed in the Certificate Services, which is a part of the Platform Services Controller. The Certificate Services manages the VMware Certificate Authority (VMCA) and the VMware Endpoint Certificate Store (VECS).

The ESXi Host gets a new certificate, which is used to communicate with vCenter
Server. It is not the vCenter Server that is issuing the certificate for the host. Specifically, it is the VMware Certificate Authority (VMCA), which runs on the vCenter
Server that is issuing the certificate. The VMCA issues certificates to all VMware
services that need them, and it uses a self-signed root certificate. It can issue certificates for the vCenter Server, ESXi, and other VMware components. The VECS is
where the certificates are stored.

Perform Update as Prescribed for Appliance or Installable

Before you run the upgrade for a vCenter Server, whether you are running a Windows server or Linux server, there are a couple things you need to do ahead of time,
as described in the following sections.

Pre-Upgrade Updates for Linux vCenter Appliance

Before you upgrade the vCenter Server Appliance, you need to complete a few updates. For the Linux Appliance, you need to download both an installer and a plug-
in, but they are both in the same download image. Once it is downloaded, you need
to set it up. Follow these steps:

Step 1.   Download the vCenter Server Appliance installer and Client Integration
Plug-In ISO file from the VMware website, at `https://my.vmware.com/`
`web/vmware/downloads`.

Step 2.   Mount the ISO image to a Windows VM and then configure the ISO image as a datastore for the CD/DVD drive of the virtual machine.

Step 3.   Install the Client Integration Plug-in by navigating to the `vcsa` directory and double-clicking `VMware-ClientIntegrationPlugin-6.0.0.exe`. The Client Integration Plug-In Installation Wizard appears. Complete its steps, and when the installation is complete, click **Finish**.

The next step is to perform the upgrade of the Linux vCenter Server Appliance, as discussed shortly.

Pre-Upgrade Updates for Windows Installer

Before you upgrade the Windows vCenter Server installer, you need to complete a few updates. For the Linux Appliance, you need to download a plug-in and then mount it for the upgrade. Follow these steps:

Step 1.   Download the vCenter Server Appliance installer and Client Integration Plug-In ISO file from the VMware website, at `https://my.vmware.com/web/vmware/downloads`.

Step 2.   Mount the ISO image to a Windows VM and then configure the ISO image as a datastore for the CD/DVD drive of the virtual machine.

The next step is to perform the upgrade of the Windows vCenter Server, as discussed shortly.

Upgrade vCenter Server Appliance (vCSA)

There is a new upgrade method for the Linux vCenter Server Appliance to version 6. The new method involves using a browser with the Client Integration Plug-In. You start off by deploying a new vCenter Server Appliance with temporary network settings. The temporary networking is needed because the old vCSA 5.x will be copying data to the new vCSA 6.0. Once the data and settings are finished copying to the new vCenter Server Appliance, the old vCSA can power down. The new vCSA then assumes the vCenter's IP address and identity.

NOTE   Upgrading a vCenter Server Appliance that is registered with an external vCenter Single Sign-On server is supported for vCenter Server Appliance 5.1 Update 3 and 5.5.x to version 6.0 Update 1.

Consider the following prerequisites to upgrading vCSA:

- The versions of existing vCenter Server Appliance that can be directly upgraded are vCSA 5.1 Update 3 and vCenter Server Appliance 5.5.

- vCenter Server Appliance can be deployed only on ESXi Hosts that are running version ESXi 5.0 or later.

- If clocks become unsynchronized, you might have authentications problems, and the vCenter Server may not start after the upgrade.

- Be sure to verify that there is additional disk space to accommodate the vCenter Server upgrade.

- Be sure to verify that the SSL certificate for the existing vCenter Server Appliance is configured correctly.

- Be sure to create a snapshot of the vCenter Server Appliance before you upgrade it.

- Be sure to upgrade the Client Integration Plug-In.

NOTE If you do not deploy vCenter Server Appliance with the correct FQDNs, you must regenerate the certificates.

Follow these steps to perform the upgrade of the vCenter Server Appliance:

Step 1. Upgrade the Client Integration Plug-In by double-clicking `vcsa-setup.html` in the software directory.

Step 2. Wait up to 3 seconds for the browser to detect the Client Integration Plug-In and allow the plug-in to run on the browser when prompted.

Step 3. On the Home page, click **Upgrade**.

Step 4. When you get a warning about upgrading, click **OK** to begin the upgrade of the vCenter Server Appliance.

Step 5. Read and accept the license agreement and click **Next**.

Step 6. In the vCenter Server Appliance Deployment window that appears, enter the FQDN or IP address of the ESXi Host where the vCenter Server Appliance will be installed. Also enter the username `root` and password for the `root` user on the ESXi Host.

Step 7. Accept any certificate warning by clicking **Yes**.

Step 8. Enter the name of the vCenter Server Appliance 6.0 and authentication information for the ESXi Host.

Step 9. On the Select Appliance Size page of the wizard, select the vCenter Server Appliance size for the vSphere inventory size and click **Next**. Table 7-2 lists the options and descriptions for this field.

Table 7-2 vCenter Server Appliance CPU and Memory Choices

Option	Description
Tiny (up to 10 hosts, 100 VMs)	Deploys appliance with 2 CPUs and 8 GB of memory
Small (up to 100 hosts, 1000 VMs)	Deploys appliance with 4 CPUs and 16 GB of memory
Medium (up to 400 hosts, 4000 VMs)	Deploys appliance with 8 CPUs and 24 GB of memory
Large (up to 1000 hosts, 10,000 VMs)	Deploys appliance with 16 CPUs and 32 GB of memory

Step 10. Select the datastore where all the virtual machine configuration files and virtual disks will be stored.

Step 11. On the Setup Temporary Network page, set up a temporary network. The new appliance requires temporary network settings during the migration as data is migrated from the existing appliance to the new appliance. After the migration completes, the new appliance assumes the network identity of the existing appliance.

Step 12. On the Ready to Complete page, click **Finish** to complete the process.

Given a Scenario, Determine the Upgrade Compatibility of an Environment

Company ABCD wants to upgrade to vCenter Server 6.0. The company has a large environment with almost 700 ESXi Hosts and 7000 virtual machines. You want to run the vCenter Server on a Virtual Machine server and have an embedded Platform Services Controller. Therefore, you want only one virtual machine to run both the vCenter Server Services and Platform Services Controller.

Here are the planned components for vCenter Server:

- OS = Microsoft Windows Server 2008 R2
- vCPUs = 8
- RAM = 24 GB

For the Windows OS, vCenter Server requires a 64-bit operating system, and the earliest Windows Server version that vCenter Server supports is Windows Server 2008 SP2. The conclusion is that the planned VM's OS will meet the minimum software requirements.

The hardware must meet the minimum specific requirements for the vCenter Server to run on either a virtual machine or physical server running Microsoft Windows.

In addition, the vCenter Server can be embedded with both the Platform Services Controller and vCenter Server Service on the same machine. If both components are on the same machine, you need to add an additional 2 CPUs and 2 GB of RAM to the minimum hardware requirements. When you install vCenter Server, the minimum hardware requirements are based on the expected size of the vSphere environment. Table 7-3 shows the virtual CPU and virtual RAM of the Windows vCenter Server, depending on the environment size you select.

Table 7-3 Minimum Hardware Requirements for Windows vCenter Server

	Tiny Environment (up to 10 Hosts, 100 VMs)	Small Environment (up to 100 Hosts, 1000 VMs)	Medium Environment (up to 400 Hosts, 4000 VMs)	Large Environment (up to 1000 Hosts, 10,000 VMs)
CPUs	2	4	8	16
Memory	8 GB RAM	16 GB RAM	24 GB RAM	32 GB RAM

Scenario Conclusion

Based on the minimum recommended hardware requirements for running vCenter Server on a Windows Machine, the ABCD Company would be classified as a large environment. In addition, the Platform Services Controller will add an additional 2 CPUs and 2 GB of RAM. Therefore, the Windows vCenter Server needs at least 18 CPUs and 34 GB of RAM. The conclusion is that the proposed VM does not meet the minimum hardware requirements because the proposed VM has only 8 vCPUs and 24 GB of RAM.

Determine Correct Order of Steps to Upgrade a vSphere Implementation

When upgrading vSphere, it is important to follow a particular order, and it is different from the order in which vSphere is installed. There are a few steps to take before upgrading:

Step 1. Read the vSphere release notes.

Step 2. Verify that your systems meet the vSphere hardware and software requirements.

Step 3. If your vSphere system includes VMware solutions or plug-ins, verify that they are compatible with vSphere 6.0.

Step 4. Verify that you have backed up your environment.

Step 5.   Upgrade vCenter Server.

Step 6.   Upgrade vSphere Update Manager.

Step 7.   Upgrade ESXi Hosts.

Step 8.   Reconnect the hosts to the vCenter Server system and apply a new license.

Step 9.   Upgrade to the latest version of VMware Tools on the VM's guest OS.

Step 10.   Upgrade the virtual machine's hardware version.

The process is important when it comes to upgrading vSphere from an existing version to vSphere 6.0. Following these steps as listed will help ensure a successful upgrade. It is important that as you complete each step, you check the functionality before continuing to the next step. For example, the vCenter Server must not only be upgraded in step 5, but it also needs to be working before you upgrade Update Manager. You might need to stop and restart the vCenter Server before going to the next step.

Summary

You have now read the chapter covering exam topics related to upgrading vSphere to version 6.0. This chapter discusses two objectives. The first one is Objective 4.1—Perform ESXi Host and Virtual Machine Upgrades. The second one is Objective 4.2—Perform vCenter Server Upgrades. Understanding both of these objectives will help prepare you for the certification exam.

Exam Preparation Tasks

Review All the Key Topics

Table 7-4 provides a reference to each of the key topics identified in this chapter. Take a few moments to review each of these specific items.

Table 7-4   Key Topics for Chapter 7

Key Topic Element	Description	Pages
List	Update Manager tasks	263
Note	Ensure that the Update Manager server and client plug-ins are the same version	263

Key Topic Element	Description	Pages
Figure 7-1	Download vSphere upgrade sources	265
Note	Cannot download update sources and use shared repository together	265
List	ESXi requirements	265
Figure 7-2	Import ESXi image	266
Figure 7-3	Create ESXi Host baseline	267
Figure 7-4	Switch to the compliance view	267
Figure 7-5	Attach baseline to a host or cluster	268
Figure 7-6	Baseline attached to the lab cluster	268
Figure 7-7	After scanning ESXi Hosts are non-compliant	269
Figure 7-8	Remediation selection	270
Figure 7-9	Upgrade vSphere Distributed Switch	271
Note	Automated VMware Tools only supported for Windows or Linux guest operating systems	271
Figure 7-10	VMware Tools version information	272
List	Prerequisites upgrade VM hardware version	273
List	Upgrade methods for vSphere 6.0	273
List	Upgrade script locations	275
List	Different upgrade versions deployment models	277
Figure 7-11	Embedded deployment option	278
Figure 7-12	External deployment option	278
Note	Upgrade vCenter Server Appliance supported for versions 5.1 Update 3 and 6.0 Update 1	281
Note	Regenerate certificates if vCenter Server is not deployed with the correct FQDNs	282

Complete the Tables and Lists from Memory

Print a copy of Appendix B, "Memory Tables" (found on the CD), or at least the section for this chapter, and complete the tables and lists from memory. Appendix C, "Memory Tables Answer Key," also on the CD, includes completed tables and lists to check your work.

Definitions of Key Terms

Define the following key terms from this chapter and check your answers in the glossary.

vSphere Update Manager (VUM), vSphere Update Manager Download Service (UMDS), baseline, baseline group, vCenter Server Appliance (vCSA)

Answer Review Questions

The answers to these review questions can be found in Appendix A.

1. Which of the following statements about upgrading vCenter Server Appliance is incorrect?

   a. If you do not deploy vCenter Server Appliance with the correct FQDNs, you must regenerate the certificates.

   b. An existing vCenter Server with version 5.1 Update 2 is supported for upgrading to vCenter Server 6.0.

   c. A prerequisite to upgrading vCSA is to synchronize the clocks in the vSphere environment.

   d. A prerequisite to upgrading vCSA is to verify that the SSL certificate for the existing vCenter Server Appliance is configured correctly.

2. Which of the following is not a requirement to upgrade an ESXi Host to version 6.0?

   a. Boot device with a minimum 1 GB

   b. A minimum of 4 GB of physical RAM

   c. At least two CPU cores

   d. 32-bit x86 CPU processor

3. Which of the following commands is used to upgrade an ESXi Host?

   a. `viupgrade`

   b. `esxupdate`

   c. `esxcfg-upgrade`

   d. `esxcli`

This chapter covers the following objective:

- **Objective 5.1—Configure Advanced/Multilevel Resource Pools**

  - Understand/apply

  - Determine the effect of the Expandable Reservation parameter on resource allocation

  - Create a resource pool hierarchical structure

  - Configure custom resource pool attributes

  - Determine how resource pools apply to vApps

  - Describe vFlash architecture

  - Create/remove a resource pool

  - Add/remove virtual machines from a resource pool

  - Create/delete vFlash resource pool

  - Assign vFlash resources to VMDKs

  - Given a scenario, determine appropriate shares, reservations, and limits for hierarchical resource pools

## CHAPTER 8

Resource Pools

Resource pools ease management of resource allocations in a way that does not happen by default and is not possible on a per-VM basis. The problem with attempting to manage individual virtual machine's resource controls is that it becomes an administrative near impossibility. Resource pools provide a much easier way of managing large numbers of VM resource allocations and provide predictable allocation of resources during periods of resource competition.

"Do I Know This Already?" Quiz

The "Do I Know This Already?" quiz allows you to assess whether you should study this entire chapter or move quickly to the "Exam Preparation Tasks" section. Regardless, the authors recommend that you read the entire chapter at least once. Table 8-1 outlines the major headings in this chapter and the corresponding "Do I Know This Already?" quiz questions. You can find the answers in Appendix A, "Answers to the 'Do I Know This Already?' Quizzes and Review Questions."

Table 8-1 "Do I Know This Already?" Foundation Topics Section-to-Question Mapping

Foundation Topics Section	Questions Covered in This Section
Understand/Apply	1, 3, 5
Determine the Effect of the Expandable Reservation Parameter on Resource Allocation	7
Create a Resource Pool Hierarchical Structure	2
Configure Custom Resource Pool Attributes	8
Determine How Resource Pools Apply to vApps	6
Describe vFlash Architecture	4
Create/Remove a Resource Pool	9
Add/Remove Virtual Machines from a Resource Pool	10
Assign vFlash Resources to VMDKs	11

1. Which of the following is configured for virtual machines by default?

   a. Reservations

   b. Limits

   c. Shares

   d. Expandable reservations

2. From where does a resource pool expand when an expandable reservation is used?

   a. From the resource pool's children pools

   b. From the resource pool's parent pool

   c. From the resource pool's sibling pools

   d. From other ESXi Hosts

3. In which places can resource pools be created? (Choose two.)

   a. Standalone ESXi Hosts

   b. HA cluster

   c. DRS cluster

   d. vSAN cluster

4. In which ways does vFRC benefit vSphere environments? (Choose two.)

   a. It speeds up vMotion migrations.

   b. It speeds up VM provisioning operations.

   c. It utilizes local SSD on ESXi Hosts as a read cache for VM disk I/O.

   d. It allows the ESXi Hosts to swap to cache during periods of contention.

5. When would a limit be used?

   a. To prevent a VM from monopolizing memory resources

   b. To prevent a VM from powering on

   c. To limit the number of virtual machines in a resource pool

   d. When a server owner requests a VM with more RAM than an application needs

6. Which of the following could be a child object of a resource pool? (Choose three.)

   a. DRS cluster

   b. VM

   c. Resource pool

   d. ESXi Host

   e. vApps

7. If a virtual machine's collective reservations exceed the resource pool's unreserved capacity, and expandable reservations are enabled, from where can the resource pool borrow the extra capacity? (Choose two.)

   a. From its parent

   b. From its grandparent

   c. From its sibling resource pool

   d. From its child objects

   e. From another ESXi Host

8. When defining a custom value for a virtual machine's CPU shares, what is the maximum value an administrator can define?

   a. 10,000

   b. 100,000

   c. 1,000,000

   d. 20,000

9. If a resource pool containing virtual machines is deleted, what happens to the virtual machines in the resource pool?

   a. They are removed from the inventory.

   b. They are deleted from disk.

   c. They are evenly distributed between the sibling resource pools.

   d. They are placed in the resource pool's parent.

10. How can you place virtual machines in a resource pool? (Choose two.)

   a. Drag them from the Navigator pane one at a time.

   b. Hold down the **Shift** key and select multiple VMs from the Navigator pane and then drag them into the pool.

   c. Select a higher inventory object, select the **Related Objects** > **Virtual Machines** tab, and hold down the **Shift** key and select multiple VMs and drag them into the Navigator pane.

   d. Right-click the resource pool from the Navigator pane and select **Add Virtual Machines**.

   e. Right-click the resource pool from the Navigator pane, select **Edit Settings**, and select **Add Virtual Machines**.

11. Which of the following is *not* an available setting when defining vFRC for a virtual machine?

   a. Enabling vFRC for one of the virtual disks

   b. Enabling vFRC for all of the virtual disks

   c. Defining the block size of the vFRC

   d. Defining the vFRC scan time

Foundation Topics

Objective 5.1—Configure Advanced/Multilevel Resource Pools

There are default resource allocation definitions for all virtual machines, but the default mechanism treats all like-configured virtual machines the same. In reality, VMs and their applications have multiple different priorities and relative importance, and it doesn't make sense to treat them as equal. Some people assume that they will never have resource contention, but planning for resource contention is like an insurance policy. It's nice to not need it, but when it is needed, it's nice to have planned for it beforehand.

Understand/Apply

Resource pools allow the prioritization of resources to more important virtual machines when resources are under constraint. They can also be used to limit access to resources or guarantee access to resources. Resource pools can be created either on a standalone ESXi Host (one that is not a member of a DRS cluster object) or on a DRS cluster object. Resource pools can be nested within one another, but you cannot define any more than 8 pools deep. However, each host can support up to 1600 resource pools (which is also the maximum number of resource pools per cluster) and 1100 child resource pools.

If resource pools exist on a DRS cluster, and DRS is turned off for the cluster object, the resource pools and their hierarchy disappear, but they can be backed up and restored later if needed. This is explored in more detail in Chapter 13, "Troubleshoot Clusters."

Resource pools have three attributes, much like individual virtual machine resource controls:

- **Shares:** Shares determine relative priority when resources are under contention. If there is competition, VMs or resource pools with more shares will get more of the resource than VMs or resource pools with fewer shares. Share values have four possible settings: high, normal, low, or custom. Shares always maintain a 4:2:1 ratio by default for high, normal, and low. Table 8-2 shows a breakdown of how shares are defined for CPU and memory for virtual machines versus resource pools. By default, all shares are set to normal shares for both VMs and resource pools, illustrating how everything is set to be more-or-less equal by default.

- **Reservations:** Reservations determine a minimum guaranteed amount of the resource that must be available at time of power on, and if that amount is not available, the virtual machine is not allowed to power on. Reservations can never be taken away, so if they are set too high and a virtual machine is not using its reservation, no other virtual machine can use any of that resource; this limits access to the physical resource. If too many reservations are set too high, too often, virtual machines may not be able to be powered on. By default, there are no reservations set for VMs or resource pools, and reservations are expandable, so if the VMs' reservations inside the resource pool exceed the reservation of the pool, the VMs can potentially borrow resources from the resource pool's parent. We will discuss expandable reservations in more detail in the next section, "Determine the Effect of the Expandable Reservation Parameter on Resource Allocation." For resource pools, reservations are set aside and cannot exceed the current unreserved capacity. So, even if a resource pool is empty, its reservations cannot be used by other VMs or resource pools. If reservations are to be used, they should be set to the minimum amount of resource a virtual machine needs 100% of the time because if there is a percentage of the time that a virtual machine is not using the resource, no other VM can use it.

- **Limits:** You can place an upper limit, or cap, on how much of a resource can be consumed by a virtual machine or group of virtual machines. Limits are typically used in response to a misconfigured virtual machine or resource pool that is consuming too much of a resource and negatively impacting more important virtual machines. By default, there are no limits set for VMs or resource pools, and limits are set to unlimited (that is, the **Unlimited** check box is selected). Setting too many limits effectively limits access to the physical resources, preventing full resource utilization. Since a VM or resource pool can never consume more than the limit, it doesn't matter if no other VM or resource pool is using the extra resource. As a result, typically limits are set in response to a misconfigured or oversized VM or resource pool consuming too much of a resource, negatively impacting more important VMs or resource pools.

Table 8-2   Share Allocations for VMs Versus Resource Pools

	VM CPU Share Values	VM Memory Share Values	Resource Pool CPU Share Values	Resource Pool Memory Share Values
High	2000 shares per vCPU	20 shares per MB of configured RAM	8000	327680
Normal	1000 shares per vCPU	10 shares per MB of configured RAM	4000	163840
Low	500 shares per vCPU	5 shares per MB of configured RAM	2000	81920

NOTE   It is best practice to not allow VMs and resource pools to be siblings. Otherwise, when there is contention, it is very likely for the VMs inside the pool to lose out in competition with VMs outside the pools.

Determine the Effect of the Expandable Reservation Parameter on Resource Allocation

Expandable reservations allow resource pools to grow because they allow more virtual machines to power on even if their collective reservations exceed the resource pools reservations, provided that the resource pool's parent pool has sufficient capacity to meet the reservation. Admission control checks to make sure the reservation can be met at the time of power on. If the reservation can be met, the reservation is taken, and the virtual machine is allowed to power on. If the reservation cannot be met, admission control checks to see if the resource pool is expandable. If the resource pool is expandable, admission control checks to see if the parent pool can meet the reservation. This continues until there is nowhere left to expand or until the reservation can be met. Expandable reservations could allow misconfigured virtual machines or resource pools to consume all the unused capacity, which would result in no extra resource being available to power on other VMs. As a result, they can provide more flexibility but less protection.

Consider this story to better understand expandable reservations: Envision three rooms, at three different levels: a top room, a middle room, and a lower room. Each room has four chairs, and each room is expandable, meaning it can borrow from its parent room. Four people come into the first room, each with a reservation for one chair. The room is now full, but assume it is expandable. Four more people come in, each with a reservation for one chair. The first room is full, but because it is expandable, it can use chairs from the next room. Now that room is full, but it is also expandable, so when four more people show up to the first room, each with a reservation for one chair, it is full but expandable, and it checks the second room. The second room is full as well, but it also is expandable. The four remaining people are able to get the four chairs in the last room. However, now all of the chairs in each of the three rooms have been taken, so no other people can enter the room with reservations because there are no unreserved chairs left. It is useful to note that in this analogy, the people who took the chairs also have to be the same ones to release them. In other words, the people using the chairs in the last room (or the root) have to be the ones to give them up in order for that room to reclaim its chairs—even if all the other rooms are empty.

Create a Resource Pool Hierarchical Structure

As resource pools can be nested, it may be necessary in a sufficiently large environment to provide more than just one level of resource pools (as shown in Figure 8-1). For example, there could be resource pools for different departments, and each department could have its own resource pools. It is important, then, to understand the different levels of resource pools and to identify what levels compete with each other.

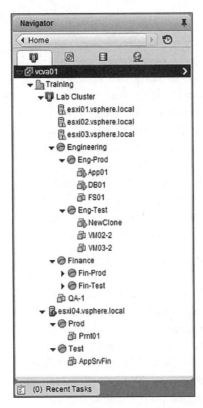

Figure 8-1   Resource Pool Hierarchy

In Figure 8-1, the resource pools are identified as follows:

- The Lab Cluster object is identified as a root resource pool.

- The Engineering and Finance pools are child resource pools and are siblings to each other.

- The Eng-Prod and Eng-Test resource pools are child pools of the Engineering pool and are siblings with each other.

- The VM QA-1 is not in a resource pool, and as such is directly in the root resource pool, and it is a sibling with the Engineering and Finance resource pools; this is a bad setup because the VM will directly compete with the resource pools. This has been done to illustrate what it would look like in the interface, and it is arguable that because the VM is powered off and stays powered off, it wouldn't pose a problem.

- The Fin-Prod and Fin-Test resource pools are child pools of the Finance pool and are siblings with each other.

- The VMs in the Eng-Prod resource pool are siblings with each other, and their direct parent is the Eng-Prod pool.

- ESXi04.vsphere.local is an ESXi Host outside the cluster, and it is another root resource pool. It has two resource pools that are siblings with each other: Prod and Test.

Be aware that the VMs in this example within the Fin-Prod pool do not directly compete with VMs in any other resource pools. They indirectly compete through their pools. VMs in each pool compete with each other for a piece of the pool's resource. As a result, it is important to understand that the way resources get divided can become quite complex when you're dealing with large numbers of VMs and hierarchical resource pools. Reservations must always be met at power on and can expand to parent pools (as explained in the section "Determine the Effect of the Expandable Reservation Parameter on Resource Allocation"). Limits are hard limits and cannot be exceeded. However, shares, which cannot be avoided, determine a relative priority. So if administrators were carving up the resource pools with the default share values but weren't paying attention to the numbers of VMs in each pool, they might find that once there is contention, the pool with the largest number of VMs may get fewer resources than otherwise expected.

For example, in Figure 8-2, we see three resource pools with the default share values for high, normal, and low, and we end up with a predictable allocation of resources in the event of contention (following the 4:2:1 ratio for high, normal, and low).

High, Normal, and Low Resource Pools

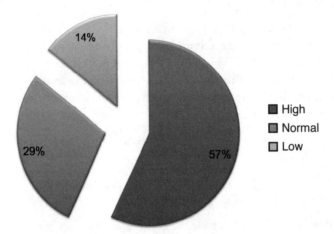

Figure 8-2   Resource Pools with Default Values

The interesting thing about this is that when you see it graphed out, it may be surprising at first that the high pool ends up getting 4/7 of the total overall resources in the event of contention (8000 shares out of 14,000 total shares), with the normal pool getting only 2/7 (4000 out of 14,000 total shares), and the low pool getting only 1/7 (2000 out of 14,000 total shares). This may on the surface be acceptable, but what happens many times is that if administrators are not careful with the distribution of VMs in each pool, they could end up with an uneven distribution, with resources not distributed fairly, as illustrated in Figure 8-3.

Resource Pools With Uneven Numbers of VMs

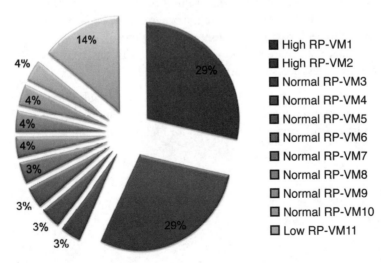

Figure 8-3   Uneven Resource Pools

In Figure 8-3, there are two VMs in the high pool, eight VMs in the normal pool, and only one VM in the low pool. This could happen, because more VMs may be categorized as normal than low or high. However, we see that the high pool VMs (High RP-VM1 and High RP-VM2) get the majority of the resource, but remember that resource pools compete with each other. So, if there is contention present, these two VMs end up each getting 1/2 of the 4/7 of the total resource, or about 29% of the total overall resource (assuming full competition). Then the interesting thing is that in this example, the one VM in the low pool (Low RP-VM11) ends up getting more resources than any of the VMs in the normal pool. This is because the low VM has a pool unto itself and doesn't directly compete with any other VMs. So the low pool VM ends up getting 1/7 of the total overall resource, or 14%. Then each VM in the normal pool would end up getting 1/8 of 2/7 of the resource, or 3% to 4% of the total overall resource, assuming full competition.

This is a good illustration of the planning required to determine how to divide up resource pools. Administrators need to further analyze the situation to reprioritize VMs and move some from the normal pool to low or high. If there is an even number or a somewhat equal number of VMs in each pool, resource distribution ends up being a lot more predictable, as illustrated in Figure 8-4. Here, there are still 11 total VMs, but now the high pool has 4 VMs, the normal pool has 4 VMs, and the low pool has 3 VMs. As a result of moving these VMs, if there is full competition for the resource, the low pool VMs get the least, the normal pool VMs get twice that of low, and the high pool VMs get twice that of the normal pool, as would be expected.

Evenly Distributed VMs in Resource Pools

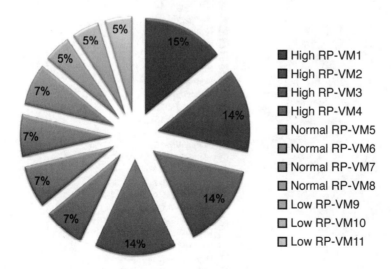

Figure 8-4 Evenly Distributed Resource Pools

Another thing to think about, as an option, is that if it is not possible to have an even number of VMs in each pool, then it can be useful to adjust the resource pool values to have custom values instead of the predefined high, normal, and low share values. This is discussed in the next section, "Configure Custom Resource Pool Attributes."

Another issue that happens often in environments is that vSphere administrators decide to slowly roll out resource pools. What happens then is that, in an effort to prioritize the most critical workloads first, the business-critical or mission-critical VMs get placed in a high-priority pool, and then no other VMs are placed in a re-source pool. This causes VMs and resource pools to be siblings in the resource pool hierarchy, which is never a good idea. To illustrate this, Figure 8-5 shows 25 total VMs, 10 of which are in the high resource pool, and 15 VMs outside the resource pool. The impact is that because there are 10 VMs in the pool, they each get 1/10 of 8000 shares. Since each VM has normal shares in this example, that's 15,000 total shares for the VMs outside the pool plus the 8000 shares for the pool, or a total of 23,000 total shares. The VMs outside the pool each get 1/23 of the total resource (around 4%), and the VMs in the pool each get 1/10 of 8/23 of the resource, or about 3%. This is a minor difference, but the point is that the VMs in the high pool that were supposed to be high priority end up getting slightly less resource than if they hadn't been placed in a pool to begin with. This may seem overly simplistic, but in reality, the number of critical VMs may end up being somewhat close to this, while the VMs outside the pool would most likely be a much larger number, further negatively affecting the performance of the critical VMs.

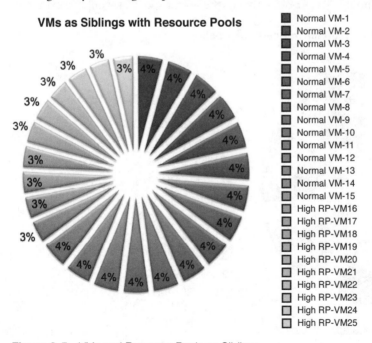

Figure 8-5   VMs and Resource Pools as Siblings

Configure Custom Resource Pool Attributes

When building or modifying a resource pool, it is possible to define custom shares as well as limits and reservations. When defining custom share values for memory and/or CPU in a resource pool, it is important to consider the total shares between all competing resource pools as well as numbers of VMs in each pool. For resource pools, the custom shares for CPU or memory can be any number between 0 and 1,000,000. Another thing to consider is to ensure that all share values be relative to each other. For example, even if one resource pool is vastly more important than another, it still wouldn't justify setting the important pool's custom share value to 1,000,000 shares, and the less important resource pool to 10. If there is any competition for the resource, the resource pool (and all VMs within it) in the low-importance resource pool would get a very small amount of resource.

It is possible to schedule changes to resource controls such as limits, reservations, and shares to address different peak usage times for applications if so desired. Administrators can define a one-time scheduled change, or even a recurring daily or weekly scheduled change. For example, Monday morning, a VM could have an increased number of shares and no limits, and on Tuesday morning, another scheduled event could lower the number of shares and impose a limit. It is important to document such a change fully because too many recurring scheduled resource changes can cause difficulty in troubleshooting whenever resources are under constraint.

Determine How Resource Pools Apply to vApps

vApps, are, in fact, resource pools. Although they offer far more functionality than resource pools, they are still resource pools. They have their own shares, reservations, and limits that can be defined for the VMs within the vApp. As a result, when placed within a resource pool, the VMs in the vApp are then in a child resource pool within the resource pool where they have just been added.

Describe vFlash Architecture

vFlash Read Cache (vFRC), introduced in vSphere 5.5, allows read caching of VM I/O requests. This essentially creates another storage tier between the ESXi servers and the physical storage (local or remote). Setting up a resource pool that utilizes vFRC and can benefit from the performance increase vFlash can provide requires multiple steps. First, ESXi servers need to have at least one SSD, and ESXi servers and vCenter must be at vSphere 5.5 (Enterprise Plus) or newer, and VMs need to be at virtual machine hardware version 10 or later.

To begin, each ESXi Host needs to have the vFlash capability enabled. To do this from the hosts and clusters view of the vSphere Web Client:

Step 1.   Right-click the ESXi Host and select **Storage** -> **Add Virtual Flash Resource Capacity** (see Figure 8-6).

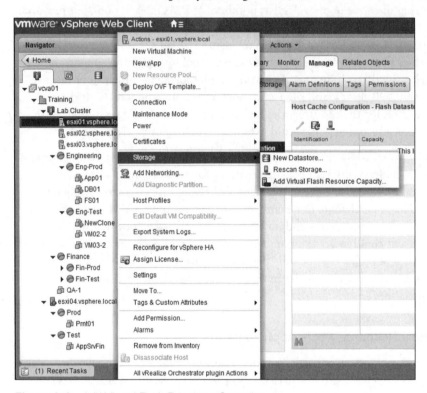

Figure 8-6   Add Virtual Flash Resource Capacity

Step 2.   Select the local disk to use for vFRC. Be aware of the warning that the chosen disk will be formatted and all existing data will be erased (see Figure 8-7).

Another way to do this is to right-click the cluster object, select **Storage -> Add Virtual Flash Resource Capacity**, and then select each disk from each ESXi Host (see Figure 8-8).

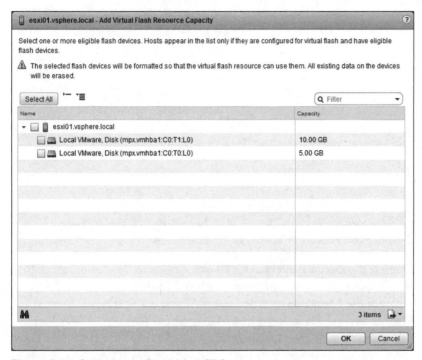

Figure 8-7   Select Virtual Disk(s) for vFRC

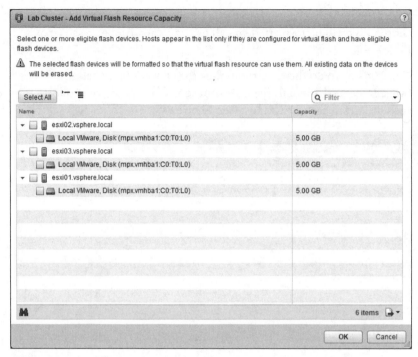

Figure 8-8   Add Virtual Flash Resource Capacity for Multiple Hosts

Step 3.   Once vFRC has been enabled for all of the hosts in the cluster, check to ensure that it has been configured per host. To do this, select an ESXi server in the Navigator pane and select **Manage > Settings > Virtual Flash > Virtual Flash Resource Management** (see Figure 8-9). Here, you can determine the capacity for the virtual Flash Read cache (see Figure 8-10). You may see space consumed for capacity if the ESXi servers have been configured for the ESXi Hosts to use this space for swapping. After vFRC has been enabled for the hosts, it then has to be configured for each VM that needs to use, or can benefit from, the read cache, as explored in the section, "Assign vFlash Resources to VMDKs."

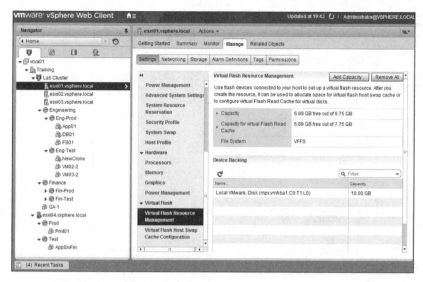

Figure 8-9   Virtual Flash Resource Management

Note that once vFRC has been configured for all hosts in the cluster, the ESXi Hosts themselves can also use this virtual flash pool for .vswp during periods of heavy contention. This is not a requirement for VMs to utilize vFRC, and it is an added benefit; if there is so much contention that memory pages have to get swapped to the .vswp files, the hypervisor can use the vFlash pool for caching the reads of the .vswp files. This dramatically reduces the negative performance caused by utilizing .vswp under extremely low memory conditions.

During vMotion migrations, the cache has to be moved with the VM. This can cause the vMotion migration to take longer, however, because the cache is also being moved, and it doesn't have to "warm up" after the migration. In other words, the cache is ready to be used on the destination host. If vFRC is turned off for the VM prior to the migration, this is not the case. When performing a vMotion migration, administrators are prompted to identify what will happen to the cache: migrate the cache contents or not (see Figure 8-11). DRS also does not migrate VMs with vFRC automatically unless a high-priority recommendation is generated as a result of affinity/anti-affinity rules, maintenance mode, or serious load imbalance. As a result, DRS considers the virtual machine with the virtual flash reservation as having a soft affinity for the host on which the VM currently resides.

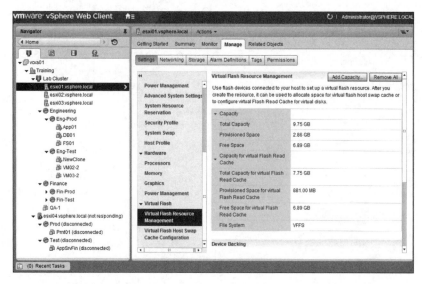

Figure 8-10   Additional Virtual Flash Resource Management Information

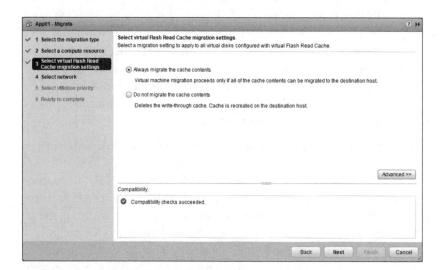

Figure 8-11   Migrate Cache Contents

Create/Remove a Resource Pool

To create a resource pool, right-click a cluster or standalone ESXi Host in the navigator pane and choose **New Resource Pool** (see Figure 8-12).

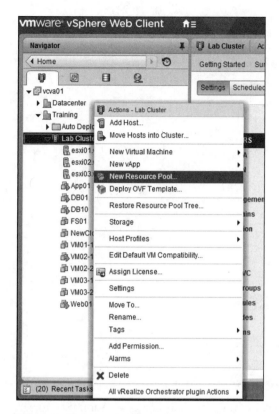

Figure 8-12   New Resource Pool

In the New Resource Pool Wizard that appears, define a name for the resource pool, as well as CPU and memory shares, reservations, and limits (see Figure 8-13).

To remove a resource pool, right-click the resource pool in the Navigator pane and select **Delete**. A popup appears, requesting confirmation on this action. When a resource pool is deleted, any VMs within that pool are placed in the parent resource pool.

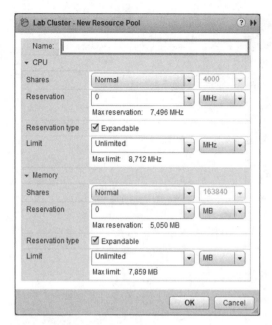

Figure 8-13   New Resource Pool Wizard

Add/Remove Virtual Machines from a Resource Pool

Adding VMs to a resource pool is a pretty straightforward process. Administrators can move one VM at a time or multiple VMs. From the Navigator pane, left-click a VM that needs to be added to the resource pool and drag it into the resource pool. All of the VM's existing shares, reservations, and limits stay with the VM, but now it gets a share of the resource pool's resources and competes with the other VMs in that pool.

> **NOTE**   The web client may not refresh when you're dragging VMs into resource pools. If they do not look like they moved, refresh the vSphere Web Client manually.

To move multiple VMs, select a higher-level inventory object in the Navigator pane, such as the cluster object, and select the **Related Objects > Virtual Machines** tab. From here, select multiple VMs by holding down either the **Ctrl** or **Shift** key and dragging the selected VMs from the Virtual Machines tab into the resource pool in the Navigator pane.

Removing a VM from a resource pool is exactly the opposite of placing the VM in the resource pool: Left-click the VM in the resource pool in the Navigator pane and drag it to a higher-inventory object, such as a parent pool or the root resource pool.

When creating virtual machines, or deploying VMs from templates, or cloning virtual machines, you can place the new virtual machines into a resource pool when prompted to choose a computing resource.

Create/Delete vFlash Resource Pool

We have discussed how to configure vFlash on a cluster object and for each ESXi Host. We have also explored how this can be used for .vswp to reduce the performance penalty that results from swapping. The next section, "Assign vFlash Resources to VMDKs," explores defining vFlash resources for individual virtual disks.

In this chapter we have explored creating resource pools and adding virtual machines to those pools. There isn't a way to create a resource pool specifically for vFlash, even once all the hosts have been configured for vFlash at the DRS cluster level. As a result, we do not explore a vFlash resource pool, since there really isn't any such thing. Instead, please refer to the sections on enabling vFlash for a cluster, hosts, and virtual disks.

Assign vFlash Resources to VMDKs

It is useful to know which virtual machines are more I/O intensive than others. It is also useful, if possible, to identify the block size that an application may require to better make use of the cache. Follow these steps to configure vFRC per VM:

Step 1.   Right-click the VM in the Navigator pane and select **Edit Settings**.

Step 2.   Expand the hard disk for which vFRC should be enabled. (It can be enabled for some or all of the virtual disks.)

Step 3.   Either enter the amount of cache this should use (see Figure 8-14) or click **Advanced**.

Step 4.   If **Advanced** was selected, select **Enable Virtual Flash Read Cache** and define the **Reservation** in GB for the virtual disk, and **Block Size** in KB (see Figure 8-15). This should align with the application I/O size requirements. The block size defined for vFRC can be between 4 KB and 1024 KB.

Figure 8-14   Define vFRC for Virtual Disk(s)

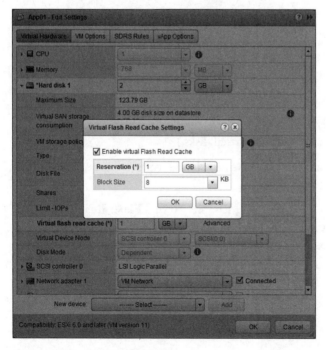

Figure 8-15   Advanced vFRC

Given a Scenario, Determine Appropriate Shares, Reservations, and Limits for Hierarchical Resource Pools

One of the most important factors in designing resource pools is understanding all the requirements and needs of an environment and doing all the planning up front. It is also important to understand the impact of the resource pools, the number of VMs in each pool, how many siblings/children there are, etc. It is important, then, to identify the relative importance of virtual machines and especially the applications within the virtual machines. vSphere administrators in many cases cannot simply ask end users, server owners, or application owners about the importance of their virtual machines because most likely they would respond that their VMs are the most important. It is important to identify business impact, criticality of the VM workload, and the sensitivity to latency of an application.

Consider a multi-tiered application consisting of a web server, an application server, and a database server. The database server may be used by multiple different applications. Some of those applications may be production, some may be testing and development applications, and some may be used by customers. In this type of scenario, it would be important to identify the number of VMs in each tier and their relative importance to each other. Once their relative importance and business criticality have been identified, you can start carving the tiers into different resource pools. You could start with one initial resource pool for the multi-tier app or apps and go from there. Since the database is probably the most important component of this multi-tier application, it would most likely need to be in a resource pool, with priority over resources during periods of contention, translating into more relative shares. Depending on the database resource consumption, it would most likely not need a limit, but perhaps a reservation may be prudent. In this case, it's useful to know how certain applications consume resources. Database servers, for example, have a tendency to consume all memory allocated to them, regardless of the size of the database(s). This is why it is so important to size VMs according to the resources they need. This server may end up with a reservation, and that reservation could possibly match the VM's memory allocation. This way, the VM would never suffer performance penalties of .vswp or ballooning. However, this could also be mitigated to some degree with vFRC. Shares would need to be defined to ensure priority during contention for CPU and memory, assuming reservations were not set to be equal to the VM's resource allocation.

The next thing to look at is the application server or servers. These VMs are reliant on the database server and are still important—but only for their specific application. If you are dealing with just two application servers, for example, and one is production and the other is test, then you could most likely put them in two separate resource pools, prioritizing production over test by using shares. It also may be prudent to define a reservation to be the lowest acceptable amount of resource the production application server requires, while not defining a reservation for the development pool application server. The test, or least important application server, may also have a limit defined on its resource pool.

Finally, there may be two or more web servers. For this example, let's say that each application has two web servers for redundancy. Because the web servers are what the users hit first, it may be useful to put them in resource pools with a small reservation so that there is some physical resource guaranteed. The reservation for the production web servers would most likely be higher than that of the resource pool for the test web servers. The production web servers' resource pool would also most likely have a higher share value than the test resource pool.

This discussion illustrates just some of the issues involved in thinking through the design for a hierarchical resource pool structure for something as simple as a multi-tier app. It could obviously become far more complex with more database servers and more different levels beyond test and production, such as QA, staging, etc. The same decisions would be made, however, regarding identifying the relative priority of each of the VMs, deciding how many pools and how many layers deep they would need to be to split them up accordingly, and whether limits, reservations, shares, or a combination of all three would be prudent and useful for each level of the resource pool hierarchy.

Summary

This chapter has discussed many of the intricacies of resource pools as well as potential issues resulting from configuring them incorrectly (or improperly). This chapter has also discussed vFRC, how to configure it for VMs and hosts, and why it may be useful. Remember to plan out a resource pool implementation fully before deploying a single resource pool; if you don't, when contention occurs, there may be a less-than-predictable allocation of resources. You should now use information in the following sections to complete your preparation for Objective 5.1.

Exam Preparation Tasks

Review All the Key Topics

Table 8-3 provides a reference to each of the key topics identified in this chapter. Take a few moments to review each of these specific items.

Table 8-3   Key Topics for Chapter 8

Key Topic Element	Description	Pages
Paragraph	Resource pool hierarchy	296
Paragraph	Determine vFlash Read Cache status	304
Paragraph	Add/remove VMs from resource pool	307

Complete the Tables and Lists from Memory

Print a copy of Appendix B, "Memory Tables" (found on the CD), or at least the section for this chapter, and complete the tables and lists from memory. Appendix C, "Memory Tables Answer Key," also on the CD, includes completed tables and lists to check your work.

Definitions of Key Terms

Define the following key terms from this chapter and check your answers in the glossary.

share, reservation, limit, expandable reservation, Virtual Flash Read Cache (vFRC)

Answer Review Questions

The answers to these review questions can be found in Appendix A.

1. On which of the following can vFRC *not* be defined?

   a. On a cluster for all hosts

   b. On a host

   c. On a virtual disk

   d. On a resource pool

2. What is the maximum depth for resource pools?

   a. 8

   b. 12

   c. 10

   d. 6

3. What happens when a resource pool that contains VMs is deleted?

  a. The VMs are deleted from inventory.

  b. The VMs are removed from inventory.

  c. The VMs are placed in the parent resource pool.

  d. The VMs are kept in the resource pool, and an error message is generated.

4. What happens when you drag a VM with existing shares, reservations, and limits defined into a new resource pool?

  a. The existing settings are removed in favor of the resource pool settings.

  b. The existing settings are retained, and the VM is placed in the new pool.

  c. A prompt asks what you want to do with the existing resource allocations.

  d. A new child resource pool is created in the resource pool, and the VM is placed in that pool.

5. What would an ESXi Host use vFlash for if no VMs are configured to use vFRC?

  a. For caching swap when memory is under heavy contention

  b. For caching frequently accessed storage blocks

  c. For caching balloon driver elements

  d. For caching VM MAC addresses

6. Which of the following should *not* be siblings of a resource pool?

  a. Hosts

  b. Resource pools

  c. vApps

  d. VMs

This chapter covers the following objective:

- **Objective 6.1—Configure and Administer a vSphere Backups/Restore/ Replication Solution**

  - Compare and contrast vSphere Replication compression methods

  - Differentiate VMware Data Protection capabilities

  - Configure recovery point objective (RPO) for a protected virtual machine

  - Explain VMware Data Protection sizing guidelines

  - Create/delete/consolidate virtual machine snapshots

  - Install and configure VMware Data Protection

  - Create a backup job with VMware Data Protection

  - Backup/restore a virtual machine with VMware Data Protection

  - Install/configure/upgrade vSphere Replication

  - Configure VMware Certificate Authority (VMCA) integration with vSphere Replication

  - Configure vSphere Replication for single/multiple VMs

  - Recover a VM using vSphere Replication

  - Perform a failback operation using vSphere Replication

  - Deploy a pair of vSphere Replication virtual appliances

## CHAPTER 9

Backup and Recovery

This chapter covers exam topics related to backup, restoration, and replication.

"Do I Know This Already?" Quiz

The "Do I Know This Already?" quiz allows you to assess whether you should study this entire chapter or move quickly to the "Exam Preparation Tasks" section. Regardless, the authors recommend that you read the entire chapter at least once. Table 9-1 outlines the major headings in this chapter and the corresponding "Do I Know This Already?" quiz questions. You can find the answers in Appendix A, "Answers to the 'Do I Know This Already?' Quizzes and Review Questions."

Table 9-1 "Do I Know This Already?" Foundation Topics Section-to-Question Mapping

Foundation Topics Section	Questions Covered in This Section
Compare and Contrast vSphere Replication Compression Methods	1
Differentiate VMware Data Protection Capabilities	2
Explain VMware Data Protection Sizing Guidelines	3
Install and Configure VMware Data Protection	4
Create a Backup Job with VMware Data Protection	5
Backup/Restore a Virtual Machine with VMware Data Protection	6, 7
Install/Configure/Upgrade vSphere Replication	8
Perform a Failback Operation Using vSphere Replication	9
Deploy a Pair of vSphere Replication Virtual Appliances	10

1. Which of the following is the compression used by vSphere Replication?

   a. LZ77

   b. LZR

   c. FastLZ

   d. PPM

2. Which of the following is *not* a VMware Data Protection feature?

   a. Support for up to 500 virtual machines per VDP appliance

   b. Ability to back up and restore virtual machine–based Platform Service Controllers (PSCs)

   c. Ability to back up and restore virtual machine–based vCenter Servers and vCenter Server Appliances

   d. Ability to replicate backups to a VDP target, an Avamar server, or a Data Domain system

3. Which of the following are valid configurations for a VMware Data Protection appliance? (Choose three.)

   a. 0.5 TB

   b. 2 TB

   c. 3 TB

   d. 6 TB

   e. 10 TB

4. Which of the following is a valid URL for accessing the VDP configuration utility?

   a. `https://VDP-IP-adrress:8543/vdp`

   b. `https://VDP-IP-adrress:8543/vdp-configure/`

   c. `https://VDP-IP-adrress:5480/vdp-configure/`

   d. `https://VDP-IP-adrress:5480/vdp`

5. Which of the following is *not* a valid retention option when creating a backup job with VDP?

   a. **Forever**

   b. **Custom Retention Schedule**

   c. **For** *a specified number of days*

   d. **Until** *the next backup job completes*

6. Which of the following is a valid scenario where you could choose the **Restore to Original Location** option?

    a. Restore to the original location and overwrite any existing VMDK files.

    b. Restore to the original location, where the original virtual machine has been deleted.

    c. Restore to the original location, where an associated virtual disk has been deleted.

    d. All of the above are valid.

7. Which of the following can be used to restore a virtual machine running the Platform Services Controller (PSC) when the vCenter Server is unavailable?

    a. vSphere Web Client

    b. VDP Configuration Utility

    c. vSphere Client

    d. `psc-restore -u username -p password`

8. Which of the following summarizes the steps that may be used to change the vCenter Server to which a vSphere Replication Appliance is registered?

    a. Use the vSphere Web Client to select the vSphere Replication Appliance and modify the **vCenter Server** setting.

    b. Use the VAMI to modify the **Connect to vCenter Server** setting.

    c. Use the VAMI to modify the **LookUp Service Address**, the **SSO Administrator** credentials, and the **vCenter Server Address**.

    d. Use the vSphere Web Client to select **Manage > vSphere Replication > Replication Servers**, select a virtual machine, and select **Register a virtual machine as VMware Replication Server**.

9. Which of the following summarizes the process for performing a failback using vSphere Replication?

    a. Reconfigure the replication in the reverse direction. Wait for replication to occur. Recover to the original source site.

    b. Right-click the virtual machine and select **vSphere Replication > Failback**.

    c. Right-click the virtual machine and select **Reprotect**.

    d. During the original process of configuring replication, select the **Allow Failback** option. After a recovery, right-click the virtual machine and select **Recover to Source**.

10. What is the maximum number of virtual appliances running the replication service per vCenter Server?

    a. 1

    b. 2

    c. 9

    d. 10

Foundation Topics

Objective 6.1—Configure and Administer a vSphere Backups/Restore/Replication Solution

The following sections describe how to back up and restore virtual machines using VMware Data Protection. They also describe how to protect and recover virtual machines using vSphere Replication.

Compare and Contrast vSphere Replication Compression Methods

VMware vSphere Replication 6 uses the FastLZ compression library, which is designed to provide a balance of solid speed, minimal CPU overhead, and good compression efficiency. When vSphere 6.0 and vSphere Replication 6 are deployed at the source and target locations, replicated data is compressed at the source and stays compressed until it is written to storage at the target. In a mixed configuration, packets may be decompressed at some point in the replication path. For example, if an ESXi 6.0 host is replicating to a vSphere Replication 5.8 virtual appliance, packets will not be compressed over the network. For another example, if an ESXi 6.0 Host is replicating to a vSphere Replication 6 virtual appliance, which is writing to vSphere 5.5 host storage, packets are compressed as they are sent from the source to the target, but they are decompressed in the appliance before being written to the target storage. Decompression in the vSphere Replication virtual appliance causes higher CPU utilization in the appliance. The greatest benefit from compression will be realized when running vSphere 6.0 and vSphere Replication 6 at both the source and target locations.

If ESXi 6.0 is used for the source and target, then compression is used end to end. If the source ESXi Host version is earlier than 6.0, then the **Enable Network Compression for VR Data** option is disabled in the replication wizard. If the source ESXi Host version is 6.0, but the version of the ESXi Host that manages the target datastore is earlier than 6.0, the source host sends compressed data to the vSphere Replication Server at the target, which decompresses the data (if no ESXi 6.0 hosts are found for the target datastore) and sends decompressed data to the ESXi Host.

If data compression is enabled and only ESXi 6.0 hosts are used (all hosts support data compression), then normal vMotion migrations can occur. If some hosts do not support compression (that is, if the ESXi version is earlier than 6.0), then vSphere Replication prevents vMotion migrations at the source of replicated virtual machines to hosts that do not support data compression (that is, if the ESXi version earlier than 6.0). In this case, to use vMotion to migrate a virtual machine to an ESXi 5.5 Host, you should reconfigure replication to disable data compression.

Differentiate VMware Data Protection Capabilities

VMware Data Protection (VDP) is a product designed to back up and restore virtual machines in vSphere environments. Specifically, VDP 6.0 has the following features and capabilities:

- Support for up to 400 virtual machines per VDP appliance
- Support for up to 20 VDP appliances per vCenter Server
- Up to 8 TB per appliance for backup data
- Image-level backups and restores
- Individual virtual disk backups and restores
- Image-level replication
- Direct-to-host recovery
- Detachable and remountable data partitions
- File-level recovery
- Support for guest-level backups and restores of Microsoft Exchange Server, SQL Server, and SharePoint servers
- Support for application-level replication
- Ability to expand datastores
- Support for backing up a Data Domain system
- Ability to restore granularly on Microsoft servers
- Automatic backup verification (ABV)
- Support for external proxies
- Support for Customer Experience Improvement Program
- Deployable to any storage supported for vSphere, including VMware Virtual SAN
- Backup agents for software applications
- Ability to back up and restore virtual machine–based Platform Service Controllers (PSCs)

- Ability to back up and restore virtual machine–based vCenter Servers and vCenter Server appliances

- Ability to replicate backups to a VDP target, an Avamar server, or a Data Domain system (Don't confuse this with vSphere Replication.)

Configure Recovery Point Objective (RPO) for a Protected Virtual Machine

Each time you configure vSphere Replication for a virtual machine or set of virtual machines, you must set the recovery point objective (RPO). To configure replication and RPO on a virtual machine in the vSphere Web Client, right-click the virtual machine, select **All vSphere Replication Actions > Configure Replication**, and use the wizard to configure the replication, including the RPO. You may use the RPO slider or text boxes to set its value between 15 minutes and 24 hours, as illustrated in Figure 9-1.

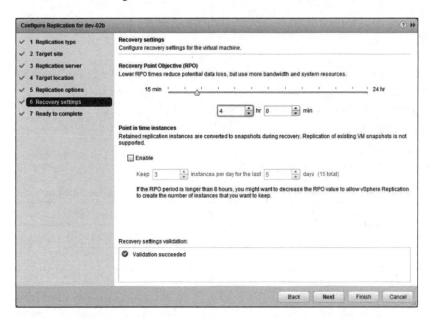

Figure 9-1 Configure RPO

In vSphere Replication 6, the minimum RPO is 15 minutes and the maximum is 24 hours. This value is used by vSphere Replication to automatically determine when to schedule upcoming changed data transfers to the target. vSphere Replication works to ensure that the data is always available to the target in a manner that does not violate the RPO. Consider an example in which the RPO for a virtual machine is 15 minutes, and vSphere Replication starts the transfer of changed data now. If the data takes 4 minutes to arrive, then it is already 4 minutes old at arrival, and the

RPO is violated if new data does not arrive within less than 11 minutes of the arrival of the first set of data. vSphere Replication determines that if the next transfer also requires 4 minutes to complete, then the next transfer needs to begin no later than 11 minutes from now. In other words, if the first transfer begins at 1:00 pm and the data arrives at 1:04 pm, the next transfer begins at 1:11 pm.

Explain VMware Data Protection Sizing Guidelines

The VDP appliance is available in the following configurations:

- 0.5 TB
- 1 TB
- 2 TB
- 4 TB
- 6 TB
- 8 TB

These configurations represent the amount of disk space that is available in the appliance for data backup. The total disk space required for the appliance is greater than the configuration size. After VDP is deployed, you may increase its size. Table 9-2 contains the minimum system requirements for VDP, based on the configuration size.

Table 9-2 Minimum System Requirements for VDP

Configuration	Number of 2 GHz Processors	Memory (GB)	Disk Space
0.5 TB	4	4	873 GB
1 TB	4	4	1600 GB
2 TB	4	4	3 TB
4 TB	4	8	6 TB
6 TB	4	10	9 TB
8 TB	4	12	12 TB

To support large and growing VMware environments, each VDP appliance can simultaneously back up 8 virtual machines if the internal proxy is used. Each VDP appliance can simultaneously back up 24 virtual machines, if 8 external proxies, which is the maximum, are deployed with the VDP appliance.

VDP backup data capacity requirements depend on many factors, such as number of protected virtual machines, amount of protected data in the virtual machines, data types, retention period, and data rate changes. VMware states that assuming average virtual machine sizes, data types, change rates, and 30-day retention, 1 TB of VDP backup data capacity supports approximately 25 virtual machines.

Create/Delete/Consolidate Virtual Machine Snapshots

A common issue that occurs with backup and recovery solutions that utilize virtual machine snapshots, such as VDP, is that a snapshot disk may fail to compress after the snapshot delete operation completes. In other words, when VDP automatically deletes a snapshot following a virtual machine backup, the operation may succeed, even if the delta disks fail to commit back to the base disk. Whenever this condition occurs, the vSphere Web Client marks the virtual disk as `Needs Consolidation`. To use the vSphere Web Client to identify virtual machines that need consolidation, select the vCenter Server in the inventory, select **Related Objects > Virtual Machines**, and examine the **Needs Consolidation** column. In order to view this column, you may first need to right-click the menu bar and select **Show/Hide** to add the column. When this condition occurs, and only when this condition occurs, you should consolidate the virtual disk. To do this using the vSphere Web Client, right-click the virtual machine and select **Snapshots > Consolidate**. This operation requires the user to have the **Virtual machine.Snapshot management.Remove Snapshot** privilege. If the task fails, check the event log for the reason, such as running out of disk space, correct the issue, and retry as necessary. Verify success by reexamining the **Needs Consolidation** value.

Although VDP does its own snapshot creation, deletion, and management, you should know how to do these tasks as well. A virtual machine snapshot is a point-in-time capture of the state of the virtual machine and its virtual disk. Optionally, the snapshot could include the state of its memory content. After a snapshot is created, you can choose to revert the virtual machine back to the captured point in time. To use the vSphere Web Client to create a snapshot, you can use this procedure:

Step 1.   Right-click the virtual machine and select **Take Snapshot**.

Step 2.   Provide a snapshot name.

Step 3.   Optionally provide a description.

Step 4.   Optionally select or deselect the **Snapshot the Virtual Machine's Memory** option. If selected, the memory contents will be captured to a file, which takes time and disk space but provides a means to revert the memory to the captured state.

Step 5.   Optionally select or deselect the **Quiesce Guest File System** option. If selected, VMware Tools is used to communicate to the guest OS to ensure that the file system contents are brought to a known consistent state prior to creating the snapshot. Do not use this option for powered-down virtual machines. Do not use it if you selected to snapshot the memory.

Step 6.   Click **OK**.

To revert a virtual machine to the most recent snapshot, right-click the virtual machine and select **Revert to Latest Snapshot**. To revert the virtual machine to any available snapshot, right-click the virtual machine, select **Manage Snapshots**, select the appropriate snapshot, and click the **Revert To** button.

As snapshots are created, files are created and modified to represent and track the snapshot, as described in Table 9-3.

Table 9-3   Virtual Machine Snapshot Files

Filename Syntax	Filename Example	Description (GB)
`vmname-###.vmdk`	`Servera-000001.vmdk`	Contains snapshot metadata, such as the name of the delta file and disk geometry.
`vmname-delta-###.vmdk`	`Servera-000001-delta.vmdk`	Contains all the virtual disk data blocks that have changed at least once following the creation of the snapshot. Each block represents the most recent state of that block.
`vmname.vsd`	`Servera.vmsd`	Contains information on all of the virtual machine's snapshots.
`vmname.Snapshot###.vmsn`	`servera.Snapshot000001.vmsn`	Contains the memory state of the of the virtual machine, if you select to snapshot the memory.

vSphere 6.0 has the following snapshot limitations:

- Snapshots of raw disks, RDM physical mode disks, or guest operating systems that use an iSCSI initiator in the guest are not supported.

- Virtual machines with independent disks must be powered off before you take a snapshot. Snapshots of powered-on or suspended virtual machines with independent disks are not supported.

- Snapshots are not supported with PCI vSphere Direct Path I/O devices.

- VMware does not support snapshots of virtual machines configured for bus sharing.

- Snapshots are not meant to be a robust method of backup and recovery.

- Snapshots can negatively affect the performance of a virtual machine.

- If a virtual machine has virtual hard disks larger than 2 TB, snapshot operations can take significant time to finish.

Install and Configure VMware Data Protection

The prerequisites that should be met prior to implementing VDP are DNS configuration, NTP configuration, and user account configuration.

The DNS server must support forward and reverse lookup for the VDP appliance and vCenter Server. Add forward (A record) and reverse (PTR record) entries to the DNS server for the VDP appliance, using its IP address and fully qualified domain name (FQDN). In addition, the VMware proxy nodes require communication to DNS over port 53 (TCP and UDP). Improperly configured DNS may cause many runtime and configuration issues. To confirm that DNS is properly configured, you can run the `nslookup` command twice on the vCenter Server, once using the FQDN of the VDP appliance and once using the FQDN of the vCenter Server.

Ensure that time synchronization is properly configured on the ESXi Hosts using NTP. Ensure that time synchronization is properly configured on the vCenter Server. The VDP appliance will leverage VMware Tools to synchronize its time with the ESXi Host, where it runs. Do not configure NTP services directly in the VDP guest OS because doing so may actually cause time synchronization issues.

In the SSO domain or in a domain that is used as an SSO identity source, prepare a user account (VDP service account) to be used to connect VDP and vCenter Server. For example, if an Active Directory domain named `mydomain` is registered as an identity source for your SSO, you could prepare an account in `mydomain` named `vdpservice`. Then use the vSphere Web Client to select the vCenter Server object in the host and clusters inventory tree and add an appropriate permission for the VDP service account on the vCenter Server object. For the previous example, you could assign the Administrator role to the `mydomain\vpdservice` account and allow it to propagate.

NOTE Ensure that you select vCenter from the root level of the hosts and clusters tree structure. If you select the vCenter virtual machine object, the configuration fails.

Instead of assigning the Administrator role (all privileges) to the VDP service account, you can configure custom role with just these required privileges:

- Alarms:
    - Create
    - Modify

- Datastore:
    - Allocate space
    - Browse datastore
    - Configure datastore (for VSAN support)
    - Low level file operations
    - Move datastore
    - Remove datastore
    - Remove file
    - Rename datastore

- Extension:
    - Register extensions
    - Update extensions

- Folder:
    - Create folder
- Global:
    - Cancel task
    - Disable methods
    - Enable methods
    - Licenses
    - Log event
    - Manage custom attributes
    - Settings

- Network:
  - Assign network
  - Configure

- Resource:
  - Assign virtual machine to resource pool
- Sessions:
  - Validate session
- Tasks:
  - Create task
  - Update task

- Virtual Machine > Configuration:
  - Add existing disk
  - Add new disk
  - Add or remove device
  - Advanced
  - Change CPU count
  - Change resource
  - Disk change tracking
  - Disk lease
  - Extend virtual disk
  - Host USB device
  - Memory
  - Modify device setting
  - Raw device
  - Reload from path
  - Remove disk
  - Rename
  - Reset guest information
  - Set annotation

- Settings
- Swap file placement
- Upgrade virtual machine compatibility

- Virtual Machine > Guest Operations:
  - Guest operation modifications
  - Guest operation program execution
  - Guest operation queries

- Virtual Machine > Interaction:
  - Console interaction
  - Device connection
  - Guest operating system management by VIX API
  - Power off
  - Power on
  - Reset
  - VMware tools install

- Virtual Machine > Inventory:
  - Create new
  - Register
  - Remove
  - Unregister

- Virtual Machine > Provisioning:
  - Allow disk access
  - Allow read-only disk access
  - Allow virtual machine download
  - Mark as template

- Virtual Machine > Snapshot Management:
  - Create snapshot
  - Remove snapshot
  - Revert to snapshot

- vApp:
  - Export
  - Import
  - vApp application configuration

Assign the role directly to the user accounts on the vCenter Server root node in hosts and clusters. Users who inherit permissions from group roles are not valid.

You should verify that you meet all system requirements, software requirements, network requirements, and client browser requirements. Verify that the VDP backup data capacity and minimum system requirements are met, as defined in the "Explain VMware Data Protection Sizing Guidelines" section. Verify that the VDP software requirements are met, including vCenter Server 5.1 (vCenter Server 5.5 and later is recommended, either Windows based or virtual appliance), vSphere Web Client, and vSphere 5.0 or later. Verify that network requirements are met, including the ability to use port 902 for VDP–to–ESXi Host connections. Verify that the client has a supported web browser, Adobe Flash, and the VMware Client Integration Plug-in. Download the VDP OVA file to a location that is accessible by the client.

NOTE   Because the VDP appliance is built on virtual hardware version 7, which cannot use vSphere Flash Read Cache, attempts to perform an image backup of a vSphere Flash Read Cache–backed virtual disk will use the network block device protocol instead of HotAdd. These backups may perform poorly.

NOTE   VDP 6.0 does not support the backup of independent, RDM independent—virtual compatibility mode, or RDM—physical compatibility mode virtual disk types.

The VDP installation involves three main steps. The first step is to deploy the OVF template. The second step is the initial configuration. The third step is to create new storage.

You can use the following procedure to deploy a VDP appliance from the OVF template:

Step 1.   Log onto the vSphere Web Client as a user with administrative privileges.

Step 2.   Right-click a datacenter object in the inventory and choose **Deploy OVF Template**.

Step 3.   Use the wizard to select the appropriate OVA file and click **Next**.

Step 4. Enter the VDP FQDN in the **VDP Appliance Name** field. (The VDP configuration uses this name to find the VDP appliance in the vCenter inventory.) Click **Next**.

Step 5. Select the folder to deploy the appliance and click **Next**.

Step 6. Select the ESXi Host to deploy the appliance and click **Next**.

Step 7. Choose a virtual disk type, select a datastore to deploy the appliance, and click **Next**.

Step 8. Select the appropriate network to connect the appliance and click **Next**.

Step 9. Specify the appropriate IP settings, gateway, and DNS. (DHCP is not supported.) Click **Next**.

Step 10. On the final page, click **Power On** and click **Finish**.

Step 11. Monitor the deployment and wait for the appliance to boot into the install mode.

You can use the following procedure to perform the initial VDP configuration:

Step 1. In the vSphere Web Client, select the VDP appliance in the VMs and templates view.

Step 2. On the **Summary** tab, select **Open Console**.

Step 3. Verify that the installation is completed, and the Welcome screen appears in the VDP console.

Step 4. From your client system, use a web browser to connect to the VDP configuration utility at `https://VDP-IP-adrress:8543/vdp-configure/`.

Step 5. On the VMware login page, provide the default username (`root`) and default password (`changeme`) and click **Login**.

Step 6. On the VDP Welcome page, click **Next**.

Step 7. In the Network Settings dialog, double-check the network settings you provided during the OVF deployment and click **Next**.

Step 8. Set the appropriate time zone and click **Next**.

Step 9. On the VDP Credentials page, provide a VDP appliance password, which must meet specific criteria. One acceptable criterion is to use at least two character classes and at least 8 total characters. Click **Next**.

Step 10. On the vCenter Registration page, provide the appropriate username, password, and FQDN to register with vCenter Server. Optionally, change the HTTP port or HTTPs port. If a vCenter Server with embedded PSC is used, select the **Use vCenter for SSO Authentication** check box. Otherwise, deselect this check box and provide the SSO FQDN and SSO ports. Click **Test Connection**.

Step 11.   If the test is unsuccessful, troubleshoot the issue. Common issues are misconfiguration of the IP settings, user credentials, or user permissions. If successful, click **Next**.

Step 12.   Verify that the Create Storage page appears.

You can use the following procedure to create new storage for VCP backup:

Step 1.   On the Create Storage page, select **Create New Storage**.

Step 2.   Select one of the appropriate capacity option, such as 2 TB, as discussed previously in this chapter. Click **Next**.

Step 3.   On the Device Allocation page, select the provisioning type. The default and recommended type is Thick-Lazy Zeroed. Click **Next**.

Step 4.   On the Ready to Complete page, choose to run a performance analysis if desired. Optionally select the **Run Performance Analysis and Storage Configuration** check box and the **Restart if Appliance Is Successful** check box and click **Next**.

Step 5.   The test often takes 30 minutes or more to complete. Also, the VDP restart, which performs a series of automated configuration steps, frequently takes up 45 minutes or more. Monitor the progress of the storage configuration and verify that it completes before using VDP.

After deploying VDP, you can use the VDP configuration utility (`https://VDP-IP-adrress:8543/vdp-configure/`) to perform configuration and administration tasks such as:

- Viewing status
- Starting and stopping services
- Collecting logs
- Modifying configuration, such as network settings and vCenter Server registration
- Configuring a backup window and a maintenance window
- Configuring email notification
- Viewing logs
- Running integrity checks

- Monitoring VDP activity

- Viewing alarms

- Viewing events

- Shutting down the VDP appliance

- Configuring an external proxy

- Storage management

Create a Backup Job with VMware Data Protection

Some key limitations of VDP backups are:

- Backup of Windows virtual machines larger than 2 TB are not supported.

- VDP cannot back up these specialized virtual machines:

  - VDP appliances

  - vSphere Storage Appliances (VSA)

  - VMware Data Recovery (VDR) Appliances

  - Templates

  - Secondary fault-tolerant nodes

  - Proxies

  - Avamar Virtual Edition (AVE) servers

- Virtual machines that contain special characters in their names cannot be added to backup jobs, but the dash (-) and an underscore (_) are accepted.

- Using snapshots to perform a backup on VMs that use SCSI bus sharing is not supported, per VMware KB 1006392.

When you create VDP backup jobs, you have choices for identifying the virtual machines. You could specify a set of virtual machines, such as all virtual machines in a datacenter or folder, which automatically covers new virtual machines that are later added to the container. In this case, if a virtual machine is later migrated from the container to a container that is not included in the backup job, the virtual machine is no longer covered in the backup job. If you select a single virtual machine, then any virtual disks that are later added to the virtual machine are automatically covered in the backup.

When you create a VDP backup job, you can specify the backup schedule and the retention policy. These are the retention policy options:

- **Forever:** The backup job never expires, and the backup data is never deleted

- **For:** The backup data is maintained for a specified number of days from the date the backup data was created.

- **Until:** The backup data is kept until a specified date, when it is automatically deleted.

- **Custom Retention Schedule:** The retention time is based on tags, such as Daily, Weekly, Monthly, and Yearly. Multiple tags can be applied to each backup.

To create a full image backup job, you can use this procedure:

Step 1.   In the vSphere Web Client, select **vSphere Data Protection** in the Navigator pane and click the **Backup** tab.

Step 2.   Select **Backup Job Actions > New**.

Step 3.   On the Job Type page, select **Guest Images** and click **Next**.

Step 4.   On the Data Type page, select **Full Image** and click **Next**.

Step 5.   On the Backup Sources page, select the virtual machine to include and click **Next**.

Step 6.   On the Schedule page, specify the backup job schedule and click **Next**.

Step 7.   On the Retention page, specify a retention period and click **Next**.

Step 8.   On the next page, provide a backup job name and click **Next**.

Step 9.   On the Ready to Complete page, click **Finish**.

Step 10. Click **OK**.

Backup/Restore a Virtual Machine with VMware Data Protection

In addition to creating a scheduled, full image backup job, as described in the previous section, you can do the following with VDP:

- Immediately back up a protected virtual machine. The virtual machine must belong to a backup job. The key step is to right-click the virtual machine and choose **All VDP Actions > Backup Now**.

- Immediately run a backup job.

- Create backup jobs on individual virtual disks rather than on entire virtual machines.

NOTE   Storage vMotion migrations of full virtual machines cause no issues for VDP backups because VDP receives notification and updates the backup jobs. But Storage vMotion migrations of individual virtual disks are troublesome to VDP backup jobs that back up individual virtual disks. In this case, you should expect to receive VDP log messages indicating that one or more VDP protected disks may have been migrated and manual intervention is needed to edit the backup job.

VDP can be used to restore one or more virtual machines from a backup. A virtual machine may be restored to the original location or to an alternate location. VDP does not allow you to select multiple restore points for the same MSApp client or to restore to virtual machines using SCSI bus sharing. Another limitation is that although previous versions of VDP may have allowed restoring virtual machines with snapshots, VDP 5.5 and later do not. Prior to restoring to a virtual machine that has snapshots, you should delete the snapshots.

When you review a list of backups, you can filter the list in various ways. For example, you can filter by "is before" on the **Backup Date** and by "contains" on the **Client Name**.

You can use the following procedure to restore a virtual machine to its original location:

Step 1.   In the vSphere Web Client, select **vSphere Data Protection** in the Navigator pane and click the **Restore** tab.

Step 2.   Optionally filter the list of backups.

Step 3.   In the Name column, select a virtual machine and expand its list of associated backups. Select a backup or select a specific virtual disk. Use the check box beside one or more specific items that you want to restore. Click **Restore**.

Step 4.   On the Select Backup page, verify that the selected list of backup items to restore is correct and make any necessary modifications. Click **Next**.

Step 5.   On the Restore Options page, leave the **Restore to Original Location** box checked and click **Next**.

Step 6.   On the Ready to Complete page, click **Finish**.

Step 7.   Click **OK**.

You can use the same procedure to restore to a new location, except that in step 5 you should deselect the **Restore to Original Location** box and provide values for **New VM Name**, **Destination**, and **Datastore**.

NOTE The Restore to Original Location option overwrites existing VMDK files as necessary, but if the original virtual disk has been deleted or removed from the virtual machine, then it cannot be restored to the original location. Instead, the virtual disk must be restored to a new location.

You can use VDP to back up virtual machines containing vCenter Server, vCenter Server Appliance, or PSC and restore them to new or original locations.

NOTE VMware recommends that you back up all vCenter Server and PSC instances at the same time.

These virtual machines must have VMware Tools installed and must use a FQDN with proper DNS resolution or use a static IP address. When using VDP, you must do full image backups and restores of the vCenter Server and PSC. For vCenter Server and PSC backups, VDP does not support incremental backups, differential backups, individual disk backups, virtual machine snapshots, or fault tolerance–protected virtual machines. You can use VDP to restore a virtual machine containing vCenter Server, vCenter Server Appliance, or PSC directly on an ESXi Host that is running the VDP appliance when vCenter Server is unavailable or the vSphere Web Client is unavailable.

The process for backing up and restoring virtual machines containing vCenter Server, vCenter Server Appliance, or PSC is the same as the process for performing a full image backup and restore for other virtual machines. After restoring a virtual machine containing PSC, you should start the virtual machine, log onto the guest OS using the virtual machine console, and run the `psc-restore` script. For a PSC appliance, you can use the `root` account to logon and run the script. For a Windows virtual machine, you can log on as a user in the local Administrators group and change the default directory to the location of the script, such as:

```
c:\Program Files\VMWare\vCenter Server
```

When running the script, you should provide the credentials on the command line, such as:

```
psc-restore  -u username -p password
```

NOTE After powering on a recovered Windows virtual machine running PSC, if Windows prompts you to restart the server, do not do so until you run the `psc-restore` script.

> **NOTE** If you do not provide user credentials on the command line with the `psc-restore` script, the script will interactively prompt you for credentials three times.

In situations where vCenter Server and PSC reside on ESXi Hosts that are managed by a separate vCenter Server, a separate VDP instance could be used for backup and recovery of vCenter Server and PSC, using the procedures described previously in this chapter. In situations where VDP and its required services are available, you can perform a full image restore of vCenter Server or PSC to the original location or new location in the same manner as previously described.

For example, in situations where two external PSC instances share the same SSO domain and you want to restore the virtual machine running the first PSC instance, you could repoint vCenter Server to the second PSC instance (if necessary), shut down the first PSC instance, and perform a full image restore of the virtual machine. To repoint a vCenter Server to another PSC, you can use this command:

```
cmsso-util repoint --repoint-psc psc-fqdn
```

In this example, replace `psc-fqdn` with the FQDN or IP address of the second PSC instance. After restoring the virtual machine for the first PSC instance, starting it, and running the `psc-restore` script, you can repoint the vCenter Server back to the first PSC instance.

> **NOTE** Repointing the connections between vCenter Server and the Platform Services Controller results in loss of all backup jobs and replication jobs. Existing restore points remain intact, but you must re-create backup jobs and replication jobs.

In many situations, the need to restore a virtual machine containing vCenter Server, vCenter Server Appliance, or PSC requires you to perform a direct-to-host emergency restore operation. If the vCenter Server where VDP is registered is unavailable or if you cannot access the VPD user interface by using the vSphere Web Client, you can only restore virtual machines containing vCenter Server or PSC with an emergency restore.

VDP provides an Emergency Restore feature that allows VDP to connect directly to an ESXi host to restore virtual machines. The main use cases are for restoring when vCenter Server is unavailable and for restoring vCenter Server. Because many VDP features are dependent on vCenter Server, the emergency restore has limitations, such as:

- The virtual machine must be restored to the ESXi Host where VDP performs the emergency restore.

- The ESXi Host cannot be part of the associated vCenter Server inventory. If necessary, remove it from the vCenter Server inventory prior to starting the emergency restore. If vCenter Server is unavailable, you should use the vSphere Client (not the vSphere Web Client) to use the **Disassociate Host from vCenter** link on the host's **Summary** tab.

- DNS must still be available, so VDP can use it to resolve the ESXi Host name.

- The restored virtual machine will be in a powered-down state.

- The restored virtual machine is treated as a new virtual machine. You should ensure that its name is not a duplicate of a virtual machine that already exists.

- MSApp clients cannot be restored.

- VDP automatically activates an internal proxy when the emergency restore is performed. If both the internal proxy and external proxy are activated, you should disable the internal proxy using the VDP configuration utility, or the emergency restore may not succeed.

To perform an emergency restore, you can use this procedure:

Step 1. Log onto the VDP configuration utility at `https://VDP-IP-adrress:8543/vdp-configure/`.

Step 2. Select the **Emergency Restore** tab and examine the list of virtual machines that are protected by VDP.

Step 3. Select the appropriate virtual machine and click **Restore**.

Step 4. In the Host Credentials dialog, provide the ESXi Host FQDN and appropriate user credentials and click **OK**.

Step 5. In the Restore a Backup dialog, enter a new name, select a datastore, and click **Restore**.

Step 6. Monitor the restore progress in the Recent Tasks dialog box.

Step 7. Choose a virtual disk type. Select a datastore to deploy the appliance and click **Next**.

Step 8. Select the appropriate network to connect the appliance and click **Next**.

Step 9. Specify the appropriate IP settings, gateway, and DNS. (DHCP is not supported.) Click **Next**.

Step 10.   On the final page, click **Power On** and click **Finish**.

Step 11.   Monitor the deployment and wait for the appliance to boot into install mode.

> **NOTE**   The restored virtual machine is listed at the vSphere host level in the inventory. Restoring to a more specific inventory path is not supported during an emergency restore.

Install/Configure/Upgrade vSphere Replication

To prepare for vSphere Replication deployment, install the VMware Client Integration Plug-in on your desktop. Use the vSphere Web Client to set the `VirtualCenter.FQDN` advanced setting (at **Manage > Settings > Advanced Settings**) to the vCenter Server FQDN, not a short name or an IP address. Download the vSphere Replication Appliance OVF file from VMware's website.

To deploy a vSphere Replication Appliance at each site, you can use the vSphere Web Client and follow this procedure:

Step 1.   Launch the Deploy OVF Template Wizard and choose the appropriate OVF file.

Step 2.   Follow the prompts in the wizard to accept the license agreement, supply a virtual machine name, and select a folder.

Step 3.   When prompted, keep or modify the default option of two virtual CPUs and click **Next**.

Step 4.   Continue following the prompts in the wizard to select the computing resource, select the datastore, and configure network settings.

Step 5.   When prompted, set a password for the `root` account and click **Next**.

Step 6.   Review the binding information for the vCenter Extension vService. (The vSphere Replication Appliance automatically binds to the vCenter Server that you are using to run the Deploy OVF Template wizard.) Click **Next**.

Step 7.   Click **Finish**.

After deploying a vSphere Replication Appliance, you can configure it by using the Virtual Appliance Management Interface (VAMI). To access the VAMI, use a web browser to log onto `https://vr-address:5480` as the `root` account, using the password you provided in the previous procedure. You can use the VAMI to change or fix its registration with vCenter Server. To change the vCenter registration, modify the **LookupService Address** setting on the **Configuration** tab (shown in Figure 9-2), provide **SSO Administrator** credentials (such as administrator@vsphere.local), provide the vCenter Server Address, and select **Save and Restart Service**.

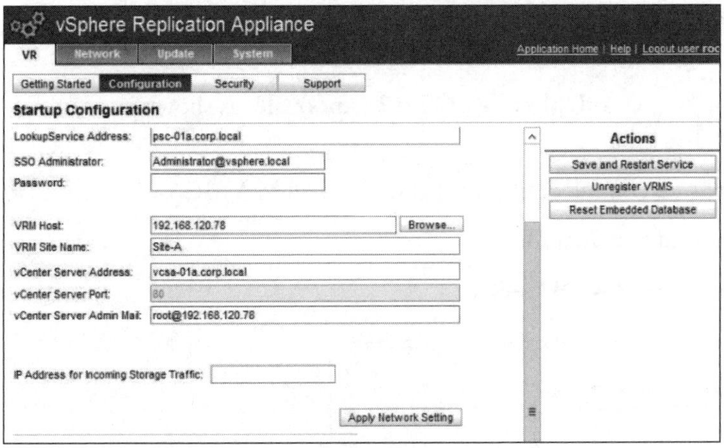

Figure 9-2 LookupService Settings in the VAMI

Next, you can use the vSphere Web Client to establish vSphere Replication connections. On the home page, select **vSphere Replication** and click **Home > Manage**. Click **Target Sites** and then click **Connect to Target Site**. Either choose **Connect to a Local Site** or choose **Connect to a Remote Site**. For a remote site, you must provide the hostname or IP address of the target site server where PSC runs and provide credentials that have the **VRM remote.Manage VRM** privilege. Finally, select the appropriate vCenter Server and click **OK**.

After deploying a vSphere Replication Appliance (VRA) at a site, you can deploy additional appliances that run just the vSphere Replication Service (VRS). The VRA runs both a management service and a replication service. The VRS appliance only runs a replication service. One VRA is required for each site to provide management for the replication. It can also be used independently to provide the actual replication. Additional VRS appliances can be deployed to assist in the replication, but not the management. To deploy additional appliances, download and use the vSphere_Replication_AddOn_OVF10.ovf file. After starting the deployed appliance, use the vSphere Web Client to select **Manage > vSphere Replication > Replication Servers**, click **Register a Virtual Machine as vSphere Replication Server**, and select the appliance from the list of virtual machines.

Configure VMware Certificate Authority (VMCA) integration with vSphere Replication

You can change the SSL certificate used by vSphere Replication to a certificate issued by VMCA. To change the certificate, you can use the following procedure:

Step 1.   Use the VMCA to generate a trusted certificate.

Step 2.   In the VAMI, select **VR > Security** and review the current certificate.

Step 3.   Select the **Configuration** tab and select the **Accept only SSL Certificates Signed by a Trusted Certificate Authority** check box.

Step 4.   Select the option to **Upload PKCS#12 (*.pfx) file**, as shown in Figure 9-3.

Step 5.   Click **Browse** and select the certificate supplied by VMCA.

Step 6.   Click **Upload and Install**.

Step 7.   Click **Save and Restart Service**.

Figure 9-3   Install a New SSL Certificate

Configure vSphere Replication for Single/Multiple VMs

You can configure replication for a set of virtual machines or for individual virtual machines. To get started, ensure that vSphere Replication is deployed at the source and target sits. Also ensure the following:

- Sufficient disk space is available on the target datastores.

- If you want to use guest OS quiescing, ensure that VMware Tools is installed in the virtual machines.

- To configure replication to a remote site (a target vCenter Server that is not the same as the source vCenter Server), you must plan to use the **Add Remote Site** option, which requires that you log onto the vSphere Web Client as a user with the **VRM remote.Manage VRM** privilege.

When you configure vSphere Replication for a virtual machine, you can choose to use VSS quiescing for virtual machines running supported versions of Windows. When you enable quiescing, vSphere Replication first attempts application-level quiescing, but the attempt is unsuccessful. Then vSphere Replication attempts file system–level quiescing. Table 9-4 provides the compatibility of application quiescing and file system quiescing for combinations of Windows guest operating system versions and vSphere Replication versions. Quiescing is not available for unsupported guest operating systems.

Table 9-4   Supported Quiescing for Windows and vSphere Replication Versions

Windows Version	Application Quiescing		File System Quiescing	
	vSphere Replication 5.8	vSphere Replication 6.0	vSphere Replication 5.8	vSphere Replication 6.0
Windows Server 2003	Yes	Discontinued support	Yes	Yes
Windows Server 2008	Yes	Yes	Yes	Yes
Windows Server 2012	Yes	Yes	Yes	Yes
Windows Vista	No	No	Yes	Yes
Windows 7	No	No	Yes	Yes
Windows 8	No	No	Yes	Yes

NOTE   vSphere Replication does not support VSS quiescing on Virtual Volumes.

When you configure vSphere Replication for a virtual machine, you must set the RPO as described in the "Configure Recovery Point Objective (RPO) for a Protected Virtual Machine" section in this chapter.

When you configure vSphere Replication for a virtual machine, you have the option to retain multiple points in times (MPIT). By default, MPIT is not enabled for a replicated virtual machine, so after recovering a virtual machine, you do not have the ability to choose a different point in time in the Snapshot Manager. If you do enable MPIT for the replication of a virtual machine, you must configure the number of instances to retain per day and the number of days of retention. For example, you can configure the retention of 3 instances per day for the last 5 days, as shown in Figure 9-4. In this example, a total of 15 snapshots (points of time) will be maintained for the replicated virtual machine. After recovering the virtual machine, you could use Snapshot Manager to revert back to any one of the 15 points in time. The maximum number of points in time that may be maintained for a virtual machine is 24. In other words, the number of instances per day times the number of days cannot exceed 24.

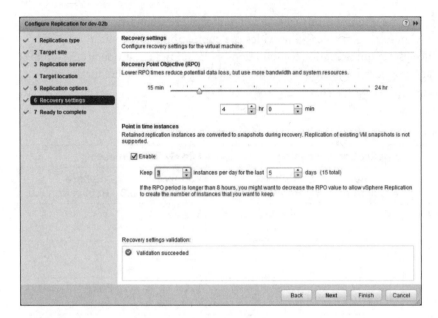

Figure 9-4   Configure Point in Time Instances

You can use the following procedure to configure vSphere Replication on a set of virtual machines between two vSphere environments managed by separate vCenter Servers:

Step 1.   In the vSphere Web Client, select **vSphere Replication** on the home page.

Step 2.   In the left pane, select the source vCenter Server.

Step 3.   In the right pane, select **Related Objects** > **Virtual Machines**.

Step 4.   Using the mouse, **Ctrl**, and **Shift** keys, select a set of virtual machines, right-click and select **All vSphere Replication Actions**> **Configure replication**, and click **Next**.

Step 5.   Select **Replicate to a vCenter Server**.

Step 6.   Click **Add Remote Site** (assuming that this the first attempt to replicate to the target vCenter Server), provide the FQDN or IP address of the target vCenter Server and user credentials that has the **VRM remote. Manage VRM** privilege, click **OK**, and click **Next**.

Step 7.   Accept or modify the automatic target vSphere Replication Server assignment.

Step 8.   Select the target datastore.

Step 9.   Optionally select **Enable Quiescing**.

Step 10.   Optionally select the **Enable Network Compression for VR Data**.

Step 11.   Set the RPO to a value between 15 minutes and 24 hours.

Step 12.   Optionally select **Enable** for the **Points in Time Instances** and set the number of instances per day and the number of days.

Step 13.   Click **Next**.

Step 14.   On the Ready to Complete page, click **Finish**.

The only method to upgrade vSphere Replication 5.5.1 to 5.8 or to 6.0 or 6.1 is to use the downloadable ISO image. You cannot upgrade to version 6.0 or 6.1 using the Update Manager or VAMI. After upgrading to 6.0 or 6.1, you can use the VAMI or Update Manager to install updates. You can also use the VAMI or Update Manager to upgrade. To upgrade from a vSphere Replication 5.5.1 or 5.8, download the ISO from VMware and use this procedure:

Step 1.   Shut down the vSphere Replication Appliance.

Step 2.   In the vSphere Web Client, edit the virtual machine properties to connect the ISO file to the virtual CD/DVD drive.

Step 3.   Power on the virtual machine.

Step 4.   Use a web browser to connect to the VAMI.

Step 5.   Select the **Update** tab, click **Settings**, select **Use CDROM Updates**, and click **Save**.

Step 6.   Click **Status** and **Check Updates**.

Step 7.   Click **Install Updates** and **OK**.

Step 8.   When the installation completes, click **System > Reboot**.

Recover a VM Using vSphere Replication

You can use the vSphere Web Client to recover virtual machines protected with vSphere Replication at the target site by using these steps:

Step 1.   Power down the source virtual machine.

Step 2.   On the **Incoming Replications** tab, right-click the virtual machine and select **Recovery**, as shown in Figure 9-5.

Step 3.   Select whether to recover with the most recent changes or with the latest available data. The former option ensures that the target is synchronized with the most recent changes but can be selected only if the source virtual machine data is accessible. The latter option should be selected if the data is inaccessible or corrupt.

Step 4.   Select the recovery folder and click **Next**.

Step 5.   Select the target computing resource and click **Next**.

Step 6.   If the virtual machine contains virtual disks that are not replicated, a page appears, requiring you to take action for each of these virtual disks. For each of these virtual disks, either attach an existing virtual disk file by using the **Browse** button or detach the virtual disk by using the **Detach** button. Click **Next**.

Step 7.   Optionally select **Power On After Recovery**.

Step 8.   Click **Finish**.

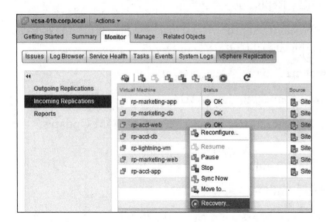

Figure 9-5   Recovering a Virtual Machine with vSphere Replication

Perform a Failback Operation Using vSphere Replication

The procedure to perform a failback operation using vSphere Replication is to manually reconfigure replication in the reverse direction and recover the virtual machine back to the original source site. The manual steps are required because vSphere Replication does not provide an automated failback. When you configure the replication in the reverse direction, vSphere Replication recognizes the original source virtual disks and uses those as replication seeds, so it does not have to copy the entire virtual disk across the network. It determines what data has changed and transfers just the changed data.

Deploy a Pair of vSphere Replication Virtual Appliances

As previously described in the "Install/Configure/Upgrade vSphere Replication" section of this chapter, you can deploy a vSphere Replication Appliance (VRA) and a vSphere Replication Service (VRS) appliance to each site. The VRA, which is required, provides a management service and a replication service. The VRS appliance provides an additional replication service, but it does not provide an additional management service. In addition to the original VRA, you can deploy up to 9 instances of the VRS appliance per site or, more specifically, per vCenter Server instance. This provides a total of 10 replication services at the site that can serve as targets for replication.

Summary

You have now read the chapter covering exam topics related to backup, restoration, and replication. You should now use information in the following sections to complete your preparation for Objective 6.1.

Exam Preparation Tasks

Review All the Key Topics

Table 9-5 provides a reference to each of the key topics identified in this chapter. Take a few moments to review each of these specific items.

Table 9-5 Key Topics for Chapter 9

Key Topic Element	Description	Pages
List	Required vCenter Server privileges for the VDP service account	328
Procedure	Initial VDP configuration	332
Paragraph	Restore vCenter Server or PSC	337
Procedure	Perform an emergency restore	339
Paragraph	Deploy vSphere Replication Service appliance and register with VRA	341
Procedure	Upgrade vSphere Replication	345

Complete the Tables and Lists from Memory

Print a copy of Appendix B, "Memory Tables" (found on the CD), or at least the section for this chapter, and complete the tables and lists from memory. Appendix C, "Memory Tables Answer Key," also on the CD, includes completed tables and lists to check your work.

Definitions of Key Terms

Define the following key terms from this chapter and check your answers in the glossary.

quiesce, VMware Data Protection (VDP), snapshot

Answer Review Questions

The answers to these review questions can be found in Appendix A.

1. Which of the following summarizes the steps to engage compression for vSphere Replication? (Choose two.)

   a. Use the VAMI to start compression.

   b. In the vSphere Web Client, select the vSphere Replication Server and set the compression option.

   c. Compression is automatically enabled for all replication when vSphere Replication detects that it is supported end to end.

   d. In the wizard to configure replication for a virtual machine, select **Enable Network Compression for VR Data**.

2. Which of the following is a scenario where application quiescing is supported for vSphere Replication?

   a. Windows 2003 virtual machines, running on NAS, protected by vSphere Replication 6.0

   b. Windows 2008 virtual machines, running on NAS, protected by vSphere Replication 6.0

   c. Windows 2012 virtual machines, running on Virtual Volumes, protected by vSphere Replication 6.0

   d. Windows 7 virtual machines, running on local VMFS datastore, protected by vSphere Replication 5.8

3. Which of the following is not a method in which VDP may be used to restore a virtual machine running vCenter Server?

    a. Direct-to-host emergency restore

    b. Restore to original location

    c. Restore to new location

    d. Direct to vCenter Server emergency restore

4. What is the maximum number of virtual appliances running the vSphere Replication management service that can be registered with a single vCenter Server?

    a. 1

    b. 2

    c. 9

    d. 10

5. Which of the following is *not* a task that you can perform using the VDP configuration utility?

    a. View status

    b. Configure SNMP notifications

    c. Collect logs

    d. Run integrity checks

This chapter covers the following objective:

- **Objective 7.1—Troubleshoot vCenter Server, ESXi Hosts, and Virtual Machines**
    - Monitor status of the vCenter Server service
    - Perform basic maintenance of a vCenter Server database
    - Monitor status of ESXi management agents
    - Determine ESXi Host stability issues and gather diagnostics information
    - Monitor ESXi system health
    - Locate and analyze vCenter Server and ESXi logs
    - Determine the appropriate command-line interface (CLI) command for a given troubleshooting task
    - Troubleshoot common issues, including:
        - vCenter Server service
        - SSO
        - vCenter Server connectivity
        - Virtual machine resource contention, configuration, and operation
        - Platform Services Controller (PSC)
        - Problems with installation
        - VMware Tools installation
        - Fault tolerant network latency

## CHAPTER 10

Troubleshoot Common Issues

This chapter covers exam topics related to troubleshooting common issues.

"Do I Know This Already?" Quiz

The "Do I Know This Already?" quiz allows you to assess whether you should study this entire chapter or move quickly to the "Exam Preparation Tasks" section. Regardless, the authors recommend that you read the entire chapter at least once. Table 10-1 outlines some of the major headings in this chapter and the corresponding "Do I Know This Already?" quiz questions. You can find the answers in Appendix A, "Answers to the 'Do I Know This Already?' Quizzes and Review Questions."

Table 10-1   "Do I Know This Already?" Foundation Topics Section-to-Question Mapping

Foundation Topics Section	Questions Covered in This Section
Monitor Status of the vCenter Server Service	1
Determine ESXi Host Stability Issues and Gather Diagnostics Information	2
Locate and Analyze vCenter Server and ESXi Logs	3
Determine the Appropriate Command-Line Interface (CLI) Command for a Given Troubleshooting Task	4, 7
Troubleshoot Common Issues	5, 6, 8, 9, 10

1. Which of the following is *not* a service that you can manage in the vSphere Web Client at **Administration > System Configuration > Services**?

   a. VMware vSphere ESXi Dump Collector

   b. VMware vSphere High Availability

   c. VMware vSphere Profile-Driven Storage Service

   d. VMware vSphere Web Client

2. Which of the following is not a useful argument for the ESXTOP utility when used in replay mode?

   a. -t

   b. -R

   c. -d

   d. -n

3. Which of the following is the appropriate ESXi Host log file that you should examine to gather information related to the connection to the vCenter Server?

   a. `/var/log/vmware.log`

   b. `/var/log/hostd.log`

   c. `/var/log/vpxd.log`

   d. `/var/log/vpxa.log`

4. Which command can be used to display information on all the virtual switches that are built and controlled directly on an ESXi Host?

   a. `esxcli network vswitch standard list`

   b. `esxcli network vswitch list`

   c. `esxcli vswitch list`

   d. `esxcli network software vswitch standard list`

5. Which of the following network ports are required for VMware Directory Service (vmdir) or Single Sign-On (SSO)? (Choose three.)

   a. 2012

   b. 11711

   c. 11712

   d. 8080

   e. 722

6. Which of the following is not a service that runs in the Platform Services Controller (PSC)?

   a. VMware Security Token Service

   b. VMware Common Logging Service

   c. VMware Storage Profiles Service

   d. VMware Syslog Health Service

7. What is the impact of not adding ESXi thumbprints to the certificate store?

   a. `esxcfg-*` commands may not work.

   b. `vicfg-*` commands may not work.

   c. ESXCLI commands may not work.

   d. The vCenter Server cannot manage the ESXi Host.

8. A virtual machine fails to start, and the error message `Insufficient memory resources` appears. Which of the following is *not* useful for solving this issue?

   a. Decrease the memory limit on the virtual machine.

   b. Decrease the memory reservation on the virtual machine.

   c. Decrease the memory reservation on other virtual machines.

   d. Increase the memory reservation on the resource pool.

9. Which of the following is true concerning legacy Fault Tolerance (FT)?

   a. You can use the Cluster Settings page in the vSphere Web client to select the version of FT to use.

   b. You cannot use both the new version of FT and legacy FT on the same ESXi Host.

   c. You can disable the new version of FT and enable the legacy version on an ESXi Host by using the command `esxcli software legacyFT true`.

   d. You can configure legacy FT on individual virtual machines by using the `vm.uselegacyft` option.

10. Which of the following parameters can be used to control the maximum number of Fault Tolerance (FT)–protected virtual machines per ESXi Host?

   a. `ft.maxvmsperhost`

   b. `das.maxftvmsperhost`

   c. `ha.maxftvmsperhost`

   d. `drs.maxftvmsperhost`

Foundation Topics

Objective 7.1—Troubleshoot vCenter Server, ESXi Hosts, and Virtual Machines

The following sections describe how to troubleshoot general vSphere issues. They explain how to monitor the status of vSphere components, analyze logs, and troubleshoot common issues. They also cover troubleshooting issues concerning the vCenter Server, ESXi Hosts, and virtual machines.

Monitor Status of the vCenter Server Service

The vCenter Server and its related components involve many services. One of these services is the vCenter Server service, which can be managed using the native operating system. For example, a Windows-based vCenter Server service can be stopped and restarted by using the Services Management Console from within Windows. This service and its related services can also be managed from the vSphere Web Client, using **Home** > **Administration** > **System Configuration** > **Services**, as shown in Figure 10-1.

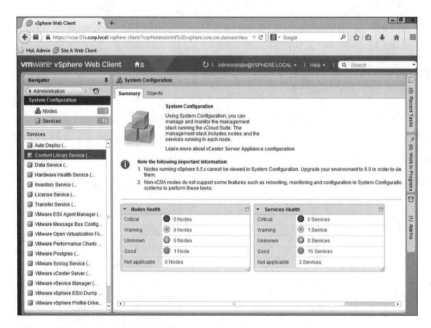

Figure 10-1   Services in the vSphere Web Client

In this example, you can determine the state of each of the services that support the vCenter Server named `vcsa-01a.orp.local`. For example, you can select the VMware vCenter Server service to examine its state and health, as shown in Figure 10-2. In this example, the vCenter Server startup type is automatic, its state is running, and its health is good. Also in this example, the Health Section indicates that the health of the vCenter Server, the vCenter Server Database, and the Workflow Manager is green, which means healthy.

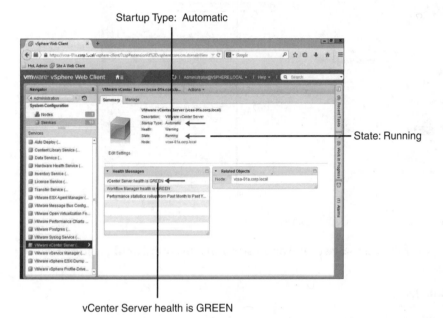

Figure 10-2   vCenter Server Service Summary

For each of these services, you can use the **Actions** drop-down to start, stop, and restart the service, as shown in Figure 10-3. On some of the services, you can also choose **Edit Startup Type** and edit the settings.

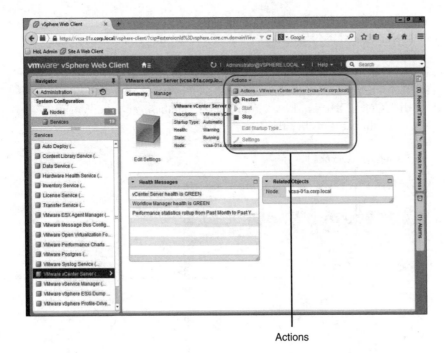

Actions

Figure 10-3   Actions for the vCenter Server Service

You find the following services at **Administration > System Configuration > Services**:

- Auto Deploy
- Content Library Service
- Data Service
- Hardware Health Service
- Inventory Service
- License Service
- Transfer Service
- VMware ESX Agent Manager

- VMware Message Bus Configuration Service

- VMware Open Virtualization Format Service

- VMware Performance Charts Service

- VMware Postgres

- VMware Syslog Service

- VMware vCenter Server

- VMware Service Manager

- VMware vSphere ESXi Dump Collector

- VMware vSphere Profile-Driven Storage Service

- VMware vSphere Web Client

- vAPI Endpoint

If you are troubleshooting vSphere feature issues that are directly related to any of these services, you can try stopping and restarting corresponding service. For example, if you are troubleshooting issues where the vSphere Web Client hangs or provides unusual messages while attempting to configure licensing, you could restart License Service. If you are troubleshooting issues where the vSphere Web Client does not successfully produce an advanced performance graph, you could restart VMware Performance Charts Service. If you are troubleshooting an issue where data is no longer accessible in the content library, you could try restarting Content Library Service.

Perform Basic Maintenance of a vCenter Server Database

You can monitor the state of the VMware Postgres database at **Home** > **Administration** > **System Configuration** > **Services**. Select the **VMware Postgres** service from the list of services and use the information in the center pane to verify that the health is good and the state is running, as shown in Figure 10-4. If necessary, you can use the **Actions** drop-down to stop and restart the service.

Health: Good   State: Running

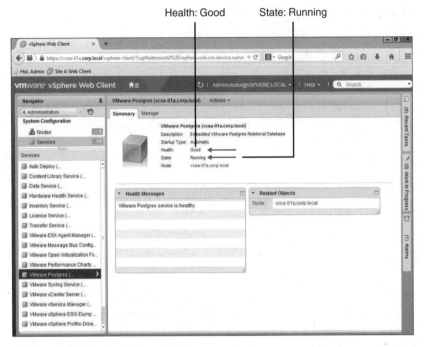

Figure 10-4   Managing the VMware Postgres Service

You should perform standard maintenance operations on the vCenter Server database, including the following items:

- Monitor the growth of the log file and compact the database log file, as needed.

- Perform regular backups of the database.

- Back up the database before any vCenter Server upgrade.

These operations are dependent on the database type. You can follow vendor-specific documentation for performing these operations.

For example, if performance graphs are not properly displaying or if they contain gaps, it could be due to rollup jobs running slowly due to the size of the vCenter Server database. If the statistics collection level is higher than 1, you could address this problem by lowering the level to 1. Another option is to have a database administrator issue these commands to truncate the VPX_HIST_STAT1 and VPX_SAMPLE_TIME1 tables:

```
truncate table VPX_HIST_STAT1;
truncate table VPX_SAMPLE_TIME1;
```

The vCenter Server service must be stopped prior to the execution of these commands and restarted following the execution.

Another optional maintenance task is to use a PostgresSQL script to reduce the amount of historical data by specifying the maximum age of task, event, and statistic records. Download the appropriate script from VMware KB 2110031. Run the script, specifying appropriate values for the parameters `TaskMaxAgeinDays`, `Event-MaxAgeinDays`, and `StatMaxAgeinDays`. The actual script name and syntax may depend on the operating system in which vCenter Server is running and the database type, but here is an example for a vCenter Server Appliance that uses a Postgres database. In this Postgres database, the username is `postgres`, the maximum number of days for each parameter is `10`, and the script resides in the `/root` directory:

```
/opt/vmware/vpostgres/current/bin/psql -U postgres -v TaskMaxAgeInDays=10
  -v EventMaxAgeInDays=10 -v StatMaxAgeInDays=10 -d database -t -q -f /
  root/2110031_Postgres_task_event_stat.sql
```

Monitor Status of ESXi Management Agents

You can use the vSphere Web Client, the vSphere Client, the Direct Console User Interface (DCUI), and the ESXi Shell to monitor and manage the ESXi management agents.

To use the vSphere Web Client to manage the ESXi management agents, use the inventory pane to select the ESXi Host and use the center pane to select **Manage** > **Settings** > **Security Profile** > **Services**, as shown in Figure 10-5. Locate a specific service and examine the **Daemon** column to determine the status of the service, such as **Stopped** or **Running**.

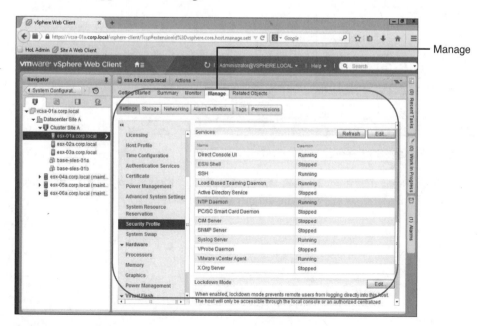

Figure 10-5 ESXi Management Services in vSphere Web Client

To change the state or settings of a service, click the **Edit** button. (You do not need to select a service before clicking the Edit button.) A window appears, listing all the services. In this interface, select the desired service and use the **Status** buttons and **Startup** drop-down list to make changes to the service. For example, Figure 10-6 shows the **SSH** service status as **Running** and includes **Stop** and **Restart** buttons. You can use the **Startup Policy** drop-down to set the SSH service to one of these values:

- **Start and Stop with Host**

- **Start and Stop with Manually**

- **Start and Stop with Port Usage**

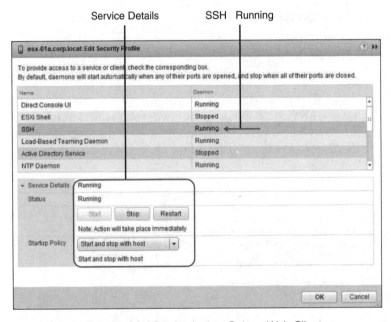

Figure 10-6   Edit the SSH Service in the vSphere Web Client

The ESXi Management agents that can be managed in the vSphere Web Client are shown in Table 10-2, along with the default status of each.

Table 10-2   ESXi Management Services

Service	Default State
Direct Console UI	Running
ESXi Shell	Stopped
SSH	Stopped
Load-Based Teaming Daemon	Running
Active Directory Service	Stopped
NTP Daemon	Stopped
PC/SC Smart Card Daemon	Stopped
CIM Server	Stopped
SNMP Server	Stopped
Syslog Server	Running
VProbe Daemon	Stopped
VMware vCenter Agent	Running
X Org Server	Stopped

Likewise, you can use **Configuration** > **Security Profile** > **Services** in the vSphere Client to manage ESXi management agents. In this case, the vSphere Client can be connected either directly to the ESXi Host or to the vCenter Server. You can also use the DCUI to control the ESXI management agents. In the DCUI menu, select **Troubleshooting Options**, select **Restart Management Agents**, and press Enter.

Determine ESXi Host Stability Issues and Gather Diagnostics Information

One method for collecting ESXi Host diagnostics data is to use the `vm-support` command, which can be run on the ESXi Host from either the ESXi Shell or an SSH session. The `vm-support` command provides many options, which you can examine by entering `vm-support -h`, as shown in Figure 10-7.

List available manifest groups

[root@esx–02a:~] vm–support –h

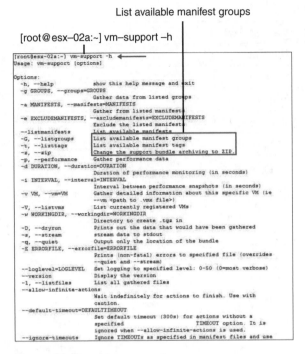

Figure 10-7 `vm-support -h`

You can simply run the `vm-support` command without adding any options, but it requires a large working directory to operate successfully, so you should typically use the `-w` parameter to identify a working directory with plenty of available space. Executing the `vm-support` command creates a TGZ file, which you may submit to VMware when reporting an incident. If you wish to analyze the data yourself, you may begin by unpacking it by using the `tar` command. For example, the following commands could be used to run `vm-support` and to unpack its data, where the working directory is set to a VMFS datastore named NFSA. In this example, assume that the `vm-support` command automatically named the resulting TGZ file `esx-esxi02-2015-10-20--22.14.tgz`:

```
vm-support -w /vmfs/volumes/NFSA
cd /vmfs/volumes/NFSA
tar -xzf esx-esxi02-2015-10-20--22.14.tgz
```

The unpacked content contains ESXi logs, configuration files, and other data that may be useful for troubleshooting.

Another use for the `vm-support` command is to collect data that you can feed into the ESXTOP utility for displaying resource usage in replay mode. To do so, run the `vm-support` command with the `-p`, `-d`, and `-i` arguments. The `-p` option indicates that performance snapshot data should be collected. The `-d` option is used to specify the duration (in seconds) for which data should be collected. The `-i` option is used to specify the interval (in seconds) between samples. For example, the following command can be used to collect performance data for 60 seconds at 2-seconds intervals, using a datastore named NFSA as the working directory:

```
vm-support -p -d 60 -i 2 -w /vmfs/volumes/NFSA
```

Next, unzip and un-`tar` the resulting output file so it can be used by ESXTOP. Then change to the newly created directory and run the `reconstruct` script by executing the following command:

./reconstruct.sh

Finally, return to the previous directory and run ESXTOP in replay mode, specifying the newly created folder. An example of issuing these commands is shown in Figure 10-8. The resulting ESXTOP results are shown in Figure 10-9.

```
esxtop -R vm-support_dir_path
```

cd/vmfs/volumes/NFSA/

tar –xzf esx-esx-02a-2015-12-28--17.09.tgz

cd esx-esx-02a-2015-12-28--17.09/

esx-esx-02a-2015-12-28--17.09] ./reconstruct.sh

esxtop -R esx-esx-02a-2015-12-28--17.09

Figure 10-8   `reconstruct.sh`

```
PCPU USED(%):  33  58 AVG:  46
PCPU UTIL(%):  34  58 AVG:  46

    ID      GID NAME              NWLD  %USED  %RUN  %SYS   %WAIT %VMWAIT   %RDY  %IDLE %OVRLP  %
     2        2 system             107   1.10  1.59  0.16 10668.32      -   7.80   0.00   1.51
221704   221704 python.66282         2   1.10  1.11  0.00   96.97      -   0.63   0.00   0.02
   793      793 vmsyslogd.32996      4   0.83  0.85  0.00  397.32      -   0.53   0.00   0.03
  8094     8094 hostd.34192         19   0.23  0.23  0.00 1894.00      -   0.25   0.00   0.00
     8        8 helper             208   0.15  0.16  0.00 4080.91      -   1.48   0.00   0.01
 16675    16675 vmtoolsd.35673       1   0.06  0.07  0.00   97.69      -   1.93   0.00   0.01
186256   186256 sshd.60017           1   0.06  0.08  0.00   99.53      -   0.04   0.00   0.02
 12665    12665 vpxa.34872          17   0.06  0.04  0.02 1694.70      -   0.15   0.00   0.00
  1746     1746 net-lacp.33186       3   0.02  0.02  0.00  298.97      -   0.07   0.00   0.00
  2545     2545 busybox.33477        1   0.02  0.00  0.02   99.64      -   0.00   0.00   0.00
  2158     2158 nfsgssd.33336        1   0.02  0.02  0.00   99.41      -   0.21   0.00   0.00
  5834     5834 net-lbt.33900        1   0.01  0.01  0.00   99.88      -   0.00   0.00   0.00
 14892    14892 openwsmand.3544      3   0.01  0.01  0.00  299.03      -   0.03   0.00   0.00
    10       10 ft                   5   0.00  0.00  0.00  498.38      -   0.01   0.00   0.00
 17538    17538 sfcb-ProviderMa     10   0.00  0.01  0.00  999.08      -   0.02   0.00   0.00
  9510     9510 dcbd.34379           1   0.00  0.01  0.00   99.39      -   0.25   0.00   0.00
  3406     3406 ntpd.33598           1   0.00  0.01  0.00   99.62      -   0.02   0.00   0.00
  5818     5818 rhttpproxy.3389      9   0.00  0.00  0.00  898.10      -   0.01   0.00   0.00
     9        9 drivers             12   0.00  0.00  0.00 1198.24      -   0.06   0.00   0.00
  9420     9420 nscd.34362           6   0.00  0.00  0.00  597.99      -   0.00   0.00   0.00
  3791     3791 swapobjd.33646       1   0.00  0.00  0.00   99.64      -   0.01   0.00   0.00
  5769     5769 sdrsInjector.33      1   0.00  0.00  0.00   99.65      -   0.00   0.00   0.00
  5885     5885 storageRM.33906      1   0.00  0.00  0.00   99.65      -   0.00   0.00   0.00
  2413     2413 busybox.33447        1   0.00  0.00  0.00   99.64      -   0.00   0.00   0.00
   970      970 vobd.33020          19   0.00  0.00  0.00 1894.03      -   0.00   0.00   0.00
  8512     8512 slpd.34249           1   0.00  0.00  0.00   99.64      -   0.00   0.00   0.00
 21685    21685 sfcb-ProviderMa      7   0.00  0.00  0.00  699.41      -   0.00   0.00   0.00
     1        1 idle                 2   0.00 200.00 0.00    0.00      - 200.00   0.00   0.68
    11       11 vmotion              1   0.00  0.00  0.00   99.64      -   0.00   0.00   0.00
 16430    16430 sh.35642             1   0.00  0.00  0.00   99.65      -   0.00   0.00   0.00
 12568    12568 sh.34860             1   0.00  0.00  0.00   99.65      -   0.00   0.00   0.00
   396      396 init.32953           1   0.00  0.00  0.00  100.00      -   0.00   0.00   0.00
 12891    12891 sh.35143             1   0.00  0.00  0.00   99.69      -   0.00   0.00   0.00
 17088    17088 cimslp.35724         1   0.00  0.00  0.00   99.69      -   0.00   0.00   0.00
 17105    17105 sfcb-sfcb.35726      1   0.00  0.00  0.00   99.65      -   0.00   0.00   0.00
 17121    17121 sfcb-sfcb.35728      1   0.00  0.00  0.00   99.69      -   0.00   0.00   0.00
 17129    17129 sfcb-sfcb.35729      1   0.00  0.00  0.00   99.69      -   0.00   0.00   0.00
```

Figure 10-9   ESXTOP Replay Mode

Table 10-3 provides details on command-line options for using ESXTOP in replay mode.

Table 10-3   ESXTOP Replay Mode Command-Line Options

Option	Description
-R	Path to the data collected by vm-support
-a	Show all statistics
-b	Run in batch mode
-c	User-defined configuration file
-d	Delay (in seconds) for the sampling period. The default is 5, and the minimum is 2.
-n	Number of iterations (samples) for ESXTOP to take prior to automatically exiting.

When troubleshooting, a common practice is to create support bundles that you can send to VMware Support. To create support bundles using the vSphere Web Client:

Step 1.   Select **Administration** > **System Configuration**.

Step 2.   In the center pane, select the **Objects** tab and select the vCenter Server.

Step 3.   In the Actions menu, select **Export Support Bundles**, as shown in Figure 10-10.

Step 4.   In the wizard, expand the **VirtualAppliance** bundle and select the specific logs to include, as shown in Figure 10-11.

Step 5.   Click the **Export Support Bundle** button.

Step 6.   Click the **OK** button.

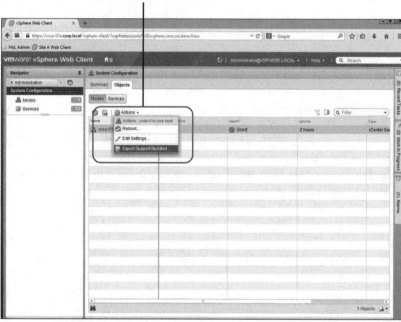

Figure 10-10   Export Support Bundle

Figure 10-11   Export Support Bundle Wizard

On Windows-based vCenter Servers, you can generate a log bundle by logging into Windows directly as an administrator and using **Start** > **All Programs** > **VMware** > **Generate vCenter Server Log Bundle**. After creating the log bundle, you should be able to locate it as a ZIP file on the administrator's desktop. This is a handy way to generate a log bundle when the vSphere Web Client is not functioning correctly. Alternatively, use the command prompt and the `cd` command to change the default directory to the vCenter Server installation directory and then to the `VMware\vCenter Server\bin` subdirectory. From there, issue the `vc-support.bat` command to generate the log bundle.

You can use the vSphere Web Client to view diagnostic data and export system log files for selected ESXi Hosts. The required privilege to view diagnostic data is **Read-Only User**. The required privilege to manage diagnostic data is **Global.Licenses**. This is the procedure for exporting the system log files:

Step 1.   In the inventory pane, select the appropriate vCenter Server in the **vCenter Servers List**.

Step 2.   In the center pane, select the **Monitor > System Logs**.

Step 3.   Click the **Export System Logs** button, as shown in Figure 10-12.

Step 4.   In the wizard, select the appropriate ESXi Hosts from which you wish to export logs.

Step 5.   Optionally, select the **Include vCenter Server and vSphere Web Client Logs** check box. Click **Next**.

Step 6.   In the next wizard page, select the specific system log files to collect, as shown in Figure 10-13. Optionally, select the **Gather Performance Data** check box.

Step 7.   Click the **Generate Log Bundle** button.

Step 8.   Click the **Download Log Bundle** button and specify a location to save the bundle. When the download completes, click **Finish**.

Export System Logs

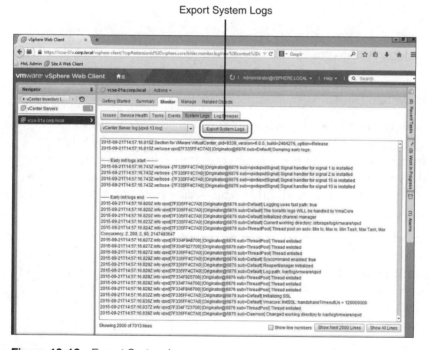

Figure 10-12   Export System Logs

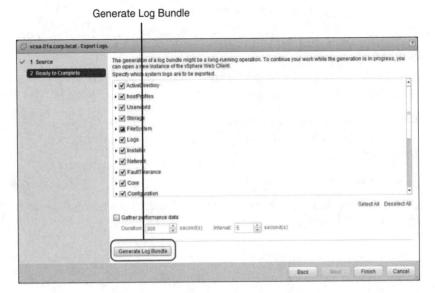

Figure 10-13   Specify System Logs

Monitor ESXi System Health

Health information for ESXi servers is visible in multiple places in the vSphere Web Client. For example, the **Summary** page for the ESXi Host shows the **State** and **Uptime** for the host. The **Monitor > Issues** page for the host provides the ability to view **All Issues** and **Triggered Alarms**. The **Hardware Status** page shows information on the health of physical components such as processor, memory, voltage, and temperature, as shown in Figure 10-14.

In addition, whenever you see a yellow warning or a red alert indicator on an ESXi Host icon, it is a sign that an alarm has triggered for the host. You can view the alert by selecting **Monitor > Issues > Triggered Alarms**. You can customize the alarms to provide actions to use SNMP and SMTP messages to automatically notify operators and administrators.

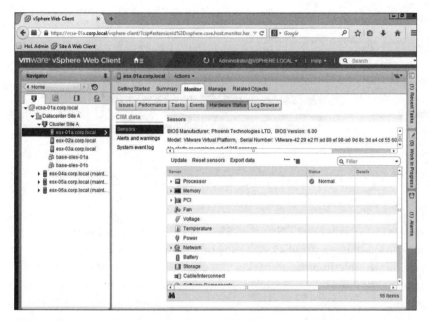

Figure 10-14 ESXi Host Hardware Health

Locate and Analyze vCenter Server and ESXi Logs

The earlier section "Determine ESXi Host Stability Issues and Gather Diagnostics Information" covers collecting and exporting log bundles from the vCenter Server and ESXi Hosts. This section covers the location of log files and analysis of log files.

The default log level setting on ESXi and vCenter Server systems is **Info**, which means errors, warnings, and informational level are logged. You can change the log level to lower levels, such as **Verbose**, which is useful for troubleshooting and debugging but not recommended for normal use in production environments. You can use the vSphere Web Client to change the logging level for vCenter Server by navigating to and selecting the vCenter Server, selecting **Manage** > **Settings** > **Edit**, and setting the **Logging Settings** to the appropriate level. The available levels are **None**, **Error**, **Warning**, **Info**, **Verbose**, and **Trivia**, as shown in Figure 10-15. You can use a text editor to modify the logging level on ESXi Hosts by modifying the appropriate `config.xml` file. For example, to change the logging level for the hostd service, modify the `/etc/vmware/hostd/config.xml` file and change the value for the *<level>* tag.

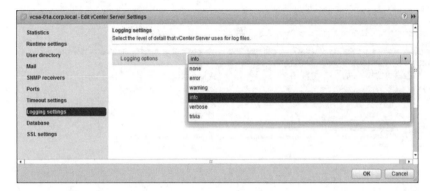

Figure 10-15   Setting the vCenter Server Log Level

Table 10-4 provides details on the ESXi log files, including the location and purpose of each. You should get familiar with each of these and learn which logs are useful for various troubleshooting scenarios. For example, when troubleshooting virtual machine issues, the only directly useful logs are `vmkernel`, `vmkwarning`, `hostd`, and the specific virtual machine's log files. When troubleshooting issues related to the connection between and ESXi Host and the vCenter Server, the `vpxa` log is most useful.

Table 10-4   ESXi Log Files

Component	Location	Purpose
VMkernel	`/var/log/vmkernel.log`	Records activities related to virtual machines and ESXi.
VMkernel warnings	`/var/log/vmkwarning.log`	Records activities related to virtual machines.
Vmkernel summary	`/var/log/vmksummary.log`	Used to determine uptime and availability statistics for ESXi.
ESXi Host agent	`/var/log/hostd.log`	Contains information about the agent that manages and configures the ESXi Host and its virtual machines.
vCenter agent	`/var/log/vpxa.log`	Contains information about the agent that communicates with vCenter Server.
ESXi Shell	`/var/log/shell.log`	Contains a record of all commands typed into the ESXi Shell as well as shell events.
Authentication	`/var/log/auth.log`	Contains all events related to authentication for the local system.

Component	Location	Purpose
System Messages	`/var/log/syslog.log`	Contains all general log messages and can be used for troubleshooting.
Virtual Machines	`vmware.log`, located in the same folder as the virtual machine configuration file	Contains virtual machine power events, system failure information, tools status and activity, time sync, virtual hardware changes, vMotion migrations, machine clones, and more.

You can use the Log Browser in the vSphere Web Client to retrieve, examine, and search logs. To get started, navigate to the desired vCenter Server or ESXi Host and select **Monitor > Log Browser**, as shown in Figure 10-16. Next, click the **Retrieve Now** link to retrieve the logs for the selected object. Optionally, click **Refresh** and select the type of log to view. You can use the **Filter** box and the **Advanced Filters** option to manage the log data to be viewed.

Monitor

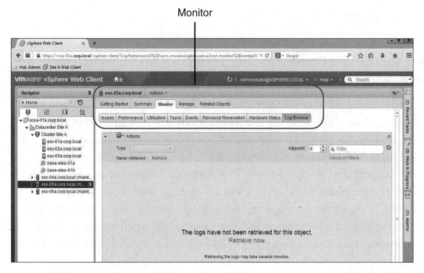

Figure 10-16 Log Browser

The major log file for the vCenter Server is `vpxd`. Other logs that are available in the vSphere Web Client Log Browser for the vCenter Server object include `Virgo-Server`, `front-desk`, `lookup Server`, and `ssoAdminServer`, as shown in Figure 10-17.

lookup Server

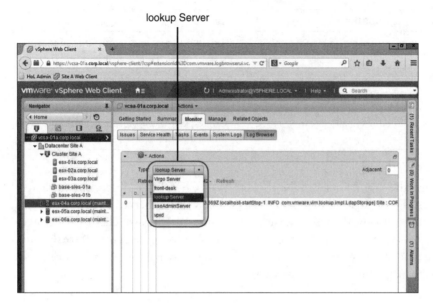

Figure 10-17   vCenter Server Log Types

Determine the Appropriate Command-Line Interface (CLI) Command for a Given Troubleshooting Task

In a vSphere environment, commands can be run directly on an ESXi Host in the ESXi Shell or via Secure Shell (SSH). Commands can also be run in the vSphere Command-Line Interface (vCLI). VMware provides a Windows version and a Linux version of the vCLI to allow you to install it on the desktop of your choice. Alternatively, you can deploy the vSphere Management Assistant (vMA), which is a Linux-based virtual appliance that includes many management tools, including the vCLI. The vMA is handy when you're running vCLI commands to configure and manage the environment. Running commands in the ESXi Shell is mostly useful for troubleshooting, especially when you're tackling issues that relate to ESXi Host connectivity.

To deploy the vMA, download the OVF file from the VMware website and use it to deploy the appliance. A trust relationship is required between vMA (or the source of vCLI) and the ESXi Host. This can be accomplished using a thumbprint. Failure to use a thumbprint results in errors, as described in VMware KB 2108416. Here is an example of the error message:

```
Connect to server-01.mydomain.com failed. Server SHA-1 thumbprint 5D:01:0
6:63:55:9D:DF:FE:38:81:6E:2C:FA:71:BC:63:82:C5:16:51 <not trusted>
```

The following command can be used from the vMA command line to add the thumbprint to the vCenter Server certificate store:

```
/usr/lib/vmware-vcli/apps/general/credstore_admin.pl add -s server -t
  thumbprint
```

Alternatively, the thumbprint can be added to each ESXCLI command.

```
esxcli --server myESXi --username user1 --password 'my_password'
  --thumbprint 5D:01:06:63:55:9D:DF:FE:38:81:6E:2C:FA:71:BC:63:82
  :C5:16:51 storage nfs list
```

Another option is to download the trusted root certificate from the vCenter Server. You can do this by using a web browser to connect to the vCenter Server fully qualified domain name or IP address and selecting **Download Trusted Root Certificates**. Save the certificates as a ZIP file. The ZIP file contains nested files that have the extensions .0 or .1, which are certificates, and nested files that have the extensions .r0 and .r1, which are associated CRL files.

The VMware recommended command-line approach is to use the ESXCLI command name space in the vCLI. The ESXi Shell provides ESXCLI as well as the legacy `esxcfg` command set. Likewise, the vMA provides the legacy `vicfg` command set. Generally speaking, you should use ESXCLI commands when available and only use `vicfg` and `esxcfg` commands when required. For example, when using a command to troubleshoot NTP configuration, you should use `vicfg-ntp` because ESXCLI has no command for configuring NTP.

The ESXCLI command set is intended to provide a single set of commands to perform all ESXi Host–based administrative tasks. It provides a collection of namespaces as a mechanism for an administrator to quickly discover the precise command necessary for a specific task. For example, all the commands to configure networking exist in the `esxcli network` namespace, and all the commands to configure storage exist in the `esxcli storage` namespace. Each namespace is further divided into child namespaces that comprise various functions performed under the parent namespace. For example, the `esxcli storage` parent namespace contains a `core` namespace that deals with storage adapters and devices and an `nmp` namespace that deals with path selection and storage array types. Therefore, a typical ESXCLI command is composed of multiple namespaces, where each additional namespace is used to narrow the scope of the command, ending with the actual operation to be performed.

You can use the following method to identify the proper ESXCLI command to perform a specific task. First, simply enter `esxcli` at the command prompt in the ESXi Shell, vCLI instance, or vMA. Because it is not a command by itself, just the entry point to the namespace hierarchy, the results will show the first level of the namespace hierarchy. The first level of available namespaces includes `esxcli`, `fcoe`, `hardware`, `iscsi`, `network`, `sched`, `software`, `storage`, `system`, and `vm`. The results include a brief description of each namespace, as shown in Figure 10-18. Next, identify which namespace is most likely to serve your need. Use the up-arrow key on the keyboard to retrieve the last entered namespace and add the name for the next namespace. For example, if you are seeking a network-related command, you could enter `esxcli network` to provide the next level of the namespace hierarchy, as shown in Figure 10-19.

Figure 10-18   First-Level Hierarchy of the ESXCLI Namespace

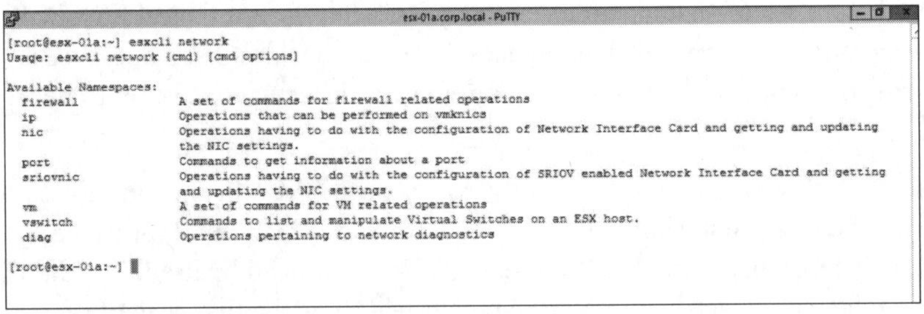

Figure 10-19   Available Namespaces at `esxcli network`

For a more thorough example, if you are seeking a command to list all standard vSwitches, you could use these steps:

Step 1. Enter `esxcli` and examine the results, which should look as shown in Figure 10-18.

Step 2. Enter `esxcli network` and examine the results, which should look as shown in Figure 10-19.

Step 3. Enter `esxcli network vswitch`, and examine the results, which should look as shown in Figure 10-20.

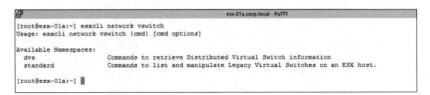

Figure 10-20 Available Namespaces at `esxcli network vswitch`

Enter `esxcli network vswitch standard` and examine the results, which should look as shown in Figure 10-21. Notice that at this level, some available commands are now displayed: `add`, `list`, `remove`, and `set`. For this example, the `list` command seems to be the most appropriate.

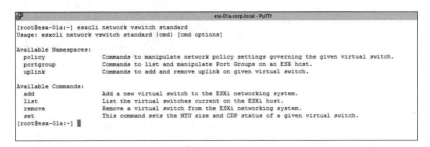

Figure 10-21 Available Namespaces at `esxcli network vswitch standard`

Enter the `esxcli network vswitch standard list` command to produces results like those shown in Figure 10-22.

```
                                                           esx-01a.corp.local - PuTTY
[root@esx-01a:~] esxcli network vswitch standard list
vSwitch0
   Name: vSwitch0
   Class: etherswitch
   Num Ports: 1536
   Used Ports: 1
   Configured Ports: 128
   MTU: 1500
   CDP Status: listen
   Beacon Enabled: false
   Beacon Interval: 1
   Beacon Threshold: 3
   Beacon Required By:
   Uplinks:
   Portgroups: Internal Network
[root@esx-01a:~]
```

Figure 10-22   Results of Command to List Standard Virtual Switches

NOTE   When using the previously discussed approach to discover the appropriate command for a given task, pay attention to commands versus namespaces. Entering a namespace at the command prompt is safe because it simply displays the next level of available namespaces and commands. However, entering a command at the command prompt executes that command. You should be careful not to enter a command without fully understanding the consequences.

Table 10-5 contains some sample ESXCLI commands.

Table 10-5   Sample ESXCLI Commands

Command	Purpose
esxcli system account add	Create an ESXi Host local user account.
esxcli system account set	Configure an ESXi Host local user account.
esxcli system account list	List ESXi Host local user accounts.
esxcli system account remove	Delete an ESXi Host local user accounts.
esxcli network ip dns server list	List DNS servers.
esxcli network nic list	List the ESXi Host physical network adapters.

Troubleshoot Common Issues

The following sections provide information on troubleshooting some common issues.

vCenter Server Service

If the vCenter Server is not working well, you should first determine whether the issue is actually a connectivity issue, which is covered in a later section of this chapter. If the issue is not connectivity, then it may be related directly to the vCenter Server service. For example, if the vCenter Server responds to pings and port tests but one or more of the following symptoms exist, then the issue may be related to the vCenter Server service:

- When you select the vCenter Server and then select **Monitor > All Issues**, a small error window appears, with the error message `Issues information is not available at this time`, as shown in Figure 10-23.

- Likewise, similar error messages indicating that information is not available appears as you navigate to other areas of the vCenter Server, including the host and clusters area.

- When you navigate to the hosts and clusters area in the vCenter server, you see the error `Unexpected status code: 503`.

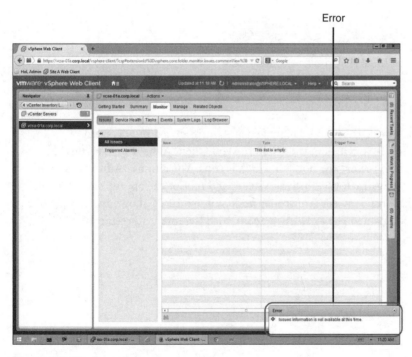

Figure 10-23   Error: `Issues information is not available at this time`

Whenever issues occur that are related to the vCenter Server service, you could first try stopping and restarting the vCenter Server service. To do so, select **Home > Administration > System Configuration > Services**, select the vCenter Server service, and use the Actions drop-down, as previously described, in the "Monitor Status of the vCenter Server Service" section in this chapter.

You can also manage the nodes in which the vCenter and related services run. You can use **Administration > System Configuration > Nodes** to identify and reboot the nodes. You can edit the nodes to enable local login, enable SSH login, and configure networking and firewall settings. For example, if you are troubleshooting a vCenter Server appliance that runs both the Platform Services Controller and vCenter Server and you want to access its command-line interface, you could edit the node to enable SSH login, as shown in Figure 10-24.

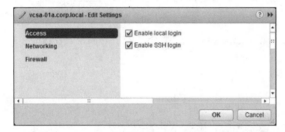

Figure 10-24   Enable SSH Login in a vCenter Node

Single Sign-On (SSO)

SSO is not a service that can be managed at **Administration > System Configuration > Services** in the vSphere Web Client. One way to restart the SSO service is to restart the node in which it runs. You can use **Administration > System Configuration > Nodes** to select and reboot the appropriate vCenter Server or Platform Services Controller node. Figure 10-25 shows an example of restarting a node named `vcsa-01a.corp.local` with the intent to restart its SSO service.

Figure 10-25 Restart Node

SSO can be configured using **Administration** > **Single Sign-On** > **Configuration**. From here you can configure policies, identity sources, certificates, and SAML providers.

Policies include password and lockout policies. The default password policy includes these requirements:

- Passwords must be changed every 90 days.

- Users cannot reuse the previous 5 passwords.

- The maximum character length is 20.

- The minimum character length is 8.

- The password must contain uppercase, lowercase, special, and numeric characters.

This information can be useful for troubleshooting. For example, if users are locked out of their accounts or have forgotten their passwords, it may be that they are struggling to comply with the password policy. When necessary, the password policy can be changed to meet new requirements. By default, 5 consecutive, recent failed attempts triggers SSO to lock the account. You can use **Administration** > **Single Sign-on** > **Users and Groups** to unlock accounts and change passwords, as shown in Figure 10-26.

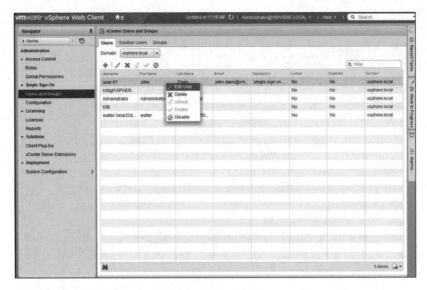

Figure 10-26   Troubleshoot SSO User Account

For example, if the administrator@vsphere.local account is the main account for
SSO administration and it is locked due to an excessive number of failed login attempts, you could simply wait until the configured Unlock time period has expired
and try again. If the unlock time period is too long or if the password is unknown,
then the issue may be very difficult to correct, if this is the sole account used for
SSO administration. Therefore, VMware recommends that you configure at least
one other account that can be used for SSO administration, which you could use to
unlock accounts and to change SSO policies.

vCenter Server Connectivity

Whenever the vCenter Server appears to be nonresponsive, it may be suffering from
connectivity issues. A common test for vCenter Server connectivity is to use the
`ping` command, but the results you get from it are actually not conclusive because
you actually need to verify connectivity using specific ports, as shown in Table 10-6.

Table 10-6   vCenter Server Ports

Port	Purpose
22	For SSH connections, when using the vCenter Server Appliance
80	For direct HTTP connections, which vCenter Server automatically redirects to port 443
88	For VMware key distribution

Port	Purpose
389	For Directory Services
443	For connections with the vSphere Web Client, SDK clients, and third-party clients
514 and 1514	For Syslog Collector connections
636	For vCenter Server Enhanced Linked Mode
902	For ESXi Host management
2012	For SSO control
2014	For VMCA API connections
2020	For authentication framework management
6500	For ESXi Dump Collection connections
6501 and 6502	For Auto Deploy service and management
7444	For Secure Token Service (STS)
9443	For vSphere Web Client HTTPS connections
11711 and 11712	For VMware Directory Service (vmdir) LDAP and LDAPS

You can use the `telnet` command to test connectivity to the vCenter Server via a specific port. For example, the following command can be used from any Windows or Linux system that provides the `telnet` utility:

```
telnet vcsa-01a.corp.local 443
```

In this example, the command is used to test the ability to connect to a server named `vcsa-01a.corp.local` using port 443.

If `telnet` successfully reaches the target server using the specified port, a blank telnet session window appears with a flashing cursor, as if it is waiting on input. Otherwise, an error message, such as `connection refused` or `connect failed`, may appear immediately.

If you discover that specific, required vCenter connections cannot be made, you must troubleshoot by focusing on the path between the specific vCenter component and the corresponding source or target component. You must verify that each point along the path provides general connectivity as well as acceptance of the specific port. For example, when troubleshooting an issue where the logs of an ESXi Host are not successfully reaching the Syslog Collector, you should verify the connectivity from the ESXi Host to the collector using port 514. If a problem is found with this connectivity, you need to verify that TCP port 514 is permitted via any firewalls in the path, including the ESXi Host firewall, and software firewalls that reside on the collector. If the Syslog Collector runs on a Windows server, verify that the Windows Firewall is configured to permit TCP port 514. To manage the ESXi firewall in the vSphere Web Client, select the ESXi Host inventory pane and select **Manage** > **Settings** > **Security Profile** > **Firewall**. Ensure that the **Syslog** box is checked, as shown in Figure 10-27.

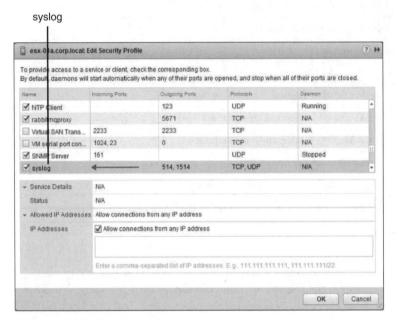

Figure 10-27   Enable Syslog in Security Profile Firewall

Alternatively, the following command can be used to examine the firewall rule settings on an ESXi Host:

```
esxcli network firewall ruleset list
```

The results provide a list of all known network services, such as `snmp`, `sshServer`, and `ntpClient`, and indicate which services are enabled.

For lower-level details, you can use the following command, which identifies the underlying rules within each rule set and provides additional fields, such as Direction, Port Type, and Protocol, as shown in Figure 10-28:

```
esxcli network firewall ruleset rule list
```

```
                                                    esx-01a.corp.local - PuTTY
[root@esx-01a:~] esxcli network firewall ruleset rule list
Ruleset              Direction   Protocol   Port Type   Port Begin   Port End
-------------------  ----------  ---------  ----------  ----------   --------
sshServer            Inbound     TCP        Dst                 22         22
sshClient            Outbound    TCP        Dst                 22         22
nfsClient            Outbound    TCP        Dst                  0      65535
nfs41Client          Outbound    TCP        Dst               2049       2049
dhcp                 Inbound     UDP        Dst                 68         68
dhcp                 Outbound    UDP        Src                 68         68
dns                  Inbound     UDP        Dst                 53         53
dns                  Outbound    UDP        Dst                 53         53
dns                  Outbound    TCP        Dst                 53         53
snmp                 Inbound     UDP        Dst                161        161
ntpClient            Outbound    UDP        Dst                123        123
CIMHttpServer        Inbound     TCP        Dst               5988       5988
CIMHttpsServer       Inbound     TCP        Dst               5989       5989
CIMSLP               Inbound     UDP        Dst                427        427
CIMSLP               Outbound    UDP        Src                427        427
CIMSLP               Inbound     TCP        Dst                427        427
CIMSLP               Outbound    TCP        Src                427        427
iSCSI                Outbound    TCP        Dst               3260       3260
vpxHeartbeats        Outbound    UDP        Dst                902        902
updateManager        Outbound    TCP        Dst                 80         80
updateManager        Outbound    TCP        Dst               9000       9100
faultTolerance       Outbound    TCP        Dst                 80         80
faultTolerance       Inbound     TCP        Dst               8100       8100
faultTolerance       Outbound    TCP        Dst               8100       8100
faultTolerance       Inbound     UDP        Dst               8200       8200
faultTolerance       Outbound    UDP        Dst               8200       8200
faultTolerance       Inbound     TCP        Dst               8300       8300
faultTolerance       Outbound    TCP        Dst               8300       8300
webAccess            Inbound     TCP        Dst                 80         80
vMotion              Inbound     TCP        Dst               8000       8000
vMotion              Outbound    TCP        Dst               8000       8000
vSphereClient        Inbound     TCP        Dst                902        902
vSphereClient        Inbound     TCP        Dst                443        443
activeDirectoryAll   Outbound    UDP        Dst                 88         88
activeDirectoryAll   Outbound    TCP        Dst                 88         88
activeDirectoryAll   Outbound    UDP        Dst                123        123
activeDirectoryAll   Outbound    UDP        Dst                137        137
activeDirectoryAll   Outbound    TCP        Dst                139        139
activeDirectoryAll   Outbound    TCP        Dst                389        389
activeDirectoryAll   Outbound    UDP        Dst                389        389
activeDirectoryAll   Outbound    TCP        Dst                445        445
```

Figure 10-28   Firewall Rule Details

ESXi Host network connectivity can be tested from the DCUI by using the **Test Management Network** option. By default, this option pings the configured gateway and DNS servers. It attempts to resolve its own hostname. It allows you to specify other IP addresses that the host will ping.

When needed, you can restart the management network services on the ESXi Host by selecting the **Restart Management Network** option in the DCUI. You can perform a similar operation per VMkernel virtual network adapter by using ESXCLI. For example, to stop and restart the management network service for the vmk0 virtual adapter, use the following commands:

```
esxcli network ip interface set -e false -i vmk0
esxcli network ip interface set -e true -i vmk0
```

Virtual Machine Resource Contention, Configuration, and Operation

See the section "Identify and Isolate CPU and Memory Contention Issues" in Chapter 12, "Troubleshoot Performance," for info on VM resource contention troubleshooting.

A common issue with virtual machines is failure to start. Many root causes can lead to this condition. Table 10-7 lists a few of them, along with potential solutions.

Table 10-7 Virtual Machine Start Failures

Symptom	Root Cause	Solution Examples
Insufficient memory resources	The required memory for starting the virtual machine is not currently available. The required memory to start the virtual machine includes the amount of memory that is directly reserved for the virtual machine plus the amount of memory automatically reserved for the virtual machine overhead. The amount of memory that is available to run the virtual machine is dependent not only on the free host memory but also on free memory in the resource pool, where the virtual machine resides.	■ Reduce the virtual machine reservation. ■ Increase the resource pool limit. ■ Reduce competing virtual machine memory reservations.
Insufficient failover resources	Whenever vSphere high availability (HA) is configured on a cluster, it may be set to effectively reserve CPU and memory resources in case of host failures. In this case, if you attempt to start a virtual machine that has CPU or memory reserved, the HA admission control may prevent it from starting because of insufficient failover resources.	■ Decrease the virtual machine reservations. ■ Change or disable the HA admission control. ■ Stop other virtual machines that have excessive reservations.
Insufficient disk space	The amount of disk space required to create the virtual machine swap file exceeds the available datastore space or the datastore lacks the space to support a snapshot, thin-provisioned virtual disk, or other virtual machine file.	■ Delete unnecessary virtual machines or files from the datastore. ■ Increase the size of the datastore. ■ Migrate the virtual machine to another datastore. ■ Migrate competing virtual machines to other datastores.

Other potential issues may occur with virtual machines. For example, some newer virtual machine features may not be available when using the vSphere Client (not the vSphere Web Client). This is because virtual machines that are configured with virtual hardware version 9 and higher are limited to version 8 features when accessed via the vSphere Client.

NOTE   The vSphere Client is frequently called the vSphere C# Client. Do not confuse this with the vSphere Web Client.

Although the VCP6-DCV Exam Blueprint does not specifically mention virtual machine 3D graphics, this is frequently an area of concern when troubleshooting virtual machine performance. For example, if a set of virtual machines suffers poor performance or uses an excessive amount of overhead memory, you may determine that you can change some virtual machines that are unnecessarily using expensive graphic features. You can use the following procedure to disable 3D graphics, disable SGVA functionality, and reduce the memory overhead:

Step 1.   Shut down the virtual machine.

Step 2.   Edit the virtual machine and disable the **Accelerate 3D Graphics** option.

Step 3.   Edit the virtual machine configuration file (VMX) using a text editor.

Step 4.   Add this line to the configuration file:

```
vga.vgaOnly=TRUE
```

Step 5.   Save the file and power on the virtual machine.

The line in step 4 is used to remove all graphics and SVGA functionality from your SVGA device, but it does not remove the settings that allow BIOS to enter VGA mode. It disables advanced graphics and leaves the `mks.enable3d` useless. You should apply this setting only to virtual machines that do not need a virtualized video card.

Another troubleshooting concern that is related to virtual machine video settings is the compatibility of specific video settings. For example, fault tolerance and HA are not supported for virtual machines that have 3D graphics enabled. For another example, the use of NVIDIA vGPU by virtual machines requires a vSphere Enterprise Plus license.

Occasionally, virtual machine troubleshooting may require you to stop and restart virtual machines. Naturally, you should typically use a graceful approach to shut down virtual machines, such as accessing the guest operating system directly to perform the shutdown. But in some cases you may need to power down virtual machines hard, which can be done in the vSphere Web Client. When necessary, you can also use an ESXCLI command to stop virtual machine processes. To do so, you begin by using this command to identify the world IDs for the running virtual machines:

```
esxcli vm process list
```

After using the results to identify the world IDs for the virtual machines that you want to stop, use the following command:

```
esxcli vm process kill --type killtype --world-id worldid
```

Replace `killtype` with `soft` (graceful shutdown), `hard` (immediate shutdown), or `force` (aggressive shutdown, last resort).

Platform Services Controller (PSC)

The following services are available in the Platform Services Controller (PSC):

- VMware Appliance Management Service (only in Appliance-based PSC)
- VMware License Service
- VMware Component Manager
- VMware Identity Management Service
- VMware HTTP Reverse Proxy
- VMware Service Control Agent
- VMware Security Token Service
- VMware Common Logging Service
- VMware Syslog Health Service
- VMware Authentication Framework
- VMware Certificate Service
- VMware Directory Service

As described in the "Monitor Status of the vCenter Server Service" section, you can use the vSphere Web Client to restart these services as needed for troubleshooting and management. Alternatively, you can restart the PSC server.

Typically, when engaging VMware Support to troubleshoot issues related to the PSC, you begin with creating a support bundle, which can be done in a variety of ways. When PSC is deployed in a virtual appliance, you can use a web browser to log on with root credentials to `https://Platform_Services_Controller_FQDN/appliance/support-bundle` and automatically download the bundle as a file named `vm-support.tgz`. Another option is to use SSH to log onto the appliance and run the command `/storage/log/ :vc-support -l` to download the bundle in a file named `vc-<FQDN_of-PSC>-<Date>.tgz`.

When PSC is deployed in a Windows virtual machine, you can create a support bundle using Windows to run the **VMware** > **Generate vCenter Server Log Bundle**. Or you can enter this on the command line:

```
install-folder\bin\vc-support.bat
```

In any case, you can use the vSphere Web Client to navigate to **Administration** > **System Configuration** > **Nodes**, select the PSC appliance, right-click, and click **Export Support Bundles**.

Problems with Installation

Various issues can occur when you're installing the PSC or vCenter Server. Table 10-8 lists some possible symptoms, root causes, and solutions.

Table 10-8 Potential PSC Installation Issues

Symptom	Root Cause	Solution Example
During the installation of a second PSC, the installation fails and leaves incomplete data on the first PSC.	During the initial failure, the second PSC was attempting to join the current SSO domain, resulting in incomplete data on the first PSC.	In the first PSC, execute the `vdcleavfed` command. In the following example, the hostname of the second PSC is `psc02`: `vdcleavefed -h psc02 -u Administrator`
A vCenter Server installation that uses a Microsoft SQL database fails, with the following message: `The DB User entered does not have the required permissions needed to install and configure vCenter Server with the selected DB.`	This could be caused by an unsupported database version or permissions. But it could also be caused when a supported database version is set for compatibility mode with an unsupported version.	Check the settings of the SQL database to determine whether the compatibility mode is set and whether it needs to be changed. For example, if the following command is used in the database configuration, then it is not compatible with vCenter Server 6.0: `ALTER DATABASE VCDB 80` In this example, the database name is `vcdb`, and the compatibility level is `80`, which corresponds to SQL Server 2000 compatibility.
The installation of vCenter Server fails.	The vCenter Server and the PSC have a time skew of more than 3 minutes.	During the installation, if you see a message that warns the time difference is greater than 2 minutes, stop the installation, correct the time synchronization, and run the installation again.

Symptom	Root Cause	Solution Example
The vCenter Server installation fails due to improper registration with the PSC.	You specified an FQDN during the PSC installation but used an IP address when registering vCenter Server with the PSC or vice versa.	Ensure that you use the same FQDN or use the same IP address when registering vCenter Server as you used when you provided a value for FQDN during the PSC installation. If you used an IP address during the PSC installation, use an IP address during the vCenter Server registration. If you used the actual FQDN during the PSC installation, use the FQDN during the vCenter Server registration.

VMware Tools Installation

One common way to install VMware Tools into a virtual machine is to use the interactive installation, which you can start by opening a console to the virtual machine, logging on with administrator privileges, and selecting **Install/Upgrade VMware Tools**. In most cases, the ESXi Host automatically mounts an ISO file containing the appropriate edition and version of VMware Tools. Table 10-9 lists some issues that you may encounter and typical fixes.

Table 10-9   Potential VMware Tools Issues

Issue	Typical Fix
VMware Tools installation fails due to wrong guest OS type setting.	Change the virtual machine properties to identify the correct guest OS that is actually installed and try the VMware Tools installation again.
The VMware Tools installation fails for a Windows virtual machine and generates this error: `The Windows Installer Service could not be accessed. This can occur if you are running Windows in safe mode or if the Windows Installer is not correctly installed.`	In the Windows guest OS, restart the Windows Installer service.
VMware Tools installation hangs.	Use the following command in the ESXi Shell: `vim-cmd vmsvc/tools.cancelinstall <vm.id>`

Issue	Typical Fix
A VMware Tools upgrade fails or VMware Tools functions improperly.	Uninstall VMware Tools and try again. In Windows, uninstall VMware Tools by using Add/Remove Programs. In Linux, use the `vmware-unintall-tools.pl` script.

You can install VMware Tools automatically and silently by following these steps:

Step 1.   Right-click the virtual machine and select **Guest OS > Install / Upgrade VMware Tools**.

Step 2.   Select **Automatic Tools Upgrade**.

Step 3.   In the Advanced Options box, enter the appropriate options.

Step 4.   Click **OK**.

The advanced options you should supply depend on the guest operating system and the desired options. For example, the following can be used to install all components of VMware Tools except shared folders while suppressing reboots:

```
/S /v "/qn /l*v ""%TEMP%\vmmsi.log"" REBOOT=R ADDLOCAL=ALL REMOVE=Hgfs"
```

In this example, `vmmsi.log` contains messages that are recorded during the VMware Tools installation. VMware Tools contains many components, so the best way to configure the installation to include only specific components is to actually include all components using `ADDLOCAL=ALL` and specifically exclude specific components using `REMOVE=`*component*.

For Linux virtual machines, you can use `--default` to silently install VMware Tools using default locations for binaries, libraries, and document files. Alternatively, you can use `prefix=binary_location,lib_location,doc_location` to change the location of these files.

Fault Tolerant Network Latency

All the information in this section refers to the new version of vSphere Fault Tolerance (FT), which is often called Symmetric Multi-Processing FT (SMP-FT). You can use Legacy FT and SMP-FT side by side. To use Legacy FT, you should configure it for specific virtual machines by adding the advanced option `vm.uselegacyft` and setting it to `TRUE`.

High network latency can lead to decreased virtual machine performance in FT-protected VMs. High network latency increases the time required for an FT-protected virtual machine to create and ship the checkpoint to the secondary virtual machine. Such increases may result in poor virtual machine performance because vSphere may slow down its processing while it waits for confirmation from the secondary virtual machine. Multi-CPU virtual machines that run latency-sensitive applications are not typically good candidates for FT protections.

The *vSphere Availability* guide states: "Use a dedicated 10-Gbit logging network for FT and verify that the network is low latency." But it does not specify a specific latency threshold.

To avoid problems with FT, consider implementing these VMware best practices:

- Provide sufficient resources for the secondary virtual machines, including CPU, memory, and disk space. By default, both the primary and secondary virtual machines reserve all the configured virtual machine memory.

- Use a dedicated 10 Gbps network for FT logging traffic. Do not place it on the same network as other vSphere traffic, such as management, vMotion, or virtual machines.

- Avoid resource contention on the ESXi Hosts running the primary and secondary virtual machines. The ESXi Host may slow the primary virtual machine to allow the secondary virtual machine to catch up to it.

- Do not place more than four FT-protected virtual machines on the same ESXi Host. Ensure that the total number of virtual CPUs in FT-protected virtual machines on the same host does not total more than eight.

- Although older CPU hardware is supported, use Intel Haswell generation and AMD Piledriver generation CPUs when feasible. (Intel Sandy Bridge or AMD Bulldozer or later is required.)

The following are some potential FT issues. These are not descriptions of default behavior but descriptions of potential issues based on specific scenarios:

- FT is not functional due to insufficient licenses for FT (vSphere Standard or higher is required).

- FT protection is functional for virtual machines with two virtual CPUs but not for virtual machines with four virtual CPUs due to insufficient licenses. (vSphere Enterprise Plus is required for FT protection of virtual machines with four virtual CPUs.)

- FT protection is functional for two virtual machines on an ESXi Host, but it does not allow protection for additional virtual machines due the value of the variable das.maxftvmsperhost, which controls the allowed number of FT-protected virtual machines per ESXi Host. Its default value is 4, but perhaps it has been changed to a lower value.

- FT protection is functional for two virtual machines with two virtual CPUs each on an ESXi Host, but it does not allow protection for additional virtual machines due the value of the variable `das.maxftvcpusperhost`, which controls the total number of allowed number of FT-protected virtual CPUs per ESXi Host. Its default value is `8`, but perhaps it has been changed to a lower value.

Summary

You have now read the chapter covering exam topics related to troubleshooting vSphere components. You should use information in the following sections to complete your preparation for Objective 7.1.

Exam Preparation Tasks

Review All the Key Topics

Table 10-10 provides a reference to each of the key topics identified in this chapter. Take a few moments to review each of these specific items.

Table 10-10 Key Topics for Chapter 10

Key Topic Element	Description	Pages
List	Services at Administration > System Configuration > Services	356
Table 10-2	ESXi Management Services	361
Procedure	Export System Log	366
Paragraph	ESXCLI thumbprint	373
Paragraph	Troubleshoot vCenter Server service	377

Complete the Tables and Lists from Memory

Print a copy of Appendix B, "Memory Tables" (found on the CD), or at least the section for this chapter, and complete the tables and lists from memory. Appendix C, "Memory Tables Answer Key," also on the CD, includes completed tables and lists to check your work.

Definitions of Key Terms

Define the following key terms from this chapter and check your answers in the glossary.

thumbprint, support bundle, ESXCLI

Answer Review Questions

The answers to these review questions can be found in Appendix A.

1. Which of the following is the correct option to provide to the ESXTOP utility to run in replay mode?

    a. `-R`

    b. `-r`

    c. `-i`

    d. `-I`

2. Which of the following is the proper command for listing virtual switches on an ESXi Host?

    a. `vicfg-vswitch standard list`

    b. `vicfg-vswitch list`

    c. `esxcli vswitch standard list`

    d. `esxcli network vswitch standard list`

3. Disabling or changing vSphere HA Admission Control may be useful when troubleshooting which of the following problems?

    a. Admission control is overcommitted

    b. Insufficient cluster space

    c. Insufficient disk space

    d. Insufficient failover resources

4. Per VMware best practices, you should not use FT to protect more than which of the following?

   a. 2 virtual machines or 4 virtual CPUs per ESXi Host

   b. 2 virtual machines or 8 virtual CPUs per ESXi Host

   c. 4 virtual machines or 8 virtual CPUs per ESXi Host

   d. 4 virtual machines or 16 virtual CPUs per ESXi Host

5. Which of the following services is directly dependent on network port 2012?

   a. Syslog Collector

   b. SSO

   c. Dump Collector

   d. Profile-driven Storage Service

This chapter covers the following objectives:

- **Objective 7.2—Troubleshoot vSphere Storage and Network Issues**

  - Identify and isolate network and storage resource contention and latency issues

  - Monitor networking and storage resources using vROps alerts and all badges

  - Verify network and storage configuration

  - Verify a given virtual machine is configured with the correct network resources

  - Monitor/troubleshoot Storage Distributed Resource Scheduler (SDRS) issues

  - Recognize the impact of Network and Storage I/O Control configurations

  - Recognize a connectivity issue caused by a VLAN/PVLAN

  - Troubleshoot common issues

- **Objective 7.3: Troubleshoot vSphere Upgrades**

  - Collect upgrade diagnostic information

  - Recognize common upgrade issues with vCenter Server and vCenter Server Appliance

  - Create/locate/analyze VMware log bundles

  - Determine alternative methods to upgrade ESXi Hosts in the event of failure

  - Configure vCenter Server logging options

## CHAPTER 11

Troubleshoot Storage, Networks, and Upgrades

This chapter covers exam topics related to troubleshooting storage, network, and upgrade issues in vSphere environments.

"Do I Know This Already?" Quiz

The "Do I Know This Already?" quiz allows you to assess whether you should study this entire chapter or move quickly to the "Exam Preparation Tasks" section. Regardless, the authors recommend that you read the entire chapter at least once. Table 11-1 outlines some of the major headings in this chapter and the corresponding "Do I Know This Already?" quiz questions. You can find the answers in Appendix A, "Answers to the 'Do I Know This Already?' Quizzes and Review Questions."

Table 11-1 "Do I Know This Already?" Foundation Topics Section-to-Question Mapping

Foundation Topics Section	Questions Covered in This Section
Verify Network and Storage Configuration	1
Recognize the Impact of Network and Storage I/O Control Configurations	2
Troubleshoot Common Issues	3-5
Collect Upgrade Diagnostic Information	7
Create/Locate/Analyze VMware Log Bundles	6, 8
Determine Alternative Methods to Upgrade ESXi Hosts in the Event of Failure	9
Configure vCenter Server Logging Options	10

1. Which of the following options is available in the DCUI, regardless of whether the management VMkernel virtual adapter is configured to use a distributed switch?

   a. Restore Network Settings

   b. Restore Standard Switch

   c. Restore vDS

   d. Restore Management Network

2. On a distributed virtual switch, where two 10 Gbps adapters on each ESXi Host are connected, NIOC is used to configure the following reservations (in Gbps): Management = 0.5, iSCSI = 1.0, Fault Tolerance = 1.0, and vMotion = 0.5. What is the maximum reservation that can be placed on the virtual machine traffic?

   a. 6.0 Gbps

   b. 16 Gbps

   c. 4.5 Gbps

   d. 12 Gbps

3. Which of the following correctly identifies the state in which the ESXi Host terminates all non-virtual machine I/O but the virtual machine I/O continues trying?

   a. APD

   b. PDL

   c. SOL

   d. PSP

4. In ESXTOP, which of the following is not a reasonable approach to avoid SCSI reservations?

   a. Implement the latest firmware and BIOS versions

   b. Reduce the number of ESXi Hosts and virtual machines sharing a datastore

   c. Implement ATS

   d. Implement ADS

5. Which of the following is a utility that is useful for directly checking for VMFS consistency?

    a. ESXCLI

    b. ESXTOP

    c. VMKFSTOOLS

    d. VOMA

6. Which of the following is a file you should examine to identify errors that occur while upgrading the vCenter Server database in-place?

    a. `vcdb.out`

    b. `vcdb_upgrade.out`

    c. `vcdb_err.out`

    d. `vcdb_inplace.out`

7. Which of the following is a required privilege for generating log bundles in vCenter Server?

    a. Global.Diagnostic

    b. Virtual_Center.manage

    c. Administrator

    d. vpxd.system

8. Which of the following scripts can be used from the Bash Shell of the vCenter Server Appliance to generate a log bundle?

    a. `vcsa-support.sh`

    b. `vpx-support.sh`

    c. `vs-support.sh`

    d. `vc-support.sh`

9. Which of the following commands can you use to upgrade to ESXi 6.0?

    a. `esxcli software profile install --depot=depot_location`
       `--profile=profile_name`

    b. `esxcli software profile update --depot=depot_location`
       `--profile=profile_name`

    c. `esxcli software image update --depot=depot_location`
       `--profile=profile_name`

    d. `esxcli software image install --depot=depot_location`
       `--profile=profile_name`

10. Which of the following is not a valid vCenter Server logging option?

   a. None

   b. Warning

   c. Normal

   d. Error

Foundation Topics

Objective 7.2—Troubleshoot vSphere Storage and Network Issues

The following sections describe how to troubleshoot storage, network, and upgrade issues in vSphere.

Identify and Isolate Network and Storage Resource Contention and Latency Issues

See the sections "Differentiate Common Metrics—Network" and "Differentiate Common Metrics—Storage" in Chapter 12, "Troubleshoot Performance," for details on storage- and network-related metrics that indicate contention and poor performance. Those sections provide guidance on troubleshooting these issues. Chapter 12 also provides details on using the VMware vSphere Web Client and ESXTOP to view and analyze resource metrics.

Monitor Networking and Storage Resources Using vROps Alerts and All Badges

You can use vRealize Operations Manager (vROps) to monitor a vSphere network and storage resources.

In the vROps user interface, in the left pane select **Environment** and select **vSphere Storage**. In the right pane, select the **Summary** tab. Examine the health, risk, and efficiency badges that appear in the right pane. In the example shown in Figure 11-1, all three badges are green, indicating that the overall health of the storage is good; however, at least one health alert exists for descendants.

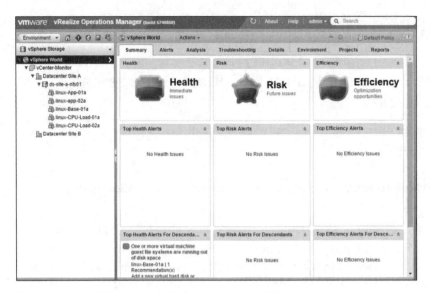

Figure 11-1 vROps vSphere Storage Summary Page

You can select any alert that appears on the Summary tab to discover root causes and recommendations. In this example, if you click on the **One or More Virtual Machine Guest Files Systems Are Running Out of Disk Space** alert, you learn that the culprit virtual machine is linux-Base-01a, as shown in Figure 11-2.

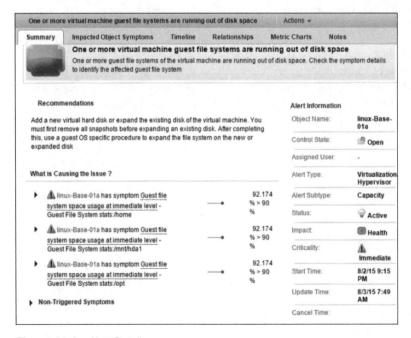

Figure 11-2 Alert Details

In vROps, you can select a specific datastore in the Environment inventory and use the **Troubleshooting**, **Analysis**, and **Details** tabs to take a closer look. You can click **Troubleshooting > All Metrics** and use the metric picker widget (in the lower-left corner of the right pane) to discover and select available datastore metrics. Double-click a metric to make it appear in the metric viewer widget immediately to the right, as shown in Figure 11-3.

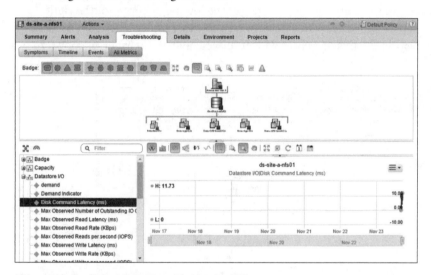

Figure 11-3   Select Datastore Metrics in vROps

You can add multiple metrics to this widget and use the provided buttons to manipulate the graphs in multiple ways, such as stacking the graphs, changing the time range, and adding trending lines. For example, you can examine the Command Latency, Observed Reads per Second, and Observed Write Rate, as shown in Figure 11-4.

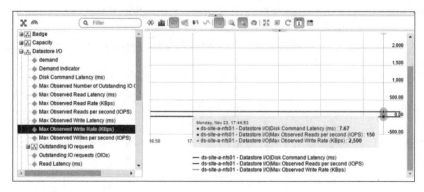

Figure 11-4   Stacked Datastore Graphs in vROps

Likewise, in the vROps user interface, select **Environment** in the left pane, below that select **vSphere Networking**, and then select the **Summary** tab. Examine the health, risk, and efficiency badges that appear in the right pane. Examine any alerts or descendant alerts that may appear. Select a specific distributed virtual switch or port group in the Environment inventory and use the **Analysis**, **Troubleshooting**, and **Details** tabs to take a closer look. You can click **Troubleshooting > All Metrics** and use the metric picker widget (in the lower-left corner of the right pane) to discover and select available network metrics. Double-click a metric to make it appear in the metric viewer widget immediately to the right, as shown in Figure 11-5.

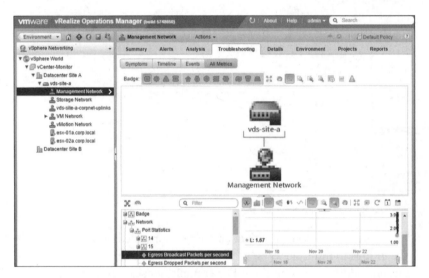

Figure 11-5 Network Metrics in vROps

For any object, such as a network port group or datastore, you can use the Analysis tab for troubleshooting performance-related issues. For example, if you are trouble-shooting an issue that may involve heavy disk I/O, you could select the datastore and examine its **Anomalies**, **Faults**, and **Time Remaining** tabs, as shown in Figures 11-6 through 11-8.

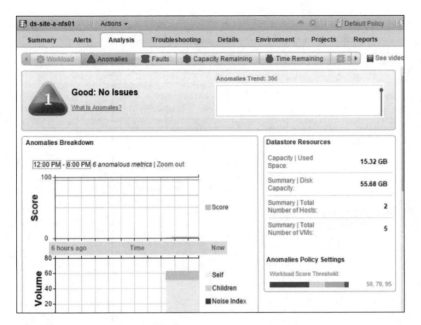

Figure 11-6   Datastore Anomalies

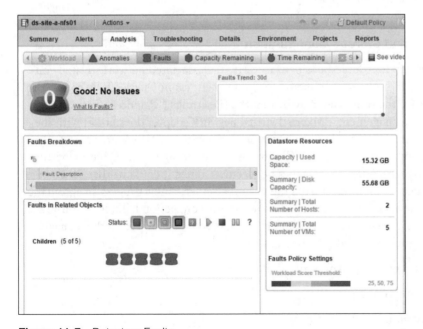

Figure 11-7   Datastore Faults

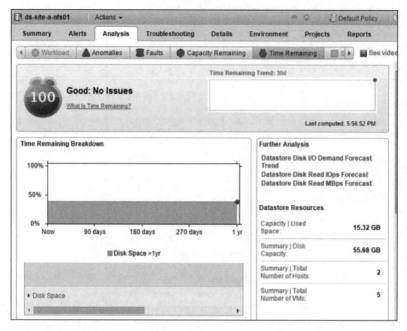

Figure 11-8   Datastore Time Remaining

Verify Network and Storage Configuration

A common step in troubleshooting is to verify the associated network-related con-figuration. If the vCenter Server and vSphere Client cannot successfully connect to an ESXi Host, the root cause may be that the IP settings (IP address, gateway, or mask) of the management VMkernel virtual network adapter does not fit with the IP subnet that is provided by the corresponding physical network switch port. If you are attempting to change the IP settings of the management VMkernel virtual network adapter but the change does not seem to apply, it could be that the change causes the host to disconnect from the vCenter Server, and it triggers an automatic rollback. Likewise, ESXi Host–to–vCenter Server connection failures or automatic rollbacks could occur due to improperly configured items impacting the manage-ment VMkernel virtual adapter, such as:

- Physical network adapter speed or duplex

- DNS and routing

- NIC teaming and failover

- VLAN

- MTU (jumbo frames)

An action that could result in a rollback or failure of the ESXi Host–to–vCenter Server connection is the removal of a management VMkernel virtual network adapter or its associated physical NIC. Another such action is the migration of a VMkernel virtual network adapter from a standard virtual switch to a distributed switch.

In cases where the host is disconnected from the vCenter Server due to a recent configuration change, you may consider using one of these network restore options in the Direct Console User Interface (DCUI):

- **Restore Network Settings:** This option is intended only for use in the worst-case scenarios because it sets the ESXi Host network settings back to factory settings, which can cause all network connections for the host and its virtual machines to fail. The last two options are available only when the ESXi Host management VMkernel virtual network adapter uses a distributed virtual switch.

- **Restore Standard Switch:** When you choose this option, a new management VMkernel virtual network adapter is created, the currently used uplink is migrated to the new virtual switch, and the host reconnects to the vCenter Server.

- **Restore vDS:** When you choose this option, you are prompted in a wizard to provide the appropriate VLAN, uplink, and blocking details, which are then used to apply to a new ephemeral port on the distributed switch. The DCUI moves the management VMkernel virtual network adapter to the new port, and the host reconnects to the vCenter Server.

For more details, see the section "Recognize Behavior of vDS Auto-Rollback" in Chapter 2, "Networking, Part I."

NOTE   If the **Restore Standard Switch** option is disabled, it may be that the ESXi Host management VMkernel network interface is already configured to use a standard virtual switch.

In addition to ESXi Host–to–vCenter Server connection issues, the misconfiguration of network-related settings in vSphere or physical switches could cause issues for virtual machine migrations, host management, virtual machine backup, IP-based storage activity, and virtual machine network activity. When troubleshooting any issue, consider whether the misconfiguration of any network-related component, including the following, could be the root cause:

- Standard virtual switch or port group
- Distributed virtual switch or distributed port group

- VLAN
- MTU size
- Network security policies
- Traffic-shaping policies
- Physical switch ports
- Physical network adapter
- VMkernel virtual network adapter
- Virtual machine network adapter
- ESXi Host network adapter driver
- Virtual machine network adapter driver

Another common step in troubleshooting is to verify the associated storage-related configuration. The misconfiguration of storage-related settings in vSphere or the storage system could cause issues for virtual machine migrations, virtual machine backup, virtual machine deployment, datastore accessibility, and virtual disk accessibility. When troubleshooting any issue, consider whether the misconfiguration of any storage-related component, including the following, could be the root cause:

- iSCSI adapter
- Storage network switch
- Storage multipathing
- Zoning and masking
- VMFS datastore
- NFS datastore
- Virtual SAN
- Virtual Volumes

When troubleshooting issues involving iSCSI storage, you should closely review the associated vSphere configuration. For example, when troubleshooting an issue where the ESXi Hosts are failing to properly access storage via an iSCSI software adapter, you should verify that all of the following items are properly configured:

- The iSCSI software adapter is enabled.
- The iSCSI software adapter is bound to one or more VMkernel virtual network adapters.

- The IP configuration of the bound VMkernel virtual network adapters is properly set.

- The iSCSI software adapter dynamic discovery is properly configured with the appropriate storage array IP addresses.

- The iSCSI chap authentication is properly configured.

For more details, see the section "Configure/Edit Software ISCSI Initiator Settings" in Chapter 4, "Storage, Part 1."

Likewise, when troubleshooting an issue where the ESXi Hosts are failing to properly access storage via an iSCSI-dependent adapter, you should verify that all of the following items are properly configured:

- Ensure that the iSCSI-dependent adapter is bound to the appropriate VMkernel virtual adapter and physical network adapter. To check this, select the iSCSI adapter in the vSphere Web Client and use the **Network Port Binding** tab. For more details, see the section "Configure iSCSI Port Binding" in Chapter 4.

- Ensure that the iSCSI name and alias are properly assigned to the adapter. To check this, select the iSCSI adapter in the vSphere Web Client and click the **Properties** tab in **Adapter Details** and then click the **Edit** button to the right of General. For more details, see the section "Configure/Edit Software ISCSI Initiator Settings" in Chapter 4.

NOTE When using a dependent hardware iSCSI adapter, performance reporting for the associated NIC may show little or no activity, even when iSCSI traffic is heavy. This behavior occurs because the iSCSI traffic bypasses the regular networking stack.

NOTE When using a Broadcom iSCSI adapter, be sure to enable flow control to avoid performance degradation due the adapter's reassembly of data in a limited hardware buffer space. To enable flow control, you can use the `esxcli system module parameters` command, per VMware KB 1013413.

Table 11-2 lists potential ESXi issues whose root causes could be related to common storage misconfigurations.

Table 11-2 Storage Configuration Issues That Impact ESXi

Problem	Root Cause(s)	Solution(s)
The ESXi Host cannot access a new storage device.	In order to detect the new device, a storage rescan is required.	Use the vSphere Web Client to navigate to the ESXi Host and rescan its storage adapters.
The ESXi Host cannot access the Fibre Channel storage array.	Zoning is improperly configured on the Fibre Channel switches, preventing the ESXi Host's storage adapters from connecting to the array's storage processors.	Correct the zoning on the switches and rescan the storage adapters.
The ESXi Host does not recognize its storage adapter.	The proper storage adapter driver is not installed on the ESXi Host	Follow the hardware vendor's recommendations to ensure that the correct VMware Information Bundles (VIBs) that contain the correct drivers are installed on the ESXi Host. Ensure that only supported hardware is used.
The storage I/O performance of an ESXi Host is terrible or unusable.	The storage multipathing is misconfigured.	Follow the storage vendor's recommendation to ensure that the correct multipath settings are used. Active-passive arrays require Most Recently Used (MRU). Active-active arrays typically default to Fixed (Preferred) but may support Round Robin. Some arrays require custom Storage Array Type Plug-ins (SATPs) and Path Selection Plug-ins (PSPs)

For example, if the multipathing for a storage device is set to Fixed on an ESXi Host, but the array is active-passive, then thrashing may occur, where two hosts are accessing the LUN through different storage processors. |
| The performance of the datastore in a datastore cluster is poor. The datastores are backed by auto-tiering storage. | Storage DRS is configured to balance based on I/O, but the storage vendor does not recommend or support this. | Disable I/O load balancing on Storage DRS. Optionally, leave storage space load balancing enabled on Storage DRS. |
| An ESXi Host cannot access a specific storage device. | The LUN masking configuration in the array is not properly set. | Change the LUN masking to allow access by the ESXi host and rescan the storage adapters. |

Problem	Root Cause(s)	Solution(s)
Virtual machine performance is very poor due to increased disk I/O latency.	The current LUN queue depth is inadequate.	The queue depth is dependent on the host bus adapter (HBA) type. Use the `esxcli system module parameters set -p parameters` command, where *parameters* should be replaced, as described here:
		QLogic: `p qlfxmaxqdepth=64 -m qlnativefc`
		Emulex: `lpfc0_lun_queue_depth=64 -m lpfc`
		Brocade: `-p bfa_lun_queue_depth=64 -m bfa`
		Also change the value of `Disk.SchedNumReqOutstanding` to a value that is high enough to accommodate all the virtual machines on the host that write to the same LUN. You can use the following command for this:
		`esxcli storage core device set -O | --sched-num-req-outstanding value -d device_ID`
		If the iSCSI software adapter is used, you can use the following command to set its queue depth
		`esxcli system module parameters set -m iscsi_vmk -p iscsivmk_LunQDepth=value`
The operational state of a storage device is `Lost Communication`. The status of all paths to the device is Dead. When you analyze ESXi Host's `/var/log/vmkernel` log files, you encounter events or error messages that contain SCSI Sense codes.	The storage device is in a permanent device lost (PDL) state.	Power off and unregister all associated virtual machines on the ESXi Host. Unmount the datastore. Address any issues concerning the device within the storage array. Rescan the storage array. Register the virtual machines. Power on the virtual machines.

Problem	Root Cause(s)	Solution(s)
An ESXi Host does not automatically detect a flash disk or recognize it as a local disk.	Some flash disk vendors do not support automatic flash recognition. In these cases, the ESXi Host does not recognize the disk as flash storage or as a local device.	In the vSphere Web Client, select the ESXi Host, select **Manage > Storage,** click **Storage Devices,** select the device, and click **Mark as Flash Disks.** Alternatively, click **Mark as Local for the Host.**

Verify a Given Virtual Machine Is Configured with the Correct Network Resources

To achieve satisfactory virtual machine performance, the virtual machine must have sufficient network resources. The full network path from the virtual machine to the clients and servers to which it communicates must provide sufficient network capacity to satisfy the application. This path includes:

- Guest network adapter driver

- VM virtual network adapter

- ESXi Host network adapter driver

- ESXi Host physical network adapter

- Connection (cable) to the physical switch port

- Physical network switch port

- Physical network switch

If the network I/O performance of a virtual machine–based application is inadequate, although it uses a 10 Gbps network connection, you should consider the following:

- Verify that the network adapter and switch port are truly connected at 10 Gbps. Verify that neither is statically set for a slower speed or that the connection automatically negotiated to a slower speed.

- Verify that VMXNET3 is used, if it is supported in the guest O/S. It is the best-performing virtual network adapter. It supports performance features such as:

  - Multiple receive and transmit queues, which is often called receive-side scaling (RSS)

  - SplitRx Mode, which uses multiple physical CPUs to process network packets received in a single network queue

- TCP Segmentation Offload (TSO), which offloads the segmentation processing to the network adapter

- Jumbo frames, which are Ethernet frames that are larger than 1500 bytes.

- Large Receive Offload (LRO), which aggregates multiple incoming packets prior to processing

- Virtual interrupt coalescing

- Otherwise, use VMXNET2 or the best-performing virtual network adapter that is supported in the guest operating system.

- Implement jumbo frames, which requires the proper settings on the virtual switch (MTU=9000), network adapter, physical switch, guest O/S, and entire network path.

- Verify that TCP Segmentation Offload (TSO) is enabled. In the vSphere Web Client, select the ESXi Host and use **Manage** > **Settings** > **Advanced System Settings** to ensure that Net.UseHwTSO and Net.UseHwTSO6 are set to 1 to enable TSO in IPv4 and IPv6, respectively. By default, TSO is enabled on the ESXi Host and for virtual machines that use the E1000, E1000e, VMXNET2, or VMXNET3 virtual adapters. The ESXi Host provides TSO to virtual machines, even when the hardware does not support it.

- Verify that Large Receive Offload (LRO) is enabled. In the vSphere Web Client, select the ESXi Host and use **Manage** > **Settings** > **Advanced System Settings** to ensure that Net.Vmxnet2HwLRO or Net.Vmxnet3HwLRO are set to 1 to enable TSO for VMXNET2 or VMXNET3, respectively. Verify that LRO is enabled in the guest operating system and also ensure that you address the specific LRO requirements for the guest operating system. For example, the prerequisites for LRO in Windows are:

  - Virtual machine hardware version 11 or later

  - VMXNET3 and guest driver version 1.6.6.0 or later

  - Windows 2012 or Windows 8.0 or later

  - Receive Segment Coalescing (RSC) enabled in Windows

- Verify that virtual network coalescing is set appropriately for the virtual machine. This feature is enabled by default for all virtual network adapters in ESXi 6.0, but it can be disabled or modified for VMXNET3 adapters. To do so, use the vSphere Web Client to edit the virtual machine, select the **VM Options** tab, and use **Advanced** > **Configuration Parameters** to set values for these parameters (where X identifies a specific virtual network adapter) and click **Add Row**:

- `ethernetX.coalescingScheme`, which is used to enable or disable coalescing

- `ethernetX.coalescingParams`, which can be used to set the number of packets to a value between 1 and 64

NOTE   If a physical network adapter experiences issues with TSO, you can temporarily enable TSO software simulation in the VMkernel while you troubleshoot. For example, you can use the following commands to enable software TSO for IPv4 and IPv6 on `vmnic1`:

```
esxcli network nic software set --ipv4tso=0 -n vmnic1
esxcli network nic software set --ipv6tso=0 -n vmnic1
```

This setting persists across ESXi reboots.

Virtual machines may experience difficulties with network connectivity if the virtual machine, virtual switch port group, physical network adapter, or physical switch port is misconfigured. Table 11-3 lists some common network configuration issues (but not a comprehensive set) that impact virtual machines.

Table 11-3   Network Configuration Issues That Impact Virtual Machines

Problem	Root Cause(s)	Solution(s)
A virtual machine is able to communicate with other virtual machines on the same virtual switch port group and ESXi Host, but it cannot communicate with any other server.	The virtual switch port group VLAN setting does not match the physical switch port setting.	Ensure that the physical switch ports where the virtual switch uplinks connect are trunked with a set of VLAN IDs that includes the VLAN ID assigned to the virtual switch port group. For example, if a virtual switch port group is assigned VLAN 10, but the physical switch port where it connects is trunked with VLANs 100 to 110, modify the trunking to include VLAN 10 or change the virtual port group to use a VLAN ID between 100 and 110.

Problem	Root Cause(s)	Solution(s)
A set of virtual machines lost connectivity to the network during a maintenance procedure, where you deliberately disconnected just one of two host network adapters in a team. Because you have NIC teaming set up, you expected the virtual switch to fail over the impacted virtual machine connections to the other network adapter.	The NIC teaming on the virtual switch port group is misconfigured. One of the two available paths is inadvertently configured as Unused instead of Active or Standby. In this case, the virtual machine may still be connected to the network if at least one active path is healthy, but a single path failure may cause the virtual machine connection to drop.	Change the virtual switch port group NIC teaming such that the currently unused path is set to Active or Standby.
A set of virtual machines on the same virtual switch port group cannot communicate with external devices.	The virtual switch port group NIC teaming is set to Route-Based on IP Hash, but then the physical switch ports are not configured for Etherchannel.	Change the NIC teaming to use Route-Based on Originating Virtual Port or Route-Based on Source MAC Hash.
A set of virtual machines that requires jumbo frames and is connected to a specific distributed switch port group is not performing well.	Jumbo frame support is not properly configured on the distributed virtual switch.	You should set the distributed virtual switch MTU to 9000.
One specific virtual machine cannot communicate with any device on the network, including virtual machines on the same host and connected to the same virtual switch port group.	A virtual machine guest OS is configured with the wrong IP settings.	Correct the IP address, gateway, and mask in the guest O/S.
One specific virtual machine cannot communicate with any device on the network. The guest O/S reports issues with the network adapter.	A virtual machine is configured with the wrong virtual NIC.	Edit the virtual machine and change the network adapter to a type that the guest O/S supports and that has a valid driver. Or install a valid network adapter driver in the guest O/S. For example, if the network adapter type is VMXNET3, then ensure that VMware Tools, which includes the guest driver for VMXNET3, is installed in the virtual machine.

Problem	Root Cause(s)	Solution(s)
A set of virtual machines is able to communicate well with other virtual machines on the same virtual switch port group and ESXi Host but experiences terrible performance when communicating with other servers.	The physical NIC settings, such as speed or duplex, are improperly configured.	Use the vSphere Web Client to properly set the speed and duplex of the network adapter, or modify the associated physical switch port speed and duplex.
The network performance of a set of virtual machines is poor when the workload is significant but the physical network adapter bandwidth is not being saturated.	Network traffic shaping is misconfigured. The average bandwidth, peak bandwidth, or burst size is set too low on a virtual switch port group.	Modify the network traffic settings to increase the underlying values or disable traffic shaping on the virtual switch port group.
A virtual machine running network analyzer software (such as Wireshark) is unable to successfully monitor network traffic.	The security settings for the standard virtual switch port group are misconfigured. Promiscuous mode is rejected.	Modify the security settings on the virtual switch port group to allow promiscuous mode.
Microsoft Network Load Balancing (NLB) is not working in unicast mode for a specific virtual machine.	The associated virtual switch port group is misconfigured. The virtual switch is rejecting forged transmits and is notifying the physical switch.	To support Microsoft Network Load Balancing (NLB) in unicast mode, change the virtual switch port group's **Forged Transmits** setting to `Allow` and set the **Notify Switch** setting to `No`.

Monitor/Troubleshoot Storage Distributed Resource Scheduler (SDRS) Issues

As you troubleshoot issues concerning Storage DRS datastore clusters, ensure that the associated hosts and datastores meet the appropriate requirements:

- Ensure that only similar, interchangeable datastores are used.
  - NFS and VMFS datastores cannot be mixed in the same datastore cluster.
  - Replicated and non-replicated datastores cannot be mixed in the same datastore cluster.
- Ensure that each host is ESXi 5.0 or later.
- Ensure that datastores are not shared across multiple data centers.

- As a best practice, but not necessarily a requirement, ensure that all the datastores in the cluster have a consistent hardware acceleration configuration. Either all the datastores should have hardware acceleration enabled or all datastores should have hardware acceleration disabled.

One common problem after enabling Storage DRS on a datastore cluster is that it may be disabled on some virtual disks. The following are some reasons Storage DRS may be disabled on a virtual disk, although it is enabled on the datastore cluster:

- A virtual machine's swap file is stored in a local datastore on the ESXi host, so Storage DRS is disabled for the swap file.

- A virtual machine's VMX swap file is stored in a local datastore on the ESXi Host, so Storage DRS is disabled for the VMX swap file.

- Storage vMotion is disabled on the virtual machine due to another vCenter Server operation in progress on the same virtual machine. This causes Storage DRS to be disabled on the virtual machine until vCenter completes its running task.

- The home disk of a virtual machine is protected by vSphere HA, and relocating it causes loss of vSphere HA protection.

- If the disk is an independent disk, Storage DRS is disabled, except in the case of relocation or clone placement.

- If the virtual machine has system files on a separate datastore from the home datastore, Storage DRS is disabled on the home disk. To correct this, use Storage vMotion to migrate the home disk to a new target, which also migrates the system files to the target and enables Storage DRS on the home disk.

- If the virtual machine has a disk whose base and redo files are spread across separate datastores, Storage DRS is disabled on the disk. To correct this, use Storage vMotion to migrate the disk to a new target, which migrates the base and redo files to the target and enables Storage DRS on the disk.

- The virtual machine has hidden disks, such as disks in previous snapshots, that are not in the current snapshot.

- The virtual machine is actually a template.

- The virtual machine is vSphere fault tolerance enabled.

- The virtual machine is sharing files between its disks.

When troubleshooting an issue where Storage DRS is not functioning for a virtual disk, you should determine which of these reasons is the root cause and address the situation accordingly.

Table 11-4 lists some other Storage DRS potential problems and solutions.

Table 11-4   Potential Storage DRS Problems and Solutions

Problem	Root Cause(s)	Solution(s)
Attempts for a datastore in a datastore cluster to enter maintenance mode are not successful. The status hangs at 1%.	Storage DRS is disabled on at least one virtual disk in the datastore. Storage DRS rules prevent Storage DRS from performing the required migrations.	If Storage DRS is disabled for the cluster or for associated virtual machines, enable it. If Storage DRS rules are preventing the migrations, either remove the rules or set the advanced Storage DRS configuration parameter `IgnoreAffinityRulesFor Maintenance` to 1.
Storage DRS generates an event and an alarm that it cannot operate on a specific datastore.	ESXi Hosts that reside in different virtual datacenters share the datastore. The datastore is connected to an unsupported ESXi Host, such as a host running ESXi 4.1.	Migrate all the ESXi Hosts that share the datacenter to the same virtual datacenter. Alternatively, unmount the datastore from some ESXi Hosts that reside in other virtual datacenters. Upgrade all associated ESXi Hosts to 5.0 or higher.
When migrating virtual machines into a datastore cluster, not all virtual machines migrate successfully, and the error message `Insufficient Disk Space on Datastore` appears.	During the placement of each virtual machine, Storage DRS does not account for the space that will be consumed upon completion, so it may attempt to allocate the space for subsequent placement requests.	Retry the failed migrations again, but one at a time, allowing each migration to complete prior to requesting the next.
When you create or clone a virtual machine in a datastore cluster, the error message `Operation Not Allowed in the Current State` is received.	A Storage DRS rule cannot check the new virtual machine's disk for compliance, and it generates a fault.	Revise, remove, or disable the rule until the operation is complete.

Problem	Root Cause(s)	Solution(s)
When you deploy an OVF template that has Storage DRS disabled, the deployed virtual machine actually has Storage DRS enabled.	By design, Storage DRS applies the automation level of the datastore to the deployed virtual machine.	Use the vSphere Web Client to edit the datastore cluster: use **VM Overrides** to set **Keep VMDKs Together** to **NO.**
Multiple instances of the same affinity or anti-affinity rule violation appear in the Faults dialog box when you attempt to put a datastore into maintenance mode.	Actually, each fault refers to a different datastore, but because the datastore names are not displayed, the faults appear to be redundant.	Remove the rule that is preventing the necessary migrations.
Affinity or anti-affinity rules still apply to a virtual machine after the virtual machine was migrated from a datastore cluster.	Rules remain with a virtual machine that is removed from a datastore cluster if the virtual machine remains in the associated vCenter Server inventory.	Use the vSphere Web Client to remove the rule.
Attempts to apply Storage DRS recommendations fail.	The thin-provisioning-threshold-crossed alarm may be triggered, which indicates that the datastore is low on free space. The target datastore may be in or entering maintenance mode.	If an alarm was raised, address the specific issue that triggered the alarm. Verify that the target datastore is not in or entering maintenance mode.
When you create, clone, or relocate a virtual machine in a datastore cluster, Storage DRS provides only one recommendation.	The ESXi Host specifies the virtual machine swap file location as a datastore in the target datastore cluster, so the disks to be placed in the cluster do not form a single affinity group. Storage DRS does not generate alternative recommendations in cases where a single affinity group is not used.	Often in these cases, it is acceptable to allow a single recommendation. Otherwise, you could change the host configuration such that it does not specify a virtual machine swap file location.

Recognize the Impact of Network and Storage I/O Control Configurations

When troubleshooting network performance, you should be able to identify the impact of the Network I/O Control (NIOC) configuration. NIOC version 3 introduced the ability to reserve network bandwidth. NIOC must be enabled on a distributed virtual switch before you configure network reservations. Minimum software versions for configuring network reservations are vSphere Distributed Switch version 6.0.0 and NIOC version 3.

In NIOC version 3, the reservation for a system network traffic type is the minimum bandwidth that is guaranteed on a single physical adapter. The total bandwidth reserved by all system traffic types cannot exceed 75% of the bandwidth provided by the lowest-capacity physical network adapter. For example, for a distributed switch with two uplinks using 10 Gbps network adapters, the total of the reservations for all system traffic types on the distributed virtual switch cannot exceed 7.5 Gbps. If one of the uplinks used a 1.0 Gbps network adapters, then the total reservation cannot exceed 0.75 Gbps.

For example, consider this scenario:

- Only 10 Gbps network adapters are used as uplinks on a distributed virtual switch.

- NIOC is enabled and used to configure the reservations for system traffic types as follows:

    - Management: 1.0 Gbps

    - iSCSI: 1.0 Gbps

    - Fault tolerance: 1.0 Gbps

    - vMotion: 1.0 Gbps

The total bandwidth reservation for all system traffic types cannot exceed 75% of the bandwidth of a single network adapter. In this scenario, each adapter provides 10 Gbps, and the maximum bandwidth that is available for reservations is 7.5 Gbps. Currently 4.0 Gbps is reserved, leaving 3.5 Gbps that can be reserved for other purposes, such as virtual machine system traffic.

In vSphere 6, NIOC version 2 and NIOC version 3 can coexist. Upgrading from NIOC version 2 to NIOC version 3 is supported, but the process may be disruptive. NIOC version 3.0 requires distributed virtual switch 6.0 and ESXi 6.0. See Chapter 3, "Networking, Part 2," for more details on upgrading NIOC.

During an upgrade of a distributed virtual switch to vSphere 6.0, NIOC is also upgraded, to NIOC version 3. So if some features are currently used that are not available in NIOC version 3, such as CoS tagging or user-defined network resource pools, then a non-disruptive upgrade is not permitted. In NIOC version 2, network bandwidth is allocated at the physical adapter level. In NIOC version 3, network bandwidth is allocated at the distributed virtual switch level.

When addressing issues concerning upgrading NIOC, you should understand that the following functionality would be removed during the upgrade to NIOC version 3:

- User-defined network resource pools

- Associations between ports and user-defined network resource pools

- CoS tagging of traffic that is associated with network resource pools

See Chapter 3 for details.

In NIOC version 3, the shares for each type of system traffic can be set from 1 to 100. During periods of network contention, the amount of available network bandwidth that a specific system traffic type receives is dependent on its assigned share. By default, the value for the virtual machine system traffic shares is already set to High (100), which is the maximum. The shares for all other system traffic types are set to Normal (50). So if the performance of virtual machines is unsatisfactory during times of network contention, you could consider decreasing the shares for other types of system traffic.

Consider a case where 100 shares are assigned to vSphere FT traffic and to iSCSI traffic and 50 shares are assigned to vMotion traffic. These three traffic types are configured to share the same physical adapter. During times when all three traffic types are contending for network resources, but the adapter bandwidth cannot handle the current demand, the vMotion traffic type obtains 20% of the available bandwidth, while each of the other two traffic types obtains 40%. During times when just the vSphere FT and iSCSI traffic types are contending for network resources and the adapter bandwidth cannot handle the current demand, each of the two traffic types obtains 40%.

By default, each distributed virtual switch port group is assigned to a network resource pool named default. The total bandwidth reservation of the virtual machines on a host cannot exceed the reserved bandwidth that is configured for the virtual machine system traffic. The actual limit and reservation also depend on the traffic-shaping policy for the distributed port group the adapter is connected to. For example, if a VM network adapter requires a limit of 200 Mbps and the average bandwidth configured in the traffic-shaping policy is 100 Mbps, the effective limit is 100 Mbps.

Network resource pools can be used on a distributed virtual switch to reserve bandwidth for a set of virtual machines. Each pool can provide a reservation quota to its associated virtual machines that is a portion of the amount reserved for virtual machine system traffic. You can do this using the vSphere Web Client by selecting the distributed switch, selecting **Manage > Resource Allocation > Network Resource Pools**, clicking **Add** (the green plus sign), and providing a reservation quota. The maximum amount of the reservation quota for a new network pool is the aggregated reservation for virtual machine system traffic minus the quotas assigned to other network resource pools. In order for a distributed switch to apply bandwidth admission control, a network resource pool must be implemented.

For example, if the virtual machine system traffic reservation is set to 0.5 Gbps on each 10 Gbps uplink on a distributed switch that has 10 uplinks, the total aggregated bandwidth available for VM reservation on this switch is 5 Gbps. Each network resource pool can reserve a quota of this 5 Gbps capacity. If you create a network resource pool with a quota set to 3 Gbps, the maximum quota that you may set for the next network resource pool is 2 Gbps.

If a virtual machine does not start, it could be due to its NIOC network reservation. To guarantee sufficient network bandwidth to a virtual machine, vSphere implements admission control at the host and cluster levels, based on reservation and teaming settings. When you power on a virtual machine, NIOC verifies that the physical network adapter can provide the minimum bandwidth to the virtual machine based on teaming and reservation. NIOC also verifies that the VM reservation is less than the free quota in the network resource pool. If these conditions are not met, the virtual machine does not start. If you change the network reservation of a running virtual machine network, NIOC applies the same checks and prevents the change if it cannot be satisfied. To use admission control in a distributed virtual switch, configure bandwidth allocation for virtual machine system traffic, configure a network resource pool with a quota of the virtual machine system allocation, associate the pool with the appropriate distributed port group, and configure the bandwidth requirements of the virtual machine.

If DRS unexpectedly migrates a virtual machine, although the CPU and memory workload appears to be balanced, it could be due to a need to balance based on virtual machine network bandwidth reservation. DRS migrates a virtual machine in cases where the virtual machine network reservation is increased to a point that the current ESXi Host cannot satisfy it or when a physical network adapter on the host is offline. In this case and in cases where DRS needs to place a virtual machine that is starting, DRS applies bandwidth admission control to ensure that the virtual machine is placed on a host that has the capacity to guarantee the bandwidth based on teaming and reservation. Likewise, vSphere HA applies bandwidth admission control whenever an ESXi Host fails or becomes isolated to ensure that the virtual machine is started on a host that has the capacity to guarantee the bandwidth based on teaming and reservation. To use bandwidth admission control in DRS or HA, allocate bandwidth for the virtual machine system traffic and configure the bandwidth requirements for a virtual machine that is connected to a distributed switch.

When troubleshooting issues concerning Storage I/O Control (SIOC), you should know the requirements and limitations:

- The associated datastores must be managed by a single vCenter Server.

- SIOC is not supported for Raw Device Mapping (RDM).

- SIOC is not supported for datastores that use multiple extents.

- Ensure that SIOC is supported for the storage devices backing the datastores, especially if auto-tiering is enabled in the storage array.

If SIOC is not applying shares and limits as expected during storage resource contention, you may need to examine the congestion threshold. In most cases, the default congestion threshold, which is based on the measured latency when the storage is undergoing a workload that is 90% of its capacity, works well and does not need to be changed. But if you suspect that the threshold is too high, such that SIOC is not applying shares when some contention occurs, then you modify it, but you should consider the following:

- A higher value typically provides higher aggregate throughput.

- If throughput is more important than latency, avoid lowering the threshold.

- A lower value typically results in lower device latency and more frequent enforcement of shares.

If you want to ensure that the IOPS of some virtual machines suffer less than those of other virtual machines on the same datastore when I/O contention exists on the datastore, you can apply shares using SIOC. For example, you can set SIOC shares to High on higher-priority virtual machines and set shares to Low on lower-priority virtual machines. When applying SIOC shares to virtual machines, you should understand the impact. For example, consider this scenario:

- Two nearly identical virtual machines reside alone on the same datastore.

- When both virtual machines are concurrently under their peak workload, where the underlying storage device cannot keep up with the demand, they each achieve 1500 I/Os per second and experience 20 ms latency.

- You enable SIOC, set shares to 1000 on the first virtual machine, and set shares to 2000 on the second virtual machine.

- You should expect the first virtual machine's IOPS to drop to 1000 and the second virtual machine's IOPS to rise to 2000 IOPS.

- You should expect the first virtual machine's latency to rise and the second virtual machine's latency to drop.

If you want to limit the I/O of a virtual machine in terms of data size over time, such as MB per second, then you may be able to apply a mathematical conversion. For example, if you want to limit a virtual machine that has a steady network I/O size of 64 KB to 10 MB per second, you should set the limit to 160 IOPS (10 MB per second * 1024 KB per MB / 64 KB per I/O).

VMware recommends that you not place non-vSphere workloads in SIOC-enabled datastores. In cases where non-vSphere workloads or workloads from virtual machines running on ESXi Hosts that are not managed by the vCenter Server delivering the SIOC, vCenter Server raises the alarm Unmanaged workload is detected on the datastore. Whenever this alarm is raised, identify the unmanaged workload and migrate from the datastore. Likewise, vCenter Server raises the alarm Pre-4.1 host connected to SIOC-enabled datastore whenever a supported host is connected to the datastore. Whenever this alarm is raised, disconnect the datastore from the host or upgrade the host. In cases where at least one ESXi 4.1 or earlier host is connected to datastore, you will be unable to configure SIOC on the datastore.

For more details on SIOC, see the section "Objective 3.5—Set Up and Configure Storage I/O Control" in Chapter 6, "Storage, Part 3."

Recognize a Connectivity Issue Caused by a VLAN/PVLAN

If the VLAN setting of a virtual switch port group is improperly configured, you may have connectivity issues. For example, if a virtual switch port group is tagged with a VLAN ID that is not included in the VLAN trunk on the associated physical switch port, the virtual machines that connect to the port group can connect to other virtual machines on the same port group and ESXi Host, but they cannot connect to virtual machines on other ESXi Hosts. For another example, say that you configure traffic-sniffing software in a virtual machine on a standard virtual switch port group where promiscuous mode is enabled, but it fails to successfully monitor network packets from multiple VLANs. In this case, you may need to configure the virtual switch port group for VLAN 4095.

If VMkernel virtual network adapters or virtual machines' virtual network adapters that are connected to a distributed virtual switch port group that is configured with a secondary PVLAN cannot successfully communicate on the network, it could be because of misconfiguration on the port group or physical network switch. Verify that the primary and secondary PVLAN IDs are configured on the virtual switch. Verify that the type of secondary PVLAN (promiscuous, community, or isolated) is correct. Likewise, verify that the PVLAN IDs are properly configured on the external physical switch and upstream switches. If a physical switch is not PVLAN aware, it will have a problem because the MAC address of each virtual machine may appear to be connected to two separate VLANs.

Troubleshoot Common Issues

In addition to the troubleshooting items discussed up to this point, you should prepare yourself for troubleshooting other common issues.

Storage and Network

If a storage device status is shown as Dead or Error, the storage device may be in the all paths down (APD) state. The root cause may be a failed switch or a disconnected cable. The ESXi Host treats this as a temporary state and continues to retry any issued commands. You should check the status of the physical connections and the switch and correct any issues. The APD timeout is 140 seconds by default. If the root cause is corrected within this period, the host and virtual machines should recover nicely. If the APD timeout expires, the device is marked Dead or Error. All paths to the device are shown as Dead. All datastores on the device are shown as dimmed. The host terminates all non-virtual machine I/O, but the virtual machine I/O continues trying. If the problem is eventually corrected, the virtual machine I/O should resume automatically. Rather than wait, you can migrate the virtual machines to another ESXi Host that is successfully accessing the storage device.

If you wish, you can change the APD timeout to any value between 20 and 99,999 seconds by setting the Misc.APDTimeout parameter on the ESXi Host.

If a storage device status is Lost Communication, all paths are shown as Dead, and the associated datastores are dimmed, the device is in a permanent device lost (PDL) state. The ESXi Host treats this as a permanent state and no longer tries to access the device. Whenever the storage array determines that a device is permanently unavailable and sends SCSI sense codes to the ESXi Host, the device is in the PDL state. After you correct the issue in the array, the host is able to discover the device but treats it as a new device. To recover from a PDL state, follow this procedure:

Step 1.   Power off and unregister the associated virtual machines.

Step 2.   Unmount the datastore.

Step 3.   Correct the device problem within the array.

Step 4.   Rescan the storage.

Step 5.   Register (add to inventory) the virtual machines.

For more details on APD and PDL, see the section "Differentiate APD and PDL States" in Chapter 5, "Storage, Part 2."

If Fibre Channel storage devices do not appear correctly in the vSphere Web Client, you should check the following:

- Cable connectivity
- Zoning
- Access control (masking)
- Storage processor configuration

After remediating any of these items, you should use the vSphere Web Client to rescan the storage adapter.

If iSCSI storage devices do not appear correctly in the vSphere Web Client, you should check the following:

- Cable network connectivity
- Network routing configuration
- Access control (masking)
- Storage processor configuration
- CHAP configuration

In addition, for software and dependent iSCSI adapters, check the configuration of the associated virtual switch, port group, and VMkernel virtual adapter. After remediating any of these items, use the vSphere Web Client to rescan the iSCSI initiator.

Storage performance issues could be caused by excessive SCSI reservations. The following operations often cause VMFS to use SCSI reservations:

- Creating, resignaturing, and expanding a VMFS datastore
- Powering on a virtual machine
- Creating or deleting a file
- Creating a template
- Deploying a new virtual machine
- Migrating with vMotion
- Growing a file, such as growing a thin-provisioned virtual disk or snapshot (redo) file

Typically, these operations do not have a severe impact on the performance of the datastore, but to eliminate the potential of SCSI reservation conflicts, follow these guidelines:

- Use storage devices with hardware acceleration, which use atomic test and set (ATS), instead of SCSI reservations, to lock the LUN.

- Limit the number of concurrent operations from the previous list on the same datastore.

- Reduce the number of virtual machines and ESXi Hosts per LUN.

- Limit the use of snapshots.

- Use the latest storage adapter firmware.

- Use the latest host BIOS.

- Ensure that the Host Mode setting is correctly set on the array.

In addition to addressing the network-related issues discussed elsewhere in this chapter, you should prepare to address the following issues.

After upgrading a distributed virtual switch to version 5.5 or later, when you attempt to convert the Link Aggregate Control Protocol (LACP) configuration to the enhanced LACP support, the conversion fails. The root cause for this could be that some of the ESXi Hosts were disconnected during the conversion. In this case, the LACP conversion may have failed at some stage in the process. To identify the stage where the conversion failed and complete the conversion process, follow these steps:

Step 1. Check for the existence of a link aggregate group (LAG) on the distributed switch. If none exists, create a new LAG.

Step 2. Check the teaming configuration of the distributed port group(s) to determine whether the LAG is set as `standby`. If not, set the LAG as `standby`.

Step 3. Check the LAG settings to determine which physical network adapters are assigned to it. Ensure that at least one physical network adapter is assigned to the LAG.

Step 4. Configure the teaming of the distributed port group(s) again but now set **Active** to just the LAG (no other uplinks), set **Standby** to empty (no LAGs or uplinks), and set **Unused** to the remaining uplinks that are not part of the LAG.

A common network-related problem is that attempts to remove an ESXi Host from a vSphere distributed switch fail and produce an error similar to this example:

```
The resource '16' is in use.
vDS DSwitch port 16 is still on host 10.23.112.2 connected
to MyVM nic=4000 type=vmVnic
```

You determine that a host proxy switch still appears on the host, but your attempts to remove the host proxy switch fail. The root cause is that a virtual network adapter is still using a virtual port on the switch. To fix this issue, use this procedure:

Step 1. Use the vSphere Web Client to select the distributed virtual switch and select **Manage > Ports**.

Step 2. Identify all ports that are still in use.

Step 3. For each used port, migrate or delete the VMkernel virtual network adapter or virtual machine virtual adapter that is using the port.

Step 4. Try again to remove the ESXi Host from the distributed switch or to delete the host proxy switch.

Another common network-related problem occurs when two virtual machines that run on different hosts but use the same distributed virtual port group cannot communicate with each other. In this case, misconfiguration of the distributed virtual switch or port group is not a likely root cause because the virtual machines are using the same port group, so they share the same settings. A likely cause is that the physical network ports used by the associated uplinks are not assigned the same VLAN configuration. The solution is to check the VLAN settings of the associated physical ports and set them identically.

Virtual Switch and Port Group Configuration

Network communication problems involving virtual machines or ESXi Hosts are often caused by poor configuration of the associated virtual switch and virtual port groups. Generally speaking, any setting associated with a standard virtual switch, standard virtual port groups, distributed virtual switch, distributed virtual port groups, or individual ports can be misconfigured. Such misconfigurations could lead to no communication, poor communication, or intermittent communication.

Table 11-5 lists some potential problems and solutions involving virtual switch and port group misconfiguration.

Table 11-5   Potential Virtual Switch and Port Group Problems and Solutions

Problem	Root Cause(s)	Solution(s)
The virtual machines that are connected to a specific distributed port group can only communicate with other virtual machines on the same ESXi Host and port group. They cannot communicate with virtual machines on other ESXi Hosts.	The port group settings are not compatible with the physical switch ports. For example, the problem could be: ■ The port group is configured to use load-based teaming (LBT), but the physical switch port group is configured to use Etherchannel. ■ The port group is configured to use a VLAN ID that is not trunked on the physical switch port.	Determine whether the misconfiguration was made on the virtual switch port group or on the physical port. Correct the misconfiguration such that the VLAN on the virtual switch port group is included in the VLAN trunk on the physical port.
Two ESXi Hosts that are configured to use standard virtual switches for vMotion migrations are failing to complete migrations using vMotion. The operations hang at 10% and eventually fail.	The settings for the associated VMkernel port could be misconfigured on one of the hosts.	Check and correct the IP configuration, VLAN setting, and NIC teaming settings of each associated VMkernel port. Note that in cases where vMotion is not enabled on any VMkernel virtual adapter on an ESXi Host, a different symptom would occur: An error message would be produced, indicating that vMotion is not enabled on an ESXi Host.

Physical Network Adapter Configuration

Improperly configured physical network adapters can cause network connectivity issues for associated virtual machines. For example, if the speed or duplex is set on a physical network adapter that does not match the speed or duplex on the physical switch port, the associated virtual machines may not successfully connect to the network.

Per VMware KB 1004089, VMware recommends setting physical network adapter speed and duplex to `Auto-negotiate`. VMware does not recommend setting a network adapter for a static speed and duplex when it connects to a switch port that is set to `Auto-negotiate`. But it some cases, it may be necessary and supported to manually set the speed and duplex on a network adapter. You can use the vSphere Web Client to navigate directly to a physical network adapter and to edit its speed and duplex. In cases where the ESXi Host cannot be connected to the vCenter Server until the speed and duplex are changed, you can use the vSphere Client to edit the network adapter, but it must first be connected to a virtual switch. Alternatively, you can use the following command to set the speed and duplex:

```
esxcli network nic set -n vmnic# -S speed -D duplex
```

The use of improper network adapter drivers in the ESXi Host may cause connectivity issues. For example, if a specific network adapter requires a custom driver provided by the vendor in a VMware Installation Bundle (VIB), failure to install the VIB may render the adapter unusable by the host. Likewise, the use of unsupported firmware may render the adapter unusable by the host.

Use this command to determine whether TCP segmentation offload (TSO) is enabled on a physical network adapter:

```
esxcli network nic tso get
```

The performance of virtual machines or VMkernel services, such as vMotion, may be impacted by the configuration or limitations of physical network adapters. For example, if you configure jumbo frames on the standard virtual switches, VMkernel ports, and physical switch ports that are used for vMotion, but an associated physical network adapter does not support jumbo frames, the time required for vMotion migrations may suffer. In this case, the VMkernel and virtual switch may attempt to use jumbo frames, only to have to rend the packets, after they are rejected by the network adapter.

VMFS Metadata Consistency

In rare cases, when troubleshooting issues involving VMFS datastores or virtual flash resources, you might want to perform a metadata consistency check. For example, you may choose to check metadata consistency in these circumstances:

- Following a storage outage
- Following a disk replacement or RAID rebuild
- When you discover metadata errors in a `vmkernel.log` file
- When you are unable to access files in a VMFS datastore
- When you discover entries in an Events tab in the vSphere Web Client that indicate corruption

You can use the vSphere On-disk Metadata Analyzer (VOMA) to identify and fix metadata corruption. VOMA can be executed from the command-line interface of an ESXi Host. It cannot be used on VMFS datastores that span multiple extents.

Use VOMA only on single-extent datastores. You should not use VOMA on datastores where virtual machines are running. You should stop or migrate the virtual machines from a datastore prior to using VOMA.

The following procedure demonstrates how to use VOMA to check for VMFS metadata consistency:

Step 1. Use this command to identify the name and partition number of the device that backs the VMFS datastore:

```
esxcli storage vmfs extent list
```

Record the values of the Device_Name and Partition fields for the datastore.

Step 2. Run VOMA to check for VMFS errors in the partition. Use the -d parameter to identify the device and partition by using the values you recorded in step 1. In the following example, the value for the Device _ Name is /vmfs/devices/disks/

```
naa.600508e000000000b367477b3be3d703:3
```

and the value for the Partition is 3:

```
voma -m vmfs -f check -d /vmfs/devices/disks/
naa.600508e000000000b367477b3be3d703:3
```

Step 3. Examine the output for possible errors. In this example, the output indicates that the heartbeat address is invalid:

```
Phase 2: Checking VMFS heartbeat region
ON-DISK ERROR: Invalid HB address
Phase 3: Checking all file descriptors.
Phase 4: Checking pathname and connectivity.
Phase 5: Checking resource reference counts.
```

(Only a portion of the output is shown here.)

Step 4. If you discover problems, contact VMware Support.

When using VOMA, you can use the command options shown in Table 11-6.

Table 11-6 VOMA Command Options

Logging Option	Description
-m --module	Identifies the module to run. These are the options: • vmfs: Check VMFS3 and VMFS5 datastores. (default option) • vmfs1: Check file systems that back virtual flash volumes • lvm: Check logical volumes that back VMFS datastores

Logging Option	Description
`-f` `--func`	Identifies the function to be performed. These are the options: ■ `query`: List the following functions ■ `check`: Check for errors ■ `fix`: Check and fix errors
`-d` `--device`	Identifies the device and partition.
`-s` `--logfile`	Identifies the log file to be used.
`-v` `--version`	Displays the version of VOMA.
`-h` `--help`	Provides a help message for using VOMA.

Objective 7.3—Troubleshoot vSphere Upgrades

The following sections provide details for identifying and troubleshooting issues related to upgrading vCenter Server and ESXi Hosts.

The VMware Update Manager can be used to upgrade and patch ESXi Hosts. If necessary, you can make changes to the configuration of VMware Update Manager and VMware Update Manager Download Service (UMDS) by using the VMware Update Manager Utility. This utility can be used make the following changes without reinstalling Update Manager or losing data:

■ Proxy settings

■ Database user name and password

■ vCenter Server IP address

■ SSL certificate

The VMware Update Manager Utility is automatically installed during the installations of VMware Update Manager and UMDS. You can start the utility by executing the `VMwareUpdateManagerUtility.exe` file, which is located in the VMware vCenter Installation folder.

During interactive installations and upgrades, errors and warnings may be displayed in the installer, prompting you to confirm or cancel the installation or upgrade. During scripted installations and upgrades, such issues are recorded in the installation log file. Prior to performing an upgrade, you can use the VMware

Update Manager pre-check script and review the associated log file
`vmware-vum-server-log4cpp.log`.

Collect Upgrade Diagnostic Information

In many troubleshooting scenarios, you may want to collect diagnostic information from vCenter Server, especially when you want to engage VMware Support. This information can be useful for analyzing issues related to upgrading ESXi Hosts. To collect diagnostic data, log onto the vSphere Web Client with a user account that has the **Global.Diagnostic** privilege and follow these steps:

Step 1.   In the hosts and clusters inventory, select a vCenter instance or an ESXi Host.

Step 2.   Select **Actions** > **Export System Logs**.

Step 3.   If prompted, select the appropriate ESXi Hosts and click **Next**.

Step 4.   In the System Log pane, click **Select All**.

Step 5.   Optionally select **Gather Performance Data** and provide duration and interval parameters.

Step 6.   Click **Generate Log Bundle**.

Step 7.   Click **Download Log Bundle**.

Step 8.   Upload the bundle to the VMware per VMware KB 1008525.

When troubleshooting upgrades, you may want to gather diagnostic data from VMware Update Manager. To do so, log into Windows on the VMware Update Manager server, select **Start** > **All Programs** > **VMware** > **Generate Update Manager Log Bundle**, and locate the ZIP file. The file is named `vum-support-xxxxx.zip`, where *xxxxx* represents the user, date, and time associated with the bundle generation.

Recognize Common Upgrade Issues with vCenter Server and vCenter Server Appliance

A common issue with upgrading vCenter Server concerns the configuration for the Platform Services Controller (PSC). Perhaps your intention is to upgrade vCenter Server such that an external PSC is implemented, but following the upgrade, you see that the result is vCenter Server with embedded PSC. The root cause is that when you upgrade deployments where Single Sign-On (SSO) and vCenter Server are on the same machine, the upgrade uses an embedded deployment model.

Another common issue for vCenter Server upgrades is failure to meet the vCenter Server 6.0 requirements. For example, to upgrade a Windows-based vCenter Server to version 6.0 with an external PSC in an environment that supports up to 400 ESXi Hosts and 4000 virtual machines, these are some of the requirements:

- 8 CPUs

- 24 GB memory

- 6 GB for Program Files folder space

- 8 GB for ProgramData space

- 3 GB for system folder space (to cache the MSI installer)

- 64-bit system DSN

See VMware KV 2109772 for details.

To resolve a failed vCenter Server upgrade, you need to consider the phase of the upgrade at which the failure occurred. The upgrade has four phases:

- Export of vCenter Server 5.x configuration data

- Uninstallation of vCenter Server 5.x

- Installation of vCenter Server 6.0

- Import of vCenter Server 5.x services, configuration, and data into the new vCenter 6.0 deployment

During the export phase, vCenter Server registration data is preserved in the server where SSO is deployed. During the uninstallation phase, the vCenter Server 5.x instance is unregistered from the SSO server. During the import phase, the vCenter Server 6.0 instance is registered with the SSO server. If a failure occurs prior to the registration, SSO does not have an entry for the vCenter Server. You may need to revert back to the vCenter 5.x server. If a failure occurs during the import or first boot phase, after the export phase, you can re-attempt to upgrade to vCenter Server 6.0 rather than revert to vCenter Server 5.x. For more details, see VMware KB 2108938.

Create/Locate/Analyze VMware Log Bundles

Following a failed vCenter Server installation or upgrade, you can collect log files either by using the Installation Wizard or manually. To use the Installation Wizard, simply locate the **Log Collection** check box on the **Setup Interrupted** page, verify that it is selected, and click **Finish**. Use native Windows utilities to locate the ZIP file, extract its contents, and examine the log files. The name of the ZIP file is `vm-ware-VCS-logs-time-of-installation-attempt.zip`.

To retrieve the log files manually, use native Windows utilities to examine the log files at `%PROGRAMDATA%\VMware\vCenterServer\logs`, which often resolves to `C:\ProgramData\VMware\vCenterServer\logs`. Also examine the log files in the `%TEMP%` location, which is frequently `C:\Users\`*username*`\AppData\Local\Temp` and contains `vminst.log`, `pkgmgr.log`, `pkgmgr-comp-msi.log`, and `vim-vcs-msi.log`.

You can also collect log files from the vCenter Server Appliance following upgrade issues. To do so, you can either connect to the appliance via its virtual machine console or remotely using Secure Shell (SSH). To use the console, press **Alt+F1** after accessing the console. In either case, provide valid user credentials and follow these steps

Step 1.   From the appliance shell, enter `pi shell` to access the Bash Shell.

Step 2.   In the Bash Shell, run the `vc-support.sh` script to generate the support bundle.

Step 3.   Export the generated TGZ file from the `/var/tmp` folder to another location, perhaps on another server, using the `scp` command, as in this example:

```
scp /var/tmp/vc-etco-vm-vlan11-dhcp-63-151.eng.vmware.com-
2014-02-28--21.11.tgz user@x.x.x.x:/tmp
```

Step 4.   Use native Linux utilities to examine the `/var/log/firstboot/firstbootStatus.json` file to determine what failed.

After upgrading vCenter Server, you can retrieve and examine the database upgrade logs. Each of these log files serves a different purpose, and they can be used for different troubleshooting purposes, as shown in Table 11-7.

Table 11-7   vCenter Server Database Upgrade Logs

Purpose	Log File
Collect errors during execution of the pre-upgrade check.	`%TEMP%\..\vcsUpgrade\vcdb_req.out`
Collect errors during the export phase of the upgrade process.	`%TEMP%\..\vcsUpgrade\vcdb_export.out file.`
Collect errors during the import phase of the upgrade process.	`ProgramData\Vmware\CIS\logs\vmware\vpx\vcdb_import.out`
Collect errors during an in-place upgrade	`ProgramData\Vmware\CIS\logs\vmware\vpx\vcdb_inplace.out`

Determine Alternative Methods to Upgrade ESXi Hosts in the Event of Failure

VMware provides multiple methods for upgrading ESXi Hosts, including:

- Use VMware Update Manager
- Interactively use the ESXi Installer
- Use scripted upgrades
- Use vSphere Auto Deploy
- Use the ESXi command line

The following sections provide brief descriptions of these methods.

VMware Update Manager

You can use VMware Update Manger to build upgrade baselines using the ESXi 6.0 installer ISO file. You can then use the baseline to perform orchestrated upgrades of ESXi by attaching the baseline to the host, scanning for compliance, and remediating. Likewise, you can use Update Manager to upgrade the VMware Tools and virtual machine hardware version of each virtual machine to match the latest version that is compatible for the ESXi Host. The two-step process to upgrade the ESXi Host and its virtual machines, which can be done with little administrator interaction, is considered an orchestrated upgrade.

For more details, see Chapter 7, "Upgrade a vSphere Deployment to 6.x."

NOTE VMware Update Manager 6.0 supports upgrades from ESXi 5.x to ESXi 6.0. It does not support host upgrades to 5.x.

NOTE Upgrades to ESXi 6.0 do not provide a rollback option. VMware recommends that you back up the host configuration prior to upgrade. If the upgrade fails, reinstall the previous ESXi 5.x version and restore the configuration.

Interactively Using the ESXi Installer

You can use the ESXi 6.0 Installer CD/DVD (or USB flash drive) to perform fresh installations or upgrades of ESXi. This method is typically suitable only for small environments. The interactive methods of installing and upgrading are nearly identical, but if you select a target disk that already contains ESXi 5.x, the installer upgrades the host to ESXi 6.0, provides you an option to migrate existing settings, and provides a method to keep any existing VMFS datastores.

In larger environments, this installation method is commonly used during initial testing and during troubleshooting. When other deployment methods are having issues, you can attempt to install interactively either as a temporary workaround or to help identify root causes of the issue.

Scripted Upgrades

You can choose to perform a scripted upgrade by invoking a script (kickstart file) to facilitate an unattended upgrade. This is an efficient method for deploying multiple hosts. You can choose from any of these scripted upgrade approaches:

- Doing a scripted upgrade using CD/DVD (or USB flash drive)
- Doing a scripted upgrade using PXE boot from the installer
- Calling the script interactively from the ESXi installer

A script should contain the settings for ESXi, which can be used to apply the script to all hosts you want to have a similar configuration. The script must contain supported commands. You can edit the script, or you can use multiple scripts to apply unique configurations to each ESXi Host. The script can reside in one of these locations:

- FTP server
- HTTP/HTTPS server
- NFS server
- USB flash drive
- CD-ROM drive

You can specify the location of the upgrade script by entering boot options for the ESXi installer. You can press **Shift+O** at boot time to edit the boot options. For PXE boot, you can specify the location of the upgrade script in the `boot.cfg` file in the `kernelopts` line. In either case, to specify the script file location, use the `ks=filepath` option, where `filepath` is the location of the script file.

Other boot options are typically required. In order to use a script file located on a web server during the boot process, IP configuration must be implemented on the host to provide network connectivity so it can reach the script. For example, the following boot options could be supplied either using by **Shift+O** or by editing the `boot.cfg` file:

```
ks=http://192.168.100.10/kickstart/script-01.cfg
nameserver=192.168.100.1 ip=192.168.100.201
netmask=255.255.255.0 gateway=192.168.100.1
```

In this example, the script file named `script-01.cfg` is located on a web server at 192.168.100.10. The gateway and DNS server is 192.168.100.1. The IP address that is temporarily assigned to the host during the boot process is 192.168.100.201.

Alternatively, the `ks` boot parameter can be used to identify the other previously stated location types:

- `ks=cdrom:`/path

- `ks=file://`/path

- `ks=nfs://host:`porturl-path (for example, `ks=nfs:192.168.1.100:`/kickstart/ks.cfg)

- `ks=https://`/path

- `ks=ftp://`/path

The script file should contain a set of commands. For upgrades, the file should contain the `upgrade` command that specifies the disk where the upgrade should occur, using the `--disk`, `--drive`, or `--firstdisk` parameter. Other commonly used commands are:

- `vmaccepteula`, which is required to accept the license agreement

- `dryrun`, which is used to parse and check the script without actually performing the installation

- `network`, which sets the IP address and configuration to when the host boots into ESXi, using parameters such as `--ip` , `--gateway`, `--nameserver`, and `--mask`.

- `rootpw`, which is used to set the root account password

- `Include`, which is used to apply a separate script file

On the ESXi 6.0 host, a sample installation script resides on the initial RAM disk at /etc/vmware/weasel/ks.cfg, which you can modify and use as you wish. Example 11-1 shows what this file contains.

Example 11-1   /etc/vmware/weasel/ks.cfg

```
#
# Sample scripted installation file
#

# Accept the VMware End User License Agreement
vmaccepteula

# Set the root password for the DCUI and Tech Support Mode
rootpw mypassword

# Install on the first local disk available on machine
install --firstdisk --overwritevmfs

# Set the network to DHCP on the first network adapter
network --bootproto=dhcp --device=vmnic0

# A sample post-install script
%post --interpreter=python --ignorefailure=true
import time
stampFile = open('/finished.stamp', mode='w')
stampFile.write( time.asctime() )
```

To use this file during boot, provide the following parameter in the boot option:

```
ks=file://etc/vmware/weasel/ks.cfg
```

vSphere Auto Deploy

In environments where hosts are deployed using Auto Deploy, you can use Auto Deploy to upgrade hosts to ESXi 6.0. You can use the ESXi Image Builder Power-CLI to create and manage the image profiles and then use Auto Deploy to reprovision the host from an ESXi 6.0 image profile.

NOTE If you are using custom certificates, you may set up the host to use the custom certificates again after the deployment.

For more details on using Auto Deploy, see the section "Deploy ESXi Hosts Using Auto Deploy" in Chapter 14, "Deploy and Consolidate."

ESXi Command Line

You can use the ESXCLI command name space to upgrade ESXi Hosts. The key command is `esxcli software profile update`. This command upgrades an ESXi Host by replacing existing VMware Information Bundles (VIBs) with newer versions, but it does not remove any VIBs from the ESXi Host that are not being replaced with newer versions. This command can be used to update all the VIBs that are stored in a ZIP bundle or an online depot. When using the ZIP bundle, it may be stored in a local directory on the target host, in a network file location accessible by the target host, or on a website. The general syntax for this command is:

```
esxcli software profile update --depot=depot_location
--profile=profile_name
```

The `--depot` parameter (or `-d`) identifies the type and location of the depot or ZIP bundle that contains the VIBs to be used during the upgrade. Acceptable formats for this parameter are:

- `http://websever/depot_name`, which uses an HTTP URL to locate the VIB files in native from an online depot (not a ZIP file)

- `file:///path_to_zip/zip_file_name`, which uses a file URL to locate the VIBs within a network-based ZIP bundle

- `[datastore_name]zip_file_name`, which uses a datastore name to locate the VIBs in a datastore- (VMFS- or NFS-) based ZIP bundle

- `/path_to_zip/zip_file_name`, which uses a standard directory path to locate the VIB in a locally stored ZIP bundle

For example, the following procedure could be used to upgrade an ESXi 5.5 Host to ESXi 6.0:

Step 1.   Use the vSphere Web Client to select an ESXi Host and enter maintenance mode or issue the `esxcli` command via an SSH session:

```
esxcli system maintenanceMode set --enable true
```

Step 2.   Configure the ESXi Host firewall to allow HTTP client traffic, using the following command or using Security Profile in the vSphere Web Client:

```
esxcli network firewall ruleset set -e true -r httpClient
```

Step 3.   Identify all the available ESXi 6.0 updates (and depots) that are available online. Effectively, this command discovers all the updates available at the specified URL, but filters for only those updates that contain ESXi-6 in their name:

```
esxcli software sources profile list -d
https://hostupdate.vmware.com/software/VUM/PRODUCTION/main/vmw-dep
```

Step 4. From the list of available ESXi 6.0 updates, identify the appropriate one for your needs, which often is the most recent standard build. Then use `esxcli software profile update` to update the ESXi Host from the associated depot. In this example, the ESXi version and build is 6.0.0-20150404001:

```
esxcli software profile update -d https://hostupdate.vmware.com/
    software/VUM/PRODUCTION/main/vmw-depot-index.xml -p
    ESXi-6.0.0-20150404001-standard
```

Step 5. When prompted, reboot the ESXi Host. Following the reboot, exit maintenance mode and change the firewall back to its former state.

NOTE In this procedure, be sure to use `esxcli software profile update`, not `esxcli software install`, to avoid removing required device drivers from the ESXi Host. VMware supports the use of only `update`, not `install`, when upgrading an ESXi Host using a ZIP bundle.

NOTE The command-line utilities `esxupdate` and `vihostupdate` are not supported for upgrading to ESXi 6.

NOTE VMware-supplied bundles tend to have a standard version, which includes VMware Tools, and a no-tools version, which does not include VMware Tools. The standard version facilitates the ability to easily upgrade VMware Tools in virtual machines to match the most recent version that is compatible with the ESXi Host. For example, in the previous procedure, the `ESXi-6.0.0-20150404001-standard` update could have been used to update the ESXi Host without including VMware Tools.

Configure vCenter Server Logging Options

You can use the vSphere Web Client to configure the amount of detail that vCenter Server collects in its log files. To do so, you must use a user account with the **Global Setting** privilege. These are the steps to configure the logging settings:

Key Topic

Step 1. In the inventory pane, locate and select the vCenter Server.

Step 2. Click on the **Manage** tab.

Step 3. Select **Settings > General > Edit**.

Step 4.   Select **Logging Settings**.

Step 5.   Select the appropriate logging option as described in Table 11-8 and click **OK**.

Table 11-8   vCenter Server Logging Options

Logging Option	Description
None (Disable logging)	No vCenter Server logging occurs.
Error (Errors Only)	The vCenter Server collects only error entries into its log files.
Warning (Warning and Errors)	The vCenter Server collects warning and error entries into its log files.
Info (Normal logging)	The vCenter Server collects information, warning, and error entries into its log files.
Verbose (Verbose)	The vCenter Server collects verbose, information, warning, and error entries into its log files.
Trivia (Extended verbose)	The vCenter Server collects trivia, verbose, information, warning, and error entries into its log files.

Although, setting the logging level to verbose or trivia may be beneficial for troubleshooting, doing so for long durations could cause noticeable vCenter Server performance degradation. VMware recommends using these levels only in rare cases and actively troubleshooting and resetting the logging level to info immediately afterward.

Changes to the logging level that are made using the vSphere Web Client are persisted in the vCenter Server configuration file vpxd.cfg. On a Windows-based vCenter Server, the default location for this file is:

`C:\ProgramData\VMware\CIS\cfg\vmware-vpx\vpxd.cfg.`

On a vCenter Server Appliances, the file is located at:

`/etc/vmware-vpx/vpxd.cfg`

If you cannot successfully use the vSphere Web Client to change the logging level to trivia and start the vCenter Server Service, you may try to do so manually. To manually set the logging level to trivia, you can use this procedure:

Step 1. Make a backup of the original `vpxd.cfg` file.

Step 2. Use a text editor to add the following lines to the `<config>` section of the `vpxd.cfg` file:

```
<log>
  <level>trivia</level>
</log>
```

Step 3. Optionally, use a text editor to make additional, complementary changes, such as setting the maximum number of logs and maximum size for each log. For example, the following lines can be used to set the maximum number of logs to 50 and the maximum files size to approximately 10 GB:

```
<log>
  <level>trivia</level>
  <maxFileNum>50</maxFileNum>
  <directory>C:\vpxlog\</directory>
  <maxFileSize>10485760</maxFileSize>
  <name>vpxd</name>
</log>
```

Step 4. Restart the vCenter Server service.

Step 5. Select the appropriate logging option as described in Table 11-8 and click **OK**.

Optionally, you make additional changes to the configuration file to add even more log details. For example, you can add the following lines to enable debug logging for the NFC process:

```
<nfc>
<loglevel>debug</loglevel>
</nfc>
```

You can add the following lines to enable vCenter Server database tracing after enabling trivia logging:

```
<trace>
 <db>
 <verbose>true</verbose>
 </db>
</trace>
```

For more details on trivia logging, see VMware KB 1001584.

Summary

You have now read the chapter covering exam topics troubleshooting vSphere and troubleshooting upgrades. You should now use information in the following sections to complete your preparation for Objectives 7.2 and 7.3.

Preparation Tasks

Review All the Key Topics

Table 11-9 provides a reference to each of the key topics identified in this chapter. Take a few moments to review each of these specific items.

Table 11-9   Key Topics for Chapter 11

Key Topic Element	Description	Pages
Procedure	Use VOMA	429
Procedure	Collect upgrade diagnostic information	431
List	Alternative methods to upgrade ESXi Hosts	434
Procedure	Configure vCenter Server logging options	439

Complete the Tables and Lists from Memory

Print a copy of Appendix B, "Memory Tables" (found on the CD), or at least the section for this chapter, and complete the tables and lists from memory. Appendix C, "Memory Tables Answer Key," also on the CD, includes completed tables and lists to check your work.

Definitions of Key Terms

Define the following key terms from this chapter and check your answers in the glossary.

vSphere On-disk Metadata Analyzer (VOMA), VMware Update Manager Utility, all paths down (APD), permanent device loss (PDL)

Answer Review Questions

The answers to these review questions can be found in Appendix A.

1. Which of the following is *not* a valid tab that can be selected when analyzing a VMFS datastore in vRealize Operations Manager?

   a. Status

   b. Troubleshooting

   c. Analysis

   d. Details

2. Which of the following is the storage device status that best indicates the PDL state?

   a. All paths down

   b. Dead

   c. Down

   d. Lost communication

3. Which of the following represents a valid use of the VOMA utility?

   a. `voma -t vmfs -f check -d /vmfs/devices/disks/naa.600508e00000000`
   `0b367477b3be3d703:3`

   b. `voma -m vmfs -f check -d /vmfs/devices/disks/naa.600508e00000000`
   `0b367477b3be3d703:3`

   c. `voma -t vmfs -o check -d /vmfs/devices/disks/naa.600508e00000000`
   `0b367477b3be3d703:3`

   d. `voma -m vmfs -o check -d /vmfs/devices/disks/naa.600508e00000000`
   `0b367477b3be3d703:3`

4. Which of the following is not a valid command that should be could be used in an installation script file, such as `ks.cfg`?

   a. `license`

   b. `vmaccepteula`

   c. `dryrun`

   d. `include`

5. Which of the following is the correct location where the setting for the vCenter Server logging level is persisted?

   a. vCenter Server database

   b. vcdb.cfg

   c. vmware.cfg

   d. vpxd.cfg

This chapter covers the following objective:

- **Objective 7.4—Troubleshoot Performance**

    - Monitor CPU and memory usage (including vRealize OM badges and alerts)

    - Identify and isolate CPU and memory contention issues

    - Recognize impact of using CPU/memory limits, reservations, and shares

    - Describe and differentiate critical performance metrics

    - Describe and differentiate common metrics, including:

        - Memory

        - CPU

        - Network

        - Storage

    - Monitor performance through esxtop

    - Troubleshoot Enhanced vMotion Compatibility (EVC) issues

    - Troubleshoot virtual machine performance with vRealize operations

    - Compare and contrast overview and advanced charts

Troubleshoot Performance

This chapter covers exam topics related to troubleshooting performance issues.

"Do I Know This Already?" Quiz

The "Do I Know This Already?" quiz allows you to assess whether you should study this entire chapter or move quickly to the "Exam Preparation Tasks" section. Regardless, the authors recommend that you read the entire chapter at least once. Table 12-1 outlines the major headings in this chapter and the corresponding "Do I Know This Already?" quiz questions. You can find the answers in Appendix A, "Answers to the 'Do I Know This Already?' Quizzes and Review Questions."

Table 12-1 "Do I Know This Already?" Foundation Topics Section-to-Question Mapping

Foundation Topics Section	Questions Covered in This Section
Describe and Differentiate Common Metrics—CPU	1
Describe and Differentiate Common Metrics—Memory	2
Identify Host Power Management Policy	3
Monitor Performance Through ESXTOP	4
Troubleshoot Enhanced vMotion Compatibility (EVC) Issues	5
Troubleshoot Virtual Machine Performance with vRealize Operations	6
Describe and Differentiate Common Metrics—Storage	7
Identify and Isolate CPU and Memory Contention Issues	8
Recognize Impact of Using CPU/Memory Limits, Reservations, and Shares	9
Compare and Contrast Overview and Advanced Charts	10

1. Which of the following is the best indicator that a virtual machine is experiencing CPU contention with other virtual machines on an ESXi Host?

   a. High CPU Wait values

   b. Low CPU Wait values

   c. Low CPU Ready values

   d. High CPU Ready values

2. In the vSphere Web client, which of the following is not directly caused by a low amount of free, available ESXi Host memory?

   a. High amount of ballooning

   b. High amount of swapping

   c. High amount of transparent page sharing

   d. High amount of compression

3. Which of the following is the default power management policy in ESXi 6.0?

   a. High Performance

   b. High Power

   c. Balanced

   d. Disabled

4. In ESXTOP, which of the following fields is used to identify the balloon size?

   a. MCTLSZ

   b. BALSZ

   c. VMMEMCTL

   d. MEMCUR

5. Which of the following is the minimal Intel EVC baseline that you should use if you need to utilize the POPCOUNT instruction set?

   a. Nehalem

   b. Ivy Bridge

   c. Sandy Bridge

   d. Merom

6. Which of the following can be customized in vRealize Operations Manager 6.0? (Choose three.)

   a. Symptoms

   b. Alarms

    c. Recommendations

    d. Actions

    e. Alerts

7. Which of the following is *not* accurate concerning storage latency?

    a. GAVG = KAVG + DAVG

    b. KAVG includes QAVG

    c. DAVG includes QAVG

    d. GAVG includes QAVG

8. In the real-time performance graphs, the CPU Swap Wait metric of a poorly performing virtual machine with a single virtual CPU is 1500 ms. Which of the following is a likely potential remedy?

    a. Migrate the virtual machine to an ESXi Host with more available memory resources.

    b. Migrate the virtual machine to an ESXi Host with more available CPU resources.

    c. Set a CPU reservation on the virtual machine.

    d. Set a memory limit on the virtual machine

9. A virtual machine cannot be started due to insufficient resources. Which of the following is a potential remedy?

    a. Increase the virtual machine memory limit

    b. Decrease the virtual machine memory limit

    c. Increase the virtual machine shares

    d. Change the memory reservation on the virtual machine

10. Which of the following metrics are included in the ESXi Overview real-time graph? (Choose three.)

    a. Memory Ballooning

    b. Memory Swap In Rate (in MBps)

    c. Memory Swap Out Rate (in KBps)

    d. Disk Rate (in KBps)

    e. Disk Rate (in MBps)

Foundation Topics

Objective 7.4—Troubleshoot and Monitor vSphere Performance

The following sections identify and describe commonly used performance metrics. They explain how to use various tools to examine the metrics and how to apply the data to troubleshooting.

Monitor CPU and Memory Usage (Including vRealize Badges and Alerts)

Details for monitoring CPU are covered later in this chapter, in the "Describe and Differentiate Common Metrics—CPU" section. The authors chose to provide details on CPU metrics, including monitoring procedures and metric explanations, in the same section. Likewise, details for monitoring memory are covered later in this chapter, in the "Describe and Differentiate Common Metrics—Memory" section.

One item that is not discussed in the upcoming sections is the VMware Performance Monitor (PerfMon) dynamic link library (DLL). In a Windows virtual machine where VMware Tools is installed, the VMware PerfMon DLL may be automatically installed. In this case, you can use the Windows Performance Monitor to monitor additional counters in the guest operating system. The additional counters are VM Memory and VM Processor. This allows you to monitor Vmware-provided counters, such as CPU Limit and CPU Reservation (which are described later in the chapter) from within the guest operating system.

Details for using vRealize Operations Manager to examine badges and alerts are covered later in this chapter, in the "Troubleshoot Virtual Machine Performance with vRealize Operations" section. That section provides guidance for reviewing badges, identifying alert root causes, and exploring recommendations. You can apply such details to badges and alerts that directly relate to CPU and memory usage as well as other use cases.

The vSphere Client (not to be confused with the vSphere Web Client) can be used to connect directly to an ESXi Host to examine performance graphs. The details are not provided in this chapter, as the preferred method to examine performance graphs is to use the vSphere Web Client. Generally speaking, the vSphere Client is a legacy tool that can be used to connect to the vCenter Server to perform administration, including monitoring performance. The use of the performance graphs in the vSphere Client is similar to its counterpart in the vSphere Web Client. One use case for the vSphere Client performance graphs is troubleshooting during times of vCenter Sever or vSphere Web Client unavailability. In this case, you can use the vSphere Client to connect directly to an ESXi Host and use the performance graphs to examine recent data. But you cannot set the Timespan to the past week or higher, because only vCenter Server provides that functionality.

Identify and Isolate CPU and Memory Contention Issues

Whenever a VM running a critical application contends for CPU or memory resources on the ESXi Host against other virtual machines or VMkernel services, any users that directly use the application tend to notice slow performance. To identify CPU and memory contention, you can use ESXTOP or vSphere Web Client performance graphs to examine the associated metrics. These metrics are discussed in other sections in this chapter. In this section, you will consider a scenario where users are reporting poor application performance, and you will follow a logical approach to analyzing the associated metrics to discover the root cause.

To use the vSphere Web Client to analyze a poorly performing virtual machine and to determine whether CPU or memory contention is the root cause, you can follow this procedure:

Step 1.   Select the virtual machine in the inventory.

Step 2.   In the middle pane, select **Monitor > Performance > Advanced**.

Step 3.   Click **Chart Options**.

Step 4.   In the Chart Metrics section, select **CPU**.

Step 5.   In the Timespan section, select **Real Time**.

Step 6.   In the Counters section, click **None** and then select **Ready, Co-stop**, and **Swap Wait**.

Step 7.   Click **OK** and verify that the graph appears.

Step 8.   In the details section beneath the graph, monitor the values of the **Ready, Co-stop**, and **Swap Wait** metrics for each virtual CPU.

Step 9.   If the Ready time is frequently greater than 1000 ms, then the virtual machine is competing for CPU resources with other virtual machines and services on the ESXi Host. You could address the problem by reducing the competing workload on the host, reserving CPU resources for this virtual machine, or migrating the virtual machine to a host with more available CPU resources.

Step 10.   If the Co-stop time is frequently greater than 1000 ms, then the virtual machine performance is suffering because at least one of its virtual CPUs is waiting on another one to be scheduled. You could address this problem by reducing the number of virtual CPUs in the virtual machine. You could also address the problem in the same manner used to address high Ready time in step 9 because if contention is eliminated for all the virtual machine virtual CPUs, then the Co-stop time is reduced.

Step 11.   If the Swap Wait time is frequently greater than 1000 ms, then the virtual machine is spending time waiting on memory to be swapped into the virtual machine. You could address this problem by reducing the competing workload on the host, reserving memory resources for this virtual machine, or migrating the virtual machine to a host with more available memory resources.

Step 12.   Modify the Chart Options again but this time select **Memory** in the **Chart Metrics** section.

Step 13.   In the Counters section, click **None** and select **Decompression Rate** and **Swap In Rate**. Monitor these metrics in the graph details.

Step 14.   If the value for either Decompression Rate or Swap In Rate is greater than zero, then the active virtual machine memory is not readily available, and the virtual machine performance is being impacted by decompression and swapping techniques. Even if the Swap Wait Stop time value was acceptable, you could still address the problem in the same manner used to treat high Swap Wait in step 11.

Step 15.   If none of the values for the metrics in the previous steps are unacceptable, then the root cause is elsewhere. It could still be related to CPU or memory. For example, if you use guest OS tools and discover high guest paging values, then the virtual machine may need to be configured with additional virtual memory.

The same metrics can be examined using ESXTOP, which is covered in the "Monitor Performance Through ESXTOP" section of this chapter.

Recognize Impact of Using CPU/Memory Limits, Reservations, and Shares

You can set reservations, limits, and shares on virtual machines to impact their access to CPU and memory. A *reservation* is a guarantee for a specific amount of resources. A *limit* is a specific maximum amount of resource. A *share* is a relative priority that is applied only during resource contention. A reservation can be used to guarantee that a virtual machine is provided sufficient CPU and memory hardware to run its workload in spite of competing virtual machine workloads. A limit can be used to prevent a virtual machine from accessing all of the CPU and memory hardware for which it is configured. A share can be used to effectively grant some virtual machines higher priority than other competing virtual machines for accessing CPU and memory hardware during times of contention.

You can set a virtual machine memory reservation if you expect the performance of the guest operating system and applications to suffer if the virtual machine cannot access a specific amount of physical memory. For example, if a virtual machine is configured with 4 GB of memory and its performance is significantly impacted whenever the virtual machine engages in memory ballooning, compressing, or swapping, then you should consider setting the memory reservation to 4 GB. In this example, when vSphere starts the virtual machine, it grants 4 GB of available memory to the virtual machine and allows it to start. If 4 GB is not available (currently unreserved), then the virtual machine does not start.

You can set a virtual machine memory limit if you are concerned that allowing the virtual machine to access all of its configured memory will negatively impact critical virtual machines. For example, you can set the memory limit to 1 GB on a test virtual machine that is configured with 4 GB with the intention of minimizing competition with production virtual machines. In this case, the limit would effectively prevent the test virtual machine from using more than 1 GB memory, although its guest operating system thinks it has access to 4 GB. The virtual machine may run very slowly because at any moment it may have only 1 GB of virtual memory in physical memory and up to 3 GB of virtual memory in the swap file.

You can configure virtual CPU shares on a virtual machine to effectively establish its priority during periods of host CPU contention. During times of CPU contention, the number of shares assigned to a virtual CPU is used to determine the amount of time the virtual CPU will be scheduled on the hardware. The VMkernel schedules each virtual CPU on the hardware based on the proportion of its assigned shares to the sum of the shares assigned to competing virtual CPUs. For example, you could set CPU shares to High for each production virtual machine and set CPU shares to Low for each non-production virtual machine. In this example, during times of CPU contention on the ESXi Host, the shares for the competing virtual machines are applied, so the production machines may effectively continue to run well, with negligible performance degradation, while the non-production virtual machines become sluggish. Each virtual CPU is assigned Normal shares by default, but you can change the shares to High, to Low, or to a custom value. Each High CPU share equals two Normal CPU shares, and each Normal CPU share equals two Low CPU shares. So during times of CPU contention on an ESXi Host, a virtual machine configured with one virtual CPU and High shares will be scheduled on the physical CPU four times as often as a competing virtual machine with one virtual CPU and Low shares.

You need to be able to recognize and understand the impact of reservations, limits, and shares on how a virtual machine accesses CPU and memory. Here are some examples:

- Say that a virtual machine will not start due to insufficient resources. This may be due to improperly configured reservations but is not caused by improperly configured shares or limits. For example, a virtual machine whose CPU reservation is 8 GHz cannot start on a host that currently has only 4 GHz unreserved CPU resources.

- Say that a virtual machine is running very slowly during periods of CPU contention with other virtual machines on the same ESXi Host; however, some of the competing virtual machines are running well. This may be due to low CPU shares on the slow virtual machine. It could also be caused by the virtual machine CPU limit set to something other than Unlimited or by significantly high CPU reservations on the competing virtual machines.

- Say that a virtual machine is running very slowly due to ESXi Host memory contention. You could consider increasing its memory shares or memory reservation. Be aware that doing so may negatively impact the performance of other virtual machines.

Describe and Differentiate Critical Performance Metrics

Some specific performance metrics tend to be clear indicators of whether the performance of the environment or specific objects is healthy or poor. Such metrics include those that indicate contention for a particular resource, such as CPU, memory, disk I/O, and network I/O. Such metrics also include those that indicate some underlying faults that may not be severe enough to result in a component failure but are significantly impacting performance.

Table 12-2 contains a list of the most widely accepted critical performance metrics as well as a description of each metric.

Table 12-2 Critical Performance Metrics

Metric	Description
Disk Latency	The amount of time that elapsed while performing a storage-related task, such as a read or write operation. Latency can be reported from various perspectives. For example, the virtual machine disk read latency is the amount of time from which the guest OS generates the read operation until it is completely fulfilled by the storage system and the data is delivered to the guest OS. High disk latency is often an indicator of slow or overworked storage devices.

Metric	Description
Network Packets Dropped	The number of network packets that were dropped during a specific sampling period. This indicates that a network queue has filled due to a processing bottleneck involving a network adapter, virtual machine, or VMkernel.
CPU Ready Time	The amount of time that a VMkernel world, such as a virtual CPU, spent waiting to be scheduled on physical CPU hardware after it announced it was ready to execute its workload. High CPU Ready Time is often an indicator of overworked CPU hardware.
Memory Swapped	The amount of data that has been swapped from a virtual machine's memory to its virtual machine swap file. It is often an indicator of overworked memory hardware.
Disk Aborts	The number of aborts issued by guest operating systems. This is often an indicator of severe problems, such as failed storage paths.

Each of these metrics is covered in more detail in the following sections.

Describe and Differentiate Common Metrics—Memory

Commonly used memory metrics include those that indicate memory contention, memory usage, memory overhead, and memory reservation.

Transparent page sharing (TPS) is a mechanism whereby the VMkernel automatically identifies identical pages of virtual memory and consolidates them to a single physical memory page, in a manner that is transparent to the virtual machine guest operating system. In vSphere 6, intra-VM TPS is enabled by default, and inter-VM TPS is disabled by default, due to some security concerns, as described in VMware KB 2080735. You can change the TPS behavior by applying the salting mechanism as described in VMware KB 2097593. A low-priority, scheduled VMkernel process uses a hashing mechanism to apply TPS by identifying matching pages in a virtual machine and other processes, depending on TPS settings. Naturally, the amount of page sharing depends on factors such as the amount of matching pages among the virtual machines and other worlds. The amount of memory pages claimed by inter-VM TPS, when enabled, can rise as the number of virtual machines running the same guest OS rises. This number is negatively impacted by the use of large pages (2 MB pages). Most modern guest operating systems use large pages, which cannot be shared by the VMkernel. Page sharing is not a direct sign of memory contention because it may be engaged regardless of the memory state; however, in the Clear memory state, the TPS service is actively called instead of waiting on the next scheduled TPS run. Also in the High memory state, the ESXi Host begins breaking large memory pages into small pages, which facilitates an increase in page sharing.

NOTE   In vSphere 5.x, only four memory states exist. When using modern guest operating systems that use large pages, the effect is that the amount of page sharing is low until the ESXi Host enters the Hard memory state, where compression and swapping are enabled. The reason is that in the Hard memory state, to enable compression and swapping, large pages are automatically broken into smaller standard 4 KB pages. These standard-size pages then become candidates for TPS, which may act on the pages instead of compression or swapping. In vSphere 5.x, TPS could be considered an indirect sign of memory contention since it tends to only engage significantly when the ESXi Host is experiencing memory pressure. Per VMware KB 2080735, VMware disabled inter-VM page sharing by default in updates for VMware 5.x.

NOTE   In ESXi 6.0, the five memory states are High, Clear, Soft, Hard, and Low; Clear is a new state in version 6.0. The states are based on a value called minFree, which is 899 MB for the first 28 GB of ESXi Host memory plus 1% of any additional host memory. For example, for a 100GB ESXi Host, minFree is 899 MB plus 1% of (100 GB – 28GB) = 1619 MB. The thresholds for each state are based on the amount of free available memory in the host compared to the minFree value. The thresholds are High equals 400% minFree, Clear equals 100% minFree, Soft equals 64% minFree, Hard equals 32%, and Low equals 16%. When the Clear threshold is crossed, large pages are broken into small pages. When the free ESXi Host memory drops below 400% minFree (the High threshold), ESXi begins breaking large pages into small pages. At the Clear threshold, TPS is actively called instead of waiting for the next TPS run. At the Soft threshold, ballooning begins. At the Hard threshold, compression and swapping begins. At the Low threshold, blocking begins, where certain virtual machines are prevented from allocating memory.

In the vSphere Web Client performance graphs, the Memory - Shared metric can be used to monitor the size in kilobytes (KB) of the amount of memory that is shared by TPS. For example, Figure 12-1 illustrates an advanced performance graph for a virtual machine that was recently rebooted and is running the Windows 2008 installer. The graph contains only one metric, Shared, which peaked at 199,500 KB and is currently at 97,204 KB. Effectively, this virtual machine is now using 97,204 KB less memory than it would have used if TPS were not available. This memory is now available to the host and reduces the need to engage memory ballooning, compression, or swapping.

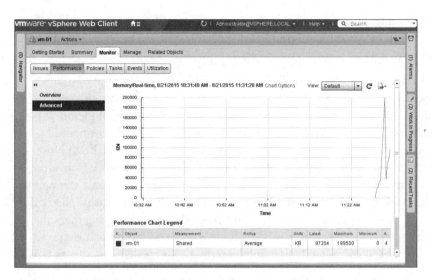

Figure 12-1 Virtual Machine Page Sharing in vSphere Web Client

Ballooning is a memory mechanism in which memory pages that were previously used by a virtual machine are reclaimed by the ESXi Host and given to another virtual machine. A main use case is when a guest OS previously used a physical memory page to store data but later marked the page as free. In this case, the underlying physical page is not automatically returned to the VMkernel for reassignment. Instead, it remains assigned to the virtual machine. When the ballooning mechanism is engaged, it may make a request to virtual machines via VMware Tools to inflate their virtual machine balloon driver. The balloon driver (vmmemctl) is deployed as part of VMWare Tools. When it is inflated, the guest OS assigns and locks virtual memory pages to it. The VMkernel identifies the underlying physical pages, reclaims the pages from the original virtual machine, and makes the pages available to other virtual machines and VMkernel worlds.

Ballooning is engaged only when sufficient memory pressure occurs on the ESXi Host, such that it enters the Soft state. Ballooning is a sign of memory contention within an ESXi Host, but it does not necessarily indicate degradation in performance. Instead, in many cases, the result of ballooning is that memory is proactively made available prior to a virtual machine demand. This means that the associated application likely performed better than it would have if ballooning were not used.

In the vSphere Web Client performance graphs, the Memory - Balloon metric can be used to monitor the size in kilobytes (KB) of the amount of memory that is claimed by the balloon driver within the virtual machine. Effectively, it indicates the amount of memory that has been reclaimed from the virtual machine by the VMkernel to be reassigned to other virtual machines and VMkernel worlds. The Memory - Balloon Target metric indicates the size of the memory that the virtual machine's balloon driver intends to claim. The target and the actual amount may be different at any moment as some time is required for the balloon driver to actually claim targeted memory pages.

Memory ballooning can be controlled using the ESXi Host setting `Mem.CtlMaxPercent` and the virtual machine setting `Sched.Mem.MaxMemCtl`. By default, `Mem.CtlMaxPercent` is set to 65%, which limits the amount of memory that can be reclaimed for any virtual machine on the host to 65% of the configured memory. Changing this value impacts all the virtual machines on the ESXi Host. For example, if you set it to zero, ballooning does not reclaim memory from any virtual machine on the ESXi Host. By default, the `Sched.Mem.MaxMemCtl` setting for a virtual machine is `-1` MB (unlimited), which means the ballooning is not limited by the virtual machine, but it still may be limited by the host. Changing this value impacts only a single virtual machine. For example, you could prevent a single virtual machine from engaging in ballooning by setting `Sched.Mem.MaxMemCtl` to 0 MB.

Compression is a memory mechanism whereby data in memory pages is compressed to save space. Like page sharing and swapping, compression works only on small memory pages. Whenever an ESXi Host is in the Hard memory state, it breaks large pages (2 MB) into small pages (4 KB) to prepare them for compression or swapping. As each page is identified, the compression algorithm is used to determine whether the data in the page can be compressed by at least 50%, such that it will fit in a 2 KB page. If it cannot, then the data is swapped to the virtual machine swap file. The virtual machine performance is expected to be impacted less by decompressing than by swapping. Compression is a sign of contention. It only engages when the ESXi Host memory state is Hard or Low.

In the vSphere Web Client performance graphs, the Memory - Compressed metric can be used to monitor the size in kilobytes (KB) of the amount of virtual machine memory that is compressed. The Memory - Compression Rate metric is the rate at which virtual machine memory is being compressed, which is an indicator of how quickly memory pages are being reclaimed from the virtual machine due to ESXi Host memory pressure. The Memory - Decompression Rate metric is the rate at which compressed virtual machine memory is being decompressed for use by the guest OS. It can be useful for determining whether a guest OS is actively reading compressed data instead of swapped data. A high decompression rate is an indicator that virtual machine's poor performance is due to memory contention on the ESXi Host.

Swapping is a memory mechanism in which pages of virtual memory are moved from physical memory to disk. Two types of swapping can occur: guest OS paging and virtual machine swapping.

Guest OS paging occurs inside a guest operating system. It is dependent on the guest operating system. For example, Windows 2012 paging involves a file named `pagefile.sys`. Some guest operating systems may wait until it is under memory pressure to utilize the paging, while others tend to use the paging more proactively to swap idle memory pages to disk. Generally speaking, the greater the guest OS paging, the greater the likelihood that memory contention exists within the guest OS, such that its applications are competing for memory. It is a sign that the virtual machine might experience greater performance if it were configured with more virtual memory.

Guest OS paging is not a direct indicator of ESXi Host memory contention. However, if a virtual machine's balloon driver is inflated, it may be more likely to cause guest OS paging within the guest OS. In this case, the paging is an indirect result of ESXi memory contention. This is not the expected, normal result of ballooning, but it is certainly possible and not necessarily a rare event.

You can use guest OS tools, such as Windows Performance Monitor and Linux TOP, to monitor and measure the guest OS paging. For example, in Windows Performance Monitor, you examine the Pages per Second metric.

Virtual machine swapping occurs within the VMkernel. The VMkernel swaps virtual memory pages from physical memory pages to a designated virtual machine swap file (VSWP file). It is an indicator of ESXi Host memory contention. It occurs when the ESXi Host memory state is Hard or Low.

In the vSphere Web Client performance graphs, the Memory - Swapped metric can be used to monitor the size in kilobytes (KB) of the virtual machine memory that is swapped into the VSWP file. The Memory - Swap Out Rate metric is the rate at which virtual machine memory is swapped to the VSWP file, which is an indicator of how quickly memory pages are being reclaimed from the virtual machine due to ESXi Host memory pressure. The Memory - Swap In Rate metric is the rate at which swapped virtual machine memory is being read from the VSWP file for use by the guest OS. It can be useful for determining whether poor VM performance may be related to memory contention with other virtual machines on the ESXi Host. For example, if the Swap In Rate metric for a poorly performing virtual machine is zero, then the problem is probably not related to memory contention on the host, even if the Swap Out Rate and Swapped metrics are nonzero. Figure 12-2 illustrates an example of a virtual machine that is actively swapping. In this example, the virtual machine named `vm-01` swapped 7140 KB of data from the VSWP file during the latest sample.

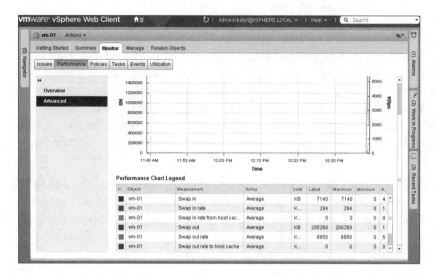

Figure 12-2 Virtual Machine Swapping in vSphere Web Client

Memory Overhead is the amount of memory that is used by the VMkernel to run and manage the virtual machine. It does not include the amount of memory that is used directly by the guest OS. It does include the memory used to run overhead services such as virtual devices and virtual machine console. It is a significant amount that can lead to unexpected memory contention on the ESXi Host, whenever it is overlooked during capacity planning. In Figure 12-3, it is about 51 MB for the selected virtual machine.

Figure 12-3 Virtual Machine Memory Overhead in vSphere Web Client

Memory Consumed, which is also called Memory Usage, is the amount of physical memory that is assigned to the virtual machine, which includes memory used by the guest OS and memory overhead. Memory Active is the amount of memory that was actively used during the sampling period. For example, if a 1 GB virtual machine is completely idle during a 20-second sampling period, then the vSphere Web Client real-time performance graph may report the active memory as 0 KB and the consumed memory as 1,024,00 KB. This indicates that although 1 GB of memory is assigned to the virtual machine, the VM did not read or write any memory pages during the sampling period.

The vSphere Web Client performance graphs include the Memory Consumed, Usage, Active, and Overhead metrics, which can be used to determine how much physical memory is used by a virtual machine and to analyze how it is used.

Memory Reservation is the amount of physical memory that is guaranteed for a virtual machine. It is an amount of memory for which the virtual machine does not have to compete with other virtual machines or VMkernel worlds. It is an amount of memory from which the VMkernel is not allowed to use ballooning, compression or swapping to reclaim physical memory pages. The vSphere Web Client performance graphs do not include a Memory Reservation metric but do include a Memory Entitlement metric and a Memory Reserved Overhead metric. Entitlement is the amount of memory to which the virtual machine is entitled based on several factors, such as shares and reservation settings. It is a good indicator of guaranteed resources, in spite of the lack of a reservation metric in the performance graphs. Memory Reserved Overhead is the amount of memory reserved for overhead services that are required to run the virtual machine. It does not include any memory that may be reserved for the guest OS. To determine the amount of memory that is reserved for the guest OS, examine the VM Hardware section of the virtual machine's Summary page. For example, the virtual machine named vm-01, which is shown in Figure 12-4, has a memory reservation of 0 MB.

Figure 12-4   Virtual Machine Reservation on the Summary Page

Table 12-3 lists a set of potential memory-related performance issues. For each potential issue, the table includes an Indicators column entry with details on using specific real-time memory counters in vSphere Web Client performance graphs to identify the issue. Also, for each potential issue, the table includes a column that contains some potential resolutions.

Table 12-3   Potential Memory Issues and Resolutions

Potential Issue	Indicators	Potential Resolutions
The VM is experiencing memory contention.	Memory Ballooning, Memory Decompression Rate, and/or Memory Swap In Rate is greater than zero. Memory latency is 5% or higher, which indicates that the VM is waiting to access swapped or compressed data.	Migrate the VM to an ESXi Host with available memory resources. Increase the Memory Shares or Memory Reservation of the VM. Stop some competing VMs or migrate the VMs to other ESXi Hosts. Decrease the Memory Shares or Memory Reservation of competing VMs.
The VM's virtual memory resources are insufficient to meet the current demand.	The Memory Usage of the VM is about 100%. The guest OS reports high paging. For example, for Windows it is reporting Pages/sec is 200.	Reconfigure the VM with additional virtual memory. Reduce the workload in the VM.
The ESXi Host's memory resources are insufficient to meet the current demand from its VMs.	Memory State is Hard or Low, which indicates that the ESXi Host is swapping and compressing memory. Memory Latency is 5% or higher.	Reduce the workload on the ESXi Host by migrating some VMs to ESXi Hosts with available memory resources. Add more memory to the ESXi Host.

Another set of useful memory metrics is related to non-uniform memory access (NUMA). Concepts and settings concerning NUMA and virtual NUMA are discussed in Chapter 16, "Virtual Machines." Some important ESXTOP metrics related to NUMA are NRMEM, GST_ND0, and N%L. NRMEM indicates the amount of memory in MB that the virtual machine is accessing from remote nodes. GST_ND0 is the amount of memory in NUMA Node 0 that is allocated to the virtual machine. GST_ND1 is the amount of memory in NUMA Node 1 that is allocated to the virtual machine. N%L is the percentage of virtual machine memory that is accessed in the local NUMA node. If N%L is less than 80%, then poor NUMA locality exists.

Describe and Differentiate Common Metrics—CPU

Commonly used memory metrics include those that indicate CPU contention, CPU usage, CPU overhead, and CPU reservation.

CPU Ready is the amount of time that a virtual machine spends in a state where it is ready to execute a workload but is waiting on the VMkernel to schedule it on the physical CPUs. It is a sign of CPU contention on the ESXi Host, where the virtual machine is competing with other virtual machines for processor time. Generally speaking, a CPU Ready value that corresponds to 5% or less of the actual sampling period duration is acceptable. CPU Ready values that exceed 10% are not acceptable, when poor performance exists. The vSphere Web Client performance graphs show Ready time as a delta in milliseconds. An acceptable CPU Ready value for a single processor virtual machine in the real time graph (20 second intervals) is 20 seconds * 1000 ms/seconds * 5% = 1000 ms.

CPU Co-stop is the amount of time that a multi-processor virtual machine spends in a state where it is ready to execute a workload but is waiting on the VMkernel to schedule other virtual CPUs from the same VM. Much like CPU Ready, an acceptable value for the Co-stop metric is 5%. If poorly running virtual machine experiences CPU Co-stop that is more than 5%, it may run better with just a single virtual CPU or on an ESXi Host with less competition.

CPU System is the amount of time spent on processing the overhead services for a virtual machine. CPU Wait is the total time the virtual machine waits on something, such as workload or disk I/O. It is not a direct sign of CPU contention because it could be a sign that the virtual machine is idle and waiting on work to be assigned. CPU Swap Wait is the amount of time a virtual machine spends waiting on data to be swapped in from the virtual machine swap file. CPU Entitlement is the amount of CPU that is guaranteed to the virtual machine due to settings such as CPU Shares and CPU Reservations.

The vSphere Web Client performance graphs include the CPU Usage, CPU Ready, CPU Co-stop, CPU System, CPU Wait, and CPU Swap Wait metrics, which can be used to determine how much CPU time is used by a virtual machine and to analyze how it is used. For example, a single-processor virtual machine with CPU Usage = 90% and CPU Ready = 1% may benefit from the addition of a second virtual CPU. Figure 12-5 shows a performance graph for a virtual machine that includes each of these metrics.

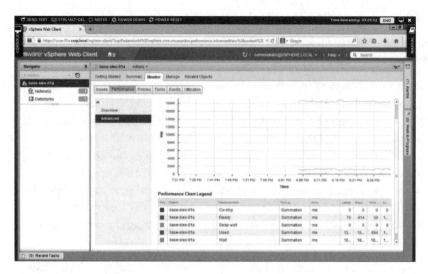

Figure 12-5   Virtual Machine Performance Graph with Common CPU Metrics

Table 12-4 contains a set of potential CPU-related performance issues. For each
potential issue, the table includes an Indicators column entry with details on using specific real-time CPU counters in vSphere Web Client performance graphs
to identify the issue. Also, for each potential issue, the table includes a column that
contains some potential resolutions.

Table 12-4   Potential CPU Issues and Resolutions

Potential Issue	Indicators	Potential Resolutions
The VM is experiencing CPU contention.	CPU Ready Time for one or more of the VM's virtual CPUs is frequently 2000 ms or more.	Migrate the VM to an ESXi Host with available CPU resources. Increase the CPU Shares or CPU Reservation of the VM. Stop some competing VMs or migrate the VMs to other ESXi Hosts. Decrease the CPU Shares or CPU Reservation of competing VMs.
The VM's virtual CPU resources are insufficient to meet the current demand.	The CPU Usage of the entire VM and of each of the VM's virtual CPUs is frequently 80% or higher.	Reconfigure the VM with additional virtual CPUs. Migrate the VM to an ESXi Host with faster CPUs. Reduce the workload in the VM.
The ESXi Host's CPU resources are insufficient to meet the current demand from its VMs.	The CPU Usage of the ESXi Host and each of its CPU cores is frequently 80% or higher. CPU Latency is 5% or higher.	Reduce the workload on the ESXi Hosts by migrating some of the VMs to less busy hosts. Add more CPUs to the ESXi Host.

NOTE Table 12-4 does not contain all potential resolutions, just a few examples. Other potential resolutions exist. Likewise, it does not contain all indicators but only a few of the strongest indicators.

Describe and Differentiate Common Metrics—Network

Commonly used network metrics include those that indicate network I/O contention, network I/O usage, and network errors.

Transmit and Receive Rates are metrics that indicate the amount of network data being transmitted and received from a virtual machine. They are indicators of the amount of network activity that involves the virtual machine. Packets Received and Packets Transmitted indicate the number of packets that are sent and received by the virtual machine. These metrics are also available for the ESXi Host and physical network adapter objects. Whenever the sum of the transmit and receive rates approaches the bandwidth of the network adapter, it is an indicator of a bottleneck.

Receive Packets Dropped and Transmit Packets Dropped are indicators of issues involving the virtual machine and network adapter. High values could result from extremely high network traffic. These values should consistently remain at zero in most cases.

In addition to monitoring these transmit and receive metrics per virtual machine, you can also monitor them per virtual machine virtual network adapter, VMkernel virtual network adapter, and physical network adapter.

Packet Receive Errors and Packet Transmit Errors are metrics that are available for the ESXi Host but not for individual virtual machines. They are indictors of packets with errors. When analyzing poor network performance, you can examine the packet errors on the ESXi Host, the packets dropped for the associated virtual machines, and the data rates for the virtual machine.

To analyze performance issues that impact a virtual machine, you could use the vSphere Web Client to examine the advanced network performance graphs for the virtual machine, as shown in Figure 12-6. Determine whether Transmit Packets Dropped is higher than zero, which indicates that outbound network contention is present. The problem could be addressed by increasing the physical network bandwidth available to the virtual machine. Determine whether the Receive Packets Dropped is higher than zero, which indicates that CPU resources are insufficient to process the inbound packets. The problem could be addressed by increasing the CPU resources available to the virtual machine and its supporting worlds.

If no packets are dropped, use the vSphere Web Client performance graphs to compare the transmit and receive rates of the virtual machine virtual network adapter with the rates on the host physical network adapter that serves as the uplink on the virtual switch where the virtual machine is connected. Determine whether the physical adapters are saturated with network I/O and determine how much of the I/O is from the troubled virtual machine. Consider migrating competing virtual machines from the virtual switch or ESXi Host and analyze the impact.

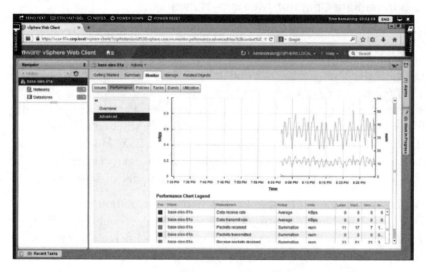

Figure 12-6   Virtual Machine Performance Graph with Network Metrics

Describe and Differentiate Common Metrics—Storage

Commonly used storage metrics include those that indicate storage contention, storage usage, storage overhead, and storage reservation.

Physical Device Latency is the amount of time for the physical storage system to process a read or write SCSI command. Generally speaking, this should be less than 10 milliseconds, on average, for a well-performing system.

Kernel Latency is the amount of time for the VMkernel to process storage commands as they travel from the virtual machine to the storage. Generally speaking, this should be less than 1 millisecond, on average, for a well-performing system. Queue Latency, which is a subset of the kernel latency, is the amount of time required to process a queued command.

Guest Latency is the total amount of time for a storage command to be completed from the moment it is used by the guest OS until the moment the operation is completed and data is returned to the guest OS. Guest latency is the sum of physical device latency plus kernel latency. Generally speaking, this should be less than 15 milliseconds, on average, for a well-performing system

Separate metrics are available in the vSphere Web Client for read latency and write latency.

Commands per Second is the number of read and write commands performed per second. It is useful for monitoring the disk I/O workload of a virtual machine. Separate metrics, Read Rate and Write Rate, provide the data rate, in KBps, for reading and writing. Figure 12-7 shows an advanced performance graph for a virtual machine containing the Read Rate, Write Rate, Read Latency, and Write Latency metrics.

Figure 12-7   Virtual Machine Performance Graph with Virtual Disk Metrics

For example, if the vSphere Web Client performance graph indicates that a poorly performing virtual machine is experiencing high values for Guest Latency and Queue Latency but low values for Commands per Second and Physical Device Latency, the issue could be I/O contention on the host storage adapter. In this case, the adapter's command queue has filled, and a spillover VMkernel command queue is filling.

Monitor Performance Through ESXTOP

The ESXTOP utility displays the real-time resource utilization of an ESXi Host. It displays CPU, memory, disk, and network usage. It can present the resource usage for the entire host as well as a detailed breakout of each of the worlds running on the host. Each world (which is similar to a process on other operating systems) performs a specific function on the host. Some worlds, such as drivers and vMotion, are used directly by the hypervisor to perform necessary tasks. Other worlds are associated with virtual machines. Some worlds represent the workload inside a VM, whereas other worlds represent virtual machine overhead, such as overhead associated with providing a console or virtual devices.

ESXTOP is very useful for examining performance and resource usage data with more granularity than what is provided by the vSphere Web Client performance graphs. By default, it updates every 5 seconds, whereas the graphs in the vSphere Web Client can only update every 20 seconds.

The concept of ESXTOP is much the same as the concept of the top command in Linux, which displays all the processes running on a Linux server in order of resource utilization, with the most resource-intensive process at the top of the list. By default, ESXTOP displays the CPU usage of all the worlds running on the ESXi Host in order of their current CPU usage, with the world utilizing the most CPU resources listed at the top and the remaining worlds listed in descending order, as illustrated in Figure 12-8.

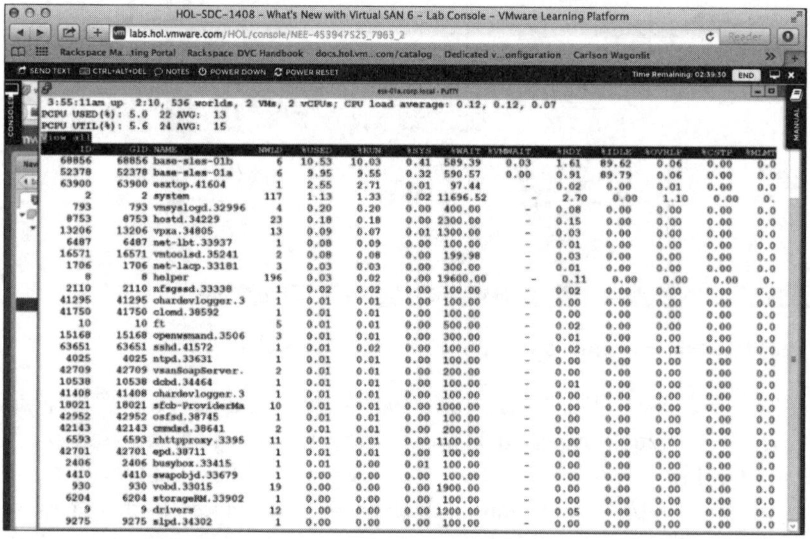

Figure 12-8   ESXTOP CPU Usage

ESXTOP is interactive. It allows you to use the keyboard to change the view from CPU usage to memory, disk, or network usage. To learn about the options and appropriate keys, press the **h** key to get help information, as shown in Figure 12-9.

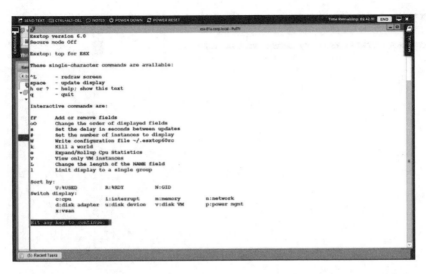

Figure 12-9   ESXTOP Help Information

The bottom of the help section indicates which resources can be monitored and the appropriate key to press to monitor each one. The main options are memory (press **m**), CPU (press **c**), network (press **n**), disk adapter (press **d**), storage device unit (press **u**), and virtual disk (press **v**). For reference, let's look at two examples. Figure 12-10 shows memory, which is displayed when you press the **m** key. Figure 12-11 shows virtual disk information, which is displayed when you press the **v** key.

Figure 12-10   ESXTOP Memory Usage

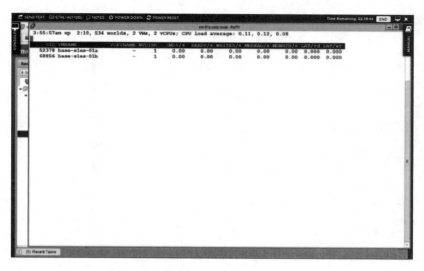

Figure 12-11   ESXTOP Virtual Disk Usage

To change the fields (columns) of a specific resource display in ESXTOP, press the **f** key while viewing that resource. For example, when displaying CPU resource usage, press the **f** key to view the CPU-related fields that may be selected. An asterisk at the beginning of the row indicates that the field is included in the current results, as shown in Figure 12-12. To add or remove a column from the current ESXTOP view, use the letter keys associated with each field. For example, pressing the **b** key toggles on or off the display of the Group ID for each world in the CPU view.

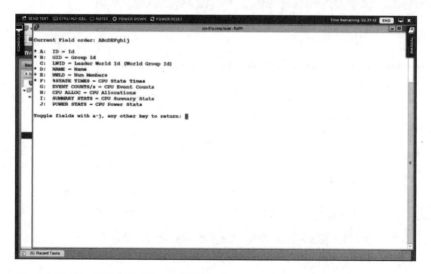

Figure 12-12   ESXTOP CPU Field Selection

Each virtual machine is assigned a Group ID (GID), which can be expanded by pressing the **e** key and entering the GID. For example, in Figure 12-13, the GID 52378 is expanded, and you can see the individual worlds that are servicing the same virtual machine. Of these expanded worlds, the world named vmx-vcpu-0:base is the world that best indicates the current CPU usage of the guest OS within this VM.

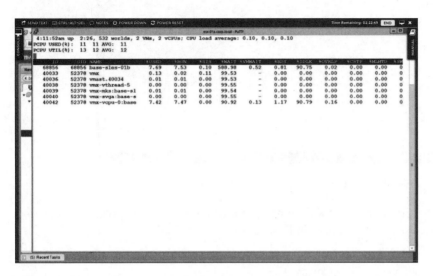

Figure 12-13   ESXTOP with an Expanded Virtual Machine

Often, when diagnosing an issue, the main concern is the resource usage of virtual machines, not the resource usage by system-related processes. You can change the ESXTOP view to display only virtual machine usage without system usage. To do so, press **Shift+V**, as shown in Figure 12-14. On a host running many VMs, this permits you to see more VMs in the display because ESXTOP provides no method by which to scroll up or down through all the available worlds.

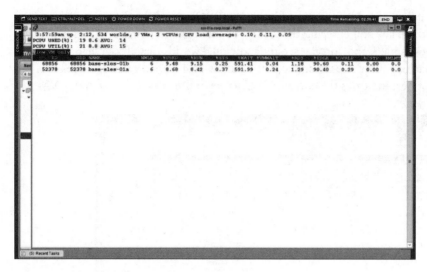

Figure 12-14   ESXTOP Virtual Machine Usage Only

Table 12-5 provides the ESXTOP names for commonly used performance metrics, which are discussed previously in this chapter.

Table 12-5   Common ESXTOP Metrics

Metric	Common Name
%RDY	CPU Ready (percentage of actual time)
%CSTP	Co-stop (percentage of actual time)
%SWPWT	Swap Wait (percentage of actual time)
MCTLSZ	Balloon Size (in MB)
SWCUR	Swapped (in MB)
SWR/s	Swap In Rate (KB per second)
UNZIP/s	Decompression Rate (KB per second)
%DRPTX	Transmit Packets Dropped (percentage of actual time)
%DRPRX	Receive Packets Dropped (percentage of actual time)
GAVG	Guest Latency (milliseconds)
DAVG	Device Latency (milliseconds)
KAVG	Kernel Latency (milliseconds)
ABRTS/s	Aborts (per second)

As an alternative to running ESXTOP interactively, you can use `esxtop -b` to run ESXTOP in batch mode. Include `>> filename` to direct the output to a file that you can examine at a later time. Using these options together allows you to collect data to a file that can be examined later using tools, such as Windows Performance Monitor, that provide more functionality. You can also use the `-d` parameter to change the sampling interval.

Here is an example of running ESXTOP in batch mode, where it collects all data at 5-minute (300 seconds) intervals and outputs the data to a file named `results01.csv`:

```
esxtop -b -a -d 300 > results.csv
```

RESXTOP is a utility that is nearly identical to ESXTOP but designed to work from the vSphere Command-Line Interface (vCLI). It requires that a connection be made to the target ESXi Host. It also requires the use of the Linux-based vCLI, which you can install in a Linux system or can access in the vSphere Management Assistant (vMA). The Windows-based vCLI does not provide RESXTOP.

Troubleshoot Enhanced vMotion Compatibility (EVC) Issues

Enhanced vMotion Compatibility (EVC) is a vSphere cluster feature that permits vMotion compatibility across a set of ESXi Hosts that contain varying generations of a specific CPU family. EVC can be used to ensure that each host in a cluster presents the same CPU features to the virtual machines to enable vMotion. Table 12-6 and 12-7 describe the currently available EVC levels and baselines. Table 12-6 shows Intel EVC baselines, and Table 12-7 shows AMD EVC baselines. The main requirement for EVC is that all hosts in the cluster support at least one common EVC level in the same table—either Intel or AMD. For example, if all the hosts in a cluster support the Intel Nehalem EVC baseline, then you configure EVC on the cluster and set its level to L2.

Table 12-6 Intel EVC Baselines

EVC Level	EVC Baseline	Description
L0	Merom	Merom generation feature set
L1	Penryn	Penryn generation (Merom plus CPU features including SSE4.1)
L2	Nehalem	Nehalem generation (Penryn plus additional CPU features including SSE4.2 and POPCOUNT)
L3	Westmere	Westmere generation (Nehalem plus additional CPU features including AES and PCLMULQDQ)

EVC Level	EVC Baseline	Description
L4	Sandy Bridge	Sandy Bridge generation (Westmere plus additional CPU features including AVX and XSAVE)
L5	Ivy Bridge	Ivy Bridge generation (Sandy Bridge Generation plus additional CPU features, including RDRAND, ENFSTRG, FSGSBASE, SMEP, and F16C)

Table 12-7   AMD EVC Baselines

EVC Level	EVC Baseline	Description
A0	Opteron Gen 1	Opteron Generation 1 Rev. E
A1	Opteron Gen 2	Opteron Generation 2 Rev. F (Opteron Gen1 plus additional CPU features, including CPMXCHG16B and RDTSCP)
A3	Opteron Gen 3	Opteron Generation 3 Greyhound (Opteron Gen 2 plus additional CPU features, including SSE4A, MisAlignSSE, POPCOUNT and ABM -LZCNT)
A2, B0	Opteron Gen 1 without 3DNow!	AMD Opteron Generation 3 (Greyhound), without 3DNow
B1	Opteron Gen 4	AMD Opteron Generation 4 Bulldozer (Opteron Gen 3 plus additional CPU features, including SSSE3, SSE4.1, AES, AVX, XSAVE, XOP, and FMA4)
B2	Opteron Piledriver	AMD Opteron Piledriver Generation (Opteron Gen 4 plus additional CPU features, including FMA, TBM, BMI1, and F16C)

In order for EVC to be supported, you must first ensure that the BIOS is properly configured on each host in the cluster, as described in VMware KB 1003212. In most cases, you configure the BIOS settings to enable hardware virtualization and execute protection. Hardware virtualization is called Intel VT on Intel processors and AMD-V on AMD processors. Execute protection is called Intel Execute Disable (XD) on Intel processors and AMD No Execute (NX) on AMD processors. These BIOS settings should be identical on each host in the cluster. For example, you should ensure that NX is either enabled on all hosts or disabled on all hosts in an Intel-based cluster.

When configuring EVC on a cluster, you can choose Disable EVC, Enable EVC for AMD Hosts, or Enable EVC for Intel Hosts. If you choose to enable EVC, you should then select one of the EVC modes from the drop-down list, which corresponds to the baselines in Tables 12-6 and 12-7. If you select a mode that is not compatible for the hosts, then an error message appears, indicating that the host(s) cannot be admitted into the cluster.

You cannot enable EVC or increase the EVC level on a host with powered-on virtual machines that are using CPU features that are not provided by the selected EVC level. Instead, you can shut down the virtual machines, configure the EVC level, and then start the virtual machines. Likewise, you cannot decrease the EVC level on hosts where virtual machines are running at a higher EVC level.

NOTE   If you experience issues while enabling EVC or setting a specific EVC level, consider shutting down the associated virtual machines.

The NX/XD feature is a frequent source of EVC and vMotion issues because it is often overlooked or because some of the hardware BIOS does not offer the ability to set it. In this case, an error may occur containing text similar to:

```
The CPU of the host is incompatible with the cpu feature require-
ments of virtual machine; problem detected at CPUID level 0x80000001
register 'edx'.
```

You can address this problem by hiding the NX/XD feature from the virtual machine regardless of the host setting. To do so, use these steps:

Step 1.   Shut down the virtual machine.

Step 2.   In the vSphere Web Client, right-click the virtual machine and click **Edit Settings**.

Step 3.   In the Virtual Hardware section, select **Hide the NX Flag from Guest** in the CPUID Mask section.

Step 4.   In the Virtual Hardware section, expand CPU, select **CPUID Mask**, and choose **Hide the NX Flag from Guest** (see Figure 12-15).

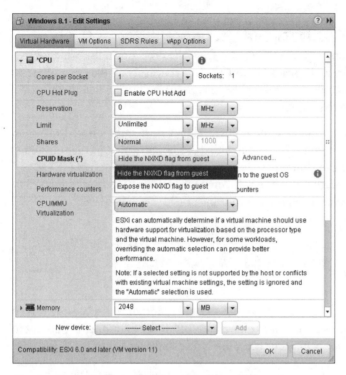

Figure 12-15 Hide the NX Flag from Guest VM

Step 5.   Click **OK**.

Step 6.   Power on the virtual machine.

Likewise, you can hide other Intel and AMD CPU features from virtual machines, although this practice should be avoided in most cases. To mask CPU features other than NX/XD, you can follow these steps:

Step 1.   Shut down the virtual machine.

Step 2.   In the vSphere Client, edit the virtual machine settings.

Step 3.   In the Virtual Hardware section, expand **CPU**, select **CPUID Mask**, and click **Advanced**.

Step 4.   In the CPU Identification Mask panel, shown in Figure 12-16, select the relevant row and click `Value (msb...lsb)` to edit the mask value.

Step 5. Click **OK**.

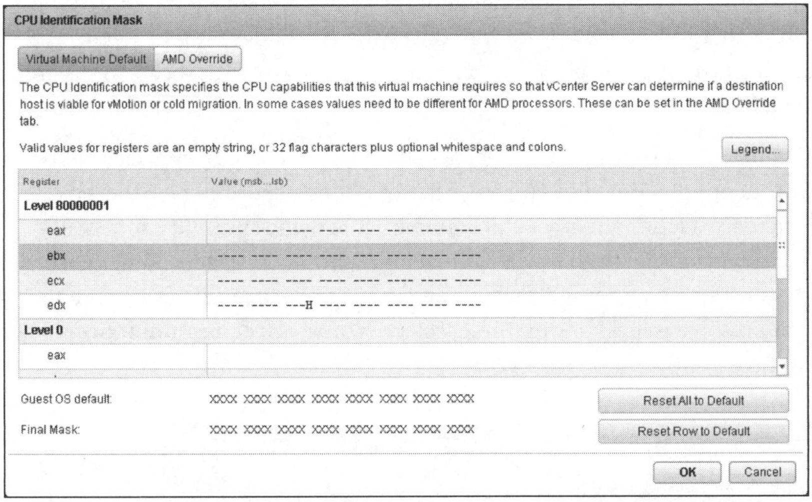

Figure 12-16 CPU Identification Mask for Guest VM

Ill-behaved applications—those that do not use Intel- or AMD-recommended methods for detecting CPU features at runtime—do not work well with EVC. A well-designed application should detect the capabilities of the CPU prior to executing instructions that may not be available, such as those in the PCLMULQDQ instruction set. If a virtual machine contains an application that requires the use of specific CPU features, such as multimedia extension, for functionality or for good performance, enabling EVC may be unacceptable. For example, if a virtual machine contains an application that requires the use of the PCLMULQDQ instruction set in order to obtain acceptable performance, running the virtual machine in an Intel cluster that is enabled for the EVC Nehalem baseline produces unacceptable performance. In this case, increase the EVC level to the Westmere baseline or migrate the virtual machine to another host that provides the PCLMULQDQ instruction set.

Troubleshoot Virtual Machine Performance via vRealize Operations

VMware vRealize Operations Manager is a management tool that provides powerful monitoring features not found in vCenter Server, such as anomalies, compliance, and recommendations. In addition, it provides analysis, troubleshooting, and capacity planning features. It can identify potential root causes for alerts and recommend remediation steps. It provides trends in resource usage and estimates the number of days remaining until a resource is exhausted. It allows you to run "what-if" capacity planning scenarios to predict the impact of growing the number of VMs or hosts.

Most of its features are customizable, including symptoms, alerts, and recommendations. Recommendations can be created and customized. Multiple recommendations can be assigned to alerts. Each recommendation can contain advice for addressing the alert, URLs that link to web pages for addressing the underlying problem, and actions to be performed at the click of a button. Several out-of-the-box actions are provided by default.

VMware vRealize Operations Manager provides a web-based user interface called the vRealize Operations Manager Console that provides a set of out-of-the-box dashboards that are useful in many environments. It provides visibility across all layers of the infrastructure, such as virtual machines, hosts, storage, and network. It provides sophisticated alerts and recommendations to reduce the mean time to investigate and resolve issues. For example, select **Home > Recommendations** to view the dashboard shown in Figure 12-17.

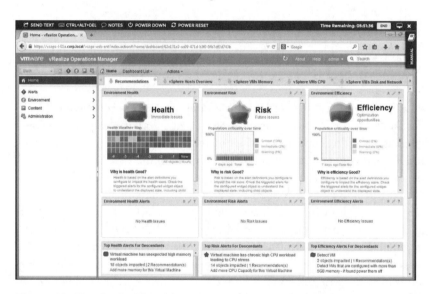

Figure 12-17 vRealize Operations Manager Main Dashboard

This dashboard could be used as the main dashboard for daily use. It provides a great means to quickly assess the overall health, risk, and efficiency of the entire environment. Health is represented by a badge that loosely resembles a cross. Risk is represented by a badge that loosely resembles a star. Efficiency is represented by a badge that loosely resembles a tilde (swirly figure). Each badge is colored green, yellow, orange, or red, with each color indicating a different level of concern. Green represents a good state with no significant concern. Yellow represents a warning state with some concern. Orange represents an elevated warning state with significant concern. Red represents an alarming state with critical concern. In the example shown in Figure 12-17, the overall health, risk, and efficiency are good because the badges are green, but some issues still exist. This dashboard enables you to quickly identify issues with underlying objects as providing heat maps, alerts, and descendant alerts. Notice that the Health Weather Map contains many red blocks, indicating issues with some objects in the environment. You can click any of these blocks to see information on the underlying object and issue. Notice that Risk contains a graph that indicates the percentage of underlying objects that are at risk.

In each of the three major badges sections (Health, Risk, Efficiency) on the **Home > Recommendations** page, sections appear that identify the related alerts and top descendant alerts. For example, in Figure 12-17, no Environment Health Alerts, Environment Risk Alerts, or Environment Efficiency Alerts appear, but Descendant Alerts do appear for each category at the bottom of the page. Another means to identify issues is to select **Home > Alerts** to see all the alerts for the entire environment, as shown in Figure 12-18. In this view, you can click on any column header, such as **Impact**, **Created On**, or **Object Type**, to sort in ascending or descending order. You can also use the **Filter** buttons and text box to identify which rows you want to see.

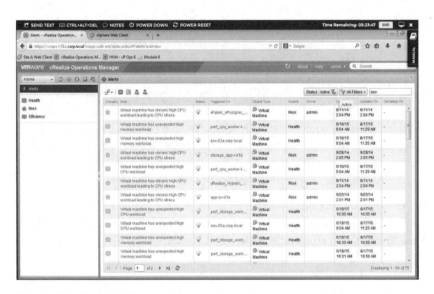

Figure 12-18   Alerts Page

Alternatively, you can select an object and then select the **Alerts** tab to view just the alerts associated with that object. To do so, use the **Environment** icon in the left pane to navigate and select the object and then select the **Alerts** tab. Figure 12-19 shows an example of the **Alerts** tab for an ESXi Host named `vesxi-1.corp.local`. In this example, the host has only one alert, which is `Host has CPU contention due to over-population of virtual machines`.

Figure 12-19   ESXi Hosts Alerts

You can click on the alert message, which is actually a hyperlink, to bring up the alert details and see the alert description, recommendations, and root causes. For example, if you click on the previous alert, you learn that the issue is caused by critical host memory usage by multiple virtual machines, as shown in Figure 12-20. You can also see that one recommendation is to identify and power down low-priority virtual machines, and an action button is provided to facilitate this. As you can see, vRealize Operations Manager is designed to actually identify the root causes of problems and provide remediation recommendations rather than trigger alarms when thresholds are exceeded, as vCenter Server alarms do. You can sort the alerts by criticality, object type, and impact by clicking on the appropriate column headers.

You can use vRealize Operations Manager to troubleshoot virtual machine performance. The first step is to select the virtual machine and select the **Summary** tab to view its health, risk, and efficiency, as shown in Figure 12-21.

Figure 12-20   Alert Details

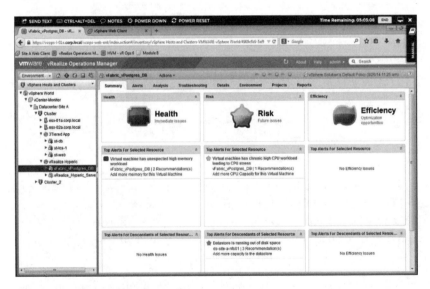

Figure 12-21   Virtual Machine Summary

In this example, you see that a virtual machine named `vFabric_vPostges_DB` has critical health issues and some risk issues, but at least its efficiency looks good. To address the virtual machine's issues, you could click on each of the alerts, beginning with critical health alerts. For example, if you click on **Virtual Machine Has Unexpected High Memory Workload**, you see a recommendation and an action button to add more memory to the virtual machine, as shown in Figure 12-22. You also see another recommendation to determine whether this is actually expected behavior.

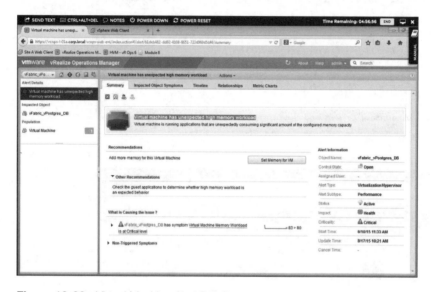

Figure 12-22   Virtual Machine Alert Details

NOTE   Like most objects in vRealize Operations Manager, recommendations are customizable. For example, you could change this alert to recommend that you first determine whether this is expected behavior and then determine whether any unnecessary services in the virtual machine should be stopped and then add memory.

Next, on the Summary tab for this virtual machine, you should investigate any noncritical health alerts and any critical risk and efficiency alerts. For example, you can click **Virtual Machine Has Chronic High CPU Workload Leading to CPU Stress Alert**. Finally, you can investigate any descendant alerts. In this example, a risk alert exists for a datastore that is used by the virtual machine. Specifically, the datastore named `ds-site-a-nfs01` is running out of disk space.

vSphere Realize Operations Manager 6.0 can be deployed as a virtual appliance, installed in a Windows server, or installed in a Linux server. It uses a few databases, such as the Global xDB database, which contains user configuration data, and a File System Database (FSDB), which contains all the statistical raw metric data. A vRealize Operations Manager cluster contains multiple nodes, including the master, master replica, data, and remote collector.

Compare and Contrast Overview and Advanced Charts

The vSphere Web Client provides overview graphs that contain some of the most commonly used metrics for an object in a single window pane. To view these graphs, select an object, such as a virtual machine or ESXi Host in the inventory, and then select **Monitor** > **Performance** > **Overview**. A set of small graphs, each containing only a few key metrics, appears. You can select the **Time Range**, such as **Realtime** or **1 Day**. For an ESXi Host, the overview graphs include CPU Usage (in percentage and MHz), Memory Usage (in MB), Memory Swap In Rate (in MBps), Memory Swap Out Rate (in MBps), Disk Latency (in ms), Disk Rate (in KBps), Network Rate (in MBps), and other metrics. The memory usage graph includes separate metrics for Balloon, Active, Swap, Granted, and Shared memory metrics. See Figure 12-23 for an example of the ESXi Host overview graphs.

Figure 12-23 ESXi Host Overview Graph

For a virtual machine, the overview graphs include many of the same metrics as the ESXi Host overview graphs. See Figure 12-24 for an example.

Figure 12-24   Virtual Machine Overview Graph

Naturally, the advanced graphs provide much more detail and flexibility than the overview graphs; however, the overview graphs tend to be much more convenient. In many cases, during troubleshooting, you can rely on the overview graphs to quickly assess the performance and resource usage of a virtual machine or ESXi Host. In the window pane, you may be able to identify which resource is likely the root cause of a performance problem. For example, when troubleshooting a performance issue, you may spend a few seconds examining the virtual machine's overview graph, and it might indicate that the problem is related to a high memory swap-in rate rather than high CPU utilization. In this case, you may then decide to take a closer look by examining the virtual machine's advanced memory graphs.

Describe How Tasks and Events Are Viewed in vCenter Server

During troubleshooting, a common step is to examine recent, associated tasks and events. In vCenter Server, *tasks* are operations that are performed by the vCenter Server, and *events* are items that occurred and were recognized by the vCenter Server. A task may trigger multiple events. An event does not have to correspond to a vCenter Server task. For example, if you use the vSphere Client to connect directly to an ESXi Host and power on a virtual machine, vCenter Server reports the event but not the task because vCenter Server did not perform the task. Tasks and events may be examined from multiple locations using the vSphere Web Client. For example, all tasks for a particular vCenter Server can be viewed by selecting the vCenter Server and navigating to **Monitor > Tasks**, as shown in Figure 12-25.

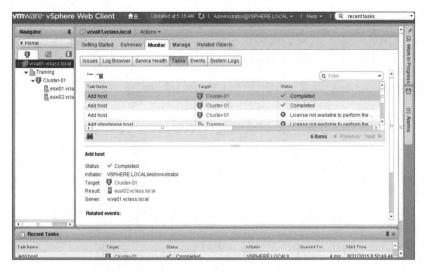

Figure 12-25   View All vCenter Server Tasks

All events for a particular vCenter Server can be viewed by selecting the vCenter Server and navigating to **Monitor** > **Events**, as shown in Figure 12-26.

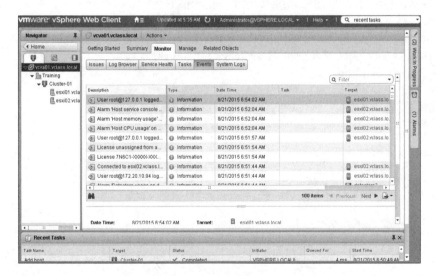

Figure 12-26   View All vCenter Server Events

You can also view all task or events for a particular object, such as an ESXi Host, as shown in Figure 12-27.

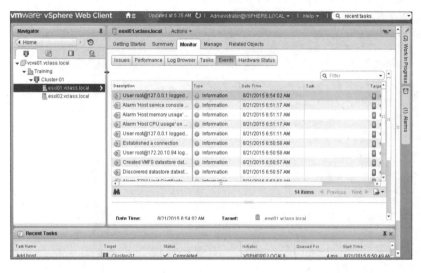

Figure 12-27   View All Virtual Machine Events

You can add and remove columns from the tasks and events views. To do so, right-click any column heading and choose **Show/Hide Columns**, as shown in Figure 12-28. In the dialog window, select the columns that you want to view, as illustrated in Figure 12-29. You can sort tasks by any of the columns. To do so, click on the column heading, such as the **Date/Time** heading, as shown in Figure 12-30, at least once. Each additional click toggles the sort order between ascending and descending.

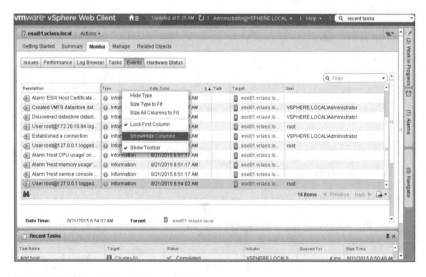

Figure 12-28   Add and Remove Columns

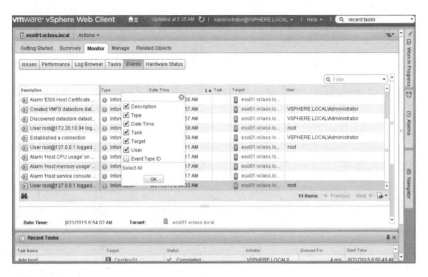

Figure 12-29   Select and Deselect Columns

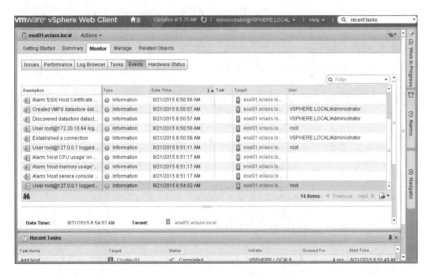

Figure 12-30   Sort on Date/Time

For example, in a situation where the performance of all the virtual machines on a specific ESXi Host has suddenly become very slow, you may wonder if memory issues are the root cause. You could select the host in the inventory, select **Monitor > Events**, and use **Filter** to search for text, such as *memory*. If you do this, you filter the list of events to include only those that contain the text *memory*, as shown in Figure 12-31.

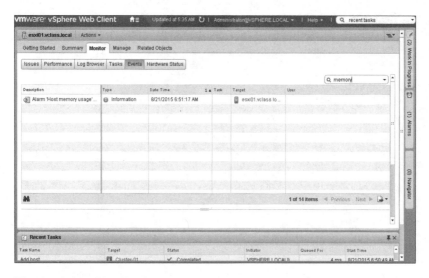

Figure 12-31   Filter Events

You can use the Recent Tasks pane at the bottom of the vSphere Web Client to
monitor the progress of current tasks and to examine details on recent tasks, as
shown in Figure 12-32. The Recent Tasks pane permits you to add, remove, and
sort by columns in the same manner as the Tasks and Events views.

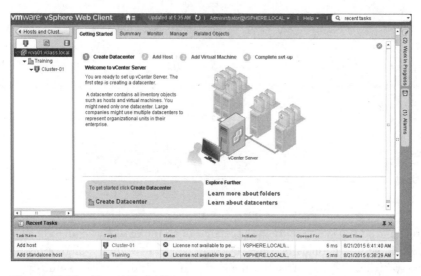

Figure 12-32   Recent Tasks Pane

In vSphere Web Client 5.x, the Recent Tasks pane is positioned on the right side.
In vSphere Web Client 6, it is positioned on the bottom by default. Its position
and docking are adjustable and may be customized to suit individual taste. You can

change the position, status, and use of each of these panes. To change the position of the Recent Tasks pane, click in its title bar and drag it to the new location. To automatically hide the pane, click on the pushpin image on the far right side of the title bar. You can also customize several other panes, such as the Navigator, Work in Progress, and Alarms panes, in the same manner.

NOTE You can click on the **More Tasks** link in the lower-right corner of the Recent Tasks pane to quickly navigate to the tasks view.

NOTE In vSphere 6, the "all users" view for recent tasks is disabled by default for performance reasons. You can click on **My Tasks > All User's Tasks**, but you may see a warning that this feature is disabled. Per VMware KB 2104914, you can enable this feature by modifying the `webclient.properties` file, setting `show.allusers.tasks` to `FALSE`, and restarting the vSphere Web Client.

Identify Host Power Management Policy

Performance issues and other issues could be triggered by the misconfiguration of the host power management. This section provides information related to power states, BIOS settings, and related vSphere Web Client settings.

vSphere provides power management by utilizing Advanced Configuration and Power Interface (ACPI) performance and power states. In VMware vSphere 5.0, the default power management policy was based on dynamic voltage and frequency scaling (DVFS), which saves power by running the processor at a lower frequency and voltage. Beginning with VMware vSphere 5.5, the default policy uses deep halt states (C-states) in addition to DVFS to significantly increase power savings over previous releases while still maintaining good performance.

The BIOS settings in the ESXi Host hardware should be configured to allow ESXi the most flexibility in using the power management features offered by the hardware. This enables you to then configure your desired power management choices using the vSphere Web Client. Generally, the best BIOS setting is OS Control Mode or the equivalent, which allows you to manage the power management via the ESXi Host. On most systems, the default setting is to only allow the firmware, not the ESXi Host, to manage power.

Ensure that you enable all C-states in the BIOS to get the best performance per watt. The ESXi Host may place the CPU into the C1 state, where the CPU hardware may determine, based on its own criteria, to deepen the state to C1E halt state, which reduces power consumption with little or no impact on performance. C-states deeper than C1/C1E are managed by software and enable further power savings. These states can sometimes increase the performance of workloads that involve some idle hardware threads, so a best practice is to enable these states in BIOS. However, in some rare cases, where some highly sensitive, multithreaded workloads are significantly negatively impacted by C-states, you can disable them in BIOS, thus sacrificing potential power savings.

NOTE If your hardware offers Processor Clocking Control (PCC) technology, do not enable it in ESXi.

In the vSphere Web Client, you can configure the host power management policy by following these steps:

Step 1.   In the inventory pane, select the ESXi Host.

Step 2.   In the middle pane, select **Manage > Settings**.

Step 3.   Select **Hardware > Power Management**.

Step 4.   Click **Edit**.

Step 5.   Select one of the four power policies:

- **High performance:** Do not use any power management features.

- **Balanced:** Reduce power consumption automatically but only with minimal performance impact. This is the default policy.

- **Low power:** Reduce power consumption automatically and aggressively, although performance may be significantly impacted.

- **Custom:** A user-defined policy that can be created using **Manage > Settings > System > Advanced System Settings**; however, this requires solid planning and testing.

Step 6.   Click OK.

VMware vSphere Distributed Power Management (DPM) can be used to power down some ESXi Hosts in a cluster whenever the current resource demand is not great enough to require all cluster resources. It can be used independently or in conjunction with hardware power management policies. Although this saves power, it could cause performance concerns, with demand growing quickly and distributed power management being unable to exit Standby Mode and power on ESXi Hosts before users notice sluggish performance. Many settings are available to configure DPM such that the performance risk is minimal. A good indicator that performance was negatively impacted by DPM standby mode is that signs of CPU or memory contention, such as CPU Ready and Swapping, occurred prior to a host exiting standby mode.

Summary

You have now read the chapter covering the exam topic of troubleshooting performance. You should use information in the following sections to complete your preparation for Objective 7.4.

Exam Preparation Tasks

Review All the Key Topics

Table 12-8 provides a reference to each of the key topics identified in this chapter. Take a few moments to review each of these specific items.

Table 12-8 Key Topics for Chapter 12

Key Topic Element	Description	Pages
Paragraph	Transparent page sharing	455
Paragraph	Ballooning	457
Table 12-3	Potential memory issues and resolutions	462
Paragraph	CPU Co-stop metric	463
Table 12-4	Potential CPU issues and resolutions	464
Paragraph	Device, Kernel, and Guest Latency metrics	466
Table 12-5	Common ESXTOP metrics	472
Table 12-7	EVC baselines	474
List	Power management options	490

Complete the Tables and Lists from Memory

Print a copy of Appendix B, "Memory Tables" (found on the CD), or at least the section for this chapter, and complete the tables and lists from memory. Appendix C, "Memory Tables Answer Key," also on the CD, includes completed tables and lists to check your work.

Definitions of Key Terms

Define the following key terms from this chapter and check your answers in the glossary.

balloning, CPU Ready, CPU Co-stop, transparent page sharing (TPS), ESXTOP

Answer Review Questions

The answers to these review questions can be found in Appendix A.

1. Which of the following keystrokes is not useful in ESXTOP to examine storage-related metrics?

   a. s

   b. u

   c. d

   d. v

2. Which of the following steps should you take to address a poorly performing single-processor virtual machine whose Ready Times is 2000 ms in the real-time vSphere Web Client performance graph?

   a. Add a second virtual CPU to the virtual machine.

   b. Increase the CPU shares on the virtual machine.

   c. Set a CPU limit on the virtual machine.

   d. Decrease the CPU limit on other virtual machines.

3. Which of the following does not directly indicate resource contention within the ESXi Host?

   a. Ready Time

   b. Latency

   c. Packets Dropped

   d. Page Sharing

4. Which of the following mechanism or metric applies to memory usage in ESXi 6.0? (Choose two.)

    a. EVC

    b. TPS

    c. MCTLSZ

    d. RDY

5. In the vSphere Web Client ESXi overview real-time graph, which of the following is not displayed in MBps?

    a. Swap In Rate

    b. Swap Out Rate

    c. Disk Rate

    d. Network Rate

This chapter covers the following objective:

- **Objective 7.5—Troubleshoot HA and DRS Configuration and Fault Tolerance**

  - Troubleshoot issues with DRS workload balancing

  - Troubleshoot issues with HA failover/redundancy, capacity, and network configuration

  - Troubleshoot issues with HA/DRS cluster configuration

  - Troubleshoot issues with vMotion/Storage vMotion configuration and/or migration

  - Troubleshoot issues with fault tolerance configuration and failover issues

  - Explain the DRS resource distribution graph and target/current host load deviation

  - Explain vMotion resource maps

## CHAPTER 13

Troubleshoot Clusters

This chapter explores the requirements for configuring vSphere High Availability (HA) and Distributed Resource Scheduling (DRS) clusters as well as potential configuration issues that could arise if you incorrectly configure these clusters. This chapter also explores troubleshooting issues with fault tolerance. Troubleshooting in general should either utilize a top-down approach or a bottom-up approach. A top-down approach involves identifying and visualizing the highest object, such as vCenter Server or a virtual machine's guest operating system, and working down to the physical layer until the problem has been identified. The bottom-up approach is just the opposite: It involves starting from the physical infrastructure and working your way up to the vCenter Server or virtual machine. Either approach gives a clear path for troubleshooting and eliminates one of the potential problems, which is not being able to clearly identify the next thing to investigate. In the case of HA or DRS clusters, administrators can start looking at the general cluster settings and work their way to more specific settings—for example, going to the ESXi server level, all the way to a virtual machine. Something as simple as a virtual machine connected to the wrong named port group or on the wrong storage device could cause HA to not successfully fail it over in the event of an ESXi server failure or isolation response. Likewise, DRS may not be able to move the virtual machine through a vMotion migration.

"Do I Know This Already?" Quiz

The "Do I Know This Already?" quiz allows you to assess whether you should study this entire chapter or move quickly to the "Exam Preparation Tasks" section. Regardless, the authors recommend that you read the entire chapter at least once. Table 13-1 outlines some of the major headings in this chapter and the corresponding "Do I Know This Already?" quiz questions. You can find the answers in Appendix A, "Answers to the 'Do I Know This Already?' Quizzes and Review Questions."

Table 13-1   "Do I Know This Already?" Foundation Topics Section-to-Question Mapping

Foundations Topics Section	Questions Covered in This Section
Troubleshoot Issues with HA Failover/Redundancy, Capacity, and Network Configuration	1
Troubleshoot Issues with HA/DRS Cluster Configuration	2, 3
Troubleshoot Issues with vMotion/Storage vMotion Configuration and/or Migration	4
Troubleshoot Issues with Fault Tolerance Configuration and Failover Issues	5

1. Which network does HA use for heartbeating?

   a. The VMkernel port enabled for vMotion

   b. The VMkernel port designated for management

   c. The VMkernel port enabled for vSAN

   d. The VMkernel port enabled for FT

2. By default, how long after a datastore has been disconnected does it take for an ESXi server to enter a PDL after an APD condition?

   a. 240 seconds

   b. 90 seconds

   c. 160 seconds

   d. 140 seconds

3. What happens to resource pools when DRS is disabled for a cluster?

   a. The resource pools stay in place.

   b. DRS cannot be disabled when resource pools are present.

   c. The resource pools disappear and all VMs are placed in the root resource pool; when DRS is reenabled, the resource pools are restored.

   d. The resource pools disappear, and all VMs are placed in the root re-source pool; when DRS is reenabled, the resource pools are not restored.

4. Which are the priorities for vMotion migrations? (Choose two.)

   a. High priority

   b. Medium priority

   c. Low priority

   d. Regular priority

5. If a virtual machine has only one vCPU and can benefit from legacy FT, how do you enable it?

    a. Right-click the VM in the Navigator pane and choose **FT** > **Turn on Legacy FT**.

    b. Use the advanced parameter `vm.legacyft = true`.

    c. Use the advanced parameter `vm.uselegacyft = true`.

    d. Use the advanced parameter `vm.enablelegacyft = true`.

    e. Use the advanced parameter `vm.disablelegacyft = false`.

Foundation Topics

Objective 7.5—Troubleshoot HA and DRS Configuration and Fault Tolerance

When troubleshooting cluster objects, like HA or DRS, it can be useful to look at the underlying components to be able to specifically identify the heart of the problem. The same could be said for fault tolerance. If HA is not restarting virtual machines in the event of an ESXi Host failure, it can be useful to identify whether virtual machines can reside on multiple hosts. Similarly, if it doesn't appear that DRS is migrating VMs, it can be useful to see whether the VMs can reside on multiple hosts. The fault tolerance technology changed in vSphere 6—in terms of more than just new maximums. The following sections look at some common problems with the configuration of HA, DRS, and fault tolerance and how to approach problems with these features.

Troubleshoot Issues with DRS Workload Balancing

When troubleshooting vSphere cluster issues, it is important to look at the requirements for those types of clusters and to ensure that the vSphere environment is configured to meet those requirements. vSphere Distributed Resource Scheduler (DRS) has three main functions:

- **Initial power on:** If set to Partially or Fully Automated, DRS decides on which ESXi server to place a virtual machine at power on.

- **Migrating virtual machines by way of vMotion:** If DRS is set to fully automated, it automatically migrates virtual machines by utilizing vMotion to achieve even resource distribution between all ESXi servers in the cluster (up to 64). If set to manual or partially automated, DRS just makes recommendations.

- **Distributed Power Management:** During off-peak hours, Distributed Power Management (DPM) can migrate as many virtual machines as possible to as few ESXi servers as possible to then be able to power off empty ESXi servers. When utilization increases, DPM would power the unused ESXi servers back up, and DRS would perform vMotion migrations to even the distribution of resources.

If DRS is not balancing the resources between ESXi servers in the cluster, you should start by looking at the cluster as a whole. One possibility that should be eliminated is determining whether DRS is performing automatic vMotion migrations to balance workloads and whether cluster resources are already balanced. To verify, click on the **Cluster** object in the Navigator pane and select the **Summary** tab (see Figure 13-1) to display a level indicating whether the cluster is balanced. The cluster's Summary tab also lists whether DRS is fully automated, what the migration threshold is currently set to, and how many vMotion migrations have taken place. To investigate further, you can select the **Monitor** tab and then select **DRS** and examine the CPU and memory distribution.

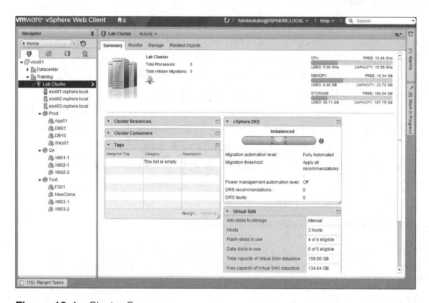

Figure 13-1   Cluster Summary

It is also useful to look at the history of automatic vMotion migrations and to determine whether there are any faults. To do this, follow these steps:

Step 1.   From the hosts and clusters inventory view, select the **Cluster** object in the Navigator pane.

Step 2.   Select the **Monitor** tab.

Step 3. Select **vSphere DRS**.

Step 4. Select **Faults** (see Figure 13-2) or **History** (see Figure 13-3).

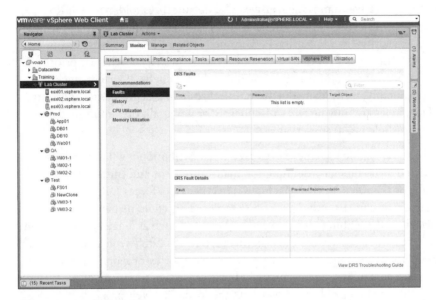

Figure 13-2 DRS Faults

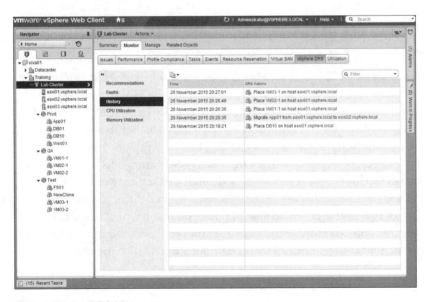

Figure 13-3 DRS History

When DRS is set to fully automated, one of the common issues experienced is too frequent or infrequent vMotion migrations as a result of misconfiguring the DRS migration threshold. The migration threshold has five settings that can be adjusted, from most conservative to most aggressive. The default threshold, where DRS performs automatic vMotion migrations, is the third and middle setting: applying all priority 1, priority 2, and priority 3 recommendations. The strongest recommendations, or the ones with the greatest benefit, are priority 1, whereas priority 5 recommendations are the lowest and provide the least benefit. If virtual machines move too frequently, most likely the migration threshold is set to be too aggressive. If virtual machines are moving very infrequently or not at all, then most likely the migration threshold is too conservative.

DRS may also be unable to achieve even resource distribution if administrators have restricted it too much by defining too many affinity or anti-affinity rules. An affinity rule, or the Keep Virtual Machines Together rule, forces DRS to keep the selected virtual machines on the same ESXi server. This could be beneficial for virtual machines that communicate to each other a lot, such as a database server, an app server, and a web server. On the other hand, an anti-affinity rule could be useful for keeping virtual machines off the same ESXi server for extra redundancy (for example, domain controllers, email servers). However, setting too many of these rules restricts DRS from being able to redistribute the load effectively and may result in virtual machines not moving and DRS not appearing to function properly.

Troubleshoot Issues with HA Failover/Redundancy, Capacity, and Network Configuration

vSphere high availability has several defaults configured when enabled, but in many cases, these defaults are not best practices. For example, the HA Admission Control setting, by default, is set to **Define Failover Capacity by Static Number of Hosts** and is configured for one failure. HA determines whether there are enough resources to tolerate one ESXi server host failing by utilizing slots. HA's slot size is equal to the largest powered-on virtual machine's reservation plus overhead. Because no virtual machine has a reservation by default, this setting works just fine. However, as soon as one virtual machine has a reservation defined, the slot size reflects this larger size, and may not be able to power on many virtual machines, even if there are ample unused resources to allow for failover. This setting is the default because it is the lowest overhead and works without additional configuration.

Because virtual machines could have various different reservations and overheads, VMware typically recommends changing this setting to the next option, which is **Define Failover Capacity by Reserving a Percentage of the Cluster Resources**. This setting looks at actual resources used and allows much better overall use of resources by not using the slot sizes. This setting also requires a little more management because if it is set to 50%, then 50% of the resources are reserved specifically for failover and cannot be used except in a failover scenario. However, although 50% may make sense for a 2-node ESXi cluster, for a 4-node, 8-node, or larger cluster, this may not be enough The percentage is still set at 50% unless an administrator changes it. Of course, as with many other recommendations, the selection depends on the environment. One vSphere environment may never use reservations, and so the default HA admission control policy may work out just fine. Other environments may use reservations extensively, so the second setting makes more sense. Still other environments may be bound by older management mandates, such as requirements of N+1 clustering or a hot spare. HA actually has two other policies as well, the first of which addresses the N+1 requirement:

- Use Dedicated Failover Hosts.

- Do Not Reserve Failover Capacity.

Typically, if environments have a legacy policy such that they require a hot spare, it may be worth revisiting and revising the policy—especially since in a vSphere environment, it might be more prudent to utilize resources from all the ESXi servers and leave a little overhead on each host to allow for failover, as opposed to having an ESXi server spend much of its life waiting for a failover event. Because an ESXi server failure is a rare event, this could translate to a lot of time being completely unutilized.

The last setting, **Do Not Reserve Failover Capacity**, probably wouldn't make sense unless you were troubleshooting HA's admission control policy because it does not allow you to power on virtual machines.

By using HA's default admission control policy, it is possible to change the slot sizes to some resource allocation less than for the largest powered-on virtual machine. Then virtual machines that are larger than the defined slot size would take up multiple slots. This is visible from the vSphere Web Client if you look closer at the HA cluster settings (see Figure 13-4).

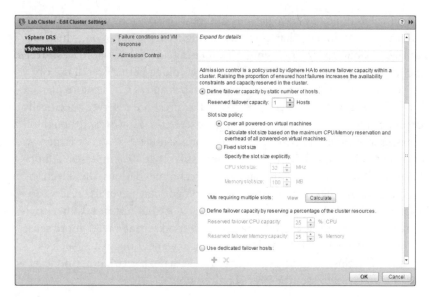

Figure 13-4   HA Cluster Settings

There are a few HA recommended settings that are not defaults:

- **Configure Management Network Redundancy:** Because there is no management network redundancy by default, HA cannot reliably detect whether an ESXi server has become isolated. The management network should be configured to be as redundant as possible, as far back as possible. This can be achieved by either configuring at least two management VMkernel ports on two virtual switches with a physical uplink attached to each vSwitch and attached to two physical switches or by having one management VMkernel port attached to a virtual switch with multiple physical uplinks attached to multiple physical switches.

- **Configure Heartbeat Datastores:** This recommendation makes sense only if the storage is on a physically different network from management. Otherwise, if it's on the same management network, it doesn't provide any additional redundancy or better detection of failure. A heartbeat datastore is a storage device that is visible from all the ESXi servers in the cluster. HA creates a directory on this datastore that the HA agents on the ESXi servers use to determine whether they are isolated. It is recommended that if heartbeat datastores are used, there should be at least two of them. To define heartbeat datastores, follow these steps:

Step 1.   Select the HA cluster from the Navigator pane.

Step 2.   Select the **Manage tab.**

Step 3. Select **Settings > HA.**

Step 4. Click **Edit.**

Step 5. Select **HA.**

Step 6. Expand the field **Datastore for Heartbeating** and choose one of the three options: Automatically Select Datastores Accessible from the Host, Use Datastores Only from the Specified List, or Use Datastores from the Specified List and Complement Automatically if Needed.

It can be useful to select datastores manually here in order to determine whether the datastores selected are in fact visible from all of the ESXi servers in the cluster. Once a datastore is selected, the section **Hosts Mounting Selected Datastore** appears at the bottom of the window (see Figure 13-5). If there is an ESXi server that is not listed, you can investigate why that ESXi server is unable to see the selected datastore(s).

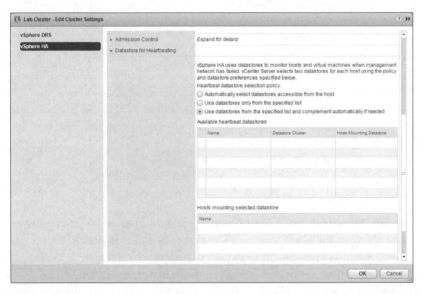

Figure 13-5 Heartbeat Datastores

- **Configure Redundant Heartbeat Addresses:** By default, HA utilizes the management VMkernel port's default gateway address to ping in order to verify whether an ESXi server is isolated. Configuring multiple addresses allows more reliable detection of failure and reduces the possibility of false positives. To define additional heartbeat addresses, follow these steps:

Step 1. Select the HA cluster from the Navigator pane.

Step 2. Select the **Manage tab.**

Step 3. Select **Settings > HA.**

Step 4. Click **Edit.**

Step 5. Select **HA.**

Step 6. Select **Advanced Options** at the bottom and add the option `das.isolationaddress0`. For the value, enter the IP address or FQDN of the address that responds to a ping. You can define 10 such addresses (`das.isolationaddress0` through `das.isolationaddress9`), and as long as one of them pings, HA does not enter an isolation response (see Figure 13-6).

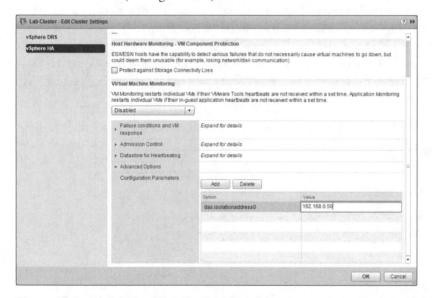

Figure 13-6 HA Additional Isolation Addresses

- **Change the Default Isolation Response:** By default, HA's isolation response is to do nothing in the event that an ESXi server becomes isolated. This is because there is no management network redundancy by default. Because simply disconnecting vmnic0 from vSwitch0 could potentially isolate an ESXi server, triggering an HA failover event, HA doesn't do anything in the event of isolation. However, if you have taken all of the above recommendations, then in order for an ESXi server to be isolated, it would have to lose access to all of its management networks, all of its heartbeat addresses, and all of its heartbeat datastores. And if all those things have occurred for this ESXi server, then things are probably bad enough to warrant shutting down the virtual machines so they can be restarted on the other ESXi servers in the cluster. Follow these steps to do this shutdown:

Step 1. In the Edit Cluster Settings window, expand **Failure Conditions and VM Response.**

Step 2.   Select **Shut Down and Restart VMs** from the Response to Host Isolation drop-down box (see Figure 13-7).

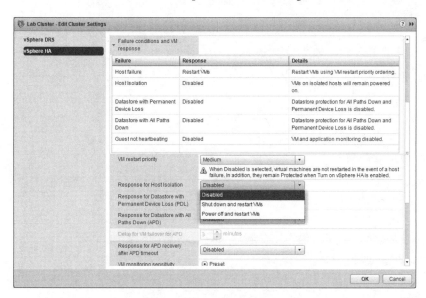

Figure 13-7   HA Isolation Response

- **Change HA's Admission Control Policy:** Change the policy from Host Failures Cluster Tolerates to Percentage of Cluster Resources Reserved as Failover Capacity, as illustrated at the beginning of this section.

You can also override HA cluster settings per virtual machine. By default, all virtual machines in the HA cluster adhere to HA's default restart priority, isolation response, and virtual machine monitoring (OS level monitoring, or OS- and application-level monitoring).

To define per-VM level overrides, follow these steps:

Step 1.   Select the HA cluster in the Navigator pane.

Step 2.   Select the **Manage** tab and select **Settings**.

Step 3.   Under Settings, select **VM Overrides** and click **Add** (see Figure 13-8).

Step 4.   Click the + button to add virtual machines to which HA cluster settings should be overridden.

Step 5.   Click **OK**. Now the automation level as well as restart priority, isolation response, and whether the virtual machine should have VM monitoring or application monitoring should differ from the cluster's setting (see Figure 13-9).

Step 6.   Click **OK**.

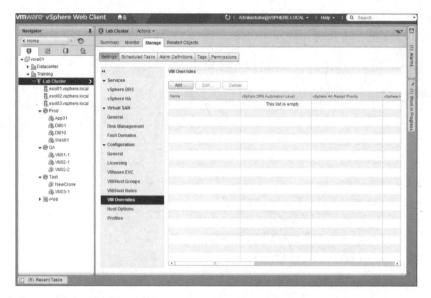

Figure 13-8   VM Overrides

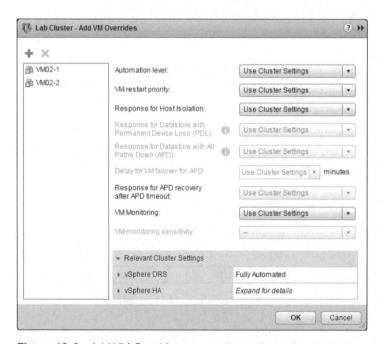

Figure 13-9   Add VM Overrides

Defining per-VM level overrides could be useful if there are certain machines that don't need to be restarted in the event of an HA failover event. One example would be a virtual machine is a test or development machine and doesn't need to be restarted in the event of an ESXi server. Another would be a virtual machine that resides on local storage.

In order to provide failover for virtual machines, the virtual machine port groups must be configured to have exactly the same name on all of the ESXi servers in the cluster, and they must all be attached to the same physical network.

NOTE When vSAN is configured, HA utilizes the VMkernel network devoted to vSAN for heartbeating instead of the VMkernel network designated as management.

If you are still having problems identifying root cause for HA-related issues, it can also be worthwhile to check the logs. The agent that HA installs on each ESXi server is called the FDM agent, or fault domain manager. In vSphere 6, HA writes to syslog. The HA log files all start with `fdm`. If there are problems pushing the FDM agent to the ESXi servers, you can check additional logs on the ESXi Hosts in `/etc/opt/vmware/fdm`. These are the main log files:

- `clusterconfig`, which contains cluster configuration information
- `compatlist`, which contains a host compatibility list for the VMs
- `hostlist`, which contains a host membership list
- `fdm.cfg`, which contains an HA configuration file
- `fdm.log`, which contains HA cluster agent logs

HA requires the following ports to be opened:

- Inbound TCP and UDP ports 8042–8045
- Outbound TCP and UDP ports 2050–2250

Troubleshoot Issues with HA/DRS Cluster Configuration

vSphere HA has fewer requirements than DRS, but the two have some similarities, such as the importance of shared storage. HA has been improved in vSphere 6, namely with Virtual Machine Component Protection (VMCP). VMCP allows the detection of storage-related failures from a single (or multiple) ESXi server and can then restart virtual machines on other ESXi servers.

VMCP can function only when the setting Protect Against Storage Connectivity Loss is selected in the Edit Cluster Settings Wizard. Once this is enabled, VMCP allows you to define when virtual machines should fail over as a result of permanent device loss (PDL) failures or all paths down (APD) events. APD is thought of as a transient condition, and connectivity is expected to resume. However, after 140 seconds, the connection enters a PDL state. Once a PDL state has been entered, the ESXi server essentially gives up trying to reach the storage device. However, if the storage has been reconnected, vSphere administrators may need to restart the ESXi management agents to be able to re-detect the storage (vpxa and hostd). These are the two conditions and their settings in the vSphere Web Client:

- Response for Datastore with Permanent Device Loss (PDL), which can be set to any of the following (see Figure 13-10):

    - Disabled

    - Issue events

    - Power off and restart VMs

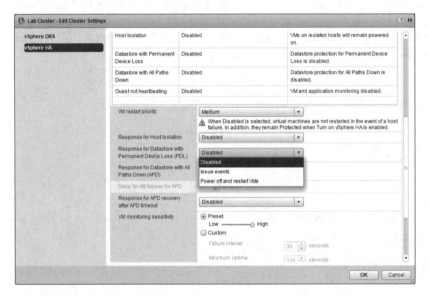

Figure 13-10 Settings for PDL

- Response for Datastore with All Paths Down (APD), which can be set to any of the following (see Figure 13-11):

    - Disabled

    - Issue events

    - Power off and restart VMs (conservative) (This setting ensures that there are enough resources available to restart virtual machines.)

    - Power off and restart VMs (aggressive) (This setting always attempts to restart virtual machines.)

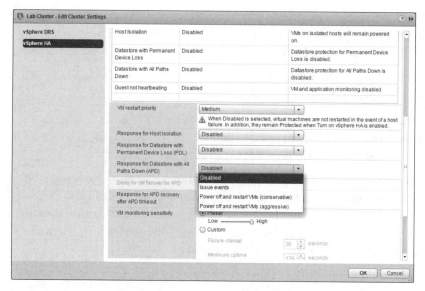

Figure 13-11 Settings for APD

You can define an immediate power off of affected virtual machines in the event that an ESXi server loses connection to a storage device so that other ESXi servers can restart the virtual machine(s), provided that they can access the storage device. You can also set a delay to restart virtual machines. Instead of powering off, a shut-down command can be attempted, but in the event that a storage device is inaccessible, the virtual machine's operating system most likely already crashed, so a power off would restart virtual machines faster.

When HA is enabled, the only thing it provides protection against is ESXi server failure. It can optionally also protect against VM failure (detecting loss of heartbeat from VMware Tools) and application failure.

It is important to be aware of the requirements for configuring HA at the cluster level:

- A vSphere cluster object must have a minimum of 2 ESXi servers in the cluster (or a maximum of 64 in vSphere 6).

- Shared storage is required: All of the ESXi servers in the cluster must be able to see the virtual machines' directories.

- All ESXi servers must have the same virtual machine networks and port groups.

- VMkernel time must be synchronized.

- A vSphere Essentials Plus license or higher is required.

- Static IP addresses must be defined for the management VMkernel ports or DHCP reservations.

The vSphere Web Client may list vSphere HA as being in a certain state. The different states that the HA is reporting can assist administrators with troubleshooting HA configuration issues. The following are the states that the HA agent can be in:

- **Unreachable:** vCenter is unable to communicate to the master host, and one or more agents has failed.

- **Uninitialized:** The host can't access any of the datastores or has lost access to its local datastore. The agent can also be in this state if the agent is inaccessible or cannot open the needed firewall port (8182).

- **Initialization Error:** vCenter cannot connect to the ESXi server when the HA agent is being installed or configured on the host. The agent can also enter this state if there is not enough space (75 MB) on the local storage to install the HA agent or when the agent successfully installed but the host doesn't become a master or slave within the timeout period.

- **Uninitialization Error:** vCenter lost connectivity to the ESXi Host at the time the HA agent was being unconfigured.

- **Host Failed:** This ESXi Host is unable to reach the master through the network and is also unable to access its heartbeat datastores (isolation).

- **Network Partitioned:** This happens when the master is unable to communicate to this host via the heartbeat network but can communicate via the heartbeat datastores and the ESXi server is not isolated.

- **Network Isolated:** An ESXi server is isolated only if all of the following are true:

  - It has lost access to its heartbeat network.

  - It has lost access to all of its isolation addresses (VMkernel default gateway and/or any additional isolation addresses).

  - It has lost access to its heartbeat datastores.

  - Its unable to reach any HA agents on any other ESXi servers in the cluster.

- **Configuration on Hosts Times Out:** The HA agent didn't completely install on the ESXi server before the timeout. This timeout can be extended by using the vCenter advanced setting `vpxd.das.electionWaitTimeSec` and changing the value to the VMware recommended value, `240`.

If you need to change license keys or downgrade a license key temporarily, you may need to disable DRS on the cluster. If this happens, any resource pools will be lost. Using the vSphere Web Client, you can snapshot the resource pool tree and import it when DRS gets turned back on. Here is how you do this:

Step 1. Select the Cluster object from the Navigator pane.

Step 2. Select the Manage tab.

Step 3. Select Settings.

Step 4. Select vSphere DRS.

Step 5. Click Edit.

Step 6. Deselect the check box Turn On vSphere DRS.

Step 7. Click OK to turn off DRS.

Step 8. Select whether the resource pool tree should be saved. If the resource pools are to be saved, you are prompted to determine the location to save the file as a snapshot file (.snapshot).

After vSphere DRS has been reenabled, you can import the resource pool tree to the cluster by following these steps:

Step 1. Right-click the **Cluster** object in the Navigator pane and select **Restore Resource Pool Tree**.

Step 2. Click **Browse**, locate the **.snapshot** file, and click **OK**.

> **NOTE**   If there are resource pools in the cluster when you attempt to restore resource pools, you receive the error message `There are resource pools in the cluster`. You then need to remove any resource pools to restore the resource pool hierarchy from the backed-up configuration file.

The vSphere Web Client has a built-in mechanism that allows you to check whether the ESXi servers are configured appropriately:

Step 1. Select the Cluster object in the Navigator pane.

Step 2. Select the Monitor tab.

Step 3. Click Profile Compliance.

Step 4. Select Check Compliance Now and check the hosts in the cluster for compliance.

Troubleshoot Issues with vMotion/Storage vMotion Configuration and/or Migration

Since vMotion is the underlying mechanism of DRS, and Storage vMotion is the underlying mechanism of Storage DRS, troubleshooting whether DRS or Storage

DRS is functioning may be as simple as ensuring that vMotion or Storage vMotion is possible.

The important thing to remember about vMotion is that there are requirements from an ESXi server host perspective as well as from a virtual machine perspective. If a virtual machine cannot be migrated through vMotion, typically the error message is helpful in identifying the problem. Otherwise, keep in mind the following requirements:

- VMs cannot be attached to an internal-only vSwitch (a virtual switch with no physical uplinks attached).

- VMs cannot be connected to a CD/DVD drive or floppy drive with a local image. In other words, a virtual machine can use an ISO or FLP image on shared storage, but if that image is on local storage, the vMotion migration is not allowed. If the virtual machine is associated with the image but the connected check box is not selected in the virtual machine's Edit Settings page, the migration is possible.

- CPU affinity cannot be utilized. CPU affinity ties a virtual machine's vCPUs to an ESXi server's LCPUs and prevents vMotion. It is also worth noting that if a virtual machine has any physical devices attached—either through Direct-Path I/O, or Single-Root I/O Virtualization (SRIOV)—the virtual machine cannot migrate through vMotion. Also, the virtual machine cannot have latency sensitivity set to high, as this bypasses the CPU scheduler and allows the virtual machine to have exclusive access to logical CPUs.

- If virtual machines are using raw device mapping (RDM), the LUN that the RDM is pointing to must be visible from the destination ESXi server.

- Virtual machines cannot have SCSI bus sharing enabled if below hardware version 11. (As of vSphere 6, if a virtual machine is at hardware version 11, and the virtual disks are SCSI controllers configured for physical SCSI bus sharing, and the disk is an RDM disk, vMotion is officially supported for that machine.)

- Virtual machines that have USB devices attached to them must have those USB devices enabled for vMotion.

NOTE   A common misconception is that virtual machines with RDM cannot be migrated through vMotion. This is not true: Virtual machines with RDM in virtual or physical compatibility mode can be migrated using vMotion. However, if the virtual machine is part of a Microsoft Clustering Services (MSCS) cluster, and if the virtual machine is below virtual hardware version 11, the virtual machine cannot migrate through vMotion because the quorum and data disks have to utilize SCSI bus sharing.

During a Storage vMotion migration, you have the option to convert a virtual compatibility mode RDM to a thick- or thin-provisioned virtual disk. To convert a physical compatibility mode RDM to a virtual disk, you must perform a cold migration.

There are also requirements for the ESXi servers to allow for vMotion migrations:

- Source and destination ESXi servers need to have VMkernel ports enabled for vMotion (and on the same network).

- If you are using standard switches for networking, ensure that the network labels used for virtual machine port groups are consistent across hosts (including case and presence of spaces; be aware that if a space is accidentally typed at the end of the port group name, that character will be accepted). During a migration with vMotion, vCenter Server assigns virtual machines to port groups based on matching network labels.

- vMotion network needs to be at least 1 Gbps.

- Source and destination ESXi servers need to be able to see the datastore where the virtual machine files are located. (Each datastore supports up to 128 simultaneous migrations.)

- Source and destination ESXi servers have to have the same manufacturer and model of CPU. Even though instruction sets differ from one generation to another, those differing instruction sets can be hidden through Enhanced vMotion Compatibility (EVC).

- vSphere Essentials Plus or higher licensing is required to be able to perform vMotion or Storage vMotion migrations.

It is also worth noting that there are two different priorities for vMotion migrations (see Figure 13-12):

- High priority
- Regular priority

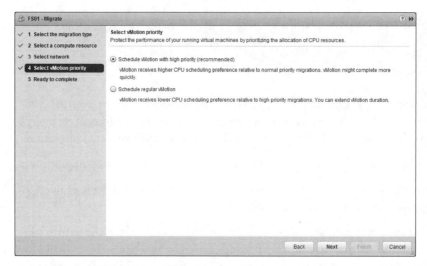

Figure 13-12 vMotion Priorities

High-priority vMotion migrations reserve resources on both the source and destination ESXi servers to ensure that the virtual machine is available during the vMotion migration. If there are not enough resources available, as a result of an overloaded or heavily utilized ESXi server, the high-priority migration will fail. The regular-priority migration will always succeed by using whatever resources are available. The end result may be that the virtual machine slows down or becomes briefly unavailable during the migration. An interesting observation from users and vSphere administrators is that the regular-priority migration may appear to complete faster than a high-priority migration. This isn't the case, however. What these people experience is that the high-priority migration seems to take a long time and then it eventually times out, resulting in no migration. When they then change the migration to regular priority, the migration completes.

Troubleshoot Issues with Fault Tolerance Configuration and Failover Issues

Most people are familiar with the major improvement to fault tolerance in vSphere 6: the ability to support four vCPU virtual machines. This is certainly a welcome improvement, but architecturally FT is also very different than in prior versions. The easiest way to visualize how the legacy FT worked—and still does, in vSphere 6, which allows legacy FT—is that it is essentially a constant, never-ending state of vMotion. However, one of the main issues or potential issues with this in prior versions is that it was just copying memory from the primary virtual machine to the secondary; they both shared all of the virtual machine files. As a result, it could be possible that the storage device where these shared files were stored could go down, bringing down the entire FT pair.

In vSphere 6, the new version of FT creates an entire second copy of the primary virtual machine that can be configured to be on a completely different datastore. FT still requires HA to be configured on the cluster object where the FT pair is going to reside. With all the advancements and failure detection possibilities with vSphere 6, the following conditions can be protected against utilizing the features of HA and FT:

- If the ESXi server the primary (or secondary) is on fails, the secondary becomes a new primary, and traffic is redirected with zero downtime and zero data loss. If there are enough ESXi servers in the cluster, a secondary gets recreated on the extra host.

NOTE   FT doesn't protect against issues like application crashes, data corruption, and other OS-level issues. These issue are replicated to the secondary VM.

- If the operating system fails, HA VM monitoring can restart the virtual machine. (This causes an outage, but the outage was most likely already experienced by end users in this case.)

- If the application fails, application HA can restart the app, service, or VM.

- If the storage device that the primary is on fails, the secondary picks up, and users are redirected—with zero downtime.

The following are requirements for FT to be enabled:

- The ESXi servers must have CPU compatibility for vMotion or EVC.

- The servers must be equipped with an Intel Sandy Bridge or newer chip or an AMD Bulldozer or newer chip.

- The ESXi servers must run on a 10 Gbps FT logging network with low network latency.

- vSphere Standard and Enterprise licensing allows up to 2 vCPUs for FT.

- vSphere Enterprise Plus licensing allows for up to 4 vCPUs for FT.

- An FT logging network must be configured, with VMkernel ports created on the same networks on each host.

- HA clustering must be enabled.

- ESXi Hosts must be certified for FT (see `http://www.vmware.com/resources/compatibility/search.php`).

- Hardware virtualization must be enabled on each ESXi server host.

- No unsupported devices can be attached to the virtual machines.

- Virtual machine files must be on shared storage.

If a virtual machine needs only one virtual CPU and can still benefit from vSphere fault tolerance, it can utilize legacy FT. Table 13-2, from the VMware vSphere 6 Documentation Center (`https://pubs.vmware.com/vsphere-60/topic/com.vmware.vsphere.avail.doc/GUID-32C39392-53FB-4928-85D6-E7222B37731E.html`), shows how to enable legacy FT.

Table 13-2   FT and Legacy FT

	Legacy FT	FT
Extended page tables/ rapid virtualization indexing (Intel EPT/ AMD RVI)	Not supported	Required
IPv6	Not supported for FT logging NICs	Supported for FT logging NICs
DRS	Fully supported for initial placement, load balancing, and maintenance mode support	Only power-on placement of secondary VM and maintenance mode are supported
vStorage APIs—data protection backups	Not supported	Supported
Eager-zeros thick .vmdk files	Required	Not required because FT supports all disk file types, including thick and thin
.vmdk redundancy	Only a single copy	Primary VMs and secondary VMs always maintain independent copies, which can be placed on different datastores to increase redundancy
NIC bandwidth	Dedicated 1 GB NIC recommended	Dedicated 10 GB NIC recommended

	Legacy FT	FT
CPU and host compatibility	Requires identical CPU model and family and nearly identical versions of vSphere on hosts	CPUs must be compatible with vSphere vMotion or EVC. Versions of vSphere on hosts must be compatible with vSphere vMotion
Turn on FT on running VM	Not always supported. You might need to power off the VM first	Supported
Storage vMotion	Supported only on powered-off VMs vCenter Server automatically turns off FT before performing a Storage vMotion action and then turns on FT again after the Storage vMotion action completes	Not supported; user must turn off FT for the VM before performing the Storage vMotion action and then turn on FT again
Vlance networking drivers	Not supported	Supported

NOTE   Upgrading ESXi servers does not upgrade FT. If VMs are configured to use FT before you upgrade the ESXi servers to vSphere 6, the VMs will be using legacy FT.

To enable legacy FT, follow these steps:

Step 1.   Right-click the virtual machine in the Navigator pane of the vSphere Web Client and select **Edit Settings**.

Step 2.   Select the **VM Options** tab.

Step 3.   Expand **Advanced**.

Step 4.   Next to Configuration Parameters, select **Edit Configuration**.

Step 5.   Click **Add Row**.

Step 6.   In the Configuration Parameters window, enter `vm.uselegacyft` in the Name field and type `true` for the Value (see Figure 13-13).

Step 7.   Click **OK**.

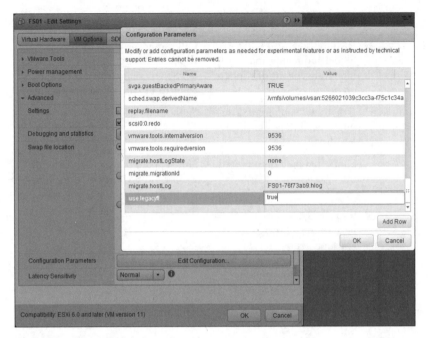

Figure 13-13   Enable Legacy FT

NOTE   Two cluster settings can be modified to adjust the default maximum number of FT VMs on an ESXi server and the maximum number of vCPUs configured for FT on a host:

```
das.maxftvmsperhost
das.maxftvcpusperhost
```

Some general problems can occur when you attempt to turn on FT for a virtual machine. In addition to making sure all the requirements are met, when you're attempting to troubleshoot the inability to turn on FT, you should be aware of some general reasons FT cannot be enabled or the secondary VM cannot be created or powered on:

- The virtual machine is on an ESXi server that is in maintenance or standby mode or disconnected.

- The permission to enable FT is not present in the user's vCenter role.

- The virtual machine's files are inaccessible.

- Hardware virtualization is not enabled on the host(s).

- There must be enough memory on the ESXi server for the full amount of the configured RAM of the VM plus overhead.

Explain DRS Resource Distribution Graph and Target/Current Host Load Deviation

The section "Troubleshoot Issues with DRS Workload Balancing" mentions the Summary tab for the DRS Cluster object, which shows how well balanced the resources are between the ESXi servers in the cluster. This section explores that in more depth, and it also gets into the memory and CPU distribution and how DRS calculates load deviation.

DRS aims to achieve close to even resource distribution between all of the ESXi servers in the cluster. DRS checks resource distribution every five minutes, so when you look at the Summary tab of the DRS cluster, you should notice that the view there doesn't update very frequently.

The Summary tab provides an overall graphical representation of the load deviation. To explore this in more depth, you can look at the resource distribution graphs for memory and CPU utilization. These graphs are visible in the vSphere Client or vSphere Web Client, although they provide the information in slightly different views. In the vSphere Web Client are boxes representing virtual machines and a percentage of entitled resources delivered to the virtual machines. From here, you can also determine whether one virtual machine is using more of a resource than other virtual machines because the size of its box is relatively larger than the other virtual machine graphical boxes (see Figures 13-14 and 13-15).

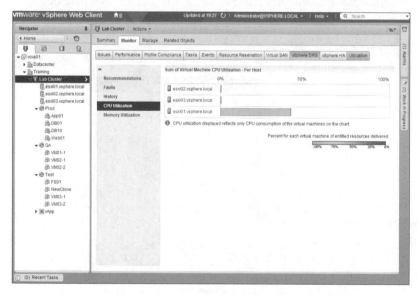

Figure 13-14   vSphere Web Client DRS CPU Resource Distribution

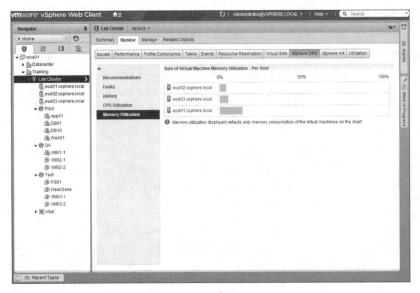

Figure 13-15   vSphere Web Client DRS Memory Distribution

The resource distribution charts in the vSphere Web Client are interesting because, while the CPU Resource Distribution chart displays individual virtual machines, the Memory Resource Distribution chart does not display anything other than memory resources consumed. In the vSphere Client, however, the memory resource distribution chart does illustrate individual virtual machines (see Figure 13-16).

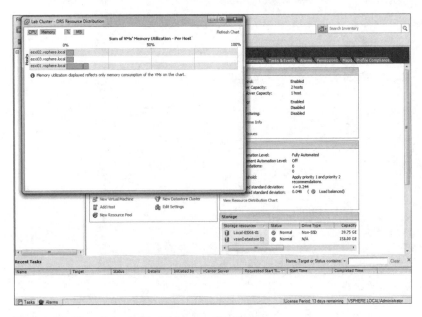

Figure 13-16   vSphere Client Memory Distribution

One of the interesting things about monitoring a DRS cluster is that you get a slightly different view of the cluster information from the vSphere Web Client than you do from the vSphere Client. The vSphere Web Client's Summary tab for the Cluster object lists information such as how well balanced (or imbalanced) the cluster is, whether DRS is fully automated or not, the migration threshold, whether Distributed Power Management is enabled, the number of outstanding DRS recommendations (which is none if the cluster is fully automated), and whether there are any DRS faults (see Figure 13-17).

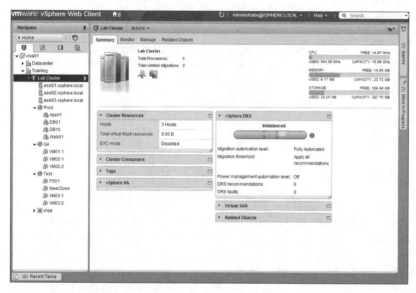

Figure 13-17   vSphere Web Client DRS Summary

The vSphere Client, on the other hand, does display some of this same information, and it also shows the following (see Figure 13-18):

- Target host load standard deviation
- Current host load standard deviation

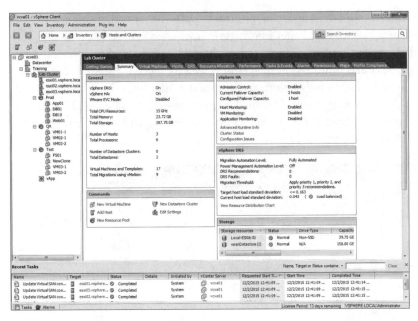

Figure 13-18   vSphere Client DRS Summary

This information tells you that if the current host load standard deviation exceeds the target host load standard deviation, DRS will make a recommendation. The target host load standard deviation can certainly change as a result of the number of ESXi servers in the cluster. In fact, you can observe this in the vSphere Client, where the target host load standard deviation is less than or equal to 0.163 for a three-node cluster, as in Figure 13-18, or less than or equal to 0.2 for a cluster of two ESXi servers. Another contributing factor to the target number is the DRS migration threshold. The numbers listed here are based on a default threshold, where DRS migrates VMs with a priority 1 through 3 recommendation. If the migration threshold were different, such as changing the DRS migration threshold to one notch more conservative, where it only applies priority 1 and 2 recommendations, the target deviation is less than or equal to 0.244. In other words, the more aggressive the threshold, the less difference there has to be between the ESXi servers in terms of resource consumption to prompt a migration.

It is useful to note that DRS determines when to move which virtual machines based on cost/benefit analysis. DRS is also aware that vMotion migrations are resource intensive, so if it can move fewer virtual machines to achieve a more balanced resource distribution, it may end up moving one big virtual machine instead of multiple small ones.

Explain vMotion Resource Maps

Before performing a vMotion migration, you can check the vMotion compatibility from a high-level overview of the environment. vMotion maps are visible only in the vSphere Client and are not present in the vSphere Web Client. To see the vMotion maps, follow these steps:

Step 1. In the hosts and clusters or VMs and templates inventory view, select the virtual machine from the inventory tree.

Step 2. Select the **Maps** tab. The maps allow you to visualize any issue with virtual machine port group consistency on the hosts, shared storage, and compatibility on the hosts (see Figure 13-19). Also, a map allows you to get a general idea of CPU consumption per host so you don't try to move a VM to an overloaded ESXi server; if the host that the virtual machine currently resides on is at a high CPU utilization, you can choose the regular-priority vMotion migration instead of the high-priority migration.

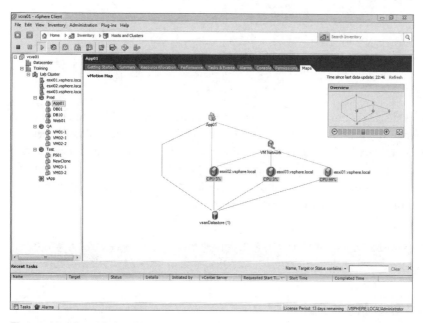

Figure 13-19 vMotion Maps

One of the nice things about the maps is that they can help you identify not just issues with interconnectivity between the vSphere components but also other issues, such as VMkernel ports not enabled for vMotion, or whether a virtual machine has an ISO image attached that is not on local storage (see Figure 13-20).

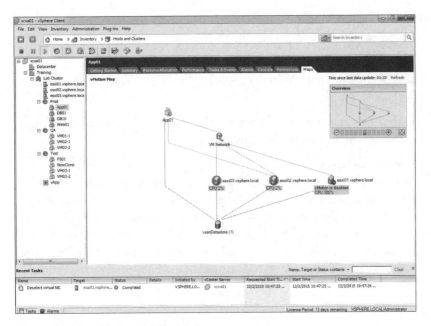

Figure 13-20   vMotion Not Enabled

Summary

This chapter discusses many of the requirements and settings you should check if you experience any problems with HA or DRS clusters and the technologies that those clusters utilize. It is useful to think about where the problems are arising and to try to either utilize the top-down approach or the bottom-up approach to identify where the problems originate. You should now use information in the following sections to complete your preparation for Objective 7.5.

Exam Preparation Tasks

Review All the Key Topics

Table 13-3 provides a reference to each of the key topics identified in this chapter. Take a few moments to review each of these specific items.

Table 13-3 Key Topics for Chapter 13

Key Topic Element	Description	Pages
Paragraph	vSphere high availability defaults and best practices	500
Paragraph	Overriding HA cluster settings	505
List	HA agent states	510
Process	How to use the vSphere Web Client to snapshot the resource pool tree and import it when DRS gets turned back on	511
List	Requirements for FT to be enabled	515
Process	How to enable Legacy FT	517
Paragraph	vMotion maps	522

Complete the Tables and Lists from Memory

Print a copy of Appendix B, "Memory Tables" (found on the CD), or at least the section for this chapter, and complete the tables and lists from memory. Appendix C, "Memory Tables Answer Key," also on the CD, includes completed tables and lists to check your work.

Definitions of Key Terms

Define the following key terms from this chapter and check your answers in the glossary.

high availability (HA), Distributed Resource Scheduler (DRS), vSphere fault tolerance (FT), vMotion, Storage vMotion

Answer Review Questions

The answers to these review questions can be found in Appendix A.

1. Which of the following is not a setting that can be defined in the event of a PDL condition?

   a. Shut Down and Restart VMs

   b. Power Off and Restart VMs

   c. Issue Events

   d. Disabled

2. Which of the following could be the reason an HA agent on a host reports an initialization error?

   a. The host is unable to reach the master host.

   b. The agent has failed.

   c. There isn't enough space on the host to install the agent.

   d. The network is isolated.

3. Which of the following prevents a hardware version 10 VM from migrating through vMotion?

   a. Physical compatibility mode RDM

   b. Virtual compatibility mode RDM

   c. vSphere license is Essentials Plus

   d. SCSI bus sharing

4. How often does DRS check resource distribution of the cluster?

   a. Every 5 minutes

   b. Every 2 minutes

   c. Every 10 minutes

   d. Every 20 seconds

5. Which piece of information is visible about a DRS cluster only in the vSphere Client and not in the vSphere Web Client? (Select two.)

   a. Target host load standard deviation

   b. Target cluster load standard deviation

   c. Past host load standard deviation

   d. Current host load standard deviation

6. Which of the following is *not* a requirement for vMotion?

   a. VMkernel port enabled for vMotion on source and destination hosts

   b. Same number of cores per host

   c. Same family/class of processor (or EVC)

   d. vSphere Essentials Plus license or higher

This chapter covers the following objectives:

- **Objective 8.1: Deploy ESXi Hosts Using Auto Deploy**
  - Describe the components and architecture of an Auto Deploy environment
  - Use Auto Deploy Image Builder and PowerCLI scripts
  - Implement host profiles with an Auto Deploy of an ESXi Host
  - Install and configure Auto Deploy
  - Understand PowerCLI cmdlets for Auto Deploy
  - Deploy multiple ESXi Hosts using Auto Deploy
  - Given a scenario, explain the Auto Deploy deployment model needed to meet a business requirement

- **Objective 8.2: Customize Host Profile Settings**
  - Edit an answer file to customize ESXi Host settings
  - Modify and apply a storage Path Selection Policy (PSP) to a device using host profiles
  - Modify and apply switch configurations across multiple hosts using a host profile
  - Create/edit/remove a host profile from an ESXi Host
  - Import/export a host profile
  - Attach and apply a host profile to ESXi Hosts in a cluster
  - Perform compliance scanning and remediation of an ESXi Host and clusters using host profiles
  - Enable or disable host profile components

- **Objective 8.3: Consolidate Physical Workloads Using VMware Converter**
  - Install a vCenter Converter standalone instance
  - Convert physical workloads using vCenter Converter
  - Modify server resources during conversion
  - Interpret and correct errors during conversion
  - Deploy a physical host as a virtual machine using vCenter Converter
  - Collect diagnostic information during conversion operation
  - Resize partitions during the conversion process
  - Given a scenario, determine which virtual disk format to use

## CHAPTER 14

Deploy and Consolidate

This chapter explores the requirements for configuring Auto Deploy to stand up new ESXi server hosts in minutes. This chapter also discusses the prerequisites to Auto Deploy and looks at configuring host profiles, as well as all the settings available when creating host profiles. Finally, this chapter explores the ability of VMware Converter to convert physical machines to virtual machines and achieve higher levels of consolidation.

"Do I Know This Already?" Quiz

The "Do I Know This Already?" quiz allows you to assess whether you should study this entire chapter or move quickly to the "Exam Preparation Tasks" section. Regardless, the authors recommend that you read the entire chapter at least once. Table 14-1 outlines the major headings in this chapter and the corresponding "Do I Know This Already?" quiz questions. You can find the answers in Appendix A, "Answers to the 'Do I Know This Already?' Quizzes and Review Questions."

Table 14-1 "Do I Know This Already?" Foundation Topics Section-to-Question Mapping

Foundations Topics Section	Questions Covered in This Section
Describe the Components and Architecture of an Auto Deploy Environment	1
Use Auto Deploy Image Builder and PowerCLI Scripts	2
Implement Host Profiles with an Auto Deploy of an ESXi Host	3
Convert Physical Workloads Using vCenter Converter	4, 7
Understand PowerCLI cmdlets for Auto Deploy	5
Deploy Multiple ESXi Hosts Using Auto Deploy	6
Import/Export a Host Profile	8
Perform Compliance Scanning and Remediation of an ESXi Host Using Host Profiles	9

Foundations Topics Section	Questions Covered in This Section
Install vCenter Standalone Instance	10

1. Which of the following is *not* required for Auto Deploy?

   a. vCenter

   b. TFTP server

   c. Auto Deploy server

   d. Static DHCP reservation

2. Which are two acceptance levels of VIBs? (Select two.)

   a. VMwareCertified

   b. PartnerCertified

   c. VMwareSupported

   d. CommunitySupported

3. Which of the following are locations where stateless caching can be used?

   a. Local storage

   b. USB drive

   c. SD card

   d. SAN LUN

4. Which of the following is *not* a location from which a virtual machine can be converted?

   a. MAC physical system

   b. Linux physical system

   c. Windows physical system

   d. Hyper-V virtual machine

5. Which of the following is *not* a PowerCLI cmdlet?

   a. `New-DeployRule`

   b. `Get-DeployRule`

   c. `Remove-DeployRule`

   d. `Delete-DeployRule`

6. What would you configure if you were worried about an Auto Deployed ESXi Host booting when the Auto Deploy server is unavailable? (Select two.)

   a. Stateless caching

   b. Stateful caching

   c. Stateless install

   d. Stateful install

   e. Stateless cached install

7. When you export a host profile, a pop-up says that _____ is not included.

   a. Passwords

   b. VMkernel port names

   c. VLAN IDs

   d. Firewall rules

8. What must be done to bring an ESXi Host into compliance with a host profile?

   a. It must be removed from a cluster.

   b. It must have its management agents stopped.

   c. It must be placed into maintenance mode.

   d. It must be rebooted.

9. Which of the following can be converted to a virtual machine using vCenter Converter? (Select three.)

   a. Physical Linux machine

   b. Physical Solaris Sparc machine

   c. Acronis True Image Backup

   d. Hyper-V virtual machine

   e. RHEV virtual machine

10. If a Windows Server 2008 server failed to convert to a virtual machine using vCenter Converter, where can you find the logs associated with the conversion?

   a. `C:\Users\All Users\Application Data\VMware\VMware Converter Enterprise\Logs`

   b. `C:\Windows\System32\VMware Converter Enterprise\Logs`

   c. `C:\Program Files (x86)\VMware\VMware Converter Enterprise\Logs`

   d. `C:\Windows\debug\VMware Converter Enterprise\Logs`

Foundation Topics

Objective 8.1—Deploy ESXi Hosts Using Auto Deploy

Auto Deploy, introduced in vSphere 5, allows the rapid provisioning of ESXi servers. In 10 minutes, it is possible to use Auto Deploy to stand up to 40 ESXi servers from a new powered-off state to running virtual machines automatically. There are obviously many pieces involved in getting Auto Deploy configured properly, and there are many different options for how to deploy. Auto Deploy was improved in vSphere 5.1 and further in vSphere 6. The following sections explore all the capabilities of Auto Deploy and all the steps required to make Auto Deploy work. Later, in the section "Objective 8.2—Customize Host Profile Settings," we explore configuring host profiles to further configure the new hosts after Auto Deploy installs the hypervisor.

There are some requirements for configuring Auto Deploy, starting with licensing. This is an Enterprise Plus feature only and requires the use of host profiles to function. The best way to start getting into the functionality and configuration of Auto Deploy is to look at the sequence of events that happen when a new ESXi server boots:

1. The new server host is powered on.

2. The new host connects to a DHCP server to get an IP address and gets redirected to a PXE server to get an initial boot image.

3. The host gets redirected to the Auto Deploy server and, based on a rules engine, gets an ESXi install image.

4. Once the hypervisor is installed, the ESXi server is visible from vCenter, and vCenter pushes a host profile to it and configures the ESXi host to match the host profile's configuration.

5. If the host profile includes adding the new host to a fully automated DRS cluster, then as soon as the host profile has been pushed to the host, it exits maintenance mode; DRS sees the new host as a new resource and automatically migrates VMs to it using vMotion.

Describe the Components and Architecture of an Auto Deploy Environment

Visualizing the entire process that occurs when a new ESXi server boots allows you to identify the components required for Auto Deploy from boot to running VMs:

- DHCP server for an IP address
- PXE boot to direct to a TFTP server

- TFTP server for the boot images

- Auto Deploy server for the rules engine and ESXi install image

- vCenter to get the host profile

- Answer file for the IP addresses needed by the VMkernel ports

Use Auto Deploy Image Builder and PowerCLI Scripts

Image Builder is a great utility that's useful not just for Auto Deploy but also for customizing any ESXi install images. Image Builder can customize the ESXi install image (ISO image) to include drivers, patches, and third-party plug-ins, such as Path Selection Plug-ins.

Image Builder is a PowerCLI utility, so we will explore the cmdlets that Image Builder utilizes. PowerCLI is a free extension to Microsoft's PowerShell that adds VMware-specific cmdlets and includes the Image Builder cmdlets, so administrators don't have to install anything other than PowerCLI to use Image Builder. PowerShell utilizes a verb-noun structure and is a great scripting and report-generation utility.

NOTE   PowerShell is beyond the scope of this book, so for further reading, please refer to the online documentation regarding PowerShell. This chapter also does not explore all the different VMware cmdlets beyond Auto Deploy and Image Builder; however, look to the online PowerCLI documentation for further information.

Before getting into the cmdlets that administrators use to configure Image Builder, it is useful to look at the different components that Image Builder utilizes:

- **vSphere Installation Bundle (VIB):** This is a collection of files that get packaged into an archive similar to a ZIP file. The VIBs have different acceptance levels that are not available for modification. These are the acceptance levels, from highest to lowest:

  - VMwareCertified

  - VMwareAccepted

  - PartnerSupported

  - CommunitySupported

The acceptance level of the VIBs to be used must be the same level or higher than the ESXi Host acceptance level. Even though the VIB acceptance levels can't be changed, an ESXi Host's level can be changed if needed.

- **Software Depot:** This is a collection of VIBs either online (accessible via HTTP) or offline (accessible via a USB drive or CD/DVD).

- **Image Profile:** This is a collection of VIBs used to install the ESXi server and saved as ZIP files or ISO images.

When starting up PowerCLI, PowerShell by default does not allow unsigned scripts to run. To determine the current execution policy (and to determine whether it is allowing unsigned scripts to run), you can enter the following command:

```
Get-ExecutionPolicy
```

If the output of this command is `Restricted`, you need to enter the following command:

```
Set-ExecutionPolicy Unrestricted
```

This command allows PowerCLI scripts to run. The next step is to connect to a vCenter Server by using the following command:

```
Connect-VIServer <vCenter Server FQDN>
```

You are then prompted for authentication. Once you're authenticated to the vCenter Server, you can begin configuring Image Builder and customizing ESXi install images for use by Auto Deploy or for keeping updated ESXi install images on hand.

There are five steps involved in creating ESXi images with Image Builder:

Step 1.   Download the software depots. These are the driver and software bundles from VMware and other vendors.

Step 2.   Import the software depots into Image Builder.

Step 3.   Create an image profile that is used to add all the VMware and third-party vendor software.

Step 4.   Add and remove VIBs. This step allows adding or removing VMware ESXi images and software as well as other vendors' software to the image profile.

Step 5.   Save the image profile to finalize the ISO or ZIP file.

Here is what you do during each of these steps:

Step 1.   Download the software depot or depots. A software depot is where the VMware VIBs and third-party software/drivers reside and is usually available via the vendors' websites. For example, VMware VIBs have to be downloaded first and can be obtained at http://www.vmware.com/ downloads. In order to include additional drivers and plug-ins from other vendors, you also have to define software depots from those other vendors' URLs as well. The vendor VIBs can then be added to the VMware VIBs as part of the image profile. A software depot can be at an online location, such as the URL listed previously, or it can be a locally saved ZIP file. For example, searching the http://www.vmware.com/ downloads site for the keywords software depot can yield a collection of already customized install images that can be downloaded for certain vendors, such as HP.

Step 2.   Import the software depots into image builder with the following cmdlet:

```
Add-EsxSoftwareDepot zip_file_name_and_location_or_URL
```

For example, if you are using HP ProLiant servers and want to use the custom install image ZIP file (offline bundle) from VMware's website that is saved in C:\images, you use this command:

```
Add-EsxSoftwareDepot C:\images\VMware-ESXi-6.0.0-Update1
  -3073146-HP-600.9.4.34-
Nov2015-depot.zip
```

Repeat this process for any additional software bundles that should be included in the install image.

You can also add individual VIBs by using the following command:

```
Get-EsxSoftwarePackage zip_file_name_and_location_or_URL
```

For example, if you want to add an individual network VIB, you use this command:

```
Get-EsxSoftwarePackage -PackageUrl C:\images\net-e1000e-
  2.3.2.x86_64.vib
```

Step 3.   Create an empty image profile, create an image profile with manually defined VMware and third-party VIBs, or clone an existing image profile. The PowerCLI cmdlet to display all currently available image profiles is:

```
Get-EsxImageProfile
```

If a VIB is being added that has a lower acceptance level than what is currently defined in the image profile, the acceptance level of the image profile can be modified with the following cmdlet:

```
Set-EsxImageProfile -ImageProfile "profile_name"
  -AcceptanceLevel Acceptance_Level
```

For example, if the current profile is Profile01, and you want to change the acceptance level to PartnerSupported, you use this cmdlet:

```
Set-EsxImageProfile -ImageProfile "Profile01" -AcceptanceLevel
  PartnerSupported
```

The cmdlet to create new profiles is `New-EsxImageProfile`, but some additional parameters are also required:

```
New-EsxImageProfile -NewProfile -Name "profile name" -vendor
"vendor name"
-SoftwarePackage esx-base, esx-xserver
```

Use the following command to get a list of available software packages (for example, `esx-base` and `esx-xserver`)

```
Get-EsxSoftwarePackage
```

This example includes the ESXi base package, which is needed when building a new image profile. The following is an example of what the script might look like without the placeholders:

```
New-EsxImageProfile -NewProfile -Name "Profile01" -vendor
  "VMware"
-SoftwarePackage esx-base, esx-xserver
```

To make a copy of an existing profile, use this:

```
New-EsxImageProfile -CloneProfile original_profile_name -Name
new_profile_name
-AcceptanceLevel AcceptanceLevel -Vendor vendor name
```

Here is an example of what this cmdlet might look like in use:

```
New-EsxImageProfile -CloneProfile ESXi-6.0.0-20151004001-standard
  -Name
NewProfile01 -AcceptanceLevel VMwareSupported -Vendor VMware
```

Step 4.   Add or remove VIBs, as needed. It is a good idea to know what VIBs are currently inside your image profile, so use this command to find out:

```
Get-EsxImageProfile -Name NewProfile01 | Select-Object
-ExpandProperty Viblist | Sort-Object
```

The cmdlets used to add or remove software packages to/from a VIB are `Add-EsxSoftwarePackage` or `Remove-EsxSoftwarePackage`. To add a software package, use this command:

```
Add-EsxSoftwarePackage -ImageProfile Profile_name
-SoftwarePackage Package_name
```

To remove a software package from a VIB, use this command:

```
Remove-EsxSoftwarePackage -ImageProfile Profile_name
-SoftwarePackage Package_name
```

Each VIB has an XML descriptor that contains information about conflicts and dependencies with/on other VIBs. To determine compatibility or dependencies, use this command:

```
Get-EsxSoftwarePackage | Format-table -Property Name,
Vendor, AcceptanceLevel, Depends, Conflicts -AutoSize
```

Step 5.   Save the image profile as a ZIP or ISO file. To export as an ISO, use this command:

```
Export-EsxImageProfile -ImageProfile Profile_name -ExportToISO
-FilePath path_to_save_iso_image
```

To export to a ZIP file, use this command:

```
Export-EsxImageProfile -ImageProfile Profile_name
-ExportToBundle -FilePath path_to_save_zip_file
```

NOTE   Though not supported, there is a VMware Fling (a tool created by a VMware developer that might become a product or part of a product) that uses a graphical interface for configuring Auto Deploy, called the Auto Deploy GUI: `https://labs.vmware.com/flings/autodeploygui`.

Implement Host Profiles with an Auto Deploy of an ESXi Host

When the hypervisor and drivers and plug-ins have been installed, the ESXi server is visible from the vCenter Server. vCenter then needs to place the new host into maintenance mode so it can push a host profile to the new host and configure it to match the profile. An answer file can be used to define additional VMkernel port IP addresses for things like IP Storage, vMotion, FT, etc. The host profile can also include options for stateless caching or stateful installs. Stateless caching allows the hosts to always boot off of the Auto Deploy server and always re-install on boot-up but then cache the install to a local drive or USB key. A stateful install, however, only boots off of the Auto Deploy server on the first boot. The software is then installed to disk, eliminating further dependence on the Auto Deploy server.

To enable stateless caching or stateful install, right-click a host profile in the Navigator pane and select **Edit Settings**. At the Edit Host Profile section of the wizard, select **Advanced Configuration Settings** > **System Image Cache Configuration** - > **System Image Cache Configuration**. From here, set one of the following settings:

- User must explicitly choose the policy option
- Enable stateless caching on the host
- Enable stateful installs on the host
- Enable stateless caching to a USB drive on the host
- Enable stateful installs to a USB drive on the host

If stateless caching or stateful installs are selected, there are additional options available:

- Arguments for first disk (`esx` and `local` defined by default)
- Check to overwrite any VMFS volumes on the selected disk (disabled by default)
- Check to ignore any SSD devices connected to the host (disabled by default)

Auto Deploy deployment rules are used to determine which ESXi image the booting hosts get as well as other configuration options, such as which host profile gets deployed to a host. To create a new deployment rule, use the following command:

```
New-DeployRule -Name Rule_Name -Item item -allhosts
```

The `-Item` rule should apply to hosts. An item can be an image profile, a host profile, or a folder or cluster or datacenter on the vCenter Server system to add the host to. For example, to put all deployed hosts into a folder called Auto Deploy, you use the following command:

```
New-DeployRule -Name "Host-Folder-Location" -Item "Auto Deploy" -allhosts
```

NOTE If the Auto Deploy service is not running, this command fails with an `Unable to connect to the remote server` error message. To resolve this on the vCenter Appliance, simply start the Auto Deploy service. Otherwise, on a Windows-based vCenter Server, verify that the Auto Deploy Windows service is running. This is discussed later in this chapter, in the section "Install and Configure Auto Deploy." Also, if you attempt to put an object defined by the `-item` field of the cmdlet that doesn't exist in vCenter inventory (such as an ESXi host, cluster, folder), the rule fails, with the error message `Could not find VIObjectCore with name 'item'`. Consider, for example, the command you ran to put all deployed hosts into the Auto Deploy folder. If that folder doesn't exist in vCenter inventory, you get the error message `Could not find VIObjectCore with name 'Auto Deploy'`.

The deploy rule can be further modified using the `Set-DeployRule` cmdlet to define things such as the IP range of the hosts to receive the image:

```
Set-DeployRule -DeployRule ImageRule -Pattern "ipv4=starting_IP_
   address-ending_ip_address"
```

If an administrator created an inventory object, such as a specific folder to be used for Auto Deployed ESXi Hosts, the profile can indicate to automatically place new hosts in that folder to place new hosts. Here is the command for this:

```
New-DeployRule -Name Rule_name -Item folder_name -allhosts
```

To see the current working set of Auto Deploy rules, you can use the `Get-Deploy-Rule` cmdlet.

Once the deployment rules have been completed, the DHCP scope needs to be defined, and possibly you need to define reservations based on the ESXi Hosts' MAC addresses. Once DHCP has been configured, TFTP needs to be set up on either the vCenter Server or a different server. The TFTP boot ZIP needs to be downloaded and extracted to the directory the TFTP server is serving. You download the TFTP boot ZIP from the vSphere Web Client as follows:

Step 1. Select the vCenter Server in the Navigator pane.

Step 2. Select the **Manage** tab.

Step 3. Select the **Settings** tab.

Step 4. Select **Auto Deploy** >

Step 5. **Download TFTP Boot Zip**.

Install and Configure Auto Deploy

Before you can use Auto Deploy, you need to install the server component or ensure that it has been installed. Auto Deploy can be installed on the same system as the Windows based vCenter Server or a separate physical or virtual machine. It also can be enabled in the vCenter Server Appliance. To install on a Windows system, the install files are on the vCenter installation media.

The Auto Deploy software does not show up in the vCenter installer splash screen. The installer can be found in the `\vCenter Server\Packages\` directory and is called `VMware-autodeploy.msi`. When you launch this MSI, you do not get a wizard. However, you get a new service called VMware vSphere Auto Deploy Waiter that is disabled. You need to enable it and start the service.

Since Auto Deploy is already part of the vCenter Appliance by default but is disabled, it must be enabled either through the vSphere Web Client or through SSH directly to the appliance, which isn't recommended.

To enable the Auto Deploy service in the vCenter Appliance, follow these steps:

Step 1. On the vSphere Web Client's home screen under Administration, select **System Configuration**.

Step 2. In the Navigator pane, select **Services** > **Auto Deploy**.

Step 3. Select the **Manage** tab.

Step 4. Select **Actions** > **Start**.

Step 5. Select the **Summary** tab and verify that the service is running.

Understand PowerCLI cmdlets for Auto Deploy

There are many PowerCLI cmdlets for Auto Deploy, as shown in Table 14-2.

Table 14-2   PowerCLI Auto Deploy cmdlets

Command	Description
Get-DeployCommand	Returns a list of Auto Deploy cmdlets.
New-DeployRule	Creates a new rule with the specified items and patterns.
Set-DeployRule	Updates an existing rule with the specified items and patterns. You cannot update a rule that is part of a rule set.
Get-DeployRule	Retrieves the rules with the specified names.
Copy-DeployRule	Clones and updates an existing rule.
Add-DeployRule	Adds one or more rules to the working rule set and, by default, also to the active rule set. Use the NoActivate parameter to add a rule only to the working rule set.
Remove-DeployRule	Removes one or more rules from the working rule set and from the active rule set. Run this command with the -Delete parameter to completely delete the rule.
Set-DeployRuleSet	Explicitly sets the list of rules in the working rule set.
Get-DeployRuleSet	Retrieves the current working rule set or the current active rule set.
Switch-ActiveDeployRuleSet	Activates a rule set so that any new requests are evaluated through the rule set.
Get-VMHostMatchingRules	Retrieves rules matching a pattern. For example, you can retrieve all rules that apply to a host or hosts. Use this cmdlet primarily for debugging.
Test-DeployRulesetCompliance	Checks whether the items associated with a specified hosts are in compliance with the active rule set.
Repair-DeployRulesetCompliance	Given the output of Test-DeployRulesetCompliance, this cmdlet updates the image profile, host profile, and location for each host in the vCenter Server inventory. The cmdlet might apply image profiles, apply host profiles, or move hosts to the prespecified folders or clusters on the vCenter Server system.
Apply-EsxImageProfile	Associates the specified image profile with the specified host.
Get-VMHostImageProfile	Retrieves the image profile in use by a specified host. This cmdlet differs from the Get-EsxImageProfile cmdlet in the Image Builder PowerCLI.

Command	Description
`Repair-DeployImageCache`	Use this cmdlet only if the Auto Deploy image cache is accidentally deleted.
`Get-VMHostAttributes`	Retrieves the attributes for a host that are used when the Auto Deploy server evaluates the rules.
`Get-DeployMachineIdentity`	Returns a string value that Auto Deploy uses to logically link an ESXi Host in vCenter to a physical machine.
`Set-DeployMachineIdentity`	Logically links a host object in the vCenter Server database to a physical machine. Use this cmdlet to add hosts without specifying rules.
`Get-DeployOption`	Retrieves the Auto Deploy global configuration options. This cmdlet currently supports the `vlan-id` option, which specifies the default VLAN ID for the ESXi Management Network of a host provisioned with Auto Deploy. Auto Deploy uses the value only if the host boots without a host profile.
`Set-DeployOption`	Sets the value of a global configuration option. Currently supports the `vlan-id` option for setting the default VLAN ID for the ESXi Management Network.

Deploy Multiple ESXi Hosts Using Auto Deploy

Since Auto Deploy installs into RAM on the ESXi server, every time the ESXi Host reboots, it begins this process all over again and has to get re-installed. The problem that could arise from this is that if the Auto Deploy server is down and the host reboots, then it won't be able to come back online because it can't reach the Auto Deploy server to re-install. As a result, vSphere 5.1 introduced Auto Deploy stateless caching and Auto Deploy stateful installs.

Stateless caching allows the host to boot off of the Auto Deploy server, but it then caches the installation on local disk. This requires the hosts to have local storage, whereas installing straight into memory doesn't require this. Each time the host reboots, it re-installs into RAM, and the local stateless cache gets updated at every install. If the host reboots and the Auto Deploy server is unreachable, it simply boots off of the local cache. This is configured entirely through host profiles.

A stateful install, on the other hand, allows a new host to install onto a local hard drive. This means that the first time the host boots, it boots off of the Auto Deploy server, but it then installs onto its local disk so it never requires the ability to reach the Auto Deploy server after the first boot. This means the speed and automation that come with Auto Deploy and host profiles allow you to stand up new hosts in minutes, and the hosts then have no further reliance on the Auto Deploy server.

The DHCP server needs to have a scope defined to reserve addresses based on ESXi server MAC addresses. However, this is only one method of allowing Auto Deploy to install hosts. If they are mostly the same and only one profile and image are being used, this may not be necessary.

Given a Scenario, Explain the Auto Deploy Deployment Model Needed to Meet a Business Requirement

Many environments have servers with local drives, but this is not always the case. Whether local drives are installed in the hosts and the level of availability required can impact how Auto Deploy is set up. For example, if an ESXi server needs to boot and the Auto Deploy server is down, the host cannot boot. In this case, stateless caching may provide an extra level of protection, but it would require each host to have at least a small local drive (or USB drive). Another option would be to have a stateful install, in which case the Auto Deploy server is used only on initial boot. There would still be a benefit of rapid provisioning of new hosts, but there would be no further reliance on the Auto Deploy servers after boot. If availability is a concern, but the servers don't have local drives, USB drives can be used for stateless caching and stateful installs. Unfortunately, however, SD cards cannot be used for these purposes.

Objective 8.2—Customize Host Profile Settings

Host profiles allow the standardization of ESXi Host configurations and allow for Auto Deploy. They are also useful for verifying that ESXi Hosts have been configured the same—for example, ensuring that port group names are identical or that VMkernel ports have been configured properly. One of the problems with using host profiles to configure ESXi Hosts and specifically to create VMkernel ports is that prior to version 5, vSphere would prompt you to provide the IP addresses needed. Now, however, you can create answer files to provide IP addresses automatically.

Edit an Answer File to Customize ESXi Host Settings

In order for Auto Deploy to work smoothly with the least amount of administrative effort, you can create an answer file to supply IP addresses for VMkernel ports.

Answer files to be used by host profiles can only be managed in the vSphere Client, not the vSphere Web Client. To create an answer file:

Step 1.   Navigate to **Home > Management > Host Profiles**.

Step 2.   Select a profile in the left pane.

Step 3.   Right-click an ESXi Host in the center pane and select **Update Answer File**.

An answer file can define IP addresses, IQNs and aliases, hostnames, etc. It can be used to automate additional configuration for a host. You can export or import an answer file by right-clicking a host from the center pane and selecting the appropriate menu option.

Answer files are manually run to configure hosts to define IP addresses, although they could also be scripted. As a result, they are usually only needed when not using DHCP reservations. If DHCP reservations are to be used, answer files aren't necessary.

Modify and Apply a Storage Path Selection Plug-in (PSP) to a Device Using Host Profiles

In the Edit Host Profiles Wizard, it is possible to define which PSP is to be used, so you can, for example, make Round Robin the default PSP. To do so, under the Storage Configuration options of the Edit Host Profile Wizard, you can select the otherwise deselected Native Multipathing option. Within the Native Multipathing Plug-in (NMP) are many options and sub-options:

- **Storage Array Type Plug-in (SATP) Configuration:** There are spots for four SATP Claimrules to be defined.

- **SATP Default PSP Configuration:** You can define default PSPs for each of the following types of SATP detected:
  - VMW_SATP_MSA
  - VMW_SATP_ALUA
  - VMW_SATP_DEFAULT_AP
  - VMW_SATP_SVC
  - VMW_SATP_EQL
  - VMW_SATP_INV
  - VMW_SATP_EVA
  - VMW_SATP_ALUA_CX
  - VMW_SATP_SYMM

- VMW_SATP_CX

- VMW_SATP_LSI

- VMW_SATP_DEFAULT_AA

- VMW_SATP_LOCAL

- **PSP and SATP Configuration for NMP Devices:** There are different PSP and SATP configuration options available for each different storage adapter.

- **Path Selection Policy (PSP) Configuration:** There are options for PSP, Fixed PSP, and Round Robin PSP.

Modify and Apply Switch Configurations Across Multiple Hosts Using a Host Profile

By default, virtual switch configuration is enabled as part of the host profiles. However, many modifications can be defined, or you can just include virtual switches, port groups, VMkernel ports, and policies. Within the Networking Configuration of the Edit Host Profiles wizard you can find the following options:

- **vSwitch:** This is where virtual switch configurations can be defined.

  - **vSwitch0:** There is one of these options for each virtual switch. Options at this level include always creating or not creating this object and defining the MTU.

  - **Link Configuration:** This allows definition of which physical uplink to attach to the virtual switch and how often beacon packets are sent (the default is every second).

  - **Number of Ports:** This option is set to 128 by default but can be modified to a higher number, up to a maximum of 4096 ports per host.

  - **Network Policy Configuration:** This setting allows the definitions of all switch policies, including security, traffic shaping, and teaming and failover policies.

- **Virtual Machine Port Group:** There is an option at this level for each VM port group on the switch. On vSwitch0, for example, it is VM Network by default. The option at this level is whether the profile should create this object. By default, Always Create the Object is selected.

  - **VLAN ID Configuration:** This allows the VLAN ID to be set at this port group. It is set to 0 by default

  - **vSwitch Selection:** This setting defines the name of the vSwitch to which this port group attaches. If there is only one virtual switch and one VM port group, this will be vSwitch0.

- **Network Policy Configuration:** Since security, traffic shaping, and teaming and failover policies can be defined at the port group level as well as the vSwitch level, this setting defines these policies for this port group.

- **Host Port Group:** VMkernel ports are at this level. On a default install, this is the VMkernel port named Management Network. Settings at this level include creating this object and defining which VMkernel port traffic will be enabled for this port, how MAC addresses get generated, name of the VMkernel port, MTU setting, and TCP/IP stack to use for this port.

  - **IP Address Settings:** Settings at this level include how the IP address is to be assigned, whether IPv6 is to be enabled, and whether IPv6 addresses are to be static or dynamically assigned.

  - **VLAN ID Configuration:** Settings at this level include the ability to define the VLAN. 0 is the default.

  - **vSwitch Selection:** As with virtual machine port groups, this defines the virtual switch to which this port will attach. For Management Network, the default is vSwitch0.

  - **Network Policy Configuration:** As with the virtual machine port groups, this setting allows you to define the configuration of the security policy, traffic shaping policy, and teaming and failover policy.

- **Physical NIC Configuration:** There is one of these settings for each physical uplink. Options at this level include whether to have the physical uplink set to auto-negotiate and which physical uplink this is (vmnic0, vmnic1, etc.).

- **vSphere Distributed Switch:** There is one selection at this level for each vDS that is defined.

  - **Uplink Port Configuration:** At this level are the settings to define the physical uplink to attach as well as uplink port names and uplink port group names.

- **Host Virtual NIC:** There is a definition at this level for each vDS that has a VMkernel port attached. Settings at this level include the name of the vDS, port group identifier, whether to create the VMkernel port, VLAN ID, network policy, active uplinks, standby uplinks, which VMkernel services are to be used, how MAC addresses are defined, names of the VMkernel ports, MTU size, and TCP/IP stack.

  - **IP Address Settings:** Settings at this level include how the IP address is assigned and IPv6 addressing.

- **NetStack Instance:** This setting allows the inclusion of VMkernel TCP/IP stacks, including the default as well as any additional TCP/IP stacks that have been defined in the reference host.

- **defaultTcpipStack:** This defines the name of the default IP stack as well as the congestion control algorithm (`newreno` by default).

- **DNS Configuration:** Settings at this level include IP addresses of the DNS servers, whether DHCP is to be used, domain name, search domain, hostname definition, and which virtual NIC to use for DNS.

- **IP route Configuration:** Settings at this level include the IPv4 and IPv6 default gateways and which device is being used for IP route gateway.

- **IP Route Config:** Settings at this level include how IP routing is being done. The default is set to Fixed Static Route. The other option is Users Must Explicitly Choose the Policy Option. Underneath this drop-down you can define the destination network address, destination prefix length, IP next hop, device name, and IP family type.

- **Network Coredump Settings:** This setting allows you to enable network core dumps, which physical uplink to use, the IP address to which core dumps should be sent, and which port is to be used.

Create/Edit/Remove a Host Profile from an ESXi Host

Creating host profiles is a fairly straightforward process:

Step 1.   To create a host profile to be used by Auto Deploy, from the home screen of the vSphere Web Client, under Monitoring, select **Host Profiles** (see Figure 14-1).

Figure 14-1   Host Profiles

Step 2. To create a new profile, click the green **Extract Profile from a Host** plus icon (see Figure 14-2).

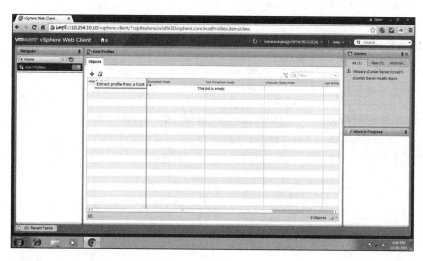

Figure 14-2 New Profile

Step 3. In the Extract Host Profile Wizard, you can define the reference ESXi Host to extract the profile from (see Figure 14-3). The complete profile that is created includes all the configurations of the selected ESXi server, including virtual switches, port groups, VLANs, load balancing policies, etc.

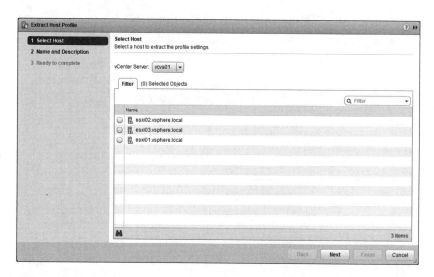

Figure 14-3 Select a Host

Step 4. The wizard then prompts for the name of the profile and a description, followed by a summary of the profile. Once the host profile has been created, it can be modified if needed.

Import/Export a Host Profile

To import a host profile, in vSphere Web Client, select the **Import Host Profile** icon under the Object tab (see Figure 14-4).

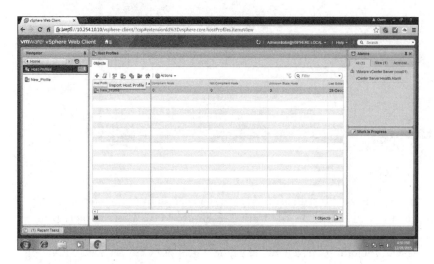

Figure 14-4 Import Host Profile

In the Import Host Profile Wizard that appears, define which vCenter Server to add the profile to, as well as the location for the profile, its name, and a description of the profile (see Figure 14-5).

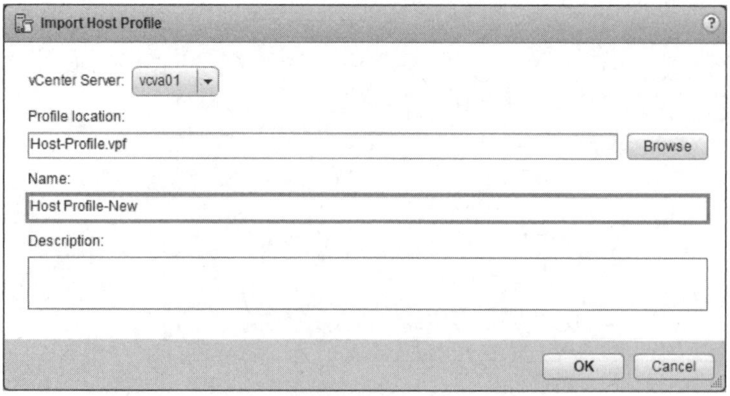

Figure 14-5 Import Host Profile Wizard

Exporting host profiles may be useful in organizations that have multiple vCenter Servers or physical locations, but it can benefit by having the standardized ESXi Host configuration available. To export a profile, right-click the host profile in the Navigator pane and select **Export Host Profile** (see Figure 14-6).

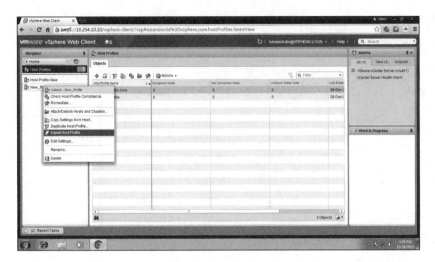

Figure 14-6   Export Host Profile

A notification screen pops up, explaining that passwords don't get exported with the profile (see Figure 14-7).

Figure 14-7   Host Profile Password Notification

Finally, the wizard prompts for a location to save the profile. Host profiles are saved as VPF files.

Attach and Apply a Host Profile to ESXi Hosts in a Cluster

There are four ways to attach a host profile to an ESXi Host (or cluster):

- Right-click the host profile in the Navigator pane and click **Attach/Detach Hosts and Clusters**.

- Select the host profile in the Navigator pane and click the **Attach/Detach Hosts and Clusters** button (see Figure 14-8).

- Select **Actions** > **Attach/Detach Hosts and Clusters** (see Figure 14-9).

- From the hosts and clusters inventory view, right-click an ESXi server or cluster and select **Host Profiles** > **Attach Host Profile**.

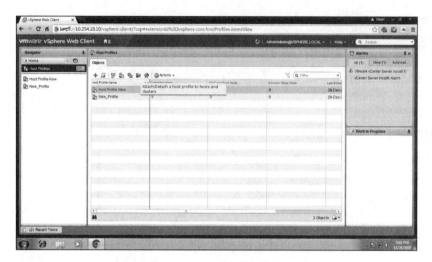

Figure 14-8 Attach/Detach Hosts and Clusters Button

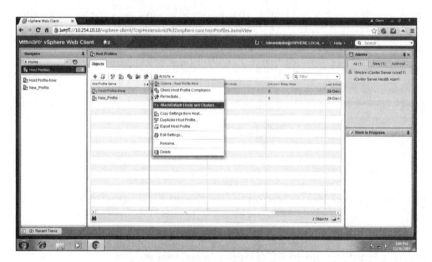

Figure 14-9 Action > Attach/Detach Hosts and Clusters

In the Attach/Detach Hosts and Clusters Wizard that appears, you can either attach the profile to an entire cluster object or, by holding the Ctrl key, select more than one host (see Figure 14-10).

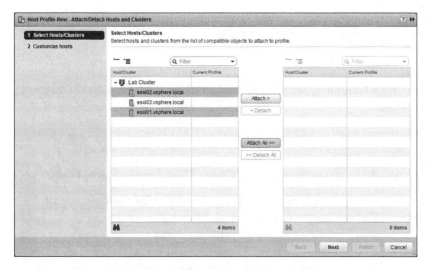

Figure 14-10   Attach/Detach Hosts and Clusters Wizard

The last screen of the wizard asks you to define things on each host, such as MAC address and IP address of VMkernel ports, enabling of iSCSI initiators, etc. (see Figure 14-11).

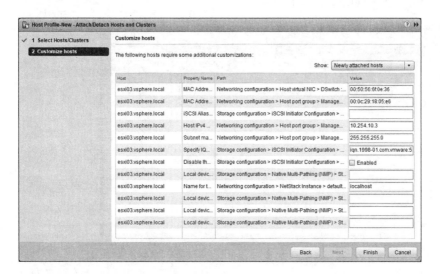

Figure 14-11   Customize Hosts

NOTE   A host profile can be attached to an ESXi server whether that server is in a cluster or not. However, it makes sense to apply a host profile at the cluster level so it can be attached to the remaining hosts.

After the host profile has been attached to a host or cluster, the number of hosts is listed under Unknown State Hosts because they have not been scanned for compliance against the host profile.

Perform Compliance Scanning and Remediation of an ESXi Host and Clusters Using Host Profiles

Just as there are four ways to attach a profile to an ESXi Host or cluster, there are four ways to scan an ESXi Host or cluster for compliance against a profile:

- Right-click the host profile and select **Check Host Profile Compliance**.

- Select the host profile and click the **Check Host Profile Compliance of Associated Entries** button (see Figure 14-12).

- Select the host profile and select **Actions > Check Host Profile Compliance**.

- From the hosts and clusters inventory view, right-click an **ESXi Host** or cluster object and select **Host Profiles > Check Host Profile Compliance**.

Once the host or cluster has been checked for compliance, you can determine whether the host or cluster object has a configuration that matches the profile from the host profiles view (see Figure 14-13).

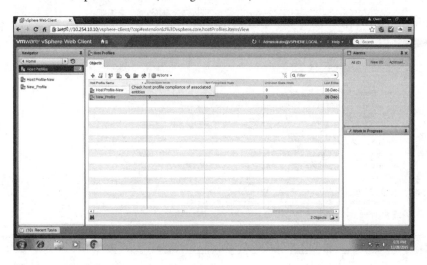

Figure 14-12   Check Host Profile Compliance

Figure 14-13   Profile Compliance Status

To get more information, select the profile from the Navigator pane and select the **Summary** tab. You can now see which hosts are not compliant with the profile. Under the **Monitor > Compliance** tab, find out why the host failed the compliance check (see Figure 14-14).

Figure 14-14   Host Profile Monitor Tab

To bring a host into compliance, the host has to be in maintenance mode. From host profiles or the hosts and clusters inventory view, the host can be entered into maintenance mode. Once in maintenance mode, right-click the ESXi Host and select **Host Profiles > Remediate**. Alternatively, you can click the **Remediate Host Based on Its Profile** button (see Figure 14-15).

Figure 14-15 Remediate Host Based on Its Host Profile

The Remediate Host(s) Based on Host Profile Wizard that appears allows the modification of profile settings such as VMkernel MAC address, IP address, subnet mask, IQNs, and other host configuration settings (see Figure 14-16).

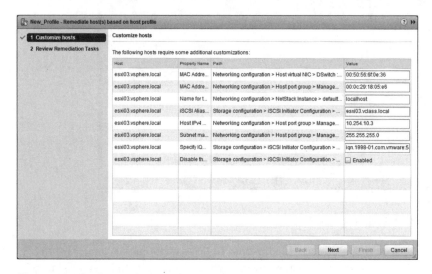

Figure 14-16 Customize Hosts

Once the host has been (re)configured to match the profile, the host can be removed from maintenance mode. If something goes wrong during the remediation, you can go back to the host profile from the Navigator pane, and select **Monitor** tab > **Compliance** to see what setting could not be modified. Then you can do some manual configuration. This is usually not a problem with new ESXi Hosts that have just been installed either manually or via Auto Deploy.

Enable or Disable Host Profile Components

To modify a profile, right-click it in the Navigator pane and select **Edit Settings** (see Figure 14-17).

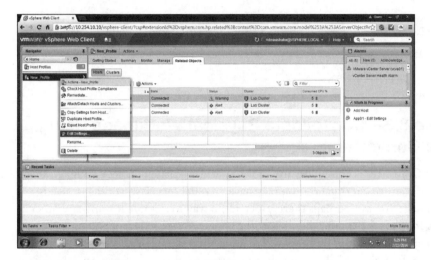

Figure 14-17   Edit Settings of Host Profiles

The first screen of the Edit Host Profile Wizard that appears allows you to change the name and description of the profile. The second screen of the wizard allows you to modify the contents of the profile (see Figure 14-18).

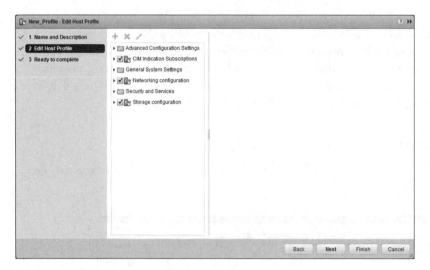

Figure 14-18   Edit Host Profile

Objective 8.3—Consolidate Physical Workloads Using VMware Converter

VMware Converter is commonly used for physical-to-virtual (or P2V) migrations. For example, an organization may have an older legacy server that it needs to continue to use but perhaps there isn't a clean way to migrate it using any other method. Perhaps the vendor didn't port the application to a new operating system, or the vendor went out of business and there is not a suitable replacement for the application. In a physical environment, this server would be kept around as long as possible, but maintaining it would become a logistical challenge. VMware Converter can allow such legacy systems to be virtualized and kept around as long as possible until a suitable replacement can be found, without worries that the hardware will die and there will be no way to repair it.

Install a vCenter Converter Standalone Instance

vCenter Converter is a free utility that allows physical Windows and Linux servers to be converted to vSphere virtual machines. vCenter Converter can convert the following to a VMware virtual machine:

- Physical machines (Windows or Linux)

- VMware virtual machines (.vmx)

- VMware Consolidated Backup (.vmx)

- Microsoft Virtual PC or Virtual Server virtual machines (.vmc)

- Symantec LiveState Recovery Image (.sv2i)

- Acronis True Image Backup (.tib)

- StorageCraft ShadowStor (.spf)

- Parallels Virtualization Products (.pvs)

- Hyper-V virtual machines

The software can be installed only on Windows systems. The installation executable is available via VMware's website (`https://my.vmware.com/group/vmware/evalcenter?p=converter`). To install it, launch the `.exe` file, which opens the install wizard. The following steps outline the install process:

Step 1.   The first screen of the install wizard is the welcome screen.

Step 2.   The second screen is the end-user patent agreement.

Step 3.   The third screen of the wizard is the end user license agreement, and you must agree to it in order to proceed through the wizard.

Step 4.   The fourth screen of the wizard asks for the install location. `C:\Program Files (x86)\VMware\VMware vCenter Converter Standalone\` is the default install location.

Step 5.   The fifth screen of the install wizard asks whether this is a local install (installed to the current machine) or a client/server install, which allows the installation of the agent, server component, or client component. If the local or server software is installed, it is this machine that processes the conversion process.

Step 6.   The last screen of the wizard begins the installation. After the install finishes, the wizard prompts to run the program.

Convert Physical Workloads Using vCenter Converter

vCenter Converter can convert a machine that the converter software itself is installed on, or another physical or virtual machine or disk image, or another virtual machine. The following steps outline the process of using the vCenter Converter wizard to convert machines:

Step 1.   When you launch the vCenter Converter, you see two main buttons:

- Convert machine
- Configure machine

Step 2.   We are going to explore the Convert machine part of this wizard. The interface in the Convert Machine Wizard is fairly straightforward. You are prompted to define the type of source machine from a drop-down that includes the following options:

- Powered-On Machine

- VMware Infrastructure Virtual Machine

- VMware Workstation or Other VMware Virtual Machine

- Backup Image or Third-Party Virtual Machine

- Hyper-V Server

Step 3.   If Powered-On Machine is selected here, the next option is whether the physical machine is the local machine or a remote machine. If a remote machine is selected, you have to define the IP address/hostname, user-name/password, and which OS is on the system (see Figure 14-19).

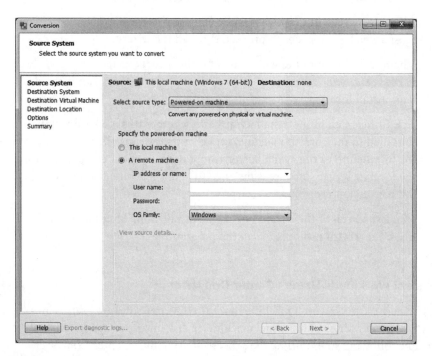

Figure 14-19   Source System

The next screen of the wizard asks for information about the destination. The only two options are VMware Infrastructure Virtual Machine (the default selection) and VMware Workstation or other VMware Virtual Machine. Below this selection are text fields to define server name and username/password (see Figure 14-20).

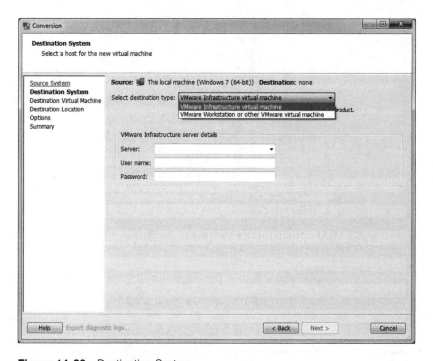

Figure 14-20 Destination System

Once you are connected to the vCenter Server, the wizard prompts for a new virtual machine name as well as VMs and templates inventory location (see Figure 14-21).

Once the inventory location has been selected, the computing resource, resource pool, datastore, and virtual machine version must be defined (see Figure 14-22).

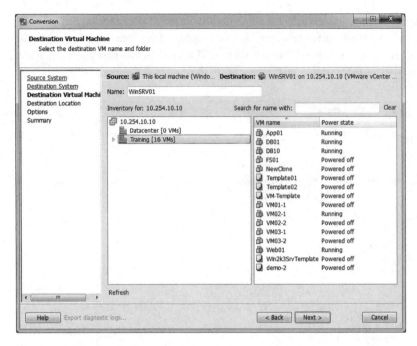

Figure 14-21   Destination Virtual Machine

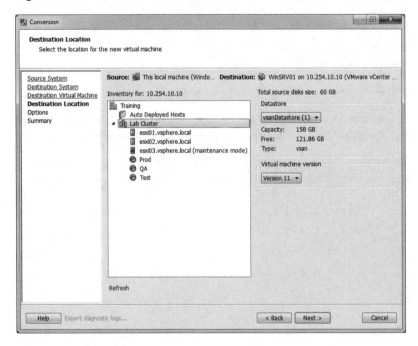

Figure 14-22   Destination Location

In the final screen of the wizard, you modify the hardware resource allocations.

Modify Server Resources During Conversion

The Conversion Wizard allows you to modify resource allocations, such as removing CPUs, reducing memory, reducing hard drive size, etc. In the second-to-last screen of the Conversion Wizard, you can see how many drives there are, as well as their sizes. You can increase or decrease these sizes, provided that they are not made smaller than the amount of consumed space (see Figure 14-23).

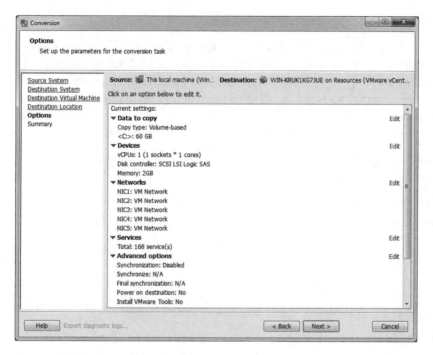

Figure 14-23   Conversion Options

You can modify all of the following settings in the second-to-last screen of the Conversion Wizard:

- **Data to Copy:** By default, all hard drives will be copied, and their current sizes will be retained. However, it is possible to modify this setting and remove certain hard drives, if needed, define different datastore locations for each individual hard drive, and change the size of the hard drives. By default, page files and hibernation files are ignored. Choosing Advanced Options allows you to define some or all drives to be thick/thin provisioned.

- **Devices:** This option allows you to modify memory allocation, number of virtual sockets, and cores per socket for vCPUs and disk controller type.

- **Networks:** This option allows you to add or remove network adapters and define to which VM port group the new NICs will connect.

- **Services:** This option allows you to see which services are enabled and running on the source and define different settings for the destination virtual machine.

Interpret and Correct Errors During Conversion

A number of issues can occur during the conversion process. The Converter's main window displays any issues and can also bring up the wizard again if an issue is found, such as inability to create the virtual machine's files. A common problem occurs when the system drive is not installed on the first partition. Such a system can still be converted, but the `init.ini` file needs to be set to read/write so that the converter can modify it, indicating that the OS is installed on the first partition.

It is also useful to be aware of which logs can be of use and their locations. The following are the log locations:

- Windows NT, Windows 2000, Windows XP, and Windows Server 2003:

  - `C:\Documents and Settings\All Users\Application Data\VMware\VMware Converter Enterprise\Logs`
  - `C:\WINDOWS\Temp\vmware-converter`
  - `C:\WINDOWS\Temp\vmware-temp`

- Windows Vista, Windows 7, and Windows Server 2008:

  - `C:\Users\All Users\Application Data\VMware\VMware Converter Enterprise\Logs`

- Windows 8 and Windows 2012:

  - `C:\ProgramData\VMware\VMware vCenter Converter Standalone\Logs`
  - `C:\WINDOWS\Temp\vmware-converter`
  - `C:\WINDOWS\Temp\vmware-temp`

- Windows NT and Windows 2000:

  - `C:\WINNT\Temp\vmware-converter`
  - `C:\WINNT\Temp\vmware-temp`

- Linux:

  - `$HOME/.vmware/VMware vCenter Converter Standalone/Logs`
  - `/var/log/vmware-vcenter-converter-standalone`

It is helpful to be aware of the TCP/IP ports required for communication, as indicated in VMware KB 1012382.

Deploy a Physical Host as a Virtual Machine Using vCenter Converter

In the Conversion Wizard, additional advanced options can facilitate a smoother transition from physical to virtual, including the following:

- **Advanced Options:** This setting has many options, broken down into two tabs:

  - **Synchronize:** This tab allows changes to be synchronized to power on the new virtual machine while powering off the source machine and ensure that the two machines are in sync before powering off the source machine. This tab also has a scheduler that defines when this operation is to occur. There is a note on this tab that you cannot synchronize the source with the destination in the following cases:

    - When FAT volumes are selected and the source is Windows Vista or later

    - When resizing FAT volumes and the source is a Windows XP or 2003

    - When shrinking NTFS volumes

    - When changing the cluster size

  - **Post-Conversion:** The options available for post-conversion are as follows:

    - Power On Destination Machine

    - Install VMware Tools on the Destination Virtual Machine

    - Customize Guest Preferences for the Virtual Machine

    - Remove System Restore Checkpoints on Destination (selected by default)

    - Reconfigure Destination Virtual Machine (selected by default)

- **Throttling:** This option allows the CPU and network throttling of the conversion process to reduce resource consumption and prevent monopolization of CPU and network resources. It is useful if other work needs to be done on the machine performing the conversion process.

Collect Diagnostic Information During Conversion Operation

In prior versions of the vCenter Converter, the user interface was the only place that logs could be found. However, as of Converter 5, there are other ways to gather information about the conversion process:

- From the job view, select **Job > Export logs**.

- From the task view, select **Task > Export logs**.

- From the computer running the Converter software, go to `C:\ProgramData\VMware\VMware vCenter Converter Standalone\logs`.

- From the computer being converted, go to `C:\ProgramData\VMware\VMware vCenter Converter Standalone Agent\logs` or `%ALLUSERSPROFILE%\Application Data\VMware\VMware vCenter Converter Standalone Client\logs`.

Resize Partitions During the Conversion Process

In the options portion of the vCenter Conversion Wizard, in the Data to Copy section, you can modify which disks are to be copied as well as on which datastore to place each disk and whether to make the disk larger or smaller than the source. There is also an advanced option to make the new virtual disk thin provisioned if required (see Figure 14-24).

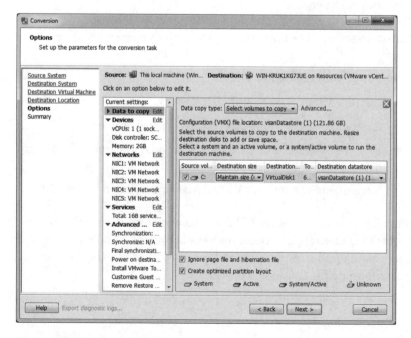

Figure 14-24 Resize Disks

Given a Scenario, Determine Which Virtual Disk Format to Use

It is important to understand the usage patterns of applications to help define the type of disk format to use. It is also important to understand any potential performance issues. If the storage device intended for use for the new virtual machine's disks supports the vSphere API for Array Integration (VAAI), the locking mechanism required to grow thin-provisioned disks, called Atomic Locking, is offloaded to the storage device. If the storage device does not support the VAAI, then the VM-kernel is responsible for locking the metadata to grow the virtual disks. This is likely to result in SCSI reservation errors on the storage device and a lower total number of thin-provisioned disks that can be used on that datastore. This locking and waiting for locking can result in degraded performance. If an array supports VAAI, there is no performance difference for thin- vs. thick-provisioned disks. With thick-provisioned disks, there is no operational performance difference between eager-zeroed thick and lazy-zeroed thick, regardless of whether the storage device supports VAAI. The only difference is when the disk files get allocated. This can translate to slow performance at first write for lazy-zeroed thick disks because these files are zeroed out at the time of first write. If this is when the disk is being formatted in the guest operating system, depending on the size of the disk, the zeroing process can take a considerable amount of time.

Whether the storage device supports the VAAI or not, it can still be useful to be able to identify disk usage rates. For example, if administrators are converting a file server with a 2 TB disk, but the server is two years old and storage usage is only 20 GB, this may be a perfect candidate for thin provisioning as the rate of usage is so slow. However, another scenario might be that a database server experiences database growth of 2 GB every week (or more frequently); here it might not make sense to thin provision as the disk grows more frequently, and thin provisioning could end up consuming the full allocated space sooner rather than later anyway.

Summary

Many pieces need to be configured correctly in order for Auto Deploy to work. It is important to understand the reliance on DHCP and TFTP servers, host profiles, Image Builder, and the Auto Deploy cmdlets covered in this chapter. As with many other VMware features that have multiple components and dependencies, it is useful to visualize all the interconnecting pieces and their relationships.

This chapter also discusses using vCenter Converter to consolidate physical workloads and some of the key areas that help you with troubleshooting, such as log file locations.

You should now use the information in the following sections to complete your preparation for Objectives 8.1, 8.2, and 8.3.

Exam Preparation Tasks

Review All the Key Topics

Table 14-3 provides a reference to each of the key topics identified in this chapter. Take a few moments to review each of these specific items.

Table 14-3 Key Topics for Chapter 14

Key Topic Element	Description	Pages
Section	Describe the components and architecture of an Auto Deploy environment	532
List	Image Builder components	533
Procedure	Steps involved in creating ESXi images	534
List	Stateless caching/stateful installs	537
List	PowerCLI Auto Deploy cmdlets	539

Complete the Tables and Lists from Memory

Print a copy of Appendix B, "Memory Tables" (found on the CD), or at least the section for this chapter, and complete the tables and lists from memory. Appendix C, "Memory Tables Answer Key," also on the CD, includes completed tables and lists to check your work.

Definitions of Key Terms

Define the following key terms from this chapter, and check your answers in the glossary.

VMware Infrastructure Bundle (VIB), Path Selection Plug-in (PSP), Storage Array Type Plug-in (SATP)

Answer Review Questions

1. Which of the following is not an acceptance level?

    a. VMwareCertified

    b. VMwareAccepted

    c. PartnerSupported

    d. CommunityAccepted

2. Which of the following is not an example of a VIB?

    a. ESXi install image ISO file

    b. ESXi install image ZIP file

    c. ESXI install image CD

    d. A third-party vendor bundle

3. Which of the following PowerCLI cmdlets would be used to create a new rule for Auto Deployed ESXi Hosts?

    a. `New-DeployRule`

    b. `Set-DeployRule`

    c. `New-AutoDeployRule`

    d. `DeployRule -New`

4. What networking settings can be modified by way of host profiles? (Choose three.)

    a. Number of Ports

    b. Traffic Shaping Policy

    c. Path Selection Plug-in

    d. LACP

    e. STP

5. How can an Auto Deployed ESXi server obtain IP addressing for VMkernel ports? (Choose two.)

    a. During the Auto Deploy process, you are prompted to define an IP address.

    b. IP addresses can be static DHCP reservations.

    c. IP addresses can be provided through an answer file.

    d. IP addresses can be defined via FDM agents.

This chapter covers the following objectives:

- **Objective 9.1: Configure Advanced vSphere HA Features**

  - Modify vSphere HA advanced cluster settings

  - Apply virtual machine monitoring for a cluster

  - Configure Virtual Machine Component Protection (VMCP) settings

  - Implement vSphere HA on a Virtual SAN cluster

  - Explain how vSphere HA communicates with Distributed Resource Scheduler and Distributed Power Management

- **Objective 9.2: Configure Advanced vSphere DRS Features**

  - Configure affinity/anti-affinity rules

  - Add/remove a host DRS group

  - Add/remove a virtual machine DRS group

  - Enable/disable Distributed Resource Scheduler (DRS) affinity rules

  - Configure the proper Distributed Resource Scheduler (DRS) automation level, based on a set of business requirements

  - Explain how DRS affinity rules affect virtual machine placement

## CHAPTER 15

Configure and Administer vSphere Availability Solutions

This chapter provides the knowledge you need to successfully perform cluster administration in a vSphere virtualized datacenter. It also ensures that you have the skills to successfully complete the cluster configuration and management tasks that might be a part of the VMware Certified Professional 6—Data Center Virtualization Exam. As you read this chapter, take time to practice the steps provided and understand how HA and DRS work.

"Do I Know This Already?" Quiz

The "Do I Know This Already?" quiz allows you to assess whether you should study this entire chapter or move quickly to the "Exam Preparation Tasks" section. Regardless, the authors recommend that you read the entire chapter at least once. Table 15-1 outlines some of the major headings in this chapter and the corresponding "Do I Know This Already?" quiz questions. You can find the answers in Appendix A, "Answers to the 'Do I Know This Already?' Quizzes and Review Questions."

Table 15-1 "Do I Know This Already?" Foundation Topics Section-to-Question Mapping

Foundations Topics Section	Questions Covered in This Section
Configure a Network for Use with HA Heartbeats	1
Apply an Admission Control Policy for HA	2
Apply Virtual Machine Monitoring for a Cluster	3
Implement vSphere HA on a Virtual SAN Cluster	4
Explain How vSphere HA Communicates with Distributed Resource Scheduler and Distributed Power Management	5
Configure Virtual Machine Component Protection (VMCP) Settings	6
Configure VM-VM Affinity/Anti-affinity Rule	7
Configure the Proper Distributed Resource Scheduler (DRS) Automation Level Based on a Set of Business Requirements	8
Configure the Proper Distributed Resource Scheduler (DRS) Automation Level Based on a Set of Business Requirements	9, 10

1. If an ESXi Host has only one management network, what two actions could be used to add an additional management network for the required redundancy? (Choose two.)

    a. Set `das.useisolationaddress=172.10.10.1`.

    b. Add another VMkernel network for heartbeats.

    c. Set `das.addvmkernelnetwork=172.10.10.1`.

    d. Set `das.isolationaddress0=172.10.10.1`.

    e. Set `das.haisolationaddress=172.10.10.1`.

2. Which statement is correct? (Choose two.)

    a. The slot size of a VM is calculated utilizing a worst-case approach. HA finds the VM with the highest CPU reservation and the VM with the highest memory reservation plus memory overhead.

    b. The default admission control policy sets the number of host failures the cluster tolerates to 2.

    c. The Use Dedicated Failover Hosts admission control policy sets aside a dedicated amount of CPU and memory resources for failover capacity.

    d. The number of host failures the cluster tolerates is an admission control policy that instructs HA to calculate and use a slot size to determine the amount of resources to reserve.

3. Which of the following is an incorrect statement?

    a. If there is no disk or network activity within the `das.iostatsinterval` of 120 seconds, HA restarts the VM on a surviving ESXi Host.

    b. If a VM has stopped sending heartbeats to HA, HA immediately checks whether there is any disk or network activity.

    c. The I/O stats interval is an advanced option variable `das.iostatsinterval` that is set at the cluster level.

    d. If the guest OS blue screens or panics, it is no longer sending heartbeats to HA.

4. Which of the following can Virtual SAN support?

    a. Up to 64 nodes with 200 VMs per host

    b. 32 datastores per cluster

    c. 3200 VMs per cluster

    d. Up to 32 nodes with 200 VMs per host

5. Which of the following DPM statements is incorrect?

   a. DRS is a subset feature within the settings of DPM.

   b. DRS must be enabled before DPM can be enabled.

   c. DPM must have the ability to wake a host from standby mode.

   d. All requirements of DRS are also requirements for DPM.

6. Which of the following is not an option for a permanent device loss (PDL)?

   a. Disabled

   b. Issue Events

   c. Power Off VMs

   d. Power Off and Restart VMs

7. Which statement about affinity and anti-affinity rules is incorrect? (Choose two.)

   a. If two VM-VM affinity rules conflict with each other, the newer one takes precedence over the older rule.

   b. If two VM-VM affinity rules conflict with each other, the older one takes precedence over the newer rule.

   c. DRS gives higher precedence to anti-affinity rules.

   d. DRS gives higher precedence to affinity rules.

8. Which statement is correct?

   a. When the Distributed Resource Scheduler is set to Fully Automated, DRS applies only recommendations that are allowed based on the migration threshold.

   b. When the Distributed Resource Scheduler is set to Manual, DRS applies only recommendations that are allowed based on the migration threshold.

   c. When the Distributed Resource Scheduler is set to Partially Automated, DRS applies only recommendations that are allowed based on the migration threshold.

   d. When the Distributed Resource Schedule is set to None, no recommendations are allowed.

9. If DRS Threshold is set to Conservative, it applies only priority 1 recommendations. The result is that DRS does not apply the DRS rules and does not
balance based on the workload. (Choose two.)

   a. If DRS Threshold is set to Conservative, it applies only priority 5
      recommendations.

   b. If DRS Threshold is set to Conservative, it applies only priority 1
      recommendations.

   c. The default threshold applies only priority 1–3 recommendations.

   d. The default threshold applies only priority 3–5 recommendations.

10. A DRS cluster has the default threshold set, which is to apply only priority 1–3
    recommendations. The DRS cluster has become unbalanced, but the VMs are
    not load balancing. Why? (Choose two.)

    a. A CD-ROM is mounted to a virtual machine.

    b. The vMotion network is enabled.

    c. An affinity rule set is keeping VMs from migrating.

    d. HA is enabled on the cluster.

Foundation Topics

Objective 9.1—Configure Advanced vSphere HA Features

VMware high availability (HA) is a vSphere cluster feature that provides automated protection for virtual machines (VMs) and applications. It provides automated recovery of VMs that fail as a result of an unplanned ESXi Host downtime event. When an ESXi Host becomes nonresponsive, VMware HA automatically cold migrates the failed VMs to a surviving ESXi Host in the cluster and restarts them. A cold migration simply involves restarting a VM on a different ESXi Host. HA requires these VMs to be hosted on shared datastores, which allows them to be immediately registered on the surviving hosts in the cluster without the need to copy any files. Typically, when a host fails, HA migrates and restarts all failed VMs within a few minutes.

VMware HA also offers other forms of protection, such as VM monitoring and application monitoring, which are not enabled by default. When configured for VM monitoring, VMware HA listens to the heartbeat of each VM, which is generated by VMware Tools. If at any point the heartbeat cannot be detected, VMware HA restarts the affected VMs. When configured for application monitoring, VMware HA listens for heartbeats that are generated by applications that are customized to interface with VMware Tools. If at any point the heartbeat cannot be detected, VMware HA restarts the affected VMs.

There are many configurable settings for vSphere HA, including Admission Control, Virtual Machine Component Protection, and Restart Priority. Although vCenter Server is required for configuration as well as for maintaining the protected VM list, VMware HA is not dependent on the vCenter Server availability for its failover operation. Instead, it uses a feature called Fault Domain Manager (FDM) to maintain the integrity of the cluster of ESXi Hosts and the ability to restart any VMs that need to be restarted even if the vCenter Server is not available. A minimum licensed edition of vSphere Essentials Plus is required to use VMware HA in a vSphere implementation.

Modify vSphere HA Advanced Cluster Settings

You can easily set up a VMware cluster by right-clicking a datacenter, selecting **New Cluster**, and clicking **OK**. You must add ESXi Hosts to the cluster to provide the resources needed for the cluster, but a default cluster has now been set up. You can add high availability (HA) by selecting the check box **Turn on vSphere HA**, which sets up the default settings for high availability. If you need to change the

VMware high availability settings, you can use a number of options in the vSphere Web Client. However, not all of the settings can be modified using the Web Client. A number of advanced HA configuration settings can be made using the HA advanced settings. In the vSphere Web Client, use the following steps to customize HA settings. With the cluster highlighted, select the **Manage** tab and click **Settings**. Under the **Settings** tab, select **vSphere HA** and click the **Edit** button. When the Edit Cluster Settings window opens, expand **Advanced Options**. If you want to change an advanced cluster setting, click **Add** and type in the name of the advanced option in the text box. You can set the value of the advanced parameter by adding the proper value of the option in the Value column. Figure 15-1 shows an example of modifying an HA advanced cluster setting. This is an example of changing a non-default isolation address to 172.16.1.5 for high availability.

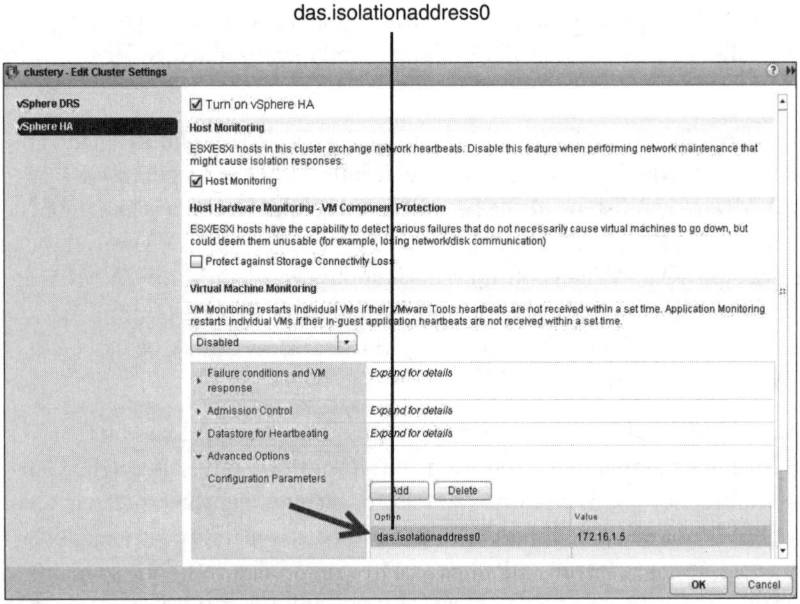

Figure 15-1   Modifying an HA Advanced Cluster Setting

Configure a Network for Use with HA Heartbeats

The VMware HA cluster uses a host-based agent known as Fault Domain Manager (FDM) that has one master node and multiple slave nodes. The master node monitors the status of the slave nodes based on heartbeats sent between the master and the slave over the heartbeat network. Each slave sends a heartbeat (an "I am alive" packet), and the master replies (an acknowledgement packet) to each one individually. This communication between the agents of the master and the slaves includes a datastore heartbeat as well as a network heartbeat. Historically, network heartbeats have been the main heartbeats between the nodes via the management network. In Figure 15-2, the ESXi Host is showing an alarm because there is only one VMkernel network set up for heartbeats. You can either add another VMkernel network for heartbeats or add an advanced HA setting.

The network for HA should be as resilient as possible. Placing additional VMkernel ports on each host and enabling them for management traffic can achieve network heartbeat redundancy. The other option is to set an HA advanced cluster setting that can override the warning message of only one HA heartbeat datastore. Modify the advanced HA parameter `das.ignoreInsufficientHbDatastore` and set the value to `true`.

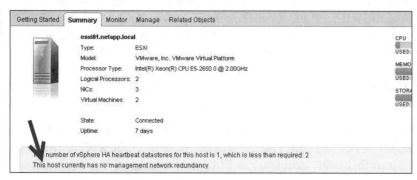

Figure 15-2   HA Network Heartbeat Alarm Messages

Apply an Admission Control Policy for HA

Admission control is an HA mechanism for controlling the number of VMs that can be powered on in a cluster. It is used to ensure that sufficient resources exist to fail over VMs if an unplanned downtime event occurs. After admission control has been configured, any attempt to power on a VM that violates the established policy setting is prevented. The admission control policy can be based on CPU and memory reservations, dedicated failover hosts, or slot size calculation. Admission control is applied as attempts are made to power on VMs, revert VMs to powered-on snapshots, increase the reservations of running VMs, and migrate VMs into the cluster. HA depends on vCenter Server for Admission Control, but if the vCenter Server goes offline, high availability continues to function, thanks to the FDM agents on the ESXi Hosts.

If admission control is enabled, HA decides whether to allow a VM to power on based on the available resources in the cluster. Resources in the cluster are diminished when an unplanned downtime event occurs and the remaining resources might be insufficient to power on all VMs. Although there are several ways to reserve spare capacity in a cluster, the preferred setting for the admission control policy is to reserve a specific percentage of CPU and memory resources. When this setting is chosen, VMs can power on successfully if sufficient unreserved CPU and memory resources exist to support VM overhead and any reservations on the VM. For example, if 25% CPU is reserved for HA spare capacity, only 75% of the cluster resources can actually be used for currently running VMs.

An alternative to reserving resources is to set the admission control policy to specify the number of host failures the cluster tolerates. This setting, and only this specific setting, instructs HA to calculate and use a slot size to determine the amount of resources to reserve. The slot size is calculated utilizing a worst-case approach that allocates a specific amount of CPU and memory resources per VM, based primarily on the currently running VMs that have the greatest CPU and memory reservation. The slot size of the VM for CPU is based on the maximum amount of the CPU reservation. The slot size for memory is based on selecting the VM with the largest memory reservation and adding the maximum memory reservation of that VM plus the amount of memory overhead for that VM. The default admission control policy sets the host failures the cluster tolerates to 1.

The option to use dedicated failover hosts is pretty self-explanatory. HA sets aside host(s) resources to protect VMs in the event that another host in the cluster fails. Hosts chosen for dedicated failover do not contribute their resource to the cluster but instead just sit there idle, waiting for an HA event to occur.

Enable/Disable Advanced vSphere HA Settings

The following are VMware's advanced HA settings that can be modified in the vSphere Web Client:

- **das.isolationaddress[...]:** Sets the address to ping to determine whether a host is isolated from the network. This address is pinged only when heartbeats are not received from any other host in the cluster. If not specified, the default gateway of the management network is used. You can specify multiple isolation addresses (up to 10) for the cluster:

  ```
  das.isolationaddressX, where X=0-9.
  ```

- **das.usedefaultisolationaddress:** By default, vSphere HA uses the default gateway of the console network as an isolation address. This option specifies whether (`true`) or not (`false`) this default is used.

- **das.isolationshutdowntimeout:** Specifies the period of time the system waits for a virtual machine to shut down before powering it off. This applies only if the host's isolation response is `Shut down VM`. The default value is 300 seconds.

- **das.slotmeminmb:** Defines the maximum memory slot size. If this option is used, the slot size is the smaller of this value or the maximum memory reservation plus memory overhead of any powered-on virtual machine in the cluster.

- **das.slotcpuinmhz:** Defines the maximum CPU slot size. If this option is used, the slot size is the smaller of this value or the maximum CPU reservation of any powered-on virtual machine in the cluster.

- **das.vmmemoryminmb:** Defines the default memory resource value assigned to a virtual machine if its memory reservation is not specified or zero. This is used for the Host Failures Cluster Tolerates admission control policy. If no value is specified, the default is 0 MB.

- **das.vmcpuminmhz:** Defines the default CPU resource value assigned to a virtual machine if its CPU reservation is not specified or is zero. This is used for the Host Failures Cluster Tolerates admission control policy. If no value is specified, the default is 32 MHz.

- **das.iostatsinterval:** Changes the default I/O stats interval for VM monitoring sensitivity. The default is 120 (seconds), but it can be set to any value greater than or equal to 0. Setting to 0 disables the check.

- **das.ignoreinsufficienthbdatastore:** Disables configuration issues created if the host does not have sufficient heartbeat datastores for vSphere HA. The default value is `false`.

- **das.heartbeatdsperhost:** Changes the number of heartbeat datastores required. Valid values can range from 2 to 5, and the default is 2.

- **fdm.isolationpolicydelaysec:** Specifies the number of seconds the system waits before executing the isolation policy once it is determined that a host is isolated. The minimum value is 30.

- **das.respectvmvmantiaffinityrules:** Determines whether vSphere HA enforces VM-VM anti-affinity rules. The default value is `false`, which means the rules are not enforced. Can also be set to `true` to have rules enforced (even if vSphere DRS is not enabled). In this case, vSphere HA does not fail over a virtual machine if doing so violates a rule, but it issues an event reporting there are insufficient resources to perform the failover.

- **das.maxresets:** Specifies the maximum number of reset attempts made by VMCP. If a reset operation on a virtual machine affected by an APD situation fails, VMCP retries the reset this many times before giving up.

- **das.maxterminates:** Specifies the maximum number of retries made by VMCP for virtual machine termination.

- **das.terminateretryintervalsec:** Specifies the number of seconds the system waits before it retries a terminate attempt after VMCP fails to terminate a virtual machine.

- **das.config.fdm.reportfailoverfailevent:** When set to 1, enables generation of a detailed per-VM event when an attempt by vSphere HA to restart a virtual machine is unsuccessful. The default value is 0.

- **vpxd.das.completemetadataupdateintervalsec:** Specifies the period of time (in seconds) after a VM-Host affinity rule is set during which vSphere HA can restart a VM in a DRS-disabled cluster, overriding the rule. The default value is 300 seconds.

- **das.config.fdm.memreservationmb:** By default, vSphere HA agents run with a configured memory limit of 250 MB. A host might not allow this reservation if it runs out of reservable capacity. You can use this advanced option to lower the memory limit to avoid this issue. Only integers 100 and greater can be specified. To prevent problems during master agent elections in a large cluster (containing 6,000 to 8,000 VMs), you should raise this limit to 325 MB.

Configure Different Heartbeat Datastores for an HA Cluster

In vSphere 5, VMware added an additional measure of resiliency for HA: the datastore heartbeat. If the master does not receive a network heartbeat response from a specific slave, it checks for a datastore heartbeat. VMFS datastores contain a heartbeat region, where each host accessing the datastore frequently updates a timestamp to indicate whether the host is healthy. On NFS datastores, HA adds a file for each host named `host-<X>-hb`, which is used for similar purposes. If needed, the master can check the timestamps on the designated HA heartbeat datastores. If no network heartbeats, no ping responses, and no datastore heartbeats are detected for a given slave node, then it is considered to have failed. If datastore heartbeats are received from a slave host, but no network heartbeats or ping responses are received, the host is considered to be isolated from the network. If a particular host is not receiving heartbeats or election traffic from any other host, it pings its set of isolation addresses. If at least one isolation address responds, the host is not isolated from the network.

Figure 15-3 shows an error message stating that there needs to be more than one heartbeat datastore for the HA cluster. You can use the vSphere Web Client to configure an additional shared datastore. You need a minimum of two shared datastores that can be accessed by every node in the cluster.

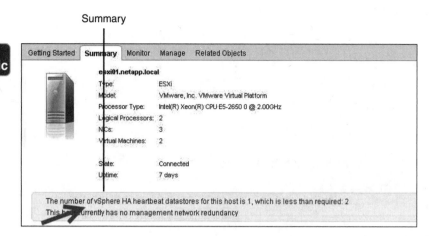

Summary

Getting Started | Summary | Monitor | Manage | Related Objects

esxi01.netapp.local

Type:	ESXi
Model:	VMware, Inc. VMware Virtual Platform
Processor Type:	Intel(R) Xeon(R) CPU E5-2650 0 @ 2.00GHz
Logical Processors:	2
NICs:	3
Virtual Machines:	2
State:	Connected
Uptime:	7 days

The number of vSphere HA heartbeat datastores for this host is 1, which is less than required: 2
This host currently has no management network redundancy

Figure 15-3   One HA Heartbeat Datastore but Should Be More Than One

Apply Virtual Machine Monitoring for a Cluster

Virtual machine monitoring is an HA cluster feature that can restart VMs if their VMware Tools heartbeats are not received within a set time. VMware Tools must be running in the guest operating system of the virtual machine in order for the VM to send regular heartbeats to the HA cluster. If the guest OS blue screens or panics, it is no longer sending heartbeats to HA. If HA encounters a situation in which a virtual machine's guest OS is no longer running, the VM is rebooted in an attempt to bring the virtual machine back online.

However, there are situations in which a virtual machine's guest OS is still functioning but has stopped sending heartbeats to HA. There is an additional HA check on the VM's guest operating system by the VM monitoring service, which can also monitor a virtual machine's I/O activity. If no heartbeats of the guest OS are received, the next check is to determine whether there is any disk or network activity in the I/O stats interval, which is 120 seconds by default. The I/O stats interval is an advanced option variable das.iostatsinterval that is set at the cluster level. By default, virtual machine monitoring is disabled when you create the cluster. Figure 15-4 shows VM monitoring being enabled in the vSphere Web Client.

Disabled

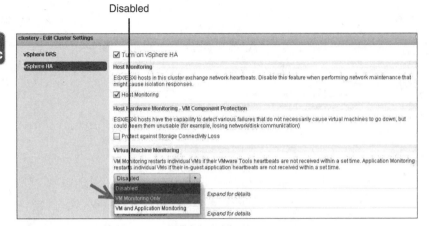

Figure 15-4   Virtual Machine Monitoring

Configure Virtual Machine Component Protection (VMCP) Settings

Virtual Machine Component Protection (VMCP) is a vSphere high availability feature that can react to permanent device loss (PDL) and all path down (APD) conditions. The response to these conditions from VMCP is based on configuration settings you make using the vSphere Web Client. You first need to enable VMCP in the HA cluster. Then you can modify the cluster's behavior when PDL and APD events occur. Figure 15-5 shows the VMCP options that can be modified using the vSphere Web Client.

Permanent Device Loss (PDL)

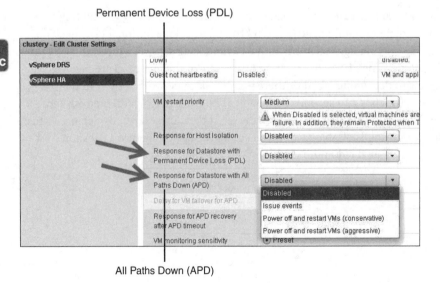

All Paths Down (APD)

Figure 15-5   VMCP Settings

Implement vSphere HA on a Virtual SAN Cluster

VMware's vSphere HA is fully supported on a Virtual SAN cluster. VSAN can support up to 64 nodes with 200 VMs per host. The ESXi Host HA agents communicate over the VSAN network. The HA communication between ESXi Host agents needs to be on the same network as the VSAN communication to avoid conflicts if there is a network partition.

Explain How vSphere HA Communicates with Distributed Resource Scheduler and Distributed Power Management

VMware's vSphere high availability (HA) integrates with both Distributed Resource Scheduler (DRS) and Distributed Power Management (DPM). HA provides failover protection, and DRS provides load balancing.

When a high availability event occurs, HA has one mission: to restart the virtual machines on the surviving nodes in the cluster. Only after all VMs have been restarted does DRS come in and load balance the cluster if necessary. The combination of both HA and DRS forms a powerful nucleus in a vSphere cluster and is recommended in most implementations.

Distributed Power Management (DPM) is used to save on power and cooling in environments that have blocks of idle time. If an HA cluster's utilization goes below a defined DPM threshold, vSphere uses the DRS algorithm to determine whether an ESXi Host should be put into standby mode. Once DRS has determined that an ESXi Host needs to be put into standby mode, it needs to migrate the powered-on VMs to other ESXi Hosts in the HA cluster. If HA is using strict admission control, which is the default, DPM needs to maintain the necessary level of powered-on capacity of resources to meet the configured HA failover capacity. In addition, HA places a constraint to prevent DPM from powering down too many ESXi Hosts if doing so would violate the admission control policy of the HA cluster.

The main prerequisites for DPM are for DRS to be enabled and for each ESXi Host to contain a network adapter capable of powering on the host. DPM appears as a subset feature within the settings of DRS. DRS must be enabled before DPM can be enabled. This implies that all requirements of DRS, such as shared storage and vMotion, are also requirements of DPM. DPM also needs the ability to wake a host from standby mode, which means it needs the ability to send a network command to the host to power on. For this feature, DPM requires iLO, IPMI, or a Wake On LAN network adapter to be present in each host of the cluster. DPM must be supplied with the proper credentials to access the interface and power on the host.

Objective 9.2—Configure Advanced vSphere DRS Features

Distributed Resource Scheduler (DRS) is a vSphere feature that provides automatic balancing of CPU and memory workloads across a cluster of ESXi Hosts. It achieves this balancing by intelligently placing VMs on hosts as they are powered on and by migrating running VMs to less-used hosts in the cluster using vMotion. The key requirements for DRS are a proper license for vSphere Enterprise Edition or higher and a properly configured vMotion network. For optimal workload balancing, each ESXi Host and each VM should meet vMotion requirements as well. DRS also provides cluster-based resource pools, allowing CPU and memory resources to be reserved for groups of VMs.

Configure VM-Host Affinity/Anti-affinity Rules

Rules can be used in DRS to control the affinity of virtual machines. By default, no rules exist, and DRS is free to put VMs on any active host in the cluster. You can create an affinity rule to force DRS to keep a set of VMs on the same host. In this case, if DRS decides to place one VM on a specific host, it places all the VMs in the rule on the same host. If you manually migrate one of the VMs to a different host, DRS is likely to migrate it back, but it could migrate the remaining VMs in the rule to the other host. You can also create an anti-affinity rule to force DRS to separate a set of VMs onto different hosts.

Before you can create a VM-Host affinity or anti-affinity rule, you need to create a VM group and a Host group. This can be done using the vSphere Web Client.

To configure a VM/Host group, follow these steps:

Step 1.   Right-click the cluster and select **Settings**.

Step 2.   Select the **Manage** tab, followed by **Settings**.

Step 3.   Under Settings select **VM/Host Groups**.

Step 4.   Click the **Add** button to open the Create VM/Host Group window.

Step 5.   Supply a name for the rule.

Step 6.   In the Type drop-down box, select either **VM Group** or **Host Group**.

Step 7.   Click the **Add** button to open the VM/Host Group Member window.

Step 8.   Check the VMs or Hosts to use and then click **OK**.

Figure 15-6 shows both a VM group and a Host group added.

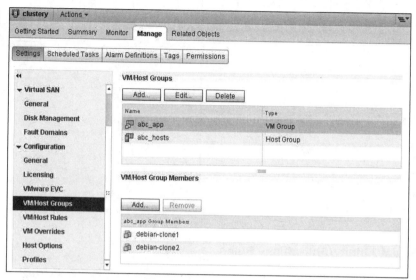

Figure 15-6   VM/Host Groups

Once you have a VM group and a Host group, you can create a VM-Host affinity or anti-affinity rule, as shown in Figure 15-7.

To configure a VM-Host affinity rule, follow these steps:

Step 1.   Right-click the cluster and select **Settings**.

Step 2.   Select the **Manage** tab, followed by **Settings**.

Step 3.   Under Settings select **VM/Host Rules**.

Step 4.   Click the **Add** button to open the Create VM/Host Rule window.

Step 5.   Supply a name for the rule.

Step 6.   In the Type drop-down box select **Virtual Machines to Hosts**.

Step 7.   In the VM Group drop-down box select **VM Group**.

Step 8.   Select **Must Run on Hosts in Group** from the drop-down box.

Step 9.   In the Host Group drop-down box select **Host Group**.

Step 10.   Click **OK**.

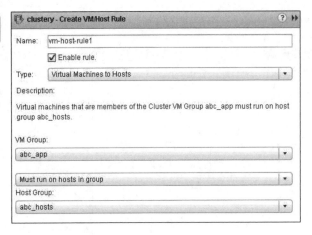

Figure 15-7   Create VM/Host Affinity/Anti-affinity Rule

Configure VM-VM Affinity/Anti-affinity Rules

A VM-VM affinity/anti-affinity rule can be created to determine whether a virtual machine should or should not run on the same host as another VM or VMs. When an affinity or anti-affinity rule is created, the Distributed Resource Scheduler (DRS) is the algorithm that enforces the rule. You should use an affinity rule when you have two or more VMs that you want to always run on the same ESXi Host. This might be needed for performance reasons. You should use an anti-affinity rule when you have two or more hosts that you do not want to run on the same ESXi Host. If two VM-VM affinity rules conflict with each other, the older one takes precedence over the newer rule. In addition, DRS gives higher precedence to anti-affinity rules. As an example of an anti-affinity rule, you might want to use a VM-VM anti-affinity rule for cached web servers. In Figure 15-8 you can see a VM-VM affinity rule being configured.

To configure a VM-VM affinity rule, follow these steps:

Step 1.   Right-click the cluster and select **Settings**.

Step 2.   Select the **Manage** tab, followed by **Settings**.

Step 3.   Under Settings select **VM/Host Rules**.

Step 4.   Click the **Add** button to open the Create VM/Host Rule window.

Step 5.   Supply a name for the rule.

Step 6.   In the Type drop-down box select **Keep VMs Together**.

Step 7.   Click the **Add** button to open the Add Rule Member window.

Step 8.   Check the VMs to use and then click **OK**.

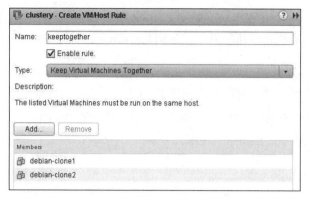

Figure 15-8   Configure VM/Host Affinity Rule

Add/Remove Host DRS Group

To add a Host DRS group, follow these steps:

Step 1.   Right-click the cluster and select **Settings**.

Step 2.   Select the **Manage** tab, followed by **Settings**.

Step 3.   Under Settings select **VM/Host Groups**.

Step 4.   Click the **Add** button to open the Create VM/Host Group window.

Step 5.   Supply a name for the rule.

Step 6.   In the Type drop-down box select **Host Group**.

Step 7.   Click the **Add** button to open the VM/Host Group Member window.

Step 8.   Check the hosts to use and then click **OK**.

To remove a Host DRS group, follow these steps:

Step 1.   Right-click the cluster and select **Settings**.

Step 2.   Select the **Manage** tab, followed by **Settings**.

Step 3.   Under Settings select **VM/Host Groups**.

Step 4.   Highlight **Host Group** and then click the **Delete** button.

Add/Remove Virtual Machine DRS Group

To add a VM/Host group, follow these steps:

Step 1.   Right-click the cluster and select **Settings**.

Step 2.   Select the **Manage** tab, followed by **Settings**.

Step 3.   Under Settings select **VM/Host Groups**.

Step 4.   Click the **Add** button to open the Create VM/Host Group window.

Step 5.   Supply a name for the rule.

Step 6.   In the Type drop-down box select **VM Group**.

Step 7.   Click the **Add** button to open the VM/Host Group Member window.

Step 8.   Check the VMs to use and then click **OK**.

To remove a VM/Host Group, follow these steps:

Step 1.   Right-click the cluster and select **Settings**.

Step 2.   Select the **Manage** tab, followed by **Settings**.

Step 3.   Under Settings select **VM/Host Groups**.

Step 4.   Highlight **VM Group** and then click the **Delete** button.

Enable/Disable Distributed Resource Scheduler (DRS) Affinity Rules

In the previous section, you learned how to configure a DRS affinity rule. In Figure 15-9 you can view the enabled DRS affinity rule. If you want to disable the DRS affinity rule, highlight the DRS rule and then select **Edit**, uncheck the box next to **Enabled Rule**, and click **OK**.

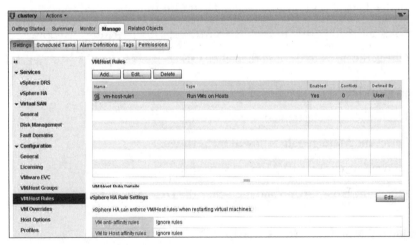

Figure 15-9   Enable/Disable DRS Affinity Rule

Configure the Proper Distributed Resource Scheduler (DRS) Automation Level Based on a Set of Business Requirements

One of the main configuration features of Distributed Resource Scheduler (DRS) is the DRS automation level, which can be set to Manual, Partially Automated, or Fully Automated. When it is set to Manual, DRS only makes recommendations, which then require manual approval to actually apply the placements or migrations. When set to Fully Automated, DRS automatically performs some placements and migrations that it recommends, dependent on a configured threshold setting. When set to Partially Automated, DRS automatically performs initial placements but only makes recommendations for migrations.

When set to Fully Automated, DRS only applies recommendations that are allowed based on the migration threshold. This setting controls how aggressively recommendations are applied. Recommendations are priority based, from priority levels 1 to 5. The most aggressive setting results in applying all recommendations. The default threshold applies only priority 1 to 3 recommendations. If the threshold is set to Conservative, it applies only priority 1 recommendations, which effectively means it applies only the DRS rules and does not balance based on workload. Each priority maps to an allowed level of deviation between the workload levels of the hosts in the cluster.

You can set the DRS automation level by highlighting the cluster, clicking the **Manage** tab, selecting the **Settings** tab, and selecting **vSphere DRS**. Then you click the **Edit** button to open the Edit Cluster Settings window, as shown in Figure 5-10.

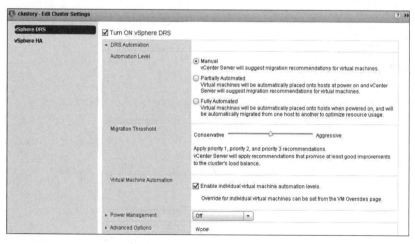

Figure 15-10   Edit Cluster Settings

Explain How DRS Affinity Rules Affect Virtual Machine Placement

DRS affinity rules affect virtual machine placement. For example, say that you have a DRS/HA cluster that contains 16 ESXi Hosts running on blade servers in two separate chassis. A DRS rule is implemented for a pair of Active Directory domain controller VMs, with the setting Separate Virtual Machines. You realize that it would be better to ensure that the domain controllers run not just on separate blades but in separate chassis. You also want to ensure that when you place all hosts in one chassis into maintenance mode, you can easily, temporarily allow both domain controllers to run in the same chassis.

To meet this requirement, you can create two Host DRS groups—one for each chassis—containing the corresponding ESXi Hosts. Create two VM DRS groups, containing one domain controller VM each. Create a VM-Host affinity rule for one of the VM DRS groups, specifying that it should run the first host DRS group, as shown in Figure 15-11. Note the setting Should Run on Hosts in Group, which satisfies the requirement of temporarily allowing both domain controllers to run on the same chassis during a maintenance window. Likewise, create a second rule for the other VM DRS group, specifying that it should run in the other Host DRS group.

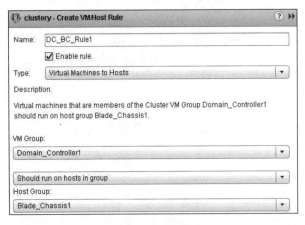

Figure 15-11   VM-Host Affinity Rule

Summary

You have now read the chapter covering exam topics related to configuring and administering vSphere availability solutions. You should now use information in the following sections to complete your preparation for exam Objectives 9.1 and 9.2.

Exam Preparation Tasks

Review All the Key Topics

Table 15-2 provides a reference to each of the key topics identified in this chapter. Take a few moments to review each of these specific items.

Table 15-2 Key Topics for Chapter 15

Key Topic Element	Description	Pages
Figure 15-1	Modifying an HA advanced cluster setting	574
Figure 15-2	HA network heartbeat alarm messages	575
List	Advanced HA settings	576
Figure 15-3	One HA heartbeat datastore but should be more than one	579
Figure 15-4	Virtual machine monitoring	580
Figure 15-5	VMCP settings	580
Figure 15-6	VM/Host groups	583
Figure 15-7	Create VM/Host affinity/anti-affinity rule	584
Figure 15-8	Configure VM/Host affinity rule	585
Figure 15-9	Enable/disable DRS affinity rule	586
Figure 15-10	Edit cluster settings	587
Figure 15-11	VM/host affinity rule	588

Complete the Tables and Lists from Memory

Print a copy of Appendix B, "Memory Tables" (found on the CD), or at least the section for this chapter, and complete the tables and lists from memory. Appendix C, "Memory Tables Answer Key," also on the CD, includes completed tables and lists to check your work.

Definitions of Key Terms

Define the following key terms from this chapter and check your answers in the glossary.

high availability (HA), fault domain manager (FDM), Virtual Machine Component Protection (VMCP), all paths down (APD), permanent device loss (PDL), Distributed Power Management (DPM), Distributed Resource Scheduler (DRS)

Answer Review Questions

The answers to these review questions can be found in Appendix A.

1. Which of the following is a correct statement?

   a. VMware's vSphere HA is fully supported on a Virtual SAN cluster.

   b. The ESXi Host HA agents communicate over the management network.

   c. VSAN can support up to 24 nodes.

   d. VMware's vSphere HA is not fully supported on a Virtual SAN cluster.

2. Which statement is correct? (Choose two.)

   a. When a high availability event occurs, vMotion restarts the VMs, while DRS load balances the virtual machines across the cluster.

   b. When a high availability event occurs, vMotion has one mission: to restart the virtual machines on the surviving nodes in the cluster.

   c. Powered-on virtual machines need to be migrated to other ESXi Hosts in the HA cluster after the host has been put into standby mode.

   d. DPM needs the ability to wake a host from standby mode, which means it needs the ability to send a network command to the host to power on.

3. Which of the following is not a DRS automation level?

   a. Partially Automated

   b. Fully Automated

   c. Manual

   d. VM Override

4. Which of the following statements is incorrect?

   a. You can create an anti-affinity rule to force DRS to keep VMs on the same host.

   b. Rules can be used in DRS to control the affinity of virtual machines.

   c. By default, no rules exist, and DRS is free to put VMs on any active host in the cluster.

   d. Before you can create a VM-Host affinity rule or a VM-Host anti-affinity rule, you need to create a VM group and a Host group.

5. Which option summarizes the minimum steps that can be taken to configure DRS Automation to automatically place and migrate VMs as necessary to enforce DRS rules but not to balance the workload?

   a. Edit the cluster settings, set the DRS automation level to **Fully Automated**, and move the **Migration Threshold** slider to the extreme left (conservative) setting.

   b. Edit the cluster settings, set the DRS automation level to **Fully Automated**, and move the **Migration Threshold** slider to the extreme right (aggressive) setting.

   c. Edit the cluster settings, set the DRS automation level to **Partially Automated**, and move the **Migration Threshold** slider to the extreme left (conservative) setting.

   d. Edit the cluster settings, set the DRS automation level to **Partially Automated**, and move the **Migration Threshold** slider to the slider to the extreme right (Aggressive) setting.

This chapter covers the following objectives:

- **Objective 10.1—Configure Advanced vSphere Virtual Machine Settings**
  - Determine how using a shared USB device impacts the environment
  - Configure virtual machines for vGPUs, DirectPath I/O, and SR-IOV
  - Configure virtual machines for multicore vCPUs
  - Differentiate virtual machine configuration settings
  - Interpret virtual machine configuration file (.vmx) settings
  - Enable/disable advanced virtual machine settings

- **Objective 10.2: Create and Manage a Multi-site Content Library**
  - Publish a content catalog
  - Subscribe to a published catalog
  - Determine which privileges are required to globally manage a content catalog
  - Compare the functionality of automatic sync and on-demand sync
  - Configure a content library to work across sites
  - Configure content library authentication
  - Set/configure content library roles
  - Add/remove content libraries

- **Objective 10.3: Configure and Maintain a vCloud Air Connection**
  - Create a VPN connection between vCloud Air and an on-premise site
  - Deploy and migrate virtual machines with vCloud Air
  - Configure connections to vCloud Air
  - Configure replicated objects in vCloud Air Disaster Recovery Service
  - Given a scenario, determine the required settings for virtual machines deployed in vCloud Air

## CHAPTER 16

Virtual Machines

This chapter covers exam topics related to virtual machines.

"Do I Know This Already?" Quiz

The "Do I Know This Already?" quiz allows you to assess whether you should study this entire chapter or move quickly to the "Exam Preparation Tasks" section. Regardless, the authors recommend that you read the entire chapter at least once. Table 16-1 outlines the major headings in this chapter and the corresponding "Do I Know This Already?" quiz questions. You can find the answers in Appendix A, "Answers to the 'Do I Know This Already?' Quizzes and Review Questions."

Table 16-1 "Do I Know This Already?" Foundation Topics Section-to-Question Mapping

Foundation Topics Section	Questions Covered in This Section
Differentiate Virtual Machine Configuration Settings	1
Interpret Virtual Machine Configuration File (.vmx) Settings	2
Configure Virtual Machines for vGPUs, DirectPath I/O, and SR-IOV	3
Differentiate Virtual Machine Configuration Settings	4
Create and Manage a Multi-site Content Library	5
Configure Content Library to Work Across Sites	6
Create and Manage a Multi-site Content Library	7
Configure vCenter Server Connection to vCloud Air	8
Configure Replicated Objects in vCloud Air Disaster Recovery Service	9
Configure vCenter Server Connection to vCloud Air	10

1. Which of the following is not a virtual machine configuration setting?

    a. `sched.mem.pshare.salt`

    b. `Mem.ShareForceSalting`

    c. `devices.hotplug`

    d. `log.rotateSize`

2. In the vSphere Web Client, a virtual machine's compatibility is displayed as `ESXi 5.5 and later (VM version 10)`. Which setting should you expect to find in the VMX file?

    a. `virtualHW.version = "10"`

    b. `virtualHW.version = "5.5"`

    c. `virtualHW.compatibility = "5.5"`

    d. `virtualHW.compatibility = "10"`

3. Which of the following actions would you take to support a virtual machine with extremely high network demand?

    a. Configure the `sched.mem.maxmemctl` parameter.

    b. Configure NPIV.

    c. Set the virtual network adapter type to `passthrough`.

    d. Configure Direct Path I/O.

4. Which of the following summarizes the steps you could use to configure a powered off virtual machine advanced configuration parameter through the vSphere Web Client?

    a. On the VM Options tab click **Advanced Configuration Parameters**. Click **Add Row** and provide the parameter name and value.

    b. Right-click the virtual machine, choose **Edit Settings**, click **Advanced**, and enter the parameter name and value.

    c. Right-click the virtual machine, select **Configuration Parameters** and click **Advanced**. Click **Add Row** and provide the parameter name and value.

    d. On the **VM Options** tab, select **Advanced**. Click **Edit Configuration**. Click **Add Row** and provide the parameter name and value.

5. Which of the following is not involved in the sequence of events associated with synchronizing content libraries when the content is changed in the publisher's content library?

    a. The data in the `lib.json` files from the publisher and subscriber are compared.

    b. vCSP is used to check for updates and request data transfer.

    c. SCP is used to transfer the data.

    d. Version numbers are updated.

6. Which of the following steps should be included to subscribe to a published library? (Choose three.)

    a. Click **Create a new library**.

    b. Select **Enable Subscription**.

    c. Select **Enable authentication**.

    d. Select **Subscribed Content Library**.

    e. Select **Synchronize Library**.

7. Which of the following is *not* a feature of the content library?

    a. Backed by multiple datastores

    b. Synchronization time and frequency can be configured through the API

    c. Synchronize an entire content library or an individual item at any time through the Web Client

    d. Can use an NFS datastore

8. Which of the following is true concerning vCloud Air and vSphere 6.0?

    a. The vCloud Connector can be used to connect vCenter Server with vCloud Air.

    b. A vCloud Air plug-in is available for the vSphere Web Client.

    c. A vCloud Connector plug-in is available for the vSphere Web Client.

    d. A vCenter Server can connect directly to vCloud Air, without using the vCloud Air plug-in or the vCloud Connector.

9. Which of the following summarizes how vCloud Air can be used as a recovery site during a disaster that impacts a vSphere 6 environment?

   a. Implement only vCloud Air Disaster Recovery Service.

   b. Implement vCloud Air Disaster Recovery Service and VMware vCenter Site Recovery Manager.

   c. Implement vCloud Air Disaster Recovery Service, vSphere Replication, and VMware vCenter Site Recovery Manager.

   d. Implement vCloud Air Disaster Recovery Service and vSphere Replication.

10. For a vCloud Connector server named `vccs.company.com`, what is the correct URL for the vCloud Connector Server Web Admin Console?

   a. `https://vccs.company.com:8283`

   b. `https://vccs.company.com:5480`

   c. `https://vccs.company.com/admin`

   d. `http://vccs.company.com:8283/admin`

Foundation Topics

Objective 10.1—Configure Advanced vSphere Virtual Machine Settings

The following sections provide details on configuring advanced virtual machine settings and related topics, such as the virtual machine configuration file and DirectPath I/O.

Determine How Using a Shared USB Device Impacts the Environment

In vSphere 6.0, virtual machines can access USB devices that are attached to an ESXi Host, attached to a client computer, or attached to a network device. ESXi Host–attached USB devices require the use of USB passthrough technology. Client-attached USB devices require the use of the virtual machine console and VMware Tools. Network-attached USB devices require the use of products such as Digi's AnywhereUSB, which connects a USB device to a guest operating system via the network.

USB passthrough technology supports adding ESXi Host–attached USB devices to virtual machines. The USB devices, such as security dongles and storage devices, must reside on the same ESXi Host as the virtual machines. Each USB device can be connected to only a single running virtual machine. If you remove the active connection of a USB device from a virtual machine, the device becomes available for connecting to other virtual machines running on the same ESXi Host. Migrations using vMotion may not be successful for virtual machines with attached USB devices. The compatibility check that is automatically run by the migration wizard may detect and report unsupported USB devices, such as:

```
Currently connected device 'USB 1' uses backing 'path:1/7/1', which
    is not accessible
```

To enable vMotion for virtual machines with host-attached USB devices, you should select `support vMotion while device is connected` as you attach each device to the virtual machine. If one or more devices are not enabled for vMotion, the migration will fail. If this occurs, remove all USB devices from the virtual machine, save the settings, re-add the USB devices while selecting the vMotion support option, and save the settings again.

USB passthrough technology uses a USB arbitrator, a USB controller, and USB devices. The arbitrator is enabled by default on ESXi Hosts. It scans the host for new USB devices, routes traffic to the correct virtual machines, and prevents access from other virtual machines. The ESXi Host, which manages the physical USB controllers, can present one or more (up to 8) virtual USB controllers to each virtual machine. The USB arbitrator can monitor up to 15 physical USB controllers. Devices that are connected to any additional physical USB controllers are not available for virtual machine use. A virtual controller must be presented to a virtual machine before a USB device can be added to the virtual machine. A maximum of 20 USB devices can be added to a virtual machine.

With ESXi 6 and virtual machine hardware version 11, you can add one virtual xHCI controller, one virtual EHCI controller, and one virtual UHCI controller per virtual machine. Each of these virtual controllers supports USB 2.0 and 1.1. In addition, the virtual xHCI controller supports USB 3.0. To add a virtual USB controller to a virtual machine, edit the virtual machine settings, add a new hardware device, select the USB Controller option, and set the controller type.

USB passthrough technology supports vMotion and vSphere DRS but does not support vSphere Distributed Power Management (DPM) or vSphere fault tolerance (FT). Following a vMotion migration, the virtual machine remains connected with the USB device on the original host, but it disconnects if the virtual machine is suspended or powered off. USB passthrough technology provides the Autoconnect feature, which allows a virtual machine to automatically reconnect to a device in cases such as virtual machine power cycle and device reconnect.

To avoid data loss involving virtual machines and ESXi Host–attached USB devices, you should follow three VMware recommendations:

- Remove USB devices from a virtual machine prior to hot-adding memory, CPU, or PCI devices.

- Ensure that USB data transfer is not in process prior to suspending a virtual machine.

- Remove USB devices from virtual machines prior to changing the state of an ESXi Host USB arbitrator.

Hot-adding and removing USB CD/DVD-ROM devices is not supported because these devices are treated as SCSI devices.

Configure Virtual Machines for vGPUs, DirectPath I/O, and SR-IOV

DirectPath I/O allows a virtual machine to directly access a physical PCI device on a host that provides an I/O memory management unit (I/O MMU). This feature remaps direct memory access (DMA) and device interrupts. This allows the virtual machine to bypass the VMkernel and gain direct access to the device, thus reducing

CPU demand by the VMkernel. The main use case is for situations involving extremely high network demand. The device must be dedicated to the virtual machine.

The following features are not available for virtual machines configured for DirectPath I/O unless they reside on Cisco Unified Computing Systems (UCS) using Cisco Virtual Machine Fabric Extender (VM-FEX) distributed switches:

- Hot-adding and hot-removing virtual devices
- Suspend and resume
- Record and replay
- Fault tolerance
- High availability
- vMotion
- Snapshots

Record and replay is not supported with DirectPath I/O, even when using UCS and VM-FEX

To configure DirectPath I/O for a virtual machine, first configure a compatible device for passthrough on the ESXi Host as shown in the following steps, using the vSphere Client:.

Step 1.   Select the ESXi Host in the inventory

Step 2.   On the Configuration tab, select **Advanced Settings** under **Hardware**.

Step 3.   Select **Configure Passthrough**, and a list of all available passthrough devices appears. Click **Edit**.

Step 4.   Select the devices to be configured for passthrough and click **OK**.

Step 5.   Reboot the host so the device can complete its configuration.

Next, configure the PCI device on a virtual machine via the vSphere Web Client:

Step 1.   Select the virtual machine in the inventory.

Step 2.   On the Manage tab, select **Settings** > **VM Hardware** > **Edit**.

Step 3.   Select **Memory** > **Limit** and then select **Unlimited**.

Step 4.   In the New Device drop-down menu, select **PCI Device** and click **Add**.

Step 5.   In the New PCI Device drop-down menu, select the previously selected passthrough device and click **OK**.

Step 6.   Power on the virtual machine.

Do not confuse DirectPath I/O with SR-IOV. SR-IOV provides similar benefits to DirectPath I/O but allows multiple virtual machines to directly access a single physical device. The main use case for SR-IOV is for situations involving high network demand, where you do not wish to dedicate the network adapter to a single virtual machine.

To configure SR-IOV, first configure the physical adapter on the ESXi Host and then configure the virtual machine, as follows:

Step 1. In the vSphere Web Client, select the ESXi Host and click the **Manage** tab.

Step 2. Click **Networking** > **Physical Adapters**. Examine the adapters and determine which adapters support SR-IOV.

Step 3. Select an adapter that supports SR-IOV and click **Edit Adapter Settings**.

Step 4. In the **SR-IOV** section, set **Status** to `Enabled`.

Step 5. Enter the number of virtual functions you want to configure for the adapter and click **OK**.

Step 6. Restart the ESXi Host.

Step 7. Select the virtual machine and select the **Manage** tab.

Step 8. Select **Settings** > **VM Hardware**.

Step 9. Click **Edit** > **Virtual Hardware**.

Step 10. In the New Device drop-down menu, select **Network** and then click **Add**.

Step 11. Expand the New Network section and select a port group for extracting network properties.

Step 12. In the Adapter Type drop-down menu, select **SR-IOV passthrough**.

Step 13. In the Physical Function drop-down, select the physical adapter that was configured previously.

Step 14. To allow changes in MTU, select from the Guest OS MTU Change drop-down menu.

Step 15. Expand the Memory section and select **Reserve All Guest Memory (All Locked)** and click **OK**.

Step 16. Power on the virtual machine.

When using DirectPath I/O or SR-IOV, device drivers for the physical PCI device must be installed directly in the virtual machine guest operating system.

Various approaches are available for configuring 3D rendering in virtual machines, some of which involve the use of a graphics processing unit (GPU) in the ESXi Host hardware. Virtual machines can use GPUs in various ways. For example, you can dedicate a GPU to a single virtual machine, share a GPU with a set of virtual machines, or implement virtual GPUs (vGPUs). Some GPU hardware may provide the ability to configure a set of vGPUs that can be accessed by a set of virtual machines, where each virtual machine is treated as if it has its own GPU. This requires the installation of special hardware and VMware Information Bundles (VIBs). For example, to implement NVIDIA vGPUs, you should install the NVIDIA VIBs on the ESXi Hosts using the `esxcli software vib install` command as instructed in VMware KB 2033434. You should configure the virtual machine virtual hardware to be compatible with ESXi 6.0, add a shared PCI device, select type NVIDIA GRID vGPU, and reserve all memory, as shown in Figure 16-1.

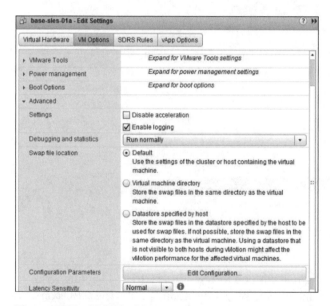

Figure 16-1   NVIDIA vGPU

To enable a virtual machine to use a dedicated GPU, you must configure a GPU for passthrough on the ESXi Host. Then edit the virtual machine settings by adding the new GPU PCI device that was previously configured for passthrough. Upon selecting the GPU, click the option **Reserve All Memory**; in order for the virtual machine to boot, it must have all its memory reserved. To allow 3D rendering in a virtual machine without implementing GPUs, select the **Enable 3D Support** option in the virtual machine settings and select **Software** from the Select a 3D Renderer drop-down.

Configure Virtual Machines for Multicore vCPUs

Virtual machines provide multicore virtual CPU functionality. Each virtual machine provides settings for the number of virtual CPU sockets and the number of virtual cores per virtual socket. This feature can be used to provide multiple cores while complying with end user license agreements that limit the number of sockets that can be used by the guest operating systems or application software. To configure multicore vCPUs for a virtual machine, edit the virtual machine settings, select the desired number of sockets from the CPU drop-down, and select the number of cores per socket, as shown in Figure 16-2. The selectable values for the number of sockets and cores per socket are automatically controlled by vSphere based on many factors, such as the guest operating system type and version. In this example, the number of sockets is set to 2, and the cores per socket may be set to 1 or 2.

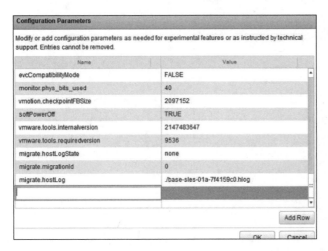

Figure 16-2 Multicore vCPUs

A virtual machine can be configured with up to 128 virtual CPUs. The number of virtual CPUs per virtual machine cannot exceed the number of logical CPUs on the ESXi Host. The number of logical CPUs on the ESXi Host is dependent on the number of physical CPU sockets and the use of hyperthreading. The number of CPU cores on an ESXi Host is equal to the number of hardware CPU sockets times the cores per socket. If hyperthreading is used, the number of logical CPUs is equal to the number of cores per host times two. Otherwise, the number of logical CPUs equals the number of CPU cores. For example, an ESXi Host with 4 sockets, 8 cores per socket, and hyperthreading has 64 logical CPUs. In this example, the virtual machines cannot be configured with more than 64 virtual CPUs.

More details related to configuring virtual machines for multicore CPU and virtual NUMA are provided in this chapter in the next section.

Differentiate Virtual Machine Configuration Settings

Virtual machines provide many advanced settings in addition to the many commonly used virtual machines settings with which you should already be familiar. You can use the vSphere Web Client to view and modify these settings. A virtual machine's guest operating system and its ESXi Host must support each setting, so not all settings are available to every virtual machine.

To view a virtual machine's options via the vSphere Web Client, right-click the virtual machine and select **Edit Settings**. Then select the **VM Options** tab, where you can view and modify the categories of options shown in Table 16-2.

Table 16-2 Virtual Machine Option Categories

Category	Description
General Options	Common virtual machine attributes such as name, location, working folder, and guest operating system.
VMware Remote Console Options	Settings, such as locking behavior, that control multiple simultaneous connections to the virtual machine's remote console.
VMware Tools	Settings that impact virtual machine management via VMware Tools, such as time synchronization, automatic upgrade, and scripts.
Power Management	Virtual machine behavior for suspend operations and wake on LAN.
Boot Options	Virtual machine boot options, such as pre-boot delay and forced entry into BIOS.
Advanced	Advanced virtual machine options, as described immediately following this table.
Fibre Channel NPIV	Options for sharing a single physical Fibre Channel HBA port among multiple virtual ports, each with unique identifiers.

To view and modify advanced options, via the vSphere Web Client, right-click the virtual machine and select **Edit Settings**. Then click the **VM Options** tab and select **Advanced**, as shown in Figure 16-3.

Figure 16-3 Virtual Machine Tools Advanced Settings

Configure any of the following settings:

- **Disable acceleration:** In some rare occasions, you may encounter an issue where installing a program in a guest operating system stalls or reports an error such as `Cannot run under a debugger`. In such cases, you may want to try to temporarily stop hardware acceleration for the virtual machine by selecting this option. After the program is installed, you should deselect this option to improve the virtual machine's performance.

- **Enable logging:** You can select this option to collect log files for troubleshooting virtual machine issues, which, by default, are stored in the same directory as the virtual machine's configuration files. Alternatively, you can deselect this option to prevent collection of these logs for purposes such as saving disk space or hardening.

- **Debugging and statistics:** You can select **Run Normally**, **Record Debugging Information**, **Record Statistics**, or **Record Statistics and Debugging Information**. Typically, you should run virtual machines normally, but you can choose to record debugging information. This option should be selected only temporarily for troubleshooting purposes because it slows down the virtual machine's performance. A typical use case is whenever you make a service request to VMware Support to troubleshoot issues such as crashes or unusual behavior. VMware Support may ask you to collect debugging information. After the collection is complete, VMware Support will ask you to generate a log bundle. Likewise, VMware Support may ask you to collect additional virtual machine statistics when tackling some performance-related issues. In this case, you should choose to record statistics.

- **Swapfile Location:** You can use this option to control where the virtual machine swapfile is located. When this option is set to **Default**, the virtual machine swapfile is stored in a default location established at the ESXi Host or cluster level. When it is set to **Always Store with the Virtual Machine**, the swapfile is stored in the same folder as the virtual machine configuration file. When it is set to **Store in the Host's Swapfile Datastore**, the swapfile is stored in a datastore designated at the host or cluster level, if designated.

- **Latency Sensitivity:** You can adjust the latency sensitivity of a virtual machine to optimize the scheduling delay for latency-sensitive applications. By default, the option is set to **Normal**. other options include **Low**, **Medium**, and **High**. Currently, **Low** and **Medium** should not be used with ESXi Hosts 6.0 and later.

- **Configuration Parameters:** You can use this option to define advanced configuration parameters that are not available elsewhere in the vSphere Web Client. These settings tend to be less frequently used than other virtual machine settings. The main use case for setting these parameters is when you are directed by VMware Support or by VMware documentation to configure a specific parameter to resolve a specific problem. By using this option, you are effectively adding advanced parameters to the virtual machine's configuration file (VMX file). To be successful, you must correctly enter the name of the configuration parameter and successfully supply an appropriate value.

The following steps explain the process for using the vSphere Web Client to configure a virtual machine's advanced configuration parameters:

Step 1.   Power off the virtual machine.

Step 2.   Right-click the virtual machine and select **Edit Settings**.

Step 3.   Click the **VM Options** tab.

Step 4.   Expand **Advanced**.

Step 5.   In the **Configuration Parameters** section, click the **Edit Configuration** button.

Step 6.   In the dialog box that appears, click **Add Row**.

Step 7.   Enter a parameter name and its value, as shown in Figure 16-4.

Step 8.   Optionally, add more rows containing parameter names and values.

Step 9.   Click **OK**.

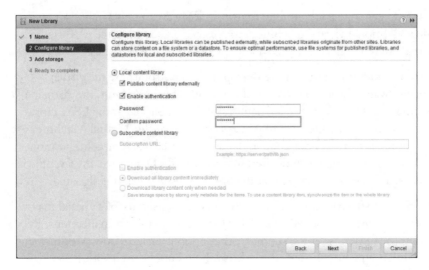

Figure 16-4   Configuration Parameters

Table 16-3 lists a few sample virtual machine advanced configuration parameters. Unless otherwise noted, for each setting to be applied, the virtual machine must power cycle.

Table 16-3   Advanced Configuration Parameters

Parameter	Description
devices.hotplug	Controls the ability to hot-add virtual devices, such as virtual network adapters, to the virtual machine. A value of FALSE disallows hot-add, and a value of TRUE enables hot-add.
log.rotateSize	Controls the maximum size to which a virtual machine's log file can grow before it is closed and a new log file is started. For example, you can set its value to 1000000 to ensure that the log is rotated when its size reaches 1,000,000 bytes.
log.keepOld	Controls the number of closed log files that are kept for the virtual machine. For example, you can set its value to 3 to ensure that no more than three closed log files are kept.

Parameter	Description
`keyboard.typematic.MinDelay`	Instructs the virtual machine console to wait a specified amount of time for a key to be held before triggering auto-repeat. For example, you can set this value to `2000000` to ensure that a key is held for two seconds before it is repeated when using the virtual machine console. The main use case for this is to prevent unintentional character repeats that are common when accessing Linux virtual machines via the virtual machine console.
`sched.mem.maxmemctl`	Controls the maximum amount of memory, in megabytes (MB), that can be reclaimed from the virtual machine via ballooning. The default value is `-1`, which indicates that the amount is unlimited. You should carefully set this value because it could lead to virtual machine swapping, which typically degrades the virtual machine's performance more than ballooning.
`sched.mem.pshare.salt`	Controls the virtual machine's ability to participate in transparent page sharing. ESXi 6.0 and recent patches to ESXi 5.x introduced the concept of salting to address recent security concerns associated with transparent page sharing (TPS). TPS is allowed only within a virtual machine (intra-VM TPS) by default. Because the ESXi Host configuration option `Mem.ShareForceSalting` is set to `2`, the `sched.mem.pshare.salt` is not present in the virtual machine configuration file, and thus the virtual machine salt value is set to a unique value. In this case, to allow TPS among a specific set of virtual machines, set `sched.mem.pshare.salt` for each virtual machine in the set to an identical value. Alternatively, to enable TPS among all virtual machines (inter-VM TPS), you can set `Mem.ShareForceSalting` to `0`. In this case, the value of `sched.mem.pshare.salt` is ignored and has no impact. Or to enable inter-VM TPS as the default but yet allow the use of `sched.mem.pshare.salt` to control the effect of TPS per virtual machine, set the value of `Mem.ShareForceSalting` to `1`. In this case, change the value of `sched.mem.pshare.salt` per virtual machine to prevent it from sharing with all virtual machines and restrict it to sharing only with those that have an identical setting.
`sched.swap.persist`	Specifies whether a virtual machine swapfile should be deleted when the VM is powered off. The default behavior is to delete the swapfile. You can set this parameter to `TRUE` to persist the swapfile during power-off.

Parameter	Description
sched.swap.dir	Specifies the location of the virtual machine swapfile. The default location is the working directory that contains the configuration file. You can change this value to another directory path that is available on the ESXi Host. For example, to place the swapfile in a folder named swapfiles in a VMFS datastore named VMFS-01, set the value to /vmfs/VMFS-01/swapfiles.
isolation.tools.copy.disable isolation.tools.paste.disable	Prevents the use of copy and paste operations within the virtual machine console. You should consider setting these values to TRUE when hardening the environment.
vm.uselegacyft	Controls the version of fault tolerance (FT) that is available for the virtual machine. When this option is set to TRUE, the legacy FT is used for the virtual machine when FT protection is configured. See Chapter 13, "Troubleshoot Clusters," for more details.

One good use case for configuring virtual machine advanced settings is to control the use of virtual NUMA. Non-uniform memory access (NUMA) is a hardware feature that links several nodes of CPU cores and memory into a single entity. The cores within a NUMA node can quickly access memory within the same node (local memory). The cores within a NUMA node can access memory in other nodes (remote memory), but the data must be transferred over the NUMA connection, which slows the processing. Virtual NUMA, which was introduced in vSphere 5.0, is the NUMA architecture that the VMkernel presents to the virtual machine's guest operating system. The size of the virtual NUMA node can be different than the size of the physical NUMA node. This is particularly helpful in cases where the size of the virtual machine is larger than the size of the physical NUMA node.

Table 16-4 is a list of virtual machine advanced settings that impact NUMA.

Table 16-4   NUMA-Related Attributes

Attribute	Description
cpuid.coresPerSocket	For virtual machines with a virtual NUMA topology, this value, which defines the number of virtual cores per virtual CPU socket, can also impact the size of the virtual NUMA node. In this case, if the value is greater than 1, it is also used as the number of virtual cores per virtual node. The default value is 1. You can only set this to powers of 2, such as 2, 4, and 8.

Attribute	Description
`numa.autosize`	When this attribute is set to TRUE, the number of virtual cores per node in the virtual NUMA topology is automatically set to match the number of cores in each physical node. The default value is FALSE.
`numa.autosize.once`	When this attribute is set to TRUE, this attribute ensures that the automatically assigned virtual node size remains unchanged during future power-on operations, unless the number of virtual CPUs in the virtual machine is modified. The default value is TRUE.
`numa.vcpu.maxPerVirtualNode`	This setting can be used instead of `cupid.coresPerSocket`. It assigns the maximum number of virtual cores per virtual node, which must be a power of 2. The default value is 8.
`numa.vcpu.min`	This setting is the minimum number of virtual CPUs in a virtual machine required for generating a virtual NUMA topology. The default value is 9.
`numa.vcpu.maxPerClient`	This setting specifies the maximum number of virtual CPUs in a NUMA client, which is a set of virtual CPUs that are managed as a single entity. You can set this when the size of the virtual NUMA node exceeds the size of the physical NUMA node. The default value is equal to `numa.vcpu.maxPerVirtualNode`.
`numa.nodeAffinity`	This setting specifies the set of NUMA nodes on which the virtual machine can execute. You should avoid using this setting except when necessary because it negatively impacts the ability of the NUMA scheduler to rebalance workload. When configuring this parameter, set its value to a comma-delimited list indicating the acceptable NUMA nodes. For example, to allow the virtual machine to only execute on NUMA nodes 0 and 1, enter `0,1`.
`numa.mem.interleave`	This setting specifies whether the virtual machine memory is statically interleaved across all the NUMA nodes on which its corresponding NUMA clients are running when no virtual NUMA topology is exposed.

NOTE ESXi actually does a good job of managing virtual machine execution on NUMA hardware without the need to configure any advanced settings, especially if you size the virtual machine based on the size of the physical server's NUMA node. For example, if the physical server has 6 cores per NUMA node, then size the virtual machines as 1, 2, 3, or 6, which are factors of 6.

> **NOTE** By default, virtual NUMA is enabled on virtual machines having 9 virtual cores or more due to the default value of **numa.vcpu.min**. In cases where virtual machines have 8 or fewer nodes but exceed the number of nodes per physical NUMA node, you should consider configuring some of the attributes in Table 16-4.

> **NOTE** Virtual NUMA is automatically disabled on virtual machines when you enable CPU hot-adding.

Interpret Virtual Machine Configuration File (.vmx) Settings

Generally speaking, you should not need to modify a virtual machine's configuration file (VMX file), unless you are troubleshooting. Instead, you can right-click the virtual machine and select **Edit Settings** > **VM Options** > **Advanced** > **Configuration Parameters** whenever you need to safely add configuration parameters to the VMX file, as described in the previous section. This is useful in situations where you want to set an advanced parameter that is not normally in the VMX file. One use case for modifying the VMX file directly is when you're troubleshooting issues when the vCenter Server is unavailable.

In situations in which you need to modify the VMX file, you should follow these guidelines:

Step 1. Power down the virtual machine prior to modifying the VMX file.

Step 2. Use the `vi` utility from an ESXi Host to modify the VMX file. Alternatively, unregister the virtual machine, download the VMX file to a desktop, modify it using a text editor, upload the modified file (overwriting the original file), and re-register the virtual machine.

Step 3. Restart the virtual machine.

The VMX file contains many entries consisting of attribute names and assigned values. Figure 16-5 shows a portion of a sample VMX file. Table 16-5 contains samples of attribute assignments that are associated with commonly used virtual machine properties. For each sample, the associated virtual machine property and value are shown in the VMware vSphere Web Client. The information in this table can be used to interpret the information from the configuration file.

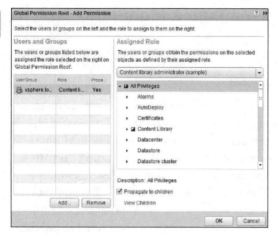

Figure 16-5 Sample Portion of a VMX File

Table 16-5 Configuration File Attribute Assignments

Attribute Assignment Example	Virtual Machine Property Details
`virtualHW.version = "10"`	This VM is compatible with ESXi 5.5 and later (VM version 10).
`displayName = "Win2008Main"`	The name of the virtual machine is `Win2008Main`.
`scsi0.virtualDev = "pvscsi"`	The type of the first storage adapter of the virtual machine is `VMware Paravirtual`.
`scsi0:0.fileName = "Win2k12-01. vmdk"`	The virtual machine contains a virtual disk whose filename is `Win2k12-01.vmdk`.
`ethernet0.virtualDev = "vmxnet3"`	The type of the first network adapter in the virtual machine is `VMXNET3`.
`ethernet0.networkName = "VM Network"`	The first network adapter in the virtual machine is connected to VM Network.
`numvcpus = "2"`	The total number of virtual cores in the virtual machine is two.
`memSize = "4096"`	The virtual machine memory size is 4 GB.

Enable/Disable Advanced Virtual Machine Settings

No option to enable or disable all virtual machine advanced settings actually exists, but some of the advanced settings can be enabled (set to TRUE) or disabled (set to FALSE). Many of these advanced settings are described in the previous sections.

Objective 10.2—Create and Manage a Multi-site Content Library

The following sections provide details on implementing content libraries for multiple sites, including publishing and subscribing.

A *content library* is a repository that can be used to share files such as virtual machine templates, vApps, and image files among a set of vCenter Servers. The content library is a new feature in vSphere 6.0 that addresses the fact that multiple vCenter Servers do not directly share associated files such as Open Virtualization Format (OVF) and image (ISO) files. A great use case is a large company that has multiple sites, each managed by a dedicated vCenter Server, where the OVF files and ISO files that are used at one site are not directly available for use at other sites. In this case, content libraries can be created at one or more sites and configured as publishers to serve the other sites. Content libraries can be created at other sites and configured as subscribers to the contents of the publisher. A subscriber can download contents from the publisher, and this content can be automatically synchronized. When used in this situation, the content library is often referenced as a multi-site content library.

A content library can be password protected during the publication procedure, such that a defined, static password must be known to subscribe to the library and download content. This mechanism does not have any integration with vCenter Single Sign-On or Active Directory.

A subscribing content library can be configured to download metadata only when it receives notification of a change. In this case, the subscribing library reflects the most recent changes, but it is not burdened with supplying the storage space for every published file. Instead, the administrator can choose whether to download the actual data for the entire item or per item.

Three types of content libraries can be used: local, published, and subscribed. A local content library is the simplest form. It allows the administrator to allow, modify, and delete content. A published library is a local library, where content is published for subscription. A subscribed library is a library whose content you cannot change or publish. It receives its content from a published library.

Each content library is built on a single storage entity, which may be a VMFS datastore, an NFS datastore, a CIFS share, or a local disk. The vCenter Server requires read and write permissions to the storage. A vCenter Server may access a maximum of 20 content libraries. Each library may contain up to 200 items and may be up to 64 TB in size. Port 443 is used for communication with the content library. Bandwidth to the library can be limited. The time and frequency at which synchronization occurs can be modified using an API. OVF templates must be used instead of traditional vCenter Server templates. Automatic synchronization occurs every 24 hours by default. The content library service, which is named `vmware-vdcs`, is installed as part of the vCenter Server installation and uses the same database as vCenter Server.

After one library is set to subscribe to another library, synchronization occurs. Simple versioning is used to keep the libraries synchronized. Version numbers are assigned to each library and to each item in the library. These numbers are incremented whenever content is added or modified. Simple versioning is used to determine when synchronization is needed. It does not store previous versions or provide rollback.

The following sequence occurs between a subscribed and published library:

1. The library service on the subscriber connects to the library services on the publisher using the VMware Content Subscription Protocol (vCSP) and checks for updates.

2. The subscriber pulls the `lib.json` file from the publisher, and each library's lib.json files are examined to determine whether discrepancies exist between the publisher and subscriber.

3. Using vCSP, the library service determines what data has changed and sends a request to the transfer service to copy the required files.

4. The subscriber updates the versioning information in the database.

Publish a Content Catalog

The details for publishing and subscribing to content across sites are provided in the section "Configure Content Library to Work Across Sites," later in this chapter.

Subscribe to a Published Catalog

The details for publishing and subscribing to content across sites are provided in the section "Configure Content Library to Work Across Sites," later in this chapter.

Determine Which Privileges Are Required to Globally Manage a Content Catalog

Content libraries are not direct children of the vCenter Server object in the vSphere inventory. Instead, content libraries are direct children of the global root. This means that permissions set on a vCenter Server do not apply to content libraries even if they are set to propagate to child objects. Global permissions, which are used to assign privileges across solutions, must be used to set permissions on content libraries. If a user is granted the Read Only role as a global permission and the Administrator role at a vCenter Server level, the user can manage the vCenter Server's content libraries and content but can only view content libraries belonging to other vCenter Servers. If a user is granted the Content Library Administrator role as a global permission, the user can manage all content libraries and content in all vCenter Server instances. If a user is not granted any global permission but is granted the Administrator role at a vCenter Server level, the user cannot view or manage any libraries or content, including the vCenter Server's content libraries, because the user must have at least Read Only defined as a global permission.

More details related to permissions are covered later in this chapter, in the section "Set/Configure Content Library Roles."

Compare the Functionality of Automatic Sync and On-Demand Sync

The following section provides details on configuring content libraries to work across sites, where one library can subscribe to the contents of another library. When configuring the subscribing library, you can choose either to download all libraries' content immediately or download library content only when needed. The first option starts the full synchronization process immediately. It includes the full content, including the metadata and actual data. The latter option starts the synchronization process for just the metadata immediately. The metadata contains information about the actual content data, allowing users to view and select the associated templates and ISOs. In this case, the actual data is synchronized only as needed when subscribed library objects are demanded. The impact of the on-demand synchronization is that storage space may be saved for the subscribing library, but a delay may exist each time a library item is selected.

Configure Content Library to Work Across Sites

The main steps to configuring a content library for multiple sites are to create the library, add content, publish the library, and create and configure other libraries that subscribe to the published library.

The following procedure can be used to create and publish a local content library:

Step 1.   Use the vSphere Web Client to navigate to the home page in the left pane and click **vCenter Inventory Lists**.

Step 2.   In the left pane, click **Content Libraries**.

Step 3.   In the center pane, click the **Create a New Content Library** icon, provide a name, and select a vCenter Server. Then click **Next**.

Step 4.   Click **Local Content Library**.

Step 5. As shown in Figure 16-6, select the **Publish Content Library Externally** check box to create a URL to the library. Optionally, select the **Enable Authentication** check box and enter a password in the **Password** and **Confirm Password** text boxes. Click **Next**.

Step 6. On the **Add Storage** page, click **Select a Datastore**.

Step 7. Select the appropriate datastore and click **Next**.

Step 8. Navigate to **vCenter Inventory Lists** > **Content Libraries**, click **Create a New Content Library**, provide a name, and select the second vCenter Server.

Step 9. On the Ready to Complete page, click **Finish**.

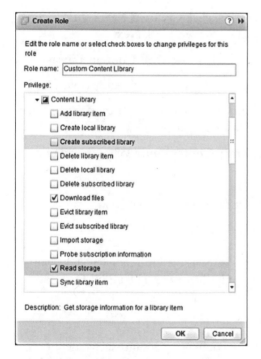

Figure 16-6   Publish Content Library Externally

After creating a content library, you can upload data files to the library by using the following procedure:

Step 1. In the center of the Contents Library page, right-click the content library and choose **Import Item**.

Step 2. In the import window, click **Local file**.

Step 3. Click **Browse**.

Step 4. In the window that opens, locate and select the desired file for upload. Click **Open**.

Step 5. Provide a name in the **Item Name** text box and click **OK**.

Finally, you can create a content library that subscribes to the published library by using these steps:

Step 1. In the center of the Contents Library page, double-click the published content library.

Step 2. In the **Summary** tab, locate the **Publication** panel and click the **Copy Link** button.

Step 3. Navigate back to **Content Libraries**, click **Create a New Library** icon, provide a name, and select a vCenter Server. Click **Next**.

Step 4. On the **Configure Library** page, click **Subscribed Content Library**.

Step 5. Click the **Subscription URL** text box and paste the recently copied URL.

Step 6. Select the **Enable Authentication** check box and enter the password that was previously assigned to the published content library.

Step 7. Optionally, click **Download Library Content only When Needed**.

Step 8. Click **Next**.

Step 9. On the Add Storage page, select a datastore and click **Next**.

Step 10. On the Ready to Complete page, click **OK**.

The transfer service on the vCenter Server is responsible for importing and exporting content between the subscriber and the publisher, using HTTP NFC.

Configure Content Library Authentication

The previous section provides a procedure for configuring a multi-site content library. One optional but frequently used step is to enable authentication, which allows you to set credentials for library access. You can enable authentication in the New Library Wizard or by modifying the library settings. You can set the password for the static username `vcsp`, but you cannot change the user account. This user account and password are not associated with vCenter Single Sign-on or Active Directory.

Set/Configure Content Library Roles

You can set permissions related to a content library. You cannot set permissions on a content library directly, but you can assign content library permissions to the global permissions root. To do so, use the vSphere Web Client to select **Home** > **Roles** > **Global Permissions**. Here, you can add a new permission to assign the **Content Library Administrator Role** to a user group, as shown in Figure 16-7. Effectively, this role provides the user with all privileges associated with content libraries. Or you can use **Administration** > **Roles** to create a custom role containing content library–related privileges and use it to assign permissions to users and groups on the global permissions root. In other words, you can set permissions for the content library in the same manner as you set permissions on other vSphere objects, except that the permissions need to be assigned on the global permission root object rather than on the content library. In the example in Figure 16-8, a custom role is being created that allows the download files and read storage privileges, but no other content library privileges, such as adding library items.

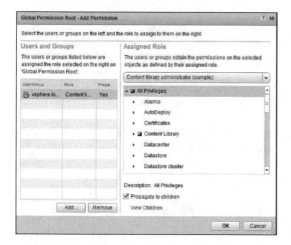

Figure 16-7   Assign Content Library Permissions to Global Permission Root

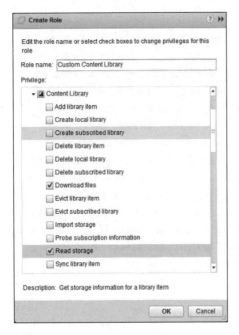

Figure 16-8 Create a Custom Content Library Role

Add/Remove Content Libraries

As described previously, you can use the Create a New Content Library icon to add a new content library. The following procedure can be used to remove a content library:

Step 1. Log onto the vSphere Web Client with a user account that has sufficient privileges, including **Content library.Delete subscribed library** or **Content library.Delete local library**.

Step 2. In the left pane, select **vCenter Inventory Lists > Content Libraries**.

Step 3. Right-click the library and click **Delete**.

Step 4. In the dialog box that appears, click **Yes**.

Objective 10.3—Configure and Maintain a vCloud Air Connection

The following sections provide details on configuring and maintaining vCloud Air connections and related topics, such as requirements and connection types.

A *hybrid cloud* is a cloud that includes some public cloud components and some private cloud components. VMware vCloud Air is a public cloud to which you can connect your private cloud to form a hybrid cloud. It is built on the trusted foundation of vSphere and is designed to easily allow you to migrate virtual machine–based workloads to and from your private cloud.

You can use vCloud Connector to link your vSphere environment to vCloud Air. This allows the transfer of workloads from your site to the cloud. You can use the Offline Data Transfer feature to migrate large numbers of virtual machines from your on-premise site to vCloud Air. You can use the Content Sync feature to ensure site-to-site consistency so you can manage a single content catalog for both your private site and for vCloud Air. You can extend your datacenter such that virtual machine–based workloads can be transferred to vCloud Air without the need to reconfigure network settings of the virtual machines. One use case for this is to accommodate seasonal workloads that are common to some businesses.

Create a VPN Connection Between vCloud Air and On-premise Site

You can connect an on-premise site to vCloud Air by using an Internet Protocol Security (IPsec) virtual private network (VPN) connection. IPsec is a protocol suite for securing communication sessions that can be used by vCloud Air to secure VPN connections between it and on-premise datacenters. To configure an IPsec VPN connection, you must configure the following:

- **Peer Networks:** Remote networks, identified in CIDR format (such as 192.168.99.0/24), to which the VPN connects

- **Local Endpoint:** The network in vCloud Air on which the gateway transmits

- **Peer ID:** The public IP address of the remote device terminating the VPN connection, which is either the peer's native IP address or, in cases where NAT is configured, the private peer IP

- **Local ID:** The public IP address of the gateway

Figure 16-9 contains a diagram from the VMware vCloud Air Documentation Center that illustrates an IPsec VPN connection between vCloud Air and a remote site.

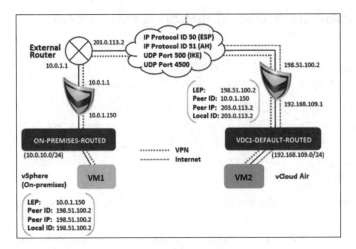

Figure 16-9 IPsec VPN

The procedure to configure an IPsec VPN connection between vCloud Air and a remote site is:

Step 1. Use vCloud Director to configure the IPsec VPN connection as part of configuring gateway services.

Step 2. In vCloud Air, click the **Gateways** tab and select the gateway that should be used for the IPsec VPN connection.

Step 3. Select **Manage Advanced Gateway Settings**.

Step 4. Select **Administration > Edge Gateway** and right-click the appropriate gateway.

Step 5. Select **Edge Gateway Services > VPN** and check the **Enable VPN** box.

Step 6. If necessary, select **Configure Public IPs** and set a public IP address for the external network.

Step 7. Click **Add** and use the **Add a Site to Site VPN** configuration window to appropriately configure each of the following settings:

- Name

- Description

- Enable this VPN Configuration

- Establish VPN to

- Local Networks

- Peer Networks

- Local Endpoint

- Local ID

- Peer ID

- Peer IP

- Encryption Protocol

- Shared Key

- MTU

Step 8.   Click **OK**.

For more details, see VMware KB 20151370.

It may take up to 10 minutes to establish a secure connection. You should monitor the Configure Services VPN tab for the appearance of a green check mark in the Status Row to indicate success.

Deploy a Virtual Machine Using vCloud Air

To deploy new virtual machines in vCloud Air, you can navigate to the **Virtual Machines** tab in a virtual datacenter in your vCloud Air portal, click **Add One**, click **Create My Virtual Machine from Scratch**, and use the interface to build a new vApp in the same manner as you would use the vCloud Director user interface to build a new vApp. Within the New vApp Wizard, you can use the New Virtual Machine button to create new virtual machines from scratch.

Alternatively, you can deploy new virtual machines from the VMware catalog or private catalogs. In this case, rather than choose to create the virtual machine from scratch, simply select a template from the **VMware Catalog** or **My Catalog** and configure the appropriate options.

Migrate a Virtual Machine to vCloud Air

You can migrate a virtual machine from an on-premise vSphere environment to vCloud Air using the vCloud Connector by using the following procedure:

Step 1.   Use the vSphere Client to log in and choose **Solutions and Applications > vCloud Connector**.

Step 2.   In the browser pane, navigate to the on-premise environment and select a virtual machine or template.

Step 3.   From the Actions list, select **Copy**, as shown in Figure 16-10, and click **Next**.

Step 4.   In the Select a Target window, select the target cloud and catalog and specify an appropriate name and description, as shown in Figure 16-11, and click **Next**.

Step 5.   Complete the wizard by specifying the appropriate virtual datacenter and deployment options.

Figure 16-10   Select Virtual Machine to Copy to vCloud Air

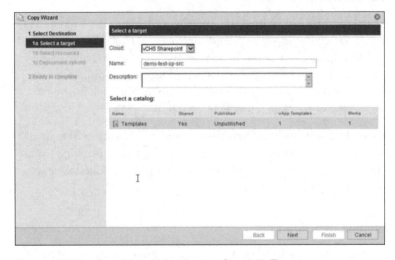

Figure 16-11   Copy Virtual Machine to vCloud Air Target

After using this method to add templates to the vCloud Air catalog, you can use the information in the previous section to deploy a virtual machine from a template in the catalog.

Verify VPN Connection Configuration to vCloud Air

To verify a VPN connection, navigate to the **Configure Services VPN** tab and examine the **Status Row**. For a valid connection, a green check mark appears, as described earlier in this chapter, in the section "Configure a VPN Connection Between vCloud Air and On-premise Site."

Configure vCenter Server Connection to vCloud Air

The vCloud Air vSphere Client plug-in is not available for use in vSphere 6.0. Previous versions of the plug-in cannot be updated for use with vSphere 6.0. Instead, vSphere 6.0 users can manage vCloud Air workloads by using the vCloud Air portal (http://vchs.vmware.com). See VMware KB article 2074778 for information on how to monitor any future changes to the compatibility of the plug-in.

The only means to connect your vSphere 6 environment to vCloud Air is to use the vCloud Connector. To get started, you need a My VMware account and a vCenter Server administrator account. You need to use the vSphere Client, not the vSphere Web Client. You also need a supported browser, such as Internet Explorer version 9 or Chrome version 23, which must be configured to accept third-party cookies. Download the vCloud Connector server and vCloud Connector node virtual appliance zip files, VCCServer.zip and VCCNode.zip, from the vCloud Connector product page (http://www.vmware.com/products/vcloud-connector). Unzip the files into separate folders.

The main steps to configure the vCloud Connector are to deploy a connector server, deploy a connector node, and register the components. The following procedure can be used to install the vCloud Connection Server in a vSphere environment:

Step 1.   Use the vSphere Client to log onto the vCenter Server.

Step 2.   Select **File** > **Deploy OVF Template**.

Step 3.   Use the wizard to deploy the vCloud Connector Server appliance into the vSphere inventory. When prompted, assign a static IP address to the appliance.

Step 4.   In the vCenter Server inventory, right-click the appliance and select **Power** > **Power on**.

Step 5.   Log on using the admin account to the vCloud Connector Server Admin Web Console by using a web browser to connect to https://<VCC-Server-IP-address>:5480. Use the console to make any required changes to time zone, networking, administrator account, or logs.

Step 6. Likewise, use **File > Deploy OVF Template** in the vSphere Client to deploy a vCloud Connector node virtual appliance from the OVF file that was extracted from `VCCNode.zip`. Assign a static IP address. Power on the appliance.

Step 7. Log on using the admin account to the vCloud Connector Server Admin Web Console by using a web browser to connect to `https://<VCCNode-IP-address>:5480`. Use the console to make any required changes to time zone, networking, administrator account, or logs.

Step 8. In the vCloud Connector Node Web Console, select **Node > Cloud**. Select **vSphere** in the Cloud Type field and set the Cloud URL to an appropriate URL that contains `https` and your cloud's fully qualified domain name or IP address.

Step 9. Click **Update Configuration**.

Step 10. In the vCloud Connector Server Admin Web Console, select **Server > vSphere Client**. Enter the IP address or fully qualified domain name of the vCenter Server. Provide a vCenter Server username and password. Click **Register**.

Step 11. In the vCloud Connector Server Admin Web Console, use **Nodes > Register Node** to register the vCloud Connector Node with the vCloud Connector server.

Step 12. Click **OK**.

Although a vCloud Air plug-in is available for vSphere 5.5, no plug-in is available for vSphere 6 at this writing. So the only currently available method for connecting your private vSphere environment or your private cloud with vCloud Air is to use the vCloud Connector for vCloud Air. You can use vCloud Connector for vCloud Air to connect clouds, perform offline data transfers, synchronize content, and extend the datacenter.

The requirements to install the vCloud Connector, which can be used to connect vCenter Server with vCloud Air, are:

- vSphere version 4.0 update 3 or later
- vSphere Client version 4.0 update 3 or later
- Internet Explorer 8 or later or Chrome 22 or later

The vSphere Client is required for the vCloud Connector user interface, which needs to be registered as a plug-in in the vSphere Client. These are the required network ports:

- **443:** For communication between vCloud Server and vCloud nodes when SSL is enabled

- **80:** For communication between vCloud Server and vCloud nodes when SSL is not enabled

- **8190:** For copying data between the private cloud and public cloud

- **548:** For the vCloud Connector Server and vCloud Connector Node Admin Web Consoles

These are the requirements for the vCloud Air vSphere Client Plug-in 1.5:

- vSphere Web Client 5.5 Update 1 or Update 2 (not vSphere Web Client 6.0)

- A supported vSphere Web Client browser

- A vCloud Air user account with Account Administrator user role

- A vCenter Server account with vCenter Server Single Sign-on administrator privileges

- Port 443

Configure Replicated Objects in vCloud Air Disaster Recovery Service

The vCloud Air Disaster Recovery Service is a new feature in vCloud Air that allows you to replicate virtual machines running in your vSphere environment to vCloud Air for potential recovery following a disaster.

To get started, you must have the following:

- Licensed instances of vSphere 5.1 or later (Check the "Disaster Recovery to Cloud System Requirements and Compatibility" list at http://tinyurl.com/os8x2o8.)

- A My VMware account

Follow these steps to configure vSphere Replication:

Step 1.   Purchase a subscription to the vCloud Air Disaster Recovery service.

Step 2.   Wait for VMware to set up your virtual datacenter, enabled for disaster recovery, and send login credentials via email. The virtual datacenter, which is designated by a Reserved for Disaster Recovery icon, serves as your replication target and recovery site.

Step 3.   Log into My VMware and download the vSphere Replication 5.6 appliance, which is distributed as an OVF virtual appliance.

Step 4.   Use the vSphere Web Client at your source site to deploy the vSphere Replication appliance, using the standard vSphere OVF Deployment wizard. Select the vCenter hosts and clusters where you will deploy the OVF template for the vSphere Replication appliance.

Step 5.   To create a cloud connection, in the vSphere Web Client, navigate to **Manage > vSphere Replication** and click on the cloud connection icon and verify that the **Connect to a Cloud Provider** wizard opens.

Step 6.   In the Connection Settings page, enter your vCloud Air address, the organization name, and credentials. Optionally, if you do not want to store these credentials in the vSphere Replication database, select the **Use a Different Account for System Monitoring** check box and provide the credentials to be used for system monitoring. These credentials are encrypted and stored in the vSphere Replication database. Click **Next**.

Step 7.   In the wizard, review the list of available virtual datacenters and select the appropriate virtual datacenter. If a virtual datacenter is already connected to the vCenter Server, that datacenter does not appear in the list. Click **Next**.

Step 8.   Review your settings and click **Finish**.

Step 9.   The connection to the cloud organization appears in the list of target sites. The status of the connection is **Missing Network Settings**.

Step 10.   In the vCloud Air Dashboard, click **Users**.

Step 11.   Select an appropriate user and select **More > View and Edit Details**.

Step 12.   In the Roles section, assign the Virtual Infrastructure role the use account. This role permits the ability to manage replications, manage recovered virtual machines, and other permissions.

Once the replication components are configured, you can use the remaining steps to configure replication for a set of virtual machines.

Step 13.   Continue to navigate through the wizard and right-click a group of virtual machines and select **All vSphere Replication Actions > Configure Replication**.

Step 14.   Continue in the wizard to select the option to replicate to a cloud provider, select the target site and target virtual datacenter, and select the storage policy.

Step 15. Continue in the wizard to configure the quiescing and Recovery Point Objective (RPO) settings.

Step 16. On the final wizard page, click **Finish**.

After you configure Replication for a set of virtual machines, you can monitor the progress by selecting **Monitor > vSphere Replication** in the vSphere Web Client.

Given a Scenario, Determine the Required Settings for Virtual Machines Deployed in vCloud Air

When deploying virtual machines in vCloud Air, as described earlier in this chapter, you should configure settings based on key items in the scenario, such as:

- **Virtual datacenter:** In scenarios involving multiple virtual datacenters, you should identify the appropriate virtual datacenter to deploy each virtual machine.

- **Catalog:** The scenario may require that you deploy a new virtual machine from a template that VMware provides in the VMware catalog or a custom template in My Catalog.

- **Template:** In scenarios where My Catalog contains many templates having the same guest operating system but unique configurations, you should ensure that you identify the template that best fits. In cases where no template fits, you may need to deploy a new virtual machine from scratch.

- **Name:** If your scenario already includes a proper naming convention, be sure to apply it as you assign a name to the virtual machine. Otherwise, you should consider creating a naming convention to use from this point forward. Commonly used conventions tend to use some characters to identify the guest operating system version, configuration, and purpose.

- **Virtual Hardware:** The scenario may explicitly call for specific hardware configuration, such as eight vCPUs and 8 GB memory. Otherwise, you should use other factors to determine whether any changes should be made to the virtual hardware as you deploy a virtual machine from the catalog. Common factors to consider are the intended application and workload for the virtual machine. You should typically follow the software vendor's recommendations for sizing the virtual machine.

Summary

You have now read the chapter covering exam topics on advanced virtual machine settings, multi-site content libraries, and vCloud Air connections. You should now use information in the following sections to complete you preparation for Objectives 10.1, 10.2, and 10.3.

Preparation Tasks

Review All the Key Topics

Table 16-6 provides a reference to each of the key topics identified in this chapter. Take a few moments to review each of these specific items.

Table 16-6   Key Topics for Chapter 16

Key Topic Element	Description	Pages
Procedure	Configure Virtual Machine DirectPath I/O	599
Table 16-3	Advanced Configuration Parameters	604
Table 16-5	Configuration File Attribute Assignments	611
Paragraph	Configure Content Library to Work Across Sites	614
Paragraph	Configure Replicated Objects in vCloud Air Disaster Recovery	625

Complete the Tables and Lists from Memory

Print a copy of Appendix B, "Memory Tables" (found on the CD), or at least the section for this chapter, and complete the tables and lists from memory. Appendix C, "Memory Tables Answer Key," also on the CD, includes completed tables and lists to check your work.

Definitions of Key Terms

Define the following key terms from this chapter and check your answers in the glossary.

Direct I/O, content library, vCloud Air, hybrid cloud

Answer Review Questions

The answers to these review questions can be found in Appendix A.

1. Which of the following is not a virtual machine configuration setting?

    a. `sched.mem.pshare.salt`

    b. `sched.mem.maxmemctl`

    c. `devices.hotAddMemory`

    d. `log.rotateSize`

2. Which of the following steps would you take to support a virtual machine with extremely high network demand? (Choose two.)

    a. Configure the `sched.mem.maxmemctl` parameter.

    b. Configure NPIV.

    c. Configure an ESXi Host network adapter for passthrough.

    d. Configure DirectPath I/O.

3. Which of the following is involved in the sequence of events associated with synchronizing content libraries when the content is changed in the publisher's content library?

    a. The `lib.json` files are rotated and renamed to reflect a timestamp.

    b. vCSP is used to check for updates and request data transfer.

    c. SCP is used to transfer the data.

    d. Data is compressed.

4. Which of the following is true concerning vCloud Air and vCenter Server?

    a. The vCloud Connector cannot be used to connect vCenter Server 6.0 with vCloud Air.

    b. A vCloud Air plug-in is available for the vSphere Web Client 6.0.

    c. The vSphere Client is required to use the vCloud Connector.

    d. A vCenter Server can connect directly to vCloud Air without using the vCloud Air plug-in or the vCloud Connector.

5. Which of the following is a valid name of an available vCloud Air service?

    a. vCloud Air Disaster Recovery Service

    b. vCloud Air vSphere Replication Service

    c. vCloud Air Site Recovery Manager Service

    d. vCloud Air Failover Service

## CHAPTER 17

Final Preparation

Congratulations on making it through all the technical chapters in this book. Now you are ready for your final preparation for taking the VCP6-DCV exam. This chapter contains two sections, "Getting Ready" and "Taking the Exam."

Getting Ready

Here is a list of actions and considerations that you should address prior to taking the exam:

- Gain hands-on experience with vSphere 6. If you have not done so already, you should access a vSphere 6 environment and use it to practice performing the procedures described in this book. If you do not have a suitable vSphere 6 environment, consider launching a hosted lab at `https://my.vmware.com/web/vmware/evalcenter?p=vsphere-hol`. If you are challenged with gaining hands-on access to vSphere environments with specific features, such as Virtual SAN, then you should take a look at VMware Hands-on Labs (`http://labs.hol.vmware.com`). Here you should be able to access virtual labs at no cost. For example, the labs *HOL-SDC-1608, Virtual SAN 6 from A to Z* and *HOL-SDC-1627 VVol, Virtual SAN and Storage Policy Based Management* should be very useful if you cannot readily implement Virtual SAN or Virtual Volumes in your own lab environment.

- Although the exam is multiple choice, one of its goals is to verify that you have hands-on experience with software. Be prepared to answer questions that are aimed at determining whether you know how to use a specific user interface to accomplish a specific task. For example, the correct choice for a question could depend on your knowledge of the exact text that appears on a link or button in the interface. The authors recommend that you at least practice performing the procedures that are described in this book.

- Because VMware may change the requirements for certifications and exams at any time, you should closely examine the VCP6-DCV requirements on the VMware Certification website, at `https://mylearn.vmware.com/mgrReg/plan.cfm?plan=64178&ui=www_cert` just prior to registering for the exam. The details listed in this chapter are accurate at the time of this book's writing but are subject to change at VMware's discretion.

- Candidates who are preparing for the VCP6-DCV exam fall into one of two categories: those who currently hold a VMware Certified Professional (VCP) certification and those who are new to VMware certification (or hold only expired VCP certifications). New candidates are required to take a qualifying course and pass the vSphere 6 Foundation exam.

- Candidates who are holders of current VCP certification in any track (data center virtualization, desktop/mobility, cloud management, or networking) and new candidates who already passed the vSphere 6 Foundations exam are good candidates for taking the VCP6-DCV exam and are the expected readers of this book.

- Candidates who are holders of the VCP5-DCV certification may take the VCP6-DCV *delta* exam rather than the standard VCP6-DCV exam. The stated objectives of both exams are identical, but the following differences exist between the exams:

  - The delta exam is more condensed and does not include all the same stated sub-objectives as the standard exam.

  - The delta exam is a bit shorter, at 90 minutes and 65 questions versus 100 minutes and 85 questions.

  - Although it is not officially stated, you may expect to see that the questions in the delta exam focus more on new features in vSphere 6 and differences between vSphere 5.x and vSphere 6. The authors recommend that as you study for either exam, pay extra attention to details on new features and changes in vSphere 6.

- VMware Press/Pearson does not provide a separate certification guide for the delta exam. Instead, this book is useful for preparing for both the standard and delta versions of the VCP6-DCV exams. The authors recommend that you study all the material in this book at a minimum prior to taking either exam.

- On the VMware Certification website, select either the **New Candidate Requirements** tab or the **Existing Candidate Requirements** tab and navigate into the path description that best fits your current status. The path will identify all the requirements for the candidate, such as any qualifying courses and exams. For example, a candidate who holds a current VCP5-DT certi-fication but no other VCP certification should select **Existing Candidate Requirements > Path 2**, which calls for the candidate to pass the standard VCP6-DCV exam (not the delta exam).

- On the VMware Certification website, use the links that are provided to ex-amine the details for your required exam. Select the **Exam Topics** tab, expand each section, expand each exam objective, and examine the **Knowledge** items. For convenience, the outline of this book closely matches the exam objectives and knowledge items. Carefully compare the exam objectives and knowledge items in the Table of Contents in this book to identify any items that may have been recently added and are not covered in the book. To address any recently added items, begin by examining the online content for this book, which may include updates and bonus content for premium editions.

- In addition to the exam topics, objectives, and knowledge items, review other exam details. For example, the details for the VCP6-DCV exam are:

  - **Exam number:** 2V0-621

  - **Duration:** 100 minutes

  - **Questions:** 85 multiple choice

  - **Passing score:** 300

  - **Recommended training:** vSphere Optimize and Scale (V6)

  - **Language:** English

- Use the **How to Prepare** tab to examine the recommended training details. If you feel that your knowledge and skillset are weak, consider some of the pro-vided training courses.

- In the **Practice Exam** section on the **How to Prepare** tab, use the link to request access to the practice exam. The practice exam contains 20 questions. You may take the exam multiple times. At the end of each attempt, review your **Test Status** (failed or passed), your **Percent Correct**, and your **Missed Questions**. If you missed any questions, read the provided explanation and ex-amine the related section in this book or the sources stated in the explanation. Continue taking the practice exam until you pass it, answering all the ques-tions correctly at least once.

- Review the following items in each chapter in this book until you have them committed to memory.

  - "Do I Know This Already" questions at the beginning of each chapter

  - The memory table at the end of each chapter

- "Definitions of Key Terms" at the end of each chapter
- "Review Questions" at the end of each chapter

- Take the practice exam(s) included with the book. The standard edition includes two exams, and the premium edition includes two more exams. If you miss any questions, read the provided explanation and the related section in this book. Continue taking the practice exam(s) until you feel you know and can explain each answer.

- Prior to registering for the VCP6-DCV exam, you must request authorization. To do so, click the **Request Exam Authorization** link at `https://mylearn.vmware.com/mgrReg/plan.cfm?plan=64180&ui=www_cert`.

- After VMware provides the requested authorization, you can register for the exam at `https://www1.pearsonvue.com/testtaker/signin/SignInPage/VMWA-REINC`. Sign in with your account (or create a new account if necessary), select the appropriate exam in the **Pre-approved Exams** section, and use the wizard to schedule the date, time, and location.

Taking the Exam

Here is a list of considerations and actions for the day of the exam:

- Bring two forms of identification that include your photo and signature. You cannot bring personal items such as laptops, tablets, phones, watches, pagers, wallets, or notes into the examination room. You may be able to place some of these items into a locker, but you should avoid bringing larger items into the training facility.

- Arrive at the exam center 30 minutes prior to the scheduled start time to provide ample time to complete the sign-in procedure and address personal needs. During the sign-in procedure, you should expect to place personal belongings in a locker, provide credentials, review the test regulations, and sign the agreement.

- Be sure to pay attention to the rules and regulations concerning the exam. For example, follow the venue's protocol for requesting help during the exam and for signaling your completion of the exam. Each venue's rules may be unique.

- The exam format is multiple choice, provided via a web-based user interface.

- Pay close attention to the wording of each question and each choice. The following are some examples of what to expect:

    - Some questions may ask you to select "which statement is correct," and some questions may ask you to select "which statement is incorrect."

    - Most questions call for you to select a single choice from a list of multiple choices. Whenever a question calls for you to select more than one choice, it will do so explicitly by including a phrase such as "Choose two."

    - Read each question carefully enough to ensure that you successfully interpret feature names and terminology. For example, when a question contains the word *heartbeat*, you need to carefully determine if it is referring to an HA network heartbeat, an HA datastore heartbeat, a VMFS heartbeat, a VMware Tools heartbeat, or some other heartbeat.

    - Questions tend to be written in a concise manner, and at first glance you may think that insufficient details are provided. For example, a question could provide a symptom and ask you to select three actions that you should take to troubleshoot the issue. Your first thought may be that you would take analytical steps or remediation steps that are not provided as choices for the question. You may even consider the provided choices to be unpractical or insufficient. Do not get frustrated. Just select the appropriate choices that fit the question.

    - Questions that ask you to identify more than one choice to accomplish a specific configuration or troubleshooting task may not always clearly state whether the steps in all the selected choices must be performed or whether just the steps in any one of the choices must be performed. Although you may wish the question contained better clarity, you should see that only one solution actually fits the question.

- Strive for good time management during the exam. For the 2V0-621 exam, you need to cover 85 questions in 100 minutes, so you should allow an average of 70 seconds per question. A timer is provided in the top-right corner of the exam user interface, along with the number of remaining questions. You might want to watch for the following milestones, ensure that the targeted time still remains, and pick up your pace when necessary:

    - 60 questions remaining: at least 70 minutes

    - 30 questions remaining: at least 35 minutes

    - 10 questions remaining: at least 12 minutes

    - 5 questions remaining: at least 6 minutes

- Don't allow yourself to get stuck on a question for too long. If a question is tricky—for example, if more than one choice seems to fit on a question that calls for a single choice, determine which choice is most likely the choice that VMware wants. You may find some questions easier to answer by focusing on which choices to eliminate.

  Be sure to answer all questions. You will not be penalized for incorrect answers. Guessing provides opportunity for a higher score.

- Whenever you are unsure of an answer or feel rushed to make a decision, use the web interface to mark the question for review.

- After answering all the questions, a **Review Page** is provided that identifies all questions that you marked for review and all questions that are incomplete. If sufficient time remains, use the provided links on the review page to return to any questions that you marked or any questions that are identified as incomplete.

Glossary

All Paths Down (APD)   A situation that can occur when an ESXi Host cannot access a storage path and the ESXi Host does not know if the storage device loss is going to be temporary or permanent.

Asymmetrical Logical Unit Access (ALUA)   A SCSI standard in which one storage processor can send I/O (optimized path) to the LUN, but both controllers can receive I/O. The controller that cannot issue I/O is the non-optimized path.

ballooning   A situation that occurs when the host's memory begins to get low and it starts reclaiming memory not used by the virtual machines by leveraging the balloon driver (vmmemctl) to prevent itself from paging to disk.

baseline   An ESXi Hosts patch or ESXi upgrade used for updating or upgrading and ESXi Host.

baseline group   A group of baselines that can be attached to an ESXi Host or a cluster of ESXi Hosts.

Challenge Handshake Authentication Protocol (CHAP)   A method for authenticating the ESXi Host and a storage device using password authentication.

Class of Service (CoS)   A classification used to define a priority on the network for upstream Layer 2 devices.

content library   A repository that can be used to share files such as virtual machine templates, vApps, and image files among a set of vCenter Servers.

CPU Co-stop   The amount of time that a multi-processor virtual machine spends in a state where it is ready to execute a workload but is waiting on the VMkernel to schedule other virtual CPUs from the same VM.

CPU Ready   The amount of time that a VMkernel world, such as a virtual CPU, spends waiting to be scheduled on physical CPU hardware after it announces it was ready to execute its workload.

dependent hardware iSCSI initiator   An adapter that depends on VMware networking and on iSCSI configuration and management interfaces that are provided by VMware. This type of adapter presents a standard network adapter and iSCSI offload function for the same port.

DES-CBC-MD5   An encryption method that encrypts packets using the Cipher Block Chaining mode. An MD5 checksum is applied and placed in the cksum field. DES blocks are 8 bytes.

DirectPath I/O   A feature by which ESXi allows a virtual machine to have direct access to a network adapter, by passing the VMkernel.

Distributed Power Management (DPM)   A DRS feature that is designed to save on power and cooling by putting ESXi Hosts into standby mode during idle time.

Distributed Resource Scheduler (DRS)   A cluster technology that is responsible for the initial placement of virtual machines and for migrating them through vMotion to achieve even resource distribution between all ESXi servers in a cluster.

distributed virtual uplink (dvUplink)   A port group used specifically by physical uplinks defined on the ESXi Hosts.

dvPort group   A distributed virtual port group that can be used by virtual machines or VMkernel ports and exists only on vDS.

ESXCLI   A command set that provides a hierarchal namespace for managing ESXi Hosts.

ESXTOP   A command set that displays the real-time resource utilization of an ESXi Host.

expandable reservation   A reservation at a resource pool level, that can grow beyond the resource pool and borrow from the parent pool to meet the higher reservation's demand, provided the parent pool has the unreserved resource.

Fault Domain Manager (FDM)   An ESXi Host–based agent system that has one master node and multiple slave nodes. The master agent monitors the status of the slave nodes by acknowledging the heartbeat packets sent over the heartbeat network.

Fibre Channel (FC)   A transport layer that can be used to transmit data on a SAN. FC encapsulates SCSI commands, which are transmitted between FC nodes.

Fibre Channel over Ethernet (FCoE)   A protocol that takes Fibre Channel frames and puts them over an Ethernet network of 10 Gbps or higher speed.

Fixed   A designated preferred path that the ESXi Host uses.

high availability (HA)   A setting defined at a cluster object level that provides restart of virtual machines in the event of hardware or OS failure.

hybrid cloud A cloud that includes some public cloud components and some private cloud components.

independent hardware iSCSI initiator A specialized third-party adapter capable of accessing iSCSI storage over TCP/IP.

Internet Small Computer System Interface (iSCSI) A protocol that provides access to storage devices over an Ethernet-based TCP/IP network.

Kerberos A secure method for authenticating a request for a service in a computer network.

limit A cap on physical resource utilization.

Managed Object Browser (MOB) A tool that can be used to explore the VMkernel object model.

Most Recently Used (MRU) An algorithm used by the ESXi Host to select the active path. If the active path fails, an alternate path becomes the active path. However, when the original path comes back online, it becomes the alternate path.

Multipathing Plug-in (MPP) The top-level plug-in for PSA. The MPP can be either the internal NMP or a third-party MPP supplied by a storage vendor.

Native Multipathing Plug-in (NMP) The default MPP that is used for storage devices that have not been claimed by a claim rule. One of the tasks of NMP is to associate physical storage paths with an SATP and associate a PSP that chooses the best available path.

Network File System (NFS) A service that lets you share files over a network between a storage device and an ESXi Host.

Network I/O Control (NIOC) A feature available only on vSphere Distributed Switches that enables you to define shares and limits for bandwidth control. NIOC version 3, introduced in vSphere 6, allows you to define reservations.

Parallel NFS (pNFS) Part of the NFS v4.1 standard that allows clients to access storage devices directly and in parallel.

Path Selection Plug-in (PSP) A plug-in that is part of the VMware Pluggable Storage Architecture and is primarily responsible for path selection and load balancing.

Permanent Device Loss (PDL) A situation that occurs when a storage device sends a SCSI sense code to the ESXi Host, specifying that the storage device has become unavailable and thus the ESXi Host stops sending I/O requests to the storage array.

Pluggable Storage Architecture (PSA)   A set of APIs that third-party vendors can use to add their multipathing software to vSphere to manage multipathing and access to storage. PSA is used to handle I/O queueing to the logical devices and physical path discovery and removal.

private virtual local area network (PVLAN)   An extension of the VLAN standard that allows further segmentation of VLANs and more flexibility and extensibility than standard VLANs.

protocol endpoint (PE)   The logical path the ESXi Host uses to communicate between a Virtual Volume and a virtual machine.

quiesce   To bring a guest file system or application option to a known consistent state prior to performing an operation such as a snapshot.

reservation   A guaranteed resource that must be physical and can never be taken away.

Round Robin   An algorithm that the ESXi Host uses to rotate through all the active paths.

share   An attribute that defines relative priority when resources are under constraint.

Small Computer Systems Interface (SCSI) An upper-layer protocol that is encrypted in each FC frame.

snapshot   A point-in-time capture of the state of a virtual machine and its virtual disk.

software iSCSI initiator   A standard 1 GbE or 10 GbE NIC, with the VMware code built into the VMkernel. A software iSCSI initiator handles iSCSI processing while communicating with the network adapter.

Storage Array Type Plug-in (SATP)   A plug-in that is part of the VMware Pluggable Storage Architecture and is primarily responsible for path failover and failure detection.

Storage I/O Control (SIOC)   A feature that provides storage I/O performance isolation for virtual machines.

storage provider (SP)   A software plug-in developed by third parties that communicates to the vCenter Server the underlying capabilities of the storage.

Storage vMotion   VMware's utility for migrating a virtual machine's files to a different datastore while the VM is powered on.

support bundle   A set of diagnostic information, such as logs and configuration data, that is collected from vCenter Server. It can be useful to support staff for troubleshooting problems.

thumbprint   A cryptographic hash of a certificate that is used to determine whether one certificate matches another.

transparent page sharing (TPS)   A mechanism whereby the VMkernel automatically identifies identical pages of virtual memory and consolidates them to a single physical memory page, in a manner that is transparent to the virtual machine guest operating system.

vCenter Server Appliance (vCSA)   A Linux-based version of vCenter.

vCenter Server storage filters   Filters that are provided to avoid presenting storage that should be avoided due to performance problems or unsupported storage devices.

vCloud Air   A public cloud to which you can connect a private cloud to form a hybrid cloud.

Virtual Flash Read Cache (vFRC)   The use of ESXi Hosts' SSDs for caching I/O for VMs and/or caching .vswp during periods of memory contention.

Virtual Machine Communication Interface (VMCI)   A high-speed communication mechanism for virtual machine–to–ESXi Host communication.

Virtual Machine Component Protection (VMCP)   A vSphere high availability feature that is used to protect VMs from failure.

Virtual Machine File System (VMFS)   A cluster file system that provides storage virtualization optimized for virtual machines.

Virtual SAN (VSAN)   A distributed layer of software that runs on the ESXi hypervisor and uses direct-attached storage across ESXi Hosts to form a virtual datastore.

Virtual Volume (VVOL)   A unique way of presenting storage that involves encapsulating virtual machine files, virtual disks, and configuration files. Each object is a VVOL that is independent of the underlying storage.

vMotion   VMware's tool for migrating powered-on virtual machines to other ESXi servers with zero downtime and zero data loss.

VMware Data Protection (VDP)   A product designed to back up and restore virtual machines in vSphere environments.

VMware Directory Service (vmdir)   A multi-tenanted, multi-mastered directory service that stores SSO data and is included in each PSC instance.

VMware Endpoint Certificate Store (VECS)   A local repository for certificates and private keys.

VMware Infrastructure Bundle (VIB)   A group of files used in an ESXi installation.

VMware Update Manager Utility   A utility used to make configuration changes to VMware Update Manager and VMware Update Manager Download Service (UMDS) that otherwise could be made only during installation.

vSphere APIs for Array Integration (VAAI)   Also referred to as hardware acceleration or hardware offload APIs, a set of APIs and SCSI commands used to offload certain functions that are performed more efficiently on the storage array.

vSphere APIs for Storage Awareness (VASA)   A set of vSphere APIs designed to allow storage vendors to advertise proprietary features and capabilities of the storage device to the hypervisor, as well as the ability to verify if the VM requirements are being met by the storage policy.

vSphere Distributed Switch (vDS)   A Layer 2 virtual switch that is owned and managed by vCenter Server.

vSphere Fault Tolerance (FT)   A setting that provides zero downtime and zero data loss to virtual machines in the event of ESXi server failure.

vSphere On-disk Metadata Analyzer (VOMA)   A utility for identifying and fixing metadata corruption.

vSphere Standard Switch (vSS)   A Layer 2 virtual switch that is owned and managed by each individual ESXi Host.

vSphere Update Manager (VUM)   A Windows-based application designed to centralize and automate patch and version management.

vSphere Update Manager Download Service (UMDS)   An optional module for Update Manager that is located in the DMZ. This separate system is used to obtain patches and upgrades from the Internet.

Answers to the "Do I Know This Already?" Quizzes and Review Questions

Answers to the "Do I Know This Already?" Quizzes

Chapter 1

1. b and c
2. d
3. a and b
4. c
5. d
6. d
7. c
8. a
9. c
10. b

Chapter 2

1. d
2. c
3. b
4. b
5. c
6. a
7. d

8. b

9. b

10. c

11. d

12. a

Chapter 3

1. a

2. c

3. a, b, and e

4. b

5. a

6. b

7. d

8. a, b, and c

9. a

Chapter 4

1. b

2. c

3. b

4. d

5. a

6. c

7. a and c

8. b and c

9. c

10. d

Chapter 5

1. b

2. c

3. b

4. d

5. a

6. c

7. a and c

8. b and c

9. c

10. d

Chapter 6

1. a

2. c

3. a, b, and c

4. c

5. d

6. a

7. d

8. b

9. b

10. b

11. d

12. b

Chapter 7

1. d

2. b

3. a

4. c

5. a

6. d

7. a

8. a

9. a

10. c

Chapter 8

1. c

2. b

3. a and c

4. c and d

5. a

6. b, c, and e

7. a and b

8. c

9. d

10. a and c

11. d

Chapter 9

1. c

2. a

3. a, b, and d

4. b

5. d

6. a

7. b

8. c

9. a

10. d

Chapter 10

1. b

2. a

3. d

4. a

5. a, b, and c

6. c

7. c

8. a

9. d

10. b

Chapter 11

1. a

2. c

3. a

4. d

5. d

6. d

7. a

8. d

9. b

10. c

Chapter 12

1. d

2. c

3. c

4. a

5. a

6. a, c, and e

7. c

8. a

9. d

10. a, b, and d

Chapter 13

1. b
2. d
3. d
4. a and d
5. c

Chapter 14

1. d
2. a and d
3. b
4. a
5. d
6. a and d
7. a
8. c
9. a, c, and d
10. a

Chapter 15

1. b and d
2. a and d
3. b
4. a
5. a
6. c
7. a and d
8. a
9. b and c
10. a and c

Chapter 16

1. b
2. a
3. d
4. d
5. c
6. a, c, and d
7. a
8. a
9. d
10. b

Answers to the Review Questions

Chapter 1

1. b
2. d
3. a
4. d
5. a,b, and d

Chapter 2

1. b
2. a
3. d
4. c
5. d

Chapter 3

1. d
2. d
3. b
4. c
5. b

Chapter 4

1. d
2. b
3. d
4. b and d
5. b

Chapter 5

1. b
2. c
3. a
4. a
5. a

Chapter 6

1. a
2. b
3. b
4. a
5. a

Chapter 7

1. b
2. d
3. d

Chapter 8

1. d
2. a
3. c
4. b
5. a
6. d

Chapter 9

1. a and d
2. b
3. d
4. a
5. b

Chapter 10

1. a
2. d
3. d
4. c
5. b

Chapter 11

1. a
2. d
3. b
4. a
5. d

Chapter 12

1. a
2. b
3. d
4. b and c
5. c

Chapter 13

1. a
2. c
3. d

4. a
5. a and d
6. b

Chapter 14

1. d
2. c
3. a
4. a, b, and c
5. b and c

Chapter 15

1. a
2. b and d
3. d
4. a
5. a

Chapter 16

1. c
2. c and d
3. b
4. c
5. a

Memory Tables

Chapter 1

Table 1-2 Required Permissions for Common Tasks

Task	Required Privileges
Create a virtual machine	

Task	Required Privileges
Deploy a virtual machine from a template	On the destination folder or datacenter: **Virtual Machine.Inventory.Create from Existing** **Virtual Machine.Configuration.Add New Disk** On a template or template folder: **Virtual Machine.Provisioning.Deploy Template** On the destination host, cluster, or resource pool: **Resource.Assign Virtual Machine to Resource Pool** On the destination datastore or folder of datastores: **Datastore.Allocate Space** On the network that the virtual machine will be assigned to: **Network.Assign Network**
Take a virtual machine snapshot	
Move a virtual machine into a resource pool	On the virtual machine or folder of virtual machines: **Resource.Assign Virtual Machine to Resource Pool** **Virtual Machine.Inventory.Move** On the destination resource pool: **Resource.Assign Virtual Machine to Resource Pool**

Task	Required Privileges
Install a guest operating system on a virtual machine	On the virtual machine or folder of virtual machines: **Virtual Machine.Interaction.Answer Question** **Virtual Machine.Interaction.Console Interaction** **Virtual Machine.Interaction.Device Connection** **Virtual Machine.Interaction.Power Off** **Virtual Machine.Interaction.Power On** **Virtual Machine.Interaction.Reset** **Virtual Machine.Interaction.Configure CD Media** **Virtual Machine.Interaction.Configure Floppy Media** **Virtual Machine.Interaction.Tools Install** On a datastore containing the installation media ISO image: **Datastore.Browse Datastore** On the datastore to which you upload the installation media ISO image: **Datastore.Browse Datastore** **Datastore.Low Level File Operations**
Migrate a virtual machine with vMotion	

Task	Required Privileges
Cold migrate (relocate) a virtual machine	On the virtual machine or folder of virtual machines: **Resource.Migrate Powered Off Virtual Machine** **Resource.Assign Virtual Machine to Resource Pool** On the destination host, cluster, or resource pool: **Resource.Assign Virtual Machine to Resource Pool** On the destination datastore: **Datastore.Allocate Space**
Migrate a virtual machine with Storage vMotion	On the virtual machine or folder of virtual machines: **Resource.Migrate Powered On Virtual Machine** On the destination datastore: **Datastore.Allocate Space**
Move a host into a cluster	On the host: **Host.Inventory.Add Host to Cluster** On the destination cluster: **Host.Inventory.Add Host to Cluster**

Specifically, it includes only these privileges:

- Virtual Machine > _____ > Disk Lease

- Virtual Machine > Provisioning > _____

- Virtual Machine > _____ > Allow Virtual Machine Download

- Virtual Machine > _____ > _____

- Virtual Machine > Snapshot Management > _____

Table 1-3 Virtual Machine Compatibility Options

Compatibility	Description	Maximum Virtual Cores	Maximum Memory (GB)
ESXi 6.0 and later			
ESXi 5.5 and later			
ESXi 5.1 and later			
ESXi 5.0 and later			
ESX/ESXi 4.0 and later			
ESX/ESXi 3.5 and later			

Table 1-6 Typical ESXi Firewall Services and Ports

Firewall Service	Incoming Port(s)	Outgoing Port(s)
CIM Server	5988 (TCP)	
CIM Secure Server	5989 (TCP)	
CIM SLP	427 (TCP, UDP)	427 (TCP, UDP)

Firewall Service	Incoming Port(s)	Outgoing Port(s)
DHCPv6	546 (TCP, UDP)	547 (TCP, UDP)
DVSSync	8301, 8302 (UDP)	8301, 8302 (UDP)
HBR		44046, 31031 (TCP)
NFC	902 (TCP)	902 (TCP)
WOL		9 (UDP)
Virtual SAN Clustering Service	12345, 23451 (UDP)	12345, 23451 (UDP)
DCHP Client	68 (UDP)	68 (UDP)
DNS Client	53 (UDP)	53 (TCP, UDP)
Fault Tolerance		
NSX Distributed Logical Router Service	6999 (UDP)	6999 (UDP)
rabbitmqproxy		5671 (TCP)
Virtual SAN Transport		
SNMP Server	161 (UDP)	
SSH Server	22 (TCP)	
vMotion		
VMware vCenter Agent		902 (UDP)
vSphere Web Client		
vsanvp	8080 (TCP)	8080 (TCP)

The SSO domain contains many predefined groups, including the following:

- **Users:** Contains all users in the SSO domain.

- _____: Members can perform domain controller administrator actions on the VMware Directory Service.

- _____: Each solution user authenticates individually to vCenter Single Sign-On with a certificate. By default, VMCA provisions solution users with certificates. Do not add members to this group explicitly.

- _____: Members have administrator privileges for VMCA. Adding members to this group is not usually recommended, but a user must be a member of this group to perform most certificate management operations, such as using the `certool` command.

- **SystemConfiguration.BashShellAdministrators:** Only applies to vCenter Server appliance deployments. Members can enable and disable access to the BASH Shell.

- _____: Members can view and manage the system configuration and perform tasks such as restarting services.

- _____: Members have full write access to all licensing-related data and can add, remove, assign, and unassign serial keys for all product assets registered in the licensing service.

- _____: Members can perform SSO administration tasks for the VMware Directory Service (vmdir).

Table 1-7 SSO Policies and Parameters

SSO Policy Type	Policy Parameter	Details
Password policy		Password policy description.
		Maximum number of days that a password can exist before the user must change it.
		Number of the user's previous passwords that cannot be selected.
		Maximum number of characters that are allowed in the password.
		Minimum number of characters that are allowed in the password, which must be no less than the combined minimum of alphabetic, numeric, and special character requirements.
		Minimum number of different character types that are required in the password. The types include special, alphabetic, uppercase, lowercase, and numeric.
		The number of identical adjacent characters that are supported in a password. The value must be greater than 0.
Lockout policy		Description of the lockout policy.
		Maximum number of failed login attempts that are allowed before the account is locked.
		Time period in which failed login attempts must occur to trigger a lockout.
		The amount of time the account stays locked. The value 0 specifies that an administrator must explicitly unlock the account.

SSO Policy Type	Policy Parameter	Details
Token policy		Time difference in milliseconds that SSO tolerates between a client clock and a domain controller clock. If the time difference is greater than the specified value, SSO declares the token to be invalid.
		Maximum number of times a token may be renewed before a new security token is required.
		Maximum number of times a single holder-of-key token can be delegated.
		The lifetime value of a bearer token before the token has to be reissued.
	Maximum holder-of-key token lifetime	The lifetime value of a holder-of-key token before the token is marked invalid.

Chapter 2

Table 2-2   vSphere Standard Switches Versus vSphere Distributed Switches

Feature	vSS	vDS
Layer 2	×	×
VLAN tagging (802.1q)	×	×
Datacenter level management		×
Network vMotion		×
Per-port policy settings		×
Port state monitoring		×
NetFlow		×

Feature	vSS	vDS
Port mirroring		×
Network I/O Control		×

Chapter 3

System traffic allows the definition of shares, reservations, and limits for all types of VMkernel traffic:

- Fault tolerance
- Management
- _____
- _____
- _____
- _____
- _____
- _____
- _____

Chapter 4

Table 4-2   vCenter Server Storage Filters

Filter	Advanced Setting Key
RDM	config.vpxd.filter.rdmFilter
VMFS	config.vpxd.filter.vmfsFilter
Host Rescan	
Same Host and Transports	

Table 4-3 CHAP Security Levels

CHAP Security Level	Description	Supported
None	CHAP authentication is not used. Select this option to disable authentication if it is currently enabled.	Software iSCSI Dependent hardware iSCSI Independent hardware iSCSI
Use Unidirectional CHAP if Required by Target	Host prefers non-CHAP connection but can use CHAP if required by the target.	
Use Unidirectional CHAP Unless Prohibited by Target	Host prefers CHAP but can use non-CHAP if the target does not support CHAP.	
Use Unidirectional CHAP	Host requires CHAP authentication. The connection fails if CHAP negotiation fails.	
Use Bidirectional CHAP	Host and target both support bidirectional CHAP.	Software iSCSI Dependent hardware iSCSI

Chapter 5

Claim rules can be created based on the following elements:

- `vendor` string: A claim rule can be set up using the `vendor` string, which must be an exact match. An example would be `vendor=DELL`.

- _____

- _____

- _____

Chapter 6

Table 6-2 Comparing Upgraded and Newly Formatted VMFS5 Datastores

Characteristic	Upgraded VMFS5	Formatted VMFS5
File block size		1 MB
Sub-block size		8 KB

Characteristic	Upgraded VMFS5	Formatted VMFS5
Partition format		GPT format
Datastore limits		Utilizes the new VMFS5 limits.
VMFS locking mechanism		Uses ATS only on hardware that supports ATS. Uses ATS and SCSI on hardware that does not support ATS.

Chapter 7

Table 7-2   vCenter Server Appliance CPU and Memory Choices

Option	Description
Tiny (up to 10 hosts, 100 VMs)	Deploys appliance with 2 CPUs and 8 GB of memory
Small (up to 100 hosts, 1000 VMs)	
Medium (up to 400 hosts, 4000 VMs)	
Large (up to 1000 hosts, 10,000 VMs)	

Chapter 8

Table 8-2   Share Allocations for VMs Versus Resource Pools

	VM CPU Share Values	VM Memory Share Values	Resource Pool CPU Share Values	Resource Pool Memory Share Values
High				
Normal	1000 shares per vCPU	10 shares per MB of configured RAM	4000	163840
Low				

Chapter 9

Table 9-2 Minimum System Requirements for VDP

Configuration	Number of 2 GHz Processors	Memory (GB)	Disk Space
0.5 TB	4	4	873 GB
1 TB	4	4	1600 GB
2 TB	4	4	3 TB

Table 9-3 Virtual Machine Snapshot Files

Filename Syntax	Filename Example	Description (GB)
		Contains snapshot metadata, such as the name of the delta file and disk geometry.
		Contains all the virtual disk data blocks that have changed at least once following the creation of the snapshot. Each block represents the most recent state of that block.
		Contains information on all of the virtual machine's snapshots.
		Contains the memory state of the of the virtual machine, if you select to snapshot the memory.

Table 9-4 Supported Quiescing for Windows and vSphere Replication Versions

Windows Version	Application Quiescing		File System Quiescing	
	vSphere Replication 5.8	vSphere Replication 6.0	vSphere Replication 5.8	vSphere Replication 6.0
Windows Server 2003				
Windows Server 2008				
Windows Server 2012	Yes	Yes	Yes	Yes
Windows Vista				
Windows 7				
Windows 8				

Chapter 10

You find the following services at **Administration > System Configuration > Services**:

- Auto Deploy

- _____

- _____

- Hardware Health Service

- _____

- _____

- Transfer Service

- _____

- _____

- VMware Open Virtualization Format Service

- _____

- VMware Postgres

- VMware Syslog Service

- VMware vCenter Server

- VMware Service Manager

- VMware vSphere ESXi Dump Collector
- VMware vSphere Profile-Driven Storage Service
- VMware vSphere Web Client
- _____

Table 10-3   ESXTOP Replay Mode Command-Line Options

Option	Description
	Path to the data collected by `vm-support`
	Show all statistics
	Run in batch mode
	User-defined configuration file
	Delay (in seconds) for the sampling period. The default is 5, and the minimum is 2.
	Number of iterations (samples) for ESXTOP to take prior to automatically exiting.

Table 10-4   ESXi Log Files

Component	Location	Purpose
VMkernel		Records activities related to virtual machines and ESXi.
VMkernel warnings		Records activities related to virtual machines.
Vmkernel summary		Used to determine uptime and availability statistics for ESXi.
ESXi Host agent		Contains information about the agent that manages and configures the ESXi Host and its virtual machines.
vCenter agent		Contains information about the agent that communicates with vCenter Server.
ESXi Shell		Contains a record of all commands typed into the ESXi Shell as well as shell events.

Component	Location	Purpose
Authentication		Contains all events related to authentication for the local system.
System Messages		Contains all general log messages and can be used for troubleshooting.
Virtual Machines		Contains virtual machine power events, system failure information, tools status and activity, time sync, virtual hardware changes, vMotion migrations, machine clones, and more.

Table 10-6   vCenter Server Ports

Port	Purpose
	For SSH connections, when using the vCenter Server Appliance
	For direct HTTP connections, which vCenter Server automatically redirects to port 443
	For VMware key distribution
	For Directory Services
	For connections with the vSphere Web Client, SDK clients, and third-party clients
	For Syslog Collector connections
	For vCenter Server Enhanced Linked Mode
	For ESXi Host management
	For SSO control
	For VMCA API connections
	For authentication framework management
	For ESXi Dump Collection connections
	For Auto Deploy service and management
	For Secure Token Service (STS)
	For vSphere Web Client HTTPS connections
	For VMware Directory Service (vmdir) LDAP and LDAPS

Table 10-8   Potential PSC Installation Issues

Symptom	Root Cause	Solution Example
During the installation of a second PSC, the installation fails and leaves incomplete data on the first PSC.	During the initial failure, the second PSC was attempting to join the current SSO domain, resulting in incomplete data on the first PSC.	
A vCenter Server installation that uses a Microsoft SQL database fails, with the following message: `The DB User entered does not have the required permissions needed to install and configure vCenter Server with the selected DB.`	This could be caused by an unsupported database version or permissions. But it could also be caused when a supported database version is set for compatibility mode with an unsupported version.	
The installation of vCenter Server fails.	The vCenter Server and the PSC have a time skew of more than 3 minutes.	
The vCenter Server installation fails due to improper registration with the PSC.	You specified an FQDN during the PSC installation but used an IP address when registering vCenter Server with the PSC or vice versa.	

Chapter 11

Table 11-2   Storage Configuration Issues That Impact ESXi

Problem	Root Cause(s)	Solution(s)
The ESXi Host cannot access a new storage device.	In order to detect the new device, a storage rescan is required.	
The ESXi Host cannot access the Fibre Channel storage array.	Zoning is improperly configured on the Fibre Channel switches, preventing the ESXi Host's storage adapters from connecting to the array's storage processors.	

Problem	Root Cause(s)	Solution(s)
The ESXi Host does not recognize its storage adapter.	The proper storage adapter driver is not installed on the ESXi Host.	
The storage I/O performance of an ESXi Host is terrible or unusable.	The storage multipathing is misconfigured.	
The performance of the datastore in a datastore cluster is poor. The datastores are backed by auto-tiering storage.	Storage DRS is configured to balance based on I/O, but the storage vendor does not recommend or support this.	
An ESXi Host cannot access a specific storage device.	The LUN masking configuration in the array is not properly set.	
Virtual machine performance is very poor due to increased disk I/O latency.	The current LUN queue depth is inadequate.	

Problem	Root Cause(s)	Solution(s)
The operational state of a storage device is `Lost Communication`. The status of all paths to the device is Dead. When you analyze ESXi Host's `/var/log/vmkernel` log files, you encounter events or error messages that contain SCSI Sense codes.	The storage device is in a permanent device lost (PDL) state.	
An ESXi Host does not automatically detect a flash disk or recognize it as a local disk.	Some flash disk vendors do not support automatic flash recognition. In these cases, the ESXi Host does not recognize the disk as flash storage or as a local device.	

Table 11-3 Network Configuration Issues That Impact Virtual Machines

Problem	Root Cause(s)	Solution(s)
A virtual machine is able to communicate with other virtual machines on the same virtual switch port group and ESXi Host, but it cannot communicate with any other server.	The virtual switch port group VLAN setting does not match the physical switch port setting.	

Problem	Root Cause(s)	Solution(s)
A set of virtual machines lost connectivity to the network during a maintenance procedure, where you deliberately disconnected just one of two host network adapters in a team. Because you have NIC teaming set up, you expected the virtual switch to fail over the impacted virtual machine connections to the other network adapter.	The NIC teaming on the virtual switch port group is misconfigured. One of the two available paths is inadvertently configured as Unused instead of Active or Standby. In this case, the virtual machine may still be connected to the network if at least one active path is healthy, but a single path failure may cause the virtual machine connection to drop.	
A set of virtual machines on the same virtual switch port group cannot communicate with external devices.	The virtual switch port group NIC teaming is set to Route-Based on IP Hash, but then the physical switch ports are not configured for Etherchannel.	
A set of virtual machines that requires jumbo frames and is connected to a specific distributed switch port group is not performing well.	Jumbo frame support is not properly configured on the distributed virtual switch.	
One specific virtual machine cannot communicate with any device on the network, including virtual machines on the same host and connected to the same virtual switch port group.	A virtual machine guest OS is configured with the wrong IP settings.	
One specific virtual machine cannot communicate with any device on the network. The guest O/S reports issues with the network adapter.	A virtual machine is configured with the wrong virtual NIC.	

Problem	Root Cause(s)	Solution(s)
A set of virtual machines is able to communicate well with other virtual machines on the same virtual switch port group and ESXi Host but experiences terrible performance when communicating with other servers.	The physical NIC settings, such as speed or duplex, are improperly configured.	
The network performance of a set of virtual machines is poor when the workload is significant but the physical network adapter bandwidth is not being saturated.	Network traffic shaping is misconfigured. The average bandwidth, peak bandwidth, or burst size is set too low on a virtual switch port group.	
A virtual machine running network analyzer software (such as Wireshark) is unable to successfully monitor network traffic.	The security settings for the standard virtual switch port group are misconfigured. Promiscuous mode is rejected.	
Microsoft Network Load Balancing (NLB) is not working in unicast mode for a specific virtual machine.	The associated virtual switch port group is misconfigured. The virtual switch is rejecting forged transmits and is notifying the physical switch.	

Table 11-4   Potential Storage DRS Problems and Solutions

Problem	Root Cause(s)	Solution(s)
Attempts for a datastore in a datastore cluster to enter maintenance mode are not successful. The status hangs at 1%.	Storage DRS is disabled on at least one virtual disk in the datastore. Storage DRS rules prevent Storage DRS from performing the required migrations	

Problem	Root Cause(s)	Solution(s)
Storage DRS generates an event and an alarm that it cannot operate on a specific datastore.	ESXi Hosts that reside in different virtual datacenters share the datastore. Or the datastore is connected to an unsupported ESXi Host, such as a host running ESXi 4.1.	
When migrating virtual machines into a datastore cluster, not all virtual machines migrate successfully, and the error message Insufficient Disk Space on Datastore appears.	During the placement of each virtual machine, Storage DRS does not account for the space that will be consumed upon completion, so it may attempt to allocate the space for subsequent placement requests.	
When you create or clone a virtual machine in a datastore cluster, the error message Operation Not Allowed in the Current State is received.	A Storage DRS rule cannot check the new virtual machine's disk for compliance, and it generates a fault.	
When you deploy an OVF template that has Storage DRS disabled, the deployed virtual machine actually has Storage DRS enabled.	By design, Storage DRS applies the automation level of the datastore to the deployed virtual machine.	
Multiple instances of the same affinity or anti-affinity rule violation appear in the Faults dialog box when you attempt to put a datastore into maintenance mode.	Actually, each fault refers to a different datastore, but because the datastore names are not displayed, the faults appear to be redundant.	
Affinity or anti-affinity rules still apply to a virtual machine after the virtual machine was migrated from a datastore cluster.	Rules remain with a virtual machine that is removed from a datastore cluster if the virtual machine remains in the associated vCenter Server inventory.	

Problem	Root Cause(s)	Solution(s)
Attempts to apply Storage DRS recommendations fail.	The thin-provisioning-threshold-crossed alarm may be triggered, which indicates that the datastore is low on free space. The target datastore may be in or entering maintenance mode.	
When you create, clone, or relocate a virtual machine in a datastore cluster, Storage DRS provides only one recommendation.	The ESXi Host specifies the virtual machine swap file location as a datastore in the target datastore cluster, so the disks to be placed in the cluster do not form a single affinity group. Storage DRS does not generate alternative recommendations in cases where a single affinity group is not used.	

Storage performance issues could be caused by excessive SCSI reservations. The following operations often cause VMFS to use SCSI reservations:

- _____

- Powering on a virtual machine

- _____

- Creating a template

- _____

- Migrating with vMotion

- Growing a file, such as growing a thin-provisioned virtual disk or snapshot (redo) file

Table 11-7   vCenter Server Database Upgrade Logs

Purpose	Log File
Collect errors during execution of the pre-upgrade check.	
Collect errors during the export phase of the upgrade process.	

Purpose	Log File
Collect errors during the import phase of the upgrade process.	
Collect errors during an in-place upgrade	

Table 11-8 vCenter Server Logging Options

Logging Option	Description
	No vCenter Server logging occurs.
	The vCenter Server collects only error entries into its log files.
Warning (Warning and Errors)	The vCenter Server collects warning and error entries into its log files.
Info (Normal logging)	The vCenter Server collects information, warning, and error entries into its log files.
Verbose (Verbose)	The vCenter Server collects verbose, information, warning, and error entries into its log files.
Trivia (Extended verbose)	

Chapter 12

Table 12-2 Critical Performance Metrics

Metric	Description
Disk Latency	The amount of time that elapsed while performing a storage-related task, such as a read or write operation. Latency can be reported from various perspectives. For example, the virtual machine disk read latency is the amount of time from which the guest OS generates the read operation until it is completely fulfilled by the storage system and the data is delivered to the guest OS. High disk latency is often an indicator of slow or overworked storage devices.

Metric	Description
Memory Swapped	The amount of data that has been swapped from a virtual machine's memory to its virtual machine swap file. It is often an indicator of overworked memory hardware.

Table 12-3   Potential Memory Issues and Resolutions

Potential Issue	Indicators	Potential Resolutions
The VM is experiencing memory contention.	Memory Ballooning, Memory Decompression Rate, and/or Memory Swap In Rate is greater than zero. Memory latency is 5% or higher, which indicates that the VM is waiting to access swapped or compressed data.	

Potential Issue	Indicators	Potential Resolutions
The VM's virtual memory resources are insufficient to meet the current demand.	The Memory Usage of the VM is about 100%. The guest OS reports high paging. For example, for Windows it is reporting Pages/sec is 200.	
The ESXi Host's memory resources are insufficient to meet the current demand from its VMs.	Memory State is Hard or Low, which indicates that the ESXi Host is swapping and compressing memory. Memory Latency is 5% or higher.	

Table 12-4   Potential CPU Issues and Resolutions

Potential Issue	Indicators	Potential Resolutions
The VM is experiencing CPU contention.	CPU Ready Time for one or more of the VM's virtual CPUs is frequently 2000 ms or more.	
The VM's virtual CPU resources are insufficient to meet the current demand.	The CPU Usage of the entire VM and of each of the VM's virtual CPUs is frequently 80% or higher.	
The ESXi Host's CPU resources are insufficient to meet the current demand from its VMs.	The CPU Usage of the ESXi Host and each of its CPU cores is frequently 80% or higher. CPU Latency is 5% or higher.	

Table 12-5 Common ESXTOP Metrics

Metric	Common Name
MCTLSZ	Balloon Size (in MB)
SWCUR	Swapped (in MB)
UNZIP/s	Decompression Rate (KB per second)
GAVG	Guest Latency (milliseconds)
DAVG	Device Latency (milliseconds)
ABRTS/s	Aborts (per second)

Table 12-6 Intel EVC Baselines

EVC Level	EVC Baseline	Description
L0	Merom	Merom generation feature set
L1	Penryn	Penryn generation (Merom plus CPU features including SSE4.1)
L2	Nehalem	Nehalem generation (Penryn plus additional CPU features including SSE4.2 and POPCOUNT)
L3		
L4		
L5	Ivy Bridge	Ivy Bridge generation (Sandy Bridge Generation plus additional CPU features, including RDRAND, ENFSTRG, FSGSBASE, SMEP, and F16C)

Chapter 13

Table 13-2   FT and Legacy FT

	Legacy FT	**FT**
Extended page tables/rapid virtualization indexing (Intel EPT/AMD RVI)	Not supported	Required
IPv6	Not supported for FT logging NICs	Supported for FT logging NICs
DRS	Fully supported for initial placement, load balancing, and maintenance mode support	Only power-on placement of secondary VM and maintenance mode are supported
vStorage APIs—data protection backups	Not supported	
Eager-zeros thick .vmdk files	Required	
.vmdk redundancy	Only a single copy	
NIC bandwidth	Dedicated 1 GB NIC recommended	
CPU and host compatibility	Requires identical CPU model and family and nearly identical versions of vSphere on hosts	
Turn on FT on running VM	Not always supported. You might need to power off the VM first	
Storage vMotion	Supported only on powered-off VMs vCenter Server automatically turns off FT before performing a Storage vMotion action and then turns on FT again after the Storage vMotion action completes	
Vlance networking drivers	Not supported	

Chapter 14

Table 14-2 PowerCLI Auto Deploy cmdlets

Command	Description
`Get-DeployCommand`	Returns a list of Auto Deploy cmdlets.
`New-DeployRule`	Creates a new rule with the specified items and patterns.
	Updates an existing rule with the specified items and patterns. You cannot update a rule that is part of a rule set.
	Retrieves the rules with the specified names.
	Clones and updates an existing rule.
	Adds one or more rules to the working rule set and, by default, also to the active rule set. Use the `NoActivate` parameter to add a rule only to the working rule set.
	Removes one or more rules from the working rule set and from the active rule set. Run this command with the `-Delete` parameter to completely delete the rule.
	Explicitly sets the list of rules in the working rule set.
	Retrieves the current working rule set or the current active rule set.
	Activates a rule set so that any new requests are evaluated through the rule set.
	Retrieves rules matching a pattern. For example, you can retrieve all rules that apply to a host or hosts. Use this cmdlet primarily for debugging.
	Checks whether the items associated with a specified hosts are in compliance with the active rule set.
	Given the output of `Test-DeployRulesetCompliance`, this cmdlet updates the image profile, host profile, and location for each host in the vCenter Server inventory. The cmdlet might apply image profiles, apply host profiles, or move hosts to the prespecified folders or clusters on the vCenter Server system.
	Retrieves the image profile in use by a specified host. This cmdlet differs from the `Get-EsxImageProfile` cmdlet in the Image Builder PowerCLI.

Command	Description
	Use this cmdlet only if the Auto Deploy image cache is accidentally deleted.
	Retrieves the attributes for a host that are used when the Auto Deploy server evaluates the rules.
	Returns a string value that Auto Deploy uses to logically link an ESXi Host in vCenter to a physical machine.
	Logically links a host object in the vCenter Server database to a physical machine. Use this cmdlet to add hosts without specifying rules.
	Retrieves the Auto Deploy global configuration options. This cmdlet currently supports the vlan-id option, which specifies the default VLAN ID for the ESXi Management Network of a host provisioned with Auto Deploy. Auto Deploy uses the value only if the host boots without a host profile.
	Sets the value of a global configuration option. Currently supports the vlan-id option for setting the default VLAN ID for the ESXi Management Network.

Chapter 15

The following are VMware's advanced HA settings that can be modified in the vSphere Web Client:

- **das.isolationaddress[...]:** Sets the address to ping to determine whether a host is isolated from the network. This address is pinged only when heartbeats are not received from any other host in the cluster. If not specified, the default gateway of the management network is used. You can specify multiple isolation addresses (up to 10) for the cluster:

  das.isolationaddressX, where X=0-9.

- **das.usedefaultisolationaddress:** By default, vSphere HA uses the default gateway of the console network as an isolation address. This option specifies whether (true) or not (false) this default is used.

- _____: Specifies the period of time the system waits for a virtual machine to shut down before powering it off. This applies only if the host's isolation response is shut down VM. The default value is 300 seconds.

- _____: Defines the maximum memory slot size. If this option is used, the slot size is the smaller of this value or the maximum memory reservation plus memory overhead of any powered-on virtual machine in the cluster.

- _____: Defines the maximum CPU slot size. If this option is used, the slot size is the smaller of this value or the maximum CPU reservation of any powered-on virtual machine in the cluster.

- _____: Defines the default memory resource value assigned to a virtual machine if its memory reservation is not specified or zero. This is used for the Host Failures Cluster Tolerates admission control policy. If no value is specified, the default is 0 MB.

- _____: Defines the default CPU resource value assigned to a virtual machine if its CPU reservation is not specified or is zero. This is used for the Host Failures Cluster Tolerates admission control policy. If no value is specified, the default is 32 MHz.

- _____: Changes the default I/O stats interval for VM monitoring sensitivity. The default is 120 (seconds), but it can be set to any value greater than or equal to 0. Setting to 0 disables the check.

- _____: Disables configuration issues created if the host does not have sufficient heartbeat datastores for vSphere HA. The default value is `false`.

- _____: Changes the number of heartbeat datastores required. Valid values can range from 2 to 5, and the default is 2.

- _____: Specifies the number of seconds the system waits before executing the isolation policy once it is determined that a host is isolated. The minimum value is 30.

- _____: Determines whether vSphere HA enforces VM-VM anti-affinity rules. The default value is `false`, which means the rules are not enforced. Can also be set to `true` to have rules enforced (even if vSphere DRS is not enabled). In this case, vSphere HA does not fail over a virtual machine if doing so violates a rule, but it issues an event reporting there are insufficient resources to perform the failover.

- _____: Specifies the maximum number of reset attempts made by VMCP. If a reset operation on a virtual machine affected by an APD situation fails, VMCP retries the reset this many times before giving up.

- _____: Specifies the maximum number of retries made by VMCP for virtual machine termination.

- _____: Specifies the number of seconds the system waits before it retries a terminate attempt after VMCP fails to terminate a virtual machine.

- _____: When set to 1, enables generation of a detailed per-VM event when an attempt by vSphere HA to restart a virtual machine is unsuccessful. The default value is 0.

- _____: Specifies the period of time (in seconds) after a VM-Host affinity rule is set during which vSphere HA can restart a VM in a DRS-disabled cluster, overriding the rule. The default value is 300 seconds.

- _____: By default, vSphere HA agents run with a configured memory limit of 250 MB. A host might not allow this reservation if it runs out of reservable capacity. You can use this advanced option to lower the memory limit to avoid this issue. Only integers 100 and greater can be specified. To prevent problems during master agent elections in a large cluster (containing 6,000 to 8,000 VMs), you should raise this limit to 325 MB.

Chapter 16

Table 16-2 Virtual Machine Option Categories

Category	Description
General Options	Common virtual machine attributes such as name, location, working folder, and guest operating system.
VMware Remote Console Options	Settings, such as locking behavior, that control multiple simultaneous connections to the virtual machine's remote console.
VMware Tools	Settings that impact virtual machine management via VMware Tools, such as time synchronization, automatic upgrade, and scripts.
Power Management	Virtual machine behavior for suspend operations and wake on LAN.

Table 16-4 NUMA-Related Attributes

Attribute	Description
	For virtual machines with a virtual NUMA topology, this value, which defines the number of virtual cores per virtual CPU socket, can also impact the size of the virtual NUMA node. In this case, if the value is greater than 1, it is also used as the number of virtual cores per virtual node. The default value is 1. You can only set this to powers of 2, such as 2, 4, and 8.
	When this attribute is set to TRUE, the number of virtual cores per node in the virtual NUMA topology is automatically set to match the number of cores in each physical node. The default value is FALSE.
	When this attribute is set to TRUE, this attribute ensures that the automatically assigned virtual node size remains unchanged during future power-on operations, unless the number of virtual CPUs in the virtual machine is modified. The default value is TRUE.
	This setting can be used instead of cupid.coresPerSocket. It assigns the maximum number of virtual cores per virtual node, which must be a power of 2. The default value is 8.
	This setting is the minimum number of virtual CPUs in a virtual machine required for generating a virtual NUMA topology. The default value is 9.
	This setting specifies the maximum number of virtual CPUs in a NUMA client, which is a set of virtual CPUs that are managed as a single entity. You can set this when the size of the virtual NUMA node exceeds the size of the physical NUMA node. The default value is equal to numa.vcpu.maxPerVirtualNode.

Attribute	Description
	This setting specifies the set of NUMA nodes on which the virtual machine can execute. You should avoid using this setting except when necessary because it negatively impacts the ability of the NUMA scheduler to rebalance workload. When configuring this parameter, set its value to a comma-delimited list indicating the acceptable NUMA nodes. For example, to allow the virtual machine to only execute on NUMA nodes 0 and 1, enter `0,1`.
	This setting specifies whether the virtual machine memory is statically interleaved across all the NUMA nodes on which its corresponding NUMA clients are running when no virtual NUMA topology is exposed.

Memory Tables Answer Key

Chapter 1

Table 1-2   Required Permissions for Common Tasks

Task	Required Privileges
Create a virtual machine	On the destination folder or datacenter:
	Virtual Machine.Inventory.Raw Create New
	Virtual Machine.Configuration.Add New Disk
	Virtual Machine.Configuration.Add Existing Disk
	Virtual Machine.Configuration.Raw Device
	On the destination host, cluster, or resource pool:
	Resource. Assign Virtual Machine to Resource Pool
	On the destination datastore or datastore folder:
	Datastore.Allocate Space
	On the network:
	Network.Assign Network

Task	Required Privileges
Deploy a virtual machine from a template	On the destination folder or datacenter:
	Virtual Machine.Inventory.Create from Existing
	Virtual Machine.Configuration.Add New Disk
	On a template or template folder:
	Virtual Machine.Provisioning.Deploy Template
	On the destination host, cluster, or resource pool:
	Resource.Assign Virtual Machine to Resource Pool
	On the destination datastore or folder of datastores:
	Datastore.Allocate Space
	On the network that the virtual machine will be assigned to:
	Network.Assign Network
Take a virtual machine snapshot	On the virtual machine or a folder of virtual machines:
	Virtual Machine.Snapshot Management.Create Snapshot
	On the destination datastore or folder of datastores:
	Datastore.Allocate Space
Move a virtual machine into a resource pool	On the virtual machine or folder of virtual machines:
	Resource.Assign Virtual Machine to Resource Pool
	Virtual Machine.Inventory.Move
	On the destination resource pool:
	Resource.Assign Virtual Machine to Resource Pool

Task	Required Privileges
Install a guest operating system on a virtual machine	On the virtual machine or folder of virtual machines:
	Virtual Machine.Interaction.Answer Question
	Virtual Machine.Interaction.Console Interaction
	Virtual Machine.Interaction.Device Connection
	Virtual Machine.Interaction.Power Off
	Virtual Machine.Interaction.Power On
	Virtual Machine.Interaction.Reset
	Virtual Machine.Interaction.Configure CD Media
	Virtual Machine.Interaction.Configure Floppy Media
	Virtual Machine.Interaction.Tools Install
	On a datastore containing the installation media ISO image:
	Datastore.Browse Datastore
	On the datastore to which you upload the installation media ISO image:
	Datastore.Browse Datastore
	Datastore.Low Level File Operations
Migrate a virtual machine with vMotion	On the virtual machine or folder of virtual machines:
	Resource.Migrate Powered on Virtual Machine
	Resource.Assign Virtual Machine to Resource Pool
	On the destination host, cluster, or resource pool:
	Resource.Assign Virtual Machine to Resource Pool
Cold migrate (relocate) a virtual machine	On the virtual machine or folder of virtual machines:
	Resource.Migrate Powered Off Virtual Machine
	Resource.Assign Virtual Machine to Resource Pool
	On the destination host, cluster, or resource pool:
	Resource.Assign Virtual Machine to Resource Pool
	On the destination datastore:
	Datastore.Allocate Space

Task	Required Privileges
Migrate a virtual machine with Storage vMotion	On the virtual machine or folder of virtual machines: **Resource.Migrate Powered On Virtual Machine** On the destination datastore: **Datastore.Allocate Space**
Move a host into a cluster	On the host: **Host.Inventory.Add Host to Cluster** On the destination cluster: **Host.Inventory.Add Host to Cluster**

Specifically, it includes only these privileges:

- Virtual Machine > Configuration > Disk Lease
- Virtual Machine > Provisioning > Allow Read-Only Disk Access
- Virtual Machine > Provisioning > Allow Virtual Machine Download
- Virtual Machine > Snapshot Management > Create Snapshot
- Virtual Machine > Snapshot Management > Remove Snapshot

Table 1-3 Virtual Machine Compatibility Options

Compatibility	Description	Maximum Virtual Cores	Maximum Memory (GB)
ESXi 6.0 and later	This virtual machine (hardware version 11) is compatible with ESXi 6.0 and later.	128	4080
ESXi 5.5 and later	This virtual machine (hardware version 10) is compatible with ESXi 5.5 and later.	64	1011
ESXi 5.1 and later	This virtual machine (hardware version 9) is compatible with ESXi 5.1 and later.	64	1011

Compatibility	Description	Maximum Virtual Cores	Maximum Memory (GB)
ESXi 5.0 and later	This virtual machine (hardware version 8) is compatible with ESXi 5.0 and 5.1.	32	1011
ESX/ESXi 4.0 and later	This virtual machine (hardware version 7) is compatible with ESX/ESXi 4.x, ESXi 5.0, and ESXi 5.1.	8	255
ESX/ESXi 3.5 and later	This virtual machine (hardware version 4) is compatible with ESX/ESX 3.5, ESX/ESX 4.x, and ESXi 5.1. It is also compatible with VMware Server 1.0 and later. You cannot create a virtual machine with ESX/ESXi 3.5 compatibility on ESXi 5.0.	4	64

Table 1-6   Typical ESXi Firewall Services and Ports

Firewall Service	Incoming Port(s)	Outgoing Port(s)
CIM Server	5988 (TCP)	
CIM Secure Server	5989 (TCP)	
CIM SLP	427 (TCP, UDP)	427 (TCP, UDP)
DHCPv6	546 (TCP, UDP)	547 (TCP, UDP)
DVSSync	8301, 8302 (UDP)	8301, 8302 (UDP)
HBR		44046, 31031 (TCP)
NFC	902 (TCP)	902 (TCP)
WOL		9 (UDP)
Virtual SAN Clustering Service	12345, 23451 (UDP)	12345, 23451 (UDP)
DCHP Client	68 (UDP)	68 (UDP)
DNS Client	53 (UDP)	53 (TCP, UDP)
Fault Tolerance	8100, 8200, 8300 (TCP, UDP)	8100, 8200, 8300 (TCP, UDP)
NSX Distributed Logical Router Service	6999 (UDP)	6999 (UDP)

Firewall Service	Incoming Port(s)	Outgoing Port(s)
rabbitmqproxy		5671 (TCP)
Virtual SAN Transport	2233 (TCP)	2233 (TCP)
SNMP Server	161 (UDP)	
SSH Server	22 (TCP)	
vMotion	8000 (TCP)	8000 (TCP)
VMware vCenter Agent		902 (UDP)
vSphere Web Client	902, 443 (TCP)	
vsanvp	8080 (TCP)	8080 (TCP)

The SSO domain contains many predefined groups, including the following:

- **Users:** Contains all users in the SSO domain.

- **DCAdmins:** Members can perform domain controller administrator actions on the VMware Directory Service.

- **SolutionUsers:** Each solution user authenticates individually to vCenter Single Sign-On with a certificate. By default, VMCA provisions solution users with certificates. Do not add members to this group explicitly.

- **CAAdmins:** Members have administrator privileges for VMCA. Adding members to this group is not usually recommended, but a user must be a member of this group to perform most certificate management operations, such as using the `certool` command.

- **SystemConfiguration.BashShellAdministrators:** Only applies to vCenter Server appliance deployments. Members can enable and disable access to the BASH Shell.

- **SystemConfiguration.Administrators:** Members can view and manage the system configuration and perform tasks such as restarting services.

- **LicenseSevice.Administrators:** Members have full write access to all licensing-related data and can add, remove, assign, and unassign serial keys for all product assets registered in the licensing service.

- **Administrators:** Members can perform SSO administration tasks for the VMware Directory Service (vmdir).

Table 1-7 SSO Policies and Parameters

SSO Policy Type	Policy Parameter	Details
Password policy	Description	Password policy description.
	Maximum lifetime	Maximum number of days that a password can exist before the user must change it.
	Restrict reuse	Number of the user's previous passwords that cannot be selected.
	Maximum length	Maximum number of characters that are allowed in the password.
	Minimum length	Minimum number of characters that are allowed in the password, which must be no less than the combined minimum of alphabetic, numeric, and special character requirements.
	Character requirements	Minimum number of different character types that are required in the password. The types include special, alphabetic, uppercase, lowercase, and numeric.
	Identical adjacent characters	The number of identical adjacent characters that are supported in a password. The value must be greater than 0.
Lockout policy	Description	Description of the lockout policy.
	Max number of failed login attempts	Maximum number of failed login attempts that are allowed before the account is locked.
	Time interval between failures	Time period in which failed login attempts must occur to trigger a lockout.
	Unlock time	The amount of time the account stays locked. The value 0 specifies that an administrator must explicitly unlock the account.

SSO Policy Type	Policy Parameter	Details
Token policy	Clock tolerance	Time difference in milliseconds that SSO tolerates between a client clock and a domain controller clock. If the time difference is greater than the specified value, SSO declares the token to be invalid.
	Maximum token renewal count	Maximum number of times a token may be renewed before a new security token is required.
	Maximum token delegation count	Maximum number of times a single holder-of-key token can be delegated.
	Maximum bearer token lifetime	The lifetime value of a bearer token before the token has to be reissued.
	Maximum holder-of-key token lifetime	The lifetime value of a holder-of-key token before the token is marked invalid.

Chapter 2

Table 2-2   vSphere Standard Switches Versus vSphere Distributed Switches

Feature	vSS	vDS
Layer 2	×	×
VLAN tagging (802.1q)	×	×
IPv6	×	×
NIC teaming	×	×
Outbound traffic shaping	×	×
Inbound traffic shaping		×
VM network port block		×
Private VLANs		×
Load-based teaming		×
Datacenter level management		×
Network vMotion		×
Per-port policy settings		×
Port state monitoring		×
NetFlow		×
Port mirroring		×
Network I/O Control		×

Chapter 3

System traffic allows the definition of shares, reservations, and limits for all types of VMkernel traffic:

- Fault tolerance

- Management

- NFS

- Virtual machines

- vSAN

- iSCSI

- vMotion

- vSphere data protection

- vSphere replication

Chapter 4

Table 4-2   vCenter Server Storage Filters

Filter	Advanced Setting Key
RDM	`config.vpxd.filter.rdmFilter`
VMFS	`config.vpxd.filter.vmfsFilter`
Host Rescan	`config.vpxd.filter.hostRescanFilter`
Same Host and Transports	`config.vpxd.filter.SameHostAndTransportsFilter`

Table 4-3   CHAP Security Levels

CHAP Security Level	Description	Supported
None	CHAP authentication is not used. Select this option to disable authentication if it is currently enabled.	Software iSCSI Dependent hardware iSCSI Independent hardware iSCSI
Use Unidirectional CHAP if Required by Target	Host prefers non-CHAP connection but can use CHAP if required by the target.	Software iSCSI Dependent hardware iSCSI

CHAP Security Level	Description	Supported
Use Unidirectional CHAP Unless Prohibited by Target	Host prefers CHAP but can use non-CHAP if the target does not support CHAP.	Software iSCSI Dependent hardware iSCSI Independent hardware iSCSI
Use Unidirectional CHAP	Host requires CHAP authentication. The connection fails if CHAP negotiation fails.	Software iSCSI Dependent hardware iSCSI Independent hardware iSCSI
Use Bidirectional CHAP	Host and target both support bidirectional CHAP.	Software iSCSI Dependent hardware iSCSI

Chapter 5

Claim rules can be created based on the following elements:

- **vendor string:** A claim rule can be set up using the vendor string, which must be an exact match. An example would be vendor=DELL.

- **model string:** A claim rule can be set up using the model string, which must be an exact match. An example would be model=Universal Xport.

- **transport type:** A claim rule can be created to mask all LUNs based on the transport type. Valid transport types are block, fc, iscsi, iscsivendor, ide, sas, sata, usb, parallel, and unknown.

- **Driver type:** A driver name can be used to create a claim rule. Figure 5-18 lists all the drivers that can be used in a claim rule. You can set up a claim rule masking all paths to devices attached to an HBA using a driver such as the iscsi_vmk driver:

Chapter 6

Table 6-2 Comparing Upgraded and Newly Formatted VMFS5 Datastores

Characteristic	Upgraded VMFS5	Formatted VMFS5
File block size	1 MB, 2 MB, 4 MB, and 8 MB	1 MB
Sub-block size	64 KB	8 KB

Characteristic	Upgraded VMFS5	Formatted VMFS5
Partition format	Originally MBR format. The datastore size needs to expand beyond 2 TB for conversion to GPT format.	GPT format
Datastore limits	Retains limitations of the original VMFS3 file system.	Utilizes the new VMFS5 limits.
VMFS locking mechanism	Uses ATS and SCSI	Uses ATS only on hardware that supports ATS. Uses ATS and SCSI on hardware that does not support ATS.

Chapter 7

Table 7-2 vCenter Server Appliance CPU and Memory Choices

Option	Description
Tiny (up to 10 hosts, 100 VMs)	Deploys appliance with 2 CPUs and 8 GB of memory
Small (up to 100 hosts, 1000 VMs)	Deploys appliance with 4 CPUs and 16 GB of memory
Medium (up to 400 hosts, 4000 VMs)	Deploys appliance with 8 CPUs and 24 GB of memory
Large (up to 1000 hosts, 10,000 VMs)	Deploys appliance with 16 CPUs and 32 GB of memory

Chapter 8

Table 8-2 Share Allocations for VMs Versus Resource Pools

	VM CPU Share Values	VM Memory Share Values	Resource Pool CPU Share Values	Resource Pool Memory Share Values
High	2000 shares per vCPU	20 shares per MB of configured RAM	8000	327680
Normal	1000 shares per vCPU	10 shares per MB of configured RAM	4000	163840
Low	500 shares per vCPU	5 shares per MB of configured RAM	2000	81920

Chapter 9

Table 9-2 Minimum System Requirements for VDP

Configuration	Number of 2 GHz Processors	Memory (GB)	Disk Space
0.5 TB	4	4	873 GB
1 TB	4	4	1600 GB
2 TB	4	4	3 TB
4 TB	4	8	6 TB
6 TB	4	10	9 TB
8 TB	4	12	12 TB

Table 9-3 Virtual Machine Snapshot Files

Filename Syntax	Filename Example	Description (GB)
`vmname-###.vmdk`	`Servera-000001.vmdk`	Contains snapshot metadata, such as the name of the delta file and disk geometry.
`vmname-delta-###.vmdk`	`Servera-000001-delta.vmdk`	Contains all the virtual disk data blocks that have changed at least once following the creation of the snapshot. Each block represents the most recent state of that block.
`vmname.vsd`	`Servera.vmsd`	Contains information on all of the virtual machine's snapshots.
`vmname.Snapshot###.vmsn`	`servera.Snapshot000001.vmsn`	Contains the memory state of the of the virtual machine, if you select to snapshot the memory.

Table 9-4 Supported Quiescing for Windows and vSphere Replication Versions

Windows Version	Application Quiescing		File System Quiescing	
	vSphere Replication 5.8	vSphere Replication 6.0	vSphere Replication 5.8	vSphere Replication 6.0
Windows Server 2003	Yes	Discontinued support	Yes	Yes
Windows Server 2008	Yes	Yes	Yes	Yes
Windows Server 2012	Yes	Yes	Yes	Yes
Windows Vista	No	No	Yes	Yes
Windows 7	No	No	Yes	Yes
Windows 8	No	No	Yes	Yes

Chapter 10

You find the following services at **Administration > System Configuration > Services**:

- Auto Deploy
- Content Library Service
- Data Service
- Hardware Health Service
- Inventory Service
- License Service
- Transfer Service
- VMware ESX Agent Manager
- VMware Message Bus Configuration Service
- VMware Open Virtualization Format Service
- VMware Performance Charts Service
- VMware Postgres
- VMware Syslog Service
- VMware vCenter Server
- VMware Service Manager

- VMware vSphere ESXi Dump Collector
- VMware vSphere Profile-Driven Storage Service
- VMware vSphere Web Client
- vAPI Endpoint

Table 10-3 ESXTOP Replay Mode Command-Line Options

Option	Description
-R	Path to the data collected by `vm-support`
-a	Show all statistics
-b	Run in batch mode
-c	User-defined configuration file
-d	Delay (in seconds) for the sampling period. The default is 5, and the minimum is 2.
-n	Number of iterations (samples) for ESXTOP to take prior to automatically exiting.

Table 10-4 ESXi Log Files

Component	Location	Purpose
VMkernel	`/var/log/vmkernel.log`	Records activities related to virtual machines and ESXi.
VMkernel warnings	`/var/log/vmkwarning.log`	Records activities related to virtual machines.
Vmkernel summary	`/var/log/vmksummary.log`	Used to determine uptime and availability statistics for ESXi.
ESXi Host agent	`/var/log/hostd.log`	Contains information about the agent that manages and configures the ESXi Host and its virtual machines.
vCenter agent	`/var/log/vpxa.log`	Contains information about the agent that communicates with vCenter Server.
ESXi Shell	`/var/log/shell.log`	Contains a record of all commands typed into the ESXi Shell as well as shell events.

Component	Location	Purpose
Authentication	`/var/log/auth.log`	Contains all events related to authentication for the local system.
System Messages	`/var/log/syslog.log`	Contains all general log messages and can be used for troubleshooting.
Virtual Machines	`vmware.log`, located in the same folder as the virtual machine configuration file	Contains virtual machine power events, system failure information, tools status and activity, time sync, virtual hardware changes, vMotion migrations, machine clones, and more.

Table 10-6   vCenter Server Ports

Port	Purpose
22	For SSH connections, when using the vCenter Server Appliance
80	For direct HTTP connections, which vCenter Server automatically redirects to port 443
88	For VMware key distribution
389	For Directory Services
443	For connections with the vSphere Web Client, SDK clients, and third-party clients
514 and 1514	For Syslog Collector connections
636	For vCenter Server Enhanced Linked Mode
902	For ESXi Host management
2012	For SSO control
2014	For VMCA API connections
2020	For authentication framework management
6500	For ESXi Dump Collection connections
6501 and 6502	For Auto Deploy service and management
7444	For Secure Token Service (STS)
9443	For vSphere Web Client HTTPS connections
11711 and 11712	For VMware Directory Service (vmdir) LDAP and LDAPS

Table 10-8   Potential PSC Installation Issues

Symptom	Root Cause	Solution Example

During the installation of a second PSC, the installation fails and leaves incomplete data on the first PSC.	During the initial failure, the second PSC was attempting to join the current SSO domain, resulting in incomplete data on the first PSC.	In the first PSC, execute the `vdcleavfed` command. In the following example, the hostname of the second PSC is `psc02`:
		
		`vdcleavefed -h psc02 -u`
		`Administrator`

A vCenter Server installation that uses a Microsoft SQL database fails, with the following message:
 	
`The DB User`
`entered does not`
`have the required`
`permissions needed`
`to install and`
`configure vCenter`
`Server with the`
`selected DB.`
	This could be caused by an unsupported database version or permissions. But it could also be caused when a supported database version is set for compatibility mode with an unsupported version.	Check the settings of the SQL database to determine whether the compatibility mode is set and whether it needs to be changed. For example, if the following command is used in the database configuration, then it is not compatible with vCenter Server 6.0:
		
		`ALTER DATABASE VCDB 80`
		
		In this example, the database name is `vcdb`, and the compatibility level is `80`, which corresponds to SQL Server 2000 compatibility.

The installation of vCenter Server fails.	The vCenter Server and the PSC have a time skew of more than 3 minutes.	During the installation, if you see a message that warns the time difference is greater than 2 minutes, stop the installation, correct the time synchronization, and run the installation again.
The vCenter Server installation fails due to improper registration with the PSC.	You specified an FQDN during the PSC installation but used an IP address when registering vCenter Server with the PSC or vice versa.	Ensure that you use the same FQDN or use the same IP address when registering vCenter Server as you used when you provided a value for FQDN during the PSC installation. If you used an IP address during the PSC installation, use an IP address during the vCenter Server registration. If you used the actual FQDN during the PSC installation, use the FQDN during the vCenter Server registration.

Chapter 11

Table 11-2 Storage Configuration Issues That Impact ESXi

Problem	Root Cause(s)	Solution(s)
The ESXi Host cannot access a new storage device.	In order to detect the new device, a storage rescan is required.	Use the vSphere Web Client to navigate to the ESXi Host and rescan its storage adapters.
The ESXi Host cannot access the Fibre Channel storage array.	Zoning is improperly configured on the Fibre Channel switches, preventing the ESXi Host's storage adapters from connecting to the array's storage processors.	Correct the zoning on the switches and rescan the storage adapters.
The ESXi Host does not recognize its storage adapter.	The proper storage adapter driver is not installed on the ESXi Host.	Follow the hardware vendor's recommendations to ensure that the correct VMware Information Bundles (VIBs) that contain the correct drivers are installed on the ESXi Host. Ensure that only supported hardware is used.
The storage I/O performance of an ESXi Host is terrible or unusable.	The storage multipathing is misconfigured.	Follow the storage vendor's recommendation to ensure that the correct multipath settings are used. Active-passive arrays require Most Recently Used (MRU). Active-active arrays typically default to Fixed (Preferred) but may support Round Robin. Some arrays require custom Storage Array Type Plug-ins (SATPs) and Path Selection Plug-ins (PSPs). For example, if the multipathing for a storage device is set to `Fixed` on an ESXi Host, but the array is active-passive, then thrashing may occur, where two hosts are accessing the LUN through different storage processors.
The performance of the datastore in a datastore cluster is poor. The datastores are backed by auto-tiering storage.	Storage DRS is configured to balance based on I/O, but the storage vendor does not recommend or support this.	Disable I/O load balancing on Storage DRS. Optionally, leave storage space load balancing enabled on Storage DRS.

Problem	Root Cause(s)	Solution(s)
An ESXi Host cannot access a specific storage device.	The LUN masking configuration in the array is not properly set.	Change the LUN masking to allow access by the ESXi host and rescan the storage adapters.

Virtual machine performance is very poor due to increased disk I/O latency.	The current LUN queue depth is inadequate.	The queue depth is dependent on the host bus adapter (HBA) type. Use the `esxcli system module parameters set -p parameters` command, where parameters should be replaced, as described here:
		
		QLogic: `p qlfxmaxqdepth=64 -m qlnativefc`
		
		Emulex: `lpfc0_lun_queue_depth=64 -m lpfc`
		
		Brocade: `-p bfa_lun_queue_depth=64 -m bfa`
		
		Also change the value of `Disk.SchedNumReqOutstanding` to a value that is high enough to accommodate all the virtual machines on the host that write to the same LUN. You can use the following command for this:
		
		`esxcli storage core device set -O | --sched-num-req-outstanding value -d device_ID`
		
		If the iSCSI software adapter is used, you can use the following command to set its queue depth
		
		`esxcli system module parameters set -m iscsi_vmk -p iscsivmk_LunQDepth=value`

The operational state of a storage device is `Lost Communication`. The status of all paths to the device is Dead. When you analyze ESXi Host's `/var/log/vmkernel` log files, you encounter events or error messages that contain SCSI Sense codes.	The storage device is in a permanent device lost (PDL) state.	Power off and unregister all associated virtual machines on the ESXi Host. Unmount the datastore. Address any issues concerning the device within the storage array. Rescan the storage array. Register the virtual machines. Power on the virtual machines.

Problem	Root Cause(s)	Solution(s)
An ESXi Host does not automatically detect a flash disk or recognize it as a local disk.	Some flash disk vendors do not support automatic flash recognition. In these cases, the ESXi Host does not recognize the disk as flash storage or as a local device.	In the vSphere Web Client, select the ESXi Host, select **Manage > Storage**, click **Storage Devices**, select the device, and click **Mark as Flash Disks**. Alternatively, click **Mark as Local for the Host**.

Table 11-3   Network Configuration Issues That Impact Virtual Machines

Problem	Root Cause(s)	Solution(s)
A virtual machine is able to communicate with other virtual machines on the same virtual switch port group and ESXi Host, but it cannot communicate with any other server.	The virtual switch port group VLAN setting does not match the physical switch port setting.	Ensure that the physical switch ports where the virtual switch uplinks connect are trunked with a set of VLAN IDs that includes the VLAN ID assigned to the virtual switch port group. For example, if a virtual switch port group is assigned VLAN 10, but the physical switch port where it connects is trunked with VLANs 100 to 110, modify the trunking to include VLAN 10 or change the virtual port group to use a VLAN ID between 100 and 110.
A set of virtual machines lost connectivity to the network during a maintenance procedure, where you deliberately disconnected just one of two host network adapters in a team. Because you have NIC teaming set up, you expected the virtual switch to fail over the impacted virtual machine connections to the other network adapter.	The NIC teaming on the virtual switch port group is misconfigured. One of the two available paths is inadvertently configured as Unused instead of Active or Standby. In this case, the virtual machine may still be connected to the network if at least one active path is healthy, but a single path failure may cause the virtual machine connection to drop.	Change the virtual switch port group NIC teaming such that the currently unused path is set to Active or Standby.

Problem	Root Cause(s)	Solution(s)
A set of virtual machines on the same virtual switch port group cannot communicate with external devices.	The virtual switch port group NIC teaming is set to Route-Based on IP Hash, but then the physical switch ports are not configured for Etherchannel.	Change the NIC teaming to use Route-Based on Originating Virtual Port or Route-Based on Source MAC Hash.
A set of virtual machines that requires jumbo frames and is connected to a specific distributed switch port group is not performing well.	Jumbo frame support is not properly configured on the distributed virtual switch.	You should set the distributed virtual switch MTU to 9000.
One specific virtual machine cannot communicate with any device on the network, including virtual machines on the same host and connected to the same virtual switch port group.	A virtual machine guest OS is configured with the wrong IP settings.	Correct the IP address, gateway, and mask in the guest O/S.
One specific virtual machine cannot communicate with any device on the network. The guest O/S reports issues with the network adapter.	A virtual machine is configured with the wrong virtual NIC.	Edit the virtual machine and change the network adapter to a type that the guest O/S supports and that has a valid driver. Or install a valid network adapter driver in the guest O/S.\n\nFor example, if the network adapter type is VMXNET3, then ensure that VMware Tools, which includes the guest driver for VMXNET3, is installed in the virtual machine.
A set of virtual machines is able to communicate well with other virtual machines on the same virtual switch port group and ESXi Host but experiences terrible performance when communicating with other servers.	The physical NIC settings, such as speed or duplex, are improperly configured.	Use the vSphere Web Client to properly set the speed and duplex of the network adapter, or modify the associated physical switch port speed and duplex.

Problem	Root Cause(s)	Solution(s)
The network performance of a set of virtual machines is poor when the workload is significant but the physical network adapter bandwidth is not being saturated.	Network traffic shaping is misconfigured. The average bandwidth, peak bandwidth, or burst size is set too low on a virtual switch port group.	Modify the network traffic settings to increase the underlying values or disable traffic shaping on the virtual switch port group.
A virtual machine running network analyzer software (such as Wireshark) is unable to successfully monitor network traffic.	The security settings for the standard virtual switch port group are misconfigured. Promiscuous mode is rejected.	Modify the security settings on the virtual switch port group to allow promiscuous mode.
Microsoft Network Load Balancing (NLB) is not working in unicast mode for a specific virtual machine.	The associated virtual switch port group is misconfigured. The virtual switch is rejecting forged transmits and is notifying the physical switch.	To support Microsoft Network Load Balancing (NLB) in unicast mode, change the virtual switch port group's **Forged Transmits** setting to `Allow` and set the **Notify Switch** setting to `No`.

Table 11-4 Potential Storage DRS Problems and Solutions

Problem	Root Cause(s)	Solution(s)
Attempts for a datastore in a datastore cluster to enter maintenance mode are not successful. The status hangs at 1%.	Storage DRS is disabled on at least one virtual disk in the datastore.	If Storage DRS is disabled for the cluster or for associated virtual machines, enable it.
	Storage DRS rules prevent Storage DRS from performing the required migrations	If Storage DRS rules are preventing the migrations, either remove the rules or set the advanced Storage DRS configuration parameter `IgnoreAffinityRulesFor Maintenance` to `1`.
Storage DRS generates an event and an alarm that it cannot operate on a specific datastore.	ESXi Hosts that reside in different virtual datacenters share the datastore. Or the datastore is connected to an unsupported ESXi Host, such as a host running ESXi 4.1.	Migrate all the ESXi Hosts that share the datacenter to the same virtual datacenter. Alternatively, unmount the datastore from some ESXi Hosts that reside in other virtual datacenters. Upgrade all associated ESXi Hosts to 5.0 or higher.

Problem	Root Cause(s)	Solution(s)
When migrating virtual machines into a datastore cluster, not all virtual machines migrate successfully, and the error message `Insufficient Disk Space on Datastore` appears.	During the placement of each virtual machine, Storage DRS does not account for the space that will be consumed upon completion, so it may attempt to allocate the space for subsequent placement requests.	Retry the failed migrations again, but one at a time, allowing each migration to complete prior to requesting the next.
When you create or clone a virtual machine in a datastore cluster, the error message `Operation Not Allowed in the Current State` is received.	A Storage DRS rule cannot check the new virtual machine's disk for compliance, and it generates a fault.	Revise, remove, or disable the rule until the operation is complete.
When you deploy an OVF template that has Storage DRS disabled, the deployed virtual machine actually has Storage DRS enabled.	By design, Storage DRS applies the automation level of the datastore to the deployed virtual machine.	Use the vSphere Web Client to edit the datastore cluster: use **VM Overrides** to set **Keep VMDKs Together** to **NO**.
Multiple instances of the same affinity or anti-affinity rule violation appear in the Faults dialog box when you attempt to put a datastore into maintenance mode.	Actually, each fault refers to a different datastore, but because the datastore names are not displayed, the faults appear to be redundant.	Remove the rule that is preventing the necessary migrations.
Affinity or anti-affinity rules still apply to a virtual machine after the virtual machine was migrated from a datastore cluster.	Rules remain with a virtual machine that is removed from a datastore cluster if the virtual machine remains in the associated vCenter Server inventory.	Use the vSphere Web Client to remove the rule.

Problem	Root Cause(s)	Solution(s)
Attempts to apply Storage DRS recommendations fail.	The thin-provisioning-threshold-crossed alarm may be triggered, which indicates that the datastore is low on free space. The target datastore may be in or entering maintenance mode.	If an alarm was raised, address the specific issue that triggered the alarm. Verify that the target datastore is not in or entering maintenance mode.
When you create, clone, or relocate a virtual machine in a datastore cluster, Storage DRS provides only one recommendation.	The ESXi Host specifies the virtual machine swap file location as a datastore in the target datastore cluster, so the disks to be placed in the cluster do not form a single affinity group. Storage DRS does not generate alternative recommendations in cases where a single affinity group is not used.	Often in these cases, it is acceptable to allow a single recommendation. Otherwise, you could change the host configuration such that it does not specify a virtual machine swap file location.

Storage performance issues could be caused by excessive SCSI reservations. The following operations often cause VMFS to use SCSI reservations:

- Creating, resignaturing, and expanding a VMFS datastore
- Powering on a virtual machine
- Creating or deleting a file
- Creating a template
- Deploying a new virtual machine
- Migrating with vMotion
- Growing a file, such as growing a thin-provisioned virtual disk or snapshot (redo) file

Table 11-7 vCenter Server Database Upgrade Logs

Purpose	Log File
Collect errors during execution of the pre-upgrade check.	`%TEMP%\..\vcsUpgrade\vcdb_req.out`
Collect errors during the export phase of the upgrade process.	`%TEMP%\..\vcsUpgrade\vcdb_export.out file.`

Purpose	Log File
Collect errors during the import phase of the upgrade process.	ProgramData\Vmware\CIS\logs\vmware\vpx\vcdb_import.out
Collect errors during an in-place upgrade	ProgramData\Vmware\CIS\logs\vmware\vpx\vcdb_inplace.out

Table 11-8   vCenter Server Logging Options

Logging Option	Description
None (Disable logging)	No vCenter Server logging occurs.
Error (Errors Only)	The vCenter Server collects only error entries into its log files.
Warning (Warning and Errors)	The vCenter Server collects warning and error entries into its log files.
Info (Normal logging)	The vCenter Server collects information, warning, and error entries into its log files.
Verbose (Verbose)	The vCenter Server collects verbose, information, warning, and error entries into its log files.
Trivia (Extended verbose)	The vCenter Server collects trivia, verbose, information, warning, and error entries into its log files.

Chapter 12

Table 12-2   Critical Performance Metrics

Metric	Description
Disk Latency	The amount of time that elapsed while performing a storage-related task, such as a read or write operation. Latency can be reported from various perspectives. For example, the virtual machine disk read latency is the amount of time from which the guest OS generates the read operation until it is completely fulfilled by the storage system and the data is delivered to the guest OS. High disk latency is often an indicator of slow or overworked storage devices.

Metric	Description
Network Packets Dropped	The number of network packets that were dropped during a specific sampling period. This indicates that a network queue has filled due to a processing bottleneck involving a network adapter, virtual machine, or VMkernel.
CPU Ready Time	The amount of time that a VMkernel world, such as a virtual CPU, spent waiting to be scheduled on physical CPU hardware after it announced it was ready to execute its workload. High CPU Ready Time is often an indicator of overworked CPU hardware.
Memory Swapped	The amount of data that has been swapped from a virtual machine's memory to its virtual machine swap file. It is often an indicator of overworked memory hardware.
Disk Aborts	The number of aborts issued by guest operating systems. This is often an indicator of severe problems, such as failed storage paths.

Table 12-3 Potential Memory Issues and Resolutions

Potential Issue	Indicators	Potential Resolutions
The VM is experiencing memory contention.	Memory Ballooning, Memory Decompression Rate, and/ or Memory Swap In Rate is greater than zero. Memory latency is 5% or higher, which indicates that the VM is waiting to access swapped or compressed data.	Migrate the VM to an ESXi Host with available memory resources. Increase the Memory Shares or Memory Reservation of the VM. Stop some competing VMs or migrate the VMs to other ESXi Hosts. Decrease the Memory Shares or Memory Reservation of competing VMs.
The VM's virtual memory resources are insufficient to meet the current demand.	The Memory Usage of the VM is about 100%. The guest OS reports high paging. For example, for Windows it is reporting Pages/ sec is 200.	Reconfigure the VM with additional virtual memory. Reduce the workload in the VM.

Potential Issue	Indicators	Potential Resolutions
The ESXi Host's memory resources are insufficient to meet the current demand from its VMs.	Memory State is Hard or Low, which indicates that the ESXi Host is swapping and compressing memory. Memory Latency is 5% or higher.	Reduce the workload on the ESXi Host by migrating some VMs to ESXi Hosts with available memory resources. Add more memory to the ESXi Host.

Table 12-4   Potential CPU Issues and Resolutions

Potential Issue	Indicators	Potential Resolutions
The VM is experiencing CPU contention.	CPU Ready Time for one or more of the VM's virtual CPUs is frequently 2000 ms or more.	Migrate the VM to an ESXi Host with available CPU resources. Increase the CPU Shares or CPU Reservation of the VM. Stop some competing VMs or migrate the VMs to other ESXi Hosts. Decrease the CPU Shares or CPU Reservation of competing VMs.
The VM's virtual CPU resources are insufficient to meet the current demand.	The CPU Usage of the entire VM and of each of the VM's virtual CPUs is frequently 80% or higher.	Reconfigure the VM with additional virtual CPUs. Migrate the VM to an ESXi Host with faster CPUs. Reduce the workload in the VM.
The ESXi Host's CPU resources are insufficient to meet the current demand from its VMs.	The CPU Usage of the ESXi Host and each of its CPU cores is frequently 80% or higher. CPU Latency is 5% or higher.	Reduce the workload on the ESXi Hosts by migrating some of the VMs to less busy hosts. Add more CPUs to the ESXi Host.

Table 12-5   Common ESXTOP Metrics

Metric	Common Name
%RDY	CPU Ready (percentage of actual time)
%CSTP	Co-stop (percentage of actual time)
%SWPWT	Swap Wait (percentage of actual time)
MCTLSZ	Balloon Size (in MB)
SWCUR	Swapped (in MB)
SWR/s	Swap In Rate (KB per second)

Metric	Common Name
UNZIP/s	Decompression Rate (KB per second)
%DRPTX	Transmit Packets Dropped (percentage of actual time)
%DRPRX	Receive Packets Dropped (percentage of actual time)
GAVG	Guest Latency (milliseconds)
DAVG	Device Latency (milliseconds)
KAVG	Kernel Latency (milliseconds)
ABRTS/s	Aborts (per second)

Table 12-6   Intel EVC Baselines

EVC Level	EVC Baseline	Description
L0	Merom	Merom generation feature set
L1	Penryn	Penryn generation (Merom plus CPU features including SSE4.1)
L2	Nehalem	Nehalem generation (Penryn plus additional CPU features including SSE4.2 and POPCOUNT)
L3	Westmere	Westmere generation (Nehalem plus additional CPU features including AES and PCLMULQDQ)
L4	Sandy Bridge	Sandy Bridge generation (Westmere plus additional CPU features including AVX and XSAVE)
L5	Ivy Bridge	Ivy Bridge generation (Sandy Bridge Generation plus additional CPU features, including RDRAND, ENFSTRG, FSGSBASE, SMEP, and F16C)

Chapter 13

Table 13-2   FT and Legacy FT

	Legacy FT	FT
Extended page tables/rapid virtualization indexing (Intel EPT/AMD RVI)	Not supported	Required
IPv6	Not supported for FT logging NICs	Supported for FT logging NICs

	Legacy FT	FT
DRS	Fully supported for initial placement, load balancing, and maintenance mode support	Only power-on placement of secondary VM and maintenance mode are supported
vStorage APIs—data protection backups	Not supported	Supported
Eager-zeros thick .vmdk files	Required	Not required because FT supports all disk file types, including thick and thin
.vmdk redundancy	Only a single copy	Primary VMs and secondary VMs always maintain independent copies, which can be placed on different datastores to increase redundancy
NIC bandwidth	Dedicated 1 GB NIC recommended	Dedicated 10 GB NIC recommended
CPU and host compatibility	Requires identical CPU model and family and nearly identical versions of vSphere on hosts	CPUs must be compatible with vSphere vMotion or EVC. Versions of vSphere on hosts must be compatible with vSphere vMotion
Turn on FT on running VM	Not always supported. You might need to power off the VM first	Supported
Storage vMotion	Supported only on powered-off VMs vCenter Server automatically turns off FT before performing a Storage vMotion action and then turns on FT again after the Storage vMotion action completes	Not supported; user must turn off FT for the VM before performing the Storage vMotion action and then turn on FT again
Vlance networking drivers	Not supported	Supported

Chapter 14

Table 14-2   PowerCLI Auto Deploy cmdlets

Command	Description
`Get-DeployCommand`	Returns a list of Auto Deploy cmdlets.
`New-DeployRule`	Creates a new rule with the specified items and patterns.
`Set-DeployRule`	Updates an existing rule with the specified items and patterns. You cannot update a rule that is part of a rule set.
`Get-DeployRule`	Retrieves the rules with the specified names.
`Copy-DeployRule`	Clones and updates an existing rule.
`Add-DeployRule`	Adds one or more rules to the working rule set and, by default, also to the active rule set. Use the `NoActivate` parameter to add a rule only to the working rule set.
`Remove-DeployRule`	Removes one or more rules from the working rule set and from the active rule set. Run this command with the `-Delete` parameter to completely delete the rule.
`Set-DeployRuleSet`	Explicitly sets the list of rules in the working rule set.
`Get-DeployRuleSet`	Retrieves the current working rule set or the current active rule set.
`Switch-ActiveDeployRuleSet`	Activates a rule set so that any new requests are evaluated through the rule set.
`Get-VMHostMatchingRules`	Retrieves rules matching a pattern. For example, you can retrieve all rules that apply to a host or hosts. Use this cmdlet primarily for debugging.
`Test-DeployRulesetCompliance`	Checks whether the items associated with a specified hosts are in compliance with the active rule set.
`Repair-DeployRulesetCompliance`	Given the output of `Test-DeployRulesetCompliance`, this cmdlet updates the image profile, host profile, and location for each host in the vCenter Server inventory. The cmdlet might apply image profiles, apply host profiles, or move hosts to the prespecified folders or clusters on the vCenter Server system.
`Apply-EsxImageProfile`	Associates the specified image profile with the specified host.
`Get-VMHostImageProfile`	Retrieves the image profile in use by a specified host. This cmdlet differs from the `Get-EsxImageProfile` cmdlet in the Image Builder PowerCLI.

Command	Description
`Repair-DeployImageCache`	Use this cmdlet only if the Auto Deploy image cache is accidentally deleted.
`Get-VMHostAttributes`	Retrieves the attributes for a host that are used when the Auto Deploy server evaluates the rules.
`Get-DeployMachineIdentity`	Returns a string value that Auto Deploy uses to logically link an ESXi Host in vCenter to a physical machine.
`Set-DeployMachineIdentity`	Logically links a host object in the vCenter Server database to a physical machine. Use this cmdlet to add hosts without specifying rules.
`Get-DeployOption`	Retrieves the Auto Deploy global configuration options. This cmdlet currently supports the `vlan-id` option, which specifies the default VLAN ID for the ESXi Management Network of a host provisioned with Auto Deploy. Auto Deploy uses the value only if the host boots without a host profile.
`Set-DeployOption`	Sets the value of a global configuration option. Currently supports the `vlan-id` option for setting the default VLAN ID for the ESXi Management Network.

Chapter 15

The following are VMware's advanced HA settings that can be modified in the vSphere Web Client:

- **das.isolationaddress[...]:** Sets the address to ping to determine whether a host is isolated from the network. This address is pinged only when heartbeats are not received from any other host in the cluster. If not specified, the default gateway of the management network is used. You can specify multiple isolation addresses (up to 10) for the cluster:

  `das.isolationaddressX, where X=0-9.`

- **das.usedefaultisolationaddress:** By default, vSphere HA uses the default gateway of the console network as an isolation address. This option specifies whether (`true`) or not (`false`) this default is used.

- **das.isolationshutdowntimeout:** Specifies the period of time the system waits for a virtual machine to shut down before powering it off. This applies only if the host's isolation response is `shut down VM`. The default value is 300 seconds.

- **das.slotmeminmb:** Defines the maximum memory slot size. If this option is used, the slot size is the smaller of this value or the maximum memory reservation plus memory overhead of any powered-on virtual machine in the cluster.

- **das.slotcpuinmhz:** Defines the maximum CPU slot size. If this option is used, the slot size is the smaller of this value or the maximum CPU reservation of any powered-on virtual machine in the cluster.

- **das.vmmemoryminmb:** Defines the default memory resource value assigned to a virtual machine if its memory reservation is not specified or zero. This is used for the Host Failures Cluster Tolerates admission control policy. If no value is specified, the default is 0 MB.

- **das.vmcpuminmhz:** Defines the default CPU resource value assigned to a virtual machine if its CPU reservation is not specified or is zero. This is used for the Host Failures Cluster Tolerates admission control policy. If no value is specified, the default is 32 MHz.

- **das.iostatsinterval:** Changes the default I/O stats interval for VM monitoring sensitivity. The default is 120 (seconds), but it can be set to any value greater than or equal to 0. Setting to 0 disables the check.

- **das.ignoreinsufficienthbdatastore:** Disables configuration issues created if the host does not have sufficient heartbeat datastores for vSphere HA. The default value is `false`.

- **das.heartbeatdsperhost:** Changes the number of heartbeat datastores required. Valid values can range from 2 to 5, and the default is 2.

- **fdm.isolationpolicydelaysec:** Specifies the number of seconds the system waits before executing the isolation policy once it is determined that a host is isolated. The minimum value is 30.

- **das.respectvmvmantiaffinityrules:** Determines whether vSphere HA enforces VM-VM anti-affinity rules. The default value is `false`, which means the rules are not enforced. Can also be set to `true` to have rules enforced (even if vSphere DRS is not enabled). In this case, vSphere HA does not fail over a virtual machine if doing so violates a rule, but it issues an event reporting there are insufficient resources to perform the failover.

- **das.maxresets:** Specifies the maximum number of reset attempts made by VMCP. If a reset operation on a virtual machine affected by an APD situation fails, VMCP retries the reset this many times before giving up.

- **das.maxterminates:** Specifies the maximum number of retries made by VMCP for virtual machine termination.

- **das.terminateretryintervalsec:** Specifies the number of seconds the system waits before it retries a terminate attempt after VMCP fails to terminate a virtual machine.

- **das.config.fdm.reportfailoverfailevent:** When set to 1, enables generation of a detailed per-VM event when an attempt by vSphere HA to restart a virtual machine is unsuccessful. The default value is 0.

- **vpxd.das.completemetadataupdateintervalsec:** Specifies the period of time (in seconds) after a VM-Host affinity rule is set during which vSphere HA can restart a VM in a DRS-disabled cluster, overriding the rule. The default value is 300 seconds.

- **das.config.fdm.memreservationmb:** By default, vSphere HA agents run with a configured memory limit of 250 MB. A host might not allow this reservation if it runs out of reservable capacity. You can use this advanced option to lower the memory limit to avoid this issue. Only integers 100 and greater can be specified. To prevent problems during master agent elections in a large cluster (containing 6,000 to 8,000 VMs), you should raise this limit to 325 MB.

Chapter 16

Table 16-2 Virtual Machine Option Categories

Category	Description
General Options	Common virtual machine attributes such as name, location, working folder, and guest operating system.
VMware Remote Console Options	Settings, such as locking behavior, that control multiple simultaneous connections to the virtual machine's remote console.
VMware Tools	Settings that impact virtual machine management via VMware Tools, such as time synchronization, automatic upgrade, and scripts.
Power Management	Virtual machine behavior for suspend operations and wake on LAN.
Boot Options	Virtual machine boot options, such as pre-boot delay and forced entry into BIOS.
Advanced	Advanced virtual machine options, as described immediately following this table.
Fibre Channel NPIV	Options for sharing a single physical Fibre Channel HBA port among multiple virtual ports, each with unique identifiers.

Table 16-4 NUMA-Related Attributes

Attribute	Description
cpuid.coresPerSocket	For virtual machines with a virtual NUMA topology, this value, which defines the number of virtual cores per virtual CPU socket, can also impact the size of the virtual NUMA node. In this case, if the value is greater than 1, it is also used as the number of virtual cores per virtual node. The default value is 1. You can only set this to powers of 2, such as 2, 4, and 8.
numa.autosize	When this attribute is set to TRUE, the number of virtual cores per node in the virtual NUMA topology is automatically set to match the number of cores in each physical node. The default value is FALSE.
numa.autosize.once	When this attribute is set to TRUE, this attribute ensures that the automatically assigned virtual node size remains unchanged during future power-on operations, unless the number of virtual CPUs in the virtual machine is modified. The default value is TRUE.
numa.vcpu.maxPerVirtualNode	This setting can be used instead of cupid.coresPerSocket. It assigns the maximum number of virtual cores per virtual node, which must be a power of 2. The default value is 8.
numa.vcpu.min	This setting is the minimum number of virtual CPUs in a virtual machine required for generating a virtual NUMA topology. The default value is 9.
numa.vcpu.maxPerClient	This setting specifies the maximum number of virtual CPUs in a NUMA client, which is a set of virtual CPUs that are managed as a single entity. You can set this when the size of the virtual NUMA node exceeds the size of the physical NUMA node. The default value is equal to numa.vcpu.maxPerVirtualNode.
numa.nodeAffinity	This setting specifies the set of NUMA nodes on which the virtual machine can execute. You should avoid using this setting except when necessary because it negatively impacts the ability of the NUMA scheduler to rebalance workload. When configuring this parameter, set its value to a comma-delimited list indicating the acceptable NUMA nodes. For example, to allow the virtual machine to only execute on NUMA nodes 0 and 1, enter 0,1.
numa.mem.interleave	This setting specifies whether the virtual machine memory is statically interleaved across all the NUMA nodes on which its corresponding NUMA clients are running when no virtual NUMA topology is exposed.

Index

C